职业教育双语教材

Bilingual Textbooks of Vocational Education

汽车电气设备检修

英汉双语教材

Automobile Electrical Equipment Maintenance

方 斌 主编

Edited by Bin Fang

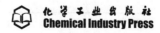

化学工业出版社

Chemical Industry Press

·北京·

BeiJing

内容简介

本书系统介绍了汽车电气基础知识、汽车电气结构、工作原理、故障诊断与排除等，共分9个项目，内容包括汽车电气设备基础、汽车蓄电池、充电系统、起动系统、点火系统、汽车灯光系统、信息显示系统、汽车辅助电气系统和汽车电气系统电路图分析等。书中突出"以能力培养为本位"的思想，采用理论实践一体化的编写模式，更加符合现代职业技术教育课程发展的需要。

本书可作为高职高专院校、职教本科院校汽车类相关专业的教材，也可作为汽车相关领域的技术人员、管理人员和科研人员的参考书和培训教材。

图书在版编目（CIP）数据

汽车电气设备检修/方斌主编．—北京：化学工业出版社，2022.5
ISBN 978-7-122-41410-6

Ⅰ.①汽… Ⅱ.①方… Ⅲ.①汽车-电气设备-车辆修理 Ⅳ.①U472.41

中国版本图书馆CIP数据核字（2022）第080307号

责任编辑：韩庆利　　　　　　　　　　　　装帧设计：刘丽华
责任校对：李雨晴

出版发行：化学工业出版社（北京市东城区青年湖南街13号　邮政编码100011）
印　　装：大厂聚鑫印刷有限责任公司
787mm×1092mm　1/16　印张27¾　字数730千字　2022年9月北京第1版第1次印刷

购书咨询：010-64518888　　　　　　　　　售后服务：010-64518899
网　　址：http://www.cip.com.cn
凡购买本书，如有缺损质量问题，本社销售中心负责调换。

定　　价：69.80元　　　　　　　　　　　　　　　　　　　　版权所有　违者必究

前言

近年来，国内汽车业快速发展，汽车保有量持续增长。高速增长的汽车保有量也带来了社会对汽车专业人才需求量的迅速增加。汽车电气设备检修是汽车维修人员必须掌握的技能，也是高等职业院校汽车维修类专业的一门必修专业核心课程。本书根据高职院校教学的要求，系统介绍了汽车维修技术人员所必须掌握的汽车电气基础知识、汽车电气结构、工作原理、维修、故障诊断与排除等知识，突出"以能力培养为本位"的思想，采用理论实践一体化的编写模式，更加符合现代职业技术教育课程发展的需要。

本书共分为9个项目，涉及汽车电气设备基础、汽车蓄电池、充电系统、起动系统、点火系统、汽车灯光系统、信息显示系统、汽车辅助电气系统和汽车电气系统电路图分析等知识。

本书根据学生的认知规律，注重职业教育的特点，以训练学生汽车电气维修技能为目标，主要内容覆盖汽车电气系统基础维修的相关知识。本书图文并茂，在介绍汽车维修知识时加入了大量的实物图片，以促进学生对所学知识的认知，提高学生的学习兴趣。

本书由天津交通职业学院方斌主编，其中天津交通职业学院方斌编写项目一、项目二、项目三、项目四，天津交通职业学院李嘉泽编写项目五、项目六、项目七，天津交通职业学院张瑞静编写项目八、项目九。

本书编者水平有限，书中难免存在不妥之处，请读者批评指正。

编　者

目录

项目一　汽车电气设备基础 ··· 001

- 一、情境引入 ···················· 001
- 二、相关知识 ···················· 001
  - （一）汽车电气设备的组成 ······ 001
  - （二）汽车电气设备的特点 ······ 002
  - （三）汽车电气设备故障的基本诊断方法 ···················· 002
  - （四）汽车电气设备维修中常用的检测仪表和工具 ············ 003
- 三、项目实施 ···················· 004
  - （一）常用检测仪表的使用 ······ 004
  - （二）实施步骤 ················ 004
- 四、知识与技能拓展 ·············· 006
  - （一）汽车电气设备基础元件 ···· 006
  - （二）汽车电路常用电子元器件 ·· 013
- 小结 ···························· 013
- 习题及思考 ······················ 013

项目二　蓄电池的检测与维护 ··· 014

- 一、情境引入 ···················· 014
- 二、相关知识 ···················· 014
  - （一）蓄电池的作用及类型 ······ 014
  - （二）蓄电池的安装位置 ········ 014
  - （三）蓄电池的结构 ············ 014
  - （四）蓄电池的工作原理 ········ 016
  - （五）蓄电池的技术参数 ········ 017
  - （六）蓄电池的型号 ············ 017
  - （七）免维护蓄电池 ············ 018
  - （八）蓄电池的常见故障及排除 ··· 019
- 三、项目实施 ···················· 020
  - （一）蓄电池安全使用、检查维护、充电与检测 ················ 020
  - （二）实施步骤 ················ 021
- 四、知识与技能拓展 ·············· 023
  - （一）蓄电池切断保护装置 ······ 023
  - （二）蓄电池监控装置 ·········· 024
- 小结 ···························· 024
- 习题及思考 ······················ 024

项目三　充电系统的检修 ··· 025

- 一、情境引入 ···················· 025
- 二、相关知识 ···················· 025
  - （一）充电系统概述 ············ 025
  - （二）交流发电机的构造 ········ 026
  - （三）交流发电机的工作原理 ···· 031
  - （四）电压调节器 ·············· 034
  - （五）交流发电机和电压调节器的使用与维护 ················ 039
  - （六）充电系统的故障诊断 ······ 039
- 三、项目实施 ···················· 042
  - （一）充电系统的检修要求 ······ 042
  - （二）实施步骤 ················ 042
- 四、知识与技能拓展 ·············· 047
  - （一）其他类型的发电机 ········ 047
  - （二）部分品牌汽车发电机电路图 ···························· 049
  - （三）电源管理系统 ············ 049
- 小结 ···························· 053
- 习题及思考 ······················ 053

项目四　起动系统的检修 ·· 054

　　一、情境引入 ······························ 054
　　二、相关知识 ······························ 054
　　　（一）起动系统概述 ················ 054
　　　（二）起动机的构造 ················ 055
　　　（三）直流电动机 ···················· 056
　　　（四）起动机的传动机构与
　　　　　　操纵机构 ······················· 059
　　　（五）起动机的控制电路 ········ 063
　　　（六）起动机的正确使用 ········ 065
　　三、项目实施 ······························ 065
　　　（一）起动系统实施要求 ········ 065
　　　（二）实施步骤 ························ 065
　　四、知识与技能拓展 ···················· 073
　　　（一）减速起动机的结构 ········ 073
　　　（二）起动/停止系统 ·············· 075
　　小结 ·· 076
　　习题及思考 ································ 077

项目五　点火系统的检修 ·· 078

　　一、情境引入 ······························ 078
　　二、相关知识 ······························ 078
　　　（一）点火系统概述 ················ 078
　　　（二）点火系统的基本构造与
　　　　　　检修 ································ 079
　　　（三）计算机控制的点火系统的
　　　　　　构造与维修 ······················ 087
　　三、项目实施 ······························ 097
　　　（一）点火系统实施要求 ········ 097
　　　（二）实施步骤 ························ 097
　　小结 ·· 097
　　习题及思考 ································ 098

项目六　汽车灯光系统的检修 ·· 099

　　一、情境引入 ······························ 099
　　二、相关知识 ······························ 099
　　　（一）照明、信号系统的作用、
　　　　　　类型和基本组成 ·············· 099
　　　（二）汽车照明系统 ················ 100
　　　（三）汽车信号系统 ················ 104
　　三、项目实施 ······························ 107
　　　（一）一汽大众宝来轿车前照灯控制
　　　　　　系统电路图分析与检修 ······ 107
　　　（二）前照灯的维护与故障诊断 ··· 113
　　　（三）电喇叭的调整 ················ 115
　　四、知识与技能拓展 ···················· 116
　　　（一）车灯主动转向系统 ········ 116
　　　（二）奥迪 A8 可变照明距离 ··· 117
　　　（三）车灯开关的 LIN 总线电路
　　　　　　 ·· 118
　　小结 ·· 119
　　习题及思考 ································ 119

项目七　信息显示系统的检修 ·· 120

　　一、情境引入 ······························ 120
　　二、相关知识 ······························ 120
　　　（一）汽车仪表系统 ················ 120
　　　（二）汽车报警信息系统 ········ 128
　　三、项目实施 ······························ 131
　　　（一）冷却液温度表的故障诊断 ··· 131
　　　（二）燃油表的故障诊断 ········ 132
　　　（三）电子式车速里程表的故障诊断
　　　　　　 ·· 132
　　四、知识与技能拓展 ···················· 133
　　　（一）奥迪多媒体交互系统 ···· 133
　　　（二）平视显示系统 ················ 133

（三）电子机油油面高度显示 …… 134
（四）电子驻车制动系统 EPB
　　（电子手刹）………………… 134
（五）触摸显示系统 ……………… 135
小结 ………………………………… 135
习题及思考 ………………………… 135

项目八　汽车辅助电气系统的检修 …………………………………………… 136

一、情境引入 ………………………… 136
二、相关知识 ………………………… 136
　（一）电动刮水器的组成与分类 … 136
　（二）刮水器系统的工作原理 …… 137
　（三）清洗器系统的组成 ………… 140
　（四）电动刮水器和清洗器的维护与
　　　　常见故障检修 …………… 141
　（五）电动车窗的组成与结构 …… 143
　（六）电动车窗的工作原理 ……… 143
　（七）电动车窗的故障诊断 ……… 147
三、项目实施 ………………………… 147
　（一）汽车辅助电气系统的检修 … 147
　（二）实施步骤 …………………… 147
四、知识与技能拓展 ………………… 152
　（一）风窗除霜装置 ……………… 152
　（二）电动座椅 …………………… 152
　（三）电动后视镜 ………………… 155
　（四）中控门锁系统 ……………… 156
小结 ………………………………… 158
习题及思考 ………………………… 158

项目九　汽车电气系统电路图的分析 ………………………………………… 159

一、情境引入 ………………………… 159
二、相关知识 ………………………… 159
　（一）汽车电路图的种类 ………… 159
　（二）常见图形符号、文字符号及
　　　　标志 ……………………… 161
　（三）汽车电路的绘制及识图要领
　　　　 ……………………………… 173
（四）汽车电路检修常识 ………… 176
三、项目实施 ………………………… 177
　（一）汽车总电路图拆画分析 …… 177
　（二）实施步骤 …………………… 177
四、知识与技能拓展 ………………… 183
小结 ………………………………… 185
习题及思考 ………………………… 185

参考文献 ………………………………………………………………………… 186

项目一

汽车电气设备基础

一、情境引入

一位客户来到维修站,反映车上点烟器无法使用,经检修发现保险丝熔断。这种情况是由于加装了电气部件后造成电路负荷增加引起的故障表现。

随着汽车制造技术的成熟,汽车机械故障越来越少,更多的故障是来自汽车电气设备与电路。对汽车电气工作原理、电路组成特点的熟练掌握,正确的诊断思路和能熟练使用诊断维修设备对机电维修工在工作中提高故障点查找的准确性及缩短排查故障的时间都起到至关重要的作用。

二、相关知识

(一)汽车电气设备的组成

汽车主要由发动机、底盘、车身和电气设备四部分组成,随着科技的发展,电气设备在汽车上越来越重要,其工作性能的优劣直接影响汽车的动力性、经济性、安全性、可靠性、舒适性等。汽车电气设备主要由电源系统、用电设备和配电装置组成。

1. 电源系统

电源系统又称充电系统,其作用是向全车用电设备提供低压直流电能。包括蓄电池、发电机及电压调节器。发电机是汽车上的主要电源,蓄电池是辅助电源。当发电机工作时,由发电机向全车用电设备供电,同时给蓄电池充电。蓄电池的作用是起动发动机时向起动机供电,同时当发电机不工作时向用电设备供电。电压调节器的作用是保持发电机的输出电压恒定。

2. 用电设备

汽车上的用电设备众多,电气设备可分为起动系统,点火系统,照明与信号系统,仪表、报警与电子显示系统,辅助电气系统及电子控制部分等。

(1)起动系统。其作用是带动发动机飞轮旋转使曲轴达到必要的起动转速,从而起动发动机。主要部件有起动机、起动继电器等。

(2)点火系统。点火系统仅用于汽油机上,其作用是将低压电转变为高压电,适时可靠点燃发动机汽缸内的可燃混合气。它分为传统点火系统、电子点火系统以及电控点火系统三种。

(3)照明与信号系统。其作用是确保车内、外一定范围内合适的亮度;告示行人车辆引起注意,指示行驶方向,指示操纵件状态,对运行性机械故障进行报警,以确保行驶和停车的安全性和可靠性。照明装置包括车内、外各种照明灯。信号装置包括电喇叭、闪光器、蜂鸣器及各种信号灯,提供安全行车所必需的信号。

（4）仪表、报警与电子显示系统。其作用是显示汽车运行参数及交通信息，监控汽车各系统的工况。仪表包括发动机转速表、车速里程表、燃油表、水温表等。

（5）辅助电气系统。其作用是为驾驶员和乘员提供良好的工作条件和舒适的乘坐环境。辅助电气系统包括电动刮水器、风窗洗涤器、空调中控门锁、电动车窗和电动座椅等。

（6）电子控制系统。其作用是更加精确地控制汽车各个系统，使经济性、动力性、安全性等得到提高。电子控制部分包括电子控制燃油喷射装置、点火装置、自动变速器和防抱死制动装置等。

3. 配电装置

配电装置，又称电源管理系统，其作用是为了规范布线，便于诊断汽车电气故障。配电装置包括中央接线盒、电路开关、保险装置、插接器、导线等。

（二）汽车电气设备的特点

现代汽车种类繁多，电气设备的数量不等、功能各异，但电路设计都遵循一定的原则，了解这些原则对汽车电路的分析和故障的检修是很有帮助的。汽车电气设备主要有下面几个特点。

1. 两个电源

汽车上有蓄电池和发电机两个供电电源。蓄电池是辅助电源，发动机未运转时向有关电气设备供电；发电机是主电源，当发动机运转到一定转速后，开始向所有电气设备供电，同时给蓄电池充电。

2. 低压直流

汽车电气设备的额定电压主要有12V和24V两种，汽油车普遍采用12V电源，柴油车采用24V电源，因为柴油机负载大，起动扭矩比汽油机大得多。如果仍采用12V电压，起动机会做得很大、很重，改用24V就可以减小起动机的体积和重量。在汽车运行中，12V电源系统电压为14V，24V电源系统电压为28V。由于蓄电池充放电均为直流电，所以汽车电气设备采用直流电。

3. 并联单线

汽车用电设备较多，采用并联电路能确保各支路的电气设备相互独立控制。布线清晰、安装方便、节约导线、排故简便，汽车电气设备一般采用单线制接线方式，即把车架、发动机、底盘等金属机体连通，并作为各种用电设备的公共并联端使用。但汽车上部分安装在钣金件上、挂车上或非金属车厢板上的电气设备仍然需要采用双线制。

4. 负极搭铁

为减少蓄电池电缆铜端子在车架、车身连接处的电化学腐蚀，提高搭铁的可靠性，采用单线制时，蓄电池的一个负电极接到车架上，俗称"负极搭铁"。

（三）汽车电气设备故障的基本诊断方法

随着现代汽车电子设备的增多，汽车电路及电气出现的故障越显复杂。发生故障后，选用合适的诊断方法是顺利排除故障的关键。为此下面介绍几种汽车电路、电气故障常用的诊断方法。

1. 直观法

当汽车电气设备的某个部分发生故障时，会出现冒烟、火花、异响、焦臭、高温等异常现象。通过人体的感觉器官，听、摸、闻、看等对汽车电气设备进行直观检查，进而判断出故障的所在部位，从而大大地提高了检修速度。

2. 试灯法

用一个汽车灯泡作为临时试灯,检查线束是否开路或短路、电器或电路有无故障等。此方法特别适合于检查不允许直接短路的带有电子元器件的电器。使用临时试灯法应注意试灯的功率不要太大,在测试电子控制器的控制(输出)端子是否有输出及是否有足够的输出时尤其要慎重,防止使控制器超载损坏。

3. 跨接法

跨接法也称短路法,即当低压电路断路时,用跨接线或螺丝刀等将某一线路或元件短路,来检验和确定故障部位。如制动灯不亮时,可在踏下制动踏板后,用螺丝刀将制动灯开关两接柱连接来检验制动灯开关是否良好。对于现代汽车的电子设备而言,应慎用短路法来诊断故障,以防止短路时因瞬间电流过大而损坏电子设备。

4. 断路法

汽车电气设备发生短路(搭铁)故障时,可用断路法判断,即将怀疑有短路故障的电路断开后,观察电气设备中短路故障是否还存在,以此来判断电路短路的部位。例如,发现车辆静电流过大,则用此方法来诊断由哪些系统引起。

5. 替换法

替换法常用于故障原因比较复杂的情况,能对可能产生故障的原因逐一进行排除。其具体做法是用一个已知是完好的零部件来替换被认为或怀疑是有故障的零部件,这样做可以试探出怀疑是否正确。若替换后故障消除,说明怀疑成立;否则,装回原件,进行新的替换,直至找到真正的故障部位。

6. 检测法

利用专用检测设备或仪器、仪表对电气元件及线路进行检测,来确定电路故障。对现代汽车上越来越多的电子设备来说,检测法有省时、省力和诊断准确的优点,但要求操作者必须能熟练应用汽车专用仪表,以及对汽车电气元件的原理、电路组成等能准确地把握。

7. 模拟法

有些故障属于偶发故障,比较难查找,因此,要进行发生条件模拟验证后再诊断故障。例如,车辆振动模拟、温度模拟(注意:不要将电气元件加热到60℃以上)、浸水模拟(注意:不得将水直接喷在电气元件上)、电负载模拟、冷起动或热起动模拟。

(四)汽车电气设备维修中常用的检测仪表和工具

1. 试灯

汽车检测试灯用于测量电路中是否存在电压。它没有内部电源,装有12V或24V灯泡。有些试灯内部装有发光二极管作为发光元件。试灯亦称无源试灯。试灯一头接地,另一头探针触到带电压的导体时,灯泡或发光二极管就会被点亮。试灯不能取代电压表。因为它只能显示是否有电压,不能显示电压的高低。

2. 跨接导线

跨接导线有时可作为故障诊断的辅助工具,可用于跨过某段被怀疑已断开的导线,而直接向某一部件供电的通路,也可用于不依赖于电路中的开关或导线而向电路加上电池电压。

注意:要定期用欧姆表对跨接导线本身进行导通性测试。跨接导线自身接头产生的电阻将影响故障诊断的正确性。

3. 数字万用表

当前轿车电控单元和电子控制元件越来越多,而汽车上的电控单元和电子元件不允许用低阻抗的指针万用表检测,因此,数字万用表在汽车电气维修中成为主要检测仪器。汽车数

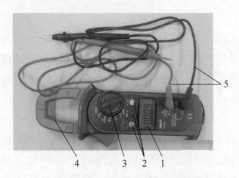

图 1-1 汽车用数字万用表(带电流测试功能)
1—数字及模拟量显示屏；2—功能按钮；
3—测试项目选择开关；4—霍尔式电流传感夹；
5—测量导线

字万用表种类繁多，功能不同。常见的数字万用表有不带电流测试功能和带电流测试功能两种。汽车用数字万用表（带电流测试功能）如图 1-1 所示。

数字万用表在许多方面都优于绝大多数型号的模拟表（指针万用表），其中最主要的方面是它更准确。大部分高质量的仪表是由表内以干电池为电源的内部电路提供已知数据。如果电池电力不足，将影响读数的精确度。大部分数字式仪表都有一个电池警告标志，用来显示电池的电位状况。

数字万用表除了能测量交、直流电压，交、直流电流及电阻外，还能测量电容量、频率、二极管正向压降，检查线路的通断。除以上测量功能外，数字万用表还有自动校零、自动显示极性、过载指示、读数保持、显示被测量单位的符号等功能。

三、项目实施

（一）常用检测仪表的使用

① 通过该项目的实施，应能够在汽车电气设备故障诊断中规范使用各种常用检测仪表和工具。

② 该项目应具备跨接导线、数字万用表等工具。

（二）实施步骤

数字万用表的使用：

根据数字万用表的功能说明进行检测。汽车用数字万用表的功能说明如图 1-2 所示。

（1）电压的测量

① 将万用表的测试导线按图 1-2 所示插入相应插孔（红表笔插入 V/Ω 插孔，黑表笔插入 COM 插孔）。

② 将万用表的功能选择开关置于电压测量挡位，并根据待测量电压的类型选择直流和交流位置（DC/AC 开关选择）。

③ 根据待测电压的大小选择量程（通过 RANGE 开关选择）。

④ 将万用表的测试导线接入待测电路，黑表笔接地，红表笔接信号线。

⑤ 闭合待测试电路，观察万用表显示区域的电压读数。

⑥ 按下 HOLD 按钮，锁定测量结果，并与标准值进行对比。

在测量高压（几百伏）时，应单手操作，即先把黑表笔固定在被测电路的公共端，再用一只手持红表笔去接触测试点，这样才比较安全。

（2）电阻的测量

① 将万用表的测试导线插入相应插孔（红表笔插入 V/Ω 插孔，黑表笔插入 COM 插孔）。

② 将万用表的功能选择开关置于电阻测量挡位，此时若不设置量程，万用表为自动量程状态。

③ 若需进行量程设置可按下 RANGE 控制键，进入手动量程设置模式，此后如再按下一次控制键，量程范围将再更换一次。若想返回自动量程，可按下该键，2s 后松开，即可返回。

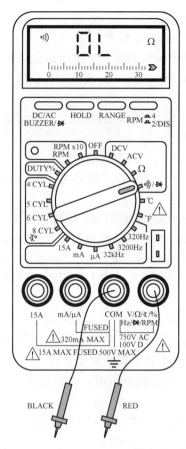

图 1-2 汽车用数字万用表的功能说明

④ 手动量程的选择范围：0～320Ω、0～3.2kΩ、0～32kΩ、0～320kΩ、0～3.2MΩ、0～32MΩ。

⑤ 将万用表的测试导线接入待测元件，黑表笔和红表笔分别连接待测元件的接线端子。

⑥ 观察万用表显示区域的数据显示。

⑦ 按下控制区域的 HOLD 按钮，锁定测量结果，与标准值进行对比。

严禁在被测线路带电的情况下测量电阻，也不允许用电阻挡测量电池的内阻。因为这相当于给数字万用表的电阻测量电路外加了一个电压，测量结果完全失去意义。而且，还有可能损坏仪表。

（3）电路通导性测试

① 将万用表的测试导线插入相应插孔（红表笔插入 V/Ω 插孔，黑表笔插入 COM 插孔）。

② 将万用表的功能选择开关置于电路导通/二极管测试挡位。

③ 将万用表的两测试导线接入被测试电路。

④ 若万用表的蜂鸣器发出报警声，表明所测电路没有断路情况。

（4）二极管的测量

注意：数字万用表红表笔是内部电池的正极，当使用其二极管挡位测量时，显示的数值表示的是二极管的正向压降值，单位是 mV。使用数字万用表测量时，质量良好的二极管正向压降一般为 500～700mV，反向电压为∞。

① 将万用表的测试导线插入相应插孔（红表笔插入 V/Ω 插孔，黑表笔插入 COM 插孔）。

② 将万用表的功能选择开关置于电路导通/二极管测试挡位。

③ 将万用表的两测试表笔接被测试二极管的 2 个管脚。

④ 将万用表的两测试表笔对调后再接被测试二极管的 2 个管脚。

⑤ 在③、④两种测试情况下，若一次测量的结果呈无值状态，另一次测量结果呈低电压状态，则表明二极管性能良好；若两次测量结果都呈低电压状态，表明二极管已击穿；若两次测量结果都呈无值状态，表明二极管已烧坏。

数字万用表属于精密电子仪表，如果使用不当，不但会引起测量失准，严重时还可造成仪表本身损坏。在使用中务必注意以下事项。

① 使用前，应仔细阅读数字万用表的说明书，了解其技术性能及特点。

② 保证数字万用表准确度的环境条件，应在清洁干燥、环境温度适宜、无外界强电磁场干扰、没有震动的条件下使用数字万用表。

③ 测量之前，需仔细检查表笔有无裂痕和引线的绝缘层是否损坏，以确保安全。

④ 尽管数字万用表内部电路有较完善的保护措施，还应避免出现误操作，例如，用电流挡去测电压，用电阻挡去测电压或电流，用电容挡去测带电的电容量，以免损坏仪表。

⑤ 测量时，假如事先无法估计被测电压（或电流）的大小，应先拨至最高量程试测一次，然后根据测试情况选择合理的量程。

⑥ 严禁在测量高电压（100V 以上）时，拨动量程开关，以免电弧烧毁触点。

⑦ 具有自动关机功能的数字万用表，在使用中如果出现 LCD 突然滑隐，不是故障现象，是仪表进入"休眠"状态（电源切断）。这只需重新起动，即可恢复正常。

⑧ 具有读数保持键（HOLD）的数字万用表，在作连续测量时，该键应置于"关断"位置。否则仪表不能正常采样，无法刷新显示数符。

⑨ 数字万用表常用的熔丝管有多种规格（如 0.2A、0.3A、0.5A、1A、2A），更换时必须选用与原规格相同的熔丝管。

⑩ 如果开机后 LCD 不显示任何数字，应首先检查是否未装电池或者电池已失效，还需检查电池引线有无断线。若显示电源低电压指示符，则应换用新电池。更换电池前，应把电源开关关闭。

四、知识与技能拓展

（一）汽车电气设备基础元件

1. 电路开关

汽车电路中，各用电设备都设有单独的控制开关，如灯光开关、灯光组合开关、雨刮器开关、转向信号灯开关、危急报警开关、倒车灯开关、制动灯开关、喇叭开关、空调开关等。开关是切断或接通电路的一种控制装置。其动作可以手控，也可以根据电路或车辆所处状况自控。开关分常开和常闭 2 种形式。常开是指开关在常态位置或静止位置时，电路是不通的；常闭是指开关在常态位置或静止位置时，电路是接通的。

开关在电路图中的表示方法有多种，常见的有结构图表示法、表格表示法和图形符号表示法等。下面以点火开关为例介绍电路开关的表示方法，如图 1-3 所示，点火开关的功能主要有锁住转向盘转轴（LOCK 挡）、接通仪表指示灯（ON 或 IG 挡）、起动发动机（ST 或 START 挡）、给附件供电（ACC 挡主要是收放机专用）、发动机预热（HEAT 挡）。其中起动、预热挡工作时消耗电流很大，开关不宜接通过久，所以这 2 个挡位在操作时必须用手克服弹簧力，扳住钥匙，一松手就弹回点火挡，不能自行定位，其他挡位均可自行定位。

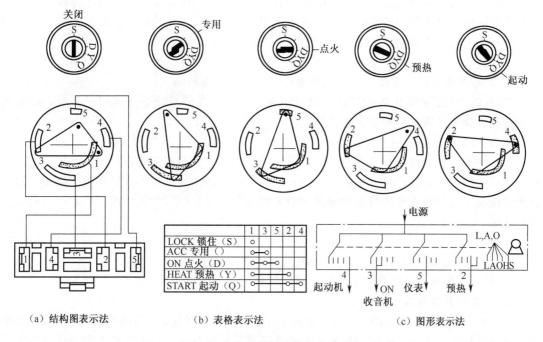

图 1-3 点火开关的结构及表示方法

2. 电路保护装置

当电路中的电流超过规定的电流时，汽车电路保护装置能够自动切断电路，从而保护电气设备和防止烧坏电路连接导线，并把故障限制在最小范围内。汽车上的电路保护装置主要有熔断器、易熔线、电路断路器和继电器。

（1）熔断器。俗称保险。熔断器是插接式装置，通过超过额定电流值就熔断（烧毁）的导体将两个端子连接。在将电路故障修复后必须更换熔断器。

有 3 种基本类型的熔断器：熔管式、缠丝式、插片式。熔断器的类型如图 1-4 所示。熔断器损坏后，可以直观地看到熔断丝断开，熔断器的检查如图 1-5 所示。插片式熔断器的应用最为广泛，并具有规定的安培值和颜色编码。熔断器一定标明额定安培值和电压值。熔断器外壳体上的 2 个小孔可以使修理工很方便地检查电压降、工作电压或通导性。

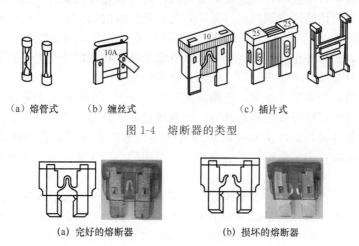

(a) 熔管式　　(b) 缠丝式　　(c) 插片式

图 1-4 熔断器的类型

(a) 完好的熔断器　　(b) 损坏的熔断器

图 1-5 熔断器的检查

熔断器的构造是当电流超过一定的程度后,金属线将熔断和烧毁,以将电路断开。电路断开后将使电路导线和部件免受过大电流的损害。熔断器按照承载安培值的能力分类。举例来说,一个10A的熔断器在电路电流超过10A至一定时间后将断开。

注意:

① 熔断丝熔断后,必须真正找到故障原因,彻底排除故障。

② 不要使用更高额定值的熔断器进行更换。一定要参阅维修手册和用户手册,以确认更换的电路保护装置负荷确切的规格规定。

③ 熔断器支架与熔断器接触不良会产生压降和发热现象,安装时要保证接触良好。

(2) 易熔线。有些车型装有易熔线。易熔线是一种大容量的熔断器,用于保护电源电路和大电流电路。易熔线直接安装在蓄电池正极位置。易熔线通常在不宜采用熔断器或电路断路器的情况下保护较大范围的车辆电路。若发生过载,易熔线较细的导线将熔断,以在发生损坏前断开电路。

注意:

① 绝对不允许换用比规定容量大的易熔线,更不允许用普通导线替代。

② 易熔线熔断,可能是主要电路短路,要仔细检查,彻底排除隐患。

③ 不能和其他导线搅在一起。

(3) 电路断路器。在电路中的作用是防止过载,通过断开电路和截断电流以防止导线和电气设备过热及由此造成的火灾等后果。电路断路器是机械装置,利用2种不同金属(双金属片)的热效应断开电路。如果额外的电流流过双金属片,双金属片弯曲,触点开路,阻止电流通过,当无电流时,双金属片冷却从而使电路重新闭合,电路断路器复位。电路断路器可以是一个单独插接的总成,或是安装在开关内或电刷支架上。若超出额定的电流值,该装置内的一组触点将瞬时断开电路。与熔断器不同,每次断开后,不必更换电路断路器。但是,在每次发生电路断开后,一定要查清造成电路过载或短路的原因并进行修理,否则,还将会造成电路损坏。

一般来说,电路断路器分为循环式和非循环式两种类型。

① 循环式电路断路器。循环式电路断路器配备一个由2种不同热膨胀系数的金属构成的双金属片。在受热后2种金属的膨胀率不同,当超过一定量的电流流过双金属片时,因为热量的积累,高膨胀率的金属将产生弯曲,并造成触点断开。因为断开电路时,没有电流流过,该金属将冷却并收缩,直到触点将电路再次接通。

在实际的运行中,触点断开的速度是很快的。若持续存在过载,电路断路器将反复循环(断开、闭合),直到该情况得到纠正。循环式电路断路器的结构如图1-6所示。

② 非循环式电路断路器。非循环式电路断路器采用由线圈缠绕的双金属片,即使在触点断开的情况下,该部件也保持为一个大电阻电流通路。在该电路的电源被断开以前,线圈所产生的热量使双金属片不能冷却至足以闭合触点的程度。

在断开电源后,双金属片冷却,电路恢复接通。对于非循环式电路断路器来说,一旦断路器断开电路,则必须断开该电路的电源,以重新设置断路器。非循环式电路断路器不能用于重要的电路,如前大灯,因为瞬间的短路将切断该电路的电压,直到断路器能够重新设置,这样便会造成在夜间如果突然失去前照灯的照明而产生灾难性的后果。非循环式电路断路器的结构如图1-7所示。

(4) 继电器。在汽车中,有许多地方应用了继电器,如燃油泵、喇叭、起动系统等。继电器是一个电气开关,其作用是用一个小电流控制一个大电流,从而可以减少控制开关的电流负荷,减少烧蚀现象的产生。继电器结构简图如图1-8所示,包括一个控制电路、一个电磁铁、一个电枢、一组触点等。

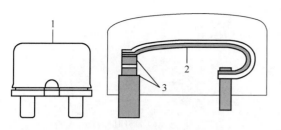
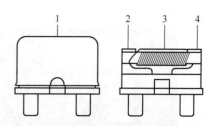

图 1-6　循环式电路断路器的结构
1—外形；2—双金属片；3—触点

图 1-7　非循环式电路断路器的结构
1—外形；2—触点；3—线圈；4—双金属臂

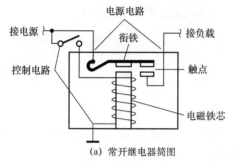
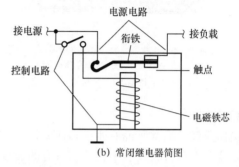

(a) 常开继电器简图　　　　　　(b) 常闭继电器简图

图 1-8　继电器结构简图

汽车上的继电器很多，常见的有 3 类，其动作状态如图 1-9 所示。第 1 类继电器平时触点是断开的，继电器动作后触点接通，第 2 类继电器平时触点是闭合的，继电器动作后触点断开，第 3 类继电器平时动断触点接通，动合触点断开，动作后变成相反状态。

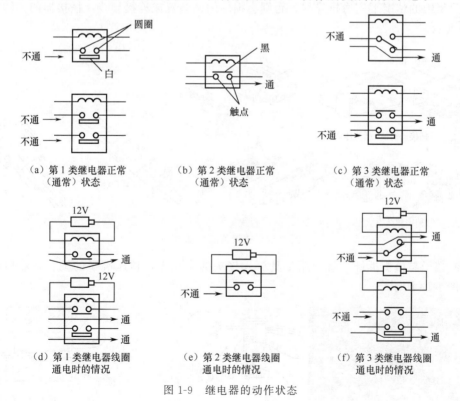

图 1-9　继电器的动作状态

集线盒中的继电器如图 1-10 所示。

图 1-10 集线盒中的继电器
1—继电器；2—保险丝

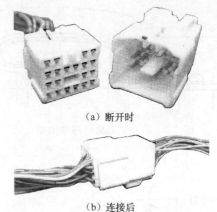

图 1-11 插接器

3. 插接器

接插器就是通常所说的插头和插座，用于导线与导线间或线束与线束间的连接。为了防止插接器在汽车行驶过程中脱开，所有的插接器均采用了闭锁装置。

（1）插接器的识别方法。插接器如图 1-11 所示。

（2）插接器的连接方法。插接器接合时，应把插接器的导向槽重叠在一起，使插头和插座对准，然后平行插入即可十分牢固地连接在一起。

（3）插接器的拆卸方法。要拆开插接器，首先要解除闭锁，然后把插接器拉开，不允许在未解除闭锁的情况下用力拉导线，否则会损坏闭锁装置或连接导线。插接器的拆卸方法如图 1-12 所示。

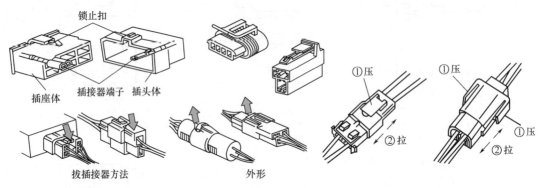

图 1-12 插接器的拆卸方法

（4）端子与接头拆卸。将专用工具深入接头的小孔中，顶压端子的锁舌，然后移动接头，如图 1-13 所示。

  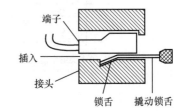

图 1-13 端子与接头拆卸

注意：用专用工具压锁舌时，用力要适当，不能用力太大，否则会损坏锁舌和接头。如果用工具压住锁舌后仍然不能移动端子，可能是压的地方不对或没有压住锁舌，而不是用力不够。如果位置正确，轻轻用力即可压住锁舌。通过维修手册可以很容易地确定锁舌的位置。另外有些插接件的背面有防水胶塞，安装时要保证防水胶塞未脱出插接件。

4. 导线

汽车用导线有低压导线和高压导线 2 种，均采用铜质多芯软线。

（1）低压导线。

① 导线截面积。导线截面积主要根据其工作电流选择，但对于一些工作电流较小的电气系统，为保证机械强度，导线截面积不小于 $0.5mm^2$。各种低压导线的标称截面积所允许的负载电流值如表 1-1 所示。

表 1-1 低压导线的标称截面积所允许的负载电流值

导线截面积/mm^2	1.0	1.5	2.5	3.0	4.0	6.0	10	13
允许载流值/A	11	14	20	22	25	35	50	60

汽车 12V 电气系统主要线路导线标称截面积如表 1-2 所示。

表 1-2 汽车 12V 电气系统主要线路导线标称截面积

用途	标称截面积/mm^2	用途	标称截面积/mm^2
后灯、顶灯、指示灯、牌照灯、仪表、刮水器等	0.5	其他 5A 以上的电路	1.5～4.0
转向灯、制动灯、停车灯、分电器	0.8	电热塞电路	4.0～6.0
前照灯的近光、电喇叭（3A 以下）	1.0	电源电路	6.0～25
前照灯的远光、电喇叭（3A 以上）	1.5	起动电路	16～95

② 导线颜色。各国汽车厂商在电路图上多以字母（英文字母）表示导线颜色及条纹颜色。部分汽车制造厂商导线颜色的代号如表 1-3 所示。

表 1-3 汽车导线颜色代号

颜色		车型							
		丰田	本田	通用	福特	克莱斯勒	宝马	奔驰	三菱
黑色	Black	B	BLK	BLK	BK	BK	BK	SW	B
棕色	Brown	BR	BRN	BRN	BR	BR	BR	BR	BR
红色	Red	R	RED	RED	R	RD	RD	RT	R
黄色	Yellow	Y	YEL	YEL	Y	YL	YL	GE	Y
绿色	Green	G	GRN	GRN	GN		GN	GN	G
蓝色	Blue	L	BLU	BLU	BL		BU	BL	L
紫罗兰色	Violet	V			VT		VI	VI	V
灰色	Grey	GR	GRY	GRY	GY	GY	GY	GR	GR
白色	White	W	WHT	WLLT	W	WT	WT	WS	W
粉红色	Pink	P	PNK	PNK	PK	PK	PK		P
橙色	Orange	O	ORN	ORN	O	OR	OR		O

续表

颜色		车型							
		丰田	本田	通用	福特	克莱斯勒	宝马	奔驰	三菱
褐色	Tan			TAN	T	TN	TN		
本色	Natural				N				
紫红色	Purple			PPL	P				
深蓝色	Dark Blue			DKBLU		DB			
深绿色	Dark Green			DKGRN		DG			
浅蓝色	Light Blue			LTBLU		LB		SB	
浅绿色	Light Green			LTGRN		LG		LG	
透明色	Clear			CLR					
象牙色	Lvorv							EI	
玫瑰色	Rose							RS	

注:"奔驰"一栏中的代码为奔驰、大众等德国车系导线颜色代码。

导线颜色要易于区别,导线上采用条纹标志要对比强烈,双色线的主色所占比例大些,辅色所占比例小些,主色条纹与辅色条纹沿圆周表面比例为 3:1～5:1。双色线标注中第一色为主色,第二色为辅色,我国规定汽车导线颜色的选用程序如表 1-4 所示。

表 1-4　汽车导线颜色的选用程序

选用程序	1	2	3	4	5	6
导线颜色	B	BW	BY	BR		
	W	WR	WB	WBi	WY	WG
	R	RW	RB	RY	RG	RBi
	G	GW	GR	GY	GB	GBi
	Y	YR	YB	YG	YBi	YW
	Br	BrW	BrR	BrY	BrB	
	Bi	BiW	BiR	BiY	BiB	BiO
	Gr	GR	GrY	GrBi	GrB	GrO

③ 线束。汽车用导线除蓄电池导线、高压线和起动机导线外,均用绝缘材料缠绕包扎成束,避免水、油的浸蚀和磨损。线束布线过程中不允许拉得太紧,线束穿过洞口或锐角处应有套管保护,线束位置确定后,应用卡簧或绊钉固定。汽车线束如图 1-14 所示。

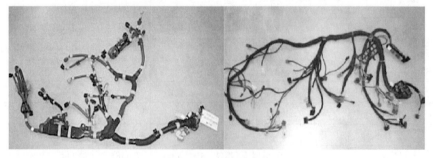

图 1-14　汽车线束

（2）高压导线。在汽车点火线圈至火花塞之间的电路使用高压导线，高压导线分为普通铜芯高压导线和高压阻尼点火导线。带阻尼的高压导线可抑制和衰减点火系统产生的高频电磁波，降低对电控装置和无线设备的干扰。

（二）汽车电路常用电子元器件

1. 电阻

当电路中不需要最大电流或电压时，可利用电阻来限制电流。电阻产生电压降并将电能转化成热能。电阻将电能转化为热能的功能在汽车上的许多地方都有应用，如后窗除霜装置、加热器和点烟器等。灯泡中的灯丝也会产生热，但它主要起照明作用。

2. 电容

电容可以吸收和储存电荷。电容是由2个或多个导体板，并在导体之间填加非导电性介质制成。电容具有通交流阻直流的功能，其所产生的微小的直流电流有助于吸收峰值电压，防止击穿断开的触点。若用于音响设备，电容也可以起到"噪声"过滤器的作用。电容的单位为法拉（F）。

3. 二极管

在电路中，二极管具有单向导电性，只允许电流从一个方向流向另一个方向，而阻止电流向相反方向的流向。二极管可用来制作逻辑电路。这种电路只有在某些条件满足一定次序时才能起作用。例如，点火开关钥匙警告蜂鸣器的电路，只有在点火开关在关闭（OFF）位置而车门打开的情况下才能被接通。

在汽车上二极管的种类很多，主要用于以下方面：整流——将交流变为直流、电压调节控制能够造成固体电路损坏的电压峰值和波动、仪表板指示灯等。

4. 三极管

三极管又称为晶体管。三极管的3个极分别是基极、集电极和发射极。将一个微小的电流或电压施加在基极上，就可以控制流经其他两极较大的电流，三极管可以当成放大器和开关来使用。

小 结

（1）汽车电气设备包括电源系统、用电设备和配电装置，汽车电气设备的特点是低压、直流、单线制、负极搭铁、2个电源和用电设备并联。

（2）汽车电气和电路故障的基本诊断方法有直观法、试灯法、跨接法、断路法、替换法、检测法和模拟法。

（3）为保证检测结果的正确，必须按规范要求正确使用通导性测试笔、试灯、跨接导线、数字万用表等汽车电气设备故障诊断的常用工具。

习题及思考

（1）汽车电气设备由哪些系统组成？

（2）汽车电气设备具有哪些特点？

（3）汽车电气设备维修中常用的检测仪表和工具有哪些？

（4）如何正确使用试灯？

（5）如何正确使用数字万用表？

项目二

蓄电池的检测与维护

一、情境引入

一辆一汽大众速腾轿车,将点火开关置于起动位置时,听到起动机运转时"哒哒"的声音,汽车仪表各指示灯在起动的瞬间连续闪烁,无法起动车辆。经检修为蓄电池电量不足。这个事例反映了汽车电源之一的蓄电池在汽车中的重要性。

二、相关知识

(一)蓄电池的作用及类型

1. 蓄电池的作用

蓄电池(俗称电瓶)作为汽车的电源之一,其作用主要是向起动机提供足够的电能以起动发动机。作为可逆直流电源,蓄电池既能储存电能,还能为车上的电气设备如驻车灯、收音机、点烟器、报警系统等提供电能。同时,由于蓄电池在电系中犹如一个低内阻、大电荷容量的容器、滤波器,在充电系统正常工作时,它可以吸收和抑制交流发电机可能出现的过电压波动,起到保护电路的作用。

2. 蓄电池的类型

蓄电池的种类很多。目前铅酸蓄电池因技术成熟、价格便宜、结构简单、起动性好,在汽车上得到广泛应用。铅酸蓄电池的电解液为稀硫酸,极板的活性物质主要成分为铅。铅酸蓄电池常见的类型有普通蓄电池、免维护蓄电池、玻璃纤维蓄电池、胶体蓄电池等。在这里所说的蓄电池都是指铅酸蓄电池。

(二)蓄电池的安装位置

蓄电池在车上的安装位置要考虑汽车部件的重量分布,还要考虑便于拆卸、防止脏污、环境温度、减震性,以及充电过程产生的有害气体等多方面的因素。上述因素通常会因为车型、用途、工作温度等的不同而不同。极端的温度条件可能需要为蓄电池加装加热器或冷却风扇。

一般来说,轿车的蓄电池多安装在发动机舱内或风挡玻璃前的流水槽内,也有的安装在行李箱侧壁或者备胎井内,还有少数蓄电池安装在乘员舱内的座椅下面。

(三)蓄电池的结构

一个单格铅酸蓄电池可以由一对正极板、负极板插入稀硫酸构成,通常设计其标称电压为2V。额定电压为12V的蓄电池,是由6个2V的单格铅酸蓄电池通过铅联条串联而成,

每个单格铅酸蓄电池由间壁相互隔开。整个铅酸蓄电池由极板、电解液、隔板、壳体等组成。蓄电池的结构如图 2-1 所示。

（1）极板。极板是蓄电池的核心部件，对蓄电池的性能有最直接的影响。极板由活性物质和栅架构成，活性物质附着在栅架上。正极板上的活性物质是深棕色二氧化铅（PbO_2），负极板上的活性物质是青灰色海绵状铅（Pb），其结构如图 2-2 所示。电能和化学能的相互转化依靠极板的活性物质和电解液中的 H_2SO_4 的化学反应来实现。

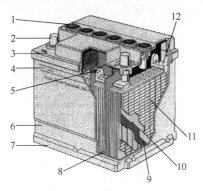 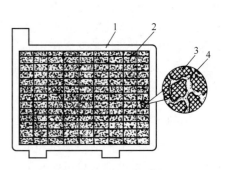

图 2-1 蓄电池的结构
1—密封塞；2—接线柱；3—密封盖；4—液面标记；
5—直接连接器；6—外壳；7—底板密封条；8—蓄电池隔板；
9—正极板；10—塑料隔板；11—负极；12—电池跨接件

图 2-2 极板的结构
1—栅架；2—活性物质；
3—活性物质颗粒；4—孔隙

栅架是极板的骨架，主要成分是铅。为了减缓栅架腐蚀、提高极板机械强度、减少蓄电池失水量和自放电、延长蓄电池使用寿命，蓄电池栅架多采用铅-锑合金、铅-锑-砷合金、铅-钙合金、铅-钙-镍-铬合金或银-铅-钙合金等。

极板的厚度影响着蓄电池的性能和使用寿命，在保证机械强度的情况下采用薄型极板可以提高蓄电池的性能。为了提高放电电流，一般将多片同极性的极板用联条连成极板组，正极板组与负极板组的极板相互交叉嵌合。一般负极板组的极板比正极板组的极板多一片，正极板夹在负极板间，可减少正极板活性物质脱落。其结构如图 2-3 所示。

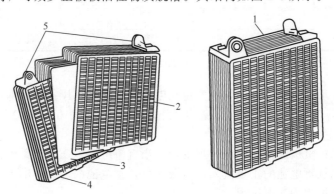

图 2-3 极板组的结构
1—极板组总成；2—负极板；3—隔板；4—正极板；5—铅联条

（2）隔板。隔板处于正负极板之间，除了要具有好的绝缘性能以防止极板短路外，还要有良好的通透性，以便电解液能自由渗透，同时还应具有耐酸和抗氧化性能。因此，隔板常用微孔橡胶、微孔塑料、玻璃纤维等材料制成。新型蓄电池多采用袋式微孔塑料隔板，将正

极板包裹，防止正极板活性物质脱落。

（3）电解液。电解液是由密度为 $1.84g/cm^3$ 的纯硫酸与蒸馏水按一定比例配制而成的稀硫酸溶液，其作用是参与化学反应，进行能量转化。电解液的密度对蓄电池性能的影响较大，密度一般为 $1.24\sim1.31g/cm^3$。另外，电解液的纯度也是影响蓄电池性能和使用寿命的重要因素。必须用纯净的专用硫酸和蒸馏水配制电解液。

（4）壳体及其他。蓄电池的壳体是用来盛放极板和电解液的容器，应耐酸、耐热、抗震，所以多采用硬橡胶或聚丙烯塑料制成由间壁分隔成多个单格容器的整体式结构。壳体上部使用相同材料的密封盖，电池盖上设有对应于每个单格电池的加液孔，用于添加电解液或补充蒸馏水。加液孔上旋有加液孔盖，以防止电解液溅出。加液孔盖上制有微型通气孔，可以排出蓄电池内部化学反应产生的气体。新型蓄电池加液孔的通气孔上安装了过滤器，以避免水蒸气逸出，减少水的消耗。蓄电池壳体的顶部或侧面有向外部提供电气连接的两个正、负极柱，旁边有（＋）、（－）标记，一般正极柱比负极柱粗。

（四）蓄电池的工作原理

蓄电池极板上的活性物质和电解液之间发生电化学反应是可逆的，所以蓄电池是一个可逆电源。铅酸蓄电池充放电时总的电化学反应方程式如下。

$$PbO_2 + Pb + 2H_2SO_4 \underset{充电}{\overset{放电}{\rightleftharpoons}} 2PbSO_4 + 2H_2O$$

蓄电池放电时，正负极板上的 PbO_2 和 Pb 与 H_2SO_4 转变为硫酸铅（$PbSO_4$），沉附在正、负极板上，极板上的活性物质减少；电解液中 H_2SO_4 不断减少，H_2O 增多，电解液密度下降；蓄电池电压降低，内阻增大，容量减小；蓄电池内部的化学能转化为电能供给用电设备。

蓄电池放电终了的特征如下。

① 单格电池电压降到放电终止电压。

② 电解液密度降到最小许可值。放电终止电压与放电电流的大小有关，见表 2-1，放电电流越大，允许的放电时间就越短，放电终止电压也就越低。

表 2-1 单格蓄电池放电电压

放电电流/A	$0.05C_{20}$	$0.1C_{20}$	$0.25C_{20}$	C_{20}	$3C_{20}$
放电时间	20h	10h	3h	25min	5min
单格电池终止电压/V	1.75	1.70	1.65	1.55	1.50

注：C_{20} 为蓄电池的额定容量。

蓄电池放电终了以后继续放电，称为过放电。此时电池电压急剧下降，同时生成不易还原的粗结晶 $PbSO_4$，造成极板硫化，蓄电池容量下降，使用寿命缩短，因此，应避免过放电。

若将直流电源正负极连接蓄电池的正负极，当直流电源电压高于蓄电池电压时，在电源力的作用下，电流从蓄电池的正极流入，负极流出，蓄电池内部发生的电化学反应将电能转化为化学能，这个过程为充电过程。

蓄电池充电时在外电力的作用下极板上的 $PbSO_4$ 转变为 PbO_2 和 Pb，极板上的活性物质增多，电解液中 H_2SO_4 不断增多，H_2O 减少，电解液密度上升；蓄电池电压升高，内阻减小，容量增大。

蓄电池充电终了以后继续充电，称为过充电，此时 $PbSO_4$ 已基本全部转化为 PbO_2 和 Pb，过剩的充电电流会将水电解生成 O_2 和 H_2 逸出。因此，蓄电池应避免长时间过充电并

且需要定期补充蒸馏水。

由于充放电过程中电解液密度和蓄电池端电压发生变化，在使用中可以通过测量电解液密度和电池端电压判断充/放电程度。

（五）蓄电池的技术参数

1. 额定电压

蓄电池的额定电压有 6V 和 12V 两种。轿车一般用额定电压为 12V 的蓄电池，电压等级为 24V 的载重卡车可以将 2 块 12V 蓄电池串联使用。

蓄电池在无充/放电，且内部电解质的运动处于平衡状态时的电动势称为静止电动势。静止电动势大小与电解液的密度和温度有关，一定程度上能够反映蓄电池的荷电状况。蓄电池工作时，电解液密度总是在 $1.12\sim1.30g/m^3$ 之间变化。选择蓄电池时，一定要选择额定电压和车上电气系统电压等级一致的蓄电池。

2. 额定容量

蓄电池的容量是蓄电池的主要性能参数，标志着蓄电池的对外供电能力。蓄电池的容量是指在放电允许的范围内输出的电量，与放电电流和电解液的温度有关。容量等于放电电流与放电时间的乘积。

额定容量是检验蓄电池质量的重要指标之一。根据规定，将充足电的新蓄电池，在电解液密度（25℃）为（1.28±0.01）g/cm^3，初始温度为（25±5）℃的条件下，以 20h 放电率的放电电流（即 C/20A），连续放电至蓄电池端电压为 10.5V 时输出的电量，输出的电量称为蓄电池的额定容量，用 C_{20} 表示，单位为 Ah。C_{20}=放电电流(A)×放电时间(h)。有的国外蓄电池标号上出现 20HR，指的是 20h 放电率，H 是 Hour（小时），R 是 Rate（比率）。例如，105Ah 充足电的蓄电池以 5.25A 电流放电至 10.5V，放电时间超过或等于 20h 则合格。

选择合适型号的蓄电池很重要，如果选择容量较大的蓄电池，会导致充电不足，而容量较小的蓄电池，容易发生过度充放电循环，会导致蓄电池使用寿命较短。

3. 储备容量

储备容量（Reserve Capacity，RC）表示在汽车充电系统失效时，蓄电池能为照明和点火系统等用电设备提供 25A 恒流的能力。根据规定，蓄电池在（25±2）℃的条件下，以 25A 的额定电流恒流放电至单格终止电压 1.75V（整个电池终止电压为 10.5V）时的放电持续时间，称为蓄电池的储备容量。单位为 min。

4. 冷起动电流

通常规定在 0℉（-18℃）时，蓄电池 30s 持续放电至端电压为 7.2V 时所能提供的电流为冷起动电流（Cold Cranking Amperage，CCA），是蓄电池对于低温起动性能的表现。蓄电池制造时根据使用地区环境温度不同，有提高耐热性或者提高耐寒性的设计，一般为热带地区设计的蓄电池 CCA 值低，为寒冷地区设计的蓄电池 CCA 值高。为寒冷地区设计的蓄电池在热带使用寿命肯定会缩短。选择蓄电池要根据当地温度去选 CCA 值适当的蓄电池，如当地气温高就要用 CCA 值低的产品，因为蓄电池对于气温很敏感，一般以气温 25℃为基准，气温每上升 10℃，寿命就会缩短一半。

（六）蓄电池的型号

有关蓄电池型号的规定，有多个标准。

虽然不同标准的规定方法不同，但其主要内容都包含蓄池额定电压、额定容量、冷起动

电流及类型、储备容量等。如有的蓄电池上面写着 CCA：700　CA：875　RC：106，表示冷起动电流 700A，起动电流 875A，储备容量 106min；也有一些蓄电池上同时标注 DIN 或 EN 标准型号，如：12 V 180 Ah 540 A（EN），表示额定电压 12V，额定容量 180Ah，冷起动电流 540A。

① 日本工业标准（JIS）：蓄电池型号为 34B19L，其含义如下。

34——蓄电池的性能，指示蓄电池中可以存储的电量（蓄电池容量）。数目越大，蓄电池可以存储的电量就越大。可通过表 2-2 查询。

$$蓄电池容量(Ah)=放电安培数×放电时间长度$$

表 2-2　蓄电池 ID 代码

蓄电池 ID 代码	蓄电池的容量(Ah)(5h 充电率)	蓄电池 ID 代码	蓄电池的容量(Ah)(5h 充电率)
34B19R/L	27	80B26R/L	55
46B24R/L	36	95B31R/L	64
55B23R/L	48		

B——蓄电池的宽度和高度，蓄电池的宽度和高度组合是由 8 个字母中的一个表示的（A 到 H）。字符越接近 H，表示电池的宽度和高度越大，如图 2-4 所示。

19——蓄电池的长，约为 19cm。

L——负极端子的位置，即正确安装蓄电池时的负极端子的位置。右侧为 R，左侧为 L。（注意靠近端子的一侧）

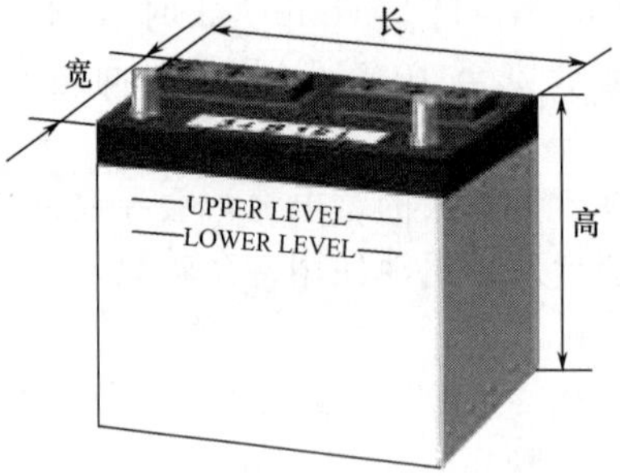

	宽/mm	高/mm
A	162	127
B	203	127 或 129
C	207	135
D	204	173
E	213	176
F	213	182
G	213	222
H	220	278

图 2-4　蓄电池的高度和宽度

② 欧洲（EN）标准：蓄电池型号为 544　059　036，其含义如下。

5——电压，1～4 表示蓄电池电压为 6V，5～7 表示蓄电池电压为 12V。

44——蓄电池的额定容量。表示以 20h 连续放电的额定容量，如蓄电池容量大于 100Ah，则首字母加 1。

059——顺序号。

036——根据 EN 标准的 1/10 冷起动测试电流，036 表示该电流为 360A。

虽然不同厂家生产的蓄电池的型号适用的标准不同，但是只要关键技术参数对照，类型和尺寸合适，是可以互相替代使用的。

（七）免维护蓄电池

免维护蓄电池的正极板栅架采用铅-钙合金或铅-锑合金，负极板栅架采用铅-钙合金，提高了氧在正极、氢在负极的析出电位，使蓄电池在使用时失水量少，在规定寿命期内不必补

充蒸馏水；免维护蓄电池一般采用超细玻璃纤维棉制作隔板或者将正极板放在袋式隔板内，有了这些结构上的改进，可以保证蓄电池自放电少，荷电保持能力增强和极板寿命延长。

免维护蓄电池通常采用极柱外露的全封闭式外壳，能够防止杂质侵入和水分蒸发。免维护蓄电池上部盖板内设有迷宫式液气分离结构且含有催化剂钯的中央通气孔和被称为"Fritte"的复燃（逆弧）保护装置。前者不但能够将充电过程中产生的水蒸气和硫酸蒸气冷却并将其收集回流，还能借助钯的催化作用将氢气和氧气还原成水回流，避免电解液的损失；后者是一个直径约为15mm，厚度为2mm的圆形玻璃纤维垫，可防止外来火花的侵入。

免维护蓄电池充电时依然会有少量气体从盖上的中央通气孔溢出，所以免维护蓄电池一般都接有通气软管将这些气体排出车外。在维修操作中注意不要拔下或阻塞该软管，以保证蓄电池的正常排气。

免维护蓄电池一般都内置温度补偿式密度计，俗称电眼，也有的叫蓄电池状态指示器。电眼的结构有两种，一种是单色小球，另一种是双色小球。单色小球的电眼是利用绿色的浮子球在不同密度的电解液中沉、浮的状态，再通过显色杆折射放大后在观察窗中显示出对应颜色的环状图形来判断蓄电池的荷电状态的。通过观察电眼的观察窗颜色可以判断蓄电池的技术状况，一般绿色表示电量充足；深绿色或黑色表示电量不足，需进行补充充电；无色或淡黄色表示电解液不足，应报废或更换。单色小球电眼结构如图2-5所示。

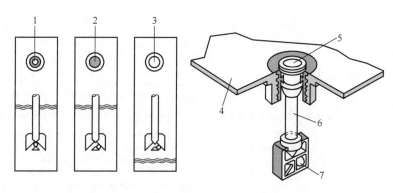

图2-5 单色小球电眼结构

1—绿色（充电程度为65%或更高）；2—黑色（充电程度低于65%）；3—无色或黄色（蓄电池有故障）；
4—蓄电池盖；5—观察窗；6—光学的荷电状况指示器；7—绿色浮子球

双色小球电眼结构如图2-6所示。这种蓄电池电眼内装有红色和蓝色两种小球，同样也是利用两种颜色的浮子球在不同密度的电解液中沉、浮的状态，再通过显色杆折射放大后在观察窗中显示出对应颜色的环状图形来判断蓄电池的荷电状态的。

（八）蓄电池的常见故障及排除

蓄电池常见的故障可分为外部故障和内部故障。外部故障明显，一般直观可以看到。外部故障有外壳裂纹、封胶干裂、极柱腐蚀或松动等。内部故障无法直观看到，在使用中可发现异常。内部故障主要有极板硫化、极板短路、自放电等。常见内部故障的故障特征、故障原因和排除方法见表2-3。

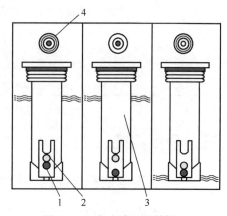

图2-6 双色小球电眼结构

1—蓝色小球；2—红色小球；
3—显色杆；4—观察窗

表 2-3 常见内部故障的故障特征、故障原因和排除方法

名称	项目	说明
极板硫化	故障特征	极板上生成难溶解的白色粗结晶硫酸铅,在正常充电时不能转化为活性物质。产生故障的蓄电池在放电时,电压急剧降低,过早降至终止电压,电池容量降低;电解液密度低于正常数值。蓄电池在充电时,单格电压上升过快,电解液温度迅速升高,但密度增加缓慢,过早产生气泡,甚至充电时就有气泡
	故障原因	①长期充电不足或放电后没有及时充电,导致极板上的硫酸铅有一部分溶解于电解液中。环境温度越高,硫酸铅溶解度越大,当环境温度降低时,溶解度减小,溶解的硫酸铅就会析出。由于蓄电池工作时温度变化,因此,析出硫酸铅在极板上再次结晶析出,形成硫化。不能将半放电的蓄电池长期搁置,尤其要注意给蓄电池定期补充充电,使之保持完全充电状态。②电解液液面过低,使极板上部与空气接触而被氧化,在行车中,电解液上下波动与极板氧化部分接触,会生成大晶粒硫酸铅硬化层,使极板上部硫化,因此,要定期检查电解液面高度和密度,发现液面降低应及时添加蒸馏水。③长期过量放电或小电流深度放电,使极板深处活性物质的孔隙内生成硫酸铅。不能让蓄电池过度放电,每次接通起动机时间不应超过 5s,避免低温大电流放电。④新蓄电池初充电不彻底,活性物质未得到充分还原。⑤电解液密度过高、成分不纯
	排除方法	轻度硫化的蓄电池,可用小电流充电和换加蒸馏水的方法予以排除;硫化较严重者采用去硫化充电方法消除硫化
活性物质脱落	故障特征	正极活性物质二氧化铅脱落,充电时从加液孔中可看到有褐色物质,电解液浑浊,会造成蓄电池容量减小
	故障原因	①蓄电池充电电流过大,电解液温度过高,使活性物质膨胀、松软而易于脱落。②蓄电池经常过充电,极板孔隙中逸出大量气体,在极板孔隙中造成压力,而使活性物质脱落。③蓄电池经常低温大电流放电使极板弯曲变形,导致活性物质脱落。④汽车行驶中的颠簸振动,这在汽车行驶过程中是不可避免的
	排除方法	若沉积物较少时,可清除后继续使用;若沉积物较多时,应更换新极板和电解液
极板短路	故障特征	蓄电池正、负极板直接接触或被其他导电物质搭接称为极板短路。此故障的现象表现为蓄电池充电时端电压回升相对缓慢,若用蓄电池放电测试端电压时,电压很低且会迅速下降为零。电解液温度迅速升高,相对密度上升很慢,充电末期气泡很少
	故障原因	①隔板损坏使正、负极板直接接触;②活性物质沉积过多,会将正、负极板连通;③极板组弯曲,铅蓄电池过量放电,或者极板活性物质脱落较多,或者蓄电池中含有杂质;④导电物体落入电解液内
	排除方法	出现极板短路时,必须将蓄电池拆开检查,找出出现极板短路的原因。或者更换破损的隔板,或消除沉积的活性物质,或校正或更换弯曲的极板组等
自放电	故障特征	蓄电池在开路搁置状态时,其容量自然损耗的现象称为自放电。一般情况下,维护良好、充足电的蓄电池在 20~30℃的环境中搁置 28 天,其容量损失超过 20%,称为自放电过大
	故障原因	①电解液不纯,杂质与极板之间及沉附于极板上的不同杂质之间形成电位差,通过电解液产生局部放电。②蓄电池长期存放,硫酸下沉,使极板上、下部产生电位差引起自放电。③蓄电池溢出的电解液堆积在电池盖的表面,使正、负极柱连通。④蓄电池活性物质脱落,下部沉积物过多使极板短路
	排除方法	应将蓄电池完全放电,倒出电解液,用蒸馏水进行清洗,再加入新的电解液,充足电后即可使用

三、项目实施

(一)蓄电池安全使用、检查维护、充电与检测

① 通过该项目的实施,应该能够对蓄电池进行安全、正确地使用,并掌握蓄电池检查和维护的方法和步骤。

② 该项目应具备常见类型蓄电池和万用表、高率放电计、充电机等检测与维护设备。

（二）实施步骤

1. 蓄电池安全、正确使用及操作的注意事项

① 有关蓄电池的警告说明和安全规程。由于蓄电池内部有酸液，充电时还会放出可燃气体，所以使用蓄电池要注意安全。一般蓄电池上标有安全警告图标，如图 2-7 所示，应按要求使用。

② 连接或断开蓄电池电缆、蓄电池充电机或跨接电缆时，点火开关必须处于 OFF（关闭）或 LOCK（锁止）位置，并且所有电气负载必须为 OFF（关闭），除非操作程序中另有说明，否则会损坏车辆上的电子设备。

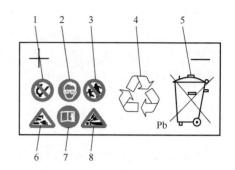

图 2-7　蓄电池警告图标
1—禁止明火；2—戴防护眼镜；3—儿童禁止接触；
4—可回收处理；5—不可作为垃圾丢弃；
6—腐蚀危险；7—参阅说明书；8—爆炸危险

③ 蓄电池电极短路产生的电流强度足以导致烧伤，所以要防止金属工具搭铁，造成蓄电池短路。

④ 避免过度的充放电循环和长时间放电。这对极板的活性物质有非常大的损害，会大大缩短蓄电池使用寿命。

⑤ 蓄电池极柱上不允许涂抹油脂，按规定扭矩拧紧蓄电池极柱螺栓，不能过度施力。

⑥ 蓄电池搭铁极性必须与发电机一致，不得接错。

⑦ 断开蓄电池接线时，应先断负极后断正极，装复时按相反顺序。

⑧ 对于带有中央排气软管的蓄电池，软管必须一直连接在蓄电池上，并保持软管畅通。

⑨ 蓄电池的大电流放电、深度充/放电和长期亏电闲置是最影响蓄电池寿命的负面因素，所以使用中应尽量避免。

2. 蓄电池的检查和维护

安装前，应检查待用蓄电池型号是否和本车型相符，电解液密度和高度是否符合规定。

保持蓄电池外表面的清洁干燥，电解液泄漏会在极柱上产生白色的硫酸铅和黄色的硫酸铁糊状物质，这些物质都有较强的腐蚀性。

及时清除极柱和电缆卡子上的氧化物。

① 极柱卡子应按规定力矩紧固，保证与极柱之间接触良好。

② 保持加液孔盖上通气孔的畅通，定期疏通。

③ 蓄电池充电时应打开加液孔盖，使气体顺利逸出，以免发生事故。

④ 定期检查并调整电解液液面高度，液面不足时，应补加蒸馏水。

⑤ 汽车每行驶 1000km 或夏季行驶 5~6 天，冬季行驶 10~15 天，应检查蓄电池的放电程度，当冬季放电超过 25%，夏季放电超过 50% 时，应及时将蓄电池从车上拆下进行补充充电。

3. 蓄电池的充电

（1）充电方法。蓄电池充电的方法有恒压充电、恒流充电和快速充电 3 种。

在汽车上，发电机对蓄电池的充电就是恒压充电。恒压充电时，充电初期电流较大，4~5h 即可达到额定容量的 90%~95%，随着蓄电池电动势的增加，充电电流逐渐减小为零。因为充电时间较短，所以不需要调整充电电流，适用于补充充电，一般单格电池充电电压为 2.5V，12V 蓄电池的充电电压为（14.8±0.05）V。

恒流充电的充电电流保持恒定。恒流充电时，随着蓄电池电动势的增加，应逐步提高充电电压。为缩短充电时间，通常将充电过程分为 2 个阶段，第 1 阶段采用较大的充电电流，

使蓄电池的容量迅速恢复。当单格电池电压达到 2.4V，开始电解水产生气泡时，转入第 2 阶段，将充电电流减小一半，直到完全充足电为止。充电电流的大小应按蓄电池容量选择，充电电流过大，会降低蓄电池的性能；充电电流过小，会使充电时间过长。

快速充电就是采用专门的快速充电机进行充电，补充充电只需 0.5~1.5h，大大缩短了充电时间，提高了充电效率，缺点是不能将蓄电池完全充足电，影响蓄电池的寿命。快速充电适用于电池集中、充电频繁、要求应急的场合。目前常用的快速充电方法有脉冲快速充电和大电流递减充电。

（2）蓄电池的充电工艺。蓄电池一般应在 5~35℃ 范围内进行充电，低于 5℃ 或高于 35℃ 都会降低寿命。充电的设定电压应在指定范围内，如超出指定范围将造成蓄电池损坏、容量降低、寿命缩短。

电池在存放、运输、安装过程中，会因自放电而失去部分容量。因此，在安装后、投入使用前，应根据电池的开路电压判断电池的剩余容量，然后采用不同的方法对蓄电池进行补充充电。对备用搁置的蓄电池，每 3 个月应进行一次补充充电。另外在汽车正常使用过程中，由于使用不当或充电系统出现故障造成的蓄电池电量不足也称为补充充电。充电时间取决于该车蓄电池缺失电量的多少。

4. 蓄电池的技术状态检测

（1）检测蓄电池电解液液面高度。检测液面高度判断电解液量是否充足。蓄电池电解液液面应高于隔板上沿 10~15mm。对于外壳有高度指示标线蓄电池，可外部观察，正常液面高度应介于两线之间。液面过低时应补充蒸馏水。

对于不透明外壳的全封闭免维护蓄电池则不能也无需进行电解液液面高度的测量。

（2）检测蓄电池电解液密度。检测电解液密度可以用来判断蓄电池的放电程度。电解液密度可用专用的吸式密度计测量。测量蓄电池电解液密度时，蓄电池应处于稳定状态。蓄电池充、放电或加注蒸馏水后，应静置 0.5h 后再测量。

对于不透明外壳的全封闭免维护蓄电池则无需进行电解液密度的测量。

电解液密度还可用专用的冰点测试仪测量，YDT-4T 冰点测试仪及其构造如图 2-8 所示。

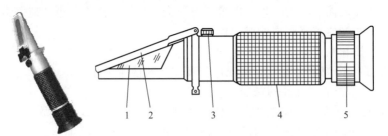

图 2-8　YDT-4T 冰点测试仪及其构造
1—棱镜；2—盖板；3—校正钉；4—把套；5—目镜

YDT-4T 冰点测试仪视场如图 2-9 所示。

YDT-4T 冰点测试仪视场说明：左侧标尺测量电解液密度（BATTERY FLUID）；1.10~1.20 表示需充电（RECHARGE）；1.20~1.25 表示电量够用（FAIR）；1.25~1.30 表示电量充足（GOOD）。中间标尺测量防冻液冰点、（ETHYLENE GLYCOL）乙二醇型防冻液冰点、（PROPYLENE GLYCOL）丙三醇型防冻液冰点；此项测试需要根据冷却液补充罐上的符号选择测试。右侧标尺测量玻璃水和玻璃清洗剂冰点。

根据电解液密度判断放电程度，密度每下降 $0.01g/cm^3$，蓄电池放电 6%，当蓄电池在夏季放电超过 50%、冬季放电超过 25% 时，应及时进行补充充电，否则会使蓄电池早期损坏。

根据各单格电池电解液密度的差值判断蓄电池是否失效。如果各单格电池具有相同的密度值，即使密度偏低，该电池一般可以通过补充充电恢复其容量。如果单格电池之间的密度相差超过 $0.05g/cm^3$，则该蓄电池失效。

(3) 检测蓄电池开路电压。测量蓄电池开路电压判断蓄电池的放电程度。检测时将蓄电池断开，万用表置于电压挡，万用表的正、负表笔分别接蓄电池的正、负极。蓄电池开路电压与蓄电池的存电状态之间的关系见表2-4。注意检测时蓄电池应处于静止状态，蓄电池充、放电或加注蒸馏水后，应静置0.5h或更长时间后再测量。

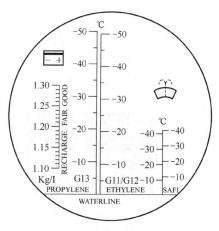

图 2-9　YDT-4T 冰点测试仪视场

(4) 检测蓄电池放电电压。检测蓄电池放电电压就是测量蓄电池以起动电流放电时的端电压，可以判断蓄电池的技术状况、放电程度和起动能力。检测时可用高率放电计检测或就车起动检测。

表 2-4　蓄电池存电状态与开路电压的关系

存电状态/%	100	75	50	25	0
开路电压/V	12.6 以上	12.4	12.2	12.0	11.9 以下

高率放电计是模拟起动机工作状态，检测蓄电池容量的仪表。它由一只电压表和一只负载电阻组成，接入蓄电池时，蓄电池对负载电阻放电，放电电流可达100A以上。检测时将高率放电计的正、负放电针分别压在蓄电池的正、负极柱上，保持15s，如果电压在9.6V以上，并保持稳定，说明性能良好；如果稳定在10.6～11.6V，说明存电充足；如果稳定在9.6～10.6V，说明存电不足，应进行补充充电；如果电压迅速下降，说明蓄电池有故障，应进行修理或更换。

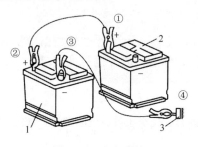

图 2-10　应急跨接
1—应急蓄电池；2—故障车蓄电池；
3—故障车上接地点

在起动汽车时，不间断地使用起动机会导致蓄电池因过度放电而损坏。正确的使用办法是每次发动车的时间总长不超过5s，再次起动间隔时间不少于15s。一旦无法起动，也可以采用临时借用其他电量充足的蓄电池应急跨接。应急跨接示意如图2-10所示，跨接安装顺序为：①、②、③、④；拆除跨接导线按相反顺序进行。

5. 蓄电池的漏电检查

一般当发现蓄电池放置数小时后就感觉电量不足时，必须进行漏电检查。检查方法：取下蓄电池的负极接头，测量蓄电池电压，并记录，若数小时后电压不变，则蓄电池正常，否则说明汽车电气系统有漏电。

四、知识与技能拓展

（一）蓄电池切断保护装置

有些轿车的蓄电池在车后部，但起动机和发电机随发动机安装在车前部，为了避免在车

辆发生碰撞时因短路而失火的危险，故装有蓄电池切断保护装置，该装置安装在蓄电池正极，通过安全气囊控制单元实现，每次安全气囊或安全带拉紧器触发时，都会一起激活蓄电池切断保护装置内部带活塞的销子，从而将起动机和发电机导线与汽车蓄电池断开。蓄电池切断保护装置如图 2-11 所示。

图 2-11 蓄电池切断保护装置
1—蓄电池正极；2—蓄电池引爆装置

图 2-12 蓄电池监控装置
1—蓄电池正极；2—蓄电池监控单元；
3—蓄电池负极

（二）蓄电池监控装置

有些轿车装有蓄电池监控装置，该装置安装在蓄电池的负极。作用是测量汽车蓄电池的充电和放电电流、电压、温度。蓄电池的电流、电压、温度可以通过专用诊断仪进行测量值读取。蓄电池监控装置如图 2-12 所示。

1. 蓄电池电流测量

在蓄电池负极上测量蓄电池电流。流入负极的总电流会流经蓄电池监控单元内部的并联电阻。这个并联电阻的阻值是毫欧级的。（此电阻值必须非常小，以保证功率损耗以及所产生的热量值尽可能小。）这个并联电阻上的压降大小与流过的电流成正比关系，CPU 可以测量电压降，并计算出流入或流出蓄电池的电流大小。

2. 蓄电池电压测量

直接在蓄电池正极上来测量蓄电池的电压，有一根测量导线从蓄电池正极接到蓄电池监控控制单元上。

3. 蓄电池温度测量

蓄电池温度的测量需要使用蓄电池模块中的 NTC 温度传感器。由于蓄电池数据模块直接固定在蓄电池上，所以在此它测得的蓄电池温度是可靠的，随后由软件进行处理。

小 结

（1）蓄电池作为汽车重要电源部件，必须掌握其相关理论知识、安全使用、检测与维护技能。

（2）要正确使用、检查维护蓄电池。

（3）蓄电池的充电需要严格执行操作规范，以免损坏蓄电池。

习题及思考

（1）简述蓄电池的组成与结构。

（2）试述蓄电池充放电过程的工作原理。

（3）蓄电池的常见技术参数都有哪些？分别是什么含义？

（4）蓄电池都有哪些常见故障？如何正确使用才能避免这些故障？

（5）蓄电池的安全使用注意事项都有哪些？

（6）蓄电池的技术状况检测都有哪些项目？

（7）如何对蓄电池进行充电？

项目三

充电系统的检修

一、情境引入

一辆帕萨特轿车,夜间行驶时大灯突然熄灭,经检修发电机工作正常,怀疑发电机调节器故障,经用检测设备对调节器进行试验,确认发电机调节器损坏。此事例中是由于充电系统电压调节器失效,造成瞬间电压过高,使汽车灯泡损坏。

很多车主对于仪表台上的充电系统指示灯都不太重视。在此讲解有关汽车电气系统中的充电系统与交流发电机的内容。

二、相关知识

随着汽车性能的不断提高,汽车上用电设备的数量也越来越多。因此,要求发电机有较大的输出功率,一般轿车发电机的输出功率可达到1200W。而蓄电池的主要作用是起动发动机及在发动机工作时充当备用电源。在发动机正常工作时,由发电机向全车用电设备供电,同时发电机还要向蓄电池进行补充充电,以保证蓄电池有足够的电力,同时电压调节器在发电机上保证其输出的电压稳定在一定范围内,防止因电压起伏过大而烧毁用电设备。充电系统的元件组成如图3-1所示。

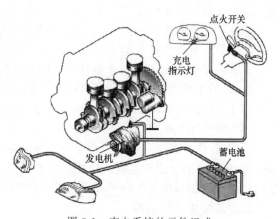

图3-1 充电系统的元件组成

(一)充电系统概述

由于当今汽车的电子装置日益增多,使充电系统迅速地显示出其重要地位。各种电控系统能否正常工作完全取决于汽车行驶时蓄电池的充电情况及所产生电流的大小。

汽车的充电系统一般由以下几部分组成:蓄电池、发电机、电压调节器、警告灯、点火开关、导线和电缆。蓄电池和发电机并联于汽车电路之中,发电机是主要电源,蓄电池是辅助电源。

当点火开关在起动位置时,蓄电池提供起动时所需的电力。在发动机起动过程中,车上所用电气系统的供电也是由蓄电池提供的。发动机起动以后,发电机不仅向蓄电池充电,保持正常充电水平,还要给车上所用电气装置供电。

汽车上所用发电机采用的是三相交流发电机，主要由三相同步交流发电机和硅二极管整流器组成，所以又称为硅整流发电机，简称交流发电机。目前汽车上所用的交流发电机，按调节器安装位置可分为两大类：一类是调节器单独安装，称为普通整流发电机，目前较少车辆在使用；另一类是调节器安装在发电机内部，称为整体式硅整流发电机，目前广泛使用。

由于发电机大多是由发动机经传动带驱动旋转的，当发动机转速变化时，发电机输出的电压也是变化的。为了满足汽车用电设备用电及向蓄电池充电的恒定电压要求，充电系统设有电压调节器，电压调节器通过调节发电机的励磁电流，保持发电机在转速和负荷变化时输出稳定的电压。如果对发电机的输出没有控制的话，它的电压将超出汽车电路的安全界限。汽车上采用电压调节器使发电机的输出在14V左右。为了使驾驶员了解发电机的情况，许多车的仪表盘上装有指示灯或电流表。

（二）交流发电机的构造

1. 交流发电机的分类

（1）按总体结构分为6类。

① 普通交流发电机（使用时需要配装电压调节器的发电机），如JF132。

② 整体式交流发机（发电机和调节器制成一个整体的发电机），如JFZ1913。

③ 带泵交流发电机（和汽车制动系统用真空助力泵安装在一起的发电机），如JFZB292。

④ 无刷交流发电机（不需要电刷的发电机），如JFW 1913。

⑤ 永磁交流发电机（磁极为永磁铁制成的发电机），如JFW1712。

⑥ 水冷交流发电机（无散热风扇，采用水冷系统，赛车一般采用）。

（2）按整流器结构分为5类。

① 6管交流发电机，如JF1522（东风汽车用）。

② 8管交流发电机，如JFZ1542（天津夏利汽车用）。

③ 9管交流发电机，如日本日立LR1140-803、北京BJ1022型用JFZ141。

④ 11管交流发电机，如JFZ1913Z（奥迪、桑塔纳汽车用）。

⑤ 12管交流发电机，如丰田汉兰达个别发动机安装。

（3）按磁场绕组搭铁形式分为2类。

① 内搭铁型交流发电机。磁场绕组的一端（负极）直接搭铁壳体相连，目前较少采用。

② 外搭铁型交流发电机。磁场绕组的一端（负极）接入调节器，通过调节器后再搭铁。目前广泛应用的整体式发电机都采用外搭铁形式。

2. 交流发电机的结构

目前，国内外生产的汽车用硅整流发电机虽然在制造工艺、局部结构及工作性能上有所改进，且形式各异，但其结构基本相同，主要由转子、定子、整流器、前端盖、后端盖、带轮及风扇组成。图3-2所示为JFZ1913Z交流发电机的组件图，图3-3所示为JF132交流发电机的结构图。

（1）转子。交流发电机的转子是发电机的磁极部分，用来产生磁场，由滑环、转子轴、爪极、磁轭、磁场绕组等部件组成，其组成如图3-4所示。

由低碳钢制成的两块六爪磁极压装在转子轴上，爪极的空腔内装有磁轭并绕有磁场绕组，磁场绕组的两端引出线分别焊接在与轴绝缘的集电环（两个铜制滑环）上，两个电刷与滑环接触，将直流电流引入磁场绕组（该电流称为发电机的励磁电流）。磁场绕组通入励磁电流后产生磁场，被磁化的爪极其中一块为N极，另一块为S极，形成相互交错的N、S磁极，于是就形成了4~8对磁极，国产交流发电机多为6对磁极。

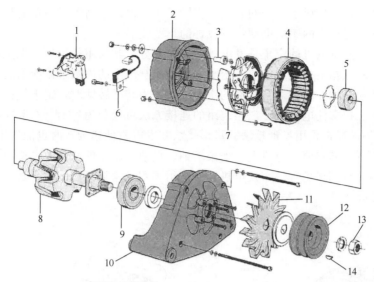

图 3-2 JFZ1913Z 交流发电机的组件

1—电压调节器与电刷；2—后端盖；3—绝缘体；4—定子；5—轴承；6—电容；7—二极管总成；8—转子；
9—轴承；10—前端盖；11—冷却风扇；12—皮带轮；13—螺母；14—半圆键

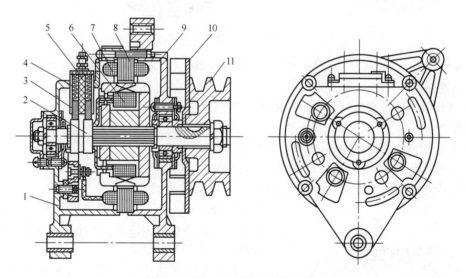

图 3-3 JF132 交流发电机的结构

1—后端盖；2—滑环；3—电刷；4—电刷弹簧；5—电刷架；6—磁场绕组；
7—电枢绕组；8—电枢铁芯；9—前端盖；10—风扇；11—带轮

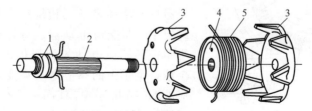

图 3-4 交流发电机的转子

1—滑环；2—转子轴；3—爪极；4—磁轭；5—磁场绕组

项目三 充电系统的检修 027

当转子转动时，就形成了旋转的磁场。将转子爪极设计成鸟嘴形的目的是使磁场呈正弦分布，以使电枢绕组产生的感应电动势有较好的正弦波形。

(2) 定子。交流发电机的定子是发电机的电枢部分，其功用是用来产生交流电动势，由定子铁芯和对称的三相电枢绕组组成。定子铁芯由相互绝缘的内圆带嵌线槽的环状硅钢片叠成，嵌线槽内嵌入三相互相独立且对称的定子线圈。当转子转动时，定子线圈切割旋转磁场的磁力线而产生三相交流电动势。三相绕组的连接方法可以分为星形（丫形）连接和三角形（△形）连接2种，通常采用星形接法。星形接法在发电机低速旋转时也能发出足够的电量，所以被广泛用在汽车硅整流发电机上。如桑塔纳、奥迪等轿车的交流发电机的定子绕组均采用星形接法；而北京切诺基等轿车发电机定子绕组采用三角形接法。定子及定子绕组的连接方式如图3-5所示。

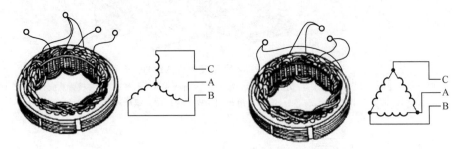

图3-5 定子及定子绕组的连接方式

为保证电枢三相绕组产生大小相等、相位差120°（电角度）的对称电动势，三相绕组的绕制应遵循以下原则。

① 每相绕组的线圈个数和每个线圈的匝数应完全相等，保证每相绕组所产生的电动势大小相等。

② 每个线圈的间距必须相同。

③ 三相绕组的起端A、B、C在定子槽内的排列必须相隔120°。

三角形绕组的每条线圈的端点与另一绕组的端点首尾相连，形成一个闭合的串联电路。而星形绕组中，每2个线圈绕组形成串联电路，3个绕组的公共点为中性点。发电机中最常使用的是星形绕组（70A发电机）。

图3-6所示为JF132型交流发电机定子绕组的结构，图3-7所示为JF132型交流发电机定子的展开图，发电机有6对磁极，定子总槽数为36，即1对磁极对应6个槽。当转子旋转时，转子磁场不断和定子三相绕组作相对运动，在定子绕组中产生交流电动势。每转过1对磁极，定子绕组中的感应电动势就变化1个周期，每转过6个槽，定子中的感应电动势变化360°，每个槽对应60°。因此，每个线圈2条有效边的位置间隔是3个槽，每相绕组相邻线圈始边之间的距离为6个槽，三相绕组的始边的相互间隔可以是2、8、14个槽等。

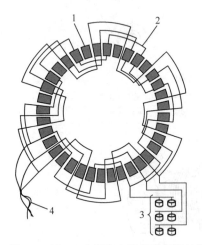

图3-6 JF132交流发电机定子绕组结构
1—定子铁芯；2—定子绕组；
3—二极管；4—定子中性接点

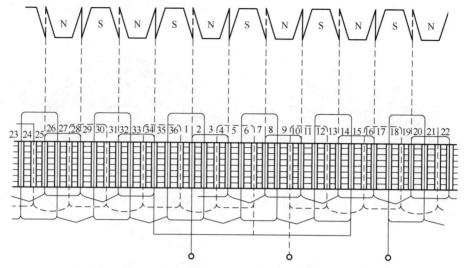

图 3-7 JF132 交流发电机定子绕组的展开

（3）整流器。由于汽车的电气系统使用直流电，所以发电机的交流电必须转变为直流电，这一过程称为整流。用很小的半导体二极管可将交流电转变为直流电。二极管只允许电流流向一个方向，它由外表掺杂的纯硅片制成。二极管可以正向连接（导电），也可以反向连接（不导电）。这些整流器连接于发电机的内部线路中，使发电机定子线圈流出的电流只流向正方向，而阻止电流流向反方向。

图 3-8 所示为由 6 只硅整流二极管组成的三相桥式整流电路。其作用是将三相绕组中产生的三相交流电转换为直流电。部分发电机还有 3 只小功率励磁二极管和 2 只中性点二极管。

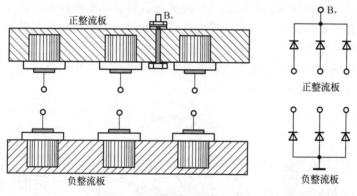

图 3-8 交流发电机的整流器

二极管的引线为二极管的一极，其壳体部分为二极管的另一极。压装在后端盖（或与外壳相通的接地散热板）上的 3 只硅二极管的壳体为二极管正极，引线为二极管负极，称之为负极管；压装在外壳绝缘散热板上的 3 只硅二极管的壳体为二极管负极，引线端为二极管正极，称之为正极管。3 只正极管和 3 只负极管的引线端通过 3 个接线柱——对应连接，并分别连接三相绕组的 A、B、C 端，就组成了三相桥式全波整流电路。

固定在散热板上的螺栓伸出发电机壳体外部，作为发电机的输出接线柱，该接线柱为发电机的正极，相应的标记为"B"（或"+"、"B+"等）。

项目三 充电系统的检修 **029**

整流板的形状各异，有马蹄形、长方形、半圆形等，其中 JF132 交流发电机整流器总成如图 3-9 所示。

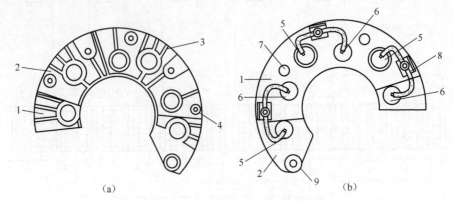

图 3-9　JF132 交流发电机整流器总成
1—负整流板；2—正整流板；3—散热片；4—连接螺栓；5—正极管；6—负极管；
7—安装孔；8—绝缘垫；9—电枢接柱安装孔

（4）端盖及电刷组件。交流发电机的前后端盖由铝合金铸成，铝合金为非导磁材料，可减少漏磁，并具有重量轻、散热性好的优点。端盖起着固定转子、定子、整流器和电刷组件的作用。前端盖铸有安装臂、调整臂与出风口，后端盖铸有安装臂与进风口。当风扇转动驱动空气从进风口流入，经发电机定子铁芯表面再从出风口流出，将定子线圈对外输出电流时产生的热量带走，达到散热的目的。整流器则装于后端盖内侧或外侧上。

在后端盖内装有电刷组件，电刷组件包括电刷、电刷架和电刷弹簧，如图 3-10 所示。电刷架有 2 种形式，一种是外装式，从发电机的外部拆下电刷弹簧盖板即可拆下电刷，如图 3-10(a) 所示；另一种是内装式，需拆开发电机后才能拆下电刷，如图 3-10(b) 所示。电刷通过弹簧与转子轴上的滑环来保持接触。外装式电刷拆装和更换在发电机外部即可进行，拆装检修方便，因此，被广泛采用；内装式电刷若需更换，必须将发电机解体，由于拆装检修不方便，因此，现在很少采用。

安装内装式电刷发电机时，先用直钢丝从外壳小孔伸入刷架压下电刷，再按普通发电机的其他步骤进行安装，如图 3-10(c) 所示。

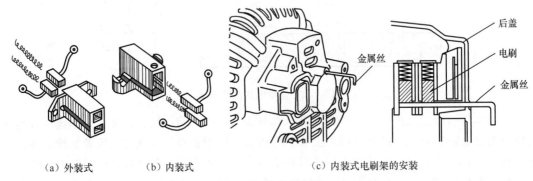

(a) 外装式　　(b) 内装式　　(c) 内装式电刷架的安装
图 3-10　发电机电刷

（5）带轮及风扇。交流发电机的前端装有带轮，由发动机通过风扇传动带驱动发电机旋转。带动交流发电机转子转动的带轮上有风扇叶片，用于对发电机的强制通风散热［叶片外装式，如图 3-11(a) 所示］。为提高发电机的效率，减小发电机的体积，有的发电机风扇叶

片设在其转子上［叶片内装式，如图3-11(b)所示］。有些内装风扇的发电机在轴的两端各装有一个风扇，散热效果更好。

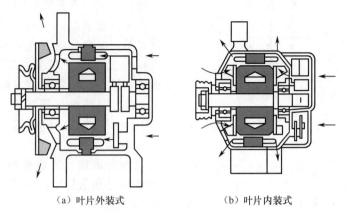

(a) 叶片外装式　　　(b) 叶片内装式

图 3-11　交流发电机的通风方式

（三）交流发电机的工作原理

1. 感应电动势产生的原理

当导体在磁场间旋转，由于电磁感应将会产生感应电动势。把导体弯成框形，会产生双倍的感应电动势；把导体做成线圈，将会产生更大的感应电动势；而且线圈中的匝数越多，产生的感应电动势越大。如图3-12所示，感应电动势越大，灯泡就越亮。

2. 交流发电机的发电原理

交流发电机产生交流电的基本原理是电磁感应原理。交流发电机是利用产生磁场的转子旋转，使穿过定子绕组的磁通量发生变化，在定子绕组内产生交流感应电动势。

当励磁绕组中有电流通过时，励磁绕组中便产生磁场，转子轴上的2个爪极分别被

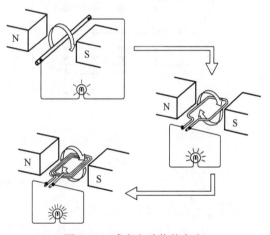

图 3-12　感应电动势的产生

磁化为N极和S极。当转子旋转时，磁极交替地在定子铁芯中穿过，形成一个旋转的磁场，磁力线和定子绕组之间产生相对运动，在三相绕组中产生交流感应电动势。

在交流发电机中，由于转子磁极呈鸟嘴形，其磁场的分布近似正弦规律分布，所以在发电机定子绕组中产生的交流感应电动势也近似正弦规律变化。

三相同步交流发电机的工作原理如图3-13所示。发电机的转子为磁极，磁极绕组通过电刷和滑环引入直流电而产生磁场；发电机的定子为电枢，三相电枢绕组按一定的规律分布在定子的槽中，彼此相差120°电角度。

当转子旋转时，产生一个旋转的磁场，使得相对静止的电枢绕组切割磁力线而产生感应电动势。通过对磁极铁芯的特殊设计使磁场近似于正弦规律分布，因此，三相电枢绕组产生的感应电动势近似按正弦规律变化，频率相同、幅值相等、相位互差120°电角度。

3. 交流发电机的整流原理

二极管具有单向导电特性。当给二极管加上正向电压时，二极管导通，呈现低阻态；当

给二极管加上反向电压时，二极管截止，呈现高阻态。汽车交流发电机定子绕组中感应产生的交流电，通过6只二极管组成的三相桥式整流电路转变为直流电输出。

桥式整流电路及电压波形如图3-14所示。

（1）由于3个正极管（VD_1、VD_3、VD_5）的正极分别接在汽车发电机三相绕组的首端（A、B、C），而它们的负极同接在元件板上。因此，

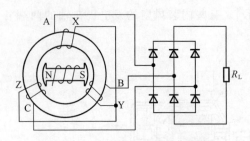

图3-13　交流发电机的工作原理

这3个正极管导通的条件是：在某一瞬间，哪一相的电压最高（相对其他两相来说正值最大），则该相的正极管导通。

（2）由于3个负极管（VD_2、VD_4、VD_6）的负极分别接在发电机的三相绕组的首端，而它们的正极同接在后端盖上。因此，这3个负极管的导通条件是：在某一瞬间，哪一相的电压最低（相对其他两相来说负值最大），则该相的负极管导通。

（3）在同一瞬间，同时导通的二极管就只有2个，即正极管、负极管各一个。三相桥式整流电路中二极管的依次循环导通，使得负载R_L两端得到一个比较平稳的脉动直流电压。

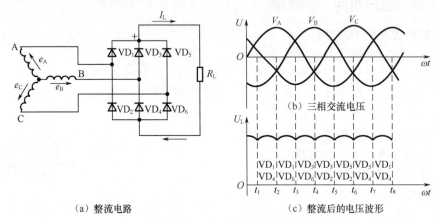

图3-14　三相桥式整流原理

根据上述原则，其整流过程如下。

在$t_1 \sim t_2$时间内，A相的电压最高，B相的电压最低，故VD_1、VD_4处于正向电压下而导通，负载R_L两端得到的电压为U_{AB}。

在$t_2 \sim t_3$时间内，A相的电压最高，C相的电压最低，故VD_1、VD_6处于正向电压下而导通，负载R_L两端得到的电压为U_{AC}。

在$t_3 \sim t_4$时间内，VD_3、VD_6导通，R_L两端的电压为U_{BC}。

以此类推，循环反复，就在R_L两端得到一个比较平稳的脉冲直流电压U_L，1个周期内有6个波形，如图3-14（c）所示。

有的发电机具有中性点接线柱。中性点接线柱是从三相绕组的末端引出，标记为"N"，输出电压为U_N。由于U_N是通过3个搭铁的负极二极管整流后得到的直流电压（即三相半波整流），所以有

$$U_N = \frac{1}{2} U$$

交流发电机的转速高到一定程度，中性点电压高过发电机输出电压。中性点电压波形如图3-15所示。部分发电机在中性点接上2只中性点二极管，对中性点电压进行全波整流，

可以有效利用中性点电压来增加发电机的功率。实验表明：加装中性点二极管的交流发电机，在结构不变的情况下可以提高发电机的功率10％～15％。交流发电机中性点电压U_N一般用来控制各种用途的继电器，如磁场继电器、充电指示灯继电器等。

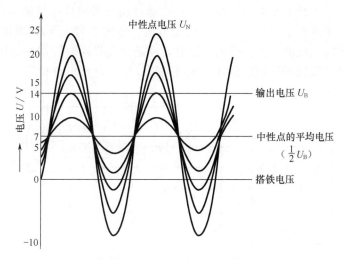

图3-15 交流发电机中性点电压

中性点二极管提高发电机功率的原理如下。

当中性点电压瞬时值高于三相绕组的最高值时，中性点正极管导通对外输出电流，电流回路为：中性点→正极二极管→负载→某一负极二极管→定子绕组→中性点。

当中性点电压瞬时值低于三相绕组的最低值时，中性点负极管导通对外输出电流，电流回路为：中性点→定子绕组→某一正极二极管→负载→中性点负极管→中性点。

4. 交流发电机的励磁方式

汽车交流发电机的磁场靠励磁产生，即必须给磁场绕组通电才会有磁场产生。由于二极管死区电压的存在，发动机转速低时交流发电机不能自励发电，所以要采用他励发电。需先由蓄电池供给励磁电流，当发电机电压达到蓄电池电压时，即由发电机自己供给励磁电流，也就是由他励转变成为自励。

在发动机起动期间，需要蓄电池供给发电机磁场电流生磁使发电机发电，这种供给磁场电流的方式称为他励发电。

随着转速的提高，发电机的电动势逐渐升高并能对外输出，一般在发动机怠速时发电机就能对外供电了。当发电机能对外供电时，就可以把自身发的电供给磁场绕组生磁发电，这种移给磁场电流的方式称为自励。

交流发电机的励磁电路如图3-16所示。

当点火开关S接通时，蓄电池便通过调节器向发电机的励磁绕组提供励磁电流，励磁电路为：蓄电池正极→点火开关S→调节器"＋"接线柱→调节器→调节器"F"接线柱→发电机"F"接线柱→发电机励磁绕组→搭铁。

当发动机起动后，发电机的输出电压略高于蓄电池电压时，发电机自己给励磁绕组提供励磁电流，励磁电路为：发电

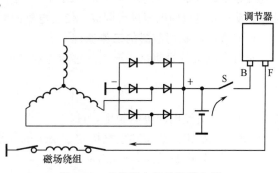

图3-16 交流发电机的励磁电路

正极→点火开关S→调节器"+"接线柱→调节器→调节器"F"接线柱→发电机"F"接线柱→发电机励磁绕组→搭铁。

以上分析的励磁电路只是一个基本电路，该电路还存在着一个缺点，即驾驶员如果在发动机熄火后忘记将点火开关S关闭，蓄电池就会通过调节器向发电机励磁线圈长时间放电。针对这一缺点，有很多车型采用了9管交流发电机。如图3-17所示，增加了3个功率较小的硅二极管，专供励磁电流，称为励磁二极管，励磁二极管同时控制充电指示灯。3只励磁二极管与3只负极二极管同样组成桥式整流电路，L点与B点电位相等。

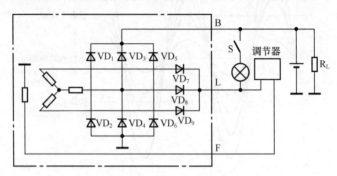

图 3-17 9管交流发电机的整流电路

如图3-17所示，电路起到警告驾驶员停车后必须关断点火开关的作用，同时电路中还连接一个充电指示灯，用来监视发电机的工作情况，指示发电机是否有故障。其工作情况如下。

在发动机起动期间，发电机电压 U_D^+ 小于蓄电池电压时，整流二极管截止，发电机不能对外输出，由蓄电池供给磁场电流。路径为蓄电池＋→点火开关→充电指示灯→调节器→磁场绕组→搭铁→蓄电池－，充电指示灯亮。

当发动机转速升高到怠速及其以上时，发电机应能正常发电并对外输出，发电机电压大于蓄电池电压，发电机自励。$U_B = U_D^+$，充电指示灯两端压降为零，充电指示灯熄灭。如果充电指示灯没有熄灭，说明发电机存在故障或充电指示灯电路有搭铁。

充电指示灯不仅可以指示发电机的工作情况，而且可在发动机停车后发亮，提醒驾驶员及时关闭点火开关。

（四）电压调节器

交流发电机的转子是由发动机通过带驱动旋转的，且发动机和交流发电机的转速比为1.7～3。汽车用交流发电机工作时其转速很不稳定且变化范围很大，若对发电机不加以调节，其端电压将随发动机转速的变化而变化，这与汽车用电设备要求电压恒定相矛盾。因此，发电机必须要有一个自动的电压调节装置。交流发电机调节器的作用就是当发动机转速变化时，自动对发电机的电压进行调节，使发电机的电压稳定，以满足汽车用电设备的要求。

1. 交流发电机调节器的工作原理

交流发电机的每相绕组产生的感应电动势的有效值为

$$E\phi = 4.44 K f N\phi = 4.44 K \frac{p_n}{60} N\phi = C_e \phi n$$

式中 f——交流电动势的频率，Hz；

K——绕组系数（和发电机定子绕组的绕线方法有关）；

n——发电机转速，r/min；

p——磁极对数；

N——每相匝数,匝;
ϕ——每极磁通,Wb;
C_e——电机结构常数。

由于发电机的电动势及端电压与磁极磁通量也成正比关系,因此,当发电机转速上升而使发电机的电压上升时,可以通过适当地减小磁极磁通量的方法使发电机电压保持稳定。

汽车用发电机电压调节器原理如图 3-18(a) 所示。

调节器动作的控制参量为发电机电压,即当发电机的电压达设定的上限值 U_2 时,调节器动作,使磁场绕组的励磁电流 I_f 下降或断流,从而减弱磁极磁通量,致使发电机电压降;当发电机电压下降至设定的下限值 U_1 时,调节器又动作,使 I_f 增大,磁通量加强,发电机电压又上升;当发电机的电压上升至 U_2 时又重复上述过程,使发电机的电压在设定的范围内波动,得到一个稳定的平均电压 U_e。发电机在某一转速下,调节器起作用后的发电机电压波形如图 3-18(b) 所示。

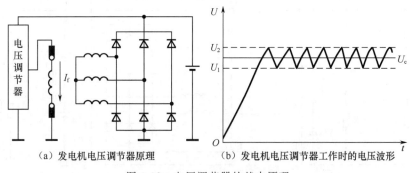

(a) 发电机电压调节器原理　　(b) 发电机电压调节器工作时的电压波形

图 3-18　电压调节器的基本原理

理论与实验表明,发电机转速不同时,磁场加强后发电机电压的上升速率和磁场减弱后的发电机电压下降速率均不同。

2. 交流发电机调节器的类型

由交流发电机的工作原理得知,对于某一发电机而言,实现对其电压的调节,只能通过改变发电机的转速和磁通量的大小来达到目的。而磁通量的大小又取决于励磁绕组电流的大小,因此,发电机的电压调节一般是通过控制励磁电流的大小来实现的。

电压调节器的类型较多,按元器件的性质来分,可分为触点式(也称电磁振动式)和电子式两大类。其中,触点式按触点的数目又可分单级和双级 2 种;电子式又分三极管式、集成电路式和可控硅式 3 种。按搭铁形式分,可分为内搭铁式(与内搭铁式交流发电机配套使用)和外搭铁式(与外搭铁式交流发电机配套使用)。目前采用较多的是外搭铁式。

电压调节器的型号举例如下。FT126C 表示 12V 的双联机械电磁振动式调节器,FT 为机械电磁振动式(FID 为电子式,JFT 为三极管式);1 为电压等级 12V(2 为电压等级 24V);2 为双联(1 为单联,4 为三极管式,5 为集成电路式);6 为第 6 次设计(指设计序号);C 为变形代号(变形代号,用字母 A、B、C 顺序表示)。

(1) 触点式电压调节器。

触点式电压调节器的基本原理。触点式电压调节器以电磁振动的方式工作,通过电磁铁控制触点的开闭来控制磁场绕组的励磁电流,实现对发电机电压的调节。因此,触点式电压调节器也为电磁振动式电压调节器。触点式电压调节器分为单级触点式电压调节器和双级触点式电压调节器。

触点式电压调节器工作时的触点火花不可能完全消除,触点容易烧蚀而使其故障率高、

使用寿命短。触点振动时产生的火花还会造成对无线电的干扰。此外，触点式电压调节器结构复杂，触点的振动频率低。因此，触点式电压调节器目前已很少在现代的汽车上使用。

（2）电子式电压调节器。

电子式电压调节器避免了触点式电压调节器的不足，目前广泛使用。

电子式电压调节器一般都是由 2～4 个三极管，1～2 个稳压管和一些电阻、电容、二极管等组成，再由印刷电路板连接成电路，然后用铝合金外壳将其封装。与触点式电压调节器相比，电子式电压调节器具有体积小、重量轻、调节反应敏捷、无触点烧蚀、使用寿命长等优点。

① 电子式电压调节器的基本原理。不同厂家生产的不同型号的电子式电压调节器的电路结构和元件组成各有不同，但基本原理相同。电子式电压调节器都是利用三极管的开关特性，通过三极管导通和截止相对时间的变化来调节发电机的励磁电流。电子式电压调节器的基本电路如图 3-19 所示。

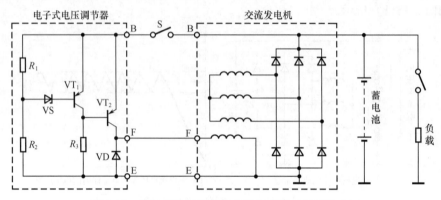

图 3-19　电子式电压调节器的基本电路（内搭铁式）

发电机电压通过 R_1、R_2 组成的分压器，将一定比例的电压加于稳压管 VD。VD 根据发电机电压的变化而导通或截止。VT_1 为小功率三极管，起放大作用，VT_1 的导通或截止由 VD 控制。大功率三极管 VT_2 用于控制励磁电流，VT_2 导通时，发电机磁场绕组回路通路，VT_2 截止时，励磁回路则断路。电路参数的设置使 VT_1、VT_2 均工作在开关状态。

工作时，在发电机电压达到调节电压以前，R_1 上的分压低于稳压管 VD 的导通电压，VD 不导通，使 VT_1 也不导通。VT_1 截止时，VT_2 的基极电位很低，使 VT_2 有足够高的正向偏压而饱和导通，发电机励磁回路通路。当发电机的电压上升至设定的调节电压时，R_1 上的分压达到了稳压管 VD 的导通电压，VD 导通，VT_1 也导通。VT_1 饱和导通后，VT_2 的基极与发射极之间被短路，VT_2 无正向偏压而截止，发电机励磁回路断路，发电机无励磁电流时，其电动势及端电压迅速下降，当降到 R_1 上的分压不足以维持 VD 导通时，VD 截止，VT_1 也截止。VT_1 截止后又使 VT_2 导通，发电机励磁回路又通路。如此反复，使发电机的电压维持在设定的调节电压值。

当发电机的转速上升时，发电机电压上升的速率增大，下降速率减小，使调节器控制 VT_2 的截止时间相对增加，发电机的平均励磁电流减小，从而使发电机的电压保持稳定。

② 三极管电压调节器。所谓三极管电压调节器，是指由分立电子元件焊接于印制电路板而制成的电子式调节器。印制电路板被固定在冲压的铁盒或铝盒内，有的在盒内还加注硅橡胶等，以利于元件的固定和三极管的散热。三极管电压调节器示例如下。

JFT106 型三极管电压调节器。JFT 106 型三极管电压调节器的电路板封装于铝合金壳体内，适用于外搭铁式交流发电机，其电路如图 3-20 所示。

JFT106 型三极管电压调节器属于外搭铁式三极管电压调节器，调节电压为 13.8～

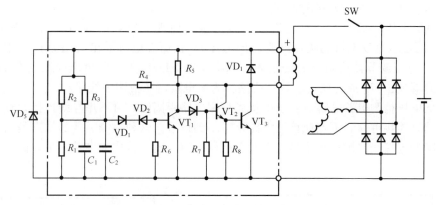

图 3-20 JFT106 型三极管电压调节器的电路

14.6V,可与 14V、750W 的外搭铁式 9 管交流发电机配套,也可与 14V、功率小于 1000W 的外搭铁式 6 管交流发电机配套。该调节器有"+""F"和"-"3 个接线柱,其中"+""F"接线柱与发电机的励磁绕组相连,"-"接线柱搭铁。

JFT106 型三极管电压调节器的工作原理是:接通点火开关 SW,蓄电池经点火开关给三极管电压调节器提供电流。首先经 R_5、VD_3 和 R_7 向复合管 VT_2、VT_3 提供电偏流,使其导通,励磁电路为(他励):蓄电池正极→点火开关 SW→励磁绕组→VT_3→蓄电池负极。发动机起动后,励磁电路由他励变为自励,励磁电路为:发电机正极→点火开关 SW→励磁绕组→VT_3→发电机负极。当发电机的输出电压达到调整值时,R_1 的端电压将反向击穿稳压管 VD_2,使 VT_1 导通,VT_2 和 VT_3 截止,励磁电流迅速下降,发电机的输出电压随之下降。发电机的输出电压下降,R_1 的端电压将下降,VD_2 截止,VT_1 又截止,VT_2 和 VT_3 又导通,发电机的输出电压又上升。当发电机的输出的电压达到调整值时,VD_2 又被反向击穿,VT_1 导通,VT_2 和 VT_3 截止,发电机的输出电压又下降。如此反复,控制发电机的输出电压保持在规定调整值上。

其他元件的作用如下。

R_3 为调整电阻,其阻值在 1.3~13kΩ,R_3 的合理选择可以提高调节器的稳定性。

C_1、C_2 为滤波电容,可以使 VD_2 两端的电压平滑过渡,减小发电机输出电压脉动影响,降低三极管的工作频率和减小损耗。

VD_1、VD_3 为温度补偿二极管,可以减少温度对三极管工作特性的影响。

VD_4 为续流二极管,可以将 VT_3 由导通进入截止时,在励磁绕组中产生的瞬时过电压短路,以保护 VT_3。

R_6 用于限制 VD_2 的击穿电流,保护 VD_2,同时又是 VT_1 的偏压电阻。

R_4 为正反馈电阻,用以提高三极管的转换速度,减少损耗。

③ 集成电路电压调节器。所谓集成电路电压调节器,是指用若干电子元件集成在基片上,具有发电机电压调节全部或部分功能的芯片所构成的电子式电压调节器。相比于分立元件的三极管电压调节器,集成电路电压调节器具有结构紧凑、体积小、电压调节精度高、故障率低等优点。集成电路电压调节器多装于发电机的内部,这种发电机也被称为整体式发电机。

集成电路电压调节器的工作原理与三极管电压调节器的工作原理完全一样,都通过稳压管感应发电机的输出电压信号,利用三极管的开关特性控制发电机的励磁电流,使发电机的输出电压保持恒定。集成电路电压调节器根据电压信号输入的方式不同,可分为发电机电压

检测方式和蓄电池电压检测方式两类。

a. 发电机电压检测方式。发电机电压检测法的原理电路如图 3-21 所示。加在分压器 R_1、R_2 上的电压是发电机励磁输出端 L 的电压 U_L，而发电机输出电压为 U_B。因为 $U_L = U_B$，因此，电压调节器检测点 P 的电压加到稳压管 VDW_1 上，其电压检测点 P 的电压 U_P 与发电机的端电压 U_B 成正比，所以该线路称为发电机电压检测法线路。

发电机电压检测电路的特点：发电机到检测电路距离近，可不用导线连接，直接接在发电机输出端，连接可靠，不致使检测电路检测不到信号。这种检测方式的缺点是当发电机与蓄电池之间的连接线路因接触不良而有较大电压降时，就会造成加在蓄电池端的电压偏低而充电不足。

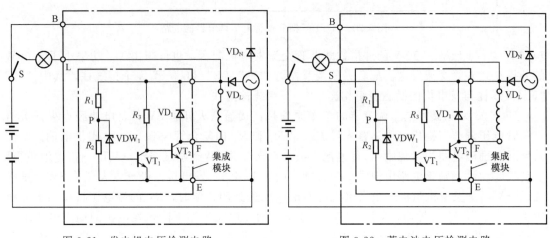

图 3-21　发电机电压检测电路　　　　图 3-22　蓄电池电压检测电路

b. 蓄电池电压检测方式。蓄电池电压检测法的原理电路如图 3-22 所示。加在分压器 R_1、R_2 上的电压为蓄电池端电压，由于通过检测点 P 加到稳压管 VDW_1 上的反向电压与蓄电池端电压成正比，所以该线路称为蓄电池电压检测法线路。

两种基本电路相比，如果采用发电机电压检测法线路，发电机的引出线可以少一根。不足之处在于，发电机电压检测原理电路中 B 点到蓄电池正极之间的电压降较大时，蓄电池的充电电压会偏低，使蓄电池充电不足。因此，一般大功率发电机要采用蓄电池电压检测法线路的调节器。

在采用蓄电池电压检测法时，当 B 点与蓄电池正极之间或 S 点与蓄电池之间断路时，由于不能检测出发电机的端电压，发电机电压将会失控。为了克服这一缺点，在线路上应采用一定的措施。图 3-23 所示为实际采用的蓄电池电压检测法的线路。在这个线路中，在调节器的分压器与发电机 B 点之间增加了一个电阻 R_4 和一个二极管 VD_2，这样，当 B 点与蓄电池正极之间出现断路时，由于 R_4 的存在，仍能检测出发电机的端电压 U_B，使调节器正常工作，可以防止出现发电机电压过高的现象。

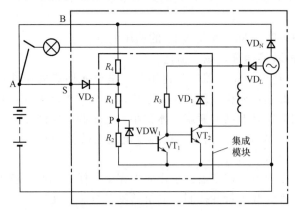

图 3-23　实际采用的蓄电池电压检测电路

（五）交流发电机和电压调节器的使用与维护

1. 交流发电机和电压调节器的使用注意事项

交流发电机与电压调节器的结构简单，维护方便。若正确使用，不仅故障少，而且寿命长；若使用不当，则会很快损坏。因此，在使用和维护中应注意以下几点。

（1）蓄电池的极性必须是负极搭铁，不能接反，否则会烧坏发电机或调节器的电子元件。

（2）发电机运转时，不能用试火的方法检查发电机是否发电，否则会烧坏二极管。

（3）整流器和定子绕组连接时，禁止用兆欧表或220V交流电源检查发电机的绝缘情况。

（4）发电机与蓄电池之间的连接要牢靠，如突然断开，会产生过电压损坏发电机或调节器的电子元件。

（5）一旦发现交流发电机或调节器有故障，应立即检修，及时排除故障，不应再连续运转。

（6）调节器必须受点火开关控制。发电机停止转动时，应将点火开关断开，否则会使发电机的磁场电路一直处于接通状态，不但会烧坏磁场线圈，还会引起蓄电池亏电。

2. 交流发电机和电压调节器的维护注意事项

交流发电机在使用中，应定期进行以下检查。

（1）检查发电机驱动带。

① 检查驱动带的外观。用肉眼观看有无裂纹或磨损现象，如有此现象应更换。

② 检查驱动带的挠度。用100N的力压在带的两个传动轮之间，新带挠度为5～10mm，旧带为7～14mm。

（2）检查导线的连接。

① 接线是否正确，是否牢靠。

② 发电机输出端接线螺丝必须加弹簧垫。

（3）检查运转时有无噪声。

（4）检查是否发电。

① 观察充电指示灯的熄灭情况。若充电指示灯一直亮着，说明发电机或调节器有故障，也可能是充电指示灯线路有故障，应及时维修。

② 用万用表直流电压挡测量电压。在发电机未转动时测量蓄电池端电压，并记录下电压值，起动发动机并将转速提高到急速以上，测量蓄电池端电压，若能高于原电压值，说明发电机正常发电，若测量电压一直不上升，说明发电机或调节器有故障，应及时维修。

（5）当发现发电机或调节器有故障需要从车上拆卸检修时，首先应关断点火开关及一切用电设备，拆下蓄电池负极电缆线，再拆卸发电机上的导线接头。

（6）就车维修检测时，最好使用专用工具。在判断不出发电故障部位是在发电机还是调节器时，将调节器短路，必须注意这时发电机的电压将失控，电压可能达到16～30V，所以要控制在很短时间内，或利用汽车电气设备作为蓄电池的负载，当线路故障没有排除时，不要更换新的调节器，这样做可能会损坏新的调节器。

（六）充电系统的故障诊断

1. 桑塔纳2000系列轿车充电系统电路介绍

桑塔纳2000系列轿车充电系统电路如图3-24所示。交流发电机的电流整流电路输出端

B_+ 用红色导线与起动机 30 端子连接。3 只磁场二极管与 6 只整流二极管组成一个三相桥式全波整流电路,成为磁场电流整流电路。其输出端 D_+ 用蓝色导线经蓄电池旁边的单端子连接器 T_1 后与中央继电器盒 D 插座的 D_4 端子连接,内部与中央继电器盒内部 A16 相连,点火开关 30 端子用红色导线经中央继电器盒的单端子插座 P 与蓄电池正极连接,点火开关 15 端子用黑色导线与仪表盘后插座中 14 端子连接(图中未标出,可参考原车线路图),再经仪表盘印刷电路中电阻 R_1、R_2 和充电指示灯和二极管接回到仪表盘后插座中 12 端子,再用蓝色导线与中央线路板 A16 相连。

充电指示灯及发电机励磁绕组电流路径为:蓄电池正极—中央继电器盒 P 端子—中央继电器盒内部—中央继电器盒插座 P 端子—点火开关 30 端子—点火开关 15 端子—电阻 R 和充电指示灯—二极管—中央继电器盒 A16 端子—中央继电器盒内部—中央继电器盒 D_4 端子—单端子连接器 T_1—交流发电机 D_+ 端子—发电机内部励磁绕组—电子调节器功率管—搭铁—蓄电池负极。

当电压高于蓄电池电压时,则由 3 只励磁二极管 D_+ 直接向励磁绕组提供电流。

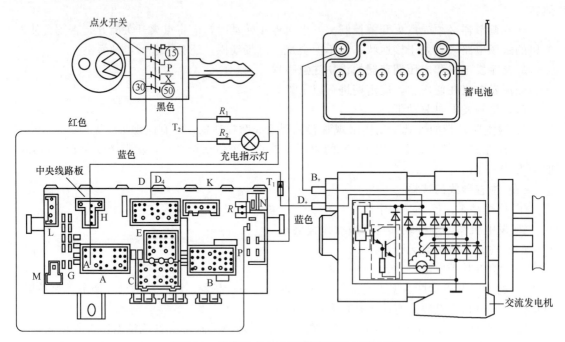

图 3-24 桑塔纳 2000 系列轿车充电系统电路

2. 充电系统故障诊断

充电系统的故障可根据车上电流表或充电指示灯的工作情况反映出来。充电系统有故障时,应及时进行检修来排除故障,以免造成更大的损失。

充电系统常见故障有不充电、充电电流过小、充电电流过大、充电不稳等。故障原因可能是发电机皮带打滑、发电机故障、调节器故障、磁场继电器故障、充电系统各连接线路有断路或短路处,以及蓄电池、电流表、充电指示灯、点火开关等有故障。诊断充电系统故障时,应综合考虑整个系统各部分之间的关系,仔细阅读说明书和线路图,按照一定的检查步骤逐步找出故障点。

(1) 不充电。发动机中速以上运转时,故障现象表现为电流表指示仍在放电或充电指示灯亮,说明为不充电故障。故障部位及原因见表 3-1。

表 3-1　不充电故障的部位及原因

故障部位		故障原因	排除方法
风扇皮带		过松或断裂	更换
电流表或指示灯		损坏	更换
发电机	定子绕组	断路或搭铁	建议更换发电机总成
	励磁绕组	断路或搭铁	建议更换发电机总成
	滑环或电刷	滑环严重烧蚀、脏污或裂纹、电刷过度磨损、卡滞	可通过焊接、机加工修复,更换电刷
	整流器	二极管脱焊	脱焊的故障可以通过补焊修复,或更换整流器总成
调节器		晶体管调节器损坏	更换调节器
外部线路		断路或接柱松脱	接通电路、拧紧接柱

（2）充电电流过小。若将发动机转速由低速逐渐升高至中速时，故障现象表现为打开大灯时灯光暗淡或按喇叭时音量过小，电流表指示放电，说明为充电电流过小故障。故障部位及原因见表 3-2。

表 3-2　充电电流过小故障部位及原因

故障部位		故障原因	排除方法
风扇皮带		张紧度不够	按要求张紧
发电机	定子绕组	匝间短路	建议更换发电机总成
	励磁绕组	匝间短路	建议更换发电机总成
	滑环或碳刷	滑环轻度烧蚀、脏污或裂纹、碳刷磨损不均、接触不良	可用细砂纸打磨滑环、更换碳刷及碳刷弹簧
	整流器	个别二极管损坏	对于压装的二极管可以个别更换,否则更换整流器总成
调节器		晶体管调节器损坏	更换调节器
外部线路		接柱松动或接触不良	拧紧接柱

（3）充电电流过大。发动机转速在中速以上，故障现象表现为电流表指示大电流充电（30A 以上），蓄电池电解液消耗过快且有气味，点火线圈过热，分电器触点易烧蚀，灯易烧坏，说明为充电电流过大故障。

故障部位及原因如下。

① 调节器调节电压过高或失控，机械式调节器低速触点烧蚀。
② 发电机"＋"接柱和磁场接柱短路。
③ 蓄电池亏电不多，蓄电池内部短路。

（4）充电不稳。发动机正常运转时，故障现象表现为汽车上的电流表指示充电，但指针左右摆动，忽大忽小，说明为充电不稳故障。

故障部位及原因如下。

① 发电机皮带过松、跳动或皮带轮失圆。
② 发电机内部接线松动、接触不良。
③ 发电机电刷磨损过度，电刷弹簧弹力减退或折断，滑环脏污或失圆。
④ 调节器触点接触不良，磁场线接触不良。

（5）充电系统的故障诊断流程。汽车发动机运转时，充电系统的工作情况是靠充电指示

灯来指示的。在汽车运行过程中,当充电指示灯指示出现异常时,说明充电系统发生故障,应该及时诊断并排除。现以尼桑颐达汽车的充电系统故障分析方法为例加以介绍。颐达汽车充电系统故障诊断流程如图 3-25 所示。

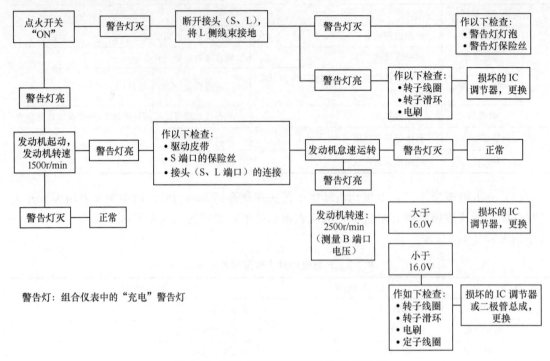

图 3-25　颐达汽车充电系统故障诊断流程

注意:
① 如果充电系统有故障而检测结果正常,检查"B"端口连接(检查拧紧力矩和电压降)。
② 检查转子线圈、转子滑环、电刷和定子线圈的状况。如果需要,更换故障零部件。

三、项目实施

(一)充电系统的检修要求

① 通过该项目的实施,应能够对充电系统的发电机及调节器进行拆装与调整,并掌握充电系统故障诊断与检测的步骤与方法。

② 该项目应具备硅整流交流发电机、发动机热试台架、电气实验台、蓄电池等设备,具备起子、扳手、台钳、油盆、毛刷等拆装和清洁工具,具备万用表、弹簧秤、百分表、V 形铁等检测仪器,具备汽车充电系统电路图等资料。

(二)实施步骤

1. 交流发电机的不解体检测

当充电系统出现故障时,如果经过检查明确交流发电机故障,就应将发电机从汽车上拆卸下来。为了判定交流发电机有无故障和故障发生在哪个部位,需做进一步检查。

(1)测量各接线柱之间的电阻或电压值。在发电机不解体时,可用数字万用表测量各接线柱之间的电阻值或电压值,可初步判断发电机是否有故障。其方法是用数字万用表电阻挡

测量发电机 F 与 E 之间的电阻值,再用数字万用表的二极管挡测量发电机 B 与 E 之间的单向导通电压。并记录所测各值,与相应的标准值进行比较。各接线柱之间的参考值见表 3-3。

表 3-3 各接线柱之间的参考值

交流发电机型号		F 与 E 之间/Ω	B 与 E 之间/mV		N 与 E 之间/mV	
			正向	反向	正向	反向
有刷	JF13、JF15、JF21	5~6	500~700	∞	500~700	∞
	JF22、JF23、JF25	19.5~21				
无刷	JFW14	3.5~3.8				
	JFW28	15~16				

① F 与 E 之间的电阻值。若超过规定值,可能是电刷与滑环接触不良;若小于规定值,可能是励磁绕组之间有匝间短路或搭铁故障;若电阻为零,可能是 2 个滑环之间有短路或 F 接线柱有搭铁故障。

② B 与 E 之间的电压值。若正反两次测得的电压值分别为 500~700mV 和 ∞,可认为无故障;若所测示值正反两次均为 ∞,则说明有失效的整流二极管,需拆检;若示值为零,则说明有不同极性的二极管击穿,需拆检。

若交流发电机有中性抽头(N)接线柱,用数字万用表二极管挡,测 N 与 E 及 N 与 B 之间的正反向电压,可进一步判断故障在正极管还是在负极管。

(2) 用示波器观察输出电压波形。当交流发电机有故障时,其输出电压的波形将出现异常。因此,根据输出电压波形可以判断交流发电机内部二极管及定子绕组是否有故障。交流发电机出现各种故障时输出电压的波形如图 3-26 所示。

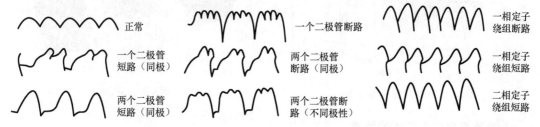

图 3-26 交流发电机出现各种故障时输出电压的波形

2. 发电机的拆解

(1) 发电机的就车拆卸。

① 断开蓄电池负极端子电缆。断开蓄电池负极电缆之前,对 ECU 等元件内保存的信息作一个记录。如 DTC(故障诊断码)、选择的收音机频道、座椅位置(带有记忆系统)、转向盘位置(带有记忆系统)等。

② 脱开发电机电缆和连接器(发电机电缆是直接从蓄电池引出的,在端子上有一个防短路罩壳),脱开发电机电缆。

③ 断开发电机连接器。断开连接器的卡爪,握住连接器,来断开连接器。

④ 拆卸发电机。拧松发电机安装螺栓,然后拆卸传动皮带。注意,拉动传动皮带来移动发电机,将损坏皮带。拆卸所有的发电机安装螺栓,然后拆卸发电机。由于发电机的安装零件带有用于定位的轴套,所以连接紧密。由于这个原因,上下摇动发电机来进行拆卸。

(2) 发电机的分解。

① 拆卸发电机皮带轮，将发电机夹在台虎钳上，采用如图 3-27 所示的方法将皮带轮拆下。

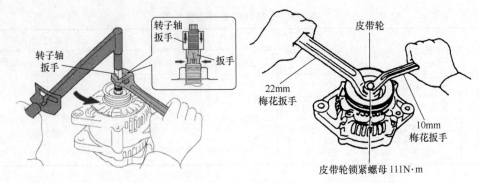

图 3-27 拆卸皮带轮

② 拆卸整流器端盖。由于机座和转子轴承是结合在一起的，所以需要专用工具来拆卸。拆卸整流器端盖时，钩住专用工具的卡爪来进行，如图 3-28 所示。

③ 拆卸发电机转子。通过用锤敲打，从主动机座一端拆卸转子。注意，用锤子敲时，转子会掉下来，所以事先应当在下面摊开一块布料，如图 3-29 所示。

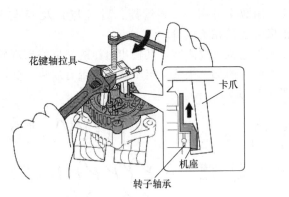

图 3-28 拆卸整流器端盖

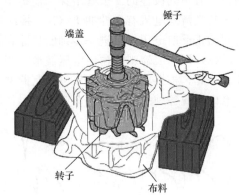

图 3-29 拆卸转子

3. 交流发电机各部件的检修

（1）转子检修。

① 目视检查。检查滑环变脏或烧蚀的程度，如图 3-30 所示。旋转时滑环和电刷接触，使电流产生。电流产生的火花会产生脏污和烧蚀。脏污和烧蚀会影响电流，使发电机的性能降低。用布料和毛刷清洁滑环和转子。如果脏污和烧蚀明显，更换转子总成。

② 滑环的检查。使用万用表，如图 3-31 所示，检查滑环之间是否导通，转子是一个旋转的电磁体，内部有一个线圈。线圈的两端都连接到滑环上。检查滑环之间是否导通可以用于探测线圈内部是否开路。如果发现在绝缘或者导通方面存在问题，更换转子。

③ 检查滑环和转子之间的绝缘。用万用表检查滑环和转子之间的绝缘，如图 3-32 所示。在滑环和转子之间存在一个切断电流的绝缘状态。如果转子线圈短路，电流会在线圈和转子之间流动。检查滑环和转子之间的绝缘可以用来检测线圈内是否存在短路。如果发现在绝缘和或者导通方面存在问题，更换转子。

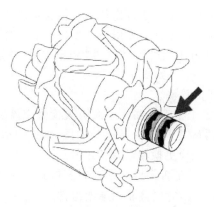

图 3-30 检查转子是否变脏或烧蚀

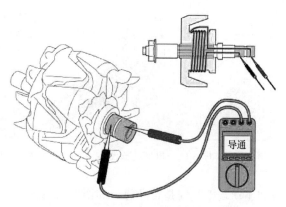

图 3-31 滑环的检测

④ 测量滑环。用游标卡尺测量滑环的外径，如图 3-33 所示。如果测量值超过规定的磨损极限，更换转子。旋转时滑环和电刷接触，使电流产生流动。因此，当滑环的外径小于规定值时，滑环和电刷之间的接触不足，有可能影响电流环流的平稳。结果可能会降低发电机的发电能力。

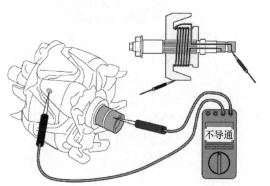

图 3-32 检查滑环和转子之间的绝缘

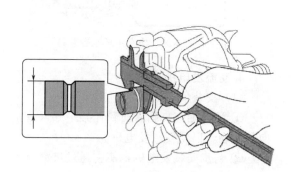

图 3-33 滑环的测量

（2）整流器的检测。使用万用表的二极管测试模式，如图 3-34 所示。在整流器的端子 B 和端子 P1 到 P4 之间测量，交换测试导线时，检查是否只能单向导通。改变端子 B 至端子 E 的连接方式，测量过程同上。

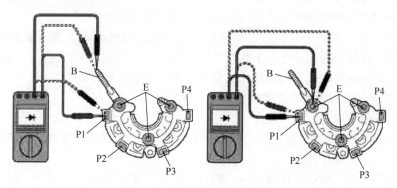

图 3-34 整流器二极管的检测

（3）电刷的检测。用游标卡尺测量电刷的长度，如图 3-35 所示。在电刷的中部测量（电刷的）长度，因为这个地方磨损最严重。滑环接触电刷，当自身旋转时接通流过电流。

因此，当电刷的长度短于规定值时，接触会恶化，影响电流的流动。因此，发电机的发电性能下降。如果测量值小于标准值，将电刷和电刷座一起更换。

（4）定子的检测。

① 检查定子是否开路。用欧姆表检查交流发电机的线圈两端之间是否导通，如图 3-36 所示。如果不导通，则应更换驱动端架组件。

② 检查定子是否接地。用欧姆表检查线圈导线和驱动端架之间是否导通，如图 3-37 所示。如果导通，则应更换驱动端架组件。

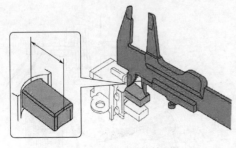

图 3-35　电刷的检测

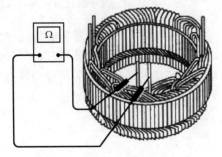

图 3-36　检查定子是否开路

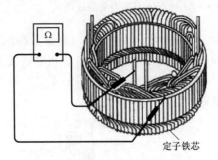

图 3-37　检查定子是否接地

定子铁芯

4. 交流发电机的装复

（1）安装发电机。

① 滑动轴套直到表面和托架平齐（管接一端），用锤子和铜棒将发电机安装部分的轴套向外滑动，以便安装发电机。

② 初步安装发电机，使它通过贯穿。

③ 初步安装螺栓。

④ 安装传动皮带。

⑤ 通过用锤子的手柄等物移动发电机来调整皮带的张紧度。

⑥ 拧紧螺栓，以牢固地安装发电机。

（2）安装传动皮带。

① 当发电机安装螺栓和贯穿螺栓松开后，将皮带安装到所有的皮带轮上。

② 用杠杆（锤子的把手或轮毂螺母扳手等）移动发电机以调节皮带松紧，然后旋紧贯穿螺栓。注意，将杠杆的尖端抵着不易变形的地方（一个足够牢固的地方），如缸盖或缸体。将杠杆放在不易导致发电机变形且比发电机中心距离调节托架更近的地方。

③ 检查传动皮带的松紧并旋紧螺栓。

（3）连接发电机电缆。

平直连接发电机的电缆，这样不会损伤发电机的端子。安装定位螺母。安装防短路罩壳。

（4）连接发电机连接器。

握住连接器主体，然后连接连接器。确认卡爪已经牢固连接。

（5）连接蓄电池负极端子电缆。

① 平直连接蓄电池负极电缆，这样不会损伤蓄电池端子。

② 恢复车辆信息。检查过程完成以后，将工作前记下的车辆信息恢复。如选择的收音

机频道、时钟设置、方向盘位置（带有记忆系统）、座椅位置（带有记忆系统）等。

5. 就车检验

交流发电机的就车检验法就是在汽车上关掉点火开关，临时拆下蓄电池搭铁线，将一块 0～40A 的电流表串接到发电机火线 B 接线柱与火线原接线之间，再将一块 0～50V 的电压表接到 B 与 E 之间，连接好蓄电池的搭铁线。起动发动机，加速发动机，当发电机转速为 2500r/min 时，电压应为 14V 或 28V 以上，电流应为 10A 左右。此时打开前照灯、雨刮器等电器，电流应为 20A 左右，则表明发电机工作正常。

6. 电压调节器的检测

为交流发电机配用调节器时，交流发电机的电压等级必须与调节器电压等级相同，交流发电机的搭铁类型必须与调节器搭铁类型一致，调节器的功率不得小于发电机的功率，否则系统不能正常工作。

（1）电压调节器搭铁类型的检测。将可调直流电源正极接调节器"B"（或"＋"）端，负极接调节器"E"（或"－"）端，将小灯泡一端接F，另一端暂时悬空，稳压电源电压调到 12V（28V 调节器则调到 24V）。

① 将小灯泡悬空的一端搭在电源"B"上，接通开关 S，若灯亮，调节器为外搭铁型。若灯不亮，关断开关 S，进入下一步。

② 将小灯泡悬空的一端搭在搭铁端"E"上，接通开关 S，若灯亮，调节器为内搭铁型。若两种情况下灯泡都不亮，便是接线有问题或调节器损坏。

（2）调节器性能好坏测试。将电压调节器按搭铁类型分类接线，如图 3-38、图 3-39 所示。连好电路后，先将可调直流电源电压调至 12V（14V 调节器）或 24V（28V 调节器）。接通开关 S，此时灯泡应发亮，然后逐渐调高电压，灯泡的亮度应随电压的升高而增强。当电压升高到调节电压时（14V 调节器为 13.5～14.5V，28V 调节器为 27～29V），若灯泡熄灭，则调节器是性能良好的，若灯泡始终发亮，则调节器是损坏的。

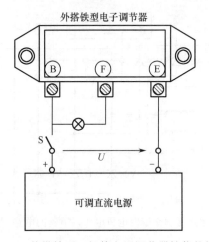
图 3-38 外搭铁型三极管电压调节器性能的检测

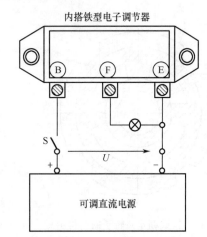
图 3-39 内搭铁型三极管电压调节器性能的检测

四、知识与技能拓展

（一）其他类型的发电机

普通交流发电机需要通过电刷与滑环将励磁电流导入旋转的磁场绕组。工作中可能出现

电刷过度磨损、电刷在架中卡滞、电刷弹簧失效、滑环脏污等，会使电刷与滑环的接触不良，这是造成发电机不发电或发电不良的故障原因之一。无刷交流发电机则可克服普通交流发电机的这一缺陷，因此，在汽车上得到了应用。

(1) 爪极式无刷交流发电机。图3-40所示为一种爪极式无刷交流发电机的结构示意。其结构特点是磁场绕组8通过1个磁轭托架固定在后端盖3上，2个爪极只有一个直接固定在转子轴上，另一爪极4则通过非导磁连接环7固定在前一爪极上。转子转动时，一个爪极就带动另一爪极转动，当固定不动的磁场绕组通入直流电后，产生的磁场使爪极磁化，一边爪极为N极，另一边爪极为S极，并经气隙和定子铁芯形成的闭合磁路。转子转动时，定子内形成交变磁场，三相电枢绕组便产生三相交流电动势，再经三相整流电路整流后输出直流电。

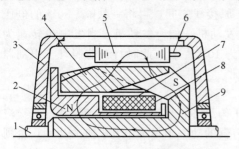

图3-40 爪极式无刷交流发电机的结构示意
1—转子轴；2—磁轭托架；3—端盖；4—爪极；
5—定子铁芯；6—定子绕组；7—非导磁连接环；
8—磁场绕组；9—转子磁轭

爪极式无刷交流发电机的主要缺点是由于磁轭托架与爪极和转子磁轭之间有附加间隙存在，漏磁较多，因此，在输出功率相同的情况下，必须增大磁场绕组的励磁能力。

(2) 永磁式无刷交流发电机。永磁式无刷交流发电机以永久磁铁为转子磁极而产生旋转磁场，常用的永磁材料有铁氧体、铬镍钴、稀土钴、钕铁硼等。图3-41所示为钕铁硼永磁转子的结构示意。

永磁式无刷交流发电机的磁场强度是固定不变的，因此，不可能像其他类型的交流发电机那样通过调节磁场绕组励磁电流的方法来达到稳定电压的目的。图3-42所示为永磁式无刷交流发电机电压调节器的电路原理。

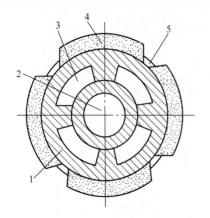

图3-41 钕铁硼永磁转子的结构示意
1—导磁轭；2—转轴；3—通风口；
4—永磁体；5—环氧树脂胶

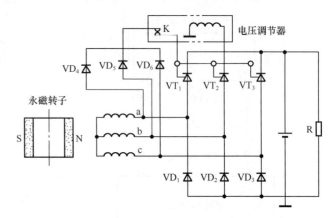

图3-42 永磁式无刷交流发电机电压调节器的电路原理

3只二极管VD_1、VD_2、VD_3与3只晶闸管VT_1、VT_2、VT_3组成的三相半控桥式整流电路向外输出直流电，而$VD_1 \sim VD_6$组成的三相桥式整流电路则向晶闸管控制极提供触发电压。其电路中串联着电压调节器的触点K，电压调节器的K为常闭触点，电磁线圈并接于发电机的输出端。电压调节原理如下。

电压调节器触点K闭合时，晶闸管控制极获得正向触发电压而导通，整流桥向外输出

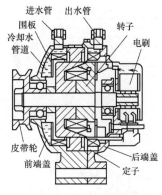

图 3-43 水冷式交流发电机

三相全波整流电压。当发电机随转速的升高，其整流电压上升至设定的上限值时，电压调节器线圈产生的磁力使触点 K 断开，晶闸管因控制极失去正向触发电压而截止，发电机的电压随之迅速下降；当发电机电压下降至下限值时，电压调节器触点因其线圈产生的磁力减弱而重新闭合，晶闸管又获得正向触发电压而导通，发电机端电压迅速上升，如此反复，使发电机的输出电压在一定的范围内波动。

永磁式无刷交流发电机具有体积小、重量轻、维护方便、比功率大、低速充电性能好等优点。

(3) 水冷式交流发电机。水冷式交流发电机利用水来代替风扇进行冷却。水冷式交流发电机如图 3-43 所示。交流发电机主要的发热部位是定子，水冷式交流发电机重点冷却部位就是定子及线圈绕组。发电机的前端盖和后端盖用铝材制造，开有水道槽。定子及线圈绕组用合成树脂固定密封，定子与转子之间有铝质围板与水道隔离。水道与进水管和出水管连通，进水管和出水管分别与发动机冷却水系统连通。这样，当发动机运转时，冷却水在发动机水泵的带动下循环流动，通过发电机壳体，可以有效地冷却定子线圈绕组、定子铁芯，同时也冷却转子、内藏式调节器和轴承等其他发热零部件。

水冷式交流发电机具有良好的低速充电特性。水冷式交流发电机大幅度抑制了定子、转子及调节器的温升，相应提高励磁电流，励磁电流越大，输出电压也越高。水冷式交流发电机省略了风扇，不存在发电机风扇发出的噪声。在 3500r/min 时，水冷式与风冷式交流发电机相比，噪声要低 15dB。水冷式交流发电机比风冷式防漏密封要求高，成本增加。同时因连接水管的问题，安装布置也受到诸多限制，自由度减少了。

(二) 部分品牌汽车发电机电路图

尼桑颐达充电系统电路如图 3-44 所示。奥迪汽车充电系统电路如图 3-45 所示。

(三) 电源管理系统

电源管理系统也称车载电网管理系统，负责电能的分配管理，使车的起动性能和蓄电池的寿命有了明显的改善和提高。随着汽车的不断发展，车辆上应用的电子和电气部件数量在不断增加，传统的中央继电器盒模式已经难以适应中高档车

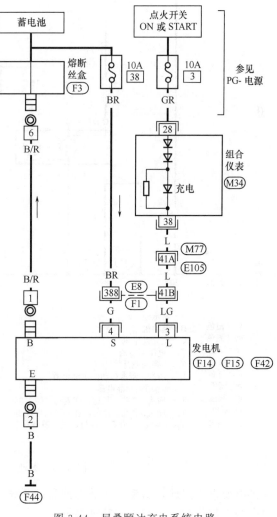

图 3-44 尼桑颐达充电系统电路

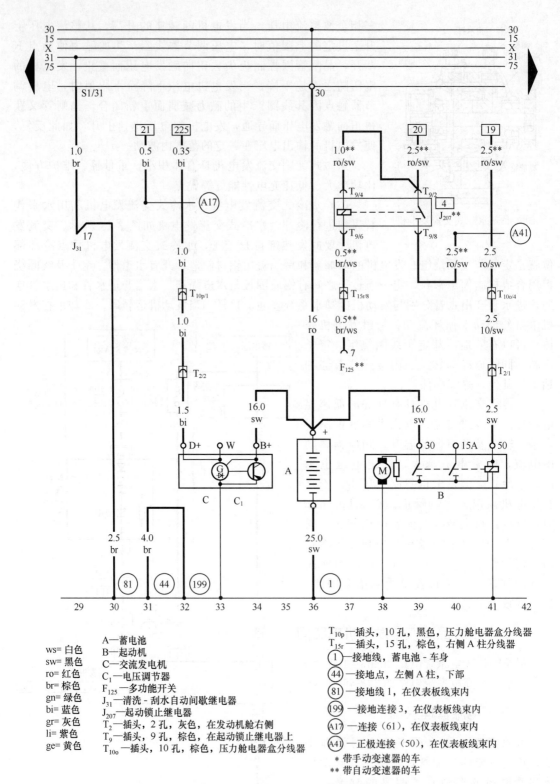

图 3-45 奥迪汽车充电系统电路

的供电要求。因此，新型的车载电网管理系统应运而生，例如，宝马、奥迪、大众等车系的中高档车都装配了车载电网管理系统。

1. 车载电网管理系统的组成

车载电网管理系统主要由保险丝盒、继电器盒和中央电器控制单元 J519 组成，如图 3-46 所示。

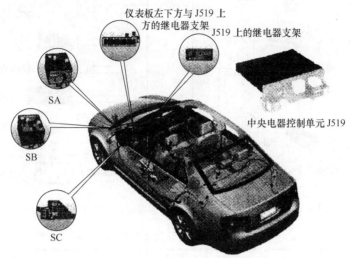

图 3-46　车载电网管理系统

2. 中央电器系统控制单元

（1）中央电器系统控制单元的主要管理功能：用电负荷管理；外部灯光的控制及灯光缺陷的检测；内部灯光的控制；后风窗加热控制；舒适灯光控制（离家、回家功能）；转向信号控制；供电端子控制（30、15、75）；燃油泵预工作控制；照明指示灯的控制（58d）；发电机励磁功能；雨刷电机。

（2）中央电器控制单元与中央继电器盒的对比优势。速腾轿车的中央电器控制单元 J519 与宝来轿车的中央继电器盒进行比较，如图 3-47 所示，J519 不仅实现了供电任务，还具备了更加强大的监控功能。具体如下：对用电器进行更强的控制；节省电量消耗；对用电器进行监控；用电器之间进行电子通信；电能管理；程序化设置；返修便利；带有自诊断功能。

（a）宝来轿车的中央继电器盒　　（b）速腾轿车的中央电器控制单元

图 3-47　宝来轿车的中央继电器盒与速腾轿车的中央电器控制单元对比

3. 用电负载（电能）管理

（1）电能管理的目标。为了确保蓄电池有足够的电能使发动机顺利起动和正常运转，控制单元根据以下的相关数据进行评估：发动机转速、电瓶电压、发电机的 DF 信号。在保证安全行驶的前提下，适当地关闭舒适功能的用电设备，如图 3-48 所示。

（2）电能管理的模式。中央电器控制单元 J519 实现电能管理的模式有 3 种，如表 3-4 所示。

（3）电能管理的工作过程。中央电器控制单元 J519 实现电能管理的工作过程如图 3-49 所示。

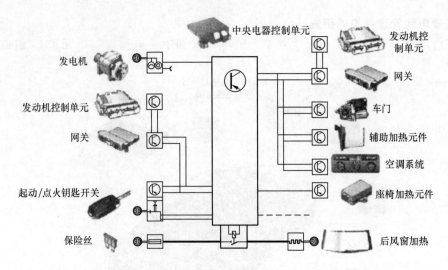

图 3-48 中央电器控制单元 J519 实现电能管理的功能电路

表 3-4 电能管理的 3 种模式

管理模式 1	管理模式 2	管理模式 3
15 号线接通并且发电机处于工作状态	15 号线接通并且发电机处于停机状态	15 号线断开并且发电机处于停机状态
如果蓄电池电压低于 12.7V，则控制单元要求发动机的急速提升 如果蓄电池的电压低于 12.2V，以下的用电器将被关闭：座椅加热、后风窗加热、后视镜加热、方向盘加热、脚坑照明、门内把手照明、全自动空调耗能降低或空调关闭、信息娱乐系统关闭并有关闭警示	如果蓄电池的电压低于 12.2V，以下的用电器将被关闭：空调耗能降低或空调关闭、脚坑照明、门内把手照明、上/下车灯、离家功能、信息娱乐系统关闭并有关闭警示	如果蓄电池的电压低于 11.8V，以下的用电器将被关闭：车内灯、脚坑照明、门内把手照明、上/下车灯、离家功能、信息娱乐系统

注：1. 这 3 种管理模式的不同之处在于，用电器被关闭的次序不同。
2. 在第 3 种模式中，一些用电器将会被立即关闭。
3. 如果关闭的条件取消，用电器将会被重新激活。
4. 如果用电器因为电能管理的原因被关闭，则 J519 中有故障存在。

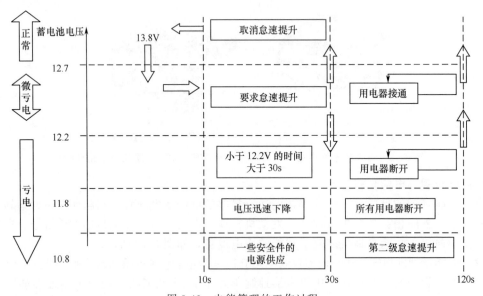

图 3-49 电能管理的工作过程

小 结

（1）交流发电机主要由转子、定子、整流器、前端盖、后端盖、带轮及风扇组成。

（2）交流发电机产生交流电的基本原理是电磁感应原理。交流发电机是利用产生磁场的转子旋转，使穿过定子绕组的磁通量发生变化，在定子绕组内产生交流感应电动势。

（3）交流发电机调节器的作用就是当发动机转速变化时，自动对发电机的电压进行调节，使发电机的电压稳定，以满足汽车用电设备的要求。

（4）发电机维修完毕需要进行空载试验和负荷试验，测出发电机在空载和满载情况下发出额定电压时对应的最小转速，从而判断发电机的工作是否正常。

习题及思考

（1）简述汽车交流发电机的组成与结构。
（2）简述硅整流发电机的励磁过程。
（3）根据奥迪汽车充电系统电路图试简述该充电系统的工作过程。
（4）如何检测汽车充电系统？请简述检测过程。

项目四 起动系统的检修

一、情境引入

一辆一汽丰田威驰轿车,接通点火开关起动挡时,只听见起动机缓慢地运转及飞轮处有"咔咔"声,而发动机不能正常起动。经检修,起动机单项离合器齿端面磨损严重,造成发动机无法起动。此事例让我们有必要对汽车起动系统与起动机常见故障进行学习。

二、相关知识

(一)起动系统概述

汽车发动机一般为内燃机。起动机向内燃机供给内燃机曲轴起动转矩,使内燃机进入自行运转状态。汽油机最低起动转速为50~70r/min。起动机(俗称马达)的作用是起动发动机。发动机起动之后,起动机便立即停止工作。发动机常用的起动方式有人力起动、辅助汽油机起动和电力起动机起动。目前大多数运输车辆都已采用电力起动机起动。电力起动机起动方式是由直流电动机通过传动机构将发动机起动,具有操作简单、体积小、重量轻、安全可靠、起动迅速并可重复起动等优点,一般将这种电力起动机简称为起动机。起动机安装在汽车发动机飞轮壳前端的座孔上,用螺栓紧固。

1. 起动系统的组成

起动系统由蓄电池、起动机和起动控制电路等组成,如图4-1所示,起动控制电路包括起动按钮或点火开关、起动继电器等。

起动机在点火开关或起动按钮的控制下,将蓄电池的电能转化为机械能,通过飞轮齿环带动发动机曲轴转动。为增大转矩,便于起动,起动机与曲轴的传动比:汽油机一般为13~17,柴油机一般为8~10。

2. 起动机的分类

(1) 按磁场产生的方式分类。

① 激磁式起动机。磁场是由激磁线圈产生的,起动大中型发动机时采用。

② 永磁式起动机。永磁式起动机以永磁材料(铁氧体或铁硼)为磁极。由于电动机中无磁极绕组,故可使起动机结构简化,体积和质量都可相应减小。起动中小型发动机时采用。

(2) 按操纵机构分类。

① 直接操纵式起动机。直接操纵式起动机是由脚踏或手拉杠杆联动机构直接控制起动机的主电路开关来接通或切断主电路,也称机械式起动机。这种方式虽然结构简单、工作可靠,但由于要求起动机、蓄电池靠近驾驶室,受安装布局的限制,且操作不便,已很少采用。

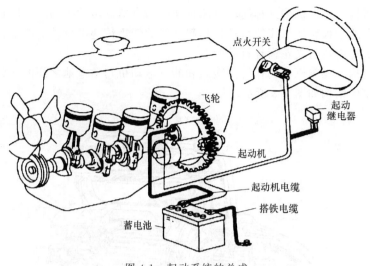

图 4-1　起动系统的总成

② 电磁操纵式起动机。电磁操纵式起动机是由起动按钮或点火开关控制继电器，再由继电器控制起动机的主开关来接通或切断主电路，也称电磁控制式起动机。这种方式可实现远距离控制，操作方便，目前在汽车上广泛采用。

（3）按传动机构的啮合方式分类。

① 惯性啮合式起动机。起动机旋转时，其啮合小齿轮靠惯性力自动啮入飞轮齿环。起动后，小齿轮又借惯性力自动与飞轮齿环脱离。这种啮合机构结构简单，但不能传递较大的转矩，且可靠性较差，已很少采用。

② 强制啮合式起动机。强制啮合式起动机是靠人力或电磁力拉动杠杆强制小齿轮啮入飞轮齿环的。这种啮合机构结构简单、动作可靠、操作方便，当今仍被采用。

③ 电枢移动式起动机。电枢移动式起动机是靠起动机磁极磁通的吸力，使电枢沿轴向移动而使小齿轮啮入飞轮齿环的，起动后再由回位弹簧使电枢回位，让驱动齿轮退出飞轮齿环。这种啮合机构多用于大功率的柴油汽车上。

④ 齿轮移动式起动机。齿轮移动式起动机是电磁开关推动安装在电枢轴孔内的啮合杆，而使小齿轮啮入飞轮齿环的。

⑤ 减速式起动机。减速式起动机也是靠电磁吸力推动单向离合器使小齿轮啮入飞轮齿环的。减速式起动机的结构特点是在电枢和驱动齿轮之间装有一级减速齿轮（一般速比为 3~4），它的优点是可采用小型高速低转矩的电动机，使起动机的体积减小、质量约减少 35%，并便于安装；提高了起动机的起动转矩，有利于发动机的起动；电枢轴较短，不易弯曲；减速齿轮的结构简单、效率高，保证了良好的机械性能，同时拆装修理方便。

（二）起动机的构造

起动机由串励直流电动机、传动机构和操纵机构 3 个部分组成，如图 4-2 所示。

（1）串励直流电动机。电动机的作用是将蓄电池输入的电能转换为机械能，产生电磁转矩。

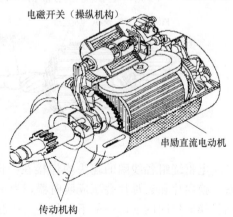

图 4-2　起动机的组成

（2）传动机构。传动机构又称起动机离合器、啮合器。传动机构的作用是在发动机起动时使起动机轴上的小齿轮啮入飞轮齿环，将起动机的转矩传递给发动机曲轴；在发动机起动后又能使起动机小齿轮与飞轮齿环自动脱开。

（3）操纵机构。操纵机构的作用是接通和断开电动机与蓄电池之间的电路。

起动机的整体结构如图 4-3 所示。

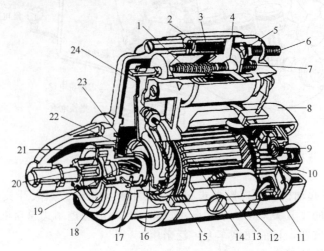

图 4-3　起动机的整体结构

1—回位弹簧；2—保持线圈；3—吸拉线圈；4—电磁开关壳体；5—触点；6—接线柱；7—接触盘；8—后端盖；
9—电刷弹簧；10—换向器；11—电刷；12—磁极；13—磁极铁芯；14—电枢；15—励磁绕组；
16—移动衬套；17—缓冲弹簧；18—单向离合器；19—电枢轴花键；20—驱动齿轮；
21—罩盖；22—制动盘；23—传动套筒；24—拨叉

（三）直流电动机

1. 串励直流电动机的构造

串励直流电动机是起动机最主要的组成部件，它的工作原理和特性决定了起动机的工作原理和特性。串励直流电动机主要由电枢（转子）、磁极（定子）、电刷架与机壳等部件构成。

（1）电枢。电枢是电动机的转子部分，作用是产生电枢转矩，包括电枢轴、换向器、电枢铁芯、电枢绕组，如图 4-4 所示。为了获得足够的转矩，通过电枢绕组的电流一般为 200～600A，因此，电枢绕组用很粗的矩形截面的铜线采用波绕法绕制而成。

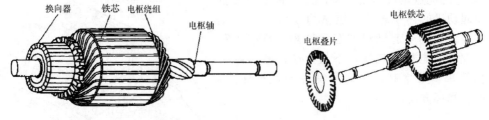

图 4-4　电枢

电枢绕组各线圈的端头均焊接在换向器片上，通过换向器和电刷将蓄电池的电流引进来。换向片和云母片叠压成换向器，为了避免电刷磨损的粉末落入换向片之间造成短路，起动机换向片间的云母一般不必割低。一般进口小汽车用起动机云母片低于钢片，检修时，若换向器铜片间槽的深度小于 0.2mm，就需用锯片将云母片割低至规定的深度。

（2）磁极。磁极的作用是产生磁场，分励磁式和永磁式两类。汽车起动机通常采用 4 个磁极，2 对磁极相对交错安装在电动机定子内壳上，定子与转子铁芯形成的磁力线回路如图 4-5 所示，低碳钢板制成的机壳是磁路的一部分。

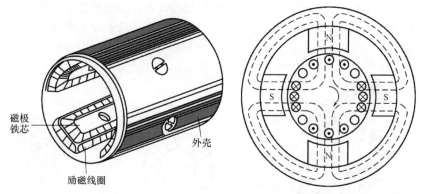

图 4-5　定子与转子铁芯形成的磁力线回路

（3）励磁式磁极。励磁绕组也是 4 个，这 4 个绕组有的是互相串联后再与电枢绕组串联，有的是每 2 个分别串联再并联后与电枢绕组串联，如图 4-6 所示。

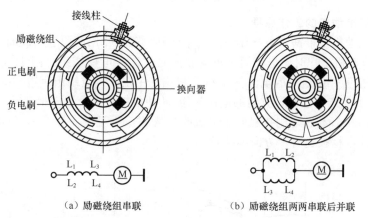

（a）励磁绕组串联　　　（b）励磁绕组两两串联后并联

图 4-6　励磁绕组的接法

如图 4-7 所示，励磁绕组一端接在外壳的绝缘接线柱上，另一端与 2 个非搭铁电刷相连，当起动开关接通时，起动机的电路为：蓄电池正极→接线柱 1→励磁绕组 4→非搭铁电刷 6→电枢绕组→搭铁电刷 5→搭铁→蓄电池负极。

（4）永磁式磁极。永磁式磁极采用永久磁铁，可节省材料，而且能使电动机磁极的径向尺寸减小，条形永久磁铁可用冷粘接法粘在机壳内壁上或用片弹簧均匀地固装在起动机机壳的内表面上。由于结构尺寸及永磁材料性能的限制，永磁起动机的功率一般不大于 2kW。

（5）电刷架与机壳。电刷架一般为框式结构，其中正极刷架与端盖绝缘固装，负极刷架直接搭铁。电刷置于电刷架中，电刷由铜粉与石墨粉压制而成，呈棕红色。刷架上装有弹性

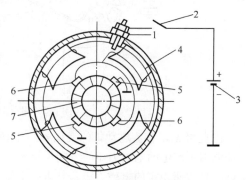

图 4-7　起动机的接线图
1—接线柱；2—起动开关；3—蓄电池；
4—励磁绕组；5—搭铁电刷；
6—非搭铁电刷；7—换向器

项目四　起动系统的检修　057

较好的盘形弹簧，电刷与刷架的组合如图 4-8 所示。

起动机机壳的一端有 4 个检查窗口，中部只有一个电流输入接线柱，并在内部与励磁绕组的一端相连。端盖分前、后 2 个，前端盖由钢板压制而成，后端盖由灰口铸铁浇制而成，呈缺口杯状。它们的中心均压装着青铜石墨轴承套或铁基含油轴承套，外围有 2 个或 4 个组装螺孔。电刷装在前端盖内，后端盖上有拨叉座，盖口有凸缘和安装螺孔，还有拧紧中间轴承板的螺钉孔。

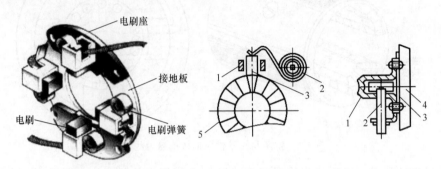

图 4-8 电刷与刷架的组合
1—框式刷架；2—盘形弹簧；3—电刷；4—前端盖；5—换向器

2. 串励直流电动机的工作原理

串励直流电动机是根据带电导体在磁场中受到电磁力作用的原理制成的。其工作原理如图 4-9 所示。电动机工作时，电流通过电刷和换向片流入电枢绕组。图 4-9（a）所示为换向片 A 与正电刷接触，绕组中的电流从 a→d，根据左手定则判定绕组匝边 ab、cd 均受到电磁力 F 的作用，由此产生逆时针方向的电磁转矩 M 使电枢转动；当电枢转动，换向片 A 与负电刷接触，换向片 B 与正电刷接触时，电流改为从 d→a［见图 4-9（b）］，但电磁转矩的方向仍保持不变，使电枢按逆时针方向继续转动。

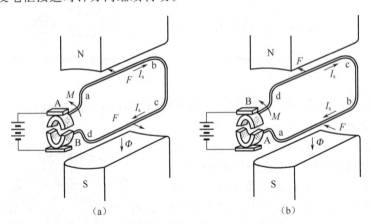

图 4-9 串励直流电动机的工作原理

由此可见，直流电动机的换向器将电源提供的直流电转换成电枢绕组所需的交流电，以保证电枢所产生的电磁力矩的方向保持不变，使其产生定向转动。实际的直流电动机为了产生足够大且转速稳定的电磁力矩，其电枢上绕有很多组线圈，换向器的铜片也随之相应增加。

3. 起动机的工作特性

（1）直流电动机工作时的特点。电动机中电流越大，电动机产生的扭矩越大。电动机的转速越高，电枢线圈中产生的反电动势就越大，电流也随之下降。

起动机在初始起动期间和起动期间各项指标的比较见表 4-1。

表 4-1　起动机在初始起动期间和起动期间各项指标

项目	阶段	
	初始起动期间	正常起动期间
电动机速度	较低	较高
电动机电流	较大	较小
电动机产生的扭矩	较大	较小
电枢中的反向电动势	较小	较大

（2）功率特性。直流串励式电动机的力矩 M、转速 n 和功率 P 随电枢电流变化的规律，称为直流串励式电动机的特性。在起动机起动的瞬间，电枢转速为零，电枢电流达到最大值，力矩也相应达到最大值，使发动机的起动变得很容易。这就是汽车起动机采用串励式电动机的主要原因。

在实际使用中，影响起动机功率的因素较多，必须对起动机进行正确保养。影响因素主要有如下 3 点。

① 接触电阻和导线电阻的影响。电刷与换向器接触不良、电刷弹簧张力减弱及导线与蓄电池接线柱连接不牢，都会使电阻增加；导线过长及导线截面积过小也会造成较大的电压降。起动机工作时电流特别大，这些都会使起动机功率减小。因此，必须保证电刷与换向器接触良好，导线接头牢固，并尽可能缩短蓄电池接至起动机的导线及蓄电池搭铁线的长度，选用截面积足够大的导线，以保证起动机的正常工作。

② 蓄电池容量的影响。蓄电池容量越小，其内阻越大，内阻上的电压降也越大，因而供给起动机的电压降低，也会使起动机功率减小。

③ 温度的影响。当温度降低时，由于蓄电池电解液黏度增大，内阻增加，会使蓄电池容量和端电压急剧下降，起动机功率将会显著降低。因此，冬季应对蓄电池采取有效的保温措施，如不要将汽车停在户外过夜等。

（四）起动机的传动机构与操纵机构

1. 起动机的传动机构

一般起动机的传动机构是指包括驱动齿轮的单向离合器和拨叉。

起动机不工作时，驱动齿轮和飞轮齿环脱离啮合，如图 4-10(a) 所示。发动机起动时，按下按钮或起动开关，线圈通电产生电磁力将铁芯吸入，带动拨叉推出离合器，使驱动齿轮啮入飞轮齿环，如图 4-10(b)、(c) 所示。发动机起动后，只要松开按钮或开关，线圈即断电，电磁力消失，在回位弹簧的作用下，铁芯退出，拨叉返回，拨叉头将打滑工况下的离合器拨回，驱动齿轮脱离飞轮齿环。

常见起动机单向离合器（超越离合器）的结构主要有滚柱式、摩擦片式和弹簧式 3 种。

（1）滚柱式离合器。滚柱式离合器的构造如图 4-11 所示，驱动齿轮与外壳制成一体，外壳内装有十字块和 4 套滚柱、压帽和弹簧。十字块与花键套筒固连，壳底与外壳相互扣合密封。花键套筒的外面装有啮合弹簧及衬圈，末端安装拨环与卡圈。整个离合器总成套装在电动机轴的花键部位上，可作轴向移动和随轴转动。在外壳与十字块之间，形成 4 个宽窄不等的楔形槽，槽内分别装有一套滚柱、压帽及弹簧。滚柱的直径略大于楔形槽的窄端，略小于楔形槽的宽端。因此，当十字块作为主动部分旋转时，滚柱滚入窄端，将十字块与外壳卡

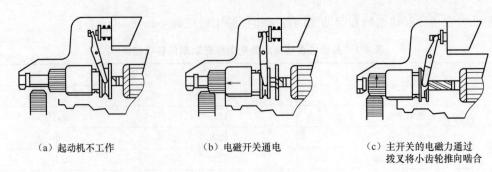

(a) 起动机不工作　　(b) 电磁开关通电　　(c) 主开关的电磁力通过拨叉将小齿轮推向啮合

图 4-10　起动机传动机构的工作过程

紧，使十字块与外壳之间能传递力矩。当外壳作为主动部分旋转时，滚柱滚入宽端，如放松打滑，则不能传递力矩。

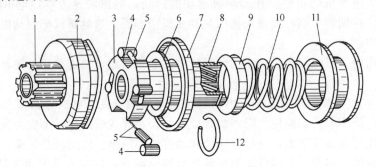

图 4-11　滚柱式离合器的构造

1—驱动齿轮；2—外壳；3—十字块；4—滚柱；5—弹簧；6—垫圈；7—护盖；8—花键套筒；
9—弹簧座；10—啮合弹簧；11—拨环；12—卡簧

滚柱式离合器的工作原理如图 4-12 所示。如图 4-12(a) 所示，发动机起动时，经拨叉将离合器沿花键推出，驱动齿轮啮入发动机飞轮齿环。由于十字块处于主动状态，随电动机电枢一起旋转，促使 4 套滚柱进入槽的窄端，将花键套筒与外壳挤紧，于是电动机电枢的转矩就可由十字块经离合器外壳传给驱动齿轮，从而达到驱动发动机飞轮齿环旋转起动发动机运转的目的。如图 4-12(b) 所示，发动机起动后，飞轮齿环的转速高于驱动齿轮，十字块处于被动状态，促使滚柱进入槽的宽端而自由滚动，只有驱动齿轮随飞轮齿环作高速旋转，起动机电枢转速并不升高，防止了电枢超速"飞散"的危险。起动完毕，由于拨叉回位弹簧的作用，经拨环使离合器退回，驱动齿轮完全脱离飞轮齿环。

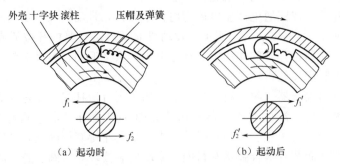

(a) 起动时　　(b) 起动后

图 4-12　滚柱式离合器的工作原理

滚柱式离合器具有结构简单、坚固耐用、体积小、重量轻、工作可靠等优点，因此，得到广泛采用。其不足是不能用到大功率起动机上。

（2）摩擦片式离合器。摩擦片式离合器具有传递大转矩、防止超载损坏起动机的优点，多用在大功率起动机上。但由于摩擦片容易磨损而影响起动性能，需要经常检查、调整或更换摩擦片。此外，这种离合器结构比较复杂，耗用材料较多，加工费时，且不便于维修。

（3）弹簧式离合器。弹簧式离合器具有结构简单、制造工艺简单、成本低等优点，但由于驱动弹簧所需圈数较多，使其轴向尺寸增大。

2. 起动机的操纵机构

起动机的电磁开关与电磁式拨叉合装在一起，利用挡铁控制，分为直接控制式电磁开关和带起动继电器控制式电磁开关。电磁开关的结构如图4-13所示。

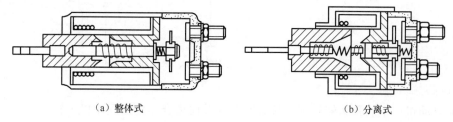

(a) 整体式　　　　　　　　(b) 分离式

图4-13　电磁开关的结构

（1）直接控制式电磁开关。在一些起动机功率小于1.2kW的轿车电路中，由点火开关直接控制起动机的吸拉线圈、保持线圈的电流，如图4-14所示。

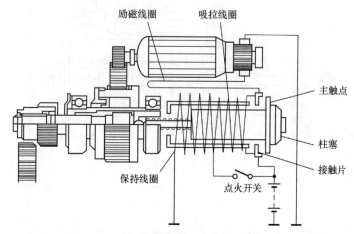

图4-14　直接控制式电磁开关电路

操纵机构的工作过程如下。

① 起动机不工作时，驱动齿轮处于与飞轮齿环脱开啮合位置，电磁开关中的接触盘与各接触点分开，如图4-14所示。

② 将起动开关接通时，分3个阶段。

第一阶段为吸引阶段，如图4-15所示，吸拉线圈（牵引线圈、吸引线圈）、保持线圈同时工作，其电流回路为：蓄电池（＋）→点火开关→吸拉线圈→励磁绕组→搭铁→蓄电池（－）→保持线圈→搭铁→蓄电池（－）。

此时，吸拉线圈和保持线圈磁场方向相同，活动铁芯在电磁力的作用下克服复位弹簧的弹力向内移动，压动推杆使起动机主开关接触盘与接触点靠近，与此同时，带动拨叉将驱动小齿轮推向啮合；当驱动小齿轮与飞轮齿环接近完全啮合时，接触盘已将触点接通，起动机主电路接通。其电流回路为：蓄电池（＋）→点火开关→电磁开关触点→励磁绕组→搭铁→

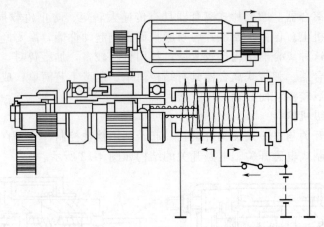

图 4-15 吸拉线圈（牵引线圈、吸引线圈）、保持线圈同时工作状态

蓄电池（一）。

直流电动机产生的强大转矩通过接合状态的单向离合器传给发动机飞轮齿环。

第二阶段为保持阶段，如图 4-16 所示，主开关接通后，吸拉线圈被主开关短路，电流消失，活动铁芯在保持线圈电磁力作用下保持在吸合位置。

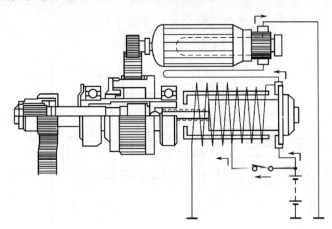

图 4-16 磁力保持阶段

发动机起动后，飞轮转动线速度超过了起动机驱动小齿轮的线速度，单向离合器打滑，避免了电枢绕组高速飞散的危险。

第三阶段为断开阶段，如图 4-17 所示，松开起动开关时，起动控制电路断开，但电磁开关内吸拉线圈和保持线圈通过仍然闭合的主开关得到电流。因吸拉线圈和保持线圈磁场方向相反，相互削弱，活动铁芯在复位弹簧的作用下迅速回位，使驱动小齿轮脱开啮合，主开关断开，起动机停止工作，起动结束。

（2）带起动继电器控制式电磁开关。带起动继电器控制式电磁开关电路如图 4-18 所示。

发动机起动时，将点火开关钥匙旋至起动挡位。起动继电器通电后，吸下可动臂使触点闭合，接通了电磁开关线圈电路，起动机投入工作。发动机起动后，只需松开点火开关钥匙，点火开关自动转回到点火工作挡位，起动继电器线圈断电触点打开，电磁开关也随即断开，起动机停止工作。

利用起动继电器控制电磁开关，能减小通过点火开关起动触点的电流，避免烧蚀触点，延长使用寿命。有些汽车上的起动继电器在改进控制电路以后，还能起到自动停止起动机工

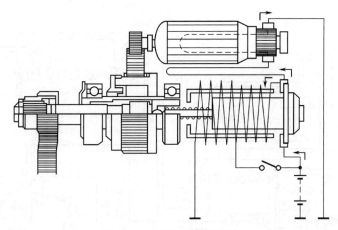

图 4-17 电磁开关断电状态

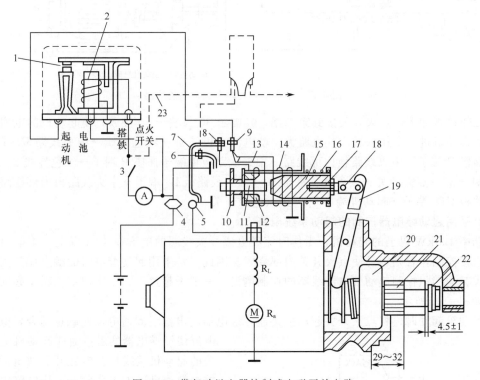

图 4-18 带起动继电器控制式电磁开关电路

1—起动继电器触点;2—起动继电器线圈;3—点火开关;4,5—主接线柱;6—附加电阻短线接线柱;
7—导电片;8—吸拉线圈接线柱;9—起动机接线柱;10—接触盘;11—推杆;12—固定铁芯;
13—吸拉线圈;14—保持线圈;15—活动铁芯;16—复位弹簧;17—调节螺钉;
18—连接叉;19—拨叉;20—滚柱式离合器;21—驱动齿轮;
22—止推螺母;23—点火线圈附加电阻线

作及安全保护的作用。

（五）起动机的控制电路

1. 点火开关直接控制的起动系统电路

桑塔纳系列轿车起动系统线路如图 4-19 所示。

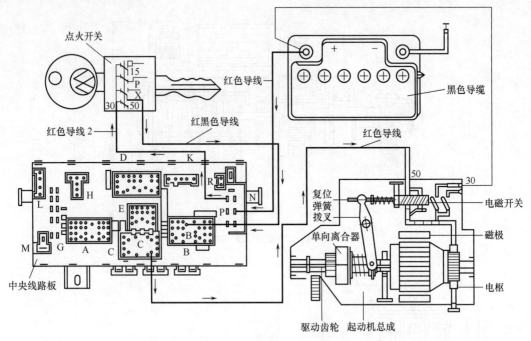

图 4-19 桑塔纳系列轿车起动系统线路

工作过程如下。点火开关拨到第二挡，其端子 30 与端子 50 接通，使起动机的电磁开关通电，起动机进入工作状态。其电路为：蓄电池正极端子→红色导线→中央线路板 16 的单端子插座 P 端子→中央线路板内部线路→中央线路板单端子插座 P 端子→红色导线 2→点火开关端子 30→点火开关→点火开关端子 50→中央线路板 B8 端子→中央线路板内部线路→中央线路板 C18 端子→起动机端子 50→进入电磁开关。

2. 采用起动继电器控制的起动系统电路

功率 1.5kW 以上的起动机，工作时流经电磁开关线圈的电流在 40A 以上，不能由点火开关直接控制，否则容易使点火开关内部烧毁。因此，常采用起动继电器的触点作开关，点火开关起动挡只控制起动继电器线圈的控制电流（一般不超过 1A）。丰田威驰轿车起动系统线路如图 4-20 所示。

发动机起动时，将点火开关起动挡接通，继电器的电磁线圈通电，使触点闭合，电源的电流便经继电器的触点通往起动机电磁开关的起动机接线柱。电磁开关通电后，便控制起动机进入工作状态。从电路中可以看出，起动期间流经点火开关起动挡和继电器线圈的电流较小，大电流经过继电器开关流入起动机，保护了点火开关。起动过程的工作原理如前所述，此处不再重复。

3. 带防盗系统的起动控制电路

有些汽车的起动继电器线圈通过防盗系统搭铁。发动机起动时，只有防盗系统发出起动信号后，继电器线圈才能搭铁，如果防盗系统没有收到起动信号，则继电器线圈中无电流，起动机就不能工作，实

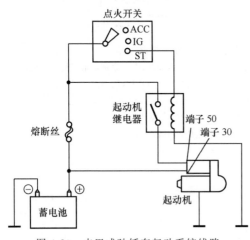

图 4-20 丰田威驰轿车起动系统线路

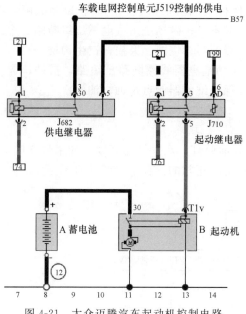

图 4-21 大众迈腾汽车起动机控制电路

现了防盗功能。

(1) 大众迈腾汽车起动机控制电路。大众迈腾汽车起动机控制线路如图 4-21 所示,起动机的电磁开关由供电继电器 J682 和起动机继电器 J710 (供电继电器 2) 两个继电器控制。供电继电器的电源来自车载电网控制单元 J519, 而车载电源控制系统又从发动机防盗系统、自动变速器挡位状态取得信号,当防盗系统未正常发出起动信号、自动变速器挡位不在 P/N 挡时,起动继电器 J682 不能接通,因而起动继电器 J710 也不能接通,因此发动机不能起动,从而实现对起动机电磁开关的控制。

(2) 工作过程。发动机起动时,在自动变速器置于 P 或 N 挡,防盗系统发出起动信号状态下,将点火开关置于起动挡,起动机继电器 J710 电磁线圈通电,继电器常开触点闭合,电源的电流便经继电器的触点通往起动机电磁开关的起动机接线柱,电磁开关通电后,起动机的主电路接通,起动机转动,同时带动发动机运转。

(六) 起动机的正确使用

(1) 起动机每次起动时间不超过 5s, 再次起动时应停止 15s, 使蓄电池得以恢复。如果有连续第 3 次起动,应在检查与排除故障的基础上停歇 15min 以后。

(2) 在冬季或低温情况下起动时,应采取保温措施。

(3) 发动机起动后,必须立即切断起动机控制电路,使起动机停止工作。

三、项目实施

(一) 起动系统实施要求

① 通过该项目的实施,应能够对起动系统进行拆装与调整,并掌握起动系统故障诊断与检测的步骤与方法。

② 该项目应具备完成项目的车辆和该车辆的电路图等资料。

③ 设备及仪器。起动机、蓄电池等设备;各类起子、尖嘴钳、扭力扳手、台钳等拆装工具;万用表、游标卡尺、百分表、V 形铁、弹簧秤等检测仪器。

(二) 实施步骤

1. 起动线路检测及起动系统的故障诊断

(1) 手动变速器车辆起动机不工作故障诊断。

① 故障现象。点火开关打至起动挡时,起动机不转动。

② 故障原因如下:

a. 供电系统故障。蓄电池储电量严重不足,亏电太多;起动机电缆线与蓄电池接线柱连接松动或接线柱氧化。

b. 起动机故障。起动机电磁开关吸拉线圈或保持线圈出现搭铁、断路、短路故障，电磁开关触点烧蚀，或因调整不当使接触盘与触点接触不良；磁场绕组或电枢绕组断路、短路或搭铁；电刷在电刷架内卡死、弹簧折断等；换向器油污、烧蚀、磨损，产生沟槽。

c. 继电器故障（用于带起动继电器的电路）。起动继电器线圈断路、短路、搭铁；起动继电器触点烧蚀、油污；铁芯与触点臂气隙过大；保护继电器触点烧蚀、油污。

d. 点火开关故障。起动挡失灵。

e. 保险丝。

③ 故障诊断方法。在未接通起动开关前，打开前照灯，观察灯光亮度。如果灯光暗淡，则可能是蓄电池亏电过多或连接线松脱所致。在蓄电池正常的情况下，起动机不工作故障诊断方法可参考图 4-22 进行。

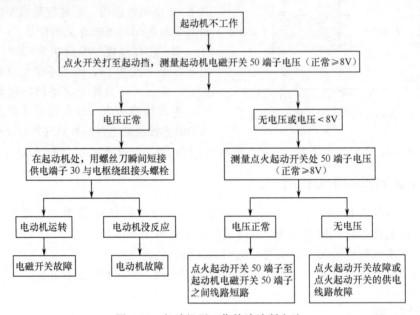

图 4-22　起动机不工作故障诊断方法

(2) 自动变速器车辆起动机不工作故障诊断。

① 故障现象：踩下制动踏板，自动变速器在 P 或 N 挡，点火开关打至起动挡，起动机没有反应。

② 故障原因。首先参考手动变速器车辆起动机不工作故障诊断的原因，另外还有以下原因：

a. 自动变速器多功能开关有故障。

b. 自动变速器控制单元有故障。

c. 相关线路接触不良或有断路处。

③ 故障诊断方法。

对于自动变速器车辆，首先要确认自动变速器是否处在 N 或 P 挡。在蓄电池有电、起动机电磁开关各接线及各搭铁线接触良好的前提下，可在起动机处用导线短接 30 与 50 端子。若起动机不工作，则说明故障在起动机自身（此时可进一步进行诊断，用较粗导线在起动机处瞬间短接 30 端子与电枢接头，若电机运转，则说明故障在电磁开关；否则说明故障在电机内部）；若起动机工作，需在起动继电器处进一步进行诊断，在确认各接线良好且点火开关起动供电正常的前提下，借助专用仪器（如大众车系使用 VAG1551 或 VAG1552）

对自动变速器的多功能开关和控制单元进行诊断，若无故障，说明故障在起动继电器。

（3）起动机运转无力故障。

① 故障现象：起动时，发动机转速太低不能起动。

② 故障原因。

a. 蓄电池亏电。

b. 线路接触不良或接线柱被氧化。

c. 起动机自身故障。

d. 发动机转动阻力太大。

③ 故障诊断方法。在正确使用发动机机油和具有合适的 V 形皮带张紧度的情况下，可按图 4-23 进行故障诊断。

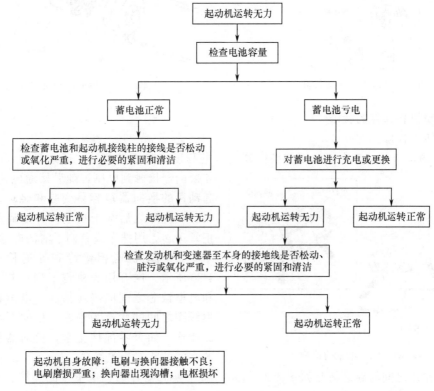

图 4-23　起动机运转无力故障诊断方法

2. 起动机的拆解

（1）起动机的就车拆卸。

① 断开蓄电池的负极电缆。断开蓄电池的负极电缆之前，对存储在 ECU 等器件内的信息做笔录。

② 拆下起动机电缆。拆下防短路盖、起动机电缆定位螺母，断开起动机端子 30 的起动机电缆。由于起动机电缆直接与电池相连，因此，带有一个防断路盖。

③ 断开起动机连接器。按压连接器的卡销，然后握住连接器机身断开连接器。

④ 拆卸起动机。拆下起动机安装螺栓，然后晃动起动机将其拆下。

（2）起动机的分解。

① 拆卸电磁开关总成，如图 4-24 所示。断开引线拆下定位螺母并断开引线。拆下 2 颗螺母并将电磁起动机开关拉到后侧。向上拉电磁起动机开关的顶端，从驱动杆中取出挂钩。

拆下电磁开关。

② 拆下起动机磁轭总成，如图 4-25 所示。拆下 2 个螺栓，拆下换向器端盖，从起动机磁轭分开起动机外壳，拆下驱动杆。

③ 拆下起动机电刷弹簧。

④ 拆卸起动机离合器。

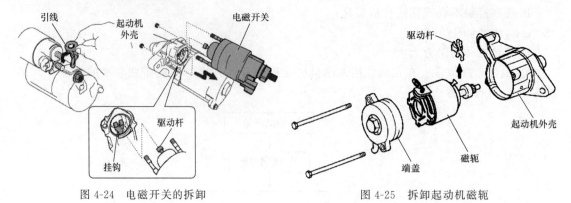

图 4-24　电磁开关的拆卸　　　　　　　　图 4-25　拆卸起动机磁轭

3. 起动机各部件的检修

（1）转子检修。

① 目测检查。检查电枢线圈和换向器变脏的程度或是否被烧坏。通过自转，电枢线圈和换向器接触到电刷，随后接通电流。因此，起动机的换向器很容易变脏和烧坏。换向器变脏和烧坏之后会干扰电流并妨碍起动机的正常运转。用抹布或者刷子清洁电枢总成。

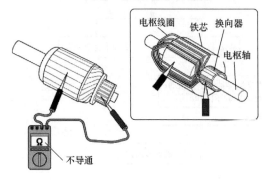

② 起动机电枢绝缘和导通检查：如图 4-26 所示。用万用表执行下列检查：换向器和电枢铁芯之间的绝缘情况。电枢铁芯和电枢线圈之间的状态为绝缘，换向器与电枢线圈相连。如果零部件正常，换向器和电枢铁芯之间的状态为绝缘。

图 4-26　电枢的检测

换向器片之间的导通情况如图 4-27 所示。每个换向器片通过电枢线圈连接。如果零部件正常，换向器片之间的状态为导通。

③ 换向器圆跳动检查。用千分表检查换向器的跳动水平，如图 4-28 所示。由于换向器的跳动量变大，换向器与电刷的接触将减弱。因此，可能会出现故障，如起动机无法运转。

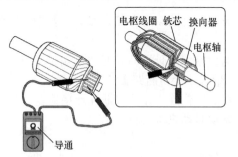 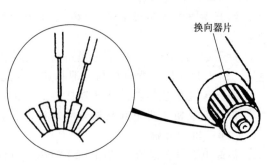

图 4-27　换向器的检测

④ 检查换向器的外径。用游标卡尺测量换向器的外径，如图 4-29 所示。由于换向器在转动时要与电刷接触，因此会受到磨损。如果测量值超出规定的磨损范围，与电刷的接触将变弱，这可能会导致电循环不良。因此，可能会发生起动机无法转动和其他故障。

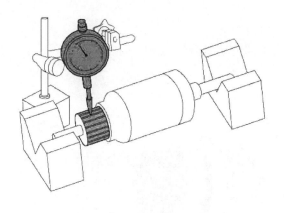

图 4-28 换向器圆跳动的检查

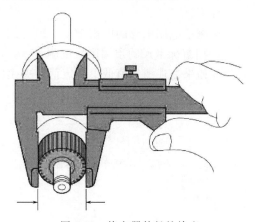

图 4-29 换向器外径的检查

⑤ 检查凹槽深度，用游标卡尺的深度杆测量换向器片之间的深度，如图 4-30 所示。

（2）定子检修。

① 检查励磁线圈。

a. 用万用表检查电刷引线（A组）和引线之间的导通情况，如图 4-31 所示。A组的2根电刷引线导通，B组的2根电刷引线不导通。检查电刷引线和引线之间的导通情况有助于确定励磁线圈中是否发生开路。检查电刷引线和起动机磁轭之间的绝缘情况有助于确定励磁线圈中是否发生短路。

b. 电刷引线（A组）和起动机磁轭之间的绝缘情况，如图 4-32 所示。检查引线和所有电刷引线之间的导通情况。A组的2根电刷引线导通，B组的两根电刷引线不导通。检查电刷引线和引线之间的

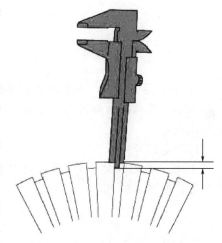

图 4-30 换向器凹槽深度检查

导通情况有助于确定励磁线圈中是否发生开路。检查电刷引线和起动机磁轭之间的绝缘情况有助于确定励磁线圈中是否发生短路。

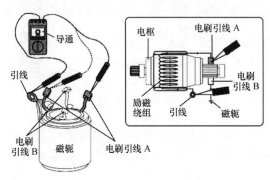

图 4-31 电刷引线的导通检查

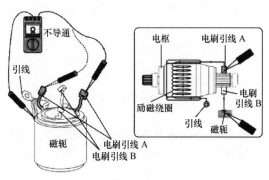

图 4-32 检查电刷引线和磁轭的绝缘情况

② 检查电刷。电刷被弹簧压在换向器上。如果电刷磨损程度超过规定限度，弹簧的夹持力将降低，与换向器的接触将变弱。这会使电流的流动不畅，起动机可能因此而无法转动。清洁电刷并用游标卡尺测量电刷长度，如图 4-33 所示。

注意：

a. 测量电刷中部的电刷长度，因为此部分磨损最严重。

b. 用游标卡尺的顶端测量电刷长度，因为磨损部位呈圆形。

c. 如果上述测量值低于规定值，更换电刷。

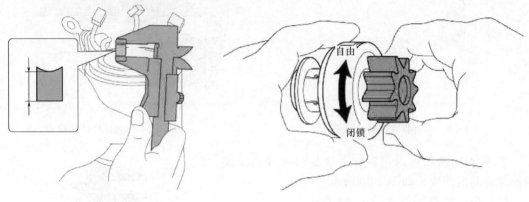

图 4-33 测量电刷的长度　　　　　　图 4-34 离合器的检查

③ 离合器的检查。用手转动起动机离合器，检查单向离合器是否处于闭锁状态，如图 4-34 所示。单向离合器仅向一个旋转方向传送扭矩。在另一个方向，离合器只是空转，不会传送扭矩。

（3）电磁开关的检查。

① 检查电磁开关，用手指按住柱塞。松开手指之后，检查柱塞是否很顺畅地返回其原来位置，如图 4-35 所示。

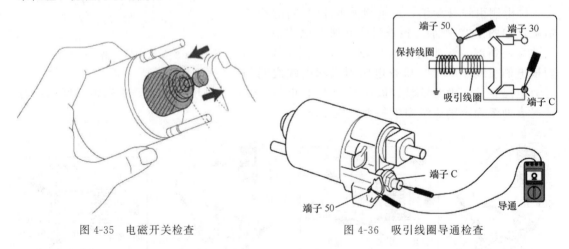

图 4-35 电磁开关检查　　　　　　图 4-36 吸引线圈导通检查

② 检查电磁开关的导通情况，如图 4-36 所示。用万用表检查端子 50 和端子 C 之间的导通情况。如果牵引线圈正常，则两个端子之间为导通。如果牵引线圈断开，柱塞无法被引入。

③ 检查端子 50 和壳体之间的导通情况，如图 4-37 所示。如果保持线圈正常，则端子

50 和开关体之间为导通。如果保持线圈断开,可牵引柱塞,但是无法保持,因此小齿轮反复伸出和返回。

4. 起动机的装复

(1) 起动机的组装。

① 安装起动机离合器分总成。

② 安装电刷弹簧。

③ 安装起动机磁轭总成。

④ 安装电磁起动机开关。将柱塞钩到驱动杆上,然后用 2 个螺栓将电磁起动机开关安装到起动机外壳上。连接引线和螺母。

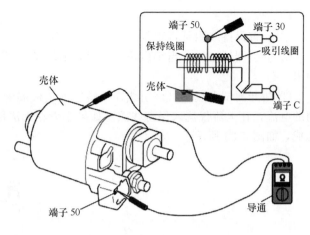

图 4-37 保持线圈的导通检查

(2) 起动机装复的注意事项。

① 注意检查各轴承的同心度。电枢轴轴承往往不易同心,若不同心度过大,就会增加电枢轴运转的阻力。检查的方法是:各轴颈与每个铜套配合时,既能转动自如又感觉不出有明显的间隙。装上前端盖后,再次转动电枢,也应转动灵活,否则为轴承不同心。

② 各铜套、电枢轴颈、键槽止推垫圈等摩擦部位,都应使用机油予以润滑。固定中间轴承支撑板的螺钉,一定要带有弹簧垫圈。否则,工作中支撑板振动,使螺钉松动,便会造成起动机不能正常工作,甚至损坏起动机。

5. 起动机的性能检验

起动机性能是否良好,也可以直接用蓄电池进行试验,但是用蓄电池给起动机长时间供电会烧坏线圈,因此,每次检查的时间限定为 3~5s。

(1) 牵引测试。检查电磁起动机开关是否正常,其连接如图 4-38 所示。

① 为防止起动机转动,从端子 C 断开励磁线圈引线。

② 将蓄电池正极(+)端子连接到端子 50 上。

③ 将蓄电池负极(-)端子连接到起动机体和端子 C(测试引线 A)上,检查小齿轮是否露出。如果小齿轮没有露出,更换电磁起动机开关总成。

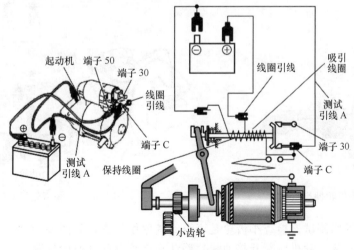

图 4-38 牵引测试

（2）保持测试。

① 检查保持线圈是否正常。

② 牵引测试之后，当小齿轮伸出时，从端子 C 断开测试引线 A。检查小齿轮是否保持伸出状态。

③ 断开测试引线 A（该引线连接蓄电池负极端子和端子 C），从端子 C 断开流入牵引线圈的电流，让电流仅流入保持线圈。如果小齿轮无法保持伸出状态，则更换电磁起动机开关总成，如图 4-39 所示。

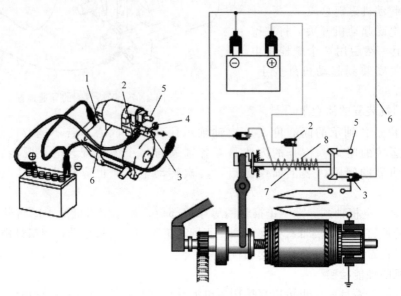

图 4-39 保持测试

1—起动机；2—端子 50 接柱；3—端子 C；4—线圈引线；5—端子 30 接柱；
6—测试线 A；7—保持线圈；8—吸引线圈

（3）检查小齿轮间隙。检查小齿轮的伸出量，如图 4-40 所示。在保持测试状态下，测量小齿轮和止动环之间的间隙。如果间隙超出规定值范围，更换电磁起动机开关总成。

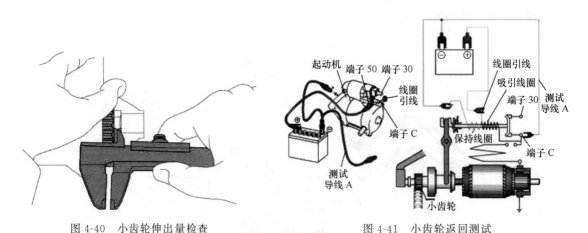

图 4-40 小齿轮伸出量检查　　图 4-41 小齿轮返回测试

（4）小齿轮返回测试。检查小齿轮是否返回其原始位置，如图 4-41 所示。保持测试后，当小齿轮伸出时，从起动机体断开接地线。确认小齿轮返回其原始位置。

（5）无负荷测试。检查电磁起动机开关的接触点及换向器和电刷之间的接触点。

① 用台钳固定住夹在铝板或者布之间的起动机。

② 将拆下的励磁线圈引线连接到端子 C。

③ 将蓄电池正极（+）端子连接到端子 30 和端子 50 上，如图 4-42 所示。

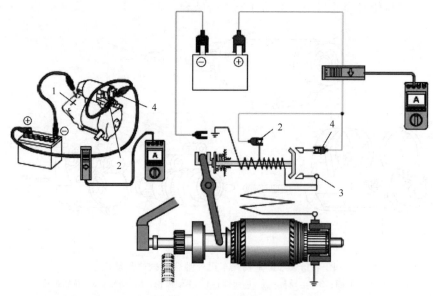

图 4-42　无负荷测试

1—起动机；2—端子 50 接柱；3—端子 C；4—端子 30

④ 将万用表连接在蓄电池正极（+）端子和端子 30 之间。

⑤ 将蓄电池负极（-）端子连接到起动机体上，然后转动起动机。

⑥ 测量流入起动机的电流。规定电流 11V 时低于 50A，如图 4-43 所示。

注意：

在无负荷测试中，电流会随起动机电机的不同而略有不同，有时甚至会用到 200～300A 的电流。预先查阅维修手册，务必使用容量足够大的安培计和引线。

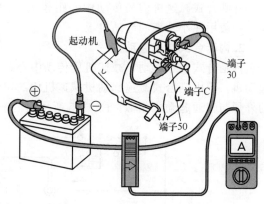

图 4-43　测量流入起动机的电流

四、知识与技能拓展

（一）减速起动机的结构

减速起动机的结构特点是在电枢与驱动齿轮之间装有减速齿轮。减速比一般为 3～4。减速齿轮使得起动机的转速降低，输出转矩增高，带动小动齿轮。因此，起动机可以采用小型、高速、低转矩的电动机，从而可以缩小起动机的外形尺寸，减轻了起动机的重量，提高起动性能的同时减轻了蓄电池的负担。减速起动机的减速机构根据结构可分为外啮合式、内啮合式和行星齿轮啮合式 3 种类型。

1. 外啮合式减速起动机

在电枢轴和起动机驱动齿轮之间利用惰轮作中间传动，且电磁开关铁芯与驱动齿轮同轴心，直接推动驱动齿轮进入啮合，无需拨叉。因此，此起动机的外形与普通的起动机有较大的差别。图 4-44 所示为丰田系列汽车用外啮合式减速起动机。有些外啮合式减速机构中间不加惰轮，驱动齿轮必须通过拨叉拨动才能进行啮合。

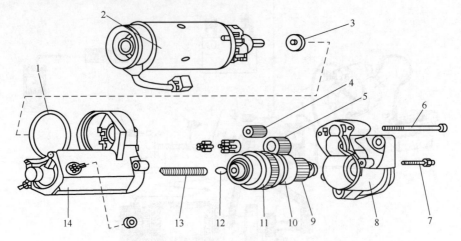

图 4-44　丰田系列汽车用外啮合式减速起动机
1—O 形橡胶圈；2—电动机；3—毡垫圈；4—主动齿轮；5—惰轮；6—拉紧螺栓；
7—螺栓；8—传动外壳；9—驱动齿轮；10—单向离合器；11—从动齿轮；
12—钢球；13—回位弹簧；14—电磁开关

外啮合式减速机构的传动中心距较大，因此，受起动机结构的限制，其减速比不能太大，一般用在小功率的起动机上。

2. 内啮合式减速起动机

内啮合式减速起动机减速机构传动中心距小，可有较大的减速比，故适用于较大功率的起动机。但内啮合式减速起动机减速机构的驱动齿轮仍需拨叉拨动进行啮合。因此，起动机的外形与普通起动机相似。图 4-45 所示为内啮合式减速起动机的工作原理。

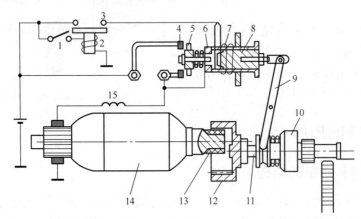

图 4-45　内啮合式减速起动机的工作原理
1—起动开关；2—起动继电器；3—起动继电器触点；4—主触点；5—接触盘；6—吸拉线圈；
7—保持线圈；8—活动铁芯；9—拨叉；10—单向离合器；11—螺旋花键轴；
12—内啮合减速齿轮；13—主动齿轮；14—电枢绕组；15—励磁绕组

3. 行星齿轮啮合式减速起动机

行星齿轮啮合式减速起动机结构紧凑、传动比大、效率高。由于输出轴与电枢轴同心、同旋向电枢轴无径向载荷，可使整机尺寸减小，除了结构上增加行星齿轮啮合式减速机构之外，由于行星齿轮啮合式减速起动机的轴向位置结构与普通起动机相同，因此，配件可通用。行星齿轮啮合式减速起动机如图4-46所示。该装置中设有3个行星齿轮，1个太阳轮（电枢轴齿轮）及1个固定的内齿圈，其啮合关系及输出路线如图4-47所示，行星齿轮支架是一个具有一定厚度的圆盘，圆盘和驱动齿轮轴制成一体。3个行星齿轮连同齿轮轴一起压装在圆盘上，行星齿轮在轴上可以灵活转动。驱动齿轮轴一端制有螺旋键齿，与离合器传动导管内的螺旋键槽配合。

太阳轮制成11个齿，压装在电枢轴上，并保持与3个行星齿轮同时啮合。塑料内齿圈制有37个齿，3个行星齿轮在其

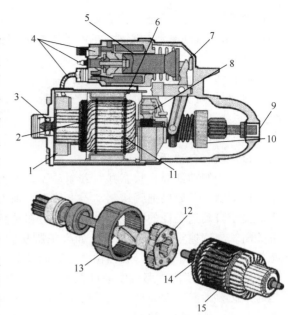

图4-46 行星齿轮啮合式减速起动机
1—电刷；2—焊接的连接；3—滚珠轴承；4—接线柱与导线；
5—活动铁芯；6—永久磁铁；7—拨叉连接机构；
8—行星齿轮减速器；9—滚柱轴承；10—离合器；11—电枢；
12—行星齿轮架；13—固定齿轮；14—太阳轮；15—电枢

上滚动。内齿圈的外缘制有凸起，嵌放在后端盖上的凹坑内，以保持固定。该齿轮的减速比为

$$i = 1 + Z_s/Z_e = 1 + 37/11 \approx 4.4$$

式中 Z_e——太阳轮齿数；
Z_s——内齿圈齿数。

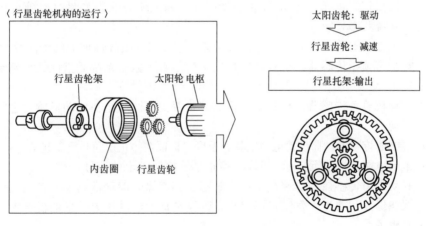

图4-47 行星齿轮内核关系及输出路线

（二）起动/停止系统

1. 起动/停止系统的作用

使用智能起动/停止系统时，如遇红灯，那么车辆静止时发动机自动关闭。点火开关在

停机阶段保持打开状态。在需要时，发动机自动再次起动。随着点火开关的打开，智能起动/停止系统自动激活。起动/停止系统在拥堵的城市道路上行驶，可帮助节省燃油并减少CO_2排放。

2. 起动/停止系统的基本使用条件

驾驶员车门必须关闭，并系上安全带。发动机舱盖关闭。车辆从上次停车至此已行驶了4公里以上。

3. 工作过程

（1）装有自动变速箱的汽车。

将车辆制动到静止状态并踩着制动器，发动机会被关闭。在组合仪表显示屏上的信息栏中出现指示灯。如果把脚从制动器上移开，那么发动机再次起动。起动/停止系统指示灯熄灭。关于自动选挡杆的其他信息：发动机在选挡杆位置 P、N 和 D/S 或 tiptronic 运行模式下关闭。当变速箱在 P 挡位时，如果把脚从制动器上移开的话，那么发动机也保持关闭状态。如果挂入一个其他行驶挡位并松开制动器，发动机才再次起动。如果在停机阶段变速箱切换到 R 倒车挡位，那么发动机再次起动。从 D/S 向 P 挡位切换要迅速，以避免在通过 R 挡时不必要地起动发动机。发动机关闭与否，可以通过降低或提高制动力量自己进行控制。在走走停停地行驶或转弯时，如果只是轻踏制动器，那么在车辆静止时不会停机。一旦重踩制动器，那么发动机即被关闭。

（2）装有手动变速箱的汽车。

车辆静止时切换到空挡状态并松开离合器，发动机会被关闭。在组合仪表显示屏上的信息栏中出现起动/停止系统指示灯。如果踩下离合器踏板，那么发动机再次起动，起动/停止系统指示灯熄灭。

4. 部件说明

（1）起动机：带起动/停止系统的车辆配备有动力强劲的起动机。

（2）发动机转速传感器：发动机转速传感器可以识别点火开关关闭位置（角度位置），这样就能够快速地重新起动发动机。

（3）发动机控制单元：起动/停止协调程序，输入所有状态变量（驾驶员操作、环境和安全状况、系统状态）。

（4）蓄电池：安装了具有更高深循环电阻的 AGM（吸收性玻璃纤维隔片）蓄电池。

（5）安全带锁扣传感器：检查驾驶员安全带是否系紧；系统凭借此结果判断驾驶员是否在座位上。

（6）发动机舱盖传感器：检查发动机舱盖是否关闭。防止在发动机舱内进行作业时，发动机意外起动。

（7）蓄电池传感器：监控蓄电池电量和温度，保证在停止期间和重新起动时有充足的电力。

（8）车载电源控制单元：接收起动/停止系统按钮发出的信号。

（9）制动压力传感器：监控制动压力状态。如红绿灯前正常刹车，发动机熄火；轻踩制动踏板，例如停止和前进，发动机不熄火；驾驶员加大制动压力，发动机熄火。

5. 注意事项

在涉水行驶时，要始终关闭起动/停止系统，以防止发动机意外熄火而再次起动使发动机气缸进水而损坏；起动/停止系统关闭按钮在汽车中控台处。

小　结

（1）起动机用直流电动机多为串励直流电动机，是因为串励直流电动机的特性可满足需

要。起动机的特性取决于直流电动机的特性，而串励直流电动机的特点是起动转矩大、机械特性软。

（2）起动机由于其轻载或空载时转速很高，容易造成"飞散"事故，故对于功率较大的串励直流电动机，不允许在轻载或空载下运行。

（3）电枢电流接近制动电流的一半时，电动机输出功率最大，最大功率作为额定功率。

（4）影响起动机功率的因素主要有接触电阻和导线电阻、蓄电池容量、温度。

习题及思考

（1）起动机装配后为什么要做空载试验和满载试验？

（2）电磁控制强制啮合式起动机电磁开关中的吸拉线圈和保持线圈，在起动前后其电流方向有无变化？为什么？

（3）滚柱式、摩擦片式和弹簧式3种离合器各有哪些优缺点？

（4）起动机上需要调整的间隙有哪些？为什么要保证这些部分的正确间隙？

（5）怎样合理使用起动机？

项目五

点火系统的检修

一、情境引入

一辆东风标致 206 轿车，冷车时车速能达到 70km/h，而热车后，车速最多能达到 40km/h。经检修，发现是由于三缸火花塞陶瓷体破裂漏电造成。这是一个典型的点火系统案例，由于一个汽缸不工作，造成发动机动力不足。

汽油机汽缸内被压缩的可燃混合气是靠高压电火花点燃的，而产生电火花的功能是由点火系统实现的。点火系统的工作直接影响燃油燃烧质量，从而对车辆的动力性、燃油经济性、工作稳定性和排放污染等产生重要影响。

二、相关知识

（一）点火系统概述

1. 点火系统的类型及发展

点火系统在汽油发动机中有重要作用。点火系统有很多类型。按所用电源不同可分为蓄电池点火系统和磁电机点火系统。在发动机工作时，由蓄电池或发电机向点火系统提供电能的称为蓄电池点火系统，而由磁电机向点火系统提供电能的称为磁电机点火系统。现代车用汽油发动机均采用蓄电池点火系统。

汽油机点火系统在产生电火花前，都必须将从电源获取的能量储存起来，以便在瞬间释放以产生高压电灭花。按储存能量的元件不同，汽油机点火系统又可分为电感储能式点火系统和电容储能式点火系统。电感储能式点火系统将点火能量以磁场能量的方式储存在电感线圈（点火线圈）中；电容储能式点火系统将点火能量以电场能量的方式储存在电容中。汽油机的点火系统一般都属电感储能式点火系统。

按汽油机点火系统对点火提前角的控制方式不同，可将点火系统的发展划分成传统点火系统、三极管电子点火系统和计算机控制的电子点火系统 3 个阶段。

（1）传统点火系统。传统点火系统又称机械触点式点火系统，它利用机械触点控制点火提前角，并利用机械离心装置和真空装置自动调节点火提前角。发动机工作时，为保证点火顺序，传统点火系统利用分电器给各缸配电。

传统点火系统的结构简单、成本低，在汽油机上应用最早。但由于机械触点的存在，导致其点火能量低、工作可靠性差、对火花塞积炭敏感且干扰大，已不能适应现代汽车发展的要求。目前，传统点火系统已被点火性能好、工作可靠、点火提前角控制精度高的电子点火系统所取代。

（2）三极管电子点火系统。三极管电子点火系统的功能和工作原理与传统点火系统基本相同，只是控制点火提前角的元件用电子点火器取代了断电器，它利用三极管的导通和截止来控制点火线圈一次绕组回路的通断，而三极管的导通与截止则用点火信号发生器产生的信号来控制。普通电子点火系统仍保留了机械离心式和真空式点火提前角自动调节装置。

汽车用汽油机电感储能式普通电子点火系统，按点火信号发生器的结构原理不同，又分为电磁式、霍尔式和光电式3种类型。电磁式电子点火系统的点火信号发生器利用电磁感应原理产生点火信号；霍尔式电子点火系统的点火信号发生器利用霍尔效应原理产生点火信号；光电式电子点火系统的点火信号发生器利用光电效应产生点火信号。

（3）计算机控制的电子点火系统。在计算机控制的电子点火系统中，由ECU（电子控制单元）来控制和修正点火提前角，甚至可取消分电器，成为全电子点火系统。由于减少甚至取消了机械装置，与其他点火系统相比，不仅点火提前角的控制精度提高，而且能量损失少、对无线电干扰小、工作更加可靠。

计算机控制的电子点火系统除点火提前角控制功能外，还具有爆燃控制、通电时间控制等功能。随着汽车电子控制技术的发展和普及，计算机控制的电子点火系统的应用也越来越多。

2. 点火系统的功能

点火系统经过多年的发展，虽然已有很多类型，现代计算机控制的电子点火系统从外表上看已与传统的触点式点火系统有了很大的不同，但是它们的功能却是相同的。点火系统主要具有下面3项功能。

（1）产生足以击穿火花塞间隙的电火花。点火系统必须能够产生足够高的击穿电压，以击穿火花塞的电极间隙，产生具有充足能量的电火花，引燃空气、燃油混合气，并维持足够长的火花时间，以保证空气、燃油混合气充分燃烧。为了保证发动机可靠点火，应保证火花塞跳火时有100MJ以上的电火花能量。

（2）控制点火提前角以适应发动机的工况。点火系统必须能随着发动机转速和负荷的变化，及其工作情况的改变，而及时调整点火提前角，使得发动机在各种情况下都能在最恰当的时间点火。

（3）分配电火花。对于多缸发动机，点火系统必须在压缩行程的适当时刻向正确的汽缸输送电火花，以便开始燃烧过程。

（二）点火系统的基本构造与检修

1. 点火系统的基本组成

点火系统的总体布局如图5-1所示。主要由电源（蓄电池）、点火开关、点火线圈、分电器等组成。如图5-2所示，这些部件构成了2个相互关联的电路：初级回路和次级回路。其中，初级回路是低压电路，次级回路是高压电路。

（1）初级回路。当点火开关接通时，电流从蓄电池流出，经点火开关和初级回路电阻，流到点火线圈的初级绕组。然后，电流流经某种开关设备后接地。开关设备是由触发设备通过电子的方式或者机械触点的方式控制的。

点火线圈初级绕组内的电流会产生磁场。开关设备或控制模块在预定的时刻切断这个电流。这时，初级绕组内的电磁场消失，从而在次级绕组上感应出高压脉冲，这时恰好接通了点火系统的次级回路。

有些点火系统在点火开关和点火线圈接线柱间串联了一个附加电阻，用来向点火线圈提供适当大小的电压和电流。现在，很多点火系统已经不使用附加电阻了，它们直接向点火线

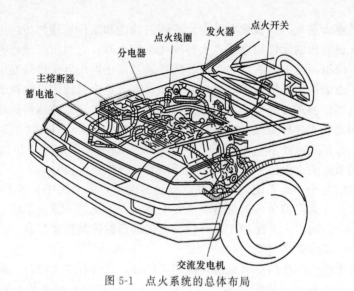

图 5-1 点火系统的总体布局

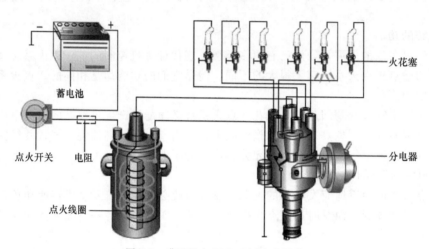

图 5-2 典型的初级和次级点火回路

圈提供 12V 电压。

（2）次级回路。次级回路用来向火花塞提供高压脉冲。过去的点火系统都使用分电器来实现这个功能，现在，为了提高燃油的经济性，减少污染排放物，大多数汽车都采用了无分电器的点火系统。

在分电器点火系统中，次级线圈产生的高压脉冲通过高压导线，从点火线圈到达分电器。分电器根据发动机的点火顺序，由一组高压分线将这个高电压分配到各个汽缸的火花塞。

2. 点火线圈的结构与检修

（1）点火线圈的结构。点火线圈是将电源的低压电转变成高压电的基本元件。按磁路的结构形式不同，点火线圈可分为开磁路点火线圈和闭磁路点火线圈。

① 开磁路点火线圈。开磁路点火线圈的结构如图 5-3 所示。点火线圈一般为二低压接线柱。二低压接线柱，分别标注 "+" "−" 符号。

开磁路点火线圈的中心是用硅钢片叠成的铁芯，在铁芯外面套有绝缘的纸板套管，点火线圈的一次绕组和二次绕组分层绕在套管上。二次绕组用直径为 0.06～0.10mm 的漆包线

绕11000～23000匝,一次绕组用直径为0.5～1.0mm的高强度漆包线绕230～270匝。由于一次绕组的通过电流大,产生的热量多,所以将其绕在二次绕组的外面,以利于散热。点火线圈绕组与外壳之间装有导磁钢套,上部有绝缘胶木盖,下部有瓷质绝缘座。为加强绝缘并防止潮气浸入点火线圈,外壳内一般都充满沥青或变压器油,所以这种开磁路点火线圈也称为湿式点火线圈。

当点火线圈的一次绕组电路接通时,铁芯被磁化,其磁路如图5-4所示。由于磁路的上、下部分需经过空气,外围需经过壳体内的导磁钢套才能形成回路,铁芯本身不能构成回路(所以称为开磁路点火线圈)。开磁路点火线圈的磁阻大,漏磁损失多,能量转换效率低。

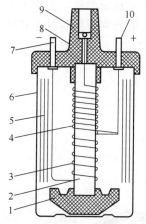
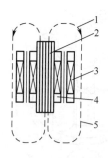

图5-3 开磁路点火线圈的结构
1—绝缘座;2—铁芯;3——次绕组;4—二次绕组;
5—导磁钢套;6—外壳;7—低压接线柱"—";
8—胶木盖;9—高压接线柱;10—低压接线柱"+"

图5-4 开磁路点火线圈的磁路
1—磁力线;2—铁芯;3——次绕组;
4—二次绕组;5—导磁钢套

② 闭磁路点火线圈。闭磁路点火线圈的结构和磁路如图5-5所示。闭磁路点火线圈的铁芯为"日"字形,本身构成闭合磁路。为减少铁芯的磁滞现象,在磁路中留有一个微小空气隙。闭磁路点火线圈的壳体内,采用热固性树脂作为填充物,所以又称为干式点火线圈。

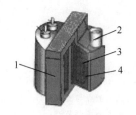
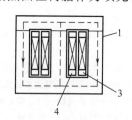
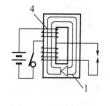

(a)"日"字形铁芯的点火线圈　　(b)"日"字形铁芯的磁路　　(c)"口"字形铁芯的磁路

图5-5 闭磁路点火线圈的结构和磁路示意
1—铁芯;2—高压插孔;3—二次绕组;4——次绕组

与开磁路点火线圈相比,闭磁路点火线圈的磁阻小,漏磁损失小,能量转换效率高。此外,闭磁路点火线圈的壳体通常以热熔性塑料注塑成型,填充物采用热固性树脂,使其绝缘性和密封性均优于开磁路点火线圈。闭磁路点火线圈体积的日益小型化,使其能直接安装在分电器盖上,不仅可省去点火线圈与分电器之间的高压线,而且使点火系统的结构更紧凑。因此,在电子点火系统中得到广泛应用。

(2) 点火线圈的检修

① 外观检查。目测观察点火线圈外表，若有脏污或接线柱锈蚀，应进行清洁后再作进一步检查；若有胶木盖裂损、接线柱松动、壳体变形、填充物外溢、高压插座接触不良等现象，应更换该点火线圈。

② 绝缘性能的检查。用万用表电阻挡测量点火线圈任一接线柱与壳体之间的电阻值，阻值应不小于 $50M\Omega$，否则说明点火线圈绝缘不良，应更换该点火线圈。

③ 绕组电阻的检查。用万用表电阻挡测量点火线圈一次绕组和二次绕组的电阻值，其阻值应符合规定，否则应更换该点火线圈。

3. 分电器的结构与检修

传统点火系统中分电器的作用是接通或切断点火线圈的初级回路，使次级点火线圈产生高压电，并按发动机的工作顺序，在最佳点火时刻将高压电分别送到各缸火花塞。传统点火系统中的分电器主要的组成结构如图 5-6 所示。

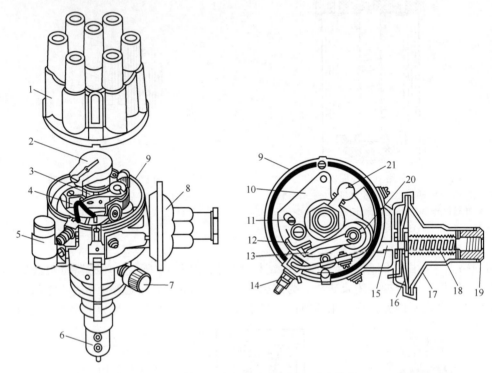

图 5-6 传统点火系统中分电器的组成结构

1—分电器盖；2—分火头；3—凸轮；4—触点及断电器底板总成；5—电容器；6—轴节；7—油环；
8—真空提前机构；9—配电器；10—活动底板；11—偏心螺钉；12—固定触点与支架；
13—活动触点臂；14—接线柱；15—拉杆；16—膜片；17—真空式点火提前角调节器；
18—弹簧；19—螺母；20—触点臂弹簧片；21—油毡及夹圈

普通电子点火系统中的分电器与传统点火系统中的分电器的结构基本相同，只是用点火信号发生器代替了断电器，分电器内仍保留有传统的配电器、机械离心式点火提前角自动调节器和真空式点火提前角自动调节器。

(1) 配电器。配电器的作用是将点火线圈产生的高压电按发动机各汽缸的点火顺序配送给火花塞，主要由分电器盖、分火头和高压线组成。配电器安装在断电器上方。分电器盖的中央有一高压线插孔，插孔内装有带弹簧的电刷，电刷靠其弹簧压在分火头的导电片上。分

电器盖中央插孔的周围均布有各缸高压分线插孔,插孔内有金属套与分电器盖内的旁电极连接,通过高压分线将各旁电极分别与各缸火花塞连接。分火头安装在凸轮的顶端的点火信号发生器转子上,发动机工作时,分火头随点火信号发生器转子一起旋转。分火头的顶端铆有铜质导电片,分火头端部与旁电极有 0.2~0.8mm 的间隙。当断电器触点打开时,点火线圈产生的高压电由分火头导电片跳至与其相对的旁电极,再经高压分线送至火花塞电极。

配电器在高压下工作,是点火系统中故障率较高的部位之一。其常见故障主要有分电器盖漏电、中央插孔电刷与分火头导电片接触不良、分火头漏电等,配电器的检修内容及方法如下。

① 目测检查分电器盖,若盖内脏污应进行清洁,若有裂纹应更换。

② 检查分电器盖绝缘性能。如图 5-7(a) 所示,用万用表电阻挡分别测量分电器盖各插孔之间的电阻值,电阻值应不小于 500 MΩ,否则说明绝缘性能不良,应更换该分电器盖。也可采用在车跳火法检查,如图 5-7(b) 所示,拔掉分电器盖上的所有高压分线,将中央高压线插到任一高压分线插孔中,并在其分线孔邻近的插孔中再插上一根高压分线,使其端头距汽缸体 3~4mm,再拨动断电器触点臂,看此分线端头与汽缸体之间是否出现火花。若有火花跳过,说明所检查的高压分线插孔之间已被击穿而漏电。然后按上述方法再检查其他高压分线插孔之间是否漏电。用此方法也可检查中央高压线插孔与各高压分线插孔是否有漏电现象存在。凡无火花跳过,说明绝缘良好;如有火花跳过,说明已被击穿而漏电,应更换。

③ 检查分电器盖中央插孔内的电刷是否有弹性、有无卡滞或磨损,必要时更换该分电器盖。

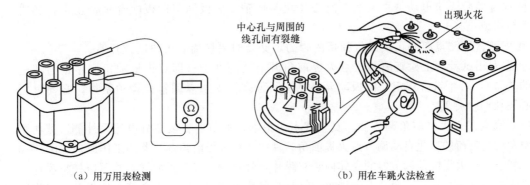

(a) 用万用表检测　　　　　　　　(b) 用在车跳火法检查

图 5-7　分电器盖绝缘性能的检测

④ 检查分火头是否有裂纹、导电片烧蚀、安装不稳固,必要时更换该分火头。

⑤ 检查分火头是否漏电,常用方法如图 5-8 所示。可用万用表检查 [见图 5-8(a)],检查方法同分电器盖,分火头极片与绝缘体间电阻不应小于 500MΩ,否则说明其漏电。也可用在车跳火法检查 [见图 5-8(b)],先将分火头反放于汽缸盖上,使其导电片(金属部分)与汽缸盖接触,然后将高压线的端头距离分火头座孔 6~8mm,同时接通点火开关,用螺丝刀拨动断电器触点,使其一开一闭。此时,高压线端头与分火头座孔之间若有火花跳过,说明分火头漏电,应换新件。

(2) 离心式点火提前角调节器。离心式点火提前角调节器的功用是根据发动机转速的变化自动调节点火提前角。离心式点火提前角调节器安装在分电器内的底板下部,其结构如图 5-9 所示。

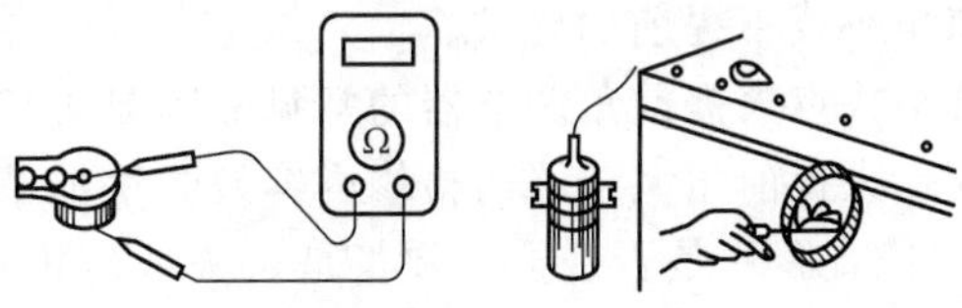

(a) 用万用表检查　　(b) 用在车跳火法检查

图 5-8　检查分火头是否漏电

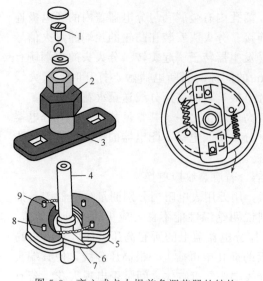

图 5-9 离心式点火提前角调节器的结构
1—凸轮固定螺钉及垫圈；2—凸轮；3—拨板；4—分电器轴；
5—离心飞块；6—弹簧；7—托板；8—销钉；9—柱销

离心式点火提前角调节器的托板固定在分电器轴上，托板上安装着 2 个离心飞块，离心飞块的一端套在托板上的销轴上，离心飞块可绕其销轴转动，飞块的另一端与托板之间装有飞块回位弹簧。2 个离心飞块上各有 1 个拨板销，可以与拨板上的孔插接以驱动点火信号发生器转子。

发动机转速提高时，离心飞块在离心力作用下绕其销轴向外甩开，离心飞块上的拨板销推动拨板连同点火信号发生器转子顺其旋转方向相对分电器轴转过一定角度，使点火信号发生器产生脉冲信号的时刻自动提前，即点火提前角增大。反之，当发动机转速降低时，由于离心飞块的离心力减小，回位弹簧将离心飞块拉拢，点火信号发生器转子逆其旋转方向相对分电器轴转过一定角度，点火提前角自动减小。

离心式点火提前角调节器常见故障是弹簧失效、离心飞块上的拨板销与拨板插孔磨损松旷或卡死等，检修内容及方法如下。

① 检查离心飞块甩动是否灵活，离心飞块与销轴、拨板销与拨板配合是否正常，必要时进行检修或更换。

② 用弹簧秤测量离心飞块回位弹簧的弹力，必要时更换离心飞块回位弹簧。

③ 在专用试验台上检查离心式点火提前角调节器的性能（即点火提前角调整量与转速之间的关系），若不符合规定，可扳动离心飞块回位弹簧支架以调整弹簧预紧力，必要时更换离心飞块回位弹簧。

（3）真空式点火提前角调节器。真空式点火提前角调节器安装在分电器壳外侧，其功用是根据发动机负荷的变化自动调节点火提前角。真空式点火提前角调节器的工作原理如图 5-10 所示。真空式点火提前角调节器的壳体内装有膜片，膜片左侧气室通大气，并用拉杆将膜片与分电器内的活动底板连接；膜片右侧气室装有膜片回位弹簧，并通过真空管与位于节气门附近的取真空口相通。发动机节气门开度（即负荷）减小时，取真空口的真空度增大，使膜片克服膜片回位弹簧作用力向右拱曲，并通过推杆拉动分电器内的活动底板使其逆时针方向转过一定角度，由于分电器内的活动底板连同点火信号发生器的定子总成一起转动，且转动方向与点火信号发生器转子旋转方向相反，所以点火信号发生器产生脉冲信号的时刻提前，点火提前角增大。反之，发动机负荷增大时，膜片在膜片弹簧作用下向左拱曲，点火提前角减小。

发动机怠速工况、节气门位于最小开度位置时，取真空口位于节气门上方，此时该处的真空度几乎为零，膜片回位弹簧推动膜片使点火提前角达到最小，以满足发动机怠速工况点火提前角小或不提前的要求。

真空式点火提前角调节器的常见故障是弹簧失效、膜片破损、断电器活动底板卡滞等，真空式点火提前角调节器的检修内容及方法如下。

① 检查膜片是否破损、弹簧是否失效、推杆与活动底板连接是否松动、活动底板转动是否卡滞、真空管接头螺纹是否完好，必要时进行检修或更换。

② 在真空管侧吹气或吸气，以检查真空点火提前角调节器的密封性，如果漏气则应更

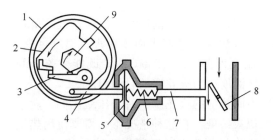 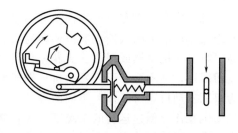

(a) 负荷减小时　　　　　　　　　　　(b) 负荷增大时

图 5-10　真空式点火提前角调节器的工作原理

1—分电器壳体；2—断电器活动底板；3—触点；4—推杆；5—膜片；
6—回位弹簧；7—真空管；8—节气门；9—凸轮

换该真空式点火提前角调节器总成。

③ 在专用试验台上检查真空式点火提前角调节器性能。在一定的转速下，用真空泵给该调节器施加一定的真空度时，其点火提前角应符合标准，否则可增减调节器真空管接头处的垫片，调节膜片回位弹簧的预紧力。

4. 火花塞的结构与检修

（1）火花塞的结构。各种类型的点火系统都使用了火花塞，其作用是将点火线圈产生的高压电流以电弧的形式引入燃烧室，并点燃混合气。火花塞主要由金属杆（钢心）、瓷绝缘体（能够导热的绝缘体），以及 1 对电极（其中一个在瓷绝缘体内被绝缘，称为中心电极，另一个在壳体上被搭铁，称为侧电极）等组成，其结构如图 5-11 所示。

图 5-11　火花塞的结构
1—插线螺母；2—连接螺纹；
3—金属杆；4—瓷绝缘体；
5—导电密封玻璃；
6—中心电极；7—侧电极

火花塞的绝缘体固定在钢制壳体内，以保证中心电极与侧电极之间绝缘。在绝缘体中心孔中装有金属杆和中心电极，金属杆顶端与分高压线插线螺母相连，金属杆底端与中心电极之间用导电密封玻璃密封。中心电极用镍-锰合金制成，具有良好的耐高温、耐腐蚀和导电性能。壳体下端是弯曲的侧电极，它与中心电极之间保持一定的间隙，间隙的大小是由汽车制造厂决定的。火花塞壳体具有螺纹，用来将火花塞安装在发动机汽缸盖上。铜制密封垫圈可起到密封和传热的功用。很多车用火花塞在其顶部的接线柱与中心电极之间有 1 个电阻器，这个电阻器能够减少射频干扰，从而避免收音机出现噪声。值得注意的是，来自射频干扰的电压也会干扰甚至损坏车载计算机。因此，如果汽车出厂时配有电阻型火花塞的话，更换火花塞时也必须选用电阻型的。

（2）火花塞的热特性。火花塞具有不同的热特性，分别用于不同的工作条件下。当发动机正在运转时，火花塞的大部分热量集中在中央电极上。因为侧电极是通过螺纹安装在缸体上的，所以侧电极的热量会快速扩散。火花塞的传热路径是从中央电极开始的，通过绝缘体传给壳体，然后由壳体传给缸盖，在缸盖内循环的冷却剂吸收这些热量。火花塞的热特性是由其绝缘体与壳体的接触点以下的绝缘体长度决定的。热型和冷型火花塞如图 5-12 所示。例如，热型火花塞的绝缘体裙部长，传热路径加长，从而电极温度较高。而冷型火花塞的绝缘体裙部短，传热路径就短，从而电极温度低。国产火花塞的热特性就是用火花塞绝缘体裙部长度标定的热值来表示，火花塞的热值代号为 1～11，热值代号为 1～3 的称热型火花塞，热值代号为 4～6 的称中型火花塞，热值代号为 7～11 的称冷型火花塞。

发动机工作时，火花塞绝缘体裙部的温度对其工作性能有很大的影响。温度过低，落在火花塞绝缘体裙部上的汽油或润滑油容易形成积炭，导致火花塞漏电而不跳火；温度过高，则容易引起发动机早燃或爆震。火花塞绝缘体裙部温度保持500～700℃时，既能使落上的油粒立即燃烧，又不至于引起发动机早燃或爆震，该温度称为火花塞的自洁温度。

为保证发动机正常工作，不同的发动机应配用不同热值的火花塞。对于压缩比低、功率小的发动机在连续低速运转的工况下，火花塞易被积炭污染。在这种情况下，需要使用热型火花塞。而对于压缩比高、功率较大的发动机，其工作过程中会长时间以极高的速度运行，为防止因温度过高而导致早燃或爆震，常采用冷型火花塞。

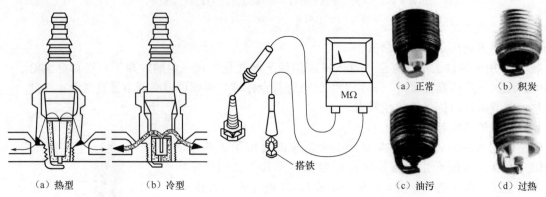

图 5-12　热型和冷型火花塞　　图 5-13　检查火花塞绝缘电阻　　图 5-14　火花塞的积炭检查

（3）火花塞的检修。火花塞在高温、高压的环境下工作，且还要受燃油中添加剂的腐蚀，是易损零件。火花塞的常见故障是绝缘体裂损、电极烧蚀、积炭、电极间隙失准等。

检查时，应注意火花塞壳体与绝缘体的连接是否牢固可靠，若发现火花塞的螺纹及绝缘体有裂纹或壳体与绝缘体连接不牢，应更换新件，或用万用表测量火花塞绝缘电阻，检查火花塞绝缘电阻如图 5-13 所示，电阻值应为 10MΩ 或更大；检查中心电极是否烧损和侧电极是否开焊或脱落，若发现有以上的现象，应更换新件；检查是否有积炭现象，火花塞的积炭检查如图 5-14 所示，火花塞积炭较轻时，可用铜丝刷或软钢丝刷进行清洁，积炭严重或绝缘体裂损、电极烧蚀时必须更换。火花塞的清理和清洗如图 5-15 所示。火花塞电极间隙一般为 0.7～1.0mm。近年来，为了适应发动机对排气净化的要求，采用稀薄燃烧，火花塞间隙有增大的趋势，有的已增大为 1.0～1.2mm，此间隙可用塞尺测量，若不符合规定标准，应更换火花塞，或用专用工具来调整。

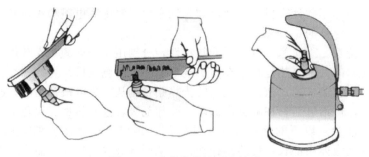

图 5-15　火花塞的清理和清洗

火花塞的工作情况检查一般都采取短路法，即：当发动机低速运转时，将被测火花塞的高压分火线与缸体间短路或断路，这时，若发动机有明显的抖动、运转不稳，说明火花塞工

作良好；否则，即为火花塞损坏。

（三）计算机控制的点火系统的构造与维修

1. 计算机控制的点火系统的功能

计算机控制的点火系统又称微机控制点火系统。计算机控制的点火系统是使用无触点电子点火系统之后，点火系统的又一大进步，其特点是将点火提前角的机械调节方式改变为电子控制方式，增加了爆震控制内容，能使发动机获得最佳的点火时刻，提高了发动机的动力性、经济性，减少了污染排放。在发动机控制系统中，点火控制包括点火提前角控制、通电时间（闭合角）控制和防爆震控制3个方面。

（1）点火提前角控制。在计算机控制点火系统中，点火提前角按发动机起动期间与正常运行期间两种基本工况实现控制，如图5-16所示。

发动机刚起动时，其转速较低（一般认为在500r/min以下），且进气管压力信号或进气量信号不稳定。此时可由ECU根据所控制的发动机工作特性预置一个固定的点火提前角，称为初始点火提前角。也就是说，ECU检测到发动机处于起动期间，就按预置的初始点火提前角控制各缸点火，此时ECU检测的控制信号主要是发动机转速信号（Ne）和起动开关信号（STA）。初始点火提前角的设定因发动机而异，但一般为压缩行程中活塞到达上止点前10°左右。

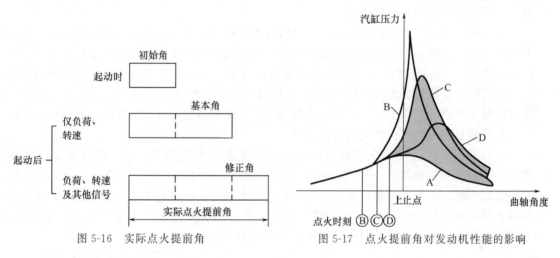

图5-16 实际点火提前角　　图5-17 点火提前角对发动机性能的影响

在汽油机的转速、负荷一定时，其功率和油耗随点火提前角的改变而变化，如图5-17所示，适当的点火提前角可使发动机每循环所做的机械功最多（C曲线下阴影部分）。为使发动机的动力性、经济性、排放性等综合性能达到最佳，应使发动机在各种工况下都在最佳点火提前角位置点火。通过试验确定不同工况下发动机的最佳点火提前角数据，并将其存储于ECU中，当发动机运转时，ECU根据发动机的转速和负荷信号，确定基本点火提前角，并根据其他相关信号进行修正，最后确定点火提前角，并向电子点火控制器输出点火指示信号，以控制点火系统的工作。

（2）通电时间控制。对通电时间进行控制就是对点火闭合角进行控制。闭合角的大小取决于发动机转速和电源供电电压的大小。在不同的转速、不同的供电电压下，都应保证有一定的初级断电电流。随着发动机转速的升高，应适当增大闭合角，以防止初级断电电流减小、点火线圈储能下降而造成次级电压下降引起的点火困难。当电源电压变化时，会影响初级断电电流的大小。当电压下降时，在相同的通电时间内初级电流所能达到的值会减小，此时应较早地将初级电路接通，即增大通电时间（闭合角），如图5-18所示。

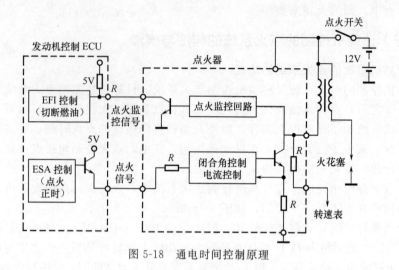

图 5-18　通电时间控制原理

ESA 系统对闭合角进行控制时，ECU 的内存中储存了根据电源电压和发动机转速确定的点火闭合角三维数据表格。在发动机的实际工况中，ECU 通过查找这个表格内的数据，就可计算确定最佳的点火闭合角。

（3）爆燃控制。爆燃也称为爆震，是汽油发动机运行中最有害的一种故障现象，轻则使发动机运行不稳定，重则将导致发动机损坏。点火提前角是影响爆燃的主要因素之一，推迟点火（即减小点火提前角）是消除爆燃的最有效措施。在点火系统中，ECU 根据爆燃传感器信号，判定有无发生爆燃及爆燃的强度，并根据其判定结果对点火提前角进行反馈控制，使发动机处于爆燃的边缘工作，既能防止爆燃发生，又能有效地提高发动机动力性和经济性。

2. 计算机控制的点火系统的基本原理

（1）基本组成。计算机控制的点火系统主要由各类传感器、电子控制单元（发动机 ECU）和点火执行器组成，如图 5-19 所示。传感器是用来检测与发动机点火有关的各种工况信息的装置。点火执行器是由电子点火器、点火线圈、分电器及火花塞组成。有些发动机无点火器，点火控制电路就在发动机（ECU）内。随着汽车生产厂家、生产年代的不同，其结构虽有所不同，但都大同小异。各部分的功能见表 5-1。

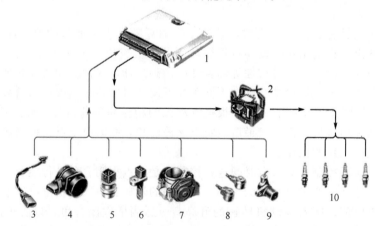

图 5-19　计算机控制的点火系统的基本组成

1—发动机 ECU；2—点火控制器和点火线圈；3—霍尔传感器；4—空气流量计；5—冷却液温度传感器；
6—进气温度传感器；7—节气门位置传感器；8—爆震传感器；9—曲轴位置传感器；10—火花塞

表 5-1　计算机控制点火系统各组成部分的功能

组成部分		功 能
传感器	空气流量计	检测进气量
	进气管绝对压力传感器	
	曲轴位置传感器	检测曲轴转角（发动机转速）
		检测曲轴角度基准位置
	节气门位置传感器	向主 ECU 输入点火提前角修正信号
	水温传感器	检测发动机的冷却水温
	起动开关	检测发动机是否处于起动状态
	空挡起动开关	检测自动变速器的选挡杆是否置于 N 位、P 位
	车速传感器	检测车速，向主 ECU 输入车速型号
	空调开关 A/C	检测空调的工作状态（ON 或 OFF）
	爆燃传感器	检测发动机爆燃信号
	电源电压传感器	向主 ECU 输入电源电压信号
执行机构	电子点火器与点火线圈	根据主 ECU 输出的点火控制信号，控制点火线圈一侧电路的通断，产生二次侧高压使火花塞点火，同时，把点火确认信号 IG_f 反馈给 ECU
	发动机控制器	根据各传感器输入的信号，计算出最佳的点火提前角，并向电子点火器输送点火控制信号

（2）基本工作原理。发动机运行时，ECU 不断采集发动机的转速、负荷、冷却水温度、进气温度等信号，并与计算机内存储器中预先储存的最佳控制参数进行比较，确定出该工况下最佳点火提前角和初级电路的最佳导通时间，并以此向点火控制模块发出指令。

点火控制模块根据 ECU 的点火指令，控制点火线圈初级回路的导通和截止。当电路导通时，有电流从点火线中的初级线圈流过，点火线圈此时将点火能量以磁场的形式储存起来。当初级线圈中的电流被切断时，在其次级线圈中将产生很高的感应电动势（15～30kV），经分电器送到工作汽缸的火花塞，点火能量被瞬间释放，并迅速点燃汽缸内的混合气，发动机完成作功过程。

此外，在具有爆燃控制功能的电控点火系统中，ECU 还根据爆燃传感器的信号来判断发动机有无爆燃及爆燃的强度，并对点火提前角进行闭环控制。

① 主要传感器信号。电控点火系统工作时，所需的主要传感器信号是曲轴位置传感器信号（Ne 信号）和凸轮轴位置传感器信号（G 信号）。

Ne 信号指发动机曲轴转角信号，它是根据曲轴位置传感器产生的信号经过整形和转换而获得的脉冲信号。在电控点火系统中，Ne 信号主要用来计量点火提前角和通电时间。ECU 计算点火提前角或通电时间时，其控制精度要求必须精确到 1°曲轴转角，而目前车用汽油发动机的最高转速高达 6000r/min 以上，发动机正常工作时，1°曲轴转角所用的时间相当短，用传感器产生 1°曲轴转角信号有一定的困难。以安装在分电器内的电磁感应式曲轴位置传感器为例，其转子一般为 24 个齿，曲轴每转 720°只能向 ECU 输送 24 个 Ne 信号，其信号周期为 30°曲轴转角，显然以此信号来直接控制点火提前角和通电时间是不能满足要求的。为此，在发动机电控系统中，通常利用具有高速运算功能的微型计算机系统，将曲轴位置传感器产生的 Ne 信号通过分频转换成 1°曲轴转角信号。

G 信号是指活塞运行到压缩上止点位置的判别信号，它是根据凸轮轴位置传感器产生的信号经过整形和转换而获得的脉冲信号。在点火系统中，G 信号主要用来确定计量点火提前

角的基准。G 信号一般为周期等于作功间隔角的脉冲信号，而且 G 信号发生时，并不是各汽缸活塞运行到压缩上止点的时刻，而是在压缩上止点前某一固定的曲轴转角，一般为上止点前 70°。部分发动机的凸轮轴位置传感器，曲轴每转 2 圈产生 2 个信号，2 个信号分别对应第 1 缸的压缩上止点和排气上止点，2 个信号分别称为 G_1 信号和 G_2 信号。

发动机工作时，ECU 如果收不到 G 信号，因无法确定计量点火提前角的基准，则无法对点火提前角进行控制。为防止造成燃油浪费或其他事故，失效保护系统将自动停止电控燃油喷射系统工作，发动机无法起动。曲轴每转 2 圈凸轮轴位置传感器产生 2 个信号的发动机，只要有一个 G 信号（G_1 信号或 G_2 信号）正常，其电控点火系统就能正常工作，所以此种发动机工作可靠性较高。

② 点火提前角控制原理。点火系统对点火提前角的控制方法，在发动机起动时和起动后是不同的。在发动机起动过程中，发动机转速变化大，且由于转速较低（一般低于 500r/min），进气管绝对压力传感器信号或空气流量计信号不稳定，ECU 无法正确计算点火提前角，一般将点火时刻固定在设定的初始点火提前角。此时的控制信号主要是发动机转速信号（Ne 信号）和起动开关信号（STA 信号）。发动机起动过程中，设定的初始点火提前角预先存储在 ECU 内，设定值随发动机而异，一般为 10° 左右。

发动机起动后正常运转时，ECU 首先根据发动机的转速信号和负荷信号，确定基本点火提前角，再根据其他有关信号进行修正，最后确定实际点火提前角，并向执行元件（点火器）输出点火控制信号，以控制点火系统的工作。ECU 确定基本点火提前角时，在发动机怠速工况与非怠速工况是不同的。

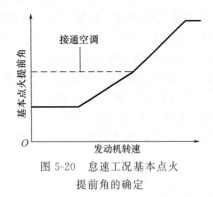

图 5-20 怠速工况基本点火提前角的确定

怠速工况基本点火提前角的确定。发动机处于怠速工况时，ECU 根据节气门位置传感器信号（IDL 信号）、发动机转速传感器信号（Ne 信号）和空调开关信号（A/C 信号）确定基本点火提前角，如图 5-20 所示。空调工作时的基本点火提前角比空调不工作时大，目的是保证发动机怠速工况运转稳定。

非怠速工况基本点火提前角的确定。发动机起动处于怠速工况以外的其他工况时，ECU 根据发动机的转速信号和负荷信号（单位转数的进气量或基本喷油量）确定基本点火提前角，不同转速和负荷时的基本点火提前角数值存储在 ECU 内的存储器中。基本点火提前角控制模型如图 5-21 所示。

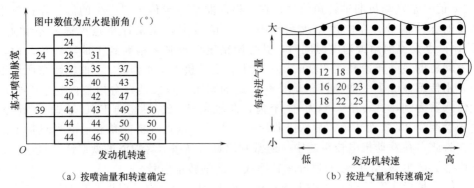

图 5-21 基本点火提前角控制模型

发动机处于怠速工况以外的其他工况时，控制点火提前角的信号主要有进气管绝对压力传感器信号（PIM 信号）或空气流量计信号（VS 信号）、发动机转速传感器信号（Ne 信号）、节气门位置传感器信号（IDL 信号）、燃油选择开关或插头信号（R-P 信号）、爆燃信号（KNK 信号）等。按燃油的辛烷值不同，在 ECU 存储器中存有 2 张基本点火提前角的数据表格时，驾驶员可根据使用燃油的辛烷值，通过燃油选择开关或插头进行选择。具有爆燃控制功能的点火系统中，ECU 内还存有专用于爆燃控制点火提前角的数据。

发动机起动后对点火提前角的修正方法：不同的发动机控制系统中，对点火提前角的修正方法是不同的，主要有以下 2 种。

a. 修正系数法。如在日本日产车系 ECCS 系统中，实际点火提前角等于基本点火提前角与点火提前角修正系数之积，即

实际点火提前角＝基本点火提前角×点火提前角修正系数

b. 修正点火提前角法。如在日本丰田车系 TCCS 系统中，实际点火提前角等于初始点火提前角、基本点火提前角和修正点火提前角之和，即

实际点火提前角＝初始点火提前角＋基本点火提前角＋修正点火提前角

修正系数或修正点火提前角都是存储在 ECU 中，发动机工作时，ECU 根据初始点火提前角、基本点火提前角和修正系数（或修正点火提前角）计算实际点火提前角。

起动后点火提前角的修正项目：发动机起动后正常运转时，对点火提前角的修正项目也随发动机而异，主要修正项目有以下 3 种。

a. 冷却水温修正。冷却水温修正又可分为暖机修正和过热修正。

发动机冷车起动后的暖机过程中，随冷却水温的提高，混合气的燃烧速度加快，燃烧过程所占的曲轴转角减小，点火提前角也应适当减小，如图 5-22 所示。修正曲线的形状与提前角的大小随车型不同而不同。暖机修正控制信号主要有冷却水温传感器信号（THW 信号）、进气管绝对压力传感器信号（PIM 信号）或空气流量计信号（VS 信号）、节气门位置传感器信号（IDL 信号）等。

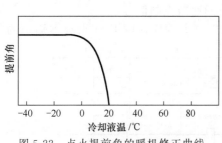

图 5-22 点火提前角的暖机修正曲线

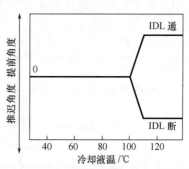

图 5-23 点火提前角的过热修正曲线

发动机工作时，随冷却水温的提高，爆燃倾向逐渐增大。冷却水温过高时，为了避免产生爆燃，必须修正点火提前角，如图 5-23 所示。发动机处于怠速工况（IDL 触点接通）时，冷却水温过高一般是燃烧速度慢、燃烧过程占的曲轴转角过大所致，所以为了避免发动机长时间过热，应增大点火提前角，以提高燃烧速度，减小散热损失。发动机处于怠速工况以外的其他工况（IDL 触点断开）时，如果冷却水温过高，为了避免产生爆燃，则应适当减小点火提前角。过热修正控制信号主要有冷却水温传感器信号（THW 信号）、节气门位置传感器信号（IDL 信号）等。

b. 怠速稳定修正。发动机在怠速运转过程中，由于负荷等因素的变化会导致转速改变，

所以 ECU 必须根据实际转速与目标转速的差值修正点火提前角，以便保持发动机在规定的急速转速下稳定运转，如图 5-24 所示。急速稳定修正控制信号主要有发动机转速传感器信号（Ne 信号）、节气门位置传感器信号（IDL 信号）、车速传感器信号（SPD 信号）、空调开关信号（A/C 信号）等。

c. 空燃比反馈修正。由于空燃比反馈控制系统是根据氧传感器的反馈信号调整喷油量的多少来实现最佳空燃比控制的，所以这种喷油量的变化必然带来发动机转速的变化。为了稳定发动机的转速，点火提前角需根据喷油量的变化进行修正，如图 5-25 所示。

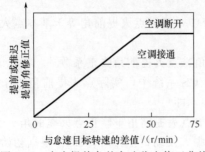
图 5-24 点火提前角的怠速稳定修正曲线

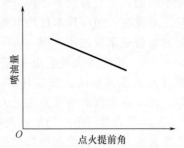
图 5-25 点火提前角的空燃比反馈修正曲线

例如，ECCS 系统在发动机的某种工况下，ECU 计算出的最佳点火提前角为上止点前 40°，点火提前角的控制原理如图 5-26 所示。根据凸轮轴位置传感器转换得到 G 信号为间隔 120°曲轴转角（6 缸发动机）的脉冲信号，G 信号设定在各汽缸活塞压缩上止点前 70°，ECU 设定的基准信号比 G 信号滞后 4°，所以实际控制点火提前角的基准为上止点前 66°。ECU 从接收到间隔 120°的 G 信号开始，即确认某汽缸活塞位于压缩上止点前 70°，由于点火基准信号滞后 G 信号 4°，所以 ECU 从压缩上止点前 66°开始，计数 26（66－40＝26）个 1°信号，此时 ECU 向点火器发出控制信号，使点火线圈一次绕组断电、二次绕组产生高压并输送给火花塞，即可保证火花塞在压缩上止点前 40°点火。

③ 控制信号。点火系统工作中，ECU 向点火器发出的控制信号有 IG_t 和 IG_d 两个信号。

IG_t 信号是 ECU 向点火器中功率三极管发出的通断控制信号。

IG_d 信号是在无分电器的点火系统中，为保证点火顺序，ECU 向点火器输送的判别汽

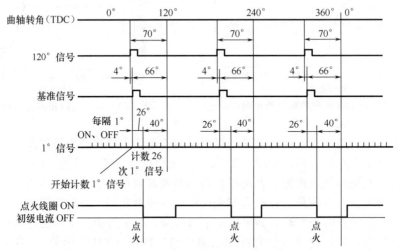
图 5-26 点火提前角的控制原理

缸的信号,以便与 G 信号共同决定需点火的汽缸。IG_d 信号存储在 ECU 内的存储器中,实际就是点火顺序信息。在采用同时点火方式的无分电器点火系统中,IG_d 信号又分为 IG_{d_A} 信号和 IG_{d_B} 信号。同时点火方式是指给接近压缩上止点的汽缸与接近排气上止点的汽缸同时点火的方式,这种点火方式应用在部分无分电器电控点火系统中,给接近压缩上止点的汽缸点火是有效的,给接近排气上止点的汽缸点火是无效的(即不起作用)。

ECU 根据 G 信号和 Ne 信号选择 IG_d 信号状态,以确定给哪个汽缸点火。以日本丰田车系无分电器计算机控制的点火系统为例,ECU 输出的点火控制信号如图 5-27 所示,IG_{d_A} 和 IG_{d_B} 信号的状态见表 5-2。

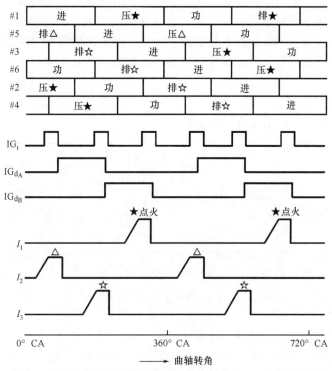

图 5-27 日本丰田车系无分电器计算机控制的点火系统中 ECU 输出的点火控制信号

表 5-2 IG_{d_A} 和 IG_{d_B} 信号的状态

序 号	信 号 状 态		点火的汽缸
	IG_{d_A} 信号	IG_{d_B} 信号	
1	0	1	1、6 缸点火
2	0	0	2、5 缸点火
3	1	0	3、4 缸点火

④ IG_f 信号。IG_f 信号是指完成点火后,点火器向 ECU 输送的点火确认信号。

由于电控燃油喷射系统中,喷油器的驱动信号也来自于曲轴位置传感器,若点火系统出故障使火花塞不能点火时,曲轴位置传感器工作正常,喷油器仍会照常喷油。为了防止因喷油过多,导致燃油浪费、发动机再起动困难或行车时三元催化反应器过热等现象的发生,特设定当完成点火过程后,点火器应及时向 ECU 返回点火确认信号(IG_f 信号)。

发动机工作时,ECU 向点火器发出点火控制信号(IG_f 信号)后,若有 3~5 次均收不

到返回的点火确认信号（IG_f信号），ECU便以此判定点火系统有故障，并强行停止电控燃油喷射系统继续喷油，使发动机熄火。

⑤ 爆燃控制。爆燃控制的过程如图5-28所示。爆燃传感器安装在汽缸体或汽缸盖上，其功用是将爆燃时传到汽缸体或汽缸盖上的机械振动转换成电压信号输送给ECU，ECU则根据此电压信号判断发动机是否发生爆燃及爆燃的强度。有爆燃时，则逐渐减小点火提前角（推迟点火），直到爆燃消失为止。无爆燃时，则逐渐增大点火提前角（提前点火）。当再次出现爆燃时，ECU又开始逐渐减小点火提前角，爆燃控制过程就是对点火提前角进行反复调整的过程。

爆燃控制实质就是对点火提前角的反馈控制，如图5-29所示。爆燃传感器向ECU输入爆燃信号时，点火系统采用闭环控制模式，并以固定的角度使点火提前角减小，若仍有爆燃存在，则再以固定的角度减小点火提前角，直到爆燃消失为止。爆燃消失后的一定时间内，点火系统使发动机维持在当前的点火提前角下工作，此时间内若无爆燃发生，则以一个固定的角度逐渐增大点火提前角，直到爆燃再次发生，然后又重复上述过程。

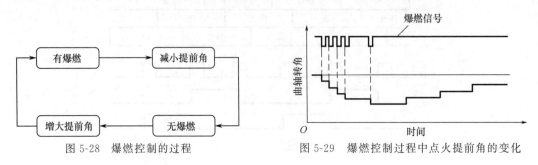

图5-28　爆燃控制的过程　　　　图5-29　爆燃控制过程中点火提前角的变化

发动机负荷较小时，发生爆燃的倾向几乎为零，所以点火系统在此负荷范围内采用开环控制模式。而当发动机的负荷超过一定值时，点火系统自动转入闭环控制模式。发动机工作时，ECU根据节气门位置传感器信号判断发动机的负荷大小，从而决定点火系统采用开环控制还是闭环控制。

（3）计算机控制点火系统的主要电路。

① 点火确认信号（IG_f信号）发生电路。当点火线圈初级电流切断时，产生反电动势触发IG_f信号发生电路，使其输出一个点火确认信号（IG_f）给ECU，IG_f信号也称为点火安全信号。

在电喷发动机中，喷油器的驱动信号来自转速与曲轴位置传感器，如果点火系统出现故障使火花塞不能点火，而该传感器工作正常时，喷油器会继续喷油。为避免这种现象的发生，当IG_f信号连续3～6次没有反馈给ECU时，ECU就判断此时发动机已熄火，并向EFI系统的喷油控制电路发出中断供油的指令，以防浪费燃油、再起动困难以及行驶时三元催化转换器过热等现象的发生。

② 过电压保护电路。当汽车电源供电电压过高时，该电路使点火器放大电路中的功率晶体管截止，以保护点火线圈与功率管。

③ 闭合角控制电路。闭合角也称接通角，是指点火线圈初级电路的通电期间曲轴转过的角度。

闭合角控制电路可控制点火器中功率管的导通时间，即控制点火线圈初级电路的通电时间，以保证次级电路产生合适的点火高压。

④ 锁止保护电路，也称发动机停转断电保护电路。如发动机熄火而点火开关仍接通，一般在点火线圈和功率管的导通时间超过预定值时，该电路控制功率管截止，切断初级电路的电流，以保护点火线圈和功率管不被烧坏，并避免不必要的电能消耗。

⑤ 恒流控制电路。保证在任何转速下，在极短的时间内，使点火线圈初级电流都能达到规定值（一般为6～7A），以减少转速对次级电压的影响，改善点火性能。同时，还可防止因初级电流过大而烧坏点火线圈，这是因为ESA系统采用了高能点火线圈，其初级电路取消了附加电阻，且初级线圈电阻很小，初级电流从通电开始到断路时可达到很大值。

⑥ 加速状态检测电路。当发动机转速急剧上升，该电路对这种加速状态进行检测，将检测到的状态信号输送给闭合角控制电路，使其中的功率管提前导通，以增大闭合角。

3. 典型计算机控制的点火系统

计算机控制的点火系统可分为两大类：有分电器式电控点火系统和无分电器式电控点火系统。

（1）有分电器式电控点火系统。有分电器式电控点火系统的主要特点是：只有一个点火线圈，点火线圈产生的高压电通过分电器按照发动机的作功顺序依次输送给各汽缸火花塞。

（2）无分电器式电控点火系统。无分电器电控点火系统又称直接点火系统，其主要特点是：用电子控制装置取代了分电器，利用电子分火控制技术将点火线圈产生的高压电直接送给火花塞进行点火，点火线圈的数量比有分电器电控点火系统多。无分电器式电控点火系统的组成如图5-30所示。

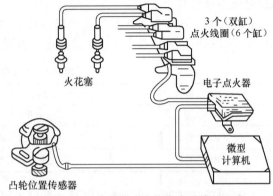

图5-30 无分电器式电控点火系统的组成

无分电器式电控点火系统与有分电器式电控点火系统的工作原理及各元件功能基本相同，不同的是无分电器式电控点火系统具有电子配电功能，即在发动机工作时，ECU除向点火器输出 IG_t 点火控制信号外，还必须输送ECU内存储的汽缸判别信号 IG_d，以便控制多个点火线圈的工作顺序，按作功顺序完成各汽缸点火的控制。

根据点火线圈的数量和高压电分配方式的不同，无分电器式电控点火系统又可分为独立点火方式、同时点火方式和二极管配电点火方式3种类型。

无分电器式独立点火方式电控点火系统的电路如图5-31所示，其特点是每个汽缸1个点火线圈，即点火线圈的数量与汽缸数相等。

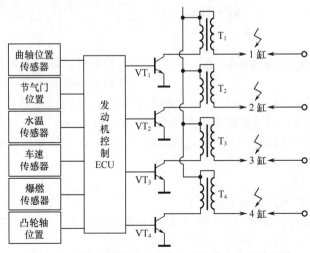

图5-31 无分电器式独立点火方式电控点火系统电路

由于每个汽缸都有各自独立的点火线圈,所以即使发动机的转速很高,点火线圈也有足够的通电时间,以保证足够高的点火能量。与有分电器式电控点火系统相比,在发动机转速和点火能量相同的情况下,单位时间内通过点火线圈一次绕组回路的电流要小得多,点火线圈不易发热,且点火线圈的体积又可以非常小,一般直接将点火线圈压装在火花塞上。

4. 计算机控制点火系统主要元件的构造与维修

计算机控制点火系统中的分电器和点火线圈与普通电子点火系统基本相同,主要区别是计算机控制点火系统的分电器中只有配电器。有关分电器和点火线圈的构造与维修在此不再详述。

(1) 点火器。在有分电器式计算机控制点火系统中,点火器和点火线圈一般都与分电器组装在一起,称为整体式点火组件。点火器的主要功能是根据 ECU 的控制信号,控制点火线圈一次绕组回路的通电或通断,并在完成点火后向 ECU 输送点火确认信号 IG_f(又称反馈信号或安全信号)。

在使用中,接好点火线圈与点火器的线束连接器,用万用表或示波器检测发动机 ECU 相应端子间的电压,应符合表 5-3 的标准,否则说明点火器或 ECU 有故障。

表 5-3 点火器检查标准

检测端子	检查条件	检查标准
+B 与搭铁	点火开关"ON"	蓄电池电压
IG_t 与搭铁	发动机工作	有脉冲
IG_f 与搭铁	发动机工作	有脉冲

(2) 爆震传感器。爆震传感器是计算机控制点火系统的主要元件之一,其功能是向发动机输入爆震信号,经过 ECU 处理后,控制点火提前角,以实现最佳点火提前角的反馈控制。

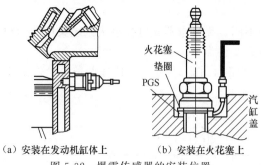

图 5-32 爆震传感器的安装位置

爆震传感器一般通过检测发动机振动的方法获取有无爆震及爆震的强度信号,根据其工作原理不同可分为 2 种类型:电感式和压电式。

爆震传感器通常安装在发动机缸体上,或安装在火花塞上,爆震传感器的安装位置如图 5-32 所示。

爆震传感器可通过检查电阻来判断其好坏。检查时,需拔下爆震传感器导线插头,用欧姆表检测爆震传感器接线端子与外壳间的电阻,应为∞(不导通);若电阻为 0(导通),则说明其内部短路,需更换爆震传感器。或在发动机怠速工况时,通过示波器检查爆震传感器工作情况,方法是:拆开传感器线束连接器,用示波器检查传感器端子与搭铁之间的信号电压,应有脉冲信号输出,否则说明传感器不良,应更换新件。

(3) 点火控制电路。

点火控制电路的检修内容及方法如下。

① 点火开关接通后,用万用表分别检查点火器+B 端子、点火线圈+端子与搭铁之间的电压值,应为蓄电池电压,否则说明电源电路有故障。

② 发动机处于怠速工况时，检查点火器 IG_t 端子与搭铁之间的电压信号，正常应有脉冲信号，否则说明控制线路或 ECU 有故障。

③ 发动机处于怠速工况时，检查 ECU 的 IG_f 端子与搭铁之间的电压信号，正常应有脉冲信号，否则说明点火器或信号线路有故障。

三、项目实施

（一）点火系统实施要求

（1）需具备桑塔纳电控发动机实训台或相关设备。一套常用工具、万用表或示波器等。

（2）项目实施过程中，一定要注意防止高压电对人身和设备的损害，选择好万用表的量程或挡位。对于点火器的检查，要注意瞬间的高压易使三极管被击穿。

（二）实施步骤

1. 点火线圈的检查

（1）通过维护，保证点火线圈绝缘盖板清洁、干燥、不漏电、接线正确。

（2）检查点火线圈电阻。拆去所有连接电线，用电阻表检查点火线圈的初级绕组和次级绕组的电阻，应符合规定值，见表5-4。若不符合，应更换点火线圈。

表 5-4　桑塔纳点火线圈的电阻额定值

项　目	初级绕组/Ω	次级绕组/kΩ
有触点式	1.7～2.1	7.0～12.0
无触点式	0.53～0.76	2.4～3.5

（3）检查点火线圈中央插孔四周是否有裂纹，若有，应更换新件。

2. 火花塞的检查

检查火花塞是否积炭，绝缘体是否损坏，电极间隙是否符合标准。必要时调整电极间隙。

3. 电子点火器的检查

检查电子点火器的接线是否正确，搭铁是否可靠，电源电压是否正常。判断电子点火器的信号输出是否正常，若不符合要求，应更换。

4. 霍尔信号发生器的检查

霍尔信号发生器与点火分电器装于一体，应先检测其输入电压是否正常，若正常，需打开点火开关，转动分电器轴，检查其信号输出端电压是否符合要求，否则应更换。

小　结

（1）点火系统能向火花塞提供极高的电压，以击穿火花塞间隙，形成电火花引燃汽缸内的空气燃油混合气。

（2）点火系统由初级回路和次级回路两个相互关联的电路组成。其中，初级回路向点火线圈的初级绕组提供低电压，以建立磁场；次级回路在初级回路断开时，形成高压脉冲，并将高压脉冲送给火花塞。

（3）传统点火系统中的分电器内容纳了离心式或真空式点火提前装置。离心式提前装置随着转速变化调节点火提前角；真空式提前装置使信号板朝着与分电器轴旋转方向相反的方

向转动。而计算机控制的点火系统取消了离心点火提前装置和真空点火提前装置，由 ECU 通过接收传感器的输入信号，并以此为基础，确定出最佳的点火时间，向点火器发送点火信号，从而在所需要的精确时刻接通次级电路。

（4）磁脉冲传感器和霍尔效应传感器是使用最广泛的曲轴位置传感器。它们在曲轴旋转的特定时刻产生电信号，这些信号触发开关设备以便控制点火正时。

习题及思考

（1）汽油机点火系统有几种类型？说出汽油机点火系统的 3 个主要功能。

（2）试说明点火线圈是如何将蓄电池电压转换为能够使火花塞跳火的高电压的？如何检查点火线圈的好坏？

（3）火花塞间隙对发动机工作有何影响？如何调整其间隙？

（4）当讨论点火系统的组成时，A 说点火器是次级电路的一部分，B 说火花塞属于次级电路。试分析他们的说法是否正确。

（5）电子点火系统的点火信号发生器有几种？各有什么特点？

（6）电子点火器有什么功用？如何检查其好坏？

项目六

汽车灯光系统的检修

一、情境引入

一辆上海大众轿车,当打开转向灯开关后,左、右转向灯均不闪亮,经检修为转向灯继电器出现故障。由于汽车灯光系统关系到自身和他人的安全,因此不能忽视对汽车灯光系统的检修。

汽车灯光系统分为照明系统和信号系统。汽车的照明、信号系统常见故障有保险烧断、灯泡损坏、继电器烧灼、开关或线插接件接触不良等,致使照明、信号系统不能正常工作。

二、相关知识

(一)照明、信号系统的作用、类型和基本组成

1. 照明、信号系统的作用

汽车照明、信号系统能够保证车辆在黑夜、恶劣天气及复杂交通状况下的行车安全。汽车照明系统是为了保证汽车在光线不好的条件下提高车辆行驶的安全性和运行速度而设置的。一般来说,汽车照明系统除了主要用于照明外,还用于汽车装饰。随着汽车电子技术应用程度的不断提高,照明系统正在向智能化方向发展。

汽车信号系统是用于汽车指示其他车辆或行人的灯光(声音)信号(或标志),通常由转向信号装置、制动信号装置、电喇叭等组成,以保证汽车行驶的安全性。

2. 照明、信号系统的类型和基本组成

汽车照明系统是保证汽车在夜间或恶劣天气安全行驶必不可少的设备。汽车照明系统根据在汽车上安装位置和作用不同,一般可分为外部照明装置和内部照明装置。外部照明装置包括前照灯、前雾灯、倒车灯及牌照灯;内部照明装置包括顶灯、阅读灯、杂物箱灯、仪表及控制按钮照明灯和行李箱照明灯等。

汽车上除照明系统外,还有用以指示车辆行驶意图或状态以保证复杂交通状态下的行车安全或者车辆自身状况的信号系统。信号系统可分为外部信号装置和内部信号装置。外部信号装置有转向灯、制动灯、尾灯、倒车灯和后雾灯、停车灯、示宽灯和发光器灯;内部信号装置泛指仪表内的指示灯,用来指示某系统工作状态或警告、报警灯信息,主要有转向、大灯远/近光、机油压力、充电、制动、水温、油量、发动机故障、安全气囊、ABS系统、关门提示等仪表内部的各种指示灯。

汽车的信号系统除了信号灯外,还包含发出声音信号的装置,如电喇叭、蜂鸣器等。电喇叭用来对外部行人或车辆发出声音信号,蜂鸣器可以提醒或警告驾驶员注意车辆的某些状

况或信息。

(二) 汽车照明系统

1. 前照灯

汽车照明系统最重要的外部灯具是前照灯,用来照亮前方路面和环境,保证汽车全天候安全行驶。汽车前照灯的照明效果直接关系着夜间行车的安全,因此,要求前照灯不仅有明亮和均匀的照明效果,还要避免使前面来车和后面来车的驾驶员引起眩目。

前照灯按照安装数量不同可分为 2 灯制前照灯和 4 灯制前照灯。前者左右各装 1 个大灯,其灯泡一般采用双丝灯泡,每只外侧采用双丝灯泡,每只具有远、近光光束;后者左右各装 2 个大灯,一般外侧为近光,内侧为远光,有的外侧采用双丝灯泡,既有远光,又有近光。

前照灯按结构的不同,又可分为可拆式前照灯、半封闭式前照灯和全封闭式前照灯。可拆式前照灯由于气密性差、反射镜易污染而降低反射能力进而降低照明效果,目前已很少采用。半封闭式前照灯的配光镜和反射镜固定结合,灯泡可从反射镜后部更换,维修方便,因此被广泛采用。全封闭式前照灯又叫真空灯,其反射镜和配光镜用玻璃制成一体,形成灯泡,灯丝焊在反射镜底座上,反射镜的反射面经真空镀铝,里面充以惰性气体。由于全封闭式前照灯完全避免反射镜被污染及不受大气的影响,因此其反射效率高,照明效果好,使用寿命长,得到了很快普及;但当灯丝烧断后,需更换整个总成,成本高,因此限制它的使用范围。

汽车前照灯一般由光源(灯泡)、反射镜、配光镜(散光玻璃)3 部分组成。

(1) 光源。目前汽车前照灯所用的光源即灯泡的类型有普通白炽灯泡、卤钨灯泡和 HID 灯泡、LED 发光二极管,如图 6-1 所示。

(a) 白炽灯泡 (b) 卤钨灯泡(一) (c) 卤钨灯泡(二) (d) HID灯泡 (e) 带有散热片的LED模块

图 6-1 前照灯的灯泡

随着汽车技术的不断发展,普通白炽灯泡已被淘汰,现在汽车的前照灯以卤钨灯泡和氙气灯泡为主。卤钨灯泡就是在灯泡内掺杂少量的卤族元素(如碘、溴),从灯丝蒸发出来的钨与碘原子相遇反应,生成碘化钨化合物,而碘化钨化合物一接触炽热的灯丝(温度超过 1450℃),又会分解还原为钨和碘,钨会重新回到灯丝中去,碘则重新进入气体中,如此循环不已,灯丝几乎不会烧断,灯泡也不会发黑,所以要比传统的白炽灯泡寿命更长,亮度更高,目前已得到广泛的应用。

HID (high intensity discharge) 灯也叫高压气体放电灯,可称为重金属灯或氙气灯。其原理是在 UV-ant 抗紫外线石英玻璃管内,以多种化学气体填充,其中大部分为氙气与碘化物等,然后再通过增压器将车上 12V 的直流电瞬间增压至 23000V,激发石英管内的氙气电离,在两电极之间产生光源,这就是所谓的气体放电。而由氙气所产生的白色超强电弧光可提高光线色温值,接近白昼的太阳光芒。氙气灯工作时所需的电流值仅为 3.5A,亮度是传统

卤钨灯泡的 3 倍，使用寿命比传统卤钨灯泡长 10 倍。氙气灯极大地增加了驾驶的安全性与舒适性，还有助于缓解驾驶员夜间行驶的紧张感与疲劳感。

LED 光源的结构和发光原理铸就了 LED 相对于常规光源拥有体积小、耗电量低（单枚耗电不超过 1W）、使用寿命长（最长可达十万小时）、高亮度（色温接近 6000K）、低热量、环保、节能和坚固耐用等无可比拟的优势。不过 LED 灯过热后会有光衰，所以作为前照灯使用时，需要加装散热片和散热风扇。

（2）反射镜。反射镜的表面形状呈旋转抛物面，一般由 0.6～0.8mm 的薄钢板冲压而成，或由玻璃或塑料制成。其内表面镀银、铝或铬，然后抛光处理。目前反射镜内表面采用真空镀铝的较多。反射镜的作用是将灯泡的反射（直射）光反射呈平行光束——使光度大大增强，增强几百乃至上千倍，以保证汽车前方 150～400m 范围内足够的照明。

（3）配光镜。配光镜又称散光玻璃，由透光玻璃压制而成，是多块特殊棱镜和透镜的组合，外形一般为圆形或矩形。配光镜的作用是将反射镜反射出的平行光束进行折射，使车前的路面有良好而均匀的照明，如图 6-2 所示。现今轿车的组合前照灯往往将反射镜和配光镜合为一体，也就是说反射镜经过计算机辅助设计，既能起到反光作用，又能进行光的合理分配。

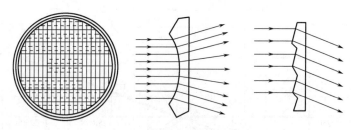

图 6-2 配光镜的结构和作用

当前照灯射出的强光束突然映进入人的眼睛时，就会对视网膜产生刺激，瞳孔来不及收缩造成视盲的现象，叫做眩目。夜间行车时，强烈光束会使对面行驶的车辆驾驶员眩目，从而容易引发交通事故。为避免此类现象的发生，前照灯采取了防眩目的措施。

① 采用带有遮光屏的双丝灯泡。图 6-3 为带有遮光屏的双丝灯泡。这种采用带有遮光屏的双丝灯泡的大灯，其远光灯丝安装于反射镜焦点的上方或前上方。根据光学原理，远光灯丝发射的光束射向远方。根据光学原理，远光灯丝发射的光线经反射镜聚光、发射后，沿光学轴线以平行光束射向远方，以此照亮车前方 150m 以上的路面；近光灯丝下方均设有遮光屏（又称遮光罩或光束偏转器），用以遮挡近光灯丝射向反射镜下部的光线，消除反射向上照射的光束；近光灯丝发射的光线经反射镜发射后，大部分光束倾斜向下射向车前的路面，从而避免了对方驾驶员眩目。其远光和近光反射的效果如图 6-4 所示。

② 采用不对称配光。为了满足既能防止眩目，又能不影响会车速度的目的，汽车的前照灯常采用不对称配光。图 6-5 所示为不对称配光方式，可以看到一条明显的明暗截止线，即上方Ⅲ区是一个明显的暗区。该区 B 点 50L 表示相距 50m 处迎面驾驶员的眼睛位置。下方区域Ⅰ、Ⅱ、Ⅳ区及右上约 15°内是一个亮区，可有效地照亮车前道路和右侧人行道。其会车时的灯光效果如图 6-6 所示。

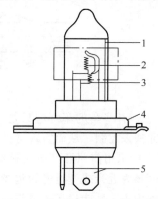

图 6-3 带有遮光屏的双丝灯泡
1—玻璃泡；2—近光灯泡；3—远光灯泡；4—灯座；5—插座

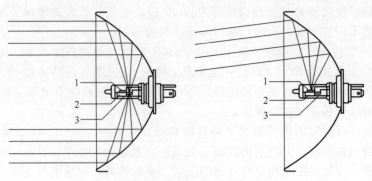

图 6-4　远光灯和近光灯的反射效果
1—近光灯丝；2—遮光屏；3—远光灯丝

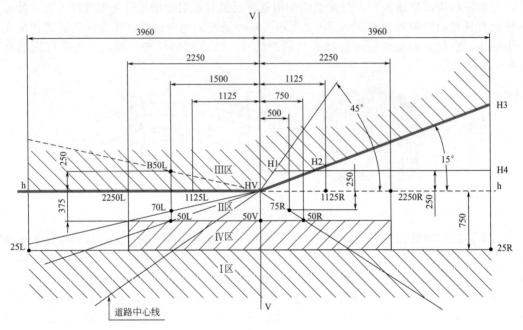

图 6-5　不对称配光方式

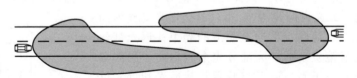

图 6-6　不对称配光方式会车时的灯光效果

③ 有些车的车灯泡只是一个灯丝，故采用遮光板的变化实现防眩目的控制。遮光板由电磁铁来控制，从而实现远光、近光的切换。

④ 采用前照灯自动控制系统。前照灯自动控制系统可以根据对方车辆灯光的亮度自动变远光为近光或变近光为远光。它的优点首先是实现了自动控制，不需要驾驶员操纵，其次是体积小、性能稳定、可靠，且灵敏度高。

前照灯自动控制系统利用车速传感器、方向盘转角传感器、车身高度传感器、红外测距传感器、光电传感器（环境光照传感器）及发动机工作状态和车门状态的检测，来判断车辆

的行驶状态、车辆行驶的道路状况、外界环境光线的强弱及光线实时变化的情况，把检测到的信号转化为电信号输入电控单元中进行判断处理，进而发出相应的指令控制车灯作出相应的调整，从而实现车灯的自动控制。同时，灯光自动控制系统在车辆行驶过程中，通过检测各处车灯供电线路的反馈电流信号及光电传感器检测输入信号两种方法，来共同检测判断各个车灯工作是否正常。

⑤ 前照灯的使用注意事项。

a. 保持前照灯配光镜清洁，尤其在雨雪天气行驶时，泥尘等污垢会使前照灯的照明性能降低50%。有的车型装有前照灯刮水器和喷水器。

b. 夜间两车会车时，要关闭前照灯远光，换用近光，以保证行车安全。

c. 为保证前照灯的各项性能，在更换前照灯后或汽车每行驶10000km后，应对前照灯光束进行检查调整。

d. 定期检查灯泡和线路插座及搭铁有无氧化和松动现象，保证插接件接触性能良好，搭铁可靠。如果接点松动，在接通前照灯时，会因电路的通断而产生电流冲击，从而烧坏灯丝，如果接点氧化，则会因接点压降增大而使灯泡亮度降低。

2. 雾灯

雾灯分为前雾灯和后雾灯，雾灯主要是用于改善大雾、大雨、大雪或尘埃弥漫情况下道路照明的灯具，不但有助于驾驶员看清楚道路，也有助于本车被其他人看到。因此，雾灯的光源需要有较强的穿透性。一般的车辆用的都是卤钨雾灯，也有少数车辆配置氙气雾灯。前雾灯安装在前照灯附近或比前照灯较低的前保险杠下方位置，为防止迎面车辆驾驶员眩目，前雾灯光束在地面的投射距离相对近光光束来说要近。

后雾灯主要是在大雾情况下，从车辆后方观察，使车辆更为易见的灯具。由于雾灯的穿透力较尾灯更强，可在很大程度上减少不良天气情况下汽车的追尾事故，预防交通事故的发生。后雾灯若采用单只时，一般安装于车辆纵向平面的左侧，与制动灯之间的距离应大于100mm，有的则安装在保险杠下方中间位置。后雾灯灯光光色为红色，灯泡功率一般为35W。

3. 其他照明灯

(1) 牌照灯。装于汽车尾部牌照上方或左右，用来照亮后牌照，功率一般为5W，确保行人在后方20m能够清楚地看见牌照上的文字。

(2) 倒车灯。倒车灯是倒车时用来照明后方道路并提醒其他车辆和行人注意的照明、信号两用灯。倒车灯的颜色是白色，驾驶员挂上倒挡，就自动接通倒车灯，灯的亮度应照亮7.5m的距离，灯泡的功率一般为28W。

(3) 车门灯。车门灯也称室内灯，一般用于轿车或旅行车。一般每个车门设置一个独立的门控开关或集成在门锁内的微型开关，当车门打开时，车门灯电路被门控开关或微型开关接通，车门灯被点亮；当车门关上时，车门灯电路被门控开关或微型开关断开，车门灯熄灭。为了便于驾驶员上、下车或打开其他设备及插入点火钥匙等操作，有的车门灯电路还设有自动延时器。

(4) 仪表及开关照明灯。仪表及开关照明灯主要用于夜间行车时仪表及开关的照明。仪表及开关照明灯为驾驶员及时查看仪表及操作开关提供了便利条件，仪表及开关照明灯由车灯开关控制。

(5) 顶灯、阅读灯。顶灯安装在驾驶室顶部，主要用于车辆的内部照明。阅读灯一般装于乘客座位旁边供乘客阅读使用，提供给乘坐人员足够的亮度，同时又不会影响驾驶员的正常驾驶、车内其他乘客的休息。目前很多汽车的顶灯可以实现剧场式亮度控制及延时熄灭控制。

(三)汽车信号系统

1. 灯光信号装置

(1) 转向信号灯。转向信号灯装在汽车的前后左右四角,其用途是在车辆转向、路边停车、变更车道、超车时,发出明暗交替的闪光信号,给前方车辆、行人、交警提供行车信号。前、后转向信号灯的灯光光色为琥珀色。转向信号灯的闪光由闪光继电器控制,其频率应控制在1~2Hz,起动时间应不大于1.5s。

汽车转向灯的闪烁是通过闪光器来实现的,通常按照结构和工作原理的不同分为电热式、电容式、翼片式、水银式、三极管式、集成电路式等。

电热式闪光器结构,由于其工作稳定性差、寿命短、信号灯的亮暗不够明显,目前已经很少使用。目前多采用结构简单、体积小、工作稳定、使用寿命长的电子闪光器,即三极管式和集成电路式两大类。

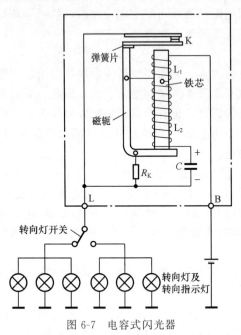

图 6-7 电容式闪光器

① 电容式闪光器。电容式闪光器由电磁式继电器连接一个电容所构成,其结构与内部电路有不同的形式,但原理基本相同,都是通过电容的充放电延时特性,控制继电器触点按某一频率开闭而使转向灯闪烁。一种典型的电容式闪光器的结构如图6-7所示。

闪光器触点K通过弹簧片使其保持常闭;串联于转向灯电路的线圈L_1其电阻较小;线圈L_2的电阻较大,L_2的一端通过继电器铁芯和磁轭与活动触点相连,另一端串接电容C后与固定触点连接,L_2、C电路与触点并联。

接通转向灯开关后,闪光器中的线圈L_1通电,电流通路为:蓄电池"+"→L_1→触点K→转向灯开关→转向灯及转向指示灯→搭铁→蓄电池"—"。此时,L_2和C电路被触点短路,而通过的L_1电流较大,其产生的电磁力使触点张开,因此,转向灯一闪亮立即变暗。

触点断开后,电源向电容C充电,充电电流通路为:蓄电池"+"→L_1→磁轭及铁芯→L_2→C→转向灯开关→转向灯及转向指示灯→搭铁→蓄电池"—"。由于L_2的电阻较大,流过转向灯的充电电流较小,故转向灯是暗的。C的充电电流虽小,但流经L_1、L_2两线圈后产生相同方向的磁力足以克服弹簧片的弹力而使触点保持张开,使转向灯保持暗的状态。

C在充电过程中,其端电压逐渐升高,充电电流随之减小。当充电电流减小至两线圈的磁力不足以克服弹簧片的弹力时,触点又闭合。这时,通过转向灯的电流增大,灯变亮。与此同时,电容通过触点放电,其放电电流通路为:C"+"→L_2→铁芯及磁轭→K→C "—"。由于C的放电电流使L_2产生的磁场与L_1相反,削弱了L_1的磁力,因此,触点不能被吸开,使转向灯保持亮的状态。

C放电过程中,其放电电流逐渐减小,L_2产生的磁场逐渐减弱。当L_2产生的磁场减弱至削弱L_1的磁场作用基本消失时,L_1的磁力又使触点张开,灯光又变暗。接着又是C充电,如此反复,C不断地充电、放电,使触点定时地开和闭,从而使转向灯按一定的频率闪光。

电容充放电回路中的R、C参数决定了转向灯的频率,使用中,R、C参数变化不大,

因此，转向灯的闪光频率也就比较稳定。电阻 R_K 与触点并联，起减小触点火花的作用。

② 三极管式闪光器。三极管式闪光器分触点式三极管闪光器和无触点三极管闪光器两种。

a. 触点式三极管闪光器。所谓触点式三极管闪光器，实际上是一种混合式闪光器，即它的振荡器主要由三极管等组成，而转向灯的驱动任务则由电磁继电器（具有触点）来完成。转向灯的闪光频率一般规定在 65~120 次/分，但以 70~90 次/分为宜；其亮灭比为 1:1；且要求其闪光清晰、工作稳定、使用寿命长。

b. 无触点三极管闪光器。无触点三极管闪光器是用大功率三极管取代了继电器，取消了触点，所以又称全电子式闪光器，其结构如图 6-8 所示。

无触点三极管闪光器的电路是一个多谐振荡器，其电路结构是对称的，即 $R_1=R_4$，$R_2=R_3$，$C_1=C_2$，VT_1 和 VT_2 是同型号的三极管。

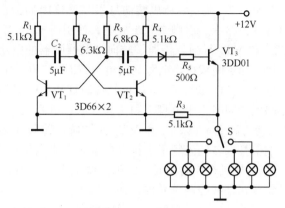

图 6-8 无触点三极管闪光器的工作原理

当接通电源开关时，VT_1 和 VT_2 都得到正向偏压，由于三极管参数的分散性，也就是说 VT_1 和 VT_2 的参数不可能完全一样，因而必然有一个先导通。若 VT_1 先导通，电容器 C_2 将 VT_1 导通时集电极的瞬间电位降低，使 VT_2 的基极电位降低，因此 VT_2 截止。同时电源经 $R_2 \rightarrow C_2 \rightarrow VT_1 \rightarrow$ 搭铁，向 C_2 充电，使 VT_2 的基极电位升高，当 VT_2 的基极电位高于其开启电压时，VT_2 便导通，电容 C_1 将 VT_2 导通时集电极电位瞬间降低，使 VT_1 的基极电位降低，VT_1 截止。同时电源通过 $R_3 \rightarrow C_1 \rightarrow VT_2 \rightarrow VT_2 \rightarrow$ 搭铁，向 C_1 充电，使 VT_1 的基极电位升高，当其电位高于开启电压时，VT_1 便导通。这样 VT_1 和 VT_2 交替导通与截止。若此时接通转向灯开关 S，当 VT_2 导通时，VT_3 的基极电位降低，VT_3 截止，转向灯不亮。当 VT_2 截止时，VT_3 的基极电位升高，产生基极电流，VT_3 导通，接通转向灯电路，转向灯亮。当 VT_2 导通时，VT_3 又截止，转向灯又熄灭。如此反复使灯光闪烁。

③ 集成电路式闪光器。集成电路式闪光器与三极管式闪光器的不同之处就是用集成电路 IC 取代了三极管振荡器，这类闪光器也分有触点式和无触点式两种。

图 6-9 所示为带有蜂鸣器的无触点式集成电路闪光器。它是用大功率三极管 VT_1 代替了有触点闪光器的继电器，利用三极管的开关作用，实现对转向灯开、关的控制。同时还增设了声响功能，构成了声光并用的转向信号装置，以引起人们对汽车转向的注意，提高了安全性。

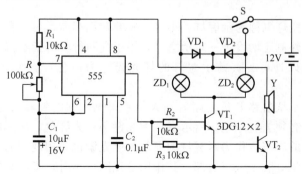

图 6-9 带有蜂鸣器的无触点式集成电路闪光器的工作原理

当转向开关 S 接通时,电源便通过 VD_1(或 VD_2)、R_1、电位器 R 向电容器 C_1 充电,使 555 集成定时器的引脚 6、2 的电位逐渐升至高电平,由 555 定时器的逻辑功能得知,引脚 6、2 为高电平时,输出端 3 为低电平。同时引脚 7 和 1 导通。反之输出端 3 转为高电平,引脚 7 和 1 截止。所以此时输出端 3 为低电平,该低电平加到 VT_1 和 VT_2 的基极上,因而 VT_1 和 VT_2 截止,所以转向灯不亮,蜂鸣器无声。同时引脚 7 和 1 间导通,电容器 C_1 便通过电位器 R、引脚 7 和 1 放电,使引脚 6、2 逐渐降为低电平,输出端转为高电平,因而 VT_1 和 VT_2 导通,接通了转向灯及蜂鸣器的电路,转向灯亮,蜂鸣器发出声响。同时由于引脚 7 和 1 间截止,电源又向电容器 C_1 充电,结果使引脚 6、2 变为高电平,输出端 3 变为低电平,VT_1 和 VT_2 又截止,转向灯和蜂鸣器的电路被切断,所以转向灯熄灭,蜂鸣器停止鸣响。同时由于引脚 7 和 1 间导通,电容又开始放电,使引脚 6、2 降为低电平,输出端 3 又变为高电平,VT_1 和 VT_2 又导通,转向灯又亮,蜂鸣器又响。如此反复,发出转向灯音响信号。若闪光频率不符合要求,可用电位器进行调整。

④ 集成在控制单元内的闪光继电器。目前很多车型的闪光继电器不再是独立式的,而是集成在某些控制单元内,如:汽车仪表控制单元、车载供电控制单元等,分别控制着左侧前、后的转向灯,右侧前、后的转向灯。此种闪光继电器不能单独更换和维修。

(2) 危险报警信号灯。危险报警信号灯用于车辆遇到紧急危险情况时,同时点亮前后左右转向灯以发出警告信号。为了安全,危险报警信号灯的供电,不受点火开关控制,在点火开关关闭状态下即可将危险报警信号灯打开。有些车型在危险报警信号灯点亮的情况下,再去开转向开关,则车灯变为单侧闪烁,这样的设计更加安全。

(3) 制动灯。制动灯用于指示车辆的制动或减速信号。制动灯安装在车尾两侧,两制动灯应与汽车的纵轴线对称并在同一高度上,制动灯光色为红光。

许多汽车将制动灯开关和制动踏板连接。当施加制动时,踏板向下运动,制动灯就亮。有些汽车的制动灯开关是一个设置在制动主缸的压敏开关,当施加制动时,制动主缸产生的压力将压敏开关接通,点亮制动灯。经过熔丝直接给制动开关施加电压,点火开关即使在 OFF 挡,制动灯也能打开。一旦制动灯开关闭合,电压便加给制动灯。汽车两侧的制动灯按并联接线,灯泡被搭铁便接通电路。

有些车型不只制动开关来点亮制动灯,同时由 ABS 防抱死控制单元内的制动压力传感器控制,当制动开关损坏后,踩制动踏板,制动灯也能点亮,但需要注意的是,如果轻踩制动踏板,制动灯不会点亮。

大多数制动灯系统采用执行多功能的双丝灯泡。通常,用于制动灯的双丝灯泡的灯丝(高亮度的灯丝)也被转向信号灯和危险报警信号灯使用。

现今汽车还装配了高位附加制动灯(又称高位刹车灯)。高位附加制动灯必须装在汽车中心线的位置。

(4) 示宽灯。示宽灯也称为示廓灯、小灯。安装在汽车前、后、左、右侧的边缘。大型车辆的中部、驾驶室外侧还增设了一对示宽灯,用于夜间行驶时指示汽车的宽度。示宽灯灯光标志在夜间 300m 以外可见。前示宽灯的灯光光色为白色,后示宽灯的灯光光色多为红色。

有了示宽灯,汽车从岔路开进公路时别人能看得见,别的驾驶员还能据此估计车的长度。前示宽灯配光镜必须为琥珀色,后示宽灯配光镜必须为红色。采用曲面拐角形配光镜的前照灯和组合式尾灯的汽车,作为示宽灯的那部分配光镜也要用规定的颜色。

(5) 后位灯。后位灯装于汽车后部,其作用是夜间行车时,指示车辆的位置,后位灯的光色为红色,一般尾灯也叫后位灯,停车时起到驻车灯的作用,用来显示车辆的存在。

(6) 倒车灯。倒车灯照亮车后路面以提醒后面的车辆和行人注意倒车。

手动变速器壳体上装备单独的倒车灯开关。自动变速器的汽车，把倒车灯开关与空挡安全开关结合起来。

2. 声音信号装置

(1) 电喇叭。电喇叭的作用是警告行人和其他车辆，电喇叭声级为90～105dB（A）。

(2) 蜂鸣器。蜂鸣器一般装在仪表板或仪表台内，可以发出声音对驾驶员进行警告或提醒，如大灯忘关、钥匙忘拔、门没锁好等信息。有的汽车蜂鸣器在倒车时，发出音响信号，警告车后行人和车辆。

三、项目实施

（一）一汽大众宝来轿车前照灯控制系统电路图分析与检修

1. 灯光的控制与检测系统

(1) 灯光控制系统的分类。

① 按供电方式可分为控制电源和控制搭铁两种。

② 按控制元件可分为灯光开关直接控制、继电器控制和带灯光故障传感器控制等。

③ 按灯光功能可分为灯光照射角度调整、灯光自动开启、灯光关闭延时、前灯清洗等。

(2) 前照灯控制系统。

① 灯光开关直接控制。图6-10所示为一汽大众宝来轿车前照灯控制系统电路。

一汽大众宝来轿车的前照灯控制系统由灯光开关直接控制。当点火开关置于第二挡ON位置，将灯光开关置于ON位置，"1#、4#"端子处于接通状态，电源经点火开关、灯光开关，加至前灯变光开关。如果此时灯光变光开关处于近光位置，则电源经近光触点分别经"21#、20#"两保险丝向两前照灯近光灯丝供电。最后形成搭铁回路，近光灯点亮。当变光开关处于远光位置时，则电源经远光触点分别经"19#、18#"两保险丝向两前照灯远光灯丝供电。最后形成搭铁回路，则远光灯点亮。当前照灯变光开关转至会车位置时（超车），远光灯电源由前照灯变光会车开关"1#"端子供电，该电源不受灯开关的控制。

② 继电器控制。继电器控制系统的电路如图6-11所示。该系统增加了前灯控制继电器、前灯变光继电器和综合继电器，灯光控制开关及变光器开关的控制均为信号线，降低了开关触点及控制回路的电流。当灯光控制开关置于HEAD挡，综合继电器接收到搭铁信号时，综合继电器控制前灯控制继电器"3#、4#"端子闭合，则蓄电池电压经前灯变光继电器内部常闭触点，再经两个保险丝分别加至左右近光灯形成回路，近光灯点亮。当变光器开关置于远光位置时，前灯变光继电器常开触点闭合，则蓄电池电压经前灯变光继电器3#端子，再经两个保险丝，分两路加至4个远光灯及远光指示灯形成回路，远光灯及远光指示灯同时点亮。

③ 带灯光故障传感器的控制。带灯光故障传感器的控制系统如图6-12所示。此系统增加了灯光故障传感器，它可监测尾灯的工作状态，当任何一尾灯出现短路或断路及所用灯泡不符合标准时，灯光故障传感器都会监测到异常的工作电压并将故障指示灯点亮来提示司机需要维修。

2. 前照灯控制装置

(1) 前照灯昏暗自动发光器。

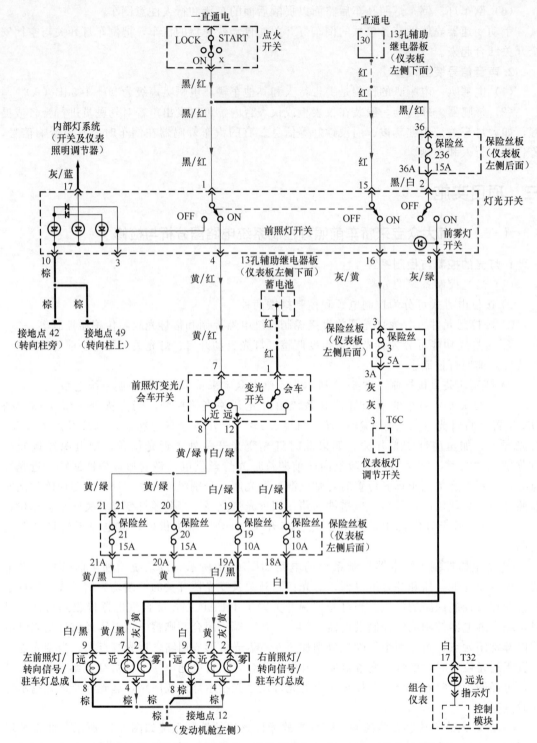

图 6-10 一汽大众宝来轿车前照灯控制系统电路（变光开关在近光位置）

① 作用与结构。这种昏暗自动发光器的作用是在汽车行驶过程中（并非夜间行驶），当汽车前方自然光的强度降低到一定程度，如汽车通过高架桥、林荫小道或树林竹林，或突然乌云密布等，发光器便自动将前照灯电路接通，开灯行驶以确保行车安全。

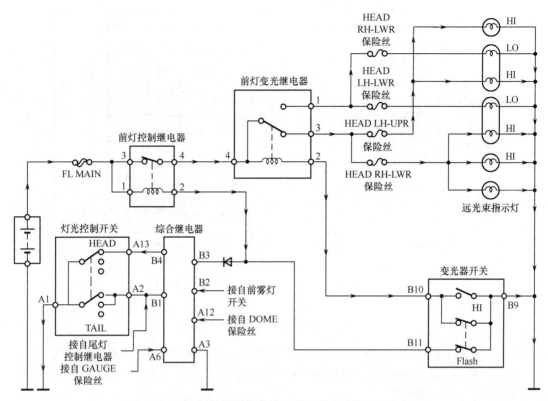

图 6-11 继电器控制系统电路（变光器开关置于远光位置）

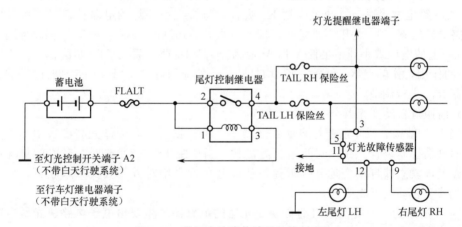

图 6-12 带灯光故障传感器的控制系统

图 6-13 所示为前照灯昏暗自动发光器的电路。该装置一般都装在汽车仪表板上，主要由光电传感器和三极管放大器两大部分组成。光电传感器由光敏元件、延时电路、控制开关等组成。在往汽车上安装光电传感器时，应注意将其感光面朝上，用以接收从汽车挡风玻璃射进来的自然光。其光通量的大小可由传感器前面的光阀进行调整，以适应各种情况（包括季节）的变化。三极管放大器主要由三极管 VT_1 和 VT_2、二极管 VD_1 和 VD_2、电阻 $R_1 \sim R_9$、电容 C_1 和 C_2，以及灵敏继电器和功率继电器等组成。

② 工作原理。

a. 汽车行驶时，当自然光的强度降低至某一程度而被光电传感器接收时，传感器中光敏

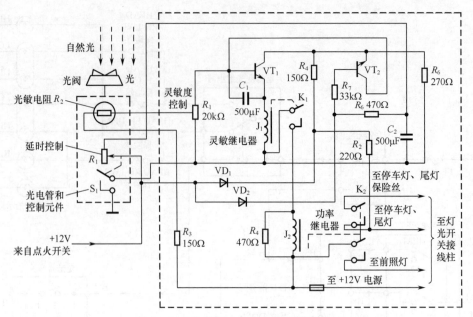

图 6-13 前照灯昏暗自动发光器电路

电阻 R_2 的阻值减小到一定数值,它便以需要发光的电压(信号)输出送往三极管放大器。

b. 当三极管放大器接收到光电传感器输出信号后,三极管 VT_1 的基极电位迅速下降,灵敏继电器 J_1 线圈被接通。

c. 当继电器 J_1 电路接通后,它便产生电磁吸力使触点 K_1 闭合,当 K_1 闭合后,功率继电器 J_2 的电路也被接通,故开关也被 K_2 吸合,将接直前照灯的电路接通,前照灯即被点亮。电路中三极管 VT_2 的作用是延时,即当点火开关切断时,VT_2 使 VT_1 保持导通,直到电容器 C_2 上的电压减小到不足使 VT_2 导通为止。VT_2 截止后,VT_1 亦截止,由于继电器 J_1 和 J_2 的作用,使触点 K_1 和开关 K_2 均打开,以使前照灯自动熄灭。其延时时间的长短可由电位器 R_{10} 进行调节。

(2) 前照灯自动变光器。

① 作用与结构。汽车前照灯自动变光器是一种根据对方车辆灯光亮度自动变光为远光或近光的自动控制装置。在夜间两车相对行驶,当相距 150~200m 时,对方的灯光照到自动变光器上,就立即自动变远光为近光,从而避免远光给对方驾驶员带来眩目,两车相会后,变光器又自动变近光为远光。

图 6-14 所示为具有光敏电阻的自动变光器的电路图。主要由电子电路、光敏电阻和继电器组成。为防止电子电路出故障后影响夜间行驶,还保留了变光开关。

② 工作过程。自动变光器的工作过程如下。

a. 在对面没有车辆驶来时,继电器 J 的线圈内没有电流通过,触点 K 和远光灯的接线柱接触,远光灯亮。当对面驶来的车辆相距 150~200m 时,灯光照射在光敏电阻 R 上,使光敏电阻的阻值突然减小,于是三极管 VT_1 获得较大的正偏压而导通,使 VT_2 也获得正向偏压也导通,VT_3 的基极电流被短路,VT_3 截止,使 VT_4 的基极电位升高,VT_4 导通。接通了 VT_5 的基极电流,VT_5 导通使继电器 J 的线圈内有电流通过,产生较大的电磁力使触点和远光灯接线柱 1 断开,而和近光灯接线柱 2 接通,灯光由远光变为近光。

b. 两车相会之后,作用到光敏电阻上的强光消失,电阻的阻值迅速增大,使三极管 VT_1 的正向偏压迅速降低,VT_1 截止,VT_2 的基极电流被断路,VT_2 也被截止。结果切断

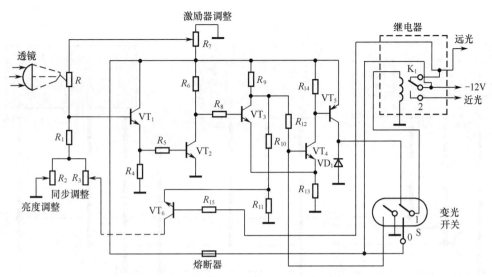

图 6-14 具有光敏电阻的自动变光器电路

了 VT_5 的基极电流，VT_5 截止，继电器 J 线圈中的电流被切断，触点 K 和近光接线柱 2 断开，又和远光接线柱 1 接触，恢复远光灯的工作。

c. 在近光状态时，VT_6 的基极电位为零，所以 VT_6 截止，并联电阻 R_3 被断路，因而使支路的电阻增大，灵敏度改变，使电路转换出现滞后现象，这样可以有效地防止杂散光的干扰。如果电子控制部分出现故障或损坏，可以使用脚踏变光器变光。当踩下脚踏变光开关 S 时，S 就由"1"位置变到"0"位置，使继电器 J 的线圈获得电流，产生电磁力，使触点 K 和接线柱 1 断开，与接线柱 2 接通，使前照灯由远光变为近光。松开脚踏变光时，S 由"0"位返回到"1"位。切断继电器线圈中的电流，触点 K 又和接线柱"1"接触，变近光为远光。

3. 前照灯高度调整系统

前照灯的高度调节也称为前照灯光束水平控制。前照灯的照明范围随着汽车的负荷变化而变化，当汽车负荷较大时，前照灯距地面变近，使照明范围变小，反之，虽然照明范围变大，但会使对面来车的驾驶员眩目，在这些情况下都容易造成安全事故。为了保证灯光照射距离不变，对灯光照射进行调节。前照灯的高度调节有两种形式，一种是手动调节形式，一种是自动调节形式。

（1）前照灯的高度手动调节。前照灯的高度手动调节开关位于前照灯开关附近，如图 6-15 所示。调节开关设定位置大致相当于以下负荷状态：0—汽车前排有人，行李箱空载；1—汽车满员，行李箱空载；2—汽车满员，行李箱满载；3—汽车只有驾驶员，行李箱满载。

图 6-15 前照灯的高度手动调节开关

扳动调节开关，两个前部大灯总成内的伺服电机则旋转至预先设置好的车灯高度。上海大众波罗车前照灯的高度手动调节电路图，如图 6-16 所示。

（2）前照灯的高度自动调节。前照灯的高度自动调节系统可以根据监测车辆前后重心等数据自动调节照射高度。速度相对平稳时，大灯自动降低，在避免造成迎面车辆眩目的情况下照亮前方；速度较快时，自动升高，获得广阔视野避免危险发生。奥迪前照灯的高度自动调节部件示意图，如图 6-17 所示。

图 6-18 所示为波许公司生产的前照灯自动调整系统的工作原理。

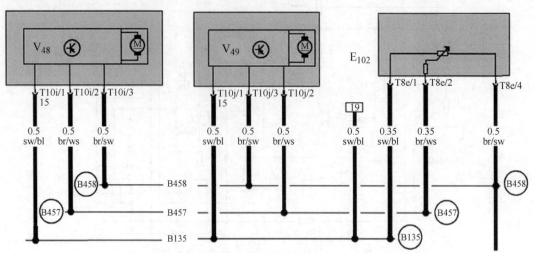

图 6-16 上海大众波罗车前照灯的高度手动调节电路图

1—左侧照明距离调整伺服马达；2—右侧照明距离调整伺服马达；3—前照灯的高度手动调节开关

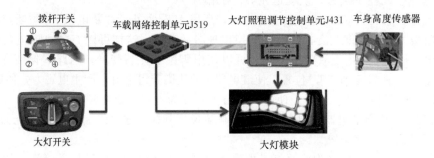

图 6-17 奥迪前照灯的高度自动调节部件示意图

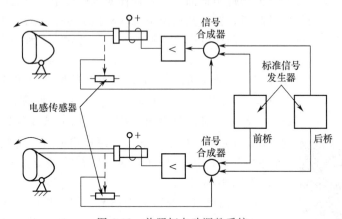

图 6-18 前照灯自动调整系统

电感传感器接收前后桥与车身的相对位移信息，并把该位移转变成表征车身实际高度的电信号，然后输送到信号合成器，与标准信号发生器传送的标准信号进行比较，得到差值信号，经放大器放大后，输送给双金属片执行机构，双金属片随失调信号的变化，得到不同的热量，产生相应的变形，作用于转动杠杆，使前照灯围绕支点转动到适当位置。

（二）前照灯的维护与故障诊断

1. 前照灯的维护

如果发现反射镜上稍有灰尘后，可用压缩空气吹干净，如果吹不干净，则应根据镀层的不同，采取不同的方法清除。

反射镜为镀铬的，可用柔软的皮蘸少量酒精，由反光镜的中心向外围成螺旋形轻轻地仔细擦拭。

如果反光镜是镀银或者是镀铝的，可用棉花蘸清水清洗（不要擦拭）。然后用压缩空气吹干。

有的反射镜表面由制造厂预先涂了一层很薄的保护层，擦拭时一定不要破坏它。如果反射镜经常有污物，应该更换橡胶密封圈。

更换大灯时由于卤钨灯泡在使用时比普通灯泡热，如果机油或润滑脂粘在其表面的话，它将会破裂。而且，人出的汗中的盐可能污染石英。因此，在换灯泡时抓住底座部分，防止手指接触玻璃。

2. 故障诊断

前照灯的故障主要有前照灯不亮、远光或近光灯不亮、灯光变暗等。这些故障一般是由于灯泡损坏、灯丝烧断、电路断路、开关损坏和控制失效等引起的，具体情况见表 6-1。

表 6-1　前照灯常见故障及原因

故障现象	故障原因
所有灯不亮	蓄电池至总开关之间的火线短路；灯总开关损坏，电源总保险丝熔断；电子自动变速器损坏（对于电子控制前照灯）；远光或近光灯的导线或接触不良；前照灯搭铁不良
远光或近光灯不亮	变光开关或自动变光器损坏；远光或近光灯的导线有一根断路；双丝灯泡的远光或近光灯丝有一根烧断；灯光继电器损坏；传感器损坏
前照灯灯光暗淡	保险丝松动；导线接头松动；前照灯开关或继电器触点接触不良；发动机输出电压低；用电设备漏电；负荷过大
一侧前照灯亮，另一侧前照灯暗	前照灯暗的一侧搭铁不良或变光开关接触不良
灯泡经常烧坏	发电机输出电压过高

3. 前照灯的调整

通常采用有关汽车前照灯的配光性能和法规有两个：一个是欧洲经济共同体 ECE 法规配光性能标准；另一个是美国 FVMSS（联邦汽车安全标准）108 号标准，它相当于 ECE 法规 76/756，也就是 SAE 法规配光性能标准。ECE 法规标准比美国 SAE 法规标准更为全面、合理。我国国家标准 GB/T 7258—2017《机动车运行安全技术条件》中，对前照灯的发光强度及光束照射位置进行如下规定。

(1) 前照灯光束照射位置要求。

① 机动车（运输用拖拉机除外）在检验前照灯的近光光束照射位置时，前照灯在距离屏幕 10m 处，光束明暗截止线转角或中心的高度应为 $(0.6 \sim 0.8)H$（H 为前照灯基准中心的高度）；在水平方向上，向左向右偏均不能超过 100mm。

② 四灯制前照灯其远光单光束灯的调整，要求在屏幕上光束中心离地高度应为 $(0.85 \sim 0.90)H$，水平位置要求左灯向左偏不得大于 100mm，向右偏不得大于 170mm；右灯向右向左偏均不得大于 170mm。

③ 机动车装用远光和近光双光束灯时以调整近光光束为主。对于只能调整远光单光束

的灯,调整远光单光束。

(2) 前照灯发光强度要求。机动车每只前照灯的远光光束发光强度应达到表 6-2 的要求。测试时,其电源系统应处于充电状态。

表 6-2　前照灯远光光束发光强度要求　　　　　　　　　　　　　　　　单位: cd

项目	新注册车			在用车		
	一灯制	两灯制	四灯制	一灯制	两灯制	四灯制[①]
汽车、无轨电车	—	15000	12000	—	12000	10000
四轮农用运输车	—	10000	8000	—	8000	6000
三轮农用运输车	8000	6000	—	6000	5000	—

① 采用四灯制的机动车其中两只对称的灯泡达到两灯制的要求时视为合格。

(3) 普通前照灯的对光调整。在调整或校准前照灯之前,应该先进行以下检查,以保证调整正确。

① 将所有轮胎气压调整到规定值。
② 确保油箱是半满状态。
③ 检查弹簧和减震器。如果弹簧或减震器受损,会影响调整结果。

(4) 屏幕检验法。前照灯光束检查可以采用屏幕检验法,下面介绍屏幕检验法。

① 将汽车停在水平地面上,并且按规定充足轮胎气压,从汽车上卸下所有负载(只允许一名驾驶员乘坐)。

距汽车前照灯 s (m) 处竖一个屏幕(注意:不同的车型要求的值也不同,具体参照维修手册。以桑塔纳车为例, $s=10$m, $D=100$mm)。在屏幕上画两条垂线(各线通过前照灯的中心)和一条水平线(与前照灯的离地高度等高),如图 6-19 所示。再画一条比 H 低 D (mm) 的水平线与两条前照灯的垂直中心线分别相交于 a、b 两点。

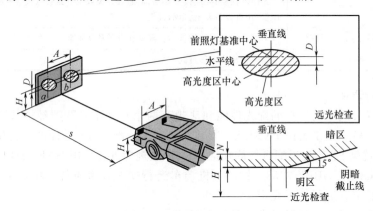

图 6-19　前照灯灯光检查

② 起动发动机,使之以 2000r/min 的速度(约为发动机转速的 60%)旋转,即在蓄电池不放电的情况下点亮前照灯远光(有些车按近光调整,参见具体的车型手册)。

③ 调整时,应该把一只灯遮住,然后检查另一只灯的光束是否对准 a 或 b 点(同一侧的光照中心)。若不符合要求,则拆下前照灯罩圈。旋出侧面的调整螺钉,可使光束作水平方向的调整,旋入或旋出上面的调整螺钉,也可作高低方向的调整(见图 6-20)。调整好一只灯后,按照同样的方法调整另一只,使其光束中心对准 b 或 a 点。

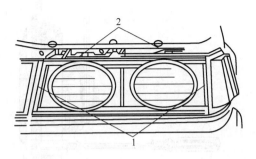 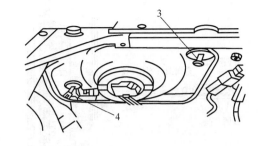

图 6-20 前照灯的调整部位

1,3—左右调整螺钉；2,4—上下调整螺钉

④ 当远光调好后，应该打开近光灯，检查屏幕上是否有明显的明暗截止线，其高度是否符合规定。一般规定是：前照灯上边缘距地面不大于 1350mm 的车，在距灯 10m 远的屏幕上明、暗截止线水平部分应比前照灯基准中心低 $H/3$ 左右。

(5) 利用集光式测试仪调整前照灯。集光式测试仪的结构如图 6-21 所示，其使用方法如下。

① 测试仪垂直放置，汽车和测试仪的相对位置应保证测试仪聚光凸透镜与前照灯配光镜之间的距离为 1m。

② 调整测试仪，使校正器对准被测汽车的纵向中心线，即对中。

③ 利用前照灯对正校正器，通过上下、左右调整测试仪，使前照灯中心与测试仪聚光凸透镜中心对中，然后将测试仪固定在支柱上。

④ 接通前照灯，将光度-光轴转换开关转到光轴位置上。左右、上下偏移指示计。转动左右、上下调整旋钮，使左右、上下偏移指示计的指针指示中央位置（0）。

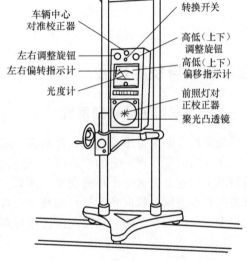

图 6-21 集光式前照灯测试仪

⑤ 将光度-光轴转换开关转到光度位置上，光度计开始工作，读取此时光度计指示值和左右、上下调整旋钮转动时的刻度值，即测出了发光强度，光轴的左右、上下偏移量。

⑥ 调节前照灯的左右、上下调节螺钉，使测试仪调整旋钮的刻度恢复到零，即调好。

（三）电喇叭的调整

(1) 将电喇叭支架固定在台虎钳上。

(2) 将导线和稳压电源连接。负极引出导线与喇叭外壳连接，正极引出导线去点触喇叭上的接线柱。

(3) 音调的调整。电喇叭音调的高低与铁芯间隙有关。间隙小时，膜片的振动频率高，音调高；反之音调低。盆形电喇叭衔铁间隙的调整如图 6-22 所示，调整时应先松开锁紧螺母，然后旋转音调调整螺栓（铁芯）进行调整。注意有些汽车喇叭没有音调调整螺栓。

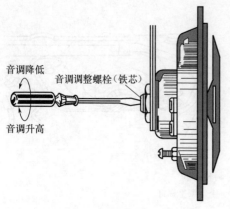
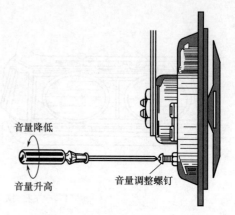

图 6-22　盆形电喇叭音调的调整　　　　　图 6-23　盆形电喇叭音量的调整

（4）音量的调整。电喇叭声音的大小与通过喇叭线圈的电流大小有关。当触点压力增大时，流入喇叭线圈的电流增大，使喇叭产生的音量增大，反之音量减小。对于图 6-23 所示的盆形电喇叭，可旋转音量调节螺钉（反时针方向转动时，音量增大）进行调整。调整时不可过急，每次只需对调整螺钉转动 1/10 圈。注意有些汽车喇叭的音量调整螺钉是用胶密封的，从喇叭背面无法直接看到。

四、知识与技能拓展

（一）车灯主动转向系统

通常汽车的大灯不论亮度如何都有一定的照明范围，当在夜间行驶转弯的时候，会因为行驶角度的问题出现一定的"盲区"，这会在一定程度上影响行车的安全，在照明光线固定的情况下，这个盲区是不可避免的，所以"AFS灯光随动转向系统"就应运而生了。它能够根据行车速度、转向角度等自动调节大灯的偏转，以便能够提前照亮"未到达"的区域，提供全方位的安全照明，确保夜间转弯行车的安全，如图 6-24 所示。

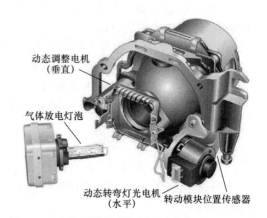

图 6-24　具有 AFS 功能的车辆转弯　　　　图 6-25　大众迈腾前照灯的动态调整电机（垂直）

自适应大灯可以在转弯时对灯光进行动态调节，这种大灯的投射模块内装有一台电机，该电机可在车辆转弯时在水平方向上改变灯光照射方向。大众迈腾前照灯的动态调整电机（垂直），如图 6-25 所示。大灯透镜和支架并不转动。灯光转动的角度在转弯方向的内侧可达约

15°，在外侧可达 7.5°，如图 6-26 所示。

这个角度变化可使车辆在转弯时得到更好的照明效果。这时灯光转弯内模块的转动角是外模块的两倍。这样就可在相同的灯光强度的情况下，得到最大的照亮范围。

车辆在静止时不回转。当车速＜6km/h 时，大灯内的投射模块不会回转。当车速超过 10km/h 时，灯光回转的角度主要取决于方向盘转动的角度。

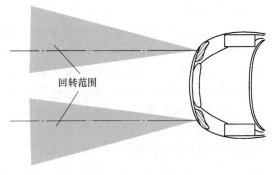

图 6-26　大灯转动的角度

这样就可以满足在车辆静止时不得摆动大灯灯光的法律规定。同时，当车在这种低速状态进行加速时，在转向角度不变的情况下，可以使得大灯的偏转均匀过渡。

（二）奥迪 A8 可变照明距离

"可变照明距离"这个功能的作用是：在夜间行车时，保证本车道能获得足够的照明，同时又不会对其他车辆司机造成眩目。该功能是在远光灯辅助系统的基础上进一步开发而来的（远光灯辅助系统在夜间行车时能自动识别当前情况下可否接通远光灯，并相应地接通或关闭远光灯）。

远光灯辅助系统与"可变照明距离"相比，工作的区别在于是纯数字式的：就是说它直接从近光灯切换为远光灯。相比之下，"可变照明距离"这个功能可根据当时的交通情况，对大灯照程进行无级调节，使照程在近光灯和远光灯之间变化。

1. 对面来车时的工作状态

如果识别出对面来车了，那么"可变照明距离"这个功能就会减小大灯照程，最多可降至近光灯的照程。这样就可避免对面司机产生眩目。对面的车辆驶过后，只要交通状况允许，大灯照程会增大，最多可增至远光灯的照程，如图 6-27 所示。

2. 前面有车时的工作状态

如果本车驶近前面的车辆时，系统的工作状态与对面来车时大致相似。在这种情况下，"可变照明距离"功能也会连续降低大灯照程，以防止对前车司机产生眩目，如图 6-28 所示。如果本车超过了前车，那么大灯照程随后会增大，最多可增至远光灯的照程。当然，前提是在交通状况允许的情况下。

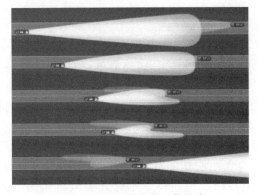

图 6-27　对面来车的工作状态

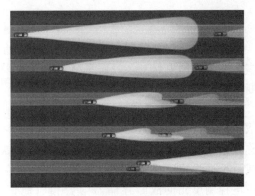

图 6-28　前面有车的工作状态

项目六　汽车灯光系统的检修　**117**

3. 基本原理

当前的交通状况由控制单元 J852 内的摄像头来识别,并在该控制单元内的运算器中进行分析处理。图像处理软件会在摄像头的图像中搜寻光源。该控制单元内的软件将识别出的光源分为:前大灯、尾灯、路灯、本功能不相关的其他光源等。

如果能准确判断出光源,那么控制单元 J852 就会在摄像头图像上确定识别出的车辆的位置,并估算与本车的距离。这两个值通过扩展 CAN 总线被送到弯道灯和照程调节控制单元 J745,如图 6-29 所示。

两个大灯中装有滚轮,用于调节照程。滚轮上有相应的轮廓形状,伺服电机工作就使滚轮转动,就可以根据需要来获得所要求的照明了。伺服电机的安装位置如图 6-30 所示。

图 6-29 基本工作原理

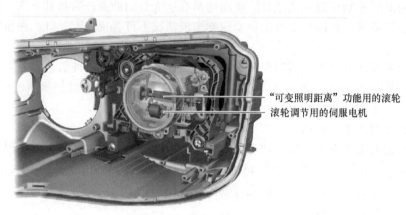

图 6-30 伺服电机的安装位置

控制单元 J745 根据被识别出车辆的位置和距离这两个输入量,来确定滚轮应在的位置。滚轮需要采用的位置信息通过专用 CAN 总线被传送到两个大灯。大灯电子系统根据 J745 的指令来启动伺服电机开始工作,于是车道就会根据实际的交通状况获得理想的照明了。

(三)车灯开关的 LIN 总线电路

传统的车灯开关集成了小灯、大灯、前雾灯、后雾灯等,所以开关背面的插接件端子很多,相关控制电路复杂,而新型车灯开关采用 LIN 总线控制后,线路简单,并且具有自诊断功能。

车灯开关内的开关、按键和调节器的所有信号,都由供电控制单元通过 LIN 总线来读取。另外,开关照明和各个功能的指示灯的指令是由供电控制单元传给灯开关的。反馈线也称冗余线,通过开关内部的电路被引至搭铁,用于校验开关位置的正确性。如果 LIN 总线或者反馈线短路或者断路,那么供电控制单元的应急照明功能就被激活了(近光灯接通),供电控制单元的故障存储器内会相应地记录一个故障。奥迪轿车车灯开关电路如图 6-31 所示。

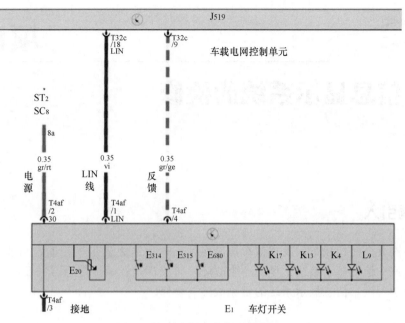

图 6-31 奥迪轿车车灯开关电路

小 结

(1) 汽车照明系统是为了保证汽车在光线不好的条件下提高车辆行驶的安全性和运行速度而设置的。一般来说，汽车照明系统除了主要用于照明外，还用于汽车装饰。随着汽车电子技术应用程度的不断提高，照明系统正在向智能化方向发展。

(2) 汽车信号系统是用于汽车指示其他车辆或行人的灯光（声音）信号（或标志），通常由转向信号装置、制动信号装置、电喇叭等组成，以保证汽车行驶的安全性。

习题及思考

(1) 前照灯的防眩目措施有哪些？
(2) 试述转向信号系统的电路工作原理。
(3) 前照灯由哪几部分组成？前照灯继电器的作用是什么？
(4) 雾灯什么时候工作？雾灯的电路有什么特点？
(5) 简述电喇叭的调整方法。

项目七

信息显示系统的检修

一、情境引入

一辆一汽大众捷达轿车,发现该车加满燃油后,燃油表显示半箱油,与实际油量不符。这个现象是汽车信息显示系统常见的一个故障,一般都是燃油量传感器失准,需要更换。在此我们将要学习汽车信息显示系统的常见故障与检修。

二、相关知识

汽车信息显示系统主要由汽车仪表系统和汽车报警信息系统两部分组成。汽车信息显示系统是汽车运行状况的动态反映,是汽车与驾驶人进行信息交流的界面,为驾驶人提供必要的汽车运行信息,同时也是维修人员发现和排除故障的重要依据。

(一)汽车仪表系统

1. 仪表的作用

为了使驾驶员随时掌握车辆的各种工作状况,保证行车安全,并及时发现和排除车辆存在的故障,现在汽车上都安装各种监控仪表和报警信息装置,这些装置一般都集成在仪表台上形成仪表总成。汽车仪表台是车辆和驾驶员进行信息沟通的最重要、最直接的人机界面。对于汽车仪表,不但要求其工作可靠、抗震、耐冲击性好,更要美观大方,指示准确、清晰,便于读取。

2. 仪表的分类

汽车仪表可按工作原理和安装方式进行分类。

汽车仪表按工作原理可分为机械式仪表、电气式仪表、模拟电路电子仪表和数字化电子仪表。传统仪表一般是指机械式仪表、电气式仪表和模拟电路电子仪表。随着现在汽车不断向信息化和电子化方向发展,数字化电子仪表相对于传统仪表具有集成度和精确度高、信息含量大、可靠性好及显示模式自由等优点,逐步取代传统仪表。

汽车仪表按安装方式可分为分装式仪表和组合式仪表两种。分装式仪表是各仪表单独安装,这在早期汽车及赛车上比较常见。组合式仪表是将各种仪表在设计时就组合在一起,结构紧凑,便于安装。现代汽车最常用的是组合式仪表。组合式仪表又分为可拆式和整体不可拆式两种。

现今轿车的仪表台总成一般是指方向盘前的主仪表板和司机旁通道上的副仪表板及仪表罩构成的平台。主仪表板上一般集中了全车的监控仪表,如车速表、发动机转速表、油压表、水温表、燃油表等。有些仪表板还设有变速挡位指示、时钟、环境温度表、路面倾斜度和海拔高度表等。按照当前流行的仪表台设计款式,一般空调、音响、导航、娱乐等设备的

显示和控制部件安装在副仪表板上，以方便驾驶员操作，同时也显得整车布局紧凑、合理。

汽车仪表装在仪表台上最便于驾驶员观察的位置，并且以最清晰、直观、简便的方式来显示信息。主仪表板上最醒目的位置都是用来指示车辆最基本也最重要的工况信息，同时也用其他指示形式来指示一些次要信息。一般汽车仪表都具备最基本、最重要的如车速、里程、发动机转速、水温、燃油量等信息的指示功能，以及发动机电控、灯光、电源、安全、润滑、制动等系统相关工况信息的指示及报警功能。例如，桑塔纳汽车的仪表及其功能如图7-1所示。

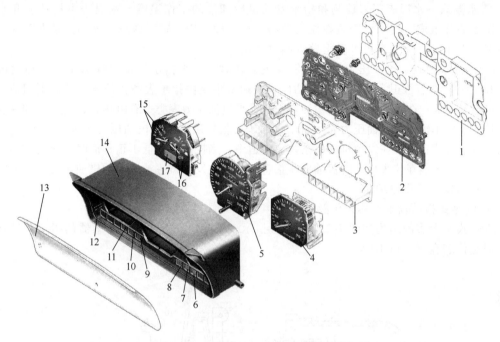

图7-1 桑塔纳汽车的仪表及其功能

1—后盖；2—线路板；3—导光板；4—发动机转速表；5—车速里程表；6—冷却液不足警告指示灯；7—后风窗电动加热器指示灯；8—前照灯指示灯；9—充电不足警告灯；10—机油警告指示灯；11—制动系统故障及驻车制动指示灯；12—数字时钟调整钮；13—透明护板；14—仪表板；15—燃油表及信号灯；16—冷却液温度表及信号灯；17—数字时钟

3. 传统汽车仪表

（1）组成与分类。传统汽车仪表中的燃油表、水温表和机油压力表（油压表），虽然测量指示的参数不同，但其均由指示表传感器组成。

指示表在原理上分为电热式（双金属片式）和电磁式。电热式指示表是利用电热线圈产生的热量加热双金属片，使之变形带动指针指示相应的示值，它需要的是断续的脉冲电流；电磁式指示表是利用垂直布置的2个电磁线圈通过不同的电流和磁场磁化转子，转子带动指针指示相应的示值，它是一种流比式表，需要的是连续的电流信号。

传感器是配合指示表使用的，其作用是提取所需的参量，将被测物理量变为电信号。为了测量不同的参数，传感器在结构上有所不同。传感器可分为电热式和可变电阻式。电热式传感器提供的是断续的脉冲电流信号，而可变电阻式传感器提供的是连续变化的电流信号。

将上述类型的指示表和传感器组合在一起，就产生了如下4种不同形式的仪表。

电热式指示表＋电热式传感器。

电热式指示表＋可变电阻式传感器。

电磁式指示表＋可变电阻式传感器。

电磁式指示表＋电热式传感器。

其中前 3 种组合形式的仪表在汽车上得到广泛应用，如常见的燃油表、水温表和机油压力表。

① 燃油表。燃油表用来检测和指示燃油箱中的燃油量。燃油表由指示表和传感器组成，指示表常见有 2 种类型，即电磁式和电热式，传感器一般使用可变电阻式的传感器。有的车型还同时设有燃油报警指示装置和燃油表配合使用。

② 水温表。水温表用来检测和指示发动机冷却液的工作温度。水温表由指示表和水温传感器 2 部分组成。指示表安装在仪表板内，有 2 种结构形式，即电热式和热敏电阻式。目前在多数汽车上，水温表与水温报警灯同时使用。

③ 机油压力表。机油压力表是在发动机运转时，用来指示发动机润滑系统主油道压力大小和系统工作是否正常的仪表。机油压力表通常也是由指示表和机油压力传感器组成，其压力传感器一般拧在机油泵后方的主油道上。常见机油压力表类型有电热式、电磁式和弹簧管式。目前很多车辆取消机油压力表，而用机油压力报警装置代替机油压力表来监控机油压力。机油压力报警装置通常在发动机润滑系统主油道中，当机油压力低于正常值时，对驾驶员发出报警信号，它由装在仪表板上的机油低压报警灯和装在发动机主油道上的机油压力开关组成。

（2）结构与工作原理。

① 电热式指示表＋电热式传感器。

电热式水温表的结构如图 7-2 所示。其指示表与电热式机油压力传感器的指示表结构相同，只是仪表盘刻度值不同。

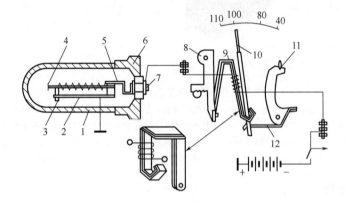

图 7-2　电热式水温表的结构

1—铜壳体；2—底板；3—固定触点；4—双金属片；5—接触片；6—壳座；7—接线柱；
8—调整齿扇；9—双金属片；10—指针；11—调整齿扇；12—弹簧片

水温传感器为一密封套管，内装有双金属片 4，上面绕有加热丝，加热丝的一端通过接触片 5 和接线柱 7 与指示表连接，另一端经固定触点 3 搭铁。

水温表的工作原理与机油压力表相似。当电路接通、水温不高时，水温传感器内的双金属片主要依靠加热丝产生变形，故双金属片需经较长时间加热，才能使触点分开。触点打开后，由于四周温度低散热快，双金属片迅速冷却又使触点闭合。当水温低时，触点在闭合时间长而断开时间短的状态下工作，使流过水温表加热线圈中的电流平均值大，双金属片变形大，带动指针向右偏转角大，指示水温低。当水温高时，双金属片周围温度高，触点的闭合时间短而断开时间长，流过水温表加热线圈的电流平均值小，双金属片变形小，指针向右偏转角小，指示高水温。

② 电磁式指示表＋可变电阻式传感器。电磁式指示表在结构上又可分为无铁芯式和有

铁芯式。

图7-3所示为有铁芯式电磁燃油表的结构及电路连接图。其指示油表有左右2个电磁线圈，其轴线互成90°，在线圈铁芯上，固装有导磁弯板，在指针轴上安装有指针转子、指针、小飞轮和配重。传感器由可变电阻、滑片和浮子等组成。当油箱内油位高低变化时，浮子带动滑片移动，从而改变电阻大小。线圈1与可变电阻串联，线圈2与可变变阻并联。

其工作原理如下。

当油箱无油时，浮子7下沉，可变电阻5被滑片6短路，线圈2同时被短路，无电流通过。此时，线圈1中的电流达到最大，产生的电磁力最强，吸引指针转子3使指针指向"0"的位置。

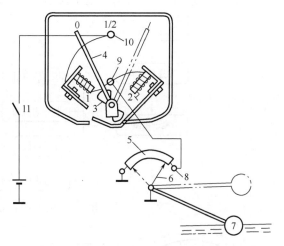

图7-3 有铁芯式电磁燃油表的结构及电路连接
1,2—线圈；3—指针转子；4—指针；5—可变电阻；
6—滑片；7—浮子；8～10—接线柱；11—点火开关

当油箱中的燃油增加时，浮子7上升，带动滑片6滑动，可变电阻5的阻值变大，使线圈2中的电流增加，而线圈1中的电流减小，在线圈1和线圈2的合成磁场作用下，指针转子带动指针向右偏转，指针指向高刻度位置。

当油箱装满油时，线圈2的电磁力最大，指针指向"1"的位置，当油箱中为半箱时，指针指向"1/2"的位置。

③ 仪表稳压器。由于电源电压的变化会对仪表指示值产生影响，造成仪表值误差，所以仪表电路一般要装有仪表稳压器。常用的仪表稳压器有双金属片型和集成电路型。

集成电路型仪表稳压器主要采用汽车专用的三端集成稳压块，具有结构简单、成本低、稳压效果好、使用寿命长等优点，因此被广泛应用。集成电路型仪表稳压器一般有电源输入、接地、输出三个端子，输出电压为9.5～10.5V。

（3）车速里程。车速里程表是用来指示汽车行驶速度和行驶里程的仪表，由车速表和里程表两部分组成。常见的车速里程表有磁感应式和电子式两种。

① 磁感应式车速里程表。磁感应式车速里程表主要利用磁感应原理工作，无电路连接。由永久磁铁、铝罩、护罩、刻度盘和表针等组成。永久磁铁与主动轴紧固在一起。主动轴由来自变速器输出轴的挠性软轴驱动，表针、铝罩固接在中心轴上，刻度盘固定在表外壳上。不工作时，铝罩在游丝的作用下，使表针定位于"0"位。当汽车行驶时，来自变速器输出轴的挠性软管驱动主动轴带动U形永久磁铁旋转，在铝罩上感应出电涡流而产生的磁场，这个磁场与永久磁铁的旋转磁场相互作用产生转矩，使铝罩向永久磁铁旋转方向转过一定角度，直到与游丝的弹力所产生的反方向转矩平衡。车速越高，产生的转矩越大，表针在刻度盘上摆动的角度就越大，即指示的车速就越高。

里程表可以指示总里程和单程数据，总里程只能累加，不能归零，单程指示可以通过回零按钮回零。传统里程表主要由蜗轮蜗杆和数字转轮组成，当汽车行驶时，主动轴经蜗轮蜗杆驱动数字轮上的最右侧的第1个数字轮（一般为1/10km），任一个数字轮与左侧相邻的数字轮传动比都为10∶1，这样显示的数字呈十进位递增，自动累计计量汽车的行驶里程。

② 电子式车速里程表。电子车速里程表由车速传感器、电子电路、步进电机、车速表

和里程表等组成。图 7-4 所示为电子式车速里程表的结构。

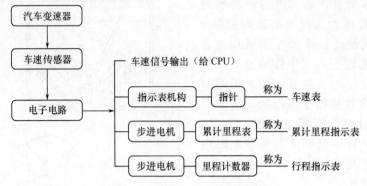

图 7-4　电子式车速里程表的结构

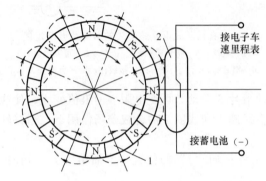

图 7-5　奥迪 100 轿车电子式车速里程表传感器
1—磁性转子；2—舌簧开关

奥迪 100 轿车的组合仪表中装有电子式车速里程表，其原理如下。

车速传感器由变速器驱动，能够产生正比于汽车行驶速度的脉冲电信号。传感器由 1 个舌簧开关和 1 个含有 4 对磁极的磁性转子组成，如图 7-5 所示。磁性转子每转一周，舌簧开关中的触点闭合 8 次，产生 8 个脉冲信号。车速越高，传感器的信号频率越高，电子电路的作用是将车速传感器送来的具有一定频率的电压，经整形、触发，输出一个与车速成正比的电流信号。该电子电路主要包括稳压电路、恒流电源驱动电路、64 分频电路和功率放大电路，如图 7-6 所示。仪表精度由电阻 R_1 调整，仪表初始工作电流由电阻 R_2 调控，电阻 R_3 和电容器 C_3 用于电源滤波。

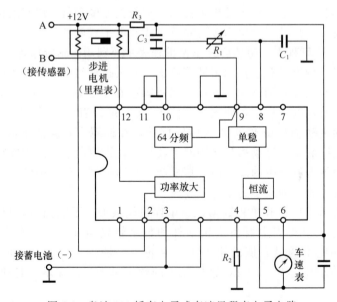

图 7-6　奥迪 100 轿车电子式车速里程表电子电路

车速表实际上是一个电磁式电流表,当汽车以不同车速行驶时,由电子电路端子 6 输出与车速成正比的电流信号驱动车速表的指针偏转,从而指示相应的车速。里程表由一个步进电机及 6 位制的十进制齿轮计数器组成,步进电机受电子电路中控制器控制来驱动计数器转动,如图 7-7 所示。

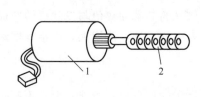

图 7-7 奥迪 100 轿车里程表的驱动
1—步进电机;2—计数器

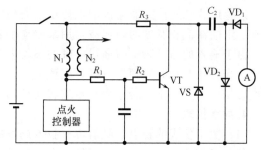

图 7-8 桑塔纳轿车电子转速表电路原理

(4) 发动机转速表。发动机转速表能够直观地显示发动机外各个工况下的转速。汽车发动机扭矩的输出和转速有着密切的关系,驾驶员知道发动机的运转情况,可以恰当地选择换挡时机,配以合适的变速器挡位和油门位置,可使车辆保持最佳的工作状态,对减小油耗、延长发动机寿命很有好处。

发动机转速表有机械式和电子式两种。机械式转速表的结构和工作原理与上述磁感应式车速表基本相同,不再赘述。电子式转速表具有指示平稳、结构简单、安装方便等优点,所以被广泛采用。

电子式转速表一般由指示表、信号处理电路组成,有的还有发动机转速传感器。电子式转速表获取发动机转速信号的方式有 3 种:从安装在飞轮边缘的转速传感器取信号,从点火线圈取脉冲信号和从交流发电机单向定子绕组取正弦交流信号,因为发动机转速和这些信号的频率成正比。

① 电容充放电式转速表。电容充放电式转速表电路(以桑塔纳轿车为例)原理如图 7-8 所示,发动机转速信号取自点火线圈初级电流中断时产生的脉冲信号。其工作原理如下。

当点火控制器使一次侧电路导通时,三极管 VT 处于截止状态,电容 C_2 被电源充电。其充电电路为:蓄电池正极→点火开关→R_1→C_2→VD_2→蓄电池负极,构成回路。当点火控制器使初级电路截止时,三极管 VT 因基极电压升高而导通,这使电容 C_2 通过导通的三极管 VT,电流表和 VD_1 构成放电回路,从而驱动电流表。当发动机工作时,初级电路不断地导通、截止,其导通、截止的次数与发动机转速成正比。因此,当一次侧电路不断地导通、截止时,对电容 C_2 不断地进行充放电,其放电电流平均值与发动机转速成正比,于是将电流平均值标定成发动机转速即可。

② 电磁感应式转速表。这种转速表由装在飞轮壳上的转速传感器和装在仪表板上的指示表(包括电子线路)组成。图 7-9 为磁感应式转速传感器的结构原理,它由永久磁铁、

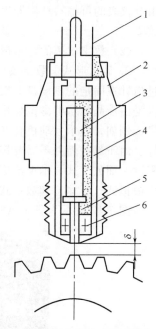

图 7-9 磁感应式转速传感器的结构原理
1—接线柱;2—壳体;3—心轴;
4—永久磁铁;5—铁芯;6—感应线圈

感应线圈、心轴、壳体等组成。

当飞轮转动时，齿顶与齿底不断地通过心轴，空气隙的大小发生周期性变化，使穿过心轴的磁通也随之发生周期性变化，于是在感应线圈中感应出变电动势。该变电动势的频率与心轴中磁通变化的频率成正比，也与通过心轴端面的飞轮齿数成正比。

磁感应式转速传感器输出的近似正弦波频率信号加在转速表线路，经电路处理后，输出具有一定的幅值和宽度的矩形波，用来驱动毫安表。

由于输入的信号频率与通过心轴的飞轮齿数成正比，信号的频率和幅值与发动机转速成正比，当转速升高时候频率升高，幅值增大，使通过毫安表中的平均电流增大，则指针摆动角度也相应增大，于是转速表指示的转速就高。

4. 数字仪表

（1）数字仪表的特点。随着电子技术的发展，以及对汽车的信息化、智能化要求不断提高，驾驶员需要更多、更快地了解汽车运行的各种信息，汽车仪表已经成为车辆和驾驶员进行信息沟通的终端。由于汽车上的各种信号转换为数字信号进行传输和处理是时代潮流，汽车仪表也自然向数字电路方向发展。数字仪表和传统仪表的基本区别就是各种信号都转化为数字信号传输、计算和处理，其仪表电路基本由集成数字电路组成。

数字仪表由实现汽车工况信息采集的传感器、单片机控制及信号处理的仪表控制单元和显示系统等组成。传感器将各种工况信号传输给仪表控制单元，这些工况信号中的模拟信号往往要经过 A/D 转换为数字信号，再经过仪表控制单元的计算处理，然后输出对应的信号驱动步进电机指示装置或利用显示设备以数据或图形显示出对应的示值。对于装备有多路传输系统的车辆，仪表只是该系统的一部分，用于仪表显示的信息往往也是发动机 ECU 需要的，所有的车辆的传感器信号送给发动机 ECU，然后再经过多路传输系统到仪表。

数字仪表都具有自诊断功能，可以进行自检。若仪表发生故障，则其故障代码会存放在组合仪表的可擦写存储器里，用专用仪器调码后，可以读出故障码，便于维修人员迅速诊断故障。

（2）数字仪表的显示形式和显示器件。

① 显示形式。数字仪表的显示形式有模拟式和数字式两种。模拟式显示形式一般是通过指针在固定的刻度盘上摆动来指示参数，该指针可以是由步进电机驱动的真实指针，也可以是由液晶显示器虚拟显示的指针。数字式显示形式则用数字或者条杠图形代替指针图形符号。例如，显示发动机转速升高与降低时，模拟式显示转速表的效果要比数字式显示转速表好。由于驾驶者并不需要知道发动机的准确转速，重要的是发动机转速达到仪表红线的快慢程度。而数字式显示形式更合适显示诸如里程、保养信息等准确数据。因而很多车速里程表将模拟式（车速）和数字式（里程）二者显示形式结合在一起。

图 7-10 所示为奥迪 A6L 轿车全数字式显示仪表。

图 7-10 奥迪 A6L 轿车全数字式显示仪表

② 显示器件。汽车上使用的仪表数字显示器件有许多不同的类型，并且各有特点。最常用的电子显示器件可分为发光型和非发光型两大类。发光型显示器自身发光，容易获得鲜艳的流行色显示，非发光型显示器靠反射环境光显示。发光型显示器主要有真空荧光管（VFD）、发光二极管（LED）、阴极射线管（CRT）、等离子显示器件（PDP）和电致变色显示器件（ECD）等。这些都可以作为汽车电子显示器件使用，既可做成数字式的，也可做成图形或模拟指针式的。

目前最常用的数字仪表显示器件有以下 3 种。

a. 发光二极管。发光二极管是应用最广泛的低压显示器件，结构如图 7-11 所示。发光二极管具有响应快、寿命长、体积小、节能等优点。发光二极管发光的颜色有红、绿、黄、橙、蓝、白等，可单独使用，也可用来组成数字、字母、发光条图使用。发光二极管在汽车上一般用作数字符号段或点数不多的光条图形显示、警示灯或者仪表盘面、公里表指针和液晶面板背光光源。图 7-12 所示为由发光二极管组成的 7 字符段显示电路。

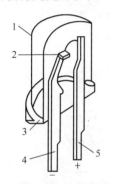

图 7-11 发光二极管的结构
1—外壳；2—芯片；3—负极标记；4—负极；5—正极

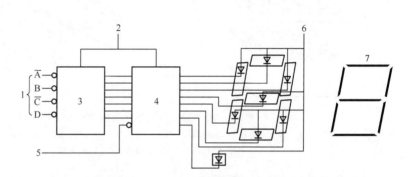

图 7-12 发光二极管组成的 7 字符段显示电路
1—输入端；2—逻辑电路；3—译码器；4—恒流源；5—小数点；
6—发光二极管电路；7—"8"字形

图 7-13 所示为由发光二极管组成的光条图形显示器。

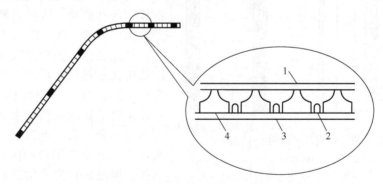

图 7-13 发光二极管组成的光条图形显示器
1—漫射器；2—LED；3—印制电路板；4—分隔器

b. 液晶显示器。其结构及工作原理如图 7-14 所示，前玻璃板和后玻璃板之间夹有一层液晶，外表面贴有垂直偏光镜和水平偏光镜，最后面是反光镜。液晶显示器的工作原理是：当液晶不加电场时，液晶的分子排列方式可将来自垂直偏光镜的垂直方向的光波旋转 90°，变成水平方向的光波，再经水平偏光镜后射到反射镜上，经反射镜后按原路回去，这时通过垂直偏光镜看液晶时，液晶呈亮的状态。当液晶加以电场时，液晶的分子排列方式改变，不

能将来自垂直偏光镜的垂直方向的光波旋转，通过液晶后是垂直方向的光波，不能通过水平偏光镜达到反射，这时通过垂直偏光镜看液晶时，液晶呈暗的状态。这样将液晶组成字符段，通过控制每个字符段的通电状态，就可显示不同的字符。

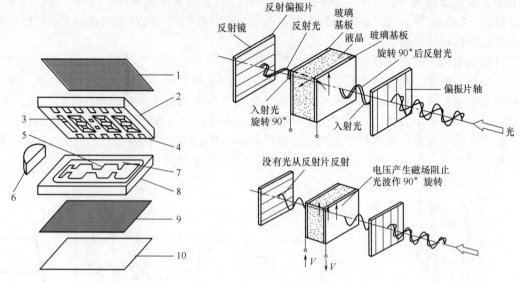

图 7-14 液晶显示器的结构及工作原理
1—前偏光板；2—前玻璃板；3—笔画电极；4—接线端；5—后板；6—端部密封件；
7—密封面；8—后玻璃板；9—后偏光板；10—反射镜

液晶显示器功耗小、显示信息灵活、示值清晰，但是由于液晶是非发光物质，所以必须要外界提供背景光源照明才可读数。液晶显示器一般用于仪表里程、时钟或者综合信息的显示。

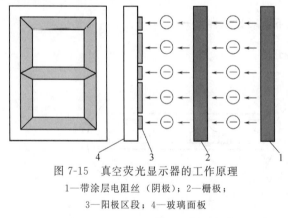

图 7-15 真空荧光显示器的工作原理
1—带涂层电阻丝（阴极）；2—栅极；
3—阳极区段；4—玻璃面板

c. 真空荧光显示器。真空荧光显示器产生的光就像电视机中的显像管发光一样，色彩鲜艳、明显清晰，是最常用的数字显示器。其工作原理如图 7-15 所示。灯丝实质上为带涂层电阻丝，电阻丝被电流加热，涂层产生自由电子。这些电子通过栅极的细丝网孔到达阳极，撞击阳极上相应区段的荧光物质后便产生蓝绿色光。高压电只施加于阳极片上要形成需显示的字符的区段，仪表电脑选择性地给需要发光信息显示的区段通电，而未通电的字符则不发光，这样仪表显示不同的数字信息。真空荧光显示器的亮度可以通过增减加速栅极电压而变化，较高的栅极电压可增加显示亮度。

（二）汽车报警信息系统

1. 汽车报警信息系统的作用和符号

汽车仪表除了指示基本的车辆行驶工况信息外，还要对其他的一些工况进行监控并向驾驶员发出指示或警告信息，这些信息通常以指示灯的形式显示在仪表板上或者以文字信息显

示在液晶显示器上，有的还伴随蜂鸣声，使驾驶员引起注意或重视。对于运用对路传输系统的汽车，它的仪表系统当然也包括指示灯，不过这些系统都是由 PCM（动力控制模块）或 BCM（车身控制模块）控制的，它们通常是多路传输系统的一部分。

汽车仪表上的指示灯系统一般由光源、刻有符号图案的透光塑料板和外电路组成。指示灯的光源以前大多采用小的白炽灯泡，损坏可以更换。目前电子仪表上更多采用体积小、亮度高、易于集成的 LED 作为光源。仪表指示灯一般都使用国际标准化组织（ISO）规定的通用符号，易于为全世界的人识别和理解，常见的符号如表 7-1 所示。

表 7-1 常用仪表指示灯与报警信息指示灯符号

符 号	描 述	符 号	描 述
	车门状态指示灯		清洗液不足报警灯
	驻车指示灯	 EPC	电子油门指示灯
	蓄电池指示灯		前后雾灯指示灯
	刹车片磨损报警灯		转向指示灯
	机油指示灯		远光指示灯
	水温指示灯		安全带指示灯
	安全气囊指示灯	 O/D OFF	O/D 挡指示灯
	ABS 指示灯		内循环指示灯
	发动机自检灯		示宽指示灯
	燃油量不足报警灯	 VSC	VSC 指示灯

驾驶员在驾驶汽车的时候，一定要养成及时关注仪表指示灯状态的好习惯，并能够根据各指示灯对应的含义和点亮或闪光的状态采取对应的措施，以做到正确使用、维护车辆和安全驾驶。

2. 常见汽车报警信息系统的意义和原理

汽车的信息指示和报警装置的组成和工作原理因车型不同而各有差异，在此对最常见、

最重要的指示灯和警告灯作一下介绍。

(1) 状态和故障指示灯。

状态指示灯最常用于灯光信号。如大灯的远/近指示灯、前/后雾灯指示灯、转向信号指示灯、示宽指示灯等。灯光信号指示灯的点亮有的是受外电路的灯关控制开关直接控制的,有的要经过继电器控制。

故障指示灯常用于与行车安全相关系统的警告指示,如轮胎气压低、安全气囊失效、制动液不足、清洗液不足等。

在轮胎充气不足或者爆胎时,轮胎气压报警灯都会点亮。有些系统设有红色和黄色报警灯,红色报警灯在轮胎压力过低或者爆胎时点亮,黄色报警灯则在轮胎压力较低时点亮,有些系统还会发出声音告知驾驶者。轮胎气压压力的检测有的是靠检测车辆直行时不同车轮轮速差异计算出来的,有的则直接通过接收安装在轮胎气门芯内的无线压力传感器发射的信号判断的。

(2) 报警灯。

① 冷却系统。冷却系统报警信息一般指冷却液不足、液位过低报警和冷却液温度高报警。冷却液温度高报警灯的作用是当发动机冷却液温度升高到一定程度时,报警灯自动点亮,以示报警。冷却液温度高报警灯的通断通常由双金属温度开关控制。当冷却液温度低于95~98℃时,双金属片上的活动触点与固定触点保持分离状态,报警灯不亮;当冷却液温度高于95~98℃时,双金属片受热变形向下弯曲程度变大,使两触点接触,将报警灯电路接通,报警灯点亮提醒驾驶员注意。

② 润滑系统。润滑系统信息指示和报警一般针对机油压力、机油温度、机油液面和机油质量等工况进行监控。

机油压力报警灯用于提醒驾驶员注意发动机的机油压力异常,指示机油泵是否以正常压力供给发动机的各部件,有的车辆上既有机油压力表又有机油压力报警灯,但多数车辆上只有机油压力报警灯。该灯由位于发动机润滑系统中的机油压力开关控制,机油压力报警灯的报警开关一般装在主油道上。

图7-16所示为膜片式机油压力报警电路。

③ 制动系统。制动系统信息指示和报警包括驻车制动指示、制动系统真空助力器真空度过低、制动管路液压低、制动液不足、刹车片磨损过度、ABS系统故障报警等。图7-17所示为常见的制动液液位报警开关结构。如果储液罐中的制动液少于规定量,浮子下降,舌簧开关在永久磁铁的磁化下闭合,报警灯在发动机运转期间点亮。这种形式的报警开关可以装在储液罐等需要检测液位并在不足时及时报警的容器内。

④ 充电系统。充电报警灯指示充电系统的状况,如果充电系统存在故障,在发动机运转时该灯会点亮。当发电机的电压达到正常充电电压时,该报警灯熄灭。如果在正常行驶时,该报警灯亮,说明充电系统有功能故障。

⑤ 燃油供给。燃油油位报警灯用

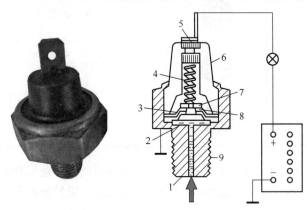

图7-16 膜片式机油压力报警电路
1—发动机润滑油;2—膜片;3—绝缘顶块;4—弹簧;5—接线柱;
6—绝缘层;7—动触点;8—静触点;9—固定螺口

于监视油箱中的燃油量,当燃油油位降至低于满箱油位高度规定值时,模块中的油位报警开关关闭,向燃油油位报警灯供电,使报警灯点亮,表明燃油剩余量不足。常见燃油油位报警灯电路如图 7-18 所示。

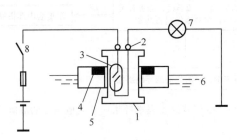

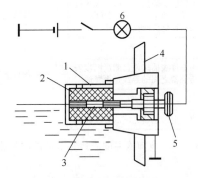

图 7-17　制动液液位报警开关结构
1—舌簧开关外壳;2—接线柱;3—舌簧开关;
4—永久磁铁;5—浮子;6—制动液面;
7—报警灯;8—点火开关

图 7-18　燃油油位报警灯电路
1—外壳;2—防爆金属网;3—热敏电阻;
4—油箱外壳;5—接线柱;6—报警灯

该装置是由负温度系数的热敏电阻式燃油油位报警传感器和报警灯组成。当油箱内油量较多时,热敏电阻原件浸没在燃油中,散热快,温度较低,电阻值较大。因此,电路中电流很小,报警灯不亮。当燃油减小到规定值以下时,热敏电阻元件露出油面,散热慢,温度较高,电阻值较小。因此,电路中电流增大,警告灯亮。

⑥ 发动机电控系统。发动机电控系统有自检功能,一旦检测到发动机电控系统有故障,仪表上的"Check Engine"(发动机故障)指示灯就会点亮,提示驾驶员及时进站维修,并在发动机电脑中存储故障码。发动机控制计算机监视着发动机的多个系统,并在发现故障时将报警灯点亮。

⑦ 变速器与底盘。变速器与底盘信息指示灯与报警灯一般有变速器指示灯、变速器挡位指示灯、驱动模式指示灯、空气悬架指示灯、牵引力及稳定性控制指示灯和巡航控制指示灯。

变速器指示灯是自动变速器控制系统的一部分,如果控制系统发现故障,将使变速器在故障安全模式下工作,并点亮指示灯告知驾驶者变速器不能正常工作。

变速器挡位指示灯可指示变速器所在挡位状态。驱动模式指示灯是指在一些四轮驱动的汽车设有驱动模式选择功能,当该灯点亮时,表示汽车在四轮驱动模式下工作。空气悬架指示灯在空气悬架存在故障时,指示灯电路搭铁,该指示灯点亮,表明系统故障。牵引力及稳定性控制指示灯是指在牵引力或稳定性控制系统中存在问题时,该灯或灯组的红灯会点亮,而在系统正在调节驱动力矩和制动力时,将黄灯点亮。巡航控制指示灯点亮说明巡航控制功能启用。

三、项目实施

(一)冷却液温度表的故障诊断

(1)指针不动。

现象:点火开关置 ON,指针不动。

原因如下:冷却液温度表电源线断路。冷却液温度表故障。传感器故障。温度表至传感

器的导线断路。

诊断：冷却液温度表指针不动的故障诊断步骤可参照图 7-19 进行。

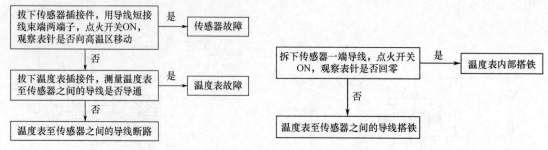

图 7-19　冷却液温度表指针不动的故障诊断　　图 7-20　冷却液温度表指针指向最大值不变的故障诊断

(2) 指针指向最大值不变。

现象：接通点火开关后，温度表指针即指向最高温度。

原因如下：温度表至传感器导线搭铁。传感器内部搭铁。温度表内部搭铁。

诊断：冷却液温度表指针指向最大值不变的故障诊断步骤可参照图 7-20 进行。

（二）燃油表的故障诊断

(1) 指针总指示"1"（油满）。

现象：点火开关置 ON 时，不论燃油量多少，燃油表指针总是指"1"（油满）。

原因如下：燃油表至传感器间导线搭铁。传感器内部断路。燃油表内部搭铁。

诊断：燃油表指针总指示"1"的故障诊断步骤可参照图 7-21 进行。

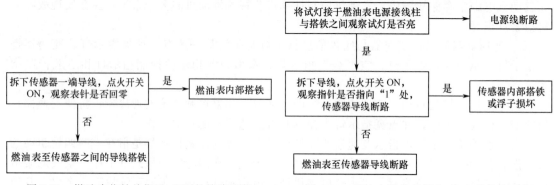

图 7-21　燃油表指针总指示"1"的故障诊断　　图 7-22　燃油表指针总指向"0"的故障诊断

(2) 指针总指向"0"（无油）。

现象：点火开关 ON，不论燃油量多少，燃油表指针总是指示"0"（无油）。

原因如下：传感器内部搭铁或浮子损坏。燃油表至电源线断路。燃油表内部故障。

诊断：燃油表指针总指向"0"的故障诊断步骤可参照图 7-22 进行。

（三）电子式车速里程表的故障诊断

电子式车速里程表常见故障是不工作。

现象：汽车行驶中车速里程表指针不动。

原因如下：传感器故障。仪表故障。线路故障。

诊断：电子式车速里程表不工作的故障诊断步骤可参照图 7-23 进行。

四、知识与技能拓展

（一）奥迪多媒体交互系统

奥迪多媒体交互系统（MMI）在一个显示屏和一个操作系统中，巧妙地融合了所有信息娱乐部件的操作。奥迪多媒体交互系统遵循简约而直观的运行理念，是一

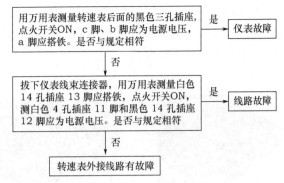

图 7-23　电子式车速里程表不工作的故障诊断

款兼具教育与娱乐功能的汽车配件。奥迪多媒体交互系统主要包括两种元素：位于中央控制台的奥迪多媒体交互系统终端及位于仪表盘的黑白或彩色奥迪多媒体交互系统显示器。

控制按钮是奥迪多媒体交互系统终端的主要部件（见图 7-24），用户可以转动或按压此按钮，按钮四周配有 4 个控制键。终端两侧共有 8 个功能键，可以直接调用主菜单（见图 7-25）。该系统的主要功能包括娱乐、通信、信息与汽车系统控制，用户可以使用 8 个永久赋值功能键实现这些功能。在各个菜单内，驾驶员可以转动/按下控制按钮以激活所需要功能。

图 7-24　奥迪多媒体交互系统旋钮控制器

图 7-25　奥迪多媒体交互系统显示屏主菜单

奥迪多媒体交互系统的第二个组成部分是奥迪多媒体交互系统显示屏。彩色屏幕位于中控台之上的仪表板中央，正处于驾驶者的最佳视野范围内。奥迪多媒体交互系统集成了车辆控制、功能设定、信息娱乐、导航系统、车载电话等多项功能，驾驶员可方便、快捷地从中查询、设置、切换车辆系统的各种信息，从而使车辆达到理想的运行和操纵状态。

（二）平视显示系统

很多高级轿车目前都采用平视显示系统，平视显示系统是指将各种车辆系统的信息投影显示到扩大的驾驶员视野中的光学系统。如果想了解这些参数，驾驶员不必明显地改变头部位置，只需在端坐的同时将目光投向道路即可。尤其是在高速公路上高速行驶时，更加安全。

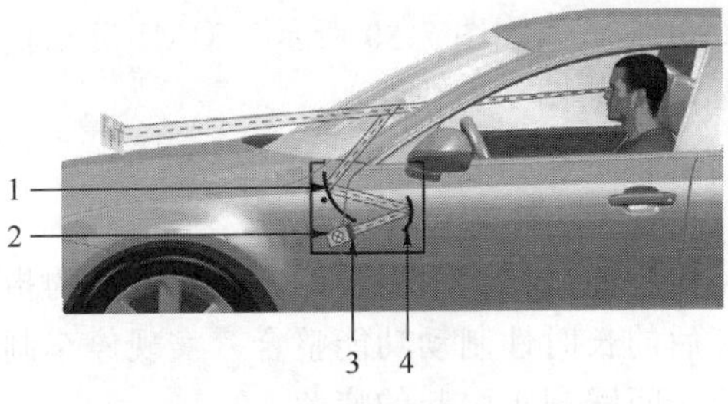

平视显示系统的显示使驾驶员能够快速、精准地获得重要的车辆信息。在带平视显示系统的车辆上使用专门的挡风玻璃可以让人产生这样的感觉：平视显示系统所显示的内容并不是出现在挡风玻璃上，而是出现在离驾驶员 2～2.5m 的舒适距离上。平视显示内容似乎悬浮在发动机罩上方。平视显示系统工作原理如图 7-26 所示。平视显示系统由可视镜面、平视显示控制单元（见图

图 7-26　平视显示系统工作原理
1—可视镜面；2—照明单元；
3—TFT 显示器；4—不可调镜面

项目七　信息显示系统的检修

7-27)、TFT 显示器、不可调镜面组成。通过光的折射把信息投射到前挡风玻璃上。通过仪表照明调节器可对显示器和仪表照明进行基本设置（见图 7-28）。改变此设置时平视显示系统的显示亮度也会发生改变。

图 7-27　平视显示控制单元

图 7-28　平视显示系统操作和设置按钮
1—平视显示位置调节器；2—显示器和仪表照明基本设置调节器

图 7-29　仪表上的机油油位高度显示

（三）电子机油油面高度显示

有些高档轿车没有设置机油尺，而是采用电子机油尺。

1. 测量方法

电子机油油面高度显示系统有两种测量方法用于计算机油油面高度。

动态测量，是在车辆行驶中进行的，重要的测量参数有：发动机转速；来自 ESP-控制单元的横向和纵向加速度；发动机舱盖接触开关信号；发动机温度。以上特定测量值满足后，即可测量出结果。

静态测量，在下述情况下进行：点火开关接通（为了尽快获得测量结果，这个测量过程在打开司机车门时就已经开始了）；发动机机油温度 >40℃；发动机停机超过 60s。在静态测量中，还要考虑 ESP-控制单元的加速度值（斜面停着的车辆）。另外，还要使用驻车制动器信号。如果机油油位低得或高得已经可能要造成发动机损坏了，那么会发出过低或者过高的提示。

2. 机油油位高度/机油温度传感器安装位置和工作原理

机油油位高度/机油温度传感器拧在油底壳上，根据超声波原理来工作。封闭式超声波液位传感器发出的超声波脉冲会被机油-空气边界层所反射，根据发出脉冲和返回脉冲的时间差，参考声速就可确定机油油位的高度。结果显示在组合仪表或者 MMI 的显示屏上。仪表上的机油油位高度显示，如图 7-29 所示。MMI 发动机机油量显示，如图 7-30 所示。

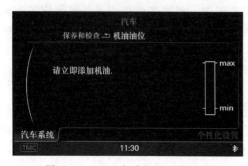

图 7-30　MMI 发动机机油量显示

（四）电子驻车制动系统 EPB（电子手刹）

目前很多车型采用的电子驻车制动系统，代替了传统的机械式手制动器，但仪表上的指示灯不变。该系统将行车过程中的临时性制动和停车后的长时性制动功能整合，实现停车制动。当驾驶者踩油门时刹车锁止自动解除，省去了长时间踩刹车引起的疲劳。

该系统主要部件为电子驻车开关、电子驻车制动控制单元（EPB）和驻车制动电机。后轮驻车制动器总成如图 7-31 所示，包含有驻车制动电机。当拉起电子驻车开关时，电子驻

车制动控制单元 J540 驱动左后和右后制动器上的驻车制动电机 V282 和 V283。驻车制动电机通过驱动轴施加制动蹄片的机械张紧力。而当释放电子手刹时，需要打开点火开关、踩下制动踏板，然后按下电子驻车开关，电子驻车制动控制单元 J540 驱动左后和右后制动器上的驻车制动电机 V282 和 V283，释放制动蹄片的机械张紧力。

使用电子驻车制动系统的车辆，在拆卸装后轮的制动盘和制动片时，需要用专用诊断仪对电子手刹进行释放。在安装后轮的制动盘和制动片时，需要用专用诊断仪对电子手刹进行复位。

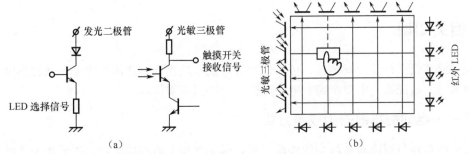

图 7-31　后轮驻车制动器总成
1—制动钳；2—制动盘；
3—电子驻车制动电机

（五）触摸显示系统

随着科技的发展，很多高档汽车采用触摸显示系统。触摸显示系统的触摸键盘通常是以模拟形式显示在屏幕上，用手指触摸键盘即可进行操作，从而简化了选择信息的过程。

触摸显示系统通常是用采用红外触摸开关来检测屏幕是否被触摸，红外触摸开关的原理如图 7-32 所示。

图 7-32　红外触摸开关的原理

在显示器的两端都有一个红外发光二极管和光敏三极管相对。在显示器键盘未被触摸时，红外发光二极管的光束到达光敏三极管促使其导通。键盘被触摸时，红外发光二极管光波被截断，光敏三极管立即截止。红外发光二极管和光敏三极管的混合体安放在显示器的多个地方，因此，屏幕上被触摸到的键盘位置由被关断的光敏三极管所在位置测定。

小　结

（1）汽车仪表按工作原理可分为机械式仪表、电气式仪表、模拟电路电子仪表和数字化电子仪表。

（2）仪表稳压器。由于电源电压的变化会对仪表指示值产生影响，造成仪表值误差，所以仪表电路一般要装有仪表稳压器。

（3）汽车仪表除了指示基本的车辆行驶工况信息外，还要对其他的一些工况进行监控并向驾驶员发出指示或警告信息，这些信息通常以指示灯的形式显示在仪表板上或者以文字信息的形式显示在液晶显示器上，有的还伴随蜂鸣声，以便引起驾驶员的注意或重视。

习题及思考

（1）汽车常见的报警信息有哪些？能够检测哪些系统的工作状况？
（2）电子组合仪表一般有哪些常见仪表？
（3）电子仪表的常见显示器件都有哪些类型？显示方式有哪些？

项目八

汽车辅助电气系统的检修

一、情境引入

一辆丰田花冠轿车，按下左前门内侧的右后玻璃升降开关，右后玻璃没有反应，但按下右后门内侧的玻璃升降开关，则此门玻璃可以升降。通过检修发现是由于左前门内侧的组合玻璃升降开关中的右后玻璃升降开关损坏。电动玻璃升降系统是汽车辅助电气系统中的一个子系统。随着汽车行业的发展，辅助电气系统所占的比重越来越大，性能也越来越完善。

二、相关知识

为了提高汽车行驶的安全性、可靠性及舒适性，现代汽车普遍配置了一些辅助电器，如电动刮水器、清洗器、电动车窗、电动座椅、中控门锁系统等。

（一）电动刮水器的组成与分类

电动刮水器与清洗器是汽车的标准配置，属于汽车上的辅助电器，主要用来清洗和刷除风窗玻璃上的雨水、雪和灰尘，以保证驾驶员的视觉效果。有的汽车前照灯也有刮水器和清洗器系统，以保证雨雪天气尤其是夜间的行车安全。电动刮水器与清洗器的元部件在汽车上的位置如图 8-1 所示。

根据动力不同，刮水器可分为电动刮水器、气动刮水器和机械式刮水器。现今汽车上广泛采用的是电动刮水器。电动刮水器的基本组成如图 8-2 所示。

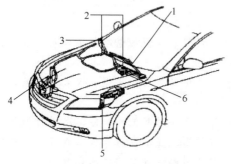

图 8-1　电动刮水器与清洗器的元部件位置
1—前挡风玻璃左刮水片总成；2—喷嘴；
3—前挡风玻璃右刮水片总成；4—储液罐和清洗泵总成；5—保险丝盒；
6—刮水器电动机总成

刮水器根据刮刷方式的不同，可分为双臂同向刮刷、双臂对向刮刷、单臂可控刮刷和普通单臂刮刷 4 种。

有些汽车刮水器的刮水臂还附带胶水管，水管接至清洗器上，按一下开关有水喷向挡风玻璃。

为了避免驾驶员关闭刮水器时，刮水臂阻碍驾驶员的视线，电动刮水器通常装有自动复位装置，它控制刮水器电动机，以便在任意时刻关闭刮水器时，都能使刮水臂停在挡风玻璃下侧的位置。

目前，汽车上使用的刮水器已经普遍具有高速、低速和间歇控制 3 个工作挡位。其中，间歇控制挡一般是利用电动机的复位开关触点与电阻

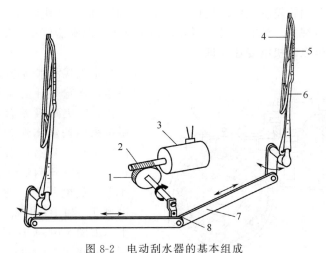

图 8-2 电动刮水器的基本组成

1—蜗轮；2—蜗杆；3—电动机；4—刮水片；5—刮水片架；6—刮水臂；7—拉杆；8—摇臂

电容的充放电功能使刮水器按照一定周期刮刷，即每动作 1 次停止 2～12s，对驾驶员的干扰更少。有些车辆的刮水器还装有电子调速器，该调速器附带雨量感应功能，能根据雨量的大小自动调节雨臂的摆动速度，雨大刮水臂转得快，雨小刮水臂转得慢，雨停刮水臂也停。奥迪 A6 汽车上使用的刮水器就具有根据雨量大小自动调节刮水臂转动速度功能，其刮水器电动机控制单元如图 8-3 所示，它将雨量传感器与雨刮电动机集成在同一个壳体内。

图 8-3 具有自动调速功能的
刮水器电动机控制单元

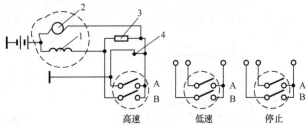

图 8-4 励磁式刮水器电动机的工作原理

1—电动机励磁绕组；2—电枢绕组；3—附加电阻；4—触点

（二）刮水器系统的工作原理

电动刮水器的变速是通过改变电动机的速度来实现的。汽车刮水器电动机是微型直流电动机，有励磁式和永磁式两种。其中，永磁式电动机具有结构简单、重量轻、噪声低、扭矩大、可靠性强等优点，因而使用更为广泛。

1. 励磁式刮水器电动机的变速原理

励磁式刮水器电动机一般有两种速度：低速和高速。它通过改变磁极的磁通来实现变速，其工作原理如图 8-4 所示。

励磁式刮水器电动机有 A、B 两个开关，用以控制刮水器实现两种不同的工作速度。当 A 闭合 B 打开时，电动机励磁绕组 1 的回路中串入了附加电阻 3，使励磁电流减小，磁通较弱，根据电动机的特性，输出转矩在一定范围以内时，磁通减小则转速升高，此时刮水器高速工作；当 A、B 均闭合时，开关 B 将附加电阻 3 短接，励磁电流不通过附加电阻，电流增大，磁通增强，转速降低，此时刮水器低速工作；当 A 打开，B 闭合，电动机的电流从触

点 4 通过，触点 4 受蜗轮轮轴上的凸块控制，蜗轮每转 1 圈，凸块将触点打开一次，通常当刮水片运动到驾驶员视界之外时，触点断开，切断电源，刮水器停止工作。

2. 永磁式刮水器电动机的变速原理

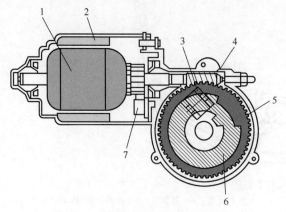

图 8-5 永磁式刮水器电动机的结构
1—电枢；2—永久磁铁；3—触点；4—蜗杆；5—蜗轮；
6—铜环；7—电刷

永磁式刮水器电动机的结构如图 8-5 所示，蜗轮蜗杆变速装置与电动机装为一体，2 块磁极粘合在电动机外壳上，磁极采用铁氧体永久磁铁，具有永不退磁的优点，其磁场强弱不可改变。电动机端部装有塑料通气管，以便将电刷由于电弧放电所产生的气体放出。1 对主电刷 B_1 和 B_3 相隔 180°压装在换向器上，如图 8-6(a) 所示，为了获得两种速度，通常在电动机内还安装了第三个电刷 B_2，通过变换电刷，改变串联在电刷间的导体数，达到变速的目的。其变速原理如图 8-6(b) 所示，图中 B_1 和 B_2 相差 60°，B_1 为低速电刷，B_2 为高速电刷，B_3 为高低速共用电刷。当直流电动机工作时，在电枢所有线圈中同时产生反电动势 $E=cn\phi$，方向与电枢电流的方向相反。

如要使电枢旋转，外加电压必须克服反电动势的作用，当电枢转速上升时，反电动势也相应上升，只有当外加电压几乎等于反电动势时，电枢的转速才趋于稳定，这一转速稳定转速。

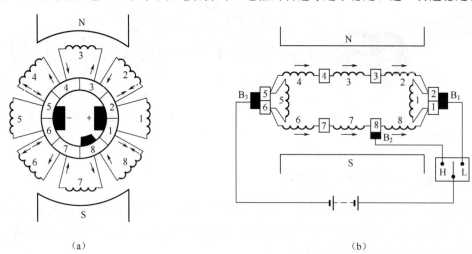

图 8-6 永磁式刮水电动机的变速原理

当刮水器开关拨向低速，即 S 与 L 接触时，电源电压加在 B_1 与 B_3 之间。在电刷 B_1 与 B_3 之间有 2 条并联支路，一条是由线圈 1、6、5 串联起来的支路；另一条是由线圈 2、4、6 串联起来的支路，即在电刷 B_1 与 B_3 之间有两条支路，各 3 个线圈。这两条支路产生的全部反电动势与电源电动势平衡后，电动机便稳定旋转。由于 3 个线圈串联的线圈的反电动势与电源电压平衡，故转速较低。

当刮水器开关拨向高速，即 S 与 H 接触时，电源电压加在 B_2 与 B_3 之间。此时，电枢绕组 1 条由 4 个线圈 2、1、6、5 串联，另一条内 2 个线圈 3、4 串联。其中，线圈 2 的反电

动势与线圈 1、6、5 的反电动势相反，互相抵消后，变为只有 2 个线圈的反电动势与电源电压平衡，因而只有使转速升高，使反电动势增大，才能得到平衡，故此时转速较高。

3. 电动刮水器的复位原理

电动刮水器的复位原理如图 8-7 所示，其刮水器开关设有 3 个挡位，0 挡为复位挡，刮水器在不工作时应该处于这个挡位置，I 挡为低速挡，II 挡为高速挡。4 个接线柱分别接到触点臂、低速电刷 B_1、搭铁和高速电刷 B_2 上。在蜗轮上，嵌有铜环，其中较大的一片与电动机的外壳相连而搭铁，触点臂用弹性材料制成，其一端铆有触点，分别与蜗轮断面或铜环接触。

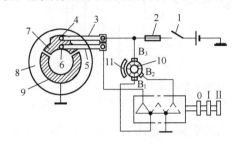

（a）刮水器回位时铜环的位置　　（b）刮水器未回位时铜环的位置

图 8-7　电动刮水器的复位原理

1—电源开关；2—熔断丝；3,5—触点臂；4,6—触点；7,9—铜环；
8—蜗轮；10—电枢；11—永久磁铁

当电源开关 1 接通，并把刮水器开关拉到 I 挡时，接线柱 2 和接线柱 3 经刮水器开关而连接在一起。此时，电流从蓄电池正极→电源开关→熔断丝→电刷 B_3→电枢绕组→电刷 B_1→接线柱 2→刮水器开关→接线柱 3→搭铁→蓄电池负极，形成回路，电动机以低速运转。

当把刮水器拉到 II 挡时，接线柱 3 和接线柱 4 经刮水器开关而连接在一起。此时，电流从蓄电池正极→电源开关→熔断丝→电刷 B_3→电枢绕组→电刷 B_2→接线柱 4→刮水器开关→接线柱 3→搭铁→蓄电池负极，形成回路，电动机以高速运转。

当刮水器开关退回到 0 挡位置，接线柱 2 和接线柱 1 经刮水器开关而连接在一起。如果此时刮水片没有停在如图 8-7(a) 所示的规定位置，而是停在如图 8-7(b) 所示的一般位置时，电流经蓄电池正极→电源开关→熔断丝→电刷 B_3→电枢绕组→电刷 B_1→接线柱 2→刮水器开关→接线柱 1→触点臂→铜环 9→搭铁，这时电动机将继续转动。当刮水器的刮水片运动到图 8-7(a) 所示的规定位置时，电路中断，但由于惯性电动机不能立刻停下来，电机以发电机方式运行，电枢绕组通过触点臂 3、5 与铜环 7 接触而构成回路，在电枢绕组产生很大的感应电流，因而产生制动扭矩，电动机迅速停止转动，使刮水器的刮水片停止在风窗玻璃规定的位置。

不同厂家生产的电动刮水器的复位盘形状不一样，但作用相同。

4. 电动刮水器的间歇工作原理

汽车在雾天或小雨雪天气中行驶时，若刮水器不间断地工作，风窗玻璃上的微量水分和灰尘就会形成一个发黏的表面，这样玻璃不仅刮不干净，反而会变得模糊，影响驾驶员的视线；同时，刮水片的刮擦阻力增大，影响刮水器的使用寿命。现今汽车上一般通过加装刮水器间歇控制系统，让刮水器按照一定的周期间歇工作，使驾驶员获得较好的视野。

刮水器间歇控制系统主要由脉冲发生电路（振荡电路）、驱动电路、继电器 3 部分组成。驱动电路在脉冲发生电路的控制下，驱动继电器定时接通和断开刮水器电动机，实现间歇工作。

常见的刮水器间隙控制电路分为不可调节式和可调节式两种。

（1）不可调节式间歇控制电路。刮水器的不可调节式间歇控制电路是利用自动复位装置和电子振荡电路实现的。图 8-8 所示为一种用集成电路形成的不可调节式间歇控制电路原理

图，NE555 与外围元件组成脉冲发生电路和驱动电路。

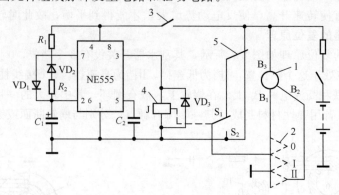

图 8-8　NE555 间歇控制电路

1—刮水器电动机；2—刮水器开关；3—间歇刮水器开关；4—继电器；5—自停开关

当间歇刮水器开关闭合时，NE555 集成块的引脚 3 输出高电位，使继电器 J 线圈通电，其常闭触点 S_1 断开，常开触点 S_2 闭合，刮水器电动机电路经蓄电池正极→电源开关→熔断丝→电刷 B_3→电枢绕组→电刷 B_1→刮水器开关→继电器常开触点 S_2→搭铁→蓄电池负极，形成回路，刮水器工作。经延时后，集成块的引脚 3 输出电位翻转为低电位，继电器断电，常闭触点 S_1 闭合，常开触点 S_2 打开，此时若刮水片为达到停止位置，则刮水器在自动停位器控制下继续工作，直至自停开关断开，刮水片停在原始位置。再经延时后，刮水器又重复上述工作过程，实现循环间歇刮刷动作。

除了由集成电路构成的刮水器间歇控制电路之外，还有一些由分立元件构成的无稳定态方波发生器、互补间歇振动电路等，如图 8-9 所示，均可实现刮水器的间歇工作。

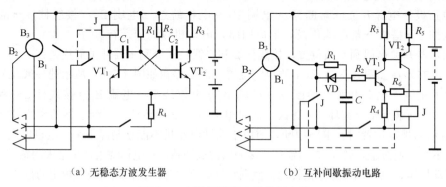

（a）无稳态方波发生器　　　　　　（b）互补间歇振动电路

图 8-9　电子间歇刮水器控制电路

（2）可调节式间歇控制电路。具有可调节式间歇控制功能的刮水器在遇到下雨时，由电子控制器驱动器驱动刮水器自动转动，在雨停止时刮水器自动停止运转，还可根据雨量的大小自动调节刮刷速度，并调节间歇时间，不需要驾驶员操心，舒适方便。可调节间歇控制电路通常由 1 个雨水传感器，加上调速控制电路构成。雨水传感器可能是 1 个流量检测电极，或者是 1 个光电雨水传感器，如图 8-10(a) 所示。光电雨水传感器发射出红外线，射在车窗上，雨水使红外线的反射量发生变化，触发接通刮水器的开关，使刮水器运转，这种刮水器还可以做到下小雨时慢刮，下大雨时快刮，如图 8-10(b) 所示。

（三）清洗器系统的组成

汽车在实际行驶过程中，会有一些灰尘飘落在挡风玻璃上，仅使用刮水器不能把玻璃刮

(a) 传感器外形

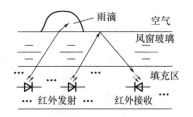
(b) 传感器工作原理

图 8-10 光电雨水传感器

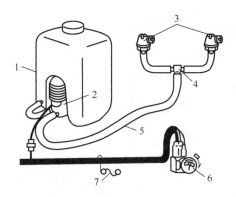

图 8-11 挡风玻璃清洗器的组成
1—储液罐；2—洗涤泵；3—喷嘴；4—三通接头；
5—输液管；6—刮水开关；7—熔断丝

刷干净。挡风玻璃清洗器与刮水器配合使用，可以使汽车挡风玻璃刮水器更好地完成刮水工作，并获得更好的刮水效果。

挡风玻璃清洗器的组成如图 8-11 所示，它主要由储液罐、洗涤泵、输液管、喷嘴等组成。洗涤泵一般由永磁直流电动机和离心叶片泵组装成为一体，喷射压力可达 70～88kPa。洗涤泵一般直接安装在储液罐上，但也有安装在管路内的。在离心泵的进口处设置有滤清器。洗涤泵喷嘴安装在挡风玻璃的下面，其喷嘴方向可以根据使用情况调整，喷水直径一般为 0.8～1.0mm，能够使洗涤液喷射在挡风玻璃的适当位置。洗涤泵的连续工作时间不应超过 1min。对于刮水和洗涤分别控制的汽车，应先开启洗涤泵，再接通刮水器。喷水停止后，刮水器应继续刮动 3～5 次，以便达到良好的清洁效果。

（四）电动刮水器和清洗器的维护与常见故障检修

根据国际驾驶安全调查显示：雨天驾车，由于刮水片老化引起视野不清而导致的交通事故率比平常高出大约 5 倍。因此，刮水器的良好维护是雨雪天气安全行驶的必要保证。刮水器推荐维护周期一般为 6 个月或 10000km，刮水片至少 1 年更换 1 次。由于清洗器时常与刮水器同时使用，所以在维护刮水器的同时，也要对清洗器进行维护。

1. 电动刮水器和清洗器的维护

（1）电动刮水器的维护。

① 检查刮水器电动机的固定及各传动机构的连接是否有松动，如图 8-12 所示，若发现松动，应予以拧紧。

② 检查刮水器橡胶刮水片的老化、磨损及其与玻璃贴附情况。当发现刮水片严重磨损或脏污时应及时更换或清洗。清洗刮水片时，可用蘸有酒精清洗剂的棉纱轻轻擦去刮水片上的污物，注意不可用汽油清洗和浸泡，否则刮水片会变形而无法使用。刮水片唇口必须与玻璃角度配合一致，否则应予以打磨或更换。

③ 用水润湿挡风玻璃后，打开刮水器开关，刮水器摇臂应摆动正常，电动机无异响。转换挡位开关，刮水器以相应的转速工作，并能自动复位。否则，应对刮水器电动机及相关线路进行检查。

④ 检查后，在各运动铰链处滴注 2～3 滴机油或涂抹润滑脂，并再次打开刮水器电动机开关使刮水器摇臂摆动，待机油或润滑脂浸到各工作面后，擦净多余的机油或润滑脂。

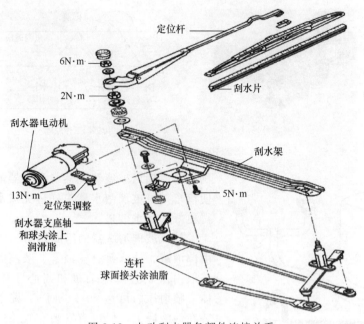

图 8-12 电动刮水器各部件连接关系

(2) 清洗器的维护。

① 检查清洗器系统的管路连接是否紧固，若有脱落或松动，应将其安装并固定好；塑料管路若有老化、折断或破裂，应予以更换。

② 检查清洗器喷嘴，脏污时可用干净的毛刷清洗喷嘴；按动喷液开关，喷嘴应将清洗液喷射到挡风玻璃上的适当位置，如图8-13所示，否则应对喷嘴位置进行调整，或对喷射部分及电路部分进行检修。

③ 清洗液应按原车要求选用，若使用普通洗涤剂、清洁剂配制的洗涤液，在进入冬季时，应予以清除，以防冻裂储液罐和塑料管路。

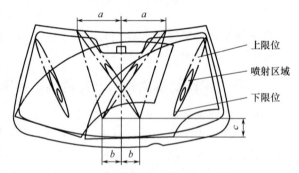

图 8-13 清洗液喷射位置示意

2. 电动刮水器和清洗器常见故障检修

电动刮水器和清洗器的常见故障有电动刮水器不工作或动作迟缓无力、不能复位、清洗系统不工作或喷射压力过低等。

(1) 电动刮水器不工作故障检修。电动刮水器的故障现象很多，但其故障原因归纳起来无外乎两个方面。从刮水器电动机上拆下机械传动装置，打开刮水器开关后，如电动机不能正常运行，说明是电动机或控制电路有故障；如电动机运行正常，则说明是机械故障。

对于电动刮水器不工作故障，先观察其故障现象是某一个速度挡不工作，还是所有挡位均不工作。如果仅是某一速度挡不工作，通常是电气方面故障，需结合该刮水器的电气原理图，确定其不工作的原因。如果是所有挡位均不工作，一般先检查是否有外来机械物品妨碍刮水器机械传动机构的动作。可接通刮水器开关，若电动机微微振动或发热，则可能是刮水片、传动机构、减速机构或电机转子卡住。根据具体情况，排除异物，或者更换局部机构零件，重新安装调整好刮水器，并加以润滑。若排除了上述故障，则应检查刮水器控制电路，如电源电压是否足够，保险丝是否熔断，搭铁及连接线是否松脱，开关接触是否良好等，若

前述各项完好,则故障可能在电动机上。

(2)清洗器不工作故障检修。

发现风窗清洗器不工作时,可先检查电源电压是否过低,清洗泵电动机接线是否良好,搭铁是否可靠,若有故障予以排除。

然后接通清洗泵开关,用手触摸电动机外壳,若电动机无反应,则说明清洗泵电动机有故障,进一步拆检电动机。

如电动机正常,接下来应检查储液罐有无清洗液、输液管路是否堵塞或泄漏等。

查清故障后,根据相应的故障进行处理,若是管道破裂,则应换上相同规格的输液管;若是喷嘴和三通阻塞,可用细钢丝疏通;若滤网堵塞,则应拆下清洗;若清洗液喷射位置不符合要求,则应对喷嘴位置进行调整;若是电动机损坏,则应更换。

(五)电动车窗的组成与结构

1. 电动车窗的组成

电动车窗可使驾驶员或乘客坐在座位上,利用开关使车门玻璃自动升降,操作简便并有利于行车安全。

电动车窗系统由车窗、车窗玻璃升降器、电动机、继电器、开关等装置组成,奥迪轿车电动车窗的结构如图8-14所示。

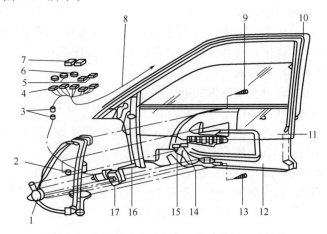

图8-14 奥迪轿车电动车窗(驾驶员侧)的结构

1—车窗玻璃升降器;2—垫;3—电机插座;4—开关总成插座;5—主开关;6—主开关的断路开关;7—插座架;8—线束;9—固定螺栓;10—车窗密封条;11—前左车窗玻璃;12—车窗附件支架;13—固定螺栓;14—垫;15—车窗锁止夹子;16—固定螺栓;17—电动机

2. 电动车窗的结构

有些汽车上的电动车窗由电动机直接作用于升降器,而有些则是通过驱动机构作用于升降器,从而把电动车的转动变换为车窗的上下移动。车窗玻璃升降器有两种形式:一种是绳轮式电动车窗玻璃升降器,如图8-15所示;另一种是交叉传动臂式电动车窗玻璃升降器,如图8-16所示。

(六)电动车窗的工作原理

电动车窗使用的电动机是双向的,有永磁型和双绕组串激型两种。每个车窗都装有一个电动机,通过开关控制它的旋转方向,使车窗玻璃上升或下降。

一般电动车窗系统都装有两套控制开关。一套装在仪表板或驾驶员侧门扶手上,为主开

关,它由驾驶员控制每个车窗的升降;另一套分别装在每一个乘客门上,为分开关,可由乘客进行操纵。一般在主开关上还装有断路开关,如果它断开,分开关就不起作用。

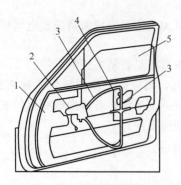 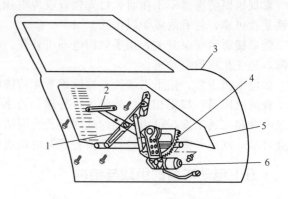

图 8-15 绳轮式电动车窗玻璃升降器　　　　图 8-16 交叉传动臂式电动车窗玻璃升降器
1—盖板;2—永磁电动机及减速器;3—导向套;　　1—调整杆;2—支架与导航;3—车门;4—驱动齿扇;
4—钢丝绳;5—车窗玻璃　　　　　　　　　　　　5—车窗玻璃;6—电动机及插座

为了防止电路过载,电路或电动机内装有 1 个或多个热敏断路开关,用以控制电流,当车窗完全关闭或由于结冰等原因使车窗玻璃不能运动自如时,即使操纵开关没有断开,热敏开关也会断路。有的车上还专门装有 1 个延迟开关,在点火开关断开后约 10min 内,或在车门打开以前,仍有电源提供,使驾驶员和乘客能有时间关闭车窗。

1. 永磁型直流电动机电动车窗

永磁型直流电动机是通过改变电枢的电流方向来改变电动机的旋转方向使车窗玻璃上升或下降。图 8-17 所示为雷克萨斯 LS400 轿车电动车窗控制系统线路。

当点火开关打至点火挡时,电动车窗主继电器工作,给电动车窗提供了电源;如将主开关上的车窗锁开关闭合,那么,所有车窗都可随时进入工作状态;若主开关的车窗锁开关断开,则只有驾驶员侧车窗可进行工作。另外,驾驶员侧的车窗开关由点触式电路控制,驾驶员要使车窗玻璃下降时,只要点触一下下降开关,车窗玻璃就会自动下降到最低点,在下降过程中,如果要使玻璃停止在某个位置时,只要再点触一下开关即可。

2. 电动天窗

电动天窗主要由天窗组件、滑动机构、驱动机构和控制系统等组成。天窗组件包括天窗框架、天窗玻璃、遮阳板、导流槽、排水槽等部分。电动车窗执行机构主要由电动机、传动机构、滑动螺杆等组成,如图 8-18 所示。工作时,电动机驱动传动机构,使得天窗滑移开启或倾斜开启。

天窗控制系统主要包括天窗控制开关、电控单元(ECU)、继电器、限位开关等。

天窗控制开关有滑动开启和倾斜开启 2 种功能,如图 8-19 所示。滑动开关有滑动打开、滑动关闭和断开 3 个位置;倾斜开关也有斜升、斜降和断开 3 个位置。通过驱动电动机实现正反转,使天窗在不同的状态下工作。

电动天窗玻璃具有遮挡视线(避免由外向内看)和前后倾斜功能。在没有打开任何车门的情况下将点火开关旋至关闭位置时,电动机仍能工作 10min,本田雅阁轿车电动天窗控制电路如图 8-20 所示。

该天窗能开启、关闭、倾斜。例如,开启电路,当开关点火开关时,电路中的电流流向为蓄电池正极→多路控制装置(前乘客席侧)→(点火开关断开定时器开关)→电动车窗继电

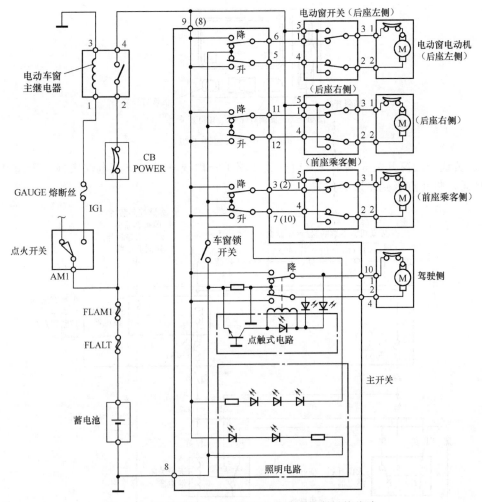

图 8-17 雷克萨斯 LS400 轿车电动车窗控制系统线路

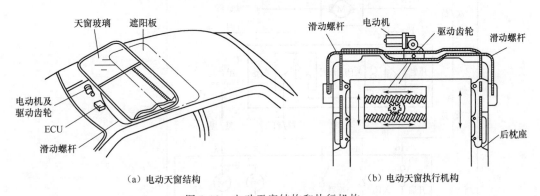

(a) 电动天窗结构　　　　　(b) 电动天窗执行机构

图 8-18 电动天窗结构和执行机构

器（前乘客席侧仪表板下熔断器/继电器盒）→黑线→搭铁→蓄电池负极,电动天窗继电器接通。

当电动天窗开关打到开启位置时,电路中的电流流向为蓄电池的正极→黑线 No.41 (100A)、No.51 (40A)（发动机盖下熔断器/继电器盒）→白/蓝线→电动车窗继电器触点→熔断丝 No.7 (20A)（前乘客席侧仪表板下熔断器/继电器盒）→白/黄线→天窗开启继电器线

项目八　汽车辅助电气系统的检修　145

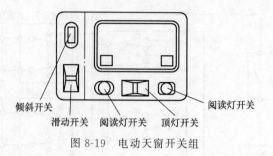

图 8-19 电动天窗开关组

圈→灰/黄线→天窗开关6端子→天窗开关2端子→黑线→搭铁→蓄电池负极，天窗开启继电器接通，将触点吸到左边的位置。

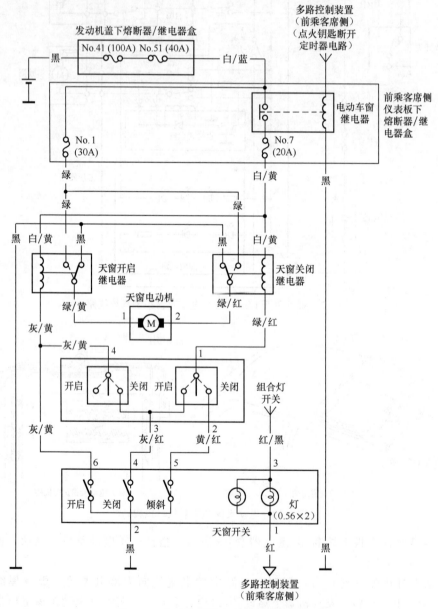

图 8-20 本田雅阁轿车电动天窗控制电路

（七）电动车窗的故障诊断

（1）所有车窗均不能升降。

① 主要故障原因：熔断器断路；有关继电器、开关损坏；电动机损坏；搭铁点锈蚀、松动。

② 诊断步骤。首先检查熔断器是否断路，若熔断器良好，则应将点火开关接通，检查有关继电器和开关火线接线柱上的电压是否正常。电压为零，则应检查搭铁线是否良好。搭铁不良时，应清洁、紧固搭铁线；若搭铁线良好，应对继电器、开关和电动机进行检测。

（2）某车窗不能升降或只能一个方向运动

① 主要故障原因：按键开关损坏，电动机损坏，连接导线断路，安全开关故障。

② 诊断步骤。如果车窗不能升降，首先检查安全开关是否工作，该车窗的按键开关工作是否正常；然后检查该车窗的电动机正反转是否运转稳定。若有故障，应检修或更换新件；若正常，则应检查连接导线。如果车窗只能一个方向运动，一般是按键开关故障或部分线路断路或接错所致，可以先检查线路连接是否正常，再检修开关。

三、项目实施

（一）汽车辅助电气系统的检修

① 通过该项目的实施，应能够对刮水器和清洗器进行拆装与调整，并掌握刮水器故障诊断与检测的步骤与方法。

② 该项目应具备汽车刮水器系统、螺丝刀、扳手、万用表等拆装与检修工具和汽车刮水器电路图等资料。

（二）实施步骤

1. 电动刮水与清洗系统的故障诊断

电动刮水与清洗系统的故障诊断流程如图 8-21 所示。

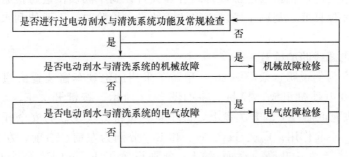

图 8-21 电动刮水与清洗系统的故障诊断流程

2. 电动刮水与清洗系统的拆卸

电动刮水器与清洗器的拆卸可以参照制造厂说明书和维修手册推荐的操作步骤进行。本项目只是种提供了奥迪 A6 轿车电动刮水器与清洗器的拆装步骤，可供参阅。

拆卸时，一般应先拆下不得不拆的有关部件，最后拆卸刮水器电动机系统，拆下线束插接器、拆下连杆机构和电动机总成连接螺栓等。拆卸时多加小心，以防损坏电动机内部的永久磁铁。

3. 电动刮水与清洗系统的检修

(1) 刮水器各联动机构的检修。

① 检查刮水片总成。刮水片是否老化,刮水臂是否变形,如老化、变形则予以更换。

② 检查传动机构。各连杆等传动部件是否弯曲变形,如变形则予以校正,不可修复的,则需更换。

③ 检查连接球等连接部位润滑是否良好,是否磨损严重。如润滑不良,则需添加润滑油脂;如磨损严重,则应予以修理或更换。

(2) 控制线路及开关的检修。可用万用表检测刮水器和清洗器组合开关处于各挡位时的通断情况。如线路问题,则对相应线路重新连接;如判断是开关内部触点接触不良或烧坏而引起的故障,则应拆开检修或更换。

(3) 刮水器电机总成检修。

① 检查蜗轮、蜗杆变速机构有无磨损,如磨损严重则予以更换。

② 检查电刷高度,一般不应低于 8mm,否则应予以更换。

③ 检查电动机换向器表面是否烧蚀,若烧蚀则用细纱布打磨,若烧蚀或磨损严重的,则需更换或重新加工,使之符合要求。

④ 检查磁场线圈有无短路、断路或搭铁故障,若有,则应更换或重新绕线。

⑤ 检查电枢轴是否弯曲,轴与轴承的配合间隙是否符合要求,否则应予以更换。

(4) 清洗器系统检修。

① 检查储液罐中清洗液是否足够,否则应补充清洗液。

② 检查输液管是否畅通,是否泄漏,否则应更换,重新连接、密封。

③ 检查喷嘴、三通、漏网是否堵塞,否则可用细钢丝疏通喷嘴和三通,滤网则需清洗。

4. 电动刮水与清洗系统的安装与调整

电动刮水与清洗系统的安装一般与拆卸步骤相反,建议参照制造厂说明书和维修手册推荐的操作步骤进行。

安装时应注意刮水片的归位;注意储液罐中的清洗液不要洒掉,如洒掉应补标准的清洗液;注意喷水管的接头要可靠;尤其要注意,根据制造厂提供的数据,调整好喷嘴的位置。

安装好后,应给电动机接通电源,将组合开关打开到不同挡位进行检验,系统应工作正常、运转平稳、复位良好、刮刷干净。值得注意的是,检验时,不要使刮水器干刮,以免造成损伤。

5. 电动车窗电源线路的检查

以桑塔纳轿车为例说明,桑塔纳 2000 型轿车采用的电动车窗装置由翘板按键开关、传动机构、升降器及电动机组成,控制电路如图 8-22 所示。按键开关 E_{39}、E_{40}、E_{41}、E_{32}、E_{53} 被安置在中央通道面板上的开关盘上,其中黄色按键开关 E_{39} 为安全开关,可以使后车窗开关 E_{53} 和 E_{55} 不起作用;E_{40}、E_{41}、E_{52} 和 E_{54} 分别为左前、右前、左后和右后玻璃升降开关。为使玻璃能独立升降,在两后门上分别设置了 E_{53} 和 E_{55} 两个按键开关。V_{14}、V_{15}、V_{26} 和 V_{27} 分别为左前、右前、左后和右后车窗电动机,电动机为永磁直流电动机,正常工作电流为 4~15A,电动机内带有过载断路保护器,以免电动机超载烧坏。延时继电器 J_{52} 是保证在点火开关断开后,使车窗电路延时约 50s 后再断开,使用方便、安全;自动继电器 J_{51} 用于控制左前门车窗电动机。

实现点动控制工作原理如下。

接通点火开关后,延时继电器 J_{52} 与 C 路电源相通,其常开触点闭合,按键开关内的 P 通过该触点接地,而 P_+ 通过熔断器 S_{37} 与 A 路电源相通,此时,按动按键开关便可使车窗

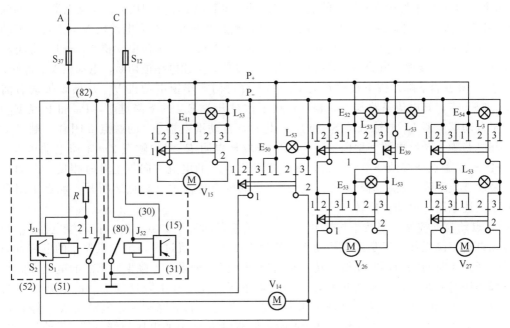

图 8-22 桑塔纳轿车电动车窗控制电路

电动机转动。

(1) 发动机熄火后的延时控制。关闭点火开关后，C 路电源断开，延时继电器 J_{52} 由 A 路电源供电，延时 50s 后，继电器触点断开，按键开关的搭铁线被割断，所有按键开关失去控制作用。

(2) 后车窗电动机的控制。左后门和右后门的车窗电动机各由 2 个按键开关 E_{52}、E_{53} 和 E_{54}、E_{55} 控制，E_{52} 和 E_{54} 安装在中央通道面板上，供驾驶员控制，E_{53} 和 E_{55} 分别安装在两后门上，供后座乘客控制。同一后门的 2 个开关采用级联方式连接，当 2 个开关被同时按下时没有控制作用，只有当某一个开关被按下时，才有控制作用，在安全开关 E_{39} 被按下的情况下，E_{39} 的常闭触点断开，切断了后车门上控制开关 E_{53} 和 E_{55} 的电源，使其失去了对各自车窗电动机的控制。因而，起到保护儿童安全的作用。

① 车窗玻璃上升。在安全开关 E_{39} 没有被按下的情况下，将 E_{52}（E_{54}）置上升位，车窗电动机 V_{26}（V_{27}）正转，带动左后（右后）车窗玻璃上升，此时电路为：A 路电源→熔断器 S_{37}→E_{52}（E_{54}）→E_{53}（E_{55}）→左后（右后）车窗电动机 V_{26}（V_{27}）→E_{53}（E_{55}）→E_{52}（E_{54}）→P→J_{52} 触点→接地→电源负极；如果按下左后（右后）车窗上 E_{53}（E_{55}）的上升键，车窗电动机 V_{26}（V_{27}）同样可带动车窗玻璃上升，此时电路为：A 路电源→熔断器 S_{37}→P_+→E_{39}→E_{53}（E_{55}）→左后（右后）→车窗电动机 V_{26}（V_{27}）→E_{53}（E_{55}）→E_{52}（E_{54}）→P→J_{52} 触点→接地→电源负极。

② 车窗玻璃下降。在安全按键开关 E_{39} 没有被按下的情况下，按下 E_{52}（E_{54}）或 E_{53}（E_{55}）的下降位，车窗电动机 V_{26}（V_{27}）电枢电流的方向与上升情况相反，电动机反转，带动左后（右后）车窗玻璃下降。

(3) 前车窗电动机的控制。右前门车窗电动机 V_{15} 由按键开关 E_{41} 控制，而左前门车窗电动机 V_{14} 由按键开关 E_{40} 和自动继电器 J_{51} 控制，且具有点动自动控制功能。

① 车窗玻璃上升。按下按键开关 E_{41} 的上升键时，车窗电动机正转，带动右前车门玻璃上升，其电路为：A 路电源→熔断器 S_{37}→P→E_{41}→车窗电动机 V_{15}→E_{41}→P→J_{52} 触点→接

地→电源负极；按下按键开关 E_{40} 的上升键时，P_+ 和 P 经 E_{40} 分别接至自动继电器 J_{51} 的输入端 S_2 和 S_1，此时，自动继电器 J_{51} 的触点闭合，触点2断开，车窗电动机 V_{14} 正转，带动左前门车窗玻璃上升，其电路为：A 路→熔断器 S_{37}→P_+→E_{40}→车窗电动机 V_{14}→J_{51} 常闭触点 1→P→J_{52} 触点→接地→电源负极，按键开关 E_{40} 复位，上述电路被切断，电动机 V_{14} 停转。

② 车窗玻璃下降。按下按键开关 E_{41} 的下降键时，车窗电动机 V_{15} 反转，带动右前门车窗玻璃下降，其电流通路与上升相反；按下按键开关 E_{40} 的下降键时，P_+ 和 P 经 E_{40} 分别接至自动继电器 J_{51} 的输入端 S_2 和 S_1，此时，自动继电器 J_{51} 的触点2闭合，触点1断开，其电路为：A 路电源→熔断器 S_{37}→P_+→取样电阻 R→J_{51} 触点2→车窗电动机 V_{14}→E_{40}→P→J_{52} 触点→接地→电源负极，流经电动机 V_{14} 的电流方向与上升时相反，电动机反转，带动玻璃下降，将手抬起时 E_{40} 复位，J_{51} 的触点也复位（触点2断开，触点1闭合），切断了上述电路，电动机停转。

③ 点动自动控制。当按下按键开关 E_{40} 下降键的时间≤300ms 时，自动继电器 J_{51} 判断为点动自动下降操作，于是继电器动作，使触点2闭合。流过车窗电动机 V_{14} 的电流方向与正常下降操作时间相同，电动机反转，车窗玻璃下降。如果在下降期间 E_{40} 的电流方向与正常下降操作时间相同，电动机反转，车窗玻璃下降。如果在下降期间 E_{40} 的上升键不被按下，继电器 J_{51} 的触点2将一直处于闭合状态，直至玻璃下降到底，电动机 V_{14} 停转，此时，电枢电流将增大，当电流增至约9A时，取样电阻 R 上的电压使继电器 J_{51} 动作，触点2断开，自动切断车窗电动机的通电回路，电动机停转；如果在下降期间，按下 E_{40} 的上升键，继电器 J_{51} 将判断为下降操作结束，触点2断开，车窗电动机 V_{14} 停转。这样，通过对按键开关 E_{40} 进行点动控制就可以使左前车窗停止在任意位置。

若出现所有车窗均不下降、某车窗不能升降或只能一个方向运动的障碍时，根据上述介绍的电路的工作过程检查相应的熔断器、有关继电器和相关的开关火线接线柱上的电压，对电动机进行检查。

6. 电动车窗机械机构的检查与维护

（1）电动车窗玻璃升降器的拆卸。电动车窗玻璃升降器的构造如图8-23所示。

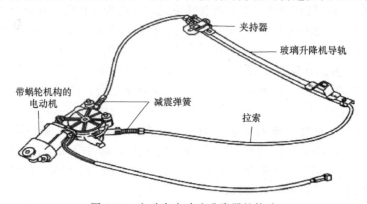

图 8-23 电动车窗玻璃升降器的构造

① 分离电动车窗玻璃升降器接线插头。

② 用扎带1将驱动器盖2和塑料轴承盖在2个钢丝出口处（箭头所指）连接固定（保险装置朝向凸起处），将驱动器盖2固定，拧紧螺栓3（箭头处），整个修理过程中，均不允许去掉扎带1，否则不可能修复，如图8-24所示。

③ 拆下驱动器盖1时，让驱动器盖1与驱动器壳2相互间稍微倾斜，用手将盘绳滚筒（在驱动器盖1内）沿箭头方向从驱动器壳2中拉出，不要损伤密封线，如图8-25所示。

（2）电动车窗玻璃升降器的组装。

① 更换新的驱动器时，沿箭头方向从新驱动器上将防尘和防止运输损伤防护盖 3 取下，注意保证法兰密封垫和 3 扇支架成形件 2 在驱动器壳 1 上（保持表面清洁，使用专用油脂，不允许沾上灰尘和污物），将 3 扇支架成形件 2 沿箭头方向从驱动轴 4 上拉出。橡胶成形垫 5 必须留在驱动器壳 1 中，如图 8-26 所示。

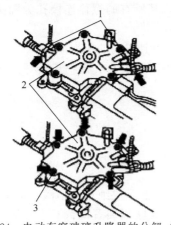   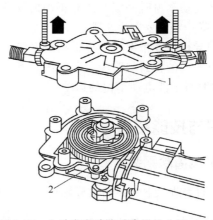

图 8-24　电动车窗玻璃升降器的分解（一）　　图 8-25　电动车窗玻璃升降器的分解（二）
　　1—扎带；2—驱动器盖；3—螺栓　　　　　　　　　　1—驱动器盖；2—驱动器壳

② 将 3 扇支架成形件 1 放入在驱动器壳 2 内的盘绳滚筒 3 内，3 个缓冲件必须小心放入盘绳滚筒 3 的空缺处，电动车窗玻璃升降器驱动器壳 4 沿箭头方向与盘绳滚筒 3 相结合。将 3 扇支架成形件 1 的 4 个卡鼻与驱动器壳 4 中的橡胶成形垫上的空缺必须对齐。安装时，法兰密封垫 5 和驱动器壳 4 中的齿轮必要时可涂一层油脂，防止其掉出来，驱动器壳 4 与盘绳滚筒 3 相接合，但不能相互接触，可稍微移动夹子 6 改变橡胶成形垫的位置，以达到相互配合（螺钉达到力矩要求），如图 8-27 所示。

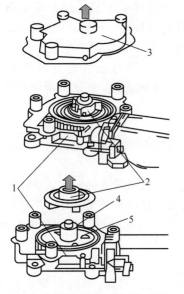   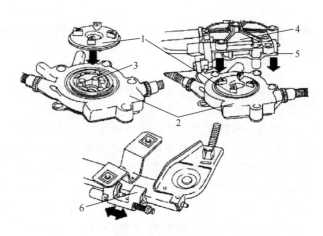

图 8-26　电动车窗玻璃升降器的组装（一）　　图 8-27　电动车窗玻璃升降器的组装（二）
1—驱动器壳；2—3 扇支架成形件；　　　　　1—3 扇支架成形件；2—驱动器壳；3—盘绳滚筒；
3—防护盖；4—驱动轴；5—橡胶成形垫　　　　4—驱动器壳；5—密封垫；6—夹子

项目八　汽车辅助电气系统的检修

③ 按规定顺序拧紧螺钉（力矩3N·m），将车窗玻璃升降器安装到定位支架之前，需进行功能检测，并割掉多余扎带（防止产生刮磨噪声）。

(3) 维修时的注意事项。

① 由于电动车窗与中央门锁、电动天线共用搭铁线，如果搭铁线处理不当，会导致中央门锁失灵。

② 拆装电动车窗时一定要注意正确的安装位置，其所有的螺栓连接孔为椭圆形孔，定位前车窗升降一定不要发生干涉。

③ 车门导槽尺寸精度将严重影响车窗玻璃升降器电动机的使用寿命。

④ 注意车门的密封与防尘，车门内板有一层塑料防护层，其破损后会导致灰尘进入车窗内，严重时将干涉电动车窗的运动。

四、知识与技能拓展

（一）风窗除霜装置

在寒冷的季节，空气中的水分容易在汽车风窗玻璃上形成细小的雨滴（即雾）或结霜。在装有空调或暖风装置的汽车上，通过除霜风门可将热风吹向前面及侧面风窗玻璃，以防止水分凝结或使冰霜融化。而后窗玻璃则需一个除霜装置进行除霜，如图8-28所示。

后窗除霜装置是一种电栅加热装置，通过加热，产生微热消除后窗玻璃上的雾和霜。图8-28中的5是1组平行的含银陶瓷输电网线，在玻璃成形过程中烧结在玻璃表面内。玻璃两侧有汇流条，各焊有1个接线柱，其中1个用以供电，1个是搭铁接线柱。这样就形成1组并联电路。由于后窗电栅消耗电流较大（可达30A），因此，电路除开关外，还需有1个定时继电器。这种继电器在通电10min后，即自动将后窗电栅电流切断。如10min后霜还没有除净，驾驶员可再次接通开关，但在此之后，每次只能通电5min。

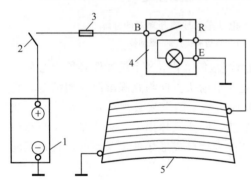

图8-28 后窗除霜装置
1—蓄电池；2—点火开关；3—熔断器；
4—除霜器开关及指示灯；5—除霜器

（二）电动座椅

汽车座椅的主要功能是为驾驶员提供便于操作、舒适而安全的驾驶位置；为乘客提供不易疲劳、舒适而又安全的乘坐位置。

作为人和汽车之间联系部件的座椅，对其要求越来越高，已从过去的固定式座椅发展到今天的多功能动力调节座椅。座椅的调节正向多功能化发展，使座椅的安全性、舒适性、操作性日益提高。其种类很多，还可以有不同的组合方式，如具有8种调节功能的电动座椅，其动作方式有座椅的前后调节与上下调节、座位前部的上下调节、靠背的倾斜调节、侧背支撑调节、腰椎支撑调节以及靠枕上下、前后调节。

电动座椅前后方向的调节量一般为100～160mm，座位前部与后部的调节量为30～50mm。全程移动所需时间为8～10s。

1. 电动座椅的结构

电动座椅一般由电动机、传动装置和座椅的控制电路组成，如图8-29所示。

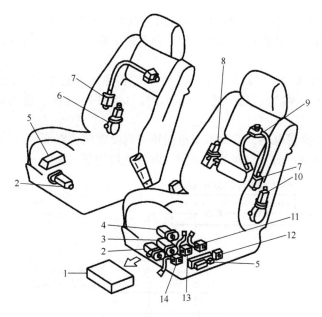

图 8-29 电动座椅的结构

1—电动座椅 ECU；2—滑动电动机；3—前垂直电动机；4—后垂直电动机；5—电动座椅开关；6—倾斜电动机；7—头枕电动机；8—腰垫电动机；9—位置传感器（头枕）；10—倾斜电动机和位置传感器；11—位置传感器（后垂直）；12—腰垫开关；13—位置传感器（前垂直）；14—位置传感器（滑动）

（1）电动机。电动机的数量取决于电动座椅的类型，通常两向移动座椅装有 2 个电动机，四向移动的座椅装有 4 个电动机，最多可达 6 个电动机。大多数电动座椅使用永磁式电动机，通过开关来操纵电动机按不同的方向运转。为防止电动机过载，大多数永磁式电动机内装有断路器。

（2）传动装置。电动机的旋转运动通过传动（机构）改变座椅的空间位置。

① 高度调整机构。如图 8-30 所示，高度调整机构由蜗杆轴、蜗轮、心轴等组成，调整时蜗杆轴在电动机的驱动下，带动蜗轮转动，从而保证心轴旋进或旋出，实现座椅的上升与下降。

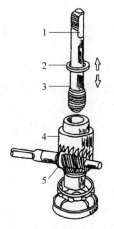 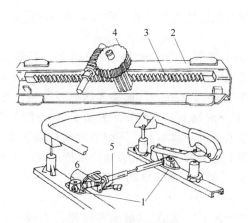

图 8-30 高度调整机构
1—铣平面；2—止推垫片；3—心轴；4—蜗轮；5—挠性驱动蜗杆轴

图 8-31 纵向调整机构
1—支承及导向元件；2—导轨；3—齿条；4—蜗轮；5—反馈信号电位计；6—调整电动机

项目八　汽车辅助电气系统的检修

② 纵向调整机构。如图 8-31 所示，纵向调整机构由蜗轮、齿条、导轨等组成，齿条装载于导轨上。调整时，电动机转矩经蜗杆传至两侧的蜗轮，经导轨上的齿条，带动座椅前后移动。

③ 靠背倾斜调整机构。该调整机构由 2 个调整齿轮与连杆组成。调整时，电动机带动两端的调整齿轮转动，调整齿轮与连杆联动，通过连杆的动作，达到调整靠背倾斜度的目的。

(3) 电动座椅的控制电路。广州本田雅阁轿车驾驶席座椅有 8 种可调方式：前端上、下调节；后端上、下调节；前、后调节；向前、向后倾斜调节，如图 8-32 所示。

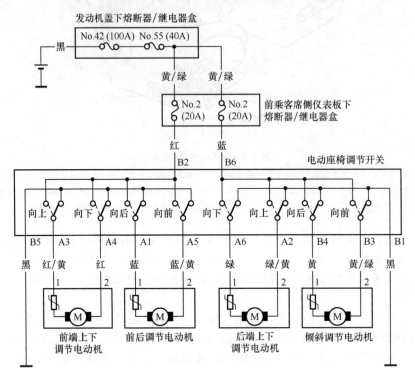

图 8-32　广州本田雅阁轿车驾驶席电动座椅电路

通过电动座椅调节开关，即可完成不同的调节功能，如电动座椅前端上、下调节，其电路如下。

① 向上调节。当将电动座椅前端上、下调节开关打到"向上"位置时，电路中的电流为：蓄电池→黑线→No.42（100A）、No.55（40A）（发动机盖下熔断器\继电器盒）→黄\绿线→No.2（20A）（前乘客席侧仪表板下熔断器\继电器盒）→红线→电动座椅开关端子端 B2→前端上、下调节开关端子 A3→红\黄线→前端上、下调节电动机端子 1→前端上下调节电动机→前端上、下调节电动机端子 2→红线→A4→B5→黑线→搭铁→蓄电池负极。前端上、下调节电动机启动。座椅前端向上移动。

② 向下调节。当将电动座椅前端上、下调节开关打到"向下"位置时，电路中电流为：蓄电池正极→黑线→No.42（100A）、No.55（40A）（发动机盖下熔断器\继电器盒）→黄\绿线→No.2（20A）（前乘客席侧仪表板下熔断器\继电器盒）→红线→电动座椅开关端子 B2→电动座椅开关 A4→红线→前端上、下调节电动端子 2→前端上下调节电动机→前端上、下调节电动机端子 1→红\黄线→A3→B5→黑线→搭铁→蓄电池负极。前端上、下调节电动机启动。座椅前端向下移动。

2. 带存储功能的电动座椅

带存储功能的电动座椅采用了微机控制，它能将选定的座椅调节位置进行储存，使用时只要按指定的按键开关，座椅就会自动地调节到预先选定的座椅位置上。带存储功能的电动座椅的控制示意如图 8-33 所示。

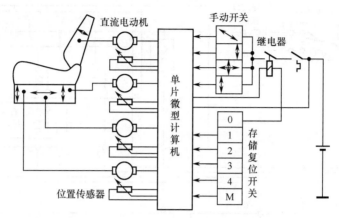

图 8-33　带存储功能的电动座椅的控制示意

该系统有 1 个存储器，存储器通过 4 个电位计来控制座椅的调定位置。只要座椅位置调定后，驾驶员按下存储器的按钮，电子控制装置就把这些电压信号存储起来，作为重新调整位置时的基准。使用时，只要一按按钮，就能按存储的座椅位置的要求调整座椅位置。

（三）电动后视镜

1. 电动后视镜的组成与功能

汽车上的后视镜位置直接关系到驾驶员能否观察到车后的情况，与行车的安全性有着密切联系。而后视镜的调整一般来说比较麻烦，采用电动后视镜，可通过开关进行调整，操作起来十分方便。

电动后视镜的结构如图 8-34 所示。电动后视镜的背后装有 2 套电动机和驱动器，可操纵反射镜上下及左右转动。通常上下方向的转动用一个电动机控制，左右方向的转动由另一个电动机控制。通过改变电动机的电流方向，即可完成后视镜的上下及左右调整。

有的电动后视镜还带有伸缩功能，由伸缩开关控制伸缩电动机工作，使整个后视镜回转伸出或缩回。

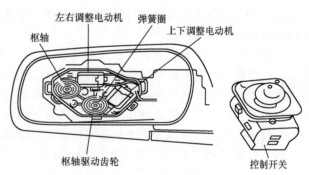

图 8-34　电动后视镜的结构

2. 电动后视镜的工作原理

图 8-35 所示为丰田皇冠轿车可伸缩式电动后视镜控制系统电路图。在进行调整时，首先通过左/右调整开关选择好要调的后视镜，如调整左镜时，开关打向左侧，此时开关分别与 7、8 接点接通，再通过控制开关即可进行该镜的上下或左右调整。如果进行向上调整时，可将控制开关推向上侧，此时控制开关分别与向上接点、左上接点结合。电路蓄电池正极→熔断器→点火开关→控制开关向上接点→左/右调整开关→7 接点→左侧镜电动机→1 接点→

电动镜开关 2 接点→控制开关左上接点→电动镜开关 3 接点→蓄电池负极，形成回路，左侧镜电动机运转，完成调整过程。其他调整过程与向上调整过程类似，通过接通不同的开关即可完成。

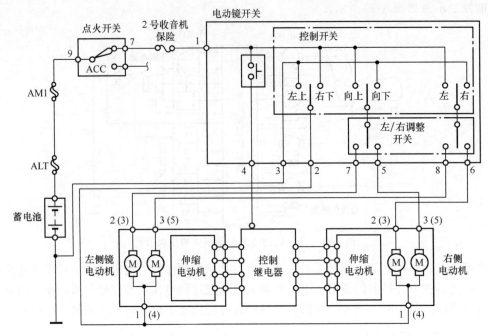

图 8-35　丰田皇冠轿车可伸缩式电动后视镜控制系统电路图

电动后视镜的伸缩是通过伸缩开关控制的，该开关控制继电器动作，使左右两镜伸缩电动机工作，来完成伸缩功能。

（四）中控门锁系统

汽车中控门锁是中央控制门锁的简称，是一种通过设在驾驶室门上的开关可以同时控制车门关闭和开启的装置。

中控门锁和防盗系统是现代汽车的重要组成部分，该系统让汽车的使用更加方便和安全。中控门锁与防盗系统是既相互联系，又有区别的两个系统，防盗功能的实现依赖于中控门锁正常工作，安装有防盗系统的车辆可以极大地减少被盗的几率。

汽车中控门锁的作用是增加汽车使用的方便性和安全性。中控门锁主要由控制部分和执行机构组成，其中控制部分主要包括门锁开关和门锁控制继电器等。

(1) 门锁控制开关。门锁控制开关一般安装在驾驶员侧前门内的扶手上，通过门锁控制开关可以同时锁上和打开所有的车门。图 8-36 所示为某丰田轿车门锁控制开关的位置图。

(2) 钥匙控制开关。钥匙控制开关装在左前门和右前门的外侧锁上，如图 8-37 所示。当从车外用车门钥匙开门或锁门时，钥匙控制开关便发出开门或锁门信号给门锁控制 ECU，实现车门打开或锁止。

(3) 门控开关。门控开关用来检测车门开闭的情况。车门打开时，门控开关接通；车门关闭时，门控开关断开。

图 8-36　门锁控制开关的位置

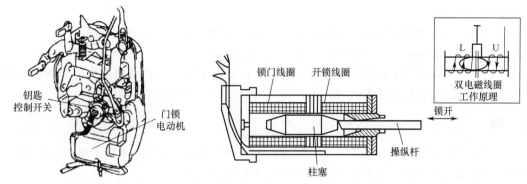

图 8-37 钥匙控制开关的位置　　　　图 8-38 电磁线圈式门锁执行器

（4）门锁执行器。中控门锁用电磁驱动方式执行门锁的关闭和开启。主要有两种形式的执行器：电磁线圈式和直流电动机式。电磁线圈式门锁执行器如图 8-38 所示，上锁时，电磁线圈 L（锁门线圈）通电，衔铁带动连杆左移，扣住门锁舌片；开锁时，电磁线圈 U（开锁线圈）通电，衔铁带动连杆右移，脱离门锁舌片。

直流电动机式执行器的连杆由可逆转的直流电动机驱动，利用电动机的正转和反转完成锁门和开门的动作。

（5）门锁连杆操纵机构。门锁连杆操纵机构如图 8-39 所示，当门锁电动机（或其他执行器）运转时，通过门锁连杆操纵门锁锁定或开启。

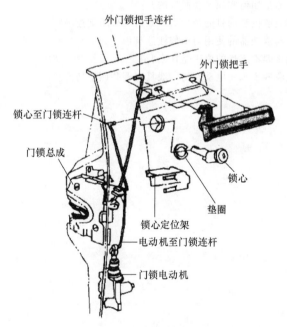

图 8-39 门锁连杆操纵机构

汽车装备中控门锁后可以实现下列功能。

① 中央控制。当驾驶员锁住车门时，其他车门同时锁住，驾驶员也可通过门锁控制开关打开所有门锁。

② 单独控制。除中央控制外，乘员仍可利用车门的机械式弹簧锁开关车门。

③ 预防功能。如果执行了锁门操作，而钥匙仍然插在点火开关内，则所有的车门会自

项目八　汽车辅助电气系统的检修　**157**

动打开。

④ 安全功能。当钥匙被拔出且车门也锁住时，不能用门锁控制开关打开车门。

此外，部分车型还具有速度控制功能、自动功能等。

遥控中控门锁系统又称为无钥匙进入系统。它的作用是给门锁系统增加一个遥控开关，通过操作无线遥控装置实现车门的开闭，为驾驶员提供一个方便的手段。

小 结

(1) 电动刮水器与清洗器是汽车的标准配置，属于汽车上的辅助电器，主要用来清洗和刷除风窗玻璃上的雨水、雪和灰尘，以保证驾驶员的视觉效果。

(2) 挡风玻璃洗涤装置主要由储液罐、洗涤泵、输液管、喷嘴等组成。

(3) 永磁型直流电动机电动车窗是通过改变永磁型直流电动机电枢的电流方向来改变电动机的旋转方向，使车窗玻璃上升或下降。

(4) 电动车窗玻璃升降器传动机构常见有钢丝滚筒式和交叉传动式2种。

(5) 电动后视镜的背后装有2套电动机和驱动器，可操纵反射镜上下及左右转动。

(6) 电动座椅一般由电动机、传动装置和座椅的控制电路组成，有的还带有存储功能。

习题及思考

(1) 简述刮水器的组成与结构。

(2) 试述刮水器用永磁电机的变速原理。

(3) 永磁式电动刮水器是如何实现自动回位的？

(4) 电动刮水器采用间歇控制的目的是什么？如何实现间歇控制？

(5) 试述电动刮水器与清洗器的使用与检修注意事项。

(6) 接通电源后，刮水器不工作的原因是什么？

(7) 汽车座椅应满足哪些要求？电动座椅一般具有哪些调整功能？

项目九

汽车电气系统电路图的分析

一、情境引入

一辆轿车,发现左后电动门锁失效,经检修发现是由于左侧 B 柱至左后门内饰板中的导线由于经常开关车门而折断引起的。如果我们不能熟练地分析电气系统电路图就不能很快地解决实际问题。

二、相关知识

(一) 汽车电路图的种类

随着汽车电子技术的发展,与之配套的汽车电路图也变得越来越复杂。因此,如何快速而准确地识读汽车电路图便越来越重要。汽车电路图有部分电路和整车电路之分。部分电路即局部电路或单元电路,通常有电源电路、起动电路、点火电路、照明电路、信号及仪表电路等;整车电路即汽车电气总电路,通常将汽车上各种用电设备按照它们各自的工作特点和相互关系,通过各种开关、保险等装置,用导线把它们合理地连接起来而构成一个整体电路。现今汽车电路图的种类繁多,电路图按车型不同,也存在一定的差别,归纳起来,汽车电路图主要有线路图(布线图)、电路原理图、线束图。

1. 汽车电气线路图

通常根据汽车电气设备的外形,用相应的图形符号进行合理布线,线路图是电气设备之间用导线相互连接的真实反映,所连接的电气设备的安装位置、外形和线路所走的路径与实际情况一致,便于对汽车电气故障进行判断与排除。通常图的左边代表汽车的前部,右边代表汽车的尾部,同时,图中的电气设备大多以实物轮廓的示意形状表示,给人以真实感。汽车电气线路图的作用是指原理图中各电气元件在电气线路图上的位置及整车走线颜色、直径及去向,供检修电路时查找,通过故障现象和对原理图的分析,在原理图上建立逻辑的检查步骤,再通过电气线路图的指示,在电气线路图上具体实施。

汽车电气线路图的优点是电气设备的外形和实际位置都和原车一致,查找线路时,导线中的分支、接点很容易找到,线路的走向和车上实际使用的线束的走向基本一致;缺点是线条密集、纵横交错,导致读图和查找、分析故障时,非常不方便,不能反映电路内部结构与工作原理。

识读线路图的要点如下。

(1) 对该车所使用的电气设备结构、原理有一定的了解,对其电气设备规范比较清楚。

(2) 通过识读认清该车所有电气设备的名称、数量及它们在汽车上的实际安装位置。

(3) 通过识读认清该车每一种电气设备的接线柱的数量、名称，了解每一接线柱的实际意义。

2. 汽车电路原理图

电路原理图是根据国家或有关部门制定的标准，用规定的图形符号绘制的较简明的电路。电路原理图也称电路简图，通常是根据电气线路图简化而来的。这种图的作用是表达电路的工作原理和连接状态，不讲究电气设备的形状、位置和导线走向的实际情况。图中电气设备均采用符号表示（较特殊的符号则辅以图例说明）。这种图对于了解电气设备的工作原理和工作过程及分析判断故障的大概部位很有用。上海大众 POLO 汽车电路原理图如图 9-1 所示。

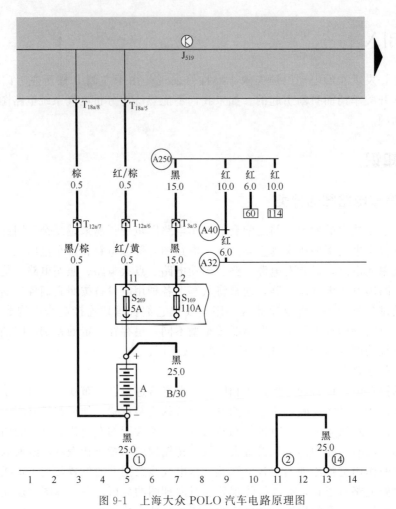

图 9-1　上海大众 POLO 汽车电路原理图

汽车电路原理图是识读汽车电气线路图、线束图及分析汽车电路工作原理和判断故障大致部位的基础图。

电路原理图描述的连接关系仅仅是功能关系，不是实际的连接导线，所以电路原理图不能代替线路图。

识读原理图的要点如下。

(1) 识读各电气设备的各接线柱分别和哪些电路设备的哪个接线柱相连。

(2) 识读电气设备所处的分线路走向。

(3)识读分线路上的开关、保险装置、继电器结构和作用。

3. 汽车线束图

汽车线束图主要用来说明哪些电气设备的导线汇合在一起组成线束,与何处进行连接等。汽车上导线的种类和数量较多,为保证安装可靠,走向相同的各类导线经常被包扎成电缆、线束。线束外形图反映的是已制成的线束外形,故也叫做线束包扎图。图中一般都标明线束中每根导线所连接的电气设备名称,有的还标注了每根导线的长度。线束图是一种突出装配记号的电路表现形式,该图有利于安装与维修,但不能说明线路的走向,线路简单。

若与线路图或电路原理图结合使用,会起到更大的作用,汽车线束图如图9-2所示。

线束图通常分为主线束图和辅助线束图。主线束图分为底盘线束图和车身线束图。辅助线束图类型较多,多用于主线束的支路,并与各种辅助电器相连(通过插接器),如空调线束、车顶线束、电动车窗线束、ABS线束、自动变速器线束、电动座椅线束等。

线束图的识读要点如下。

(1)认清整车共有几组线束、各线束名称及各线束在汽车上的实际安装位置。

图9-2 汽车线束图

(2)认清每一线束上的分支通向车上哪个电气设备,每一分支有几根导线,它们的颜色与标号及它们各连接到电气设备的哪个接线柱上。

(3)认清有哪些插接件,它们应该与哪个电气设备上的插接器相连接。

(二)常见图形符号、文字符号及标志

汽车电路图是利用图形符号和文字符号,表示汽车电路构成、连接关系和工作原理,而不考虑其实际安装位置的一种简图。为了使电路图具有通用性,便于进行技术交流,构成电路图的图形符号和文字符号,是有统一的国家标准和国际标准的。要熟练阅读和运用汽车电路图必须了解图形符号和文字符号的含义、标注原则和使用方法。因此,为了读懂汽车电路图,应熟练掌握图形符号。

1. 图形符号

图形符号(表9-1)分为基本符号、一般符号和明细符号3种。

(1)基本符号。基本符号不能单独使用,不表示独立的电气原件,只说明电路的某些特征。如"—"表示直流,"~"表示交流,"+"表示电源的正极,"—"表示电源的负极,"N"表示中性线。

(2)一般符号。一般符号用以表示一类产品和此类产品特征的一种简单符号,如⊛表示指示仪表的一般符号,▣表示传感器的一般符号。一般符号广义上代表各类元器件,另外,也可以表示没有附加信息或功能的具体原件,如一般电阻、电容等。

(3)明细符号。明细符号表示某一种具体的电气元件,它是由基本符号、一般符号、物理量符号、文字符号等组合派生出来的。例如,⊛是指示仪表的一般符号,当要表示电流、电压的种类和特点时,将"*"处换成"A""V",就成为明细符号。Ⓐ表示电流表,Ⓥ表示电压表。

表 9-1 常用图形符号

序号	名称	图形符号	序号	名称	图形符号
一、常用基本符号					
1	直流	—	6	中性点	N
2	交流	∼	7	磁场	F
3	交直流	∼	8	搭铁	⊥
4	正极	+	9	交流发电机输出接柱	B
5	负极	—	10	磁场二极管输出端	D+
二、导线端子和导线连接					
11	接点	●	17	插头的一个极	
12	端子	○	18	插头和插座	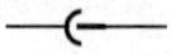
13	导线的连接	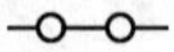	19	多极插头和插座(示出的为3极)	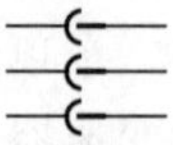
14	导线的分支连接		20	接通的连接片	
15	导线的交叉连接		21	断开的连接片	
16	插座的一个极		22	屏蔽导线	
三、触点开关					
23	动合(常开)触点		34	推动操作	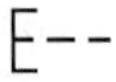
24	动断(常闭)触点		35	一般机械操作	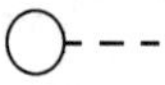
25	先断后合的触点		36	钥匙操作	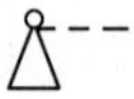
26	中间断开的双向触点		37	热执行器操作	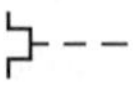
27	双动合触点		38	温度控制	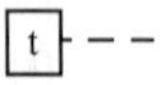 t
28	双动断触点		39	压力控制	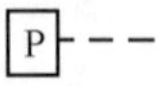 P
29	单动断双动合触点		40	制动压力控制	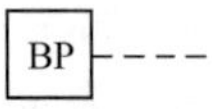 BP
30	双动断单动合触点		41	液位控制	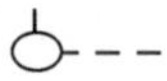
31	一般情况下手动控制	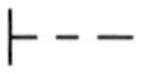	42	凸轮控制	
32	拉拔操作	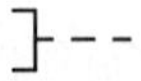	43	联动开关	
33	旋转操作	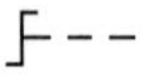	44	手动开关的一般符号	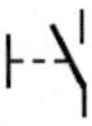

续表

序号	名　　称	图形符号	序号	名　　称	图形符号
45	定位开关（非自动复位）	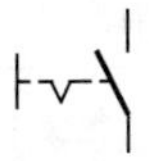	61	电阻器	
46	按钮开关	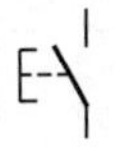	62	可变电阻器	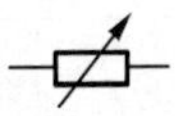
47	能定位的按钮开关		63	压敏电阻器	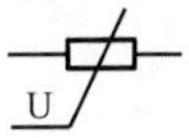
48	拉拨开关	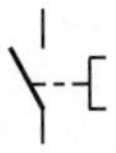	64	热敏电阻器	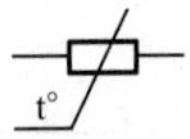
49	旋转、旋钮开关	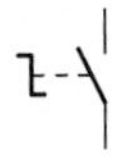	65	滑线式变阻器	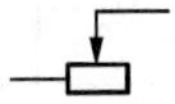
50	液位控制开关	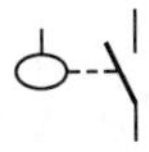	66	分路器	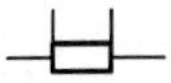
51	机油滤清器报警开关	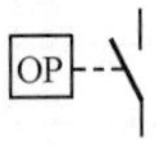	67	滑动触点电位器	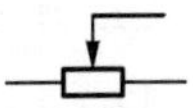
52	热敏开关动合触点		68	仪表照明调光电阻器	
53	热敏开关动断触点	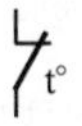	69	光敏电阻	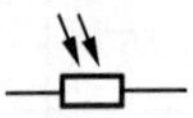
54	热敏自动开关的动断触点		70	加热元件、电热塞	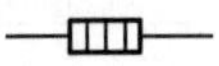
55	热继电器触点	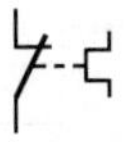	71	电容器	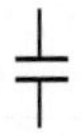
56	旋转多挡开关位置		72	可变电容器	
57	推拉多挡开关位置		73	极性电容器	
58	钥匙开关（全部定位）	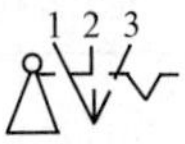	74	穿心电容器	
59	多挡开关，点火、起动开关，瞬时位置为2能自动返回到1（即2挡不能定位）	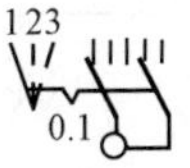	75	半导体二极管一般符号	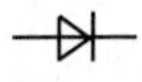
60	节流阀开关		76	稳压二极管	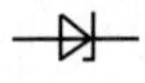

项目九　汽车电气系统电路图的分析

续表

序号	名称	图形符号	序号	名称	图形符号
四、电器元件					
77	发光二极管		88	电路断电器	
78	双向二极管（变阻二极管）	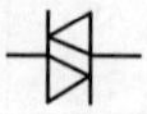	89	永久磁铁	
79	三极晶体闸流管		90	操作器件一般符号	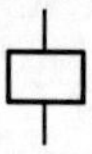
80	光电二极管		91	1个绕组电磁铁	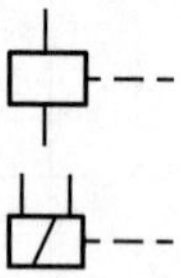
81	PNP型三极管				
82	集电极接管壳三极管（NPN）		92	2个绕组电磁铁	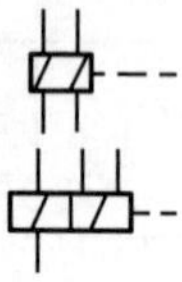
83	具有2个电极的压电晶体				
84	电感器、线圈、绕组		93	不同方向绕组电磁铁	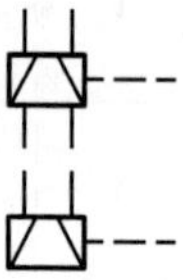
85	带铁芯的电感器				
86	熔断器		94	触点常开的继电器	
87	易熔线				
五、仪表					
95	触点常闭的继电器	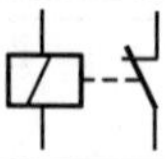	102	油压表	 OP
96	指示仪表	 *	103	转速表	 T
97	电压表	 V	104	温度表	 t°
98	电流表	 A	105	燃油表	 Q
99	电压、电流表	 A/V	106	车速里程表	 V
100	欧姆表	 Ω	107	时钟	
101	瓦特表	 W	108	数字式时钟	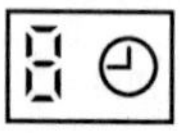

续表

序号	名　称	图形符号	序号	名　称	图形符号
六、传感器					
109	传感器的一般符号	*	116	空气流量传感器	AF
110	温度表传感器	t°	117	氧传感器	λ
111	空气温度传感器	$t_n°$	118	爆震传感器	K
112	水温传感器	$t_w°$	119	转速传感器	n
113	燃油表传感器	Q	120	速度传感器	V
114	油压表传感器	OP	121	空气压力传感器	AP
115	空气质量传感器	m	122	制动压力传感器	BP
七、电气设备					
123	照明灯、信号灯、仪表灯、指示灯		132	信号发生器	 G
124	双丝灯		133	脉冲发生器	
125	荧光灯		134	闪光器	
126	组合灯		135	霍尔信号发生器	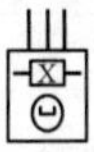
127	预热指示器	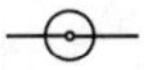	136	磁感应信号发生器	
128	电喇叭	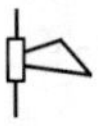	137	温度补偿器	 t° comp
129	扬声器		138	电磁阀一般符号	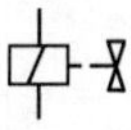
130	蜂鸣器		139	常开电磁阀	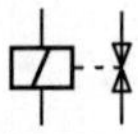
131	报警器、电警笛		140	常闭电磁阀	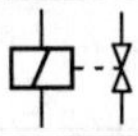

续表

序号	名　　称	图形符号	序号	名　　称	图形符号
141	电磁离合器		162	传声器一般符号	
142	过电压保护装置		163	点火线圈	
143	用电动机操纵的怠速调整装置		164	分电器	
144	过电流保护装置		165	火花塞	
145	加热器(出霜器)		166	电压调节器	
146	振荡器	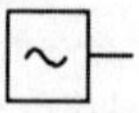	167	转速调节器	
147	变换器、转换器		168	温度调节器	
148	光电发生器		169	串励绕组	
149	空气调节器		170	并励或他励绕组	
150	滤波器		171	集电环或换向器上的电刷	
151	稳压器		172	直流电动机	
152	点烟器		173	串激直流电动机	
153	热继电器	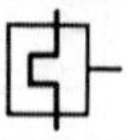	174	并激直流电动机	
154	间歇刮水继电器		175	永磁直流电动机	
155	防盗报警系统		176	起动机(带电磁开头)	
156	天线一般符号		177	燃油泵电动机、洗涤电动机	
157	发射机		178	晶体管电动汽油泵	
158	收音机		179	加热定时器	
159	内部通信联络及音乐系统		180	电子点火组件	
160	收放机		181	风扇电动机	
161	无线电话		182	刮水电动机	

续表

序号	名　称	图形符号	序号	名　称	图形符号
183	电动天线		189	定子绕组为三角形连接的交流发电机	
184	直流伺服电动机		190	外接电压调节器与交流发电机	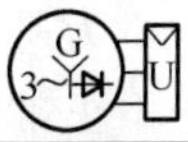
185	直流发电机		191	整体式交流发电机	
186	星形连接的三相绕组	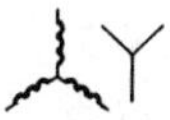	192	蓄电池	
187	三角形连接的三相绕组	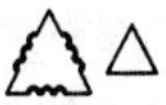	193	蓄电池组	
188	定子绕组为星形连接的交流发电机				

对标准中没有规定的符号，可以选取标准中给定的基本符号、一般符号和明细符号，按规定的组合原理进行派生，以构成完整的元件或设备的图形符号，但在图样的空白处必须加以说明。表 9-2 将天线的一般符号和直流电动机的一般符号进行组合，就构成电动天线的图形符号。

表 9-2　电动天线的图形符号组合示例

图形符号	说　明
	天线的一般符号
	直流电动机的一般符号
	电动机天线的派生符号

（4）图形符号的使用原则。
① 首先选用优选型。
② 在满足条件的情况下，首先采用最简单的形式，但图形符号必须完整。
③ 在同一幅电路图中同一图形符号采用同一种形式。
④ 符号方位不是固定的，在不改变符号意义的前提下，符号可根据图画布置的需要旋转放置，但文字和指示方向不得倒置。
⑤ 图形符号中一般无端子代号，如果端子代号是符号一部分，则端子代号必须画出。
⑥ 导线符号可以用不同宽度的线条表示，如电源线路（主电路）可用粗实线表示，控制、保护线路（辅助电路）则可用细实线表示。
⑦ 一般连接线不是图形符号的组成部分，方位可根据实际需要布置。
⑧ 符号的意义由其形式决定，可根据需要进行缩小或放大。
⑨ 图形符号表示的是在无电压、外力的常规状态。
⑩ 图形符号中的文字符号、物理量符号，应视为图形符号的组成部分。当用这些符号不能满足标注时，可按有关规定加以补充。

电路图中若未采用规定的图形符号，必须加以说明。

2. 开关和警示灯标志

汽车仪表盘和转向柱上通常装有许多开关、报警灯和指示灯。为区分功能，常用各种各样的图形符号刻印在其表面，有些进口车辆还用英文字母表示。这些图形标志国际通用，大都形象、简明，一看便知道其功能。

为避免分散驾驶员注意力，指示灯、报警灯在其所指示系统工作正常时不亮。当系统工作不正常时，代表其工况的指示灯、报警灯点亮。报警灯多用红色，表示情况紧急，需及时检修，如制动气压过低报警灯、发动机过热报警灯、机油压力报警灯等。还有一些属于正常工作状态的指示灯，如转向灯（绿色）、前照灯远光（蓝色）。

指示灯和报警灯多采用小功率灯泡（1～3.5W），也有采用发光二极管的（加合适的限流电阻）。指示灯和报警灯在正常工作状态下不点亮，如果灯泡损坏也会带来错觉。因此，在点火开关接通而不起动发动机的情况下，可检验大多数指示灯和报警灯的好坏，如充电指示灯、机油压力报警灯、SRS 指示灯等，有些需要使用专门的检验开关并加接许多隔离二极管来检验。

汽车上部分开关和报警灯标志见表 9-3。

表 9-3 开关和报警灯标志

序号	图形或文字符号	说明	序号	图形或文字符号	说明
1	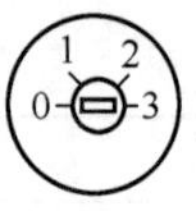 （图形）	点火开关(4挡)： 锁止方向盘 0—OFF 或(S) 附件 1—ACC 或(A) 点火、仪表 2—IGN 或(M) 起动 3—START 或(D)	6	 （图形）	阻风门关闭指示灯：冷车起动时阻风门关闭，指示灯亮，起动后应及时打开阻风门，否则发动机冒黑烟
2	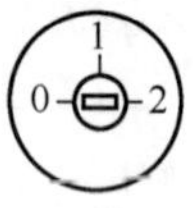 （图形）	点火开关(3挡)： 锁止 0—OFF 或(S) 工作 1—ON 或 MAR 起动 2—START 或 AVV	7	 （图形）	节气门关闭时灯亮
3	 （图形）	柴油车电源开关： 0—OFF 断开 1—ON 接通 2—START 起动 3—ACC 附件 4—PREHEAT 预热	8	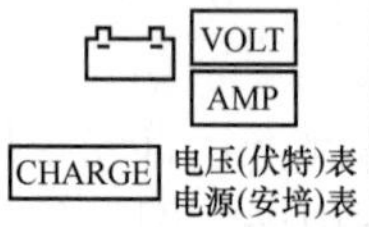 VOLT AMP CHARGE 电压(伏特)表 电源(安培)表	蓄电池充电指示灯：发电机不发电时灯亮，正常发电时灯灭
4	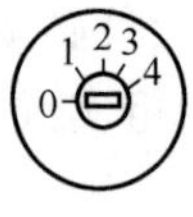 （图形）	点火开关(5挡)： 0—LOCK 锁定方向盘 1—OFF 断开 2—ACC 附件 3—ON 接通 4—START 起动	9	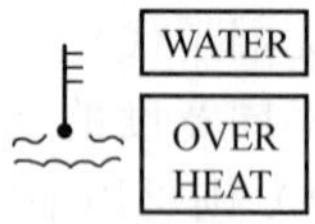 WATER OVER HEAT	水温报警灯：冷却液温度过高时报警灯亮
5	 CHECK（图形）	发动机故障代码显示灯（自诊断）：电控发动机喷油与点火的传感器与电脑出故障时灯亮，通过人工或仪器可将故障代码调出，迅速查明故障	10	 OIL-P	机油压力报警灯：当机油压力过低时灯亮

续表

序号	图形或文字符号	说　　明	序号	图形或文字符号	说　　明
11	 FUEL	燃油不足报警灯；燃油不足报警灯亮	25	AIR SUSP	电子调整空气悬挂指示灯
12	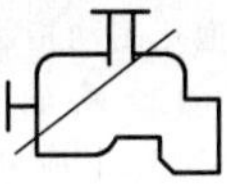	柴油机停止供油（熄火）拉杆（钮）标志	26	O/D OFF	退出超速挡时，O/D OFF//灯亮
13	 P PKB	停车制动指示灯：在手制动起作用时灯亮	27	VOLT	电压表
14	 BRAKE AIR	制动气压过低报警：制动液面低、制动系统故障报警灯亮	28	EXP TEMP	排气温度过高报警
15	r/min RPM	发动机转速表	29		转向信号灯指示灯
16	km/h	车速表	30		危急报警指示灯：当汽车遇到交通事故要呼救或需要别车避让时，左右转向灯齐闪
17	20:08	数字显示时钟	31	 BEAM	前照灯远光指示灯
18	 COOLANT LEVEL WATER LEVEL	冷却液水位指示灯：当冷却系统水位低于规定值时，报警灯亮	32		前照灯近光指示灯
			33		灯光开关指示灯：可接通示宽灯、尾灯、仪表、牌照灯等
19		机油液面指示灯：当发动机机油量少于规定值时，报警灯亮	34		汽车示宽灯开关指示
20	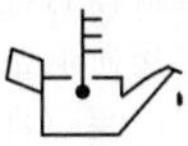	机油温度过高报警灯：机油温度超过规定值时，报警灯亮	35	 P	驻车制动灯开关指示：手制动起作用时，该指示灯亮
21	 kPa	真空度指示灯	36	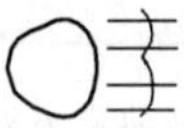	后雾灯开关指示灯
22	SRS	安全气囊指示灯	37	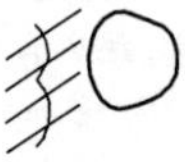	前雾灯开关指示灯
23	TRAC	牵引力控制指示灯	38	 TEST	指示灯、报警灯灯泡好坏的检查开关
24	CRUISE	巡航指示灯：装置起作用时灯亮，有故障时显示故障码	39	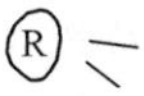 R	倒车灯开关指示

续表

序号	图形或文字符号	说　明	序号	图形或文字符号	说　明
40	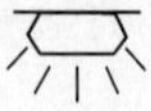	室内灯（顶灯）开关指示	51		制动蹄片磨损超限报警灯
41	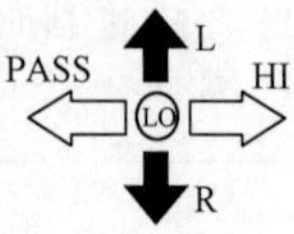 PASS L HI LO R	转向灯开关与超车灯开关：L—左转向；R—右转向；PASS—超车；HI—远光；LO—定位中间挡（近光）	52	 ABS	防抱死制动指示灯；钥匙在起动挡或车速在 5～10km/h 以下应亮，ABS 出现故障时报警灯亮，并可显示故障代码（用工具）
42		旋转灯标志；警车、救护车、消防车的车顶旋转警灯开关标志	53	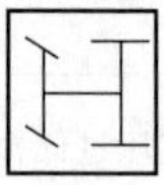	分动器前桥接入指示灯；越野车全驱动时，灯亮
43	 BELT	安全带指示灯；当点火开关接通，安全带未系时灯亮或伴有蜂鸣器	54	 kPa	空气滤清器堵塞指示灯
44	 HEAT GLOW	电热预热塞指示灯：常温下起动亮 0.3s，可直接起动；低温起动前亮 3.5s，表示"等待预热"，灯灭可起动	55		液力变扭器开关指示灯
45	 GLOW	预热塞（电热或火焰预热塞）指示灯：常温下起动 0.3s，可直接起动；低温起动前亮 3.5s，表示"等待预热"，灯灭可起动	56	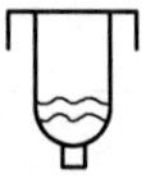	柴油粗滤器中积水超限报警灯
46	 DIFF LOCK	差速锁连锁指示灯；车辆转弯时必须脱开	57	 HORN	喇叭按钮标志
47	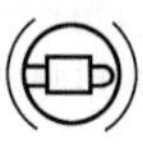	排气制动指示灯：下长坡时，堵住排气管，利用发动机阻力使汽车减速，踩离合器、加油时自动解除	58		点烟器标志：按下点烟器手柄即接通电路，发热体烧红后（约几秒）自动弹出，可供点烟用
48	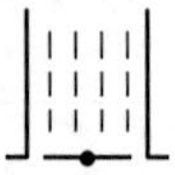 EXH-BRAKE	排气制动指示灯：下长坡时，堵住排气管，利用发动机阻力使汽车减速，踩离合器、加油时自动解除	59		发动机罩开启拉手指示
49	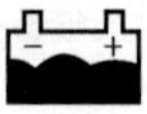	蓄电池液面指示灯	60	 TRUNK	行李舱盖开启拉手或电动按钮指示
50		拖车制动指示灯	61	 DOOR	门未关报警灯；仪表盘上设置此灯

续表

序号	图形或文字符号	说明	序号	图形或文字符号	说明
62		坐垫加热指示灯	75	 FAN	空调系统鼓风机指示
63		室内灯门控挡：当门关严后室内灯灭，此外，还有手控长明挡（ON）及断开挡（OFF）	76	 VENT	空调系统通风吹脸（FACE）挡
64	 P R N D 2 L	自动变速器挡位指示灯	77	 HEAT	空调系统加热（吹脚）挡
65	ECTPWR	电控自动变速器有2种已编好程序的换挡方式：正常模式（Normal）和动力模式（Power），用开关选择动力模式时，指示灯亮	78	 BI-LEVEL	空调系统双层（上冷下热）挡
			79	 DEF-HEAT	空调系统除霜与加热（吹脚）挡
66		增热器开关指示除霜线指示灯和开关指示：常为后窗炭粉加热	80	 DEF	挡风玻璃除霜除雾指示
67		挡风玻璃刮水开关指示	81	 Outside	车外新鲜空气循环风道开启指示（FRESH）
68	 WASHER	挡风玻璃洗涤开关指示	82	 Inside	车内空气循环风道开启指示（REC）
69		挡风玻璃刮水洗涤开关指示	83		驾驶室锁止：可倾翻的驾驶室回位时没有到达规定锁止状态，报警灯亮
70		后窗玻璃刮水指示灯和开关标志	84	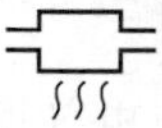 EXH TEMP	排气温度超过一定限度时此灯亮
71		后窗玻璃洗涤开关指示	85		后视镜加热指示
72		前照灯刮水洗涤开关指示	86		后视镜镜面上下调节和左右调节开关标志
73		车窗玻璃升降开关：UP—升起；DOWN—降下	87	 AIR MPa	空气压力表：常用于气压制动系统中双管路气压指示
74	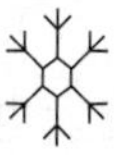 A/C	空调系统制冷压缩机开启指示	88		空气滤清器堵塞信号报警灯

3. 文字符号

文字符号是由电气设备、装置和元器件的种类（名称）字母代码和功能（与状态、特征）字母代码组成。用于电气技术领域中技术文件的编制，也可标注在电气设备、装置和元器件或其近旁，以表明电气设备、装置和元器件的名称、功能、状态和特征。此外，还可与基本图形符号和一般图形符号组合使用，以派生新的图形符号。

文字符号分为基本文字符号和辅助文字符号两大类，基本文字符号又分为单字母符号和双字母符号。

（1）基本文字符号。

① 单字母符号。单字母符号是按拉丁字母将各种电气设备、装置和元器件划分为23大类，每大类用一个专用单字母符号表示，如"C"表示电容器类，"R"表示电阻类等。

② 双字母符号。双字母符号是由一个表示种类的单字母符号与另一个字母组成，其组合形式应以单字母符号在前面另一个字母在后的次序列出，如"R"表示电阻，"RP"就表示电位器，"RT"表示热敏电阻；"G"表示电源、发动机、发生器，"GB"就表示蓄电池，"GS"表同步发电机、发生器，"GA"表示异步发电机。

（2）辅助文字符号。辅助文字符号表示电气设备、装置和元器件及线路的功能、状态和特征。例如，"SYN"表示同步，"L"表示限制左或低，"RD"表示红色，"ON"表示闭合，"OFF"表示断开等。

（3）文字符号的使用规则。

① 单字母符号应优先选用。

② 只有当用字母符号不能满足要求，需要将大类进一步划分时，才采用双字母符号，以便较详细和更具体地表述电气设备、装置和元器件等。如"F"表示保护器类，"FU"表示熔断器，"FV"表示限压保护器件。

③ 辅助文字符号也可放在表示种类的单字母符号后边组成双字母符号，如"ST"表示起动，"DC"表示直流，"AC"表示交流。为简化文字符号，若辅助文字符号由2个字母组成时，允许只采用其第1位字母进行组合，如"MS"表示同步电动机，"MS"中的"S"为辅助文字符号"SYN"（同步）的第1位字母。辅助文字符号还可以单独使用，如"QN"表示接通，"N"表示中性线，"E"表示搭铁，"PE"表示保护搭铁等。

4. 图形符号、文字符号的识读

对于基本的元器件，其图形符号、文字符号都是相同的，如电阻、电容、照明灯、蓄电池等。

由于目前国际上还没有汽车电气设备图形符号、文字符号的统一标准，各个汽车生产厂家对某些汽车电气所采用的图形符号、文字符号有所不同，与标准规定有一些差异，这给识读电路图造成一定的困难，但图形符号基本结构的组成是相似的，只要了解它们的区别，就能避免识读错误。下面通过具体示例来说明不同车型在表示同一元器件的图形符号时，在汽车电路图中的差异。

图9-3所示为导线连接的两种形式。上海桑塔纳、南京依维柯采用图9-3(a)所示的形式，神龙富康、天津夏利则采用图9-3(b)所示的形式。

图9-3 导线连接的两种表示符号

汽车都装有硅整流发电机和电压调节器，不同的是有的采用内装式，有的采用外装式，即使同一结构形式，不同的车型所采用的电路图形符号也有所不同。

图9-4所示为富康轿车内装调节器硅整流发电机图形

符号；图9-5所示为夏利轿车内装调节器硅整流发电机图形符号（国家标准规定的符号）。

现今汽车上都装有用于起动发动机的起动机，且中、小型汽车起动机的结构基本相同，但在不同车型的电路图中，所采用的符号差别很大。图9-6为天津夏利轿车起动机图形符号；图9-7为富康轿车起动机图形符号，两者与国家标准中规定图形符号差异较大。

很多车上都有3挡4接柱的点火开关，其表示方法采用方框符号，表示接线柱和挡位的符号有2种，如图9-8所示；上海桑塔纳则采用与前两者截然不同的另一种符号，如图9-9所示。

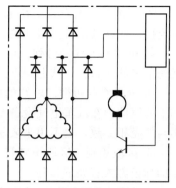

图9-4 富康轿车内装调节器硅整流发电机图形符号

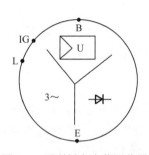

图9-5 夏利轿车内装调节器硅整流发电机图形符号

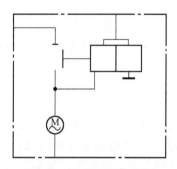

图9-6 夏利轿车起动机图形符号

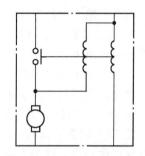

图9-7 富康轿车起动机图形符号

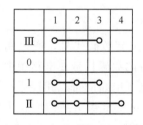

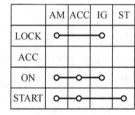

图9-8 点火开关图形符号

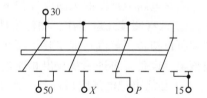

图9-9 上海桑塔纳轿车点火开关图形符号

通过上述示例可知，汽车电路图形符号目前还没有统一的标准，国产汽车制造企业大都采用电气技术行业标准，而合资汽车制造企业大都沿用国外的原标准，所以在识图过程中应不断地总结经验，找出不同的电路中采用的图形符号有哪些相同点和不同点，这样可以提高识图速度。

（三）汽车电路的绘制及识图要领

1. 汽车电路原理图的绘制及识图要领

（1）汽车电路原理图的绘制原理。

① 元器件的表示方法。电路图的一个重要特征是元器件采用国家标准规定的图形符号来表示。

为了便于对电路进行分析和检查，在电路图中除了用图形符号表示元器件，还应该在图形符号旁边注明项目代号，必要时还应该在图形符号旁边标注元器件的主要技术参数。

② 图形符号的布置。在电气系统中，有大量的元器件的驱动部分和被驱动部分采用机械连接，如继电器、按钮开关、光电耦合器等都属于这一类。

③ 电路与导线的排列。电路的安排要求有一目了然的图示效果，各个电路的排列必须优先采用从左到右、从上到下的原则，尽可能用直线无交叉点不改变方向的标记方式。

④ 分界线与边框。电路的各部分用点画线或边框线限制，以此表示仪器部件功能或结构上的属性。在汽车电气设备中，用点画线表示仪器和电器中不导电的边框，这种图示可以不与外壳相一致，也不用来表示仪器的搭铁线。

⑤ 区段识别。区段识别符号标注在电路图的下沿，有助于更方便地寻找电路部件，可能的标记方式有如下 3 种。

a. 用连续数字以相同的距离从左到右标注。

b. 标注电路区段的内容。

c. 以上两种方法的结合。

汽车电路大多数都在电路图中指明电路区段的内容。

⑥ 标注。利用字母和数码可对设备、部件或电路图中线路符号作标注，标注位于线路符号的左边或下边，如果设备的定义明确，标准内所规定的几种设备可不作标注。

(2) 汽车电路原理图的识图要领。

电路原理图的特点主要有以下几点。

① 对全车电路有完整的概念。既是一幅全车电路图，又是一幅互相联系的局部电路图。

② 图上建立了高低电位的概念。负极搭铁电位最低，用图中最下面一条导线表示；正极火线电位最高，用最上面的导线表示，电流流向基本上是从上到下。

③ 尽可能减少导线的曲折与交叉。布局合理，画面简洁清晰，图形符号兼顾元件外形和内部结构，便于分析。

④ 电路系统的相互关联关系清楚。

汽车电路原理图的识图要领如下。

① 认真阅读几遍图注。图注说明了汽车所有电气设备的名称及其数码代号，通过阅读图注可以初步了解汽车都安装了哪些电气设备，然后通过电气设备的数码代号在电路图中找出该电气设备，再进一步找出相互连线、控制关系。这样可了解汽车电路的特点和构成。

② 必须牢记电气图形符号。汽车电路原理图是利用电气图形符号来表示其构成和工作原理的。因此，必须牢记电气图形符号的含义，才能看懂电路原理图。

③ 熟记电路标记符号。为便于绘制和识读汽车电路原理图，有些电气装置或其接线柱等上面都赋予不同的标志代号。例如，接至电源端接线柱用"B"或"+"表示，接至点火开关的接线柱用"SW"表示，接至起动机的接线柱用"S"表示，接至各灯具的接线柱用"L"表示，发电机中性点接线柱用"N"表示，发电机磁场接线柱用"F"表示，励磁电压输出端接线柱用"D+"表示，发电机电枢输出端接线柱用"B+"表示等。

④ 牢记回路原则。任何一个完整的电路都是由电源、熔断器、开关、用电设备、导线等组成。电流流向必须从电源正极出发，经过熔断器、开关、导线等到达用电设备，再经过导线或搭铁回到电源负极，才能构成回路，这样的电路才是正确的，否则就是读错了或者查错了。

可以沿着电路电流的流向，由电源正极出发，顺藤摸瓜查到用电设备、开关等，回到电源负极；可以逆着电路电流的方向，由电源负极（搭铁）开始，经过用电设备、开关等回到电源正极；也可以从用电设备开始，依次查找其控制开关、连线、控制单元，到达电源正极和搭铁（或电源负极）。尤其是查询一些不太熟悉的电路，后者比前者更为方便。实际应用

时，可视具体电路选择不同思路，但有一点值得注意：随着电子控制技术在汽车上的广泛应用，大多数电路同时具有主回路和控制回路，读图时要兼顾两回路。

⑤ 牢记搭铁极性。汽车电路均为负极搭铁。

⑥ 掌握各种开关在电路图中的作用。对多层多挡接线柱开关，要按层、按挡位、按接线柱逐级分析其各层各挡功能。有的用电设备受两个以上单挡开关（或继电器）的控制，有的受两个以上多挡开关的控制，其工作状态比较复杂。当开关接线柱较多时，首先抓住从电源来的一两个接线柱，逐个分析与其他各接线柱相连的用电设备处于何种挡位，从而找出控制关系。

对于组合开关，实际线路是在一起的，而在电路图中又按其功能画在各自的局部电路中，遇到这种情况必须仔细研究识读。

⑦ 掌握开关、继电器的初始状态。在电路图中，各种开关、继电器都是按初始状态画出的，即按钮未按下，开关未接通，继电器线圈未通电，其触点未闭合（指常开触点）或未打开（指常闭触点），这种状态称为原始状态。在识图时，不能完全按原始状态分析，否则很难理解电路的工作原理，因为大多数用电设备都是通过开关按钮继电器触点的变化而改变回路的，进而实现不同的电路功能。所以，必须进行工作状态的分析。例如，刮水器就是通过刮水器开关挡位的变化来实现间歇低速高速刮水功能，必须把3种工作状态的电路走通。

⑧ 掌握电气装置在电路图中的位置。在汽车电气系统中，有大量电气装置是机电一体的，如各种继电器，还有多层多挡开关。有些电气装置在电路图上表示时，厂家为了使画法既简单又便于识图，多根据实际情况采用集中表示法、半集中表示法和分开显示法来反映电路的连接情况。

熟记各局部电路之间的相互关系。汽车全车电路基本上由电源电路、充电电路、点火电路、起动电路、照明电路、辅助电路等单元电路组成。从整车电路来讲，各局部电路除电源电路公用外，其他单元电器电路都是相对独立。但它们之间也存在着内在的联系。因此，识图时，不但要熟悉各局部电路的组成特点、工作过程和电流流经的路径，还要了解各局部电路之间的联系和相互影响。这是迅速找出故障部位、排除故障的必要条件。

⑨ 善于请教和查找资料。由于新的汽车电气设备不断出现和相应用到汽车上，汽车电路图的变化很大。对于看不懂的电路要善于请教有关人员，同时还要善于查找资料，直到看懂为止。

⑩ 先易后难各个击破。有些汽车电路图的某些局部电路可能比较复杂，一时难以看懂，可以暂时将其放一边，待其他局部电路都看懂后，结合所看懂的电路图中与该电路有联系的有关的信息，再进一步识读这部分电路。

⑪ 浏览全图，框画各个系统。要读懂汽车电路图，首先必须掌握组成电路图的各个电器元件的基本功能和特征。在大概掌握全车电路的基本原理的基础上，再将一个个单独的电气系统框出来，这样就容易抓住每一部分的主要功能及特征。

在框画各个系统时，应注意既不能漏掉各个系统中的组件，也不能多框画其他系统的组件，一般规律是，各电气系统只有电源和总开关是共用的，其他任何一个系统都应是一个完整、独立的电气回路，即包括电源、熔断器、开关、电器、导线等。并从电源的正极经导线、熔断器、开关至电器后搭铁，最后回到电源负极，否则所框画出的系统图就不正确。

2. 汽车线路图的绘制及识图要领

（1）汽车线路图的绘制原则。汽车电路线路图在画法上比较注重各电气设备在汽车上的实际位置，虽然识读比较困难，但只要掌握一定的方法，便能识图，并且能将线路图改画成电路图。线路图的特点是：由于电气设备的外形和实际位置都和原车一致，因此，查找线路时，导线中的分支、接点很容易找到，线路的走向和车上实际使用的线束的走向基本一致。

线路图的绘制原则如下。

① 线路图中的元器件、部件、组件、设备等项目，采用其简化外形（如圆形、方形、矩形）表示，为便于识图，必要时使用圆形符号表示。

② 在线路图中，接线端子用端子符号表示。

③ 导线用连续线和中断线表示。连续线是用连续的实线来表示端子之间实际存在的导线；中断线是用中断的实线来表示端子之间实际存在的导线，并在中断处标明方向。

(2) 汽车线路图的识读要领。

① 对该车所使用的电气设备结构、工作原理有一定的了解，对其电气设备规范比较清楚。

② 通过识读认清该车所有电气设备的名称、数量及在汽车上的实际安装位置。

③ 通过识读认清该车每一种电气设备的接线柱数量、名称，了解每一接线柱的实际意义。

线路图的识读可按浏览、展绘、整理3个阶段进行。

3. 汽车线束图的绘制及识图要领

(1) 汽车线束图的绘制原则。汽车线束图主要以线束的形式出现，图面的线条较少，各部件之间连接的表达是其主要内容。线束图的绘制原则如下。

① 汽车线束图由多个线束组成，有主线束、辅线束。线束图表现了每个线束上有几个分支，每个分支上有多少根导线，及导线的颜色和条纹。

② 汽车上电器数量多而复杂，为使连线准确，各个连接点都标注了接线端子的代号。

③ 线束的长度包括线束的总长、每个分支的长度和线端间隔长度。

④ 由于线束有多个，线束与线束、分支与线束、分支与电气之间都通过插接器进行连接，表示出插接器上有几根导线、每根导线位于插接器接线孔的具体位置、插接器的具体形状。

(2) 汽车线束图的识读要领。

① 认清整车共有几组线束、各线束名称及各线束在汽车上的实际安装位置。

② 认清每一线束上的分支通向车上哪个电气设备，每一分支有几根导线，它们的颜色与标号及它们各连接到电气设备的哪个接线柱上。

③ 认清有哪些插接件，它们应该与哪个电气设备上的插接件相连接。

线束图的识读与线路的识读基本一致。

（四）汽车电路检修常识

1. 汽车电路故障诊断与检修流程

汽车电路故障诊断与检修通常有以下几个步骤，其流程如图9-10所示。

(1) 听取客户陈述故障情况。详细了解故障现象及发生故障时的情况及环境，包括以下信息：车型、气候条件、故障症状、操作条件、维修保养情况及购车后是否加装其他附件等。

(2) 确认故障症状。运转系统，必要时要进行路试。查看客户所反映的情况是否属实，同时注意观察运行后的种种现象。如不能再现故障，可进行故障模拟实验。

(3) 识读系统电路，分析相关电路原理。仔细阅读该车型电路及相关资料，拆画与故障现象相关的系统电路，弄清电路的工作原理及系统工作电流走向，对系统电路进行关联性分析以缩小故障诊断范围。

(4) 分析故障原因。详细分析造成该故障现象的可能原因，根据理论分析和工作经验对故障现象可能原因，遵循由易到难进行排查。

(5) 具体诊断、修复电路。选择合适的诊断检测设备及工具确诊故障点并修复。

(6) 验证电路是否恢复正常。对电路进行系统检修之后，在所有模式下运转系统，确认系统在所有工况下运转正常，确认在诊断和修理过程中没有造成新的故障。

2. 汽车电路检修注意事项

汽车电路检修的首要原则是不要随意更换导线、电气设备和换接线路，这些操作可能会损坏汽车或因短路、过载而引起火灾。同时，应注意以下事项。

① 拆卸蓄电池时，应首先拆下蓄电池负极电缆，安装蓄电池时，最后连接蓄电池电缆。拆卸或安装蓄电池电缆时，应确保点火开关或其他开关都已关闭，切勿将蓄电池的极性接反。

② 为避免电流过载损坏三极管，应使用欧姆表及万用表的 R×100 以下低阻欧姆挡进行检测。

③ 拆卸及安装元件时，应切断电源。如无特殊说明，元件引脚距焊接点应在 10mm 以上，以免电烙铁烫坏元件，且宜使用恒温或功率小于 75W 的电烙铁。

④ 靠近震动部件的线束应用卡子固定，将松弛部分拉紧，以免由于震动造成线束与其他部件接触。

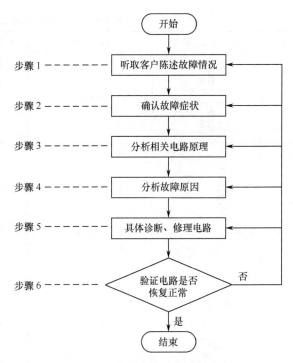

图 9-10 汽车电路故障诊断流程

⑤ 电气设备应轻拿轻放，以免过大的冲击载荷造成电气设备的损坏。

⑥ 与尖锐边缘摩擦的线束应使用胶带缠绕，以免损坏。安装固定位置时，应确保线束不被夹住或损坏，同时应确保插接件连接牢固。

⑦ 进行维护保养时，若温度超过 80℃，应先拆下对温度敏感的元件。

⑧ 通导性测试笔不能接在一个带电的电路中，否则，测试笔中的灯会被烧毁。

⑨ 要定期用欧姆表对跨接导线本身进行通导性测试。导线自身接头产生的电阻会影响故障诊断的正确性。

⑩ 熔断器熔断后，必须真正找到故障原因，彻底排除故障。一定不要使用更高规格额定值的熔断器进行更换。一定要参阅维修手册或用户手册，以确认更换的电路保护装置符合规定。

三、项目实施

（一）汽车总电路图拆画分析

（1）通过该项目的实施，应能够对各种车型的电路图进行拆画和分析。

（2）该项目应具备汽车总电路图 1 张，万用表、绘图工具及常用电路检测工具等。

（二）实施步骤

1. 大众汽车电路图中的符号含义认知

大众汽车电路图中的符号含义见表 9-4。

表 9-4　大众汽车电路图中的符号含义

序号	图形或文字符号	说　明	序号	图形或文字符号	说　明
1		熔断器	10	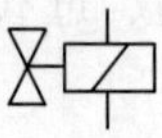	电磁阀
2	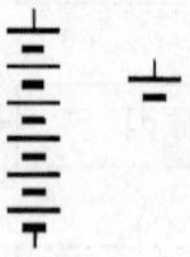	蓄电池	11		电动机
3	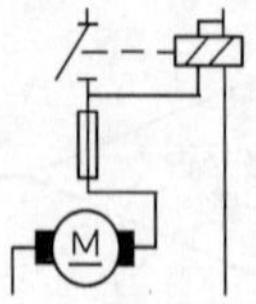	起动机	12	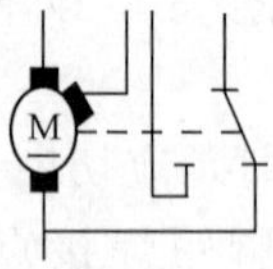	双速刮水器电机
4	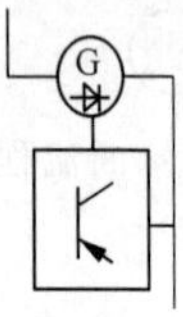	发电机	13		手动开关
5	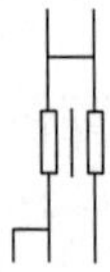	点火线圈	14	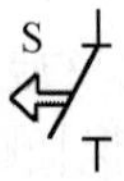	热敏开关
6	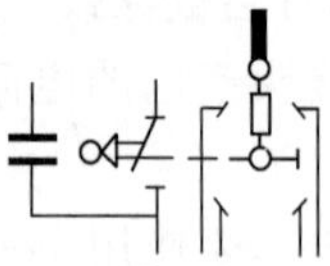	分电器（机械式）	15	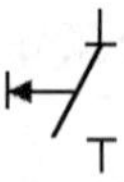	手动按钮开关
7	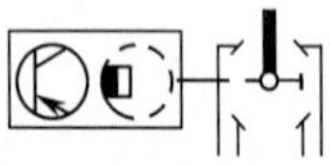	分电器（电子式）	16		机械控制开关
8		火花塞	17	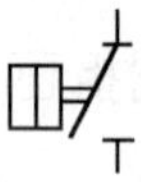	压力开关
9		加热器加热电阻	18	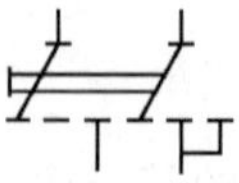	手动多挡开关

续表

序号	图形或文字符号	说　明	序号	图形或文字符号	说　明
19		可变电阻	32	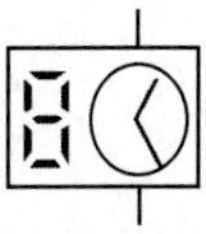	数字式时钟
20		热敏电阻	33		多功能显示器
21		电阻	34	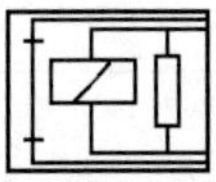	蜂鸣器
22	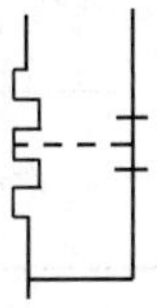	热敏时控阀	35	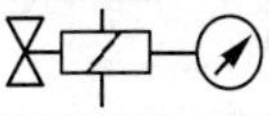	燃油指示器
			36	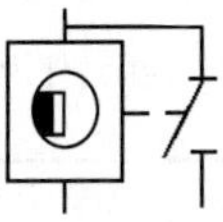	速度传感器
23	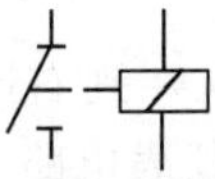	继电器	37		白炽灯
24	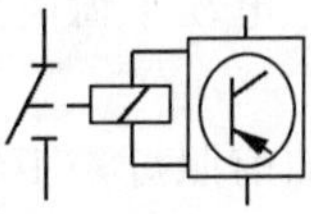	继电器（电子控制式）	38	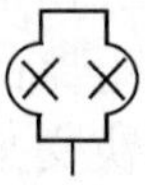	双灯丝白炽灯
25		暖风调节器附加空气阀	39	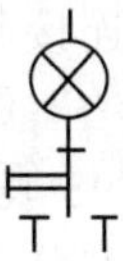	内饰灯
26		二极管	40	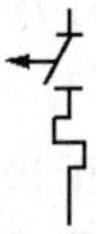	点烟器
27		稳压管			
28		发光二极管	41	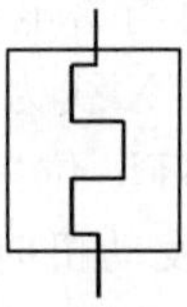	后风窗加热装置
29		指针式仪表			
30		电子式控制器	42	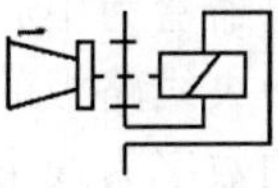	喇叭
31		指针式时钟	43		插接

项目九　汽车电气系统电路图的分析

续表

序号	图形或文字符号	说明	序号	图形或文字符号	说明
44		多孔插接	49		电阻导线
45		线路分配器			
46	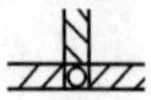	可拆式线路连接	50	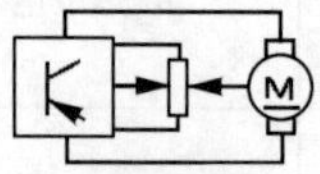	灯光调节电机
47		不可拆式线路连接	51	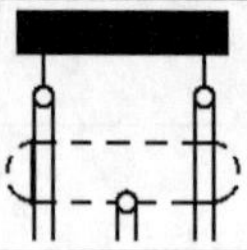	上止点传感器（感应式传感器）
48		在元件内部的连接	52	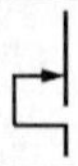	滑动触点

2. 大众汽车电路图的特点认知

（1）电路采用纵向排列，垂直布置。电源线为上"+"下"-"，从左到右同一系统的电路归纳到一起，按电源电路、起动电路、点火电路、进气预热电路、仪表电路、灯光照明电路、信号与报警装置电路、刮水与清洗装置电路、电动后视镜电路、电动车窗电路、中控门锁电路、空调电路、喇叭电路的顺序排列。

（2）采用断线代号法解决交叉问题。一些比较复杂的电气设备（如前照灯）工作时要涉及点火开关、灯光开关和变光开关等配电设备，而这3个开关不在同一条直线上，如按传统画法，要画一些横线把它们连接起来，使图面上出现较多的横线，增加读图的难度，所以在电路图中，采用"断线代号法"解决这个问题，即用导线连接端方框内的数字表明电路中与其连接导线的电路编号，如98表示与电路编号98处的导线连接。

（3）全车电路图分为3部分。最上面部分表示中央继电器盒电路，其中标明了熔断器的位置、容量和继电器位置编号及插脚号等，中间部分是车上的电气元件及连接导线，最下面的横线是搭铁线。

（4）全车电气系统电源正极分为3路（30、15、X）。30号线与蓄电池正极直接相连，称为常火线。在发动机停转时，需要工作的用电设备与30号线连接。15号线在点火开关位于"ON"和"ST"位置时与蓄电池正极连接，称为点火开关控制火线，主要为点火开关控制的小功率用电设备供电。X线为卸荷线，在点火开关位于"ON"位置时，通过中间继电器控制，点火开关置于"ST"位置时，中间继电器不工作，大功率用电设备（如雾灯、雨刮等）与X线连接，起动发动机时如果忘记关掉这些大功率的用电设备，它们会自动断电，以保证发动机顺利起动。

（5）整个电路以继电器盒为中心。汽车电气线路以中央线路板为中心进行控制，大部分熔断器和继电器安装在中央线路板的正面，插接器和插座安装在线路板的背面，英文字母为插座的位置代号，阿拉伯数字为线束插头的端子代号。根据电路图上导线与中央线路板下框线交点处的代号就能找到该导线在哪个线束中，接在第几个插孔上。

3. 大众车系电路分析范例

大众汽车电路图的识别方法如图9-11所示。

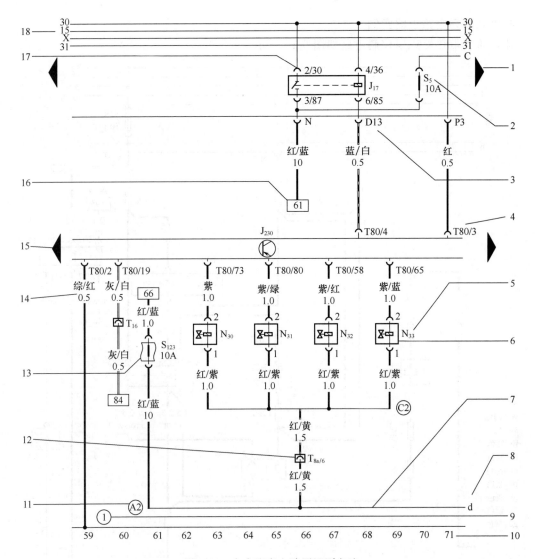

图 9-11　大众汽车电路图识别方法

1—三角箭头，表示接下一页电路图；2—熔断器代号，S_5 表示该熔断器位于熔断器座第 5 号位，10A；3—导线在中央线路板上插头连接代号，表示多针或单针插头连接和导线位置，"D13" 表示该导线在中央线路板上 D 插座 13 号位置的接线端子上；4—接线端子代号，"80/3" 表示电气元件上插接器的接线端子数位 80，3 为接线端子的位置代号；5—电气元件代号，在电路图下方可查到元件名称；6—电气元件符号，参见电路图符号说明；7—内部连接（细实线），该连接不是导线，而是表示元件的内部电路或线束的铰接点；8—指示内部接线的去向，字母表示内部接线在下一页电路图中与标有相同字母的内部接线连接；9—搭铁点代号，在电路图下方可查到该代号接地点在汽车上的位置；10—电路接续号，用此标志对电路图中的线路进行定位；11—线束内的铰接点代号，在电路图下方可查到该铰接点位于哪个线束内；12—插接器，插接器 T8a/6 表示 8 针 a 插接器上的第 6 号接线端子；13—附加熔断器代号，"S_{123}" 表示中央配电盒上第 123 号熔断器，10A；14—导线的颜色和截面积，"棕/红" 表示导线主色是棕色，辅色是红色，"2.5" 表示导线截面积为 2.5mm²；15—三角箭头指示该电气元件续接上一页电路图；16—指示导线的去向，方框内的数字 61 表明该导线与电路代码 61 的导线是同一条导线（见电路代码 61 处导线的方框内的数字是本线路的电路代码 66）；17—继电器和控制器与继电器板的接线端子代号，"2/30" 表示继电器板上该继电器插座的 2 号插孔，"30" 表示继电器上的 30 号接线端子；18—线路代码。"30" 表示常火线，"15" 为点火开关接通时的小容量火线，"X" 表示点火开关接通时，通过卸荷继电器供电的大容量火线，"31" 表示搭铁线，"C" 为中央配电盒的内部接线。

项目九　汽车电气系统电路图的分析　181

4. 大众车系电路识图实例

捷达轿车散热器风扇控制电路如图 9-12 所示。

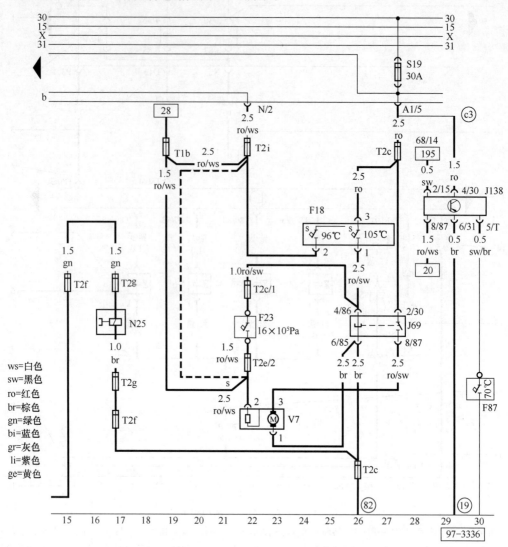

图 9-12　捷达轿车散热器风扇控制电路

F18—散热器风扇热敏开关；F23—高压开关；J69—风扇二挡继电器；J138—风扇起动控制单元；
N25—空调电磁离合器；T1b—单孔插接件；T2c—2 孔插接器（发动机舱前）；T2e—2 孔插接件
（发动机舱前）；T2f—2 孔插接器（发动机舱前）；T2g—2 孔插接件（发动机舱前）；
T2i—2 孔插接器（发动机舱前）；V7—散热器风扇；F87—风扇起动温度开关；
82—接地点，左前线束内

① 冷却水温控制。当散热器中冷却液温度达到 92～97℃时，双温开关 F18 接通一挡（96℃开关闭合）。电路为：继电器盒（30 常火线）→19 号位熔断器（30A）→继电器盒 A1/5→F18（3 号接线柱）→F18（2 号接线柱）→风扇电机 V7（2 号接线柱）→风扇电机 V7（1 号接线柱）→搭铁，形成回路，风扇低速（1600r/min）运转。当温度超过 97℃时，双温开关 F18 接通二挡（105℃开关闭合），风扇二挡继电器 J69 工作，电路为：继电器盒（30 常火线）→19 号位熔断器（30A）→J69（2/30 接线柱）→J69（8/87 接线柱）→风扇电机 V7（3 号接线柱）→风扇电机 V7（1 号接线柱）→搭铁，形成回路，风扇高速（2400r/min）运转。

② 发动机舱温度的控制。风扇起动温度开关 F87 在点火开关断开的情况下，如果机舱温度达到 70℃时，风扇起动温度开关 F87 将闭合，风扇起动控制单元 J138 工作，风扇起动控制单元 J138 的 8/87 接线柱输出电压。工作电路为：J138（8/87 接线柱）→T1b 插接件→风扇电机 V7（2 号接线柱）→风扇电机 V7（1 号接线柱）→搭铁，形成回路，风扇低速运转。

③ 空调系统工作状态控制。散热器风扇同时受空调系统工作状态的控制。当空调开关处于制冷除霜位置时，电流从继电器盒（N/2 接线柱）→风扇电机 V7（2 号接线柱）→风扇电机 V7（1 号接线柱）→搭铁，形成回路，散热器风扇低速运转。当制冷管路中压力上升到 1.6MPa 时，高压开关 F23 闭合，电流从继电器盒（N/2 接线柱）→F23→风扇二挡继电器 J69（4/86 接线柱）→风扇二挡继电器 J69（6/85 接线柱）→搭铁，形成回路，风扇二挡继电器 J69 吸合，电路为：继电器盒（30 常火线）→19 号位熔断器（30A）→J69（2/30 接线柱）→J69（8/87 接线柱）→风扇电机 V7（3 号接线柱）→风扇电机 V7（1 号接线柱）→搭铁，形成回路，风扇高速（2400r/min）运转。

四、知识与技能拓展

随着人们对汽车的安全性、乘坐舒适性、尾气排放及燃油经济性的要求越来越高，汽车控制器（电脑）之间需要交换的信息越来越多，传感器和导线的数量也迅速增加，这不仅增加了汽车的重量和成本，而且也加大了汽车的故障率及检修故障的难度。为此，必须找到一种设计优良的解决方案来使车内电子系统在不占用太大空间的情况下仍然保持其可操作性，这时 CAN 数据传输系统（又称 CAN 数据总线）应运而生，并在汽车控制系统中迅速推广和应用。国内像奥迪 A6、帕萨特 BS、波罗、宝来都采用了 CAN 数据总线。CAN 是 Controller Area Network（控制器区域网络）的缩写，意思是各个控制器通过总线相互连接并进行数据交换，通过数据总线连接发动机管理电脑、车身（如组合仪表、门控和天窗等）控制电脑、空调电脑、照明控制电脑及娱乐系统的控制电脑等，即可实现传感器数据和电脑数据的共享，简化了结构，提高了控制效率。利用 CAN 数据总线将各个控制单元连接起来，形成了车载网络系统，是计算机网络系统在现代汽车上的应用。

宝来轿车在动力传动系统和舒适系统中装用了两种 CAN 数据传输系统（见图 9-13）。

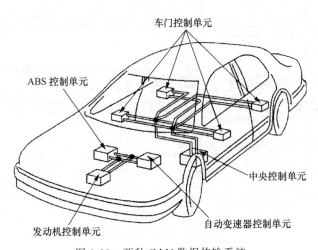

图 9-13 两种 CAN 数据传输系统

1. CAN 数据传输系统概述

CAN 数据总线是一种各控制单元间的数据传输形式，它将各个控制单元形成一个整体，所有信息都沿两条线路传输，与所参与的控制单元数及所涉及的信息量的大小无关，这样就解决了随着新增信息量的加大，线路及控制单元上的插头的数目也增加的问题，并且每条信息需要不同线路的问题也得以解决。因此，国产汽车宝来、波罗都应用了 CAN 数据总线系统，具体表现出如下优点。

（1）如果数据扩展以增加新的信息，只需升级软件即可。

（2）控制单元对所传输的信息进行实时监测，监测到故障后存储故障码。

（3）使用小型控制单元及小型控制单元插孔可节省空间。

（4）使传感器信号线减至最少，控制单元间可做到高速数据传输。

（5）CAN 数据总线符合国家标准，因此可应用不同型号控制单元间的数据传输。

2. CAN 数据总线的组成与结构

（1）组成与结构。

CAN 数据传输系统中每块电脑的内部增加了一个 CAN 控制器、一个 CAN 收发器；每块电脑外部连接了两条 CAN 数据总线。在系统中作为终端的两块电脑，其内部还装有一个数据传递终端（有时数据传递终端安装在电脑外部），如图 9-14 所示，除了数据传输线，其他元件都置于控制单元内部，控制单元功能不变（图中 J220、J104 都是不同的控制单元代号）。

（2）主要组成部分的作用。

① CAN 控制器。CAN 控制器的作用是接收控制单元中微处理器发出的数据，处理数据并传给 CAN 收发器。同时 CAN 控制器也接收收发器收到的数据，处理数据并将其传往控制单元中的微处理器。

② CAN 收发器。CAN 收发器是一个发送器和接收器的组合，它将 CAN 控制器提供的数据转化成电信号并通过数据总线发送出去，同时，它也接收总线数据，并将数据传到 CAN 控制器。

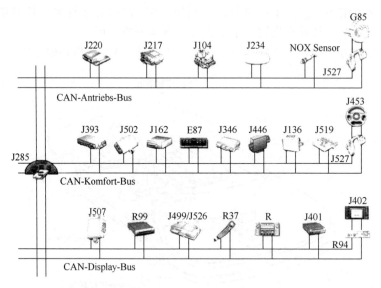

图 9-14　CAN 数据总线

③ 数据传输终端。数据传输终端实际上就是一个电阻器。它防止数据在线端被反射回

来,这会影响数据的传输。

④ 数据传输线。数据传输线是用来传输数据的双向数据线,分为 CAN 高位(CAN-high)和低位(CAN-low)数据线两种。设有指定接收器,数据通过数据总线发送给各控制单元,各控制单元接收后进行计算。为了防止外界电磁波干扰和向外辐射,CAN 总线采用两条线缠绕在一起,两线条上的电位是相反的,如果一条线的电压是 5V,另一条线就是 0V,两条线的电压和总等于常值。通过这种办法,CAN 总线得到保护而免受外界电磁场干扰,同时 CAN 总线向外辐射保持了中性,即无辐射。

3. CAN 数据总线的传输原理与过程

(1) 传输原理。CAN 数据总线的传输原理在很大程度上类似电话会议的方式。一个用户 1(控制单元 1)向网络中"说出"数据,而其他用户"收听"到这些数据。一些控制单元认为这些数据对它有用,它就接收并且应用这些数据,而其他控制单元也许不会理会这些数据。故数据总线里的数据并没有指定的接收者,而是被所有的控制单元接收及计算。

(2) 传输过程。数据的具体传输过程如图 9-15 所示。

控制单元向 CAN 控制器提供数据用于传输。CAN 收发器从 CAN 控制器处接收数据,将其转化为电信号发出。所有与 CAN 数据总线一起构成网络的控制单元成为接收器。控制单元对接收到的数据进行检测,看是不是其功能所需。如果所接收的数据是重要的,它将被认可及处理,反之将其忽略。例如,发动机电脑向某电脑 CAN 收发器发送数据,该电脑 CAN 收发器接收到由发动机电脑传来的数据,转换信号并发给本电脑的控制器。CAN 数据传输系统的其他电脑收发器均接收到此数据,但是要判断此数据是不是所需要的数据,如果不是将其忽略掉。

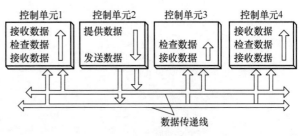

图 9-15 数据传输过程

小 结

(1) 汽车电路图全面地反映了汽车电路的原理、连接关系和位置等信息,是现今汽车维修不可缺少的维修技术资料,为维修技术人员提供了当汽车电气系统出现故障时如何进行故障诊断的逻辑诊断思路。对汽车电路图的正确识读是维修技术人员进行电气系统故障诊断与排除的一项基本技能。

(2) 汽车电路图种类繁多,自成体系,但是,只要掌握了汽车电路识图的规律,并选择一些典型的汽车全车电路进行全面、深入分析,便可全面掌握汽车电路识图的基本技能。

习题及思考

(1) 汽车线路图的识读要点有哪些?
(2) 汽车电路图中常用的电路符号有哪些?
(3) 大众车系电路图的特点有哪些?
(4) 如何进行汽车电路故障的诊断与检修?
(5) 汽车电路故障检修的注意事项有哪些?

参考文献

[1] 舒华,等. 汽车电器设备构造与维修 [M]. 2版. 北京:北京理工大学出版社,2009.
[2] Horst Gering. 现代汽车的能量管理系统 [J]. 汽车与配件,2008 (44):24-25.
[3] 曲金玉. 汽车电器与电子设备 [M]. 北京:机械工业出版社,2009.
[4] 安宗权. 汽车电气系统检修 [M]. 北京:人民邮电出版社,2009.
[5] 杨智勇. 汽车电器 [M]. 北京:人民邮电出版社,2011.
[6] Wilfried Staudt. 汽车机电技术(一)学习领域1—4 [M]. 北京:机械工业出版社,2008.
[7] 陈卫忠. 汽车诊断中心设备的配置与使用 [M]. 武汉:华中科技大学出版社,2009.
[8] Barry Hollembeak,等. 汽车电气构造与维修 [M]. 北京:北京理工大学出版社,2010.
[9] 稽伟. 新款汽车中控防盗、程序设定与保养灯归零实用手册 [M]. 北京:机械工业出版社,2009.

Bilingual Textbooks of Vocational Education
职业教育双语教材

Automobile Electrical Equipment Maintenance

汽车电气设备检修

英汉
双语教材

Edited by Bin Fang

方 斌 主编

Chemical Industry Press
化学工业出版社

BeiJing
·北京·

Preface

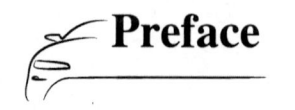

In recent years, the automobile industry in China has developed rapidly, and the automobile parc has continued to grow. What the high-speed growth of automobile parc brings about is a rapid increase in the demand for automobile professionals. Automobile electrical equipment overhaul is not only a necessary skill of automobile maintenance personnel, but also a required core course of automobile maintenance majors in higher vocational colleges. According to the teaching requirements of vocational colleges, this book systematically introduces the basic knowledge of automobile electrical system, automobile electrical structure, working principle, maintenance, fault diagnosis and elimination, etc., which must be mastered by senior automobile maintenance technicians. Highlighting the idea of "taking ability training as the first" and adopting the writing mode of integrating theory and practice is more in line with the needs of modern vocational and technical education curriculum development.

The book is divided into 9 items, involving fundamentals of automobile electrical equipment, automobile battery, charging system, starting system, ignition system, automobile lighting system, information display system, automobile auxiliary electrical system and automobile electrical system circuit diagram analysis.

This book, according to the students' cognitive law, pays attention to the characteristics of vocational education, aims at training the students' automobile electrical maintenance skills, and mainly covers the knowledge of basic maintenance of automobile electrical system. In this book, many practical pictures are added to introduce the knowledge of automobile maintenance to promote students' understanding of what they have learned and enhance their interest in learning.

This book is edited by Bin Fang of Tianjin Communications vocational college, of which Fang bin of Tianjin Communications Vocational College compiles item I, item II, item III and item IV, Jiaze Li of Tianjin Communications Vocational College compiles item V, item VI and item VII, and Ruijing Zhang of Tianjin Communications Vocational College compiles item VIII and item IX.

Due to my limited knowledge, it is inevitable that there is something improper in the book. I sincerely hope that the readers shall correct it.

Editor

Contents

Item I   Fundamentals of Automobile Electrical Equipment ······ 001

I. Scene Introduction ·· 001
II. Related Knowledge ·· 001
　(I) Composition of automobile electrical equipment ························ 001
　(II) Characteristics of the automobile electrical equipment ·············· 002
　(III) Basic methods of diagnosing the faults of automobile electrical
　　　 equipment ·· 003
　(IV) Testing instruments and tools commonly used in the maintenance of
　　　 the automobile electrical equipment ·· 004
III. Item Implementation ··· 005
　(I) Use of commonly used measuring instruments and tools ·············· 005
　(II) Implementation steps ·· 006
IV. Knowledge and Skills Expansion ·· 009
　(I) Basic components of the automobile electrical equipment ············· 009
　(II) Electronic components commonly used in automobile circuits ·········· 016
Summary ··· 017
Thinking and Practice ·· 017

Item II   Test and Maintenance of Battery ······························· 018

I. Scene Introduction ·· 018
II. Related Knowledge ·· 018
　(I) Function and type of battery ··· 018
　(II) Installation position of the battery ·· 018
　(III) Structure of the battery ··· 019
　(IV) Working principle of the battery ··· 021
　(V) Technical parameters of the battery ·· 022
　(VI) Model of battery ·· 023
　(VII) Maintenance-free battery ·· 024
　(VIII) Common failures and troubleshooting of batteries ······················· 026
III. Item Implementation ··· 028
　(I) Safe use, inspection, maintenance, charging and testing of the battery ··· 028
　(II) Implementation steps ·· 028
IV. Knowledge and Skills Expansion ·· 032
　(I) Battery cut-off protection device of the battery ······························· 032
　(II) Battery monitoring device ·· 032
Summary ··· 033

Thinking and Practice ⋯⋯⋯⋯⋯⋯⋯⋯⋯⋯⋯⋯⋯⋯⋯⋯⋯⋯⋯⋯⋯⋯⋯ 033

Item Ⅲ   Overhaul of Charging System   ⋯⋯⋯⋯⋯⋯⋯⋯⋯ 034

Ⅰ. Scene Introduction ⋯⋯⋯⋯⋯⋯⋯⋯⋯⋯⋯⋯⋯⋯⋯⋯⋯⋯⋯⋯⋯⋯⋯ 034
Ⅱ. Related Knowledge ⋯⋯⋯⋯⋯⋯⋯⋯⋯⋯⋯⋯⋯⋯⋯⋯⋯⋯⋯⋯⋯⋯⋯ 034
    (Ⅰ) Overview of charging system ⋯⋯⋯⋯⋯⋯⋯⋯⋯⋯⋯⋯⋯⋯⋯ 034
    (Ⅱ) Construction of alternator ⋯⋯⋯⋯⋯⋯⋯⋯⋯⋯⋯⋯⋯⋯⋯⋯ 035
    (Ⅲ) Working principle of alternator ⋯⋯⋯⋯⋯⋯⋯⋯⋯⋯⋯⋯⋯ 041
    (Ⅳ) Voltage regulator ⋯⋯⋯⋯⋯⋯⋯⋯⋯⋯⋯⋯⋯⋯⋯⋯⋯⋯⋯⋯⋯ 046
    (Ⅴ) Use and maintenance of alternator and voltage regulator ⋯⋯⋯⋯⋯⋯⋯ 052
    (Ⅵ) Fault diagnosis of charging system ⋯⋯⋯⋯⋯⋯⋯⋯⋯⋯⋯ 053
Ⅲ. Item Implementation ⋯⋯⋯⋯⋯⋯⋯⋯⋯⋯⋯⋯⋯⋯⋯⋯⋯⋯⋯⋯⋯ 057
    (Ⅰ) Maintenance requirements for the charging system ⋯⋯⋯⋯⋯⋯⋯ 057
    (Ⅱ) Implementation steps ⋯⋯⋯⋯⋯⋯⋯⋯⋯⋯⋯⋯⋯⋯⋯⋯⋯⋯⋯ 057
Ⅳ. Knowledge and Skills Expansion ⋯⋯⋯⋯⋯⋯⋯⋯⋯⋯⋯⋯⋯⋯ 063
    (Ⅰ) Other types of generators ⋯⋯⋯⋯⋯⋯⋯⋯⋯⋯⋯⋯⋯⋯⋯⋯ 063
    (Ⅱ) Circuit diagrams of the generators of some brand automobiles ⋯⋯⋯⋯⋯ 066
    (Ⅲ) Power management system ⋯⋯⋯⋯⋯⋯⋯⋯⋯⋯⋯⋯⋯⋯⋯⋯ 066
Summary ⋯⋯⋯⋯⋯⋯⋯⋯⋯⋯⋯⋯⋯⋯⋯⋯⋯⋯⋯⋯⋯⋯⋯⋯⋯⋯⋯⋯ 070
Thinking and Practice ⋯⋯⋯⋯⋯⋯⋯⋯⋯⋯⋯⋯⋯⋯⋯⋯⋯⋯⋯⋯⋯⋯ 070

Item Ⅳ   Maintenance of Starting System   ⋯⋯⋯⋯⋯⋯⋯⋯ 071

Ⅰ. Scene Introduction ⋯⋯⋯⋯⋯⋯⋯⋯⋯⋯⋯⋯⋯⋯⋯⋯⋯⋯⋯⋯⋯⋯⋯ 071
Ⅱ. Related Knowledge ⋯⋯⋯⋯⋯⋯⋯⋯⋯⋯⋯⋯⋯⋯⋯⋯⋯⋯⋯⋯⋯⋯⋯ 071
    (Ⅰ) Overview of starting system ⋯⋯⋯⋯⋯⋯⋯⋯⋯⋯⋯⋯⋯⋯⋯ 071
    (Ⅱ) Construction of starter ⋯⋯⋯⋯⋯⋯⋯⋯⋯⋯⋯⋯⋯⋯⋯⋯⋯⋯ 073
    (Ⅲ) DC motor ⋯⋯⋯⋯⋯⋯⋯⋯⋯⋯⋯⋯⋯⋯⋯⋯⋯⋯⋯⋯⋯⋯⋯⋯⋯ 073
    (Ⅳ) Transmission mechanism and control mechanism of starter ⋯⋯⋯⋯⋯ 078
    (Ⅴ) Control circuit of starter ⋯⋯⋯⋯⋯⋯⋯⋯⋯⋯⋯⋯⋯⋯⋯⋯ 082
    (Ⅵ) Correct use of the starter ⋯⋯⋯⋯⋯⋯⋯⋯⋯⋯⋯⋯⋯⋯⋯⋯ 085
Ⅲ. Item Implementation ⋯⋯⋯⋯⋯⋯⋯⋯⋯⋯⋯⋯⋯⋯⋯⋯⋯⋯⋯⋯⋯ 085
    (Ⅰ) Requirements for the implementation of the starting system ⋯⋯⋯⋯⋯ 085
    (Ⅱ) Implementation steps ⋯⋯⋯⋯⋯⋯⋯⋯⋯⋯⋯⋯⋯⋯⋯⋯⋯⋯⋯ 085
Ⅳ. Knowledge and Skills Expansion ⋯⋯⋯⋯⋯⋯⋯⋯⋯⋯⋯⋯⋯⋯ 095
    (Ⅰ) Structure of deceleration starter ⋯⋯⋯⋯⋯⋯⋯⋯⋯⋯⋯⋯⋯ 095
    (Ⅱ) Start/stop system ⋯⋯⋯⋯⋯⋯⋯⋯⋯⋯⋯⋯⋯⋯⋯⋯⋯⋯⋯⋯ 097
Summary ⋯⋯⋯⋯⋯⋯⋯⋯⋯⋯⋯⋯⋯⋯⋯⋯⋯⋯⋯⋯⋯⋯⋯⋯⋯⋯⋯⋯ 099
Thinking and Practice ⋯⋯⋯⋯⋯⋯⋯⋯⋯⋯⋯⋯⋯⋯⋯⋯⋯⋯⋯⋯⋯⋯ 099

Item Ⅴ   Maintenance of Ignition System   ⋯⋯⋯⋯⋯⋯⋯⋯ 100

Ⅰ. Scene Introduction ⋯⋯⋯⋯⋯⋯⋯⋯⋯⋯⋯⋯⋯⋯⋯⋯⋯⋯⋯⋯⋯⋯⋯ 100

Ⅱ. Related Knowledge ……………………………………………………………………… 100
　(Ⅰ) Overview of ignition system ……………………………………………… 100
　(Ⅱ) Basic construction and overhaul of the ignition system ……………… 102
　(Ⅲ) Construction and maintenance of computer-controlled ignition system …… 112
Ⅲ. Item Implementation ………………………………………………………………… 126
　(Ⅰ) Implementation requirements ……………………………………………… 126
　(Ⅱ) Implementation Steps …………………………………………………… 126
Summary ……………………………………………………………………………… 127
Thinking and Practice ……………………………………………………………… 127

Item Ⅵ Overhaul of Automobile Lighting System …………… 128

Ⅰ. Scene Introduction ………………………………………………………………… 128
Ⅱ. Related Knowledge ……………………………………………………………… 128
　(Ⅰ) Function，type and basic composition of the lighting and signal systems
　　……………………………………………………………………………… 128
　(Ⅱ) Automobile lighting system ……………………………………………… 129
　(Ⅲ) Automobile signaling system …………………………………………… 134
Ⅲ. Item Implementation ……………………………………………………………… 139
　(Ⅰ) Analysis of the circuit diagram of the control system for the headlight of
　　the Volkswagen Bora and overhaul ……………………………………… 139
　(Ⅱ) Maintenance and fault diagnosis of headlight ………………………… 146
　(Ⅲ) Adjustment of electric horn …………………………………………… 150
Ⅳ. Knowledge and Skills Expansion ……………………………………………… 151
　(Ⅰ) Active steering system of lights ………………………………………… 151
　(Ⅱ) Variable lighting distance of Audi A8 ………………………………… 152
　(Ⅲ) LIN bus circuit for automobile light switch ………………………… 154
Summary ……………………………………………………………………………… 154
Thinking and Practice ……………………………………………………………… 155

Item Ⅶ Maintenance of Information Display System …………… 156

Ⅰ. Scene Introduction ………………………………………………………………… 156
Ⅱ. Related Knowledge ……………………………………………………………… 156
　(Ⅰ) Automobile instrument system …………………………………………… 156
　(Ⅱ) Automobile alarm information system …………………………………… 168
Ⅲ. Item Implementation ……………………………………………………………… 172
　(Ⅰ) Fault diagnosis of coolant thermometer ……………………………… 172
　(Ⅱ) Fault diagnosis of fuel gauge ………………………………………… 173
　(Ⅲ) Fault diagnosis of electronic speedometer …………………………… 173
Ⅳ. Knowledge and Skills Expansion ……………………………………………… 174
　(Ⅰ) The Audi multimedia interactive system ……………………………… 174
　(Ⅱ) Head-up display system ………………………………………………… 174

（Ⅲ） Electronic oil level height indication ·· 175
（Ⅳ） Electronic park brake system（EPB） ·· 176
（Ⅴ） Touch display system ·· 177
Summary ·· 177
Thinking and Practice ··· 178

Item Ⅷ Overhaul of Automobile Auxiliary Electrical System   ··· 179

Ⅰ. Scene Introduction ·· 179
Ⅱ. Related Knowledge ··· 179
（Ⅰ） Composition and classification of electric wiper ····························· 179
（Ⅱ） Working principle of wiper system ·· 181
（Ⅲ） Composition of the cleaning system ··· 185
（Ⅳ） Maintenance and troubleshooting of electric wiper and cleaner ·········· 186
（Ⅴ） Composition and structure of electric windows ····························· 188
（Ⅵ） Working principle of electric window ··· 189
（Ⅶ） Fault diagnosis of electric window ·· 193
Ⅲ. Item Implementation ·· 193
（Ⅰ） Overhaul of automobile auxiliary electrical system ························· 193
（Ⅱ） Implementation steps ··· 193
Ⅳ. Knowledge and Skills Expansion ·· 200
（Ⅰ） Window defrost device ··· 200
（Ⅱ） Electric seat ··· 200
（Ⅲ） Electric rear-view mirror ·· 204
（Ⅳ） Central control door lock system ·· 205
Summary ·· 207
Thinking and Practice ··· 208

Item Ⅸ Analysis of Circuit Diagram of Automobile Electrical System ···· 209

Ⅰ. Scene Introduction ·· 209
Ⅱ. Related Knowledge ··· 209
（Ⅰ） Type of automobile circuit diagram ··· 209
（Ⅱ） Common graphic symbols，letter symbols and signs ······················· 212
（Ⅲ） Key points for drawing and reading automobile circuits ·················· 227
（Ⅳ） Common knowledge of automobile circuit overhaul ······················· 232
Ⅲ. Item Implementation ·· 234
（Ⅰ） Analysis of decomposing the general automobile circuit diagram ········· 234
（Ⅱ） Implementation steps ··· 234
Ⅳ. Knowledge and Skills Expansion ·· 240
Summary ·· 243
Thinking and Practice ··· 243

Item I

Fundamentals of Automobile Electrical Equipment

I . Scene Introduction

A customer came to the maintenance station and said that the cigarette lighter could not be used. After overhaul, it was found that the fuse had been broken. The reason is that the installation of electrical components resulted in circuit load increase.

With the maturation of automobile manufacturing technology, automobile mechanical faults are less and less, and more faults come from automobile electrical equipment and circuit. The mastery of the working principle of automobile electrical equipment, the characteristics of circuit composition, the correct diagnostic thinking and the skillful use of diagnostic maintenance devices play an important role in improving the accuracy of troubleshooting and shortening the time of troubleshooting.

II . Related Knowledge

(I) Composition of automobile electrical equipment

The automobile is mainly composed of four parts, engine, chassis, body and electrical equipment. Someone corresponds them to the four parts of a human body, With the development of science and technology, the electrical and electronic equipment is more and more important in the automobile, its working performance directly affects the power, economy, safety, reliability, travelling comfort of the automobile. Automobile electrical equipment is mainly composed of power supply system, electric devices and power distribution devices.

1. Power supply system

The power supply system, also known as the charging system, its role is to provide low-voltage DC energy to the whole automobile electric device, including battery, generator and voltage regulator. The generator is the main power supply, and the battery is the auxiliary power supply. When the generator works, the generator supplies electricity to the whole automobile and recharges the battery at the same time. The function of the battery is to supply power to the engine when the engine is started, and to the electric device when the generator is not working. The function of the voltage regulator is to keep the output voltage of the generator constant.

2. Electric devices

There are many electric devices in the automobile. The electrical equipment can be divided into starting system, ignition system, lighting and signal system, instrument, alarm and electronic display system, auxiliary electrical system and electronic control system.

(1) The starting system. Its role is to drive the engine flywheel to rotate, so that the crankshaft can achieve the necessary starting speed, thus starting the engine. The main parts are the starter, the starting relay and so on.

(2) Ignition system. The ignition system is only used in gasoline engines. Its function is to convert low-voltage electricity into high-voltage electricity, and to ignite the combustible mixture in the engine cylinder in a timely and reliable manner. It is divided into three types, traditional ignition system, electronic ignition system and electronic spark advance (ESA).

(3) Lighting and signal systems. Its function is to ensure the proper brightness in the inside and outside of the automobile, to warn pedestrians and automobiles, to indicate the direction of movement, to indicate the status of the controls, and to alarm the running mechanical faults, so as to ensure the safety and reliability of driving and parking. The lighting devices include various lights inside and outside the automobile. The signal devices include an electric horn, a flasher, a buzzer, and various signal lights to provide the necessary signals for safe driving.

(4) Instrument, alarm and electronic display systems. Its function is to display the running parameters of the automobile and the traffic information, and to monitor the working conditions of each system. Instruments include engine tachometer, speedometer, fuel meter, water thermometer, etc.

(5) Auxiliary electrical system. Its function is to provide good working conditions and comfortable environment for drivers and occupants. Auxiliary electrical system includes electric wiper, windscreen washer, air-conditioning central control door lock, electric window and electric seat, etc.

(6) Electronic control system. Its function is to control each system of the automobile more accurately, so as to improve the economy, power, safety and so on. The electronic control part includes electronic control fuel injection device, ignition device, automatic transmission and anti-lock brake device, etc.

3. Power distribution devices

Power distribution device, also known as power management system, its role is to regulate wiring, easy to diagnose automobile electrical faults. The power distribution devices include a central junction box, a circuit switch, a safety device, a connector, a conductor, etc.

(II) Characteristics of the automobile electrical equipment

In the modern, there are many kinds of automobiles, the quantity of their electrical equipment is different, the functions are different, but the circuit designs follow a certain principle. Understanding these principles is helpful to the analysis of automobile circuits and the troubleshooting. Automobile electrical equipment mainly has the following characteristics.

1. Two power supplies

There are two power supplies in an automobile, a battery and a generator. The battery is an auxiliary power supply, supplying electricity to the relevant electrical equipment when the engine is not running. The generator is a main power supply, supplying electricity to all electrical equipment when the engine is running at a certain speed and charging the battery.

2. Low voltage direct current

The rated voltage of the automobile electrical equipment is mainly 12V or 24V. The

gasoline automobile generally uses 12V power supply, and the diesel automobile uses 24V power supply, which is because the load of the diesel engine is large, and its starting torque is much larger than that of the gasoline engine. If the diesel engine still uses 12V voltage, the starter will be very large and heavy. When the diesel engine uses 24V, the volume and weight of the starter can be reduced. When the automobile is running, the voltage of 12V power supply system is 14V, and that of 24V power supply system is 28V. Because the battery charge and discharge are all direct current, so the automobile electrical equipment adopts direct current.

3. Parallel single wire

There are many electric devices in automobile. The parallel circuit can ensure that the electrical equipment of each branch can be controlled independently. The wiring is clear, easy to install, easy to save the conductor, and easy to troubleshooting. The automobile electrical equipment generally adopts the single-wire connection way, that is to connect the frame, the engine, the chassis and other metal body, and use as the common parallel end of various electric devices. But the upper part of the automobile is installed on the sheet metal parts, the electrical equipment on the trailer or the non-metal automobile board still needs to adopt the two-wire connection way.

4. Negative ground

To reduce the electrochemical corrosion of the copper terminal of the battery cable at the junction of the frame and body, and to improve the reliability of the ground, when the single-wire connection way is adopted, a negative electrode of the battery is connected to the frame, commonly known as "negative ground".

(Ⅲ) Basic methods of diagnosing the faults of automobile electrical equipment

With the increase of modern automobile electronic devices, the faults of automobile circuit and electrical system are more and more complicated. After a fault occurs, choosing a suitable diagnosis method is the key to smooth troubleshooting. For these purpose, several common methods of diagnosing automobile circuits and electrical faults are introduced in the following.

1. Direct-vision method

When a part of the electrical equipment of the automobile is out of order, there will be some abnormal phenomena such as smoke, spark, abnormal noise, burnt odour, high temperature and so on. We can directly inspect the automobile electrical appliance through our sense organs, listening, touching, smelling, seeing, etc. to judge the location of the fault, thus greatly enhancing the efficiency of the troubleshooting.

2. Test light method

Use an automobile light bulb as a temporary test light to check whether the wire harness is open or short-circuited, and the electrical appliance or circuit fails. This method is particularly suitable for checking electrical appliances with electronic components that do not allow direct short-circuit. When using the temporary test light method, we should pay attention to that the power of the test light shall not be too large. When testing whether there is output and whether there is enough output at the control (output) terminal of the electronic controller, we should be careful enough to prevent overload damage to the controller.

Item Ⅰ Fundamentals of Automobile Electrical Equipment **003**

3. Jumper connection method

Jumper connection method is also called short-circuit method, that is, when the low-voltage circuit is broken, a jumper wire or a screwdriver is used to make a circuit or a component short-circuited, to check and determine the location of the fault. If the brake light is not on, we can check whether the brake light switch is good by connecting the two wiring terminals of the brake light switch with a screwdriver after stepping on the brake pedal. For the electronic devices of a modern automobile, the short-circuit method should be used carefully to diagnose the fault, so as to prevent the damage of the electronic device due to the excessive current in the short circuit.

4. Open-circuit method

When the short-circuit (ground) fault occurs in the automobile electrical equipment, it can be judged by the open-circuit method, that is, after the circuit that may occur a short-circuit fault is disconnected, we can observe whether the short-circuit fault still exists in the electrical equipment to judge the position of the short circuit. For example, if it is found that the automobile has a large electrostatic current, this method can be used to diagnose which systems cause it.

5. Replacement method

The replacement method is often used in cases where the cause of the fault is more complicated, and it can eliminate the possible causes of the fault one by one. The practice is to replace a component that is considered or suspected to be faulty with one that is known to be intact. By this way, we can determine whether the suspicion is correct. If the fault is eliminated after the replacement, the suspicion is correct; otherwise, the original is returned and a new replacement is made until the real fault location is found.

6. Detection method

Use special testing equipment or instruments to detect electrical components and circuits to determine circuit faults. For more and more electronic devices in a modern automobile, the detection method has the advantages of time-saving, labor-saving and accurate diagnosis, but it requires the operator to be able to use the special instruments of the automobile and to grasp accurately the principle and circuit composition of the electrical components of the automobile.

7. Simulation method

Some faults are accidental and difficult to find out. Therefore, the fault should be diagnosed after the occurrence conditions are simulated and verified, such as, automobile vibration simulation, temperature simulation (Note: Do not heat electrical components above 60℃, immersion simulation (Note: Do not spray water directly on electrical components), electrical load simulation, cold start or hot start simulation.

(Ⅳ) Testing instruments and tools commonly used in the maintenance of the automobile electrical equipment

1. Test light

The automobile test light is used to measure whether there is a voltage in the circuit. It has no internal power supply and is equipped with 12V or 24V bulb. Some test lights are equipped with light-emitting diodes as light-emitting elements. Test lights are also called

passive test lights. When one end of the test light is grounded and the probe on the other end is touched with a conductor with voltage, the bulb or the light-emitting diode will be lit. A test light cannot replace a voltmeter. Because it can only show whether there is a voltage, cannot show the voltage value.

2. Jumper wire

A jumper wire can sometimes be used as an auxiliary tool for fault diagnosis. It can be used to cross a wire that is suspected to have been disconnected, to provide an electric path directly to a component, or to add a battery voltage to a circuit without relying on a switch or wire in the circuit.

Note: An ohmmeter is used to periodically test the conductivity of the jumper wire. The resistance produced by the terminal of the jumper wire will affect the correctness of the fault diagnosis.

3. Digital multimeter

At present, there are more and more electronic control units and electronic control components in automobiles, and the electronic control units and the electronic components on automobiles are not allowed to be detected with low impedance pointer multimeter, so the digital multimeter becomes the main testing instrument in the automobile electrical maintenance. There are many kinds of digital multimeters for automobiles, which have different functions. The common digital multimeter has two functions: test function without current and the test function with current. The digital multimeter (with current test function) for automobiles is shown in Figure 1-1.

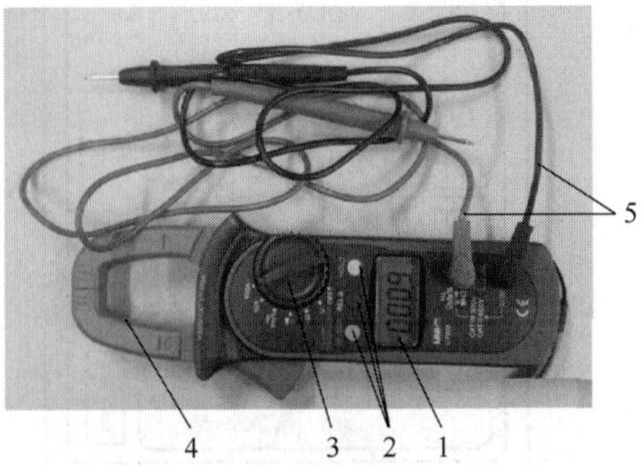

Figure 1-1　Digital Multimeter for Automobiles
(with current test function)

1—Digital and analog display screen; 2—Function button; 3—Test item selection switch; 4—Hall current sensing clip; 5—Measuring wire

The digital multimeter is superior to most analog multimeters in many ways, the most important of which is that it is more accurate. Most high-quality meters are supplied with known data from internal circuits powered by dry cells in the meters. If the battery is under-powered, it will affect the accuracy of the readings. Most digital meters have a battery warning sign that shows the potential of the battery.

In addition to measuring AC voltage, DC voltage, AC, DC, resistance, the digital multimeter can also measure the capacitance, frequency, the forward voltage drop of the diode, and check the on-off of the circuit. In addition to the above measurement functions, the digital multimeter has the functions of automatic zero reset, automatic display of polarity, overload indication, reading retention, symbol display of the unit being measured, and so on.

III. Item Implementation

(I) Use of commonly used measuring instruments and tools

① Through the implementation of this item, we should be able to standardize the use

Item I　Fundamentals of Automobile Electrical Equipment　**005**

of various commonly used measuring instruments and tools in the fault diagnosis of automobile electrical equipment.

② The item should be equipped with jumper wire, digital multimeter and other tools.

(Ⅱ) Implementation steps

Use of digital multimeter:

Carry out detection according to the function description of the digital multimeter. The function description of the digital multimeter for automobiles is shown in Figure 1-2.

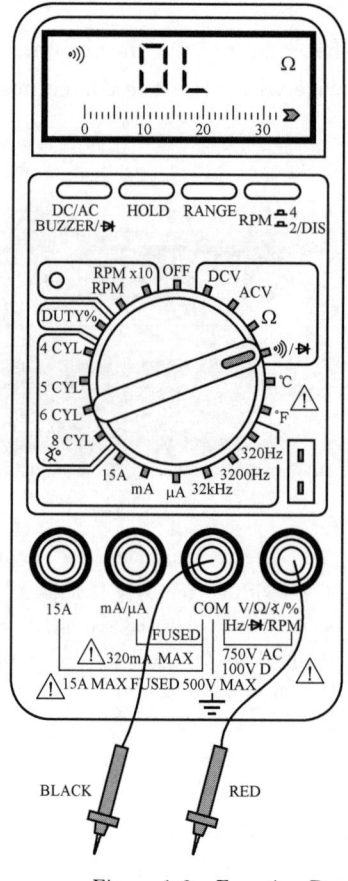

Function switch position	Function specification
V ---	DC voltage measurement
V ~	AC voltage measurement
Ω	Resistance measurement
▶⊢	Diode PN junction voltage measurement
ᵒ)))	On-off measurement of circuit
A ---	DC current measurement
A ~	AC current measurement
℃	Temperature measurement (centigrade)
hFE	Transistor measurement
DUTY	Duty ratio (%) measurement
DWELL ⤳	Motor vehicle ignition dwell angle measurement (unit: Degree)
TACHX10 ↻	Automobile engine speed measurement (unit: Rpm)
HOLD	Data hold switch
Power	Power

Figure 1-2　Function Description of Digital Multimeter for Automobiles

(1) Measurement of voltage.

① The test wire of the multimeter is inserted into the corresponding jack (the red pen is inserted into the V/Ω jack, and the black pen is inserted into the COM jack).

② The function selection switch of the multimeter is placed in the voltage measuring gear, and the DC and AC positions are selected according to the type of voltage to be measured (by DC/AC switch).

③ Select the range according to the voltage to be measured (by RANGE switch).

④ The test wire of the multimeter is connected to the circuit to be measured, the black pen is grounded, and the red pen is connected to the signal wire.

⑤ Close the circuit to be measured and observe the voltage reading in the display area of the multimeter.

006　Automobile Electrical Equipment Maintenance

⑥ Press the HOLD button to lock the measurement result and compare it with the standard value.

When measuring high voltage (hundreds of volts), it should be operated by one hand, that is, the black pen is fixed on the common end of the circuit to be tested, and then the red pen is held by a hand to touch the test point, which is safer.

(2) Measurement of resistance.

① The test wire of the multimeter shown in Figure 1-4 is inserted into the corresponding jack (the red pen is inserted into the V/Ω jack and the black pen is inserted into the COM jack).

② The function selection switch of the multimeter is placed in the resistance measuring gear. If the range is not set, the multimeter is in the automatic range state.

③ If you need to set the range, you can press the RANGE control key and enter the manual range setting mode. After that, if you press the control key one more time, the range will be replaced one more time. To return the automatic range, press the key for 2s and then release it.

④ The selection scope of manual range: $0\sim320\Omega$, $0\sim3.2k\Omega$, $0\sim32k\Omega$, $0\sim320k\Omega$, $0\sim3.2M\Omega$, $0\sim32M\Omega$.

⑤ Connect the test wire of the multimeter to the element to be tested, the black pen and the red pen are connected to the terminals of the element to be tested, respectively.

⑥ Observe the data display of the display area of the multimeter.

⑦ Press the HOLD button in the control area to lock the measurement result and compare it with the standard value.

It is strictly forbidden to measure the resistance when the circuit to be tested is electrified, nor to measure the internal resistance of the battery with the resistance gear. Because this is equivalent to adding a voltage to the resistance measurement circuit of the digital multimeter, the measurement result is completely meaningless. Also, it is possible to damage the multimeter.

(3) Circuit conductivity test.

① The test wire of the multimeter is connected to the corresponding jack as shown in Figure 1-4 (the red pen is inserted into the V/Ω jack and the black pen is inserted into the COM jack).

② The function selection switch of the multimeter is placed in the test gear of the circuit conductivity/diode.

③ Connect the two test wires of the multimeter to the circuit to be tested.

④ If the buzzer of the multimeter makes an alarm sound, it indicates that the circuit is not broken.

(4) Measurement of the diode.

Note: The red pen of the digital multimeter is the positive electrode of the internal battery. When measuring the diode with its diode gear, the value shown is the forward voltage drop of the diode and the unit is mV. When the digital multimeter is used, the forward voltage drop of the high-quality diode is $500\sim700mV$ and the reverse voltage is ∞.

① The test wire of the multimeter is connected to the corresponding jack as shown in Figure 1-4 (the red pen is inserted into the V/Ω jack and the black pen is inserted into the

COM jack).

② The function selection switch of the multimeter is placed in the test gear of the circuit conductivity/diode.

③ Connect the two test pens of the multimeter to the 2 pins of the diode to be tested.

④ The two test pens of the multimeter are exchanged and then connected to the 2 pins of the diode to be tested.

⑤ In the case of tests under ③ and ④, if the result of one measurement is of no value and the result of the other is of low voltage, it shows that the performance of the diode is good; if the results of both measurements are of low voltage, it indicates that the diode has broken down; if the results of both measurements are of no value, it indicates that the diode has burnt out.

The digital multimeter belongs to the precision electronic instrument. If it is not used properly, it will not only cause the inaccurate measurement, but also cause the damage of the instrument when it is serious. Be sure to pay attention to the following matters when using the digital multimeter.

① Before using, please read the instructions of the digital multimeter carefully to understand its technical performance and characteristics.

② The environmental conditions for ensuring the accuracy of the digital multimeter shall be that the digital multimeter shall be used under the conditions of clean and dry, suitable ambient temperature, no external strong electromagnetic interference and no vibration.

③ Before measuring, it is necessary to check carefully whether there is a crack in the pen and whether the insulation layer of the lead is damaged to ensure safety.

④ Although the internal circuit of the digital multimeter has better protection measures, misoperation shall be avoided, such as, measuring voltage with the current gear, measuring voltage or current with the resistance gear, measuring electric capacity with the capacitance gear, so as not to damage the multimeter.

⑤ When measuring, if the value of the voltage (or current) to be tested cannot be estimated in advance, the maximum range should be dialed first, and then the reasonable range should be selected according to the test situation.

⑥ Do not move the range switch when measuring high voltage (above 100V) so as not to burn the contact by arc.

⑦ If the LCD of the digital multimeter with automatic shutdown function suddenly slip to disappear under use, it is not a fault, but is the multimeter into the "body sleep" state (power is cut off). It just needs to be restarted and back to normal.

⑧ The digital multimeter with a reading HOLD key shall be placed in an "off" position for continuous measurement. Otherwise, the multimeter cannot be sampled properly and the display number cannot be refreshed.

⑨ The fuse tubes commonly used in the digital multimeter have many specifications (e. g. 0. 2 A, 0. 3 A, 0. 5 A, 1A, 2A) and must be replaced with the same fuse tubes as the original specifications.

⑩ If the LCD does not display any numbers after the boot, we should first check if the battery is not installed or if the battery has failed, and also check if the battery leads are disconnected. If the power supply low voltage indicator is displayed, the battery should be re-

placed with a new one. Turn off the power switch before replacing the battery.

Ⅳ. Knowledge and Skills Expansion

(Ⅰ) Basic components of the automobile electrical equipment

1. Circuit switch

In automobile circuits, each electric device is equipped with separate control switch, such as light switch, light combination switch, wiper switch, steering signal switch, emergency alarm switch, backup light switch, brake light switch, horn switch, air conditioning switch, etc. The motion can be manually controlled or self controlled according to the condition of the circuit or automobile. Switches are divided into normally open switch and normally closed switch. The normally open switch means that the switch is in the normal position or at rest position, and the circuit is disconnected; The normally switch means that the switch is in the normal position or at rest position, and the circuit is connected.

There are many kinds of representation methods of switch in circuit diagram, such as structure diagram representation, table representation and graphic symbol representation. We take the ignition switch as an example to introduce the representation of the circuit switch, as shown in Figure 1-3. The functions of the ignition switch are to lock the steering wheel shaft (LOCK gear), turn on the instrument indicator light (ON or IG gear), start the engine (ST or START gear), supply power to the accessories (ACC is mainly for the radio cassette player), and preheat the engine (HEAT gear). When the START gear and the HEAT gear work, the current consumed is very large, so the switch should not be connected for a long time. The two gears under operation must overcome the spring force by hand, holding the key and releasing the hand to bounce it back to the ignition gear. The two gears can not be self-positioned, but other gears can do so.

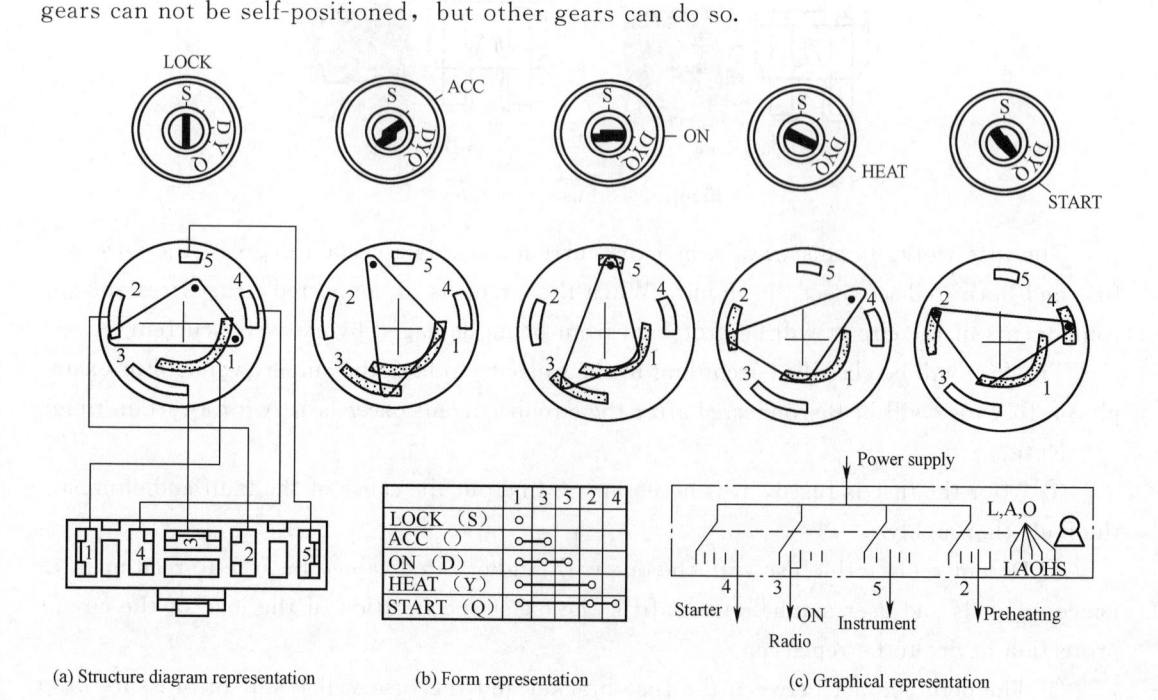

Figure 1-3   Structure and Representation of the Ignition Switch

2. Circuit protection device

When the current in the circuit exceeds the specified current, the automobile circuit protection device can automatically cut off the circuit, thereby protecting the electrical equipment, preventing the burn-out of the circuit connecting wires, and limiting the fault to a minimum. The main circuit protection devices in the automobile are fuse, fusible wire, circuit breaker and relay.

(1) Fuse. Fuse is commonly known as a safety device. The fuse is a plug-in device, connecting the two terminals by the conductor which will be fused (burnt) when the current exceeds the rated current value. The fuse must be replaced after the circuit failure has been repaired.

There are 3 basic types of fuses: fusion tube type, winding type, chip-inserted type. The types of fuses are shown in Figure 1-4. After the fuse is damaged, we can see the fuse disconnected intuitively. The fuse inspection is shown in Figure 1-5. Chip fuses are most widely used and have specified ampere values and color codes. The fuse must be marked with a rated ampere value and a voltage value. Two small holes in the outer shell of the fuse make it easy for the repairman to check the voltage drop, working voltage, or conductivity.

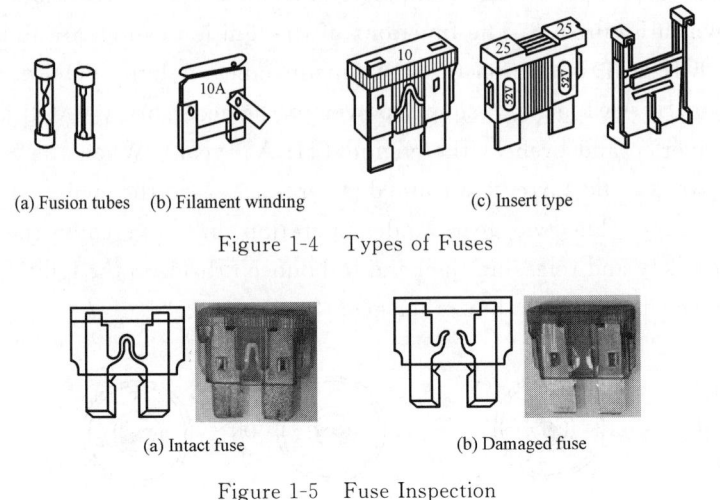

(a) Fusion tubes   (b) Filament winding   (c) Insert type

Figure 1-4   Types of Fuses

(a) Intact fuse   (b) Damaged fuse

Figure 1-5   Fuse Inspection

The fuse works in this way, when the current exceeds a certain degree, the wire will fuse and burn to disconnect the circuit. When the circuit is disconnected, the wires and the components of the circuit will be protected from being damaged by excessive current.

The fuse will be classified according to the capacity to bear the ampere value. For example, a 10A fuse will be disconnected after the circuit current exceeds 10A for a certain time.

Note:

① After the fuse is fused, it is necessary to find out the cause of the fault and eliminate the fault thoroughly.

② Do not replace the fuse with the one with higher rated value. Be sure to read maintenance manuals and user manuals to confirm the exact specification of the load of the circuit protection device to be replaced.

③ The poor contact between the fuse bracket and the fuse will result in pressure drop and heat, and a good contact shall be maintained when installing.

(2) Fusible wire. Some models are fitted with fusible wires. The fusible wire is a large-capacity fuse used to protect the power supply circuit and high-current circuit. The fusible wire is installed directly in the positive position of the battery. The fusible wires usually protect a wide range of automobile circuits when fuses or circuit breakers are not suitable. In case of overload, thin wires of the fusible wires will be fused to disconnect the circuit before damage occurs.

Note:

① It is absolutely not allowed to replace the fusible wires with the one with larger prescribed capacity, and it is not allowed to replace them with ordinary wires.

② The fusible wire is fused, the reason may be that the main circuit is short-circuited. So it must be carefully inspected to thoroughly eliminate hidden dangers.

③ Don't mix the fusible wire with other wires.

(3) Circuit breaker. The role of the circuit breaker in the circuit is to prevent overload, by disconnecting the circuit and cutting off the current to prevent wires and electrical equipment from overheating and the fire therefrom. Circuit breakers are mechanical devices that use the thermal effects of two different metals (bimetallic sheets) to disconnect the circuit. If the extra current flows through the bimetallic sheet, the bimetallic sheet bends and the contact is open-circuited to prevent the current from passing through. When there is no current, the bimetallic sheet cools to re-close the circuit and the circuit breaker resets. The circuit breaker may be a separate plug-in assembly, or it may be mounted inside the switch or on the brush holder. If the current exceeds the rated current value, a set of contacts in the device will disconnect the circuit instantaneously. Unlike fuses, circuit breakers need not be replaced after each disconnection. However, after each circuit is disconnected, we must find out the cause of circuit overload or short circuit and repair it, otherwise, it will cause circuit damage again.

In general, circuit breakers can be divided into two types: circulating type and non-circulating type.

① Circulating circuit breaker. The circulating circuit breakers are equipped with a bimetallic sheet consisting of two kinds of metals with different thermal expansion coefficients. After heating, the expansion rate of the two kinds of metals is different. When the current exceeding a certain amount flows through the bimetallic sheet, because of the accumulation of heat, the metal with high expansion rate will bend to disconnect the contact. Since no current flows through the circuit when the circuit is disconnected, the metal will cool and shrink until the contact reconnects the circuit.

In actual operation, the contact is disconnected quickly. If an overload persists, the circuit breaker will circulate repeatedly (to disconnect and to close) until the condition is corrected. The structure of the circulating circuit breaker is shown in Figure 1-6.

② Non-circulating circuit breaker. The non-circulating circuit breaker uses a bimetallic sheet wound by a coil, which remains a large resistance current path even when the contact is disconnected. Before the power supply of the circuit is disconnected, the heat generated by the coil prevents the bimetallic sheet from cooling enough to close the contact.

After disconnecting the power supply, the bimetallic sheet is cooled and the circuit is restored. For the non-circulating circuit breakers, if a circuit breaker disconnects the cir-

cuit, the power supply of the circuit must be disconnected to reset the circuit breaker. The non-circulating circuit breakers cannot be used in important circuits, such as headlights. Because an instantaneous short circuit will cut off the voltage of the circuit until the circuit breaker can be reset which may result in catastrophic consequences if the headlight suddenly goes off at night. The structure of a non-circulating circuit breaker is shown in Figure 1-7.

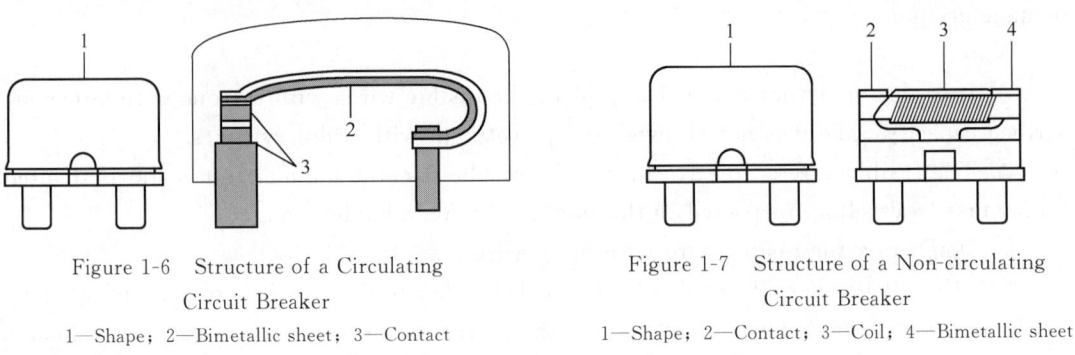

Figure 1-6　Structure of a Circulating
Circuit Breaker

1—Shape; 2—Bimetallic sheet; 3—Contact

Figure 1-7　Structure of a Non-circulating
Circuit Breaker

1—Shape; 2—Contact; 3—Coil; 4—Bimetallic sheet

(4) Relay. In automobiles, relays are used in many places, such as fuel pump, horn, starting system, etc. A relay is an electrical switch whose function is to control a large current with a small current, thereby reducing the current load of the control switch and reducing ablation. The structure diagram of the relay is shown in Figure 1-8, including a control circuit, an electromagnet, an armature, a group of contacts, etc.

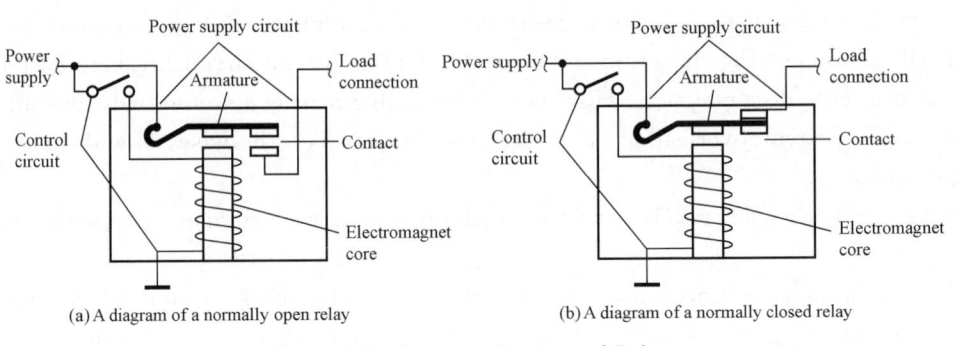

Figure 1-8　Structure Diagram of Relays

There are many relays on the automobiles, and we often see 3 kinds of relays. The action state is shown in Figure 1-9. The contact of the first kind of relay is normally disconnected, after the relay acts, the contact is connected. The contact of the second kind of relay is normally closed, after the relay acts, the contact is disconnected. The break contact of the third kind of relay is normally connected, and the make contact is normally disconnected, after the relay acts, the break contact will be disconnected and the make contact will be connected.

The relays in the junction box are shown in Figure 1-10.

3. Connector

Connectors are commonly referred to as plugs and sockets, and are used to connect a wire to a wire or a wire harness to a wire harness. In order to prevent the connector from disconnecting during the driving process of the automobile, all the connectors are equipped with locking devices.

012　Automobile Electrical Equipment Maintenance

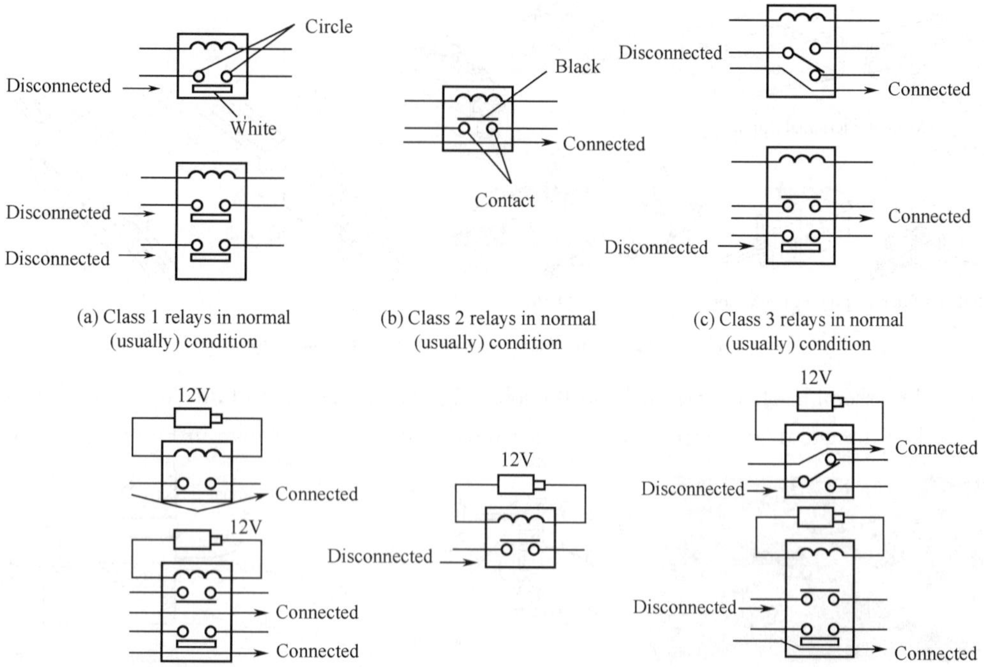

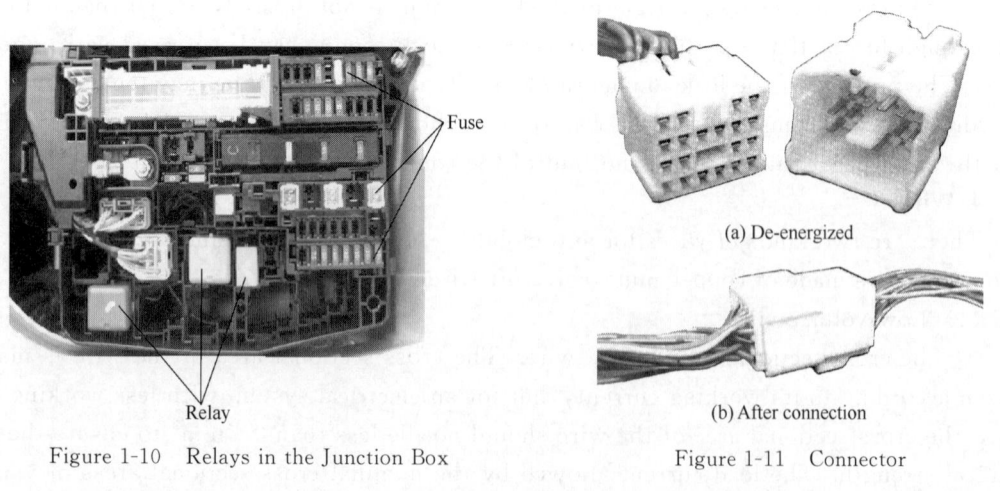

(a) Class 1 relays in normal (usually) condition

(b) Class 2 relays in normal (usually) condition

(c) Class 3 relays in normal (usually) condition

(d) When the coil of class 1 relays is energized

(e) When the coil of class 2 relays is energized

(f) When the coil of class 3 relays is energized

Figure 1-9   Action Status of Relay

(1) The way to identify the connector. The connector is shown in Figure 1-11.

(a) De-energized

(b) After connection

Figure 1-10   Relays in the Junction Box

Figure 1-11   Connector

(2) The way to connect the connector. When the connector is connected, the guide slots of the connector should be overlapped together, so that the plug and socket are aligned, and then inserted in parallel, so the connector can be connected firmly.

(3) The way to dismantle the connector. To dismantle the connector, we should first remove the lock, then pull the connector open, do not allow to pulling the wire without unlocking, otherwise it will damage the locking device or the connecting wire. The way to dismantle the connector is shown in Figure 1-12.

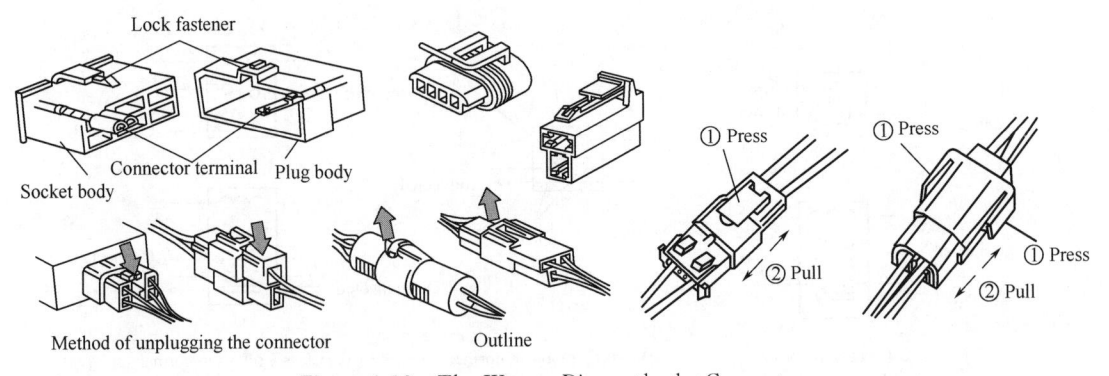

Figure 1-12   The Way to Dismantle the Connector

（4）Disassembly of the terminal and the joint. Insert the special tool into the hole of the joint，press the lock tongue of the terminal，and then move the joint，as shown in Figure 1-13.

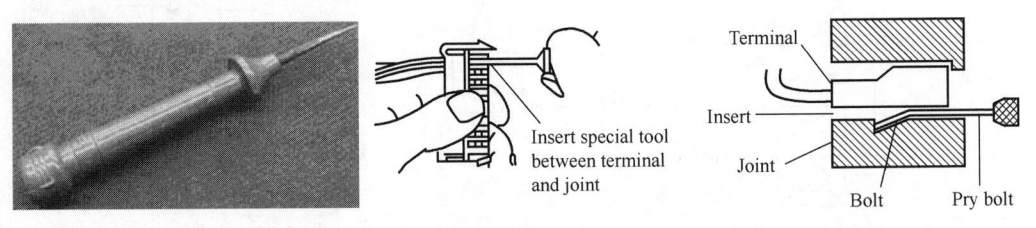

Figure 1-13   Disassembly of the Terminal and the Joint

Note：When pressing the lock tongue with the special tool，the force should be appropriate，and should not be too excessive，otherwise it will damage the lock tongue and the joint. If the terminal can not be moved after pressing the lock tongue with the tool，it may be that the pressing place is not right or the lock tongue is not pressed，rather than not exerting enough force. If the position is correct，the lock tongue can be pressed with a gentle force. The position of the lock tongue can be easily determined by the maintenance manual. In addition，some connectors have a waterproof rubber plug on the back. So we shall ensure that the waterproof rubber plug is not out of the connector when installing it.

4. Wire

There are two kinds of wires for automobiles，low voltage wire and high voltage wire，all of which are made of copper multi-core soft wires.

（1）Low voltage wire.

① The cross-sectional area of the wire. The cross-sectional area of the wire is mainly chosen according to its working current，but for an electrical system with less working current，the cross-sectional area of the wire should not be less than $0.5mm^2$ to ensure the mechanical strength. The load current allowed by the nominal cross-sectional areas of various low voltage wires is shown in Table 1-1.

Table 1-1   **Load Current Allowed by Nominal Cross-sectional Area of Low-voltage Wire**

Cross section of wire/mm^2	1.0	1.5	2.5	3.0	4.0	6.0	10	13
Allowable current value/A	11	14	20	22	25	35	50	60

The nominal cross-sectional area of the main wires of the 12V electrical system for automobiles is shown in Table 1-2.

Table 1-2　Nominal Cross-sectional Area of Main Wires of 12V Electrical System for Automobiles

Use	Nominal cross section/mm^2
Rear light，top light，indicator light，license plate light，instrument，wiper，etc	0.5
Steering light，brake light，stop light，distributor	0.8
Near light of headlight，electric horn(below 3A)	1.0
Far light of headlight，electric horn(above 3A)	1.5
Other circuits above 5A	1.5～4.0
Electric plug circuit	4.0～6.0
Power supply circuit	6.0～25
Starting circuit	16～95

② The color of the wire. Automakers across the world often use letters (English letters) to indicate the colors of wires and stripes on circuit diagrams. The color codes for the wires of some automobile manufacturers are shown in Table 1-3.

Table 1-3　Color Codes of Automobile Wires

Color		Model							
		Toyota	Honda	General Motors	Ford	Chrysler	BMW	Mercedes-Benz	Mitsubishi
Black	Black	B	BLK	BLK	BK	BK	BK	SW	B
Brown	Brown	BR	BRN	BRN	BR	BR	BR	BR	BR
Red	Red	R	RED	RED	R	RD	RD	RT	R
Yellow	Yellow	Y	YEL	YEL	Y	YL	YL	GE	Y
Green	Green	G	GRN	GRN	GN		GN	GN	G
Blue	Blue	L	BLU	BLU	BL		BU	BL	L
Violet	Violet	V				VT	VI	VI	V
Grey	Grey	GR	GRY	GRY	GY	GY	GY	GR	GR
White	White	W	WHT	WLLT	W	WT	WT	WS	W
Pink	Pink	P	PNK	PNK	PK	PK	PK		P
Orange	Orange	O	ORN	ORN	O	OR	OR		O
Tan	Tan			TAN	T	TN	TN		
Natural	Natural				N				
Purple	Purple			PPL	P				
Dark Blue	Dark Blue			DKBLU		DB			
Dark Green	Dark Green			DKGRN		DG			
Light Blue	Light Blue			LTBLU		LB			SB
Light Green	Light Green			LTGRN		LG			LG
Clear	Clear			CLR					
Ivory	Ivory							EI	
Rose	Rose							RS	

Note：The codes in the column of the "Mercedes-Benz" are wire codes for Mercedes-Benz，Volkswagen and other German automobiles.

The color of the wire should be easy to distinguish，the stripes on the wire should be contrasted strongly，the proportion of the main color of the two-color wire should be larger，

the proportion of the auxiliary color should be smaller, and the ratio of the main color stripe to the auxiliary color stripe along the circumferential surface is 3 : 1~5 : 1. The first color in the two-color wire marking is the main color and the second color is the auxiliary color. The selection procedure of the color of the automobile wire specified by China is shown in Table 1-4.

Table 1-4   The Selection Procedure of the Color of Automobile Wire

Selection procedure	1	2	3	4	5	6
Wire color	B	BW	BY	BR		
	W	WR	WB	WBi	WY	WG
	R	RW	RB	RY	RG	RBi
	G	GW	GR	GY	GB	GBi
	Y	YR	YB	YG	YBi	YW
	Br	BrW	BrR	BrY	BrB	
	Bi	BiW	BiR	BiY	BiB	BiO
	Gr	GR	GrY	GrBi	GrB	GrO

③ Wire harness. In addition to battery wire, high voltage wire and starter wire, automobile wires are wrapped with insulating materials to avoid erosion and wear of water and oil. The wiring process of the wire harness is not allowed to pull too tight. The wire harness should be protected by casings when passing through the hole or sharp angle. After the position of the wire harness is determined, the circlip or the trip nails are used to fix it. The automobile harnesses are shown in Figure 1-14.

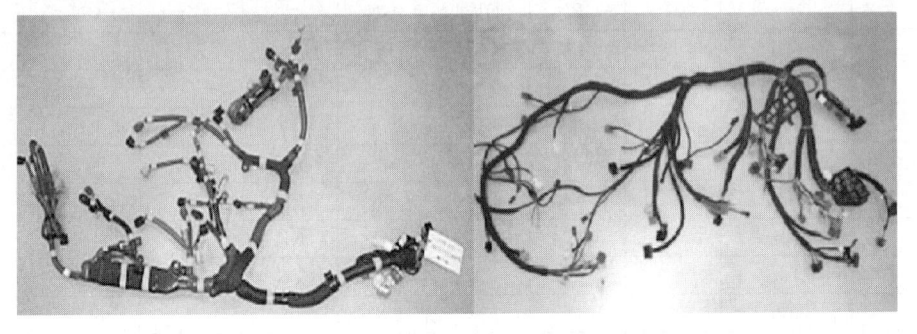

Figure 1-14   Automobile Wire Harnesses

(2) High voltage wire. High voltage wires are used in the circuit between the ignition coil and the spark plug. The high voltage wires are divided into ordinary copper-core high voltage wires and high voltage damping ignition wires. High voltage wires with damping can suppress and attenuate the high-frequency electromagnetic wave produced by the ignition system, and reduce the interference to electronic control devices and wireless equipment.

(Ⅱ) Electronic components commonly used in automobile circuits

1. Resistor

When the maximum current or voltage is not required in the circuit, the resistor can be used to limit the current. Resistor generates a voltage drop and converts electric energy into heat energy. The function of the resistor to convert electric energy into heat energy is used in many parts of the automobile, such as the rear window defrosting device, heater and ciga-

rette lighter. The filament in a light bulb also produces heat, but it mainly illuminates.

2. Capacitor

Capacitors can absorb and store charges. The capacitor is made of 2 or more conductor plates and a non-conductive medium is added between the conductors. The capacitor has the function of passing AC but blocking DC, the tiny DC current produced by it helps to absorb the peak voltage and prevent the breakdown of the disconnected contact. If the capacitor is used in audio equipment, it can also act as a "noise" filter. The unit of capacitance is Farad (F).

3. Diode

In a circuit, the diode has a unidirectional conductivity that allows the current to flow from one direction to another and prevents the current from flowing in the opposite direction. The diode can be used to make a logic circuit. This circuit works only if certain conditions satisfy a certain order. For example, the ignition switch key warning buzzer circuit can only be connected when the ignition switch is in the OFF position and the door is open.

There are many kinds of diodes in automobiles, which are mainly used in the following aspects: rectifying converting AC to DC, voltage regulation and control of voltage peaks and fluctuations that can cause damage to solid-state circuits, instrument panel indicator lights, etc.

4. Triode

A triode is also called a transistor. The three electrodes of the triode are the base electrode, collector electrode and emitter electrode, respectively. By applying a tiny current or voltage to the base electrode, the larger current flowing through the other two electrodes can be controlled, which means that the triode can be used as an amplifier and a switch.

Summary

(1) The automobile electrical equipment includes power supply system, electrical equipment and distribution devices. The characteristics of the automobile electrical equipment are low voltage, direct current, single-wire connection way, negative ground, two power supplies and electric devices in parallel.

(2) The basic methods to diagnosing automobile electrical and circuit faults are direct-vision method, test light method, jumper connection method, open-circuit method, replacement method, detection method and simulation method.

(3) To ensure the correctness of the test results, it is necessary to correctly use the common tools for fault diagnosis of automobile electrical equipment, such as conductivity test pen, test light, jumper wire, digital multimeter, etc. , as required by the specifications.

Thinking and Practice

(1) What system does the automobile electrical equipment consist of?

(2) What are the characteristics of the automobile electrical equipment?

(3) What are the common testing instruments and tools used in the maintenance of the automobile electrical equipment?

(4) How to use the test light correctly?

(5) How to use the digital multimeter correctly?

Item II

Test and Maintenance of Battery

I. Scene Introduction

When a FAW Volkswagen Suteng car sets the ignition switch to the start position, the sound of "clatter" is heard when the starter is running, and the indicator lights of the automobile instrument twinkle continuously at the starting moment, and the automobile cannot be started. Through overhaul, it found out that the battery is under-charged. This example reflects the importance of the battery, one of the automobile power supplies.

II. Related Knowledge

(I) Function and type of battery

1. Function of battery

Battery, as one of the automobile power supplies, its main function is to provide enough electricity to the starter to start the engine. As a reversible DC power supply, the battery can not only store the electric energy, but also provide the electric energy for the electrical devices such as parking light, radio, cigarette lighter, alarm system and so on. At the same time, because the battery in the electrical system is especially like a low internal resistance, high charge capacity capacitor or filter, when the charging system normally works, it can absorb and suppress the overvoltage fluctuations that alternator may appear, so as to protect the circuit.

2. Type of battery

There are many kinds of batteries. At present, lead-acid battery is widely used in automobile because of its mature technology, low price, simple structure and good starting performance. The electrolyte of lead-acid battery is dilute sulfuric acid, and the main active substance of electrode plate is lead. The common types of lead-acid batteries are common battery, maintenance-free battery, glass fiber battery, colloidal battery and so on. All the batteries mentioned here refer to lead-acid batteries.

(II) Installation position of the battery

The location of the battery in the automobile should take into account the weight distribution of the parts of the automobile, easy disassembly, dirt prevention, ambient temperature, shock absorption, and the harmful gas produced by the charging process. These factors usually vary with the model of automobile, use, working temperature, etc. Under extreme temperature conditions, it may be required to add a heater or a cooling fan to the bat-

tery.

Generally, most of the automobile batteries are installed in the running water tank in the engine compartment or in front of the windshield, some in the side wall of the trunk or in the spare tire well, and a few under the seat of the passenger compartment.

(Ⅲ) Structure of the battery

A single-cell lead-acid battery can be composed of a pair of a positive plate and a negative plate inserted into a dilute sulfuric acid, usually designed with a nominal voltage of 2V. The battery with a rated voltage of 12V is made up of 6 2V single-cell lead-acid batteries connected in series by lead bars. Each single-cell lead-acid battery is separated from each other by a wall. The whole lead-acid battery is composed of electrode plate, electrolyte, clapboard, shell and so on. The structure of the battery is shown in Figure 2-1.

(1) Electrode plate. Electrode plate is the core part of the battery, which has the most direct influence on the performance of the battery. The electrode plate is composed of active substance and grid frame, and the active substance is attached to the grid frame. The active substance on the positive plate is dark brown lead dioxide (PbO_2), and the active substance on the negative plate is blue-gray spongy lead (Pb), whose structure is shown in Figure 2-2. The mutual conversion of electric energy and chemical energy is achieved by the chemical reaction between the active substance of the electrode plate and H_2SO_4 in the electrolyte.

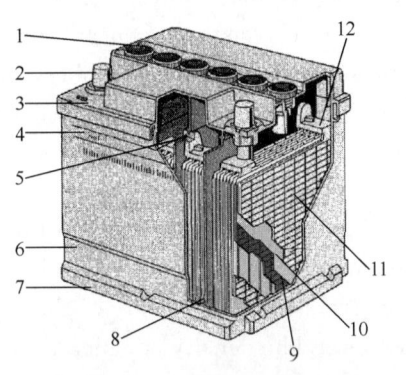

Figure 2-1   Structure of Battery

1—Sealing plug; 2—Connecting post; 3—Sealing cover;
4—Level marking; 5—Direct connector; 6—Shell;
7—Bottom plate seal; 8—Battery clapboard;
9—Positive plate; 10—Plastic clapboard;
11—Negative electrode; 12—Battery jumper

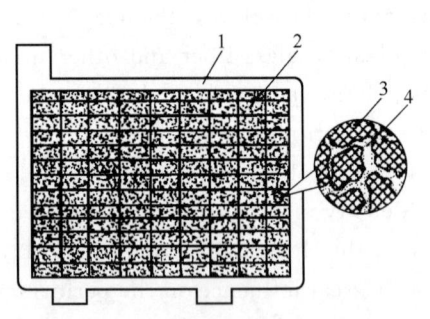

Figure 2-2   Structure of Electrode Plate

1—Grid frame; 2—Active substance;
3—Active substance particles; 4—Pore

The grid frame is the skeleton of the electrode plate, and the main component is lead. To reduce the corrosion of the grid frame, improve the mechanical strength of the electrode plate, reduce the loss of water and self-discharge of the battery, and prolong the service life of the battery, the grid frame of the battery mainly adopts lead-antimony alloy, lead-antimony-arsenic alloy, lead-calcium alloy, lead-calcium-nickel-chromium alloy or silver-lead-calcium alloy.

The thickness of the electrode plate affects the performance and service life of the battery. Using thin electrode plate can improve the performance of the battery under the condition of ensuring the mechanical strength. To improve the discharge current, several elec-

trode plates with the same polarity are connected into a group by a linking strip, and the electrode plates of the positive plate group and the negative plate group are intersected. Generally the negative plate group has one more plate than the positive plate group, and the positive plate is sandwiched between the negative plates, which can reduce the loss of active substance of the positive plate. The structure is shown in Figure 2-3.

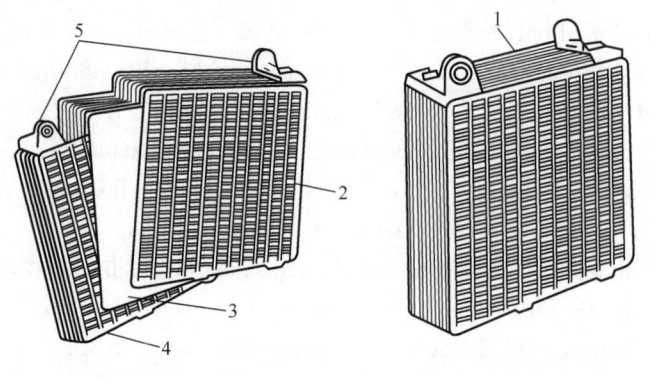

Figure 2-3   Structure of Electrode Plate Group

1—Electrode plate assembly; 2—Negative plate; 3—Clapboard; 4—Positive plate; 5—Lead linking strip

(2) Clapboard. The clapboard is located between the positive and negative plates. In addition to having good insulation to prevent short circuit of the plates, it has good permeability to make the electrolyte permeate freely, and it has acid resistance and anti-oxidation performance. Therefore, the clapboard is usually made of microporous rubber, microporous plastic, glass fiber and other materials. The new-type battery uses the bag microporous plastic clapboard, and wraps the positive plate to prevent the active substance on the positive plate from falling off.

(3) Electrolyte. Electrolyte is a dilute sulfuric acid solution made of pure sulfuric acid with a density of $1.84g/cm^3$ and distilled water in a fixed proportion. Its function is to participate in the chemical reactions and carry out energy conversion. The density of the electrolyte has a great influence on the performance of the battery. The density is generally $1.24 \sim 1.31g/cm^3$. In addition, the purity of the electrolyte is also an important factor affecting the battery performance and service life. Electrolyte must be prepared with pure special sulfuric acid and distilled water.

(4) Shell and other parts. The shell of the battery is a container for holding the electrode plates and the electrolyte. It should be acid-resistant, heat-resistant and earthquake-resistant, so it is made of hard rubber or polypropylene plastic, and is an integral structure separated by walls into several single-cell containers. The upper part of the shell is provided with a sealing cover of the same material, and the battery cover is provided with a filling hole corresponding to each single cell, which is used to add electrolyte or to replenish distilled water. The filling hole is rotated with a filling hole cover to prevent the spillage of the electrolyte. There are micro-vent holes on the filling hole cover, which can discharge the gas produced by the chemical reaction inside the battery. A filter is installed on the vent hole of the new battery filling hole to avoid water vapor escape and reduce water consumption. The top or side of the battery shell is provided with electrode terminals that provide an electrical connection to the outside, with (＋), (－) marks on the side. Generally, the positive

electrode is thicker than the negative electrode.

(Ⅳ) Working principle of the battery

Electrochemical reaction between the active substance on the battery electrode plate and the electrolyte is reversible, so the battery is a reversible power supply. The total electrochemical reaction equation of the lead-acid battery during charging and discharging is as follows.

$$PbO_2 + Pb + 2H_2SO_4 \underset{Recharge}{\overset{Discharge}{\rightleftharpoons}} 2PbSO_4 + 2H_2O$$

When the battery is discharged, the PbO_2 and Pb and H_2SO_4 on the positive and negative plates change into lead sulfate ($PbSO_4$), and attached to the positive and negative plates, and the active substance on the electrode plates decrease; the H_2SO_4 in the electrolyte decreases, the H_2O increases, and the density of the electrolyte decreases; the voltage of the battery decreases, the internal resistance increases, and the capacity decreases; the chemical energy inside the battery is converted to electric power, supplying to the electric devices.

The characteristics of the discharge end of the battery are as follows.

① The single cell voltage drops to the discharge termination voltage.

② The density of the electrolyte is reduced to the minimum permissible value. The discharge termination voltage is related to the discharge current. See Table 2-1. The larger the discharge current, the shorter the allowable discharge time and the lower the discharge termination voltage.

Table 2-1   Discharge voltage of single-cell battery

Discharge current/A	$0.05 C_{20}$	$0.1 C_{20}$	$0.25 C_{20}$	C_{20}	$3 C_{20}$
Discharge time	20h	10h	3h	25min	5min
Single-cell battery termination voltage/V	1.75	1.70	1.65	1.55	1.50

Note: C_{20} is the rated capacity of the battery.

The battery continues to discharge after discharge end, which is called over-discharge. At this time, the voltage of the battery drops sharply, and at the same time, the coarse crystalline $PbSO_4$ not easy to be reduced produces, and causes the electrode plate to be vulcanized, the storage capacity to be reduced, and the service life to be shortened. Therefore, the over-discharge should be avoided.

If the positive and negative electrodes of the DC power supply are connected to the positive and negative electrodes of the battery, when the voltage of the DC power supply is higher than the voltage of the battery, under the action of the power supply force, the current flows in from the positive electrode of the battery and flows out from the negative electrode, and the electrochemical reaction inside the battery converts electric energy into chemical energy, which is the charging process.

When the battery is charged, the $PbSO_4$ on the electrode plate changes to PbO_2 and Pb under the action of the outer power supply, the active substance on the electrode plate increases, the H_2SO_4 in the electrolyte increases, the H_2O decreases, the density of the elec-

trolyte increases, the voltage of the battery increases, the internal resistance decreases, and the capacity increases.

The battery continues to charge after charging end, which is called overcharging. At this time, $PbSO_4$ has been basically converted to PbO_2 and Pb, and the excess charging current will electrolyze water to generate O_2 and H_2. Therefore, the long-time over-charging of the battery shall be avoided and the distilled water shall be filled regularly.

Due to the change in the density of the electrolyte and the voltage at the battery terminal during charging and discharging, the degree of charging/discharging can be determined by measuring the density of the electrolyte and the voltage at the battery terminal.

(V) Technical parameters of the battery

1. Rated voltage

The rated voltage of the battery is 6V or 12V. A sedan uses a battery with a rated voltage of 12V, and the load truck with a rated voltage of 12V can use 2 12V batteries in series.

When the battery is in the state of no charge/discharge and the movement of the internal electrolyte is in equilibrium, the electromotive force at this time is called static electromotive force. The static electromotive force is related to the density and temperature of the electrolyte, which can reflect the charge state of the battery to a certain degree. The density of electrolyte always varies from 1.12 to 1.30g/m^3 when the battery is working. When selecting a battery, the rated voltage of the battery selected must have the same voltage as the automobile electrical system.

2. Rated capacity

The capacity of the battery is the main performance parameter of the battery, indicating the external power supply capacity of the battery. The capacity of a battery refers to the amount of electricity output within the permissible range of discharge, which is related to the discharge current and the temperature of the electrolyte. The capacity is equal to the product of discharge current and discharge time.

Rated capacity is an important indicator of battery quality. According to *Technical conditions*, the new battery with sufficient electricity will be discharged under the conditions that the density of the electrolyte ρ is (1.28 ± 0.01)g/cm^3 at 25℃, the initial temperature is (25 ± 5)℃, at the discharge current with 20 hours discharge rate (C/20A), when the battery is discharged to 10.5V at the battery terminal, the output power is called the rated capacity of the battery, expressed in C_{20} with the unit of Ah. C_{20} = discharge current(A) × discharge time(h). Some foreign batteries labels have 20HR, referring to the 20-hour discharge rate, of which H is Hour, R is Rate. For example, a 105Ah fully charged battery can discharge at a current of 5.25A to 10.5V, if the discharge time is more than or equal to 20h, the battery is acceptable.

It is important to select the right model of battery. If selecting a battery with the larger capacity, it will lead to insufficient charging, and if selecting a battery with the smaller capacity, it is prone to excessive charging and discharging cycle, leading to a shorter battery life.

3. Reserve capacity

Reserve Capacity (RC) means that when the charging system of an automobile fails, the battery can provide 25A constant current for electric devices, such as lighting and igni-

tion systems. According to *Technical conditions*, the discharge duration, when the battery discharges at 25A rated current constantly to the single-cell termination voltage 1.75V (the whole battery termination voltage is 10.5V) under $(25\pm2)^\circ C$, is known as the reserve capacity of the battery. The unit is min.

4. Cold cranking amperage

Cold Cranking Amperage (CCA) generally refers to the current that the battery can provide when it discharges constantly for 30s to the terminal voltage of 7.2V at $0^\circ F$ $(-18^\circ C)$, which is the performance of the battery for low temperature starting performance. When the battery is manufactured, it is designed to improve the heat-resistance or cold-resistance according to the environment temperature of the use area. The CCA value of the battery designed for the tropical area is low, and the CCA value of the battery designed for the cold area is high. When using the battery designed for cold area in the tropical area, its life is bound to be shortened. The battery with the appropriate CCA value shall be selected according to the local temperature, for example, if the local temperature is high, the battery with the low CCA value shall be selected. Because the battery is very sensitive to the temperature, generally, taking the temperature $25^\circ C$ as the base, when the temperature rises every $10^\circ C$, the life will be shortened by a half.

(VI) Model of battery

There are several standards for battery models.

Although the regulation methods of different standards are different, their main contents include the rated voltage, rated capacity, cold cranking amperage and model, reserve capacity and so on. Some batteries have CCA: 700 CA: 875 RC: 106 written on them, indicating cold cranking amperage of 700A, start current of 875A, reserve capacity of 106min; There are also some joint-venture brand batteries with GB and DIN or EN standard models, such as 6-QA-180, 12V 180 Ah 540A (EN), indicating rated voltage of 12V, rated capacity of 180Ah, cold cranking amperage of 540A.

① Japan Industrial Standard (JIS) battery model is 34B19L, its meaning is as follows:

34——the performance of a battery, indicating the amount of electricity that can be stored in the battery (battery capacity). The larger the number, the greater the amount of electricity the battery can store. You can query through Table 2-2.

Battery capacity(AH)＝discharge amperage×discharge time length

Table 2-2　Battery ID code

Battery ID code	Battery capacity(AH)(5-hour charging rate)
34B19R/L	27
46B24R/L	36
55B23R/L	48
80B26R/L	55
95B31R/L	64

B——The width and height of the battery, the width and height of the battery are represented by one of the eight letters (A to H). The closer the character is to H, the greater the width and height of the battery, as shown in Figure 2-4.

19——The length of the battery is about 19cm.

L——The position of the negative terminal, that is, the position of the negative terminal when the battery is properly installed. R is on the right and L is on the left. (Pay attention to the side near the terminal)

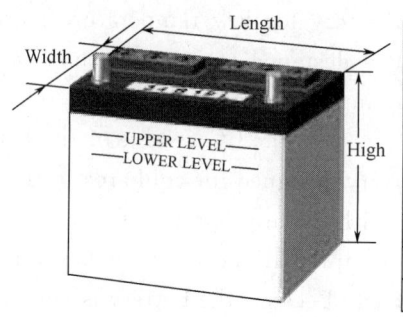

	Width /mm	High /mm
A	162	127
B	203	127 or 129
C	207	135
D	204	173
E	213	176
F	213	182
G	213	222
H	220	278

Figure 2-4   Height and Width of Battery

② European (EN) standard battery model is 544　059　036, its meaning is as follows.

5——voltage, 1~4 means the battery voltage is 6V, and 5~7 means the battery voltage is 12V.

44——the rated capacity of the battery, representing a rated capacity at 20 hours of continuous discharge. If the battery capacity is greater than 100 Ah, the first figure will add 1.

059——serial number.

036—— according to EN standard 1/10 cold start test current, 036 indicates that the current is 360A.

Although the battery models produced by different manufacturers are applicable to different standards, but as long as the key technical parameters, type and size are appropriate, they can be substituted for each other.

(Ⅶ) Maintenance-free battery

Lead-calcium alloy or lead-antimony alloy is used in the positive plate grid frame of the maintenance-free battery, and lead-calcium alloy is used in the negative plate grid frame, which improves the deposition potential of oxygen in the positive electrode and hydrogen in the negative electrode, so that the battery loses less water in use, and it is not necessary to replenish distilled water during the specified life period. The maintenance-free battery generally uses the ultra-fine glass fiber cotton to make the clapboard or put the positive plate in the bag clapboard. With the improvement of these structures, it can ensure that the battery has less self-discharge, the charge-holding capacity is enhanced and the life of the electrode plate is prolonged.

The maintenance-free battery usually uses a fully enclosed shell with the electrode outside to prevent impurities from invading and moisture from evaporating. The upper cover

plate of the maintenance-free battery is provided with a labyrinth liquid-gas separation structure with a central vent hole containing catalyst palladium and a re-ignition (reverse arc) protection device called "Fritte". The former can not only cool the water vapor and sulphuric acid vapor produced during the charging process and collect and return it, but also reduce hydrogen and oxygen to water by palladium catalysis to avoid the loss of electrolyte; the latter is a circular glass fiber mat with a diameter of about 15mm and a thickness of 2mm, which can prevent the invasion of foreign sparks.

When the maintenance-free battery is charged, a small amount of gas will still overflow from the central vent hole on the cover, so the maintenance-free battery is generally connected to the vent hose to drain the gas out of the automobile. Do not unplug or block the hose during the maintenance to ensure the normal exhaust of the battery.

Compared with the ordinary battery, the maintenance-free battery only eliminates the work of adding distilled water and adjusting the liquid level of electrolyte, and does not eliminate the work of all maintenance.

Generally, the maintenance-free battery has a built-in temperature compensation densitometer, commonly known as the electric eye, also known as the battery state indicator. There are two kinds of electric eye structures, one is a single-color ball, the other is a two-color ball. The electric eye of the single-color ball is to use the green float ball to sink and float in the electrolyte of different density, and then display the ring figure of corresponding color in the observation window through the refraction and amplification of the color bar to judge the charge state of the battery. By observing the color of the observation window of the electric eye, we can judge the technical condition of the battery. Generally, green means that the battery is enough; dark green or black means that the battery is not enough, it needs to be recharged; colorless or light yellow means that the electrolyte is not enough, it should be scrapped or replaced. The electric eye structure of the single-color ball is shown in Figure 2-5.

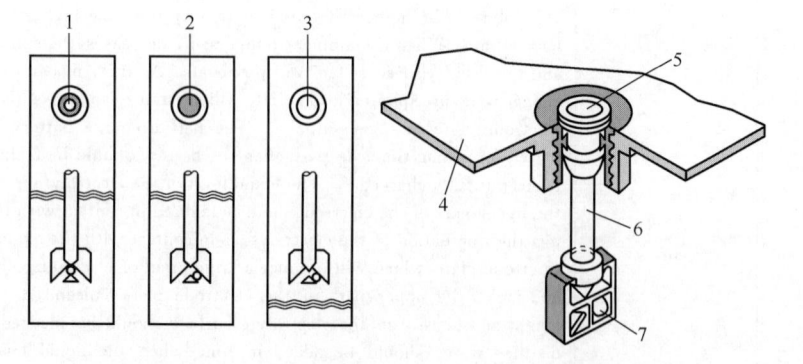

Figure 2-5　Electric Eye Structure of the Single-color Ball

1—Green (charging 65% or higher); 2—Black (charging less than 65%); 3—Colorless or yellow (battery failure);
4—Battery cover; 5—Observation window; 6—Optical charge status indicator; 7—Green float ball

The electric eye structure of the two-color ball is shown in Figure 2-6. This kind of battery electric eye is equipped with red and blue two kinds of small balls, also use two kinds of color float balls to sink or float in the electrolyte of different density, and then display the ring figure of corresponding color in the observation window through the refraction and am-

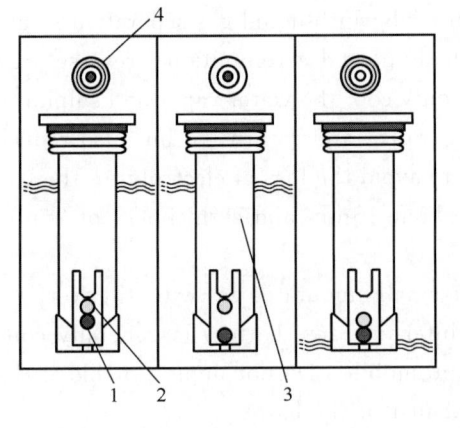

Figure 2-6　Electric Eye Structure of
the Two-color ball

1—Blue ball; 2—Red ball; 3—Color bar;
4—Observation window

plification of the color bar to judge the charge state of the battery.

(Ⅷ) Common failures and trouble-shooting of batteries

The common faults of battery can be divided into external faults and internal faults. The external faults are obvious, which can be seen directly. The external faults include shell crack, sealant dry crack, electrode column corrosion or loosening, etc. Internal faults cannot be seen visually, and can be found in use. Internal faults mainly include electrode plate vulcanization, electrode plate short circuit, self discharge and so on. The characteristics, causes and troubleshooting of common internal faults are shown in Table 2-3.

Table 2-3　Characteristics, Causes and Troubleshooting of common Internal Faults

Name	Item	Specification
Electrode plate vulcanization	Characteristics	The insoluble white coarse crystalline lead sulfate is produced on the electrode plate and cannot be converted into active substance when charged normally. When the battery with a fault is discharged, the voltage drops sharply to the termination voltage early and the battery capacity decreases. The density of the electrolyte is lower than the normal value. When the battery is charged, the single-cell voltage rises too fast, and the temperature of the electrolyte rises rapidly, but the density increases slowly, causing bubbles too early, and even bubbles when charged
	Causes	① After long-term insufficient charging or the untimely charging after the discharge, the lead sulfate on the electrode plate is partially dissolved in the electrolyte. The higher the ambient temperature, the higher the solubility of lead sulfate. When the ambient temperature decreases, the solubility decreases and the dissolved lead sulfate will precipitate. As the temperature of the battery changes, the precipitated lead sulfate will crystallize and precipitate again on the electrode plate to form sulphide. The half-discharge battery should not be placed for a long time. In particular, the battery should be recharged regularly to keep it fully charged. ② The liquid level of the electrolyte is too low, so that the upper part of the electrode plate is oxidized in contact with the air. In driving, the fluctuation of the electrolyte is in contact with the oxidized part of the electrode plate, which will produce a large grain of lead sulfate hardening layer and make the upper part of the electrode plate vulcanized. Therefore, the height and density of the electrolyte surface should be checked regularly, and distilled water should be added in time when the liquid level is lowered. ③ Long-term excessive discharge or small current deep discharge cause that lead sulfate is generated in the pores of the active substance in the deep of the electrode plate. The battery can not be excessively discharged. The time connecting the starter should not exceed 5s per time, to avoid low-temperature high-current discharge. ④ The new battery is not fully charged at first, and the active substance is not fully reduced. ⑤ The density of the electrolyte is too high, and the composition is not pure
	Troubleshooting	Mild vulcanized battery can be treated by charging with small current and changing distilled water. Devulcanized charging method can be used to eliminate vulcanization if the vulcanization is serious.

026　Automobile Electrical Equipment Maintenance

Continued

Name	Item	Specification
Active substance exfoliation	Characteristics	The positive active substance lead dioxide falls off, brown material can be seen from the filling hole when charging, and the electrolyte is turbid, which will reduce the capacity of the battery.
	Causes	① The charging current of the battery is too big, and the temperature of the electrolyte is too high, making the active substance expand, soft and easy to fall off. ② The battery is often overcharged, and a large amount of gas escapes from the pores of the electrode plate, causing pressure in the pore of the electrode plate and causing the active substance to fall off. ③ The battery is often discharged at low temperature and high current, causing the electrode plate to bend and deform, and the active substance to fall off. ④ The vibration during driving is inevitable
	Troubleshooting	If there is less sediment, it can be removed and continued to use; if there is more sediment, new electrode plate and electrolyte should be replaced
Electrode plate short circuit	Characteristics	The positive and negative plates of the battery come into direct contact or are overlapped by other conductive materials, called the electrode plate short circuit. The phenomenon of this fault is that the terminal voltage picks up relatively slowly when the battery is charged. If the terminal voltage is measured by the battery discharge, the voltage is very low and will drop rapidly to 0. The temperature of the electrolyte increases rapidly, the relative specific gravity rises slowly, and there are few bubbles at the end of charging.
	Causes	① Destruction of the clapboard makes the positive and negative plates come into direct contact; ② Excessive deposition of the active substance leads to the connection of the positive and negative plates; ③ Bend of the electrode plate group, or excessive discharge of the lead battery, or excessive loss of the active substance of the electrode plate, or containing impurities in the battery; ④ Conductive objects fall into the electrolyte.
	Troubleshooting	When the electrode plate short-circuit occurs, the battery must be taken apart and checked to find out the reason of the electrode plate short-circuit. Either replace the broken clapboard, or remove the deposited active substance, or correct or replace the bent electrode plate group, etc.
Self-discharge	Characteristics	When the battery is in open-circuit state, the phenomenon of natural loss of its capacity is called self-discharge. Generally, the well-maintained and fully-charged battery needs to be placed for 28 days at $20 \sim 30\,℃$, if its capacity loss is more than 20%, which is called too large self-discharge.
	Causes	① The electrolyte is impure, the potential difference between the impurity and the electrode plate and between the different impurities attached to the electrode plate is formed, and the partial discharge is produced by the electrolyte. ② Long-term storage of the battery and the sinking of the sulfuric acid make the upper and power parts of the electrode form a potential difference, then causing self-discharge. ③ The overflowing electrolyte accumulates on the surface of the battery cover, connecting the positive and negative electrodes. ④ The active substance of the battery falls off, and too much sediment in the lower part makes the electrode plate short-circuited
	Troubleshooting	The battery should be fully discharged, the electrolyte shall be poured out, the battery shall be cleaned with distilled water, and added with a new electrolyte, the it can be used after fully charging

Ⅲ. Item Implementation

（Ⅰ） Safe use, inspection, maintenance, charging and testing of the battery

① Through the implementation of this item, we should be able to use the battery safely and correctly, and master the methods and steps to inspect and maintain the battery.

② The item should be equipped with common types of battery and multimeter, suction densitometer, high-rate discharge meter, charger and other testing and maintenance equipment.

（Ⅱ） Implementation steps

1. Precautions for safe, correct use and operation of the battery

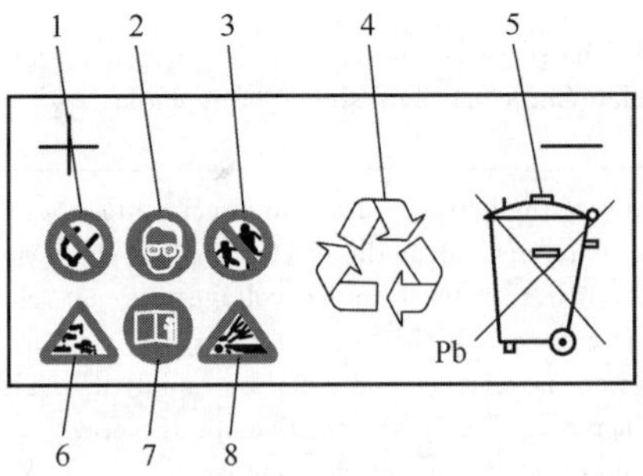

Figure 2-7　Battery Warning Icon

1—No open fire; 2—Wear protective glasses;
3—No contact with children; 4—Recyclable;
5—Can not be discarded as garbage;
6—Corrosion hazard; 7—3 Please read
instructions; 8—Explosion hazard

① Warning instructions and safety regulations for batteries. Because the inside of the battery is acid liquid, when charging, it will release combustible gas. So we should use it carefully. Generally, a battery is marked with a safety warning icon, as shown in Figure 2-7, and should be used as required.

② When connecting or disconnecting the battery cable, battery charger or jumper cable, the ignition switch must be in OFF or LOCK position, and all electrical loads must be in OFF, unless otherwise specified in the operating procedure, otherwise it will damage the electronic devices on the automobile.

③ The current intensity generated by the short circuit of the battery electrode is enough to cause burns, so it is necessary to prevent the metal tool from grounding, resulting in the battery short-circuit.

④ Avoid excessive charge and discharge cycle and long-term discharge. This has great damage to the active substance of the electrode plate, which will greatly shorten the service life of the battery.

⑤ Don't apply grease on the battery electrode, tighten the battery electrode bolt according to the required torque without applying excessive force.

⑥ The polarity of the battery ground must be with the generator, and must not be misconnected.

⑦ When disconnecting the connection of the battery, the negative electrode should be first disconnected and then the positive electrode should be disconnected. When connecting the battery, the sequence should be reverse.

⑧ For a battery with a central exhaust hose, the hose must be connected directly to the battery and keep the hose unobstructed.

⑨ High current discharge, deep charge/discharge and long-term deficit idle are the most negative factors that affect the service life of the battery, so it should be avoided.

2. Inspection and maintenance of the battery

Before installation, check whether the model of the battery to be used is in conformity with the model of the automobile, and whether the density and height of the electrolyte are in conformity with the regulations.

Keep the outer surface of the battery clean and dry. Leakage of the electrolyte will produce white lead sulfate and yellow iron sulfate paste on the electrode, which are highly corrosive.

Remove oxide from electrode and cable clip in time.

① The electrode clips shall be fastened according to the specified torque to ensure good contact with the electrode.

② Keep the air vent hole on the filling hole cover unobstructed and dredged regularly.

③ When the battery is charged, the filling hole cover should be opened to make the gas escape smoothly so as to avoid accidents.

④ Periodically check and adjust the liquid level of the electrolyte, if the liquid level is insufficient, the distilled water should be added.

⑤ If the automobile is running for 1,000km or 5～6 days in summer and 10～15 days in winter, the discharge degree of the battery should be checked. When the discharge exceeds 25% in winter and 50% in summer, the battery should be removed from the automobile in time for additional charge.

3. Battery charging

（1）Method of charging. There are three methods to charge the battery: constant voltage charging, constant current charging and fast charging.

In an automobile, the generator charges the battery at a constant voltage. When charging at constant voltage, the initial current of charging is larger, and it can reach 90%～95% of the rated capacity in 4～5 hours. With the increase of the battery electromotive force, the charging current decreases gradually to 0. Because the charging time is short, there is no need to adjust the charging current. It is suitable for additional charge. Generally, the charging voltage of the single-cell battery is 2.5V. The charging voltage of 12V battery is （14.8±0.05）V.

The charging current of constant current charging is kept constant. When charging with constant current, the charging voltage should be increased gradually with the increase of the battery electromotive force. In order to shorten the charging time, the charging process is usually divided into two stages. In the first stage, a large charging current is used to make the capacity of the battery recover rapidly. When the voltage of a single-cell battery reaches 2.4V and the electrolysis water begins to produce bubbles, then it turns to the second stage. the charging current is reduced by one-half until it is fully charged. The charging current should be chosen according to the capacity of the battery. If the charging current is too large, it will reduce the performance of the battery; if the charging current is too small, it will make the charging time too long.

Fast charging is to use a special fast charging motor for charging, it only takes 0.5～1.5 hours to recharge, which greatly shortens the charging time and improves the charging efficiency. The disadvantage is that the battery can't be fully charged and affects the life of the battery. Fast charging is suitable for battery concentration, frequent charging and emer-

gency situations. At present, the commonly used fast charging methods include pulse fast charging and large current decreasing charging.

(2) The charging process of the battery. Generally, the battery should be charged in the range of 5~35℃, below 5℃ or above 35℃ will reduce the service life. The set voltage of charging should be within the specified range. If it is beyond the specified range, the battery will be damaged, the capacity will be reduced and the service life will be shortened.

During storage, transportation and installation, the battery will lose part of its capacity due to self-discharge. Therefore, the residual capacity of the battery should be judged according to the open-circuit voltage of the battery after it is installed and before it is put into use, and then the battery should be recharged by different methods. The reserve battery should be recharged once every 3 months. In addition, in the normal use of the automobile, insufficient battery power caused by improper use or the failure of the charging system is also known as additional charge. The charging time depends on how much power is missing from the battery.

4. Technical state detection of the battery

(1) Measuring the liquid level of the battery electrolyte. Measure the liquid level to determine if the electrolyte is adequate. The liquid level of the battery electrolyte should be higher than 10~15mm on the upper of the clapboard. For a battery with a shell having height indicator lines, the liquid level can be externally observed, and the normal liquid level should be between two lines. When the liquid level is too low, the distilled water should be replenished.

For a fully enclosed maintenance-free battery with an opaque shell, the liquid level of the electrolyte cannot and does not need to be measured.

(2) Measuring the electrolyte density of the battery. Measuring the electrolyte density can be used to determine the discharge degree of the battery. Electrolyte density can be measured with a special suction densitometer, as shown in Figure 2-17. When the density of the electrolyte is measured, the battery should be in a stable state. After charging, discharging or adding distilled water, the battery should be placed for 0.5h before measuring.

It is not necessary to measure the density of the electrolyte for a fully enclosed maintenance-free battery with an opaque shell.

The density of the electrolyte can also be measured by a special freezing point tester, and YDT-4T freezing point tester and its construction is as shown in Figure 2-8.

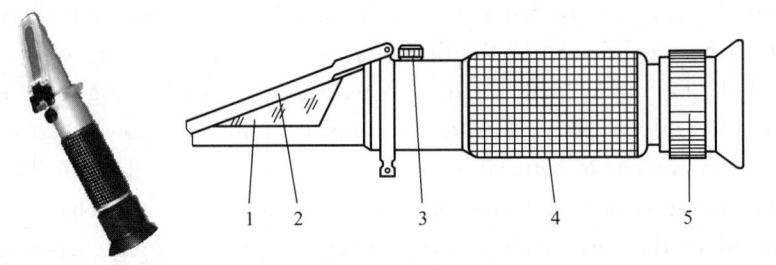

Figure 2-8　YDT-4T Freezing Point Tester

1—Prism; 2—Cover plate; 3—Correction nail; 4—Handle grip; 5—Eyepiece

The field of view of the YDT-4T freezing point tester is shown in Figure 2-9.

Description on the field of view of the YDT-4T freezing point tester: The left measur-

ing scale measures the density of the BATTERY FLUID; 1.10~1.20 denotes RECHARGE; 1.20~ 1.25 denotes FAIR; and 1.25 ~ 1.30 denotes GOOD. The intermediate scale measures the freezing point of antifreeze fluid, ETHYLENE GLYCOL antifreeze fluid, PROPYLENE GLYCOL antifreeze fluid; this test needs to be selected according to the symbol on the coolant replenishment tank. The right measuring scale measures the freezing points of glass water and glass cleaning agent.

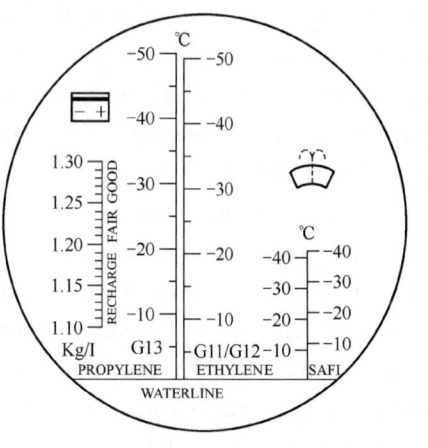

Figure 2-9　The Field of View if the YDT-4T Freezing Point Tester

According to the density of the electrolyte to determine the discharge degree, when the density drops $0.01g/cm^3$ per time, the battery discharges 6%, when the battery discharges in the summer more than 50%, in winter more than 25%, it should be timely recharged, otherwise the battery will be early damaged.

According to the difference of the electrolyte density of each single-cell battery, the failure of the battery is judged. If each single-cell battery has the same density, even if the density is low, the battery generally can be recharged to restore its capacity. If the density difference between single-cell battery is more than $0.05g/cm^3$, the battery will fail.

(3) Measuring the open-circuit voltage of the battery. The open-circuit voltage of the battery is measured to determine the discharge degree of the battery. When measuring, the battery is disconnected, the multimeter is placed in the voltage gear, and the positive and negative pens of the multimeter are respectively connected to the positive and negative electrodes of the battery. The relationship between open-circuit voltage of the battery and storage state of the battery is shown in Table 2-4. The battery should be in a static state when measuring. After charging, discharging or adding distilled water, the battery should be placed for 0.5 h or longer before measuring.

Table 2-4　Relationship between Storage State and Open-circuit Voltage of Battery

Storage state/%	100	75	50	25	0
Open-circuit voltage/V	above 12.6	12.4	12.2	12.0	under 11.9

(4) Measuring the discharge voltage of the battery. Measuring the discharge voltage of the battery is to measure the terminal voltage of the battery when it is discharged by starting current, and to judge the technical status, discharge degree and starting ability of the battery. High-rate discharge meter can be used for measurement or the on-board start-up measurement is carried out.

The high-rate discharge meter is an instrument which simulates the working state of the starter and detects the capacity of the battery. It consists of a voltmeter and a load resistor. When the high-rate discharge meter is connected to the battery, the battery discharges to the load resistor and the discharge current can reach more than 100A. The positive and negative discharge needles of the high-rate discharge meter are pressed respectively on the posi-

Item II　Test and Maintenance of Battery　**031**

tive and negative electrodes of the battery, to keep 15s. If the voltage is above 9.6V and is stable, the performance is good; if the voltage is stable from 10.6 to 11.6V, the storage is sufficient; if the voltage is stable from 9.6 to 10.6 V, the storage is insufficient, the battery should be recharged; if the voltage drops rapidly, the battery fails and should be repaired or replaced.

When starting an automobile, the uninterrupted use of the starter may cause the battery to be damaged by over-discharge. The correct method to use it is that the total length of each start-up is not more than 5s, and the interval between start-up and start-up is not less than 15s. Once the automobile can not be started, we can use another battery with sufficient power temporarily for emergency jumper connection. As shown in Figure 2-10, the sequence of the jumper connection is ①, ②, ③, ④; The removal of jumper wires is carried out in the opposite order.

5. Leakage inspection of storage battery

In general, when the battery is found to be insufficient after several hours of storage, leakage inspection must be carried out. Inspection method: remove the negative connector of the battery, measure the battery voltage, and record.

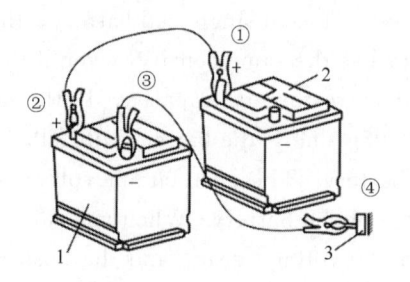

Figure 2-10　Emergency jumper connection
1—Emergency battery; 2—Fault automobile
battery; 3—Ground point of the fault automobile

Figure 2-11　Battery Cut-off Protection Device
1—Battery positive electrode;
2—Battery detonating device

IV. Knowledge and Skills Expansion

(I) Battery cut-off protection device of the battery

Some batteries are in the rear of the automobile, but the starter and the generator are installed in the front of the automobile with the engine. To avoid the danger of fire due to short circuit when the automobile collides, the cut-off protection device for the battery is installed in the positive electrode of the battery. The device is realized by the airbag control unit. Each time when the airbag or the safety belt tensioner is triggered, a pin with a piston is activated in the inside of the battery cut-off protection device. Thus the wires of the starter and the generator are disconnected from the automobile battery. The battery cut-off protection device is shown in Figure 2-11.

(II) Battery monitoring device

Some automobiles are equipped with battery monitoring device, which is installed at the negative electrode of the battery. The function is to measure the charging and discharging current, voltage and temperature of the automobile battery. The measurement values of the

current, voltage and temperature of the battery can be read by a special diagnostic instrument. The battery monitoring device is shown in Figure 2-12.

1. Current measurement of the battery

Measure the current on the negative electrode of the battery. The total current flowing into the negative electrode will flow through the shunt resistor inside the battery monitoring unit. The resistance of this shunt resistor is milliohm. (This resistance value must be very small to ensure that the power loss and the heat produced are as small as possible.) The voltage drop on this shunt resistor is proportional to the current flowing through it. The CPU can measure the voltage drop and calculate the current flowing into or out of the battery.

Figure 2-12   Battery Monitoring Device
1—Battery positive electrode;
2—Battery monitoring unit;
3—Battery negative electrode

2. Voltage measurement of the battery

Measure the voltage of the battery directly on the positive electrode of the battery. A measuring wire is connected from the positive electrode of the battery to the monitoring and control unit of the battery.

3. Temperature measurement of the battery

The measurement of the battery temperature requires the use of the NTC temperature sensor in the battery module. Because the battery data module is fixed directly on the battery, the temperature measured here is reliable and then processed by the software.

Summary

(1) The battery is an important power supply component of an automobile, we must grasp its relevant theoretical knowledge, safe use, detection and maintenance skills.

(2) To use, check and maintain the battery correctly.

(3) The charging of the battery shall be done strictly as required by the operation specifications so as not to damage the battery.

Thinking and Practice

(1) Please briefly describe the composition and structure of the battery.

(2) Please describe the working principle of the charging and discharging process of the battery.

(3) What are the common technical parameters of batteries? What do they interpret?

(4) What are the common faults of the battery? How to use correctly to avoid these faults?

(5) What are the precautions for the safe use of the battery?

(6) What are the items for testing the technical conditions of the battery?

(7) How to charge the battery?

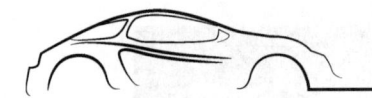

Item III

Overhaul of Charging System

I. Scene Introduction

A PASSAT, when driving at night, its headlight suddenly went out. After overhauling, the generator worked normally, so it was suspected that the generator regulator had failed. Then the regulator was tested by the testing equipment. It turned out that the regulator was damaged. In this case, the automobile bulb is damaged by the too high instantaneous voltage caused by the failure of the voltage regulator of the charging system.

Many owners do not pay attention to the indicator lights of the charging system on the dashboard. Here, let's learn about the charging system and alternator in the automobile electrical system.

II. Related Knowledge

With the continuous improvement of automobile performance, more and more electric devices are used in the automobile. Therefore, the generator is required to have a large output power. Generally, the power of the automobile generator can reach 1,200 W. The main function of the battery is to start the engine and act as a backup power source when the engine is working. In the normal operation of the engine, the generator supplies power to all electric devices of the automobile, at the same time, the generator has to recharge the battery to ensure that the battery has enough power. Meanwhile, the voltage regulator on the generator ensures that the voltage output is stable within a certain range, to prevent excessive voltage fluctuations to burn the electric devices. The positions of the components of the charging system is shown in Figure 3-1.

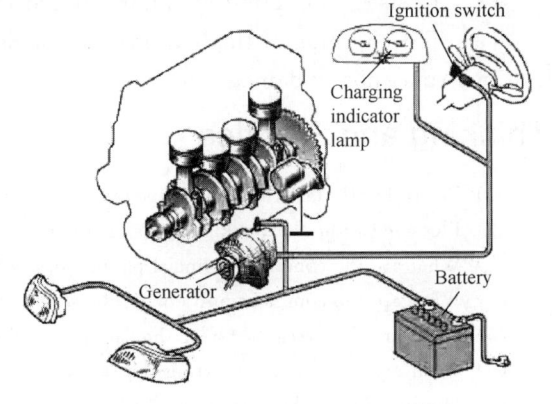

Figure 3-1 The Positions of the Components of Charging System

(I) Overview of charging system

With the increasing number of electronic devices in the automobiles, the charging system shows its importance rapidly. Whether the various electronic control systems work properly or not depends entirely on the charging condition of the battery and the current gen-

034 Automobile Electrical Equipment Maintenance

erated when the automobile is running.

The charging system of the automobile generally consists of the following parts: battery, generator, voltage regulator, warning light, ignition switch, wire and cable. The battery and the generator are parallel in the automobile circuit, the generator is the main power supply and the battery is the auxiliary power supply.

When the ignition switch is in the ON position, the battery provides the power needed for starting. During engine start-up, the power supply of the electrical system used in the automobile is also provided by the battery. After the engine starts, the generator not only charges the battery, maintains the normal charging level, but also supplies power to the electric devices used in the automobile.

The generator used in the automobile is a three-phase alternator, which is mainly composed of a three-phase synchronous alternator and a silicon diode rectifier, so it is also called a silicon rectifier generator, or alternator for short. At present, the alternator used in the automobile can be divided into two categories according to the setting position of the regulator: a category is known as the ordinary rectifier generator whose regulator is installed separately, which is currently less used in the automobiles; the other category is known as the integral silicon rectifier generator whose regulator is installed in the generator, which is currently widely used.

Since the generator is mostly driven by the engine through a drive belt, the output voltage of the generator changes as the engine speed changes. In order to meet the constant voltage requirement of electric devices and charging battery, the charging system is equipped with a voltage regulator, which can adjust the excitation current of the generator and keep the generator output stable voltage when the speed and load change. If the output of the generator is not controlled, its voltage will exceed the safety limit of the automobile circuit. A voltage regulator is applied to the automobile so that the output of the generator is about 14V. To keep the driver informed of the generator status, many automobile dashboards are equipped with indicator lights or ammeters.

(II) Construction of alternator

1. Classification of alternator

(1) Alternators are divided into 6 categories by the overall structures.

① Ordinary alternators, (need to be equipped with voltage regulators when in use) such as JF132.

② Integral alternators, (the generator and the regulator are integrated to form a whole generator) such as JFZ1913.

③ Alternators with a pump, (the generators are installed with the brake systems of automobiles by vacuum booster pumps) such as JFZB292.

④ Brushless alternators (generators without brushes), such as JFW 1913.

⑤ Permanent magnet alternators (generators made of permanent magnet poles), such as JFW1712.

⑥ Water-cooled alternators (no cooling fan, water-cooled system, generally used in race automobiles).

(2) Alternators are divided into 5 categories by the structures of the rectifiers.

① 6-pipe alternators, such as JF1522 (for Dongfeng Motor).

② 8-pipe alternators, such as JFZ1542 (for Tianjin Xiali Automobile).

③ 9-pipe alternators, such as Japan Hitachi LR1140-803, Beijing BJ1022 JFZ141.

④ 11-pipe alternators, such as JFZ1913Z (for Audi, Santana Motor).

⑤ 12-pipe alternators, such as Toyota Highlander individual engine installation.

(3) Alternators are divided into 2 categories by the form of magnetic field winding ground.

① Internal ground alternators. One terminal (negative electrode) of the magnetic field winding is grounded and connected directly with the shell, which is seldom used at present.

② External ground alternators. One terminal (negative electrode) of the magnetic field winding is connected to the regulator, and then is grounded through the regulator. At present, integral generators are widely used in the form of external ground.

2. Structure of alternator

At present, the silicon rectifier generators for automobiles produced at home and abroad have been improved in manufacturing processes, local structures and working performances, with the different forms, but the structures are basically the same, mainly composed of rotor, stator, rectifier, front end cover, back end cover, pulley and fan. Figure 3-2 shows the component diagram of the JFZ1913Z alternator, and Figure 3-3 shows the structure diagram of the JF132 alternator.

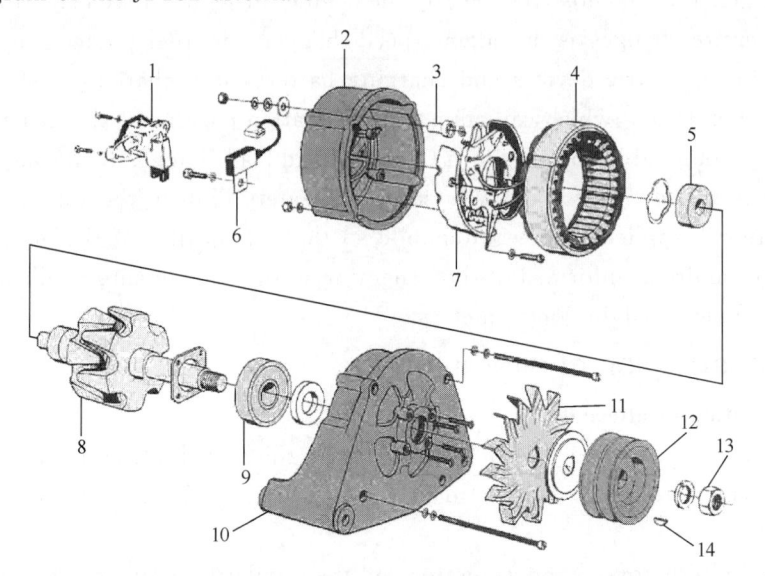

Figure 3-2　Components of JFZ1913Z Alternator

1—Voltage regulator and brush; 2—Back end cover; 3—Insulator; 4—Stator; 5—Bearing; 6—Capacitor;
7—Diode assembly; 8—Rotor; 9—Bearing; 10—Front end cover; 11—Cooling fan; 12—Belt pulley;
13—Nut; 14—Woodruff key

(1) The rotor. The rotor of an alternator is the magnetic electrode part of the generator, which is used to produce magnetic field. It is made up of slip ring, rotor shaft, claw pole, magnet yoke, magnetic field winding and so on, which is shown in Figure 3-4.

Two six-claw magnetic electrodes made of low carbon steel are pressed on the rotor shaft. The cavity of the claw pole is provided with a magnet yoke and is wound by a magnet-

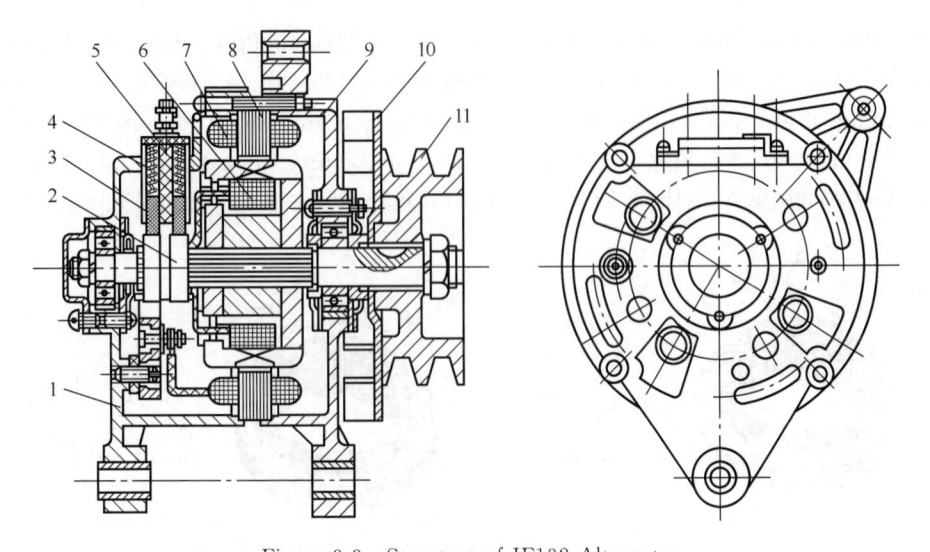

Figure 3-3　Structure of JF132 Alternator

1—Back end cover; 2—Slip ring; 3—Brush; 4—Brush spring; 5—Brush frame; 6—Magnetic field winding; 7—Armature winding; 8—Armature core; 9—Front end cover; 10—Fan; 11—Pulley

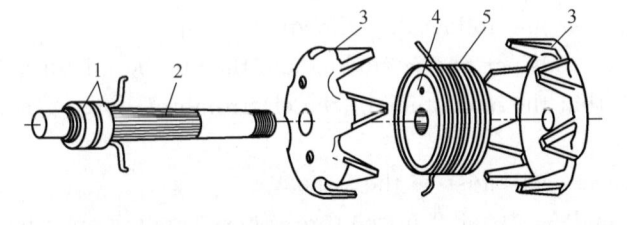

Figure 3-4　Rotor of Alternator

1—Slip ring; 2—Rotor shaft; 3—Claw pole; 4—Magnet yoke; 5—Magnetic field winding

ic field winding. The two end outgoing wires of the magnetic field winding are welded to the collector rings (two copper slip rings) insulated from the shaft. The two brushes come into contact with the slip rings and direct current is introduced into the magnetic field winding (the current is called the excitation current of the generator). When the excitation current flows into the magnetic field winding, the magnetic field winding produces a magnetic field, one of the magnetized claw poles is N, the other is S, forming alternating N, S magnetic electrodes, then formed 4~8 pairs of magnetic electrodes. Most of domestic alternators have 6 pairs of magnetic electrodes.

　　As the rotor rotates, a rotating magnetic field is formed. The aim of the design of the rotor claw pole to a beak shape is to make the magnetic field sinusoidal, so that the induction electromotive force generated by the armature winding has a good sine wave shape.

　　(2) The stator. The stator of an alternator is the armature part of the generator, and its function is to produce an AC electromotive force, which consists of a stator core and a symmetric three-phase armature winding. The stator core consists of overlapped ring-shaped silicon steel sheets with wire slots, which are insulated from each other. The three-phase independent three-phase symmetrical stator coil is embedded in the wire slot. When the rotor rotates, the stator coil cuts the magnetic line of the rotating magnetic field to produce three-phase AC electromotive force. The connection methods of three-phase winding can be divided into two kinds: star (Y-shaped) connection and triangle (△-shaped) connection, usu-

ally using star connection. Star connection can also produce enough power when the generator rotates at low speed, so it is widely used in automobile silicon rectifier generator. The stator winding of alternators of automobiles such as Santana and Audi adopts star connection, while the stator winding of automobiles such as Beijing Cherokee adopts triangle connection. The connection method of stator and stator winding is shown in Figure 3-5.

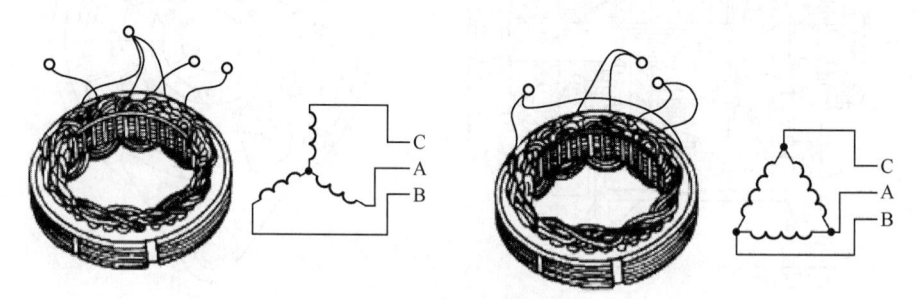

Figure 3-5   Connection Method of Stator and Stator Winding

In order to ensure that the armature three-phase winding produces the symmetric electromotive force with equal size and phase difference of 120° (electrical angle), the winding of three-phase winding should follow the following principles.

① The number of coils per phase winding and the number of turns per coil shall be exactly equal to ensure that the magnitude of the electromotive force generated by each phase winding is equal.

② The pitch of each coil must be the same.

③ The starting end A, B and C of the three-phase winding must be arranged 120° apart in the stator slot.

The end of each coil of a triangle winding is connected to the end of the other winding to form a closed series circuit. For Y-shaped winding, a series circuit is formed by every 2 coil windings, and the common point of the 3 windings is the neutral point. The Y-shaped winding is commonly used in generators (70A generators).

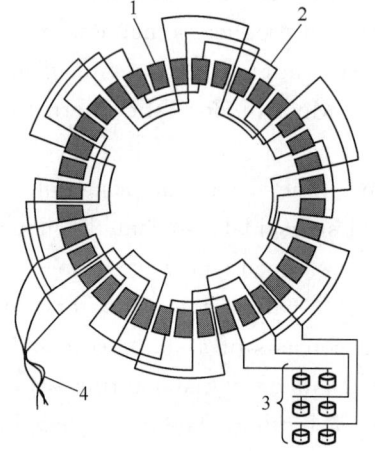

Figure 3-6   Structure of Stator Winding of JF132 Alternator

1—Stator core; 2—Stator winding;
3—Diode; 4—Stator neutral contact

Figure 3-6 shows the structure of stator winding of JF132 alternator. Figure 3-7 shows the outspread diagram of stator coils of JF132 alternator.

The generator has 6 pairs of magnetic electrodes, the total number of stator slots is 36 slots, that is, 1 pair of magnetic electrodes corresponds to 6 slots. When the rotor rotates, the rotor magnetic field continuously moves relative to the stator three-phase winding, which produces AC electromotive force in the stator winding. When winding each pair of magnetic electrodes, the induction electromotive force in the stator winding changes by one period. When winding every six slots, the induction electromotive force in the stator changes by 360°, and each slot corresponds to 60°. Therefore, the position spacing of the two effective sides of each coil is 3 slots, and the distance between the starting sides of the adjacent coils per phase

038   Automobile Electrical Equipment Maintenance

winding is 6 slots, and the mutual distance between the two starting sides of the three-phase winding can be 2, 8, 14 slots, etc.

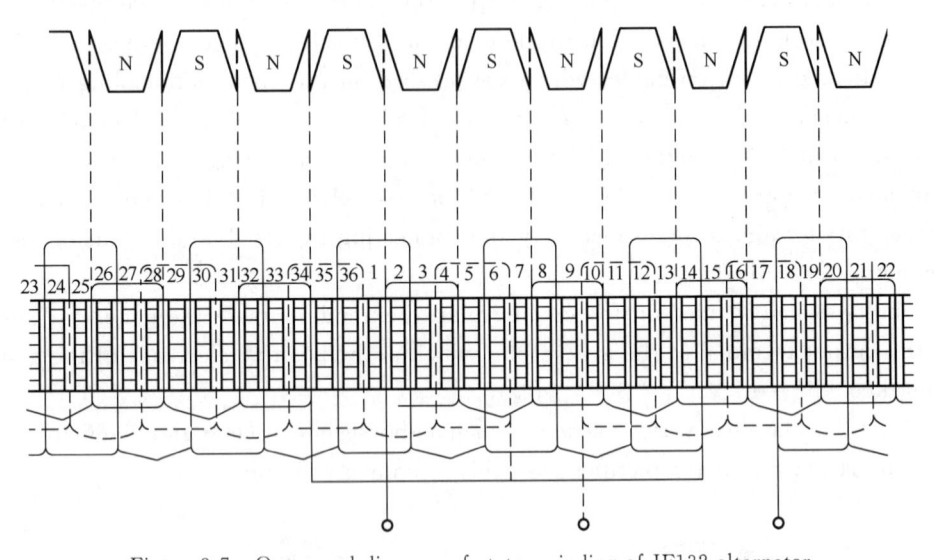

Figure 3-7　Outspread diagram of stator winding of JF132 alternator

（3）Rectifiers. Because the electrical system of the automobile uses direct current，the alternating current of the generator must be converted to direct current. This process is called rectification. It is possible to convert alternating current into direct current with a very small semiconductor diode. The diode allows the current to flow in only one direction. It is made of a pure silicon wafer that is externally doped. The diode can be either forward connected（conductive）or reverse connected（non-conductive）. These rectifiers are connected to the internal circuit of the generator so that the current flowing out of the stator coil of the generator flows only in the positive direction and prevents the current from flowing in the opposite direction.

Figure 3-8 shows a three-phase bridge rectifier circuit consisting of 6 silicon rectifier diodes. The function is to convert the three-phase alternating current generated in the three-phase winding into direct current. Some generators have 3 small-power excitation diodes and 2 neutral point diodes.

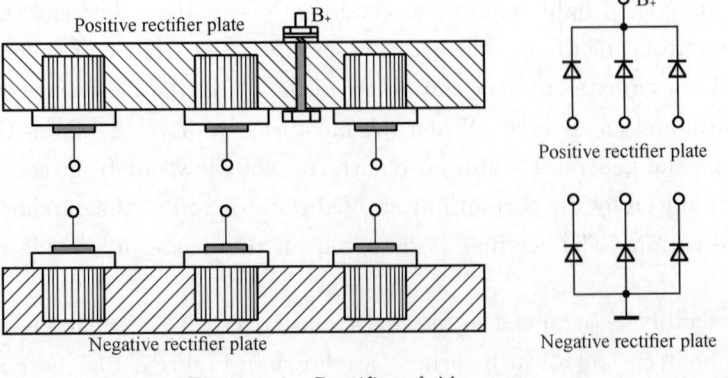

Figure 3-8　Rectifier of Alternator

Item Ⅲ　Overhaul of Charging System　**039**

The lead of the diode is one pole of the diode, and the shell part of the diode is the other pole of the diode. The shells of 3 silicon diodes which are pressed on the back end cover (or grounding cooling plate which is connected with the shell) are the positive electrode of diode, and the lead is the negative electrode of diode, which is called the negative electrode tube. The shells of 3 silicon diodes which are pressed on the insulation cooling plate of the shell are the negative electrode of diode, and the lead end is the positive electrode of the diode, which is called the positive electrode tube. A three-phase bridge full-wave rectifier circuit is formed by connecting the lead ends of 3 positive electrode tubes and 3 negative electrode tubes to 3 terminals correspondingly and connecting the A, B and C ends of the three-phase winding respectively.

The bolt, which is fixed on the cooling plate, extends outside the generator shell and acts as the output terminal of the generator, which is the positive electrode of the generator and is marked "B" (or "+", "B$_+$", etc.).

The rectifier plate has various shapes, such as horseshoe, rectangle, semicircle, etc., in which the JF132 alternator rectifier assembly is shown in Figure 3-9.

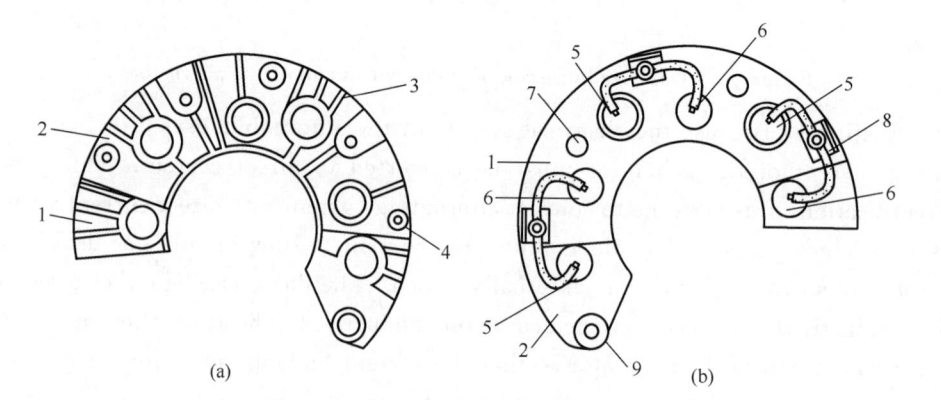

Figure 3-9　JF132 Alternator Rectifier Assembly

1—Negative rectifier plate; 2—Positive rectifier plate; 3—Cooling fin; 4—Connection bolt;
5—Positive electrode tube; 6—Negative electrode tube; 7—Installation hole; 8—Insulation pad;
9—Armature connection post mounting hole

(4) End cover and brush assembly. The front and back end covers of the alternator are made of aluminum alloy, which is a non-magnetic material, can reduce magnetic leakage and has the advantages of light weight and good heat dissipation. The end cover plays a role in fixing rotor, stator, rectifier, and brush assembly. The front end cover is cast with an installation arm, an adjustment arm and an air outlet, and the back end cover is cast with an installation arm and an air inlet. When the fan turns to drive the air to flow in from the air inlet, through the generator stator core surface, and flow out from the air outlet, take away the heat produced by the current output of the stator coil to the outside, to achieve the goal of heat dissipation. The rectifier is mounted on the inside or outside of the back end cover.

A brush assembly is arranged in the back end cover. The brush assembly includes a brush, a brush holder, and a brush spring, as shown in Figure 3-10. There are two types of brush holders, one is external type, the brush can be removed by removing the brush

spring cover from the outside of the generator, as shown in Figure 3-10(a); the other is internal type, it is necessary to remove the generator before removing the brush as shown in Figure 3-10(b). The brush is kept in contact with the slip ring on the rotor shaft by means of a spring. The external brush can be assembled, disassembled and replaced on the outside of the generator, which is convenient. Therefore, it is widely used. If the internal brush needs to be replaced, the generator must be disassembled. Because it is not convenient, it is seldom used now.

When installing the built-in brush generator, firstly, use the straight wire from the shell hole into the brush holder to press down the brush, and then follow the other steps of the ordinary generator to install, as shown in Figure 3-10(c).

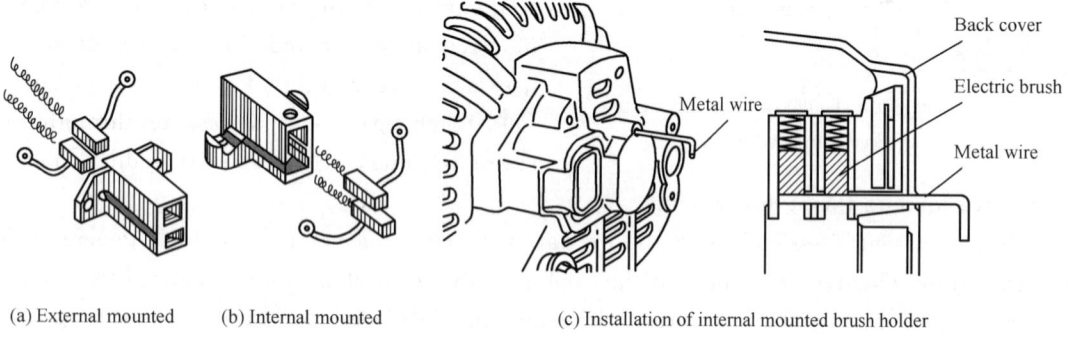

(a) External mounted   (b) Internal mounted   (c) Installation of internal mounted brush holder

Figure 3-10   Generator Brush

(5) Pulley and fan. The front end of the alternator is provided with a pulley, which is driven by the engine through a fan drive belt to drive the generator to rotate. Fan blades are arranged on the pulley that rotates the rotor of the alternator and is used for the forced ventilation and cooling of the generator [external blade type, as shown in Figure 3-11(a)]. To improve the efficiency of the generator and reduce the volume of the generator, some generator fan blades are located on its rotor [built-in blade type, as shown in Figure 3-11(b)]. Some built-in fan generators have one fan at each end of the shaft for better heat dissipation.

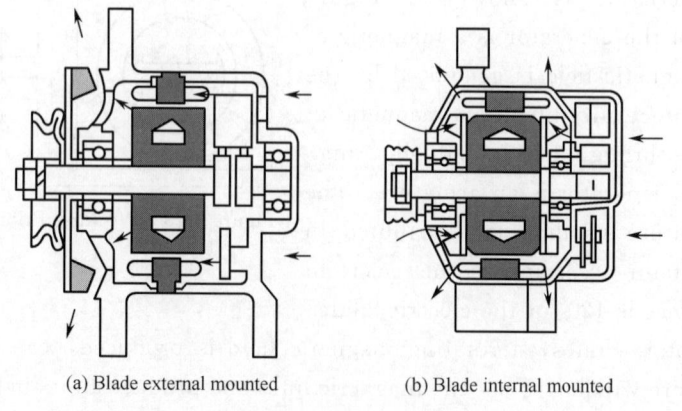

(a) Blade external mounted   (b) Blade internal mounted

Figure 3-11   Ventilation Mode of Alternator

(Ⅲ) Working principle of alternator

1. Principle of producing induction electromotive force

When a conductor rotates in the magnetic field, induction electromotive force is produced by electromagnetic induction. Bending the conductor into a frame can produce twice

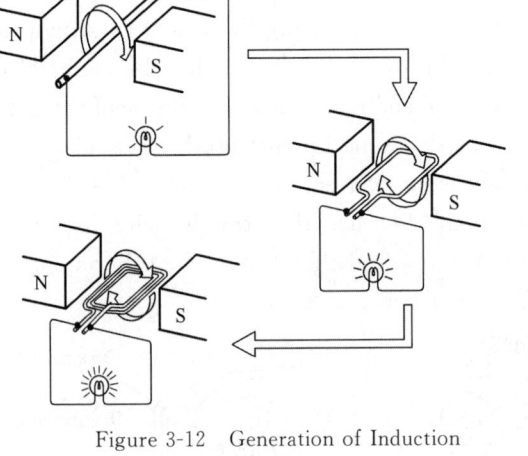

Figure 3-12　Generation of Induction Electromotive Force

the induced electromotive force; turning the conductor into a coil can produces a greater induced electromotive force; and the more turns in the coil, the greater the induction electromotive force. As shown in Figure 3-12, the larger the induction electromotive force, the brighter the bulb.

2. Power generation principle of alternator

The basic principle of generating alternating current by the alternator is the principle of electromagnetic induction. The alternator uses a rotated rotor that produces a magnetic field to change the flux passing through the stator winding, creating an AC induction electromotive force in the stator winding.

When current passes through the excitation winding, a magnetic field is generated in the excitation winding, and the two claw poles on the rotor shaft are magnetized to N and S respectively. When the rotor rotates, the magnetic electrodes alternately pass through the stator core, forming a rotating magnetic field, the relative motion between the magnetic field line and the stator winding, and the AC induced electromotive force in the three-phase winding.

In the alternator, because the rotor magnetic electrodes show like a beak shape, its magnetic field distribution is similar to sinusoidal law distribution, so the AC induction electromotive force produced in the stator winding of the generator is similar to sinusoidal law change.

The working principle of the three-phase synchronous alternator is shown in Figure 3-13. The rotor of the generator is a magnetic electrode. The magnetic field is generated by the introduction of direct current into a magnetic electrode winding through brush and slip ring. The stator of the generator is an armature. The three-phase armature winding is distributed in the slot of the stator according to the a certain rule. The difference is 120° of the electric angle.

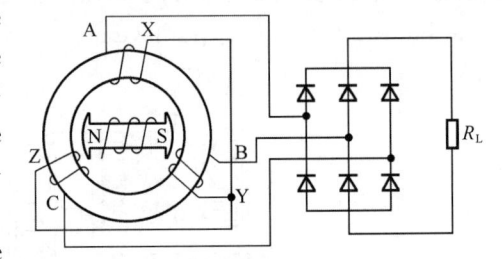

Figure 3-13　Working Principle of Alternator

When the rotor rotates, a rotating magnetic field is produced, causing the relatively stationary armature winding to cut the magnetic lines and produce an induction electromotive force. The magnetic field is approximated to the sinusoidal distribution by the special design of the magnetic electrode core. Therefore, the induction electromotive force produced by the three-phase armature winding varies approximately according to the sinusoidal law, the frequency is the same, the amplitude is the same, and the phase difference is 120° of the electric angle.

042　Automobile Electrical Equipment Maintenance

3. Rectifier principle of alternator

The diode has a one-way conduction characteristic. When the forward voltage is applied to the diode, the diode is switched on and presents a low resistance state; when the reverse voltage is applied to the diode, the diode is cut off and presents a high resistance state. The alternating current generated by induction in the stator winding of an automobile alternator is converted to DC output through a three-phase bridge rectifier circuit consisting of 6 diodes.

Bridge rectifier circuit and voltage waveform are as shown in Figure 3-14.

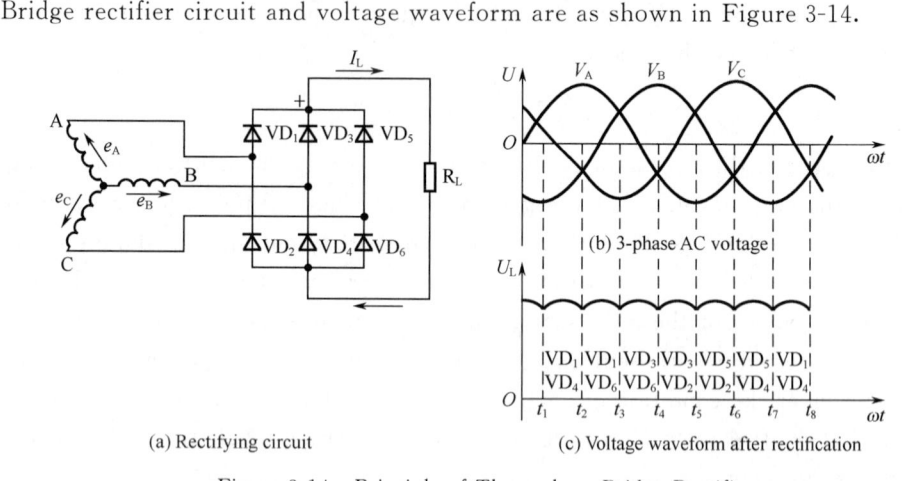

(a) Rectifying circuit

(b) 3-phase AC voltage

(c) Voltage waveform after rectification

Figure 3-14　Principle of Three-phase Bridge Rectifier

(1) Since the positive electrodes of the three positive electrode tubes (VD_1, VD_3, VD_5) are respectively connected to the first ends (A, B, C) of the three-phase winding of the generator, and their negative electrodes are connected to the component plate, the conditions for the three positive electrode tubes to be conductive are as follows: At a certain moment, which phase has the highest voltage (the positive value is the largest, relative to the other two phases), the positive electrode tube of the phase is connected.

(2) Since the negative electrodes of the three negative electrode tubes (VD_2, VD_4, VD_6) are respectively connected to the first ends of the three-phase winding of the generator, and their positive electrodes are connected to the back end cover, the conduction conditions of the three negative electrode tubes are as follows: At a certain moment, which phase has the lowest voltage (the negative value is the largest, relative to the other two phases), the negative electrode tube of the phase is connected.

(3) At the same moment, there are only two diodes connected at the same time, one positive electrode tube and one negative electrode tube. In the three-phase bridge rectifier circuit, the diodes are connected in turn, so that the two ends of the load R_L get a relatively stable pulsating DC voltage.

According to the above principles, the rectification process is as follows.

In the time of $t_1 \sim t_2$, the voltage of phase A is the highest and the voltage of phase B is the lowest, so VD_1 and VD_4 are connected at the forward voltage, and the voltage obtained at both ends of the load R_L is U_{AB}.

In the time of $t_2 \sim t_3$, the voltage of phase A is the highest and the voltage of phase C is the lowest, so VD_1 and VD_6 are connected under the forward voltage, and the voltage obtained at both ends of the load R_L is U_{AC}.

In the time of $t_3 \sim t_4$, VD_3 and VD_6 are connected, and the voltage at both ends of the R_L is U_{BC}.

In this way, a more stable pulse DC voltage U_L is obtained at both ends of the R_L, with 6 wave shapes in one cycle, as shown in Figure 3-14(c).

Some generators have neutral point terminals. The neutral point terminal is drawn from the end of the three-phase winding, marked "N", and the output voltage is U_N. Since U_N is a DC voltage obtained by rectifying a 3 ground negative electrode diodes (i. e. , a three-phase half-wave rectifier), there is

$$U_N = \frac{1}{2}U$$

When the speed of the alternator is up to a certain degree, the neutral point voltage will be higher than the output voltage of the generator. The neutral-point voltage waveform is shown in Figure 3-15. Some generators are connected with 2 neutral point diodes at the neutral point to carry out full-wave rectification of the neutral point voltage, which can effectively increase the power of the generator by using the neutral point voltage. Experiments show that: The alternator with neutral point diode can increase the power of the generator by $10\% \sim 15\%$ under the condition of constant structure. The alternator neutral point voltage U_N is used to control relays for various purposes, such as magnetic field relays, charging indicator relays, etc.

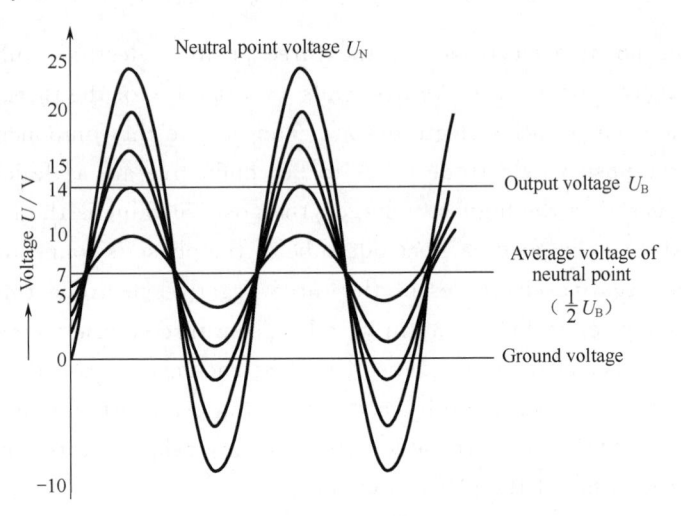

Figure 3-15   Neutral Point Voltage of Alternator

The principle of increasing generator power by neutral point diode is as follows.

When the instantaneous value of the neutral point voltage is higher than the maximum value of the three-phase winding, the neutral point positive electrode tube is connected to output current, and the current loop is: Neutral point → positive electrode diode → load → a negative electrode diode → stator winding → neutral point.

When the instantaneous value of the neutral point voltage is lower than the minimum value of the three-phase winding, the neutral point negative electrode tube is connected to output current, and the current loop is: Neutral point → stator winding → a positive electrode diode → load → neutral point negative electrode tube → neutral point.

4. Excitation mode of alternator

The magnetic field of an automobile alternator is generated by excitation, that is, the magnetic field winding must be energized to produce a magnetic field. Due to the existence of the threshold voltage of the diode, the alternator can not be self-excited to generate electricity when the speed of the engine is low, so it is necessary to use the separate excitation to generate electricity. The excitation current must be supplied by the battery first. When the voltage of the generator reaches the voltage of the battery, the excitation current is supplied by the generator itself, that is, the electricity is supplied by changing the separate excitation to self-excitation.

During starting the engine, a battery is needed to supply current to the generator magnetic field to generate electricity. This way of supplying current to the magnetic field is called separate excitation power generation.

With the increase of the speed, the electromotive force of the generator increases gradually and can output to the outside, so the generator can supply power to the outside when the engine is idle. When the generator can supply power to the outside, it can supply its own electricity to the magnetic field winding to generate electricity. This kind of transfer to the magnetic field current is called self-excitation.

The excitation circuit of an alternator is shown in Figure 3-16.

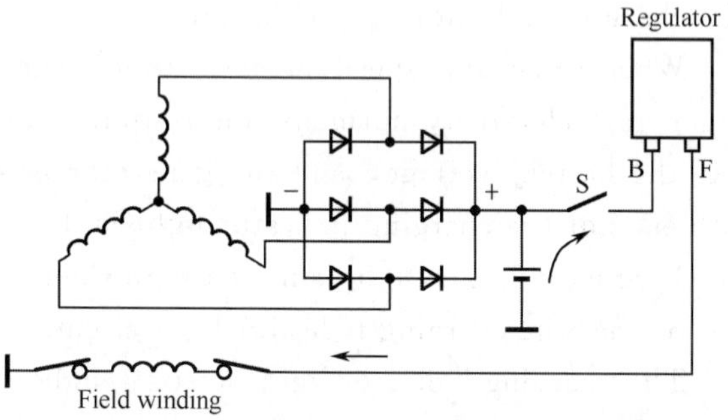

When the ignition switch S is switched on, the battery provides the excitation current through the regulator to the excitation winding of the generator. The excitation circuit is as follows: battery positive electrode → ignition switch S → regulator "+" terminal → regulator "F" terminal → generator "F" terminal → generator excitation winding → ground.

Figure 3-16   Excitation Circuit of Alternator

When the engine starts, the output voltage of the generator is slightly higher than that of the battery, the generator provides the excitation current to the excitation winding, and the excitation circuit is as follows: generator positive electrode → ignition switch S → regulator "+" terminal → regulator "F" terminal → generator "F" terminal → generator excitation winding → ground.

The excitation circuits analyzed above are only basic circuits, and there is a drawback of the such circuits, that is, if the driver forgets to turn off the ignition switch S after the engine shuts down, the battery will discharge to the generator excitation coil through the regulator for a long time. In view of this one drawback, there are many models using 9-tube alternator. As shown in Figure 3-17, 3 silicon diodes with less power are added to supply the excitation current, which are called excitation diodes, which simultaneously control the charging indicator light. 3 excitation diodes and 3 negative diodes also constitute a bridge rectifier circuit, the potential of the L-point and the potential of the B-point are equal.

As shown in Figure 3-17, the circuit serves as a warning to the driver to turn off the ig-

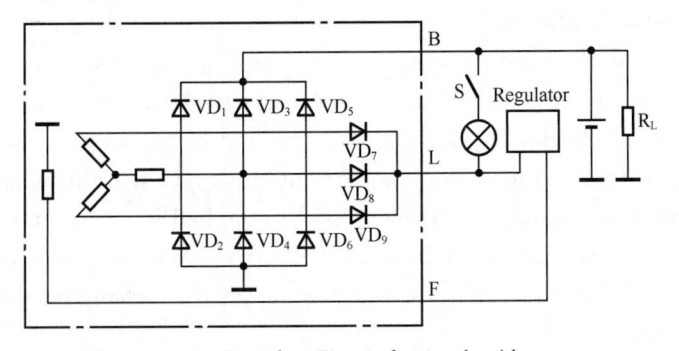

Figure 3-17 Rectifier Circuit for 9-tube Alternator

nition switch after stopping, and a charging indicator light is connected to the circuit to monitor the operation of the generator and indicate whether the generator is out of order. Its work is as follows.

During starting the engine, when the generator voltage U_D^+ is less than the battery voltage, the rectifier diode is cut-off, the generator can not output to the outside, and the battery supplies current to the magnetic field. The path is battery$+$→ ignition switch → charging indicator light → regulator → magnetic field winding → ground → storage battery$-$. The charging indicator light is bright.

When the engine speed increases to idle speed and above, the generator should be able to generate electricity normally and output to the outside, the generator voltage is higher than the battery voltage, and the generator is self-excited. $U_B = U_D^+$, the voltage drop at both ends of the charging indicator light is 0, and the charging indicator light goes out. If the charging indicator light is not extinguished, it indicates that there is a fault in the generator or that the charging indicator light circuit is grounded.

The charging indicator light not only indicates the working condition of the generator, but also lights up after the engine stops, reminding the driver to turn off the ignition switch in time.

(Ⅳ) Voltage regulator

The rotor of the alternator is rotated by the engine through the belt drive, and the speed ratio of the engine to the alternator is 1.7~3. The speed of the alternator used in the automobile is very unstable and the range of variation is very large. If the alternator is not adjusted, the terminal voltage will change with the speed change of the engine, which contradicts the requirement of constant voltage of automobile electric devices. Therefore, the alternator must have an automatic voltage regulator. The function of the alternator regulator is to adjust the voltage of the alternator automatically when the engine speed changes, so that the voltage of the alternator is stable, so as to meet the requirements of the automobile electric device.

1. Working principle of alternator regulator

The effective value of the induction electromotive force produced by each phase winding of an alternator is

$$E\phi = 4.44KfN\phi = 4.44K \frac{p_n}{60}N\phi = C_e\phi n$$

of which f ——AC electromotive force frequency, Hz;

K ——winding coefficient (related to winding method of the generator stator winding);

n ——generator speed, r/min;

p ——the number of the pairs of magnetic electrodes;

N ——the number of turns per phase, turn;

ϕ ——magnetic flux per electrode, Wb;

C_e ——Motor structure constant.

Since the electromotive force and the terminal voltage of the generator are also proportional to the magnetic flux of the magnetic electrode, the voltage of the generator can be stabilized by reducing the magnetic flux of the magnetic electrode properly when the voltage of the generator rises with the increase in the speed of the generator.

The method of regulating voltage with a generator voltage regulator is shown in Figure 3-18(a).

The control parameter of the regulator action is the generator voltage, that is, when the generator voltage reaches the set upper limit U_2, the regulator acts, causing the excitation current of the magnetic field winding I_f to drop or cut off, thus weakening the magnetic flux, causing the generator voltage to drop; When the generator voltage drops to the set lower limit U_1, the regulator acts again, causing I_f to increase, the magnetic flux to strengthen, the voltage of the generator to rise; When the voltage of the generator rises to U_2, the above process is repeated so that the voltage of the generator fluctuates within the set range and a stable average voltage U_e is obtained. Figure 3-18(b) shows the voltage waveform of the generator when the regulator acts at a certain speed.

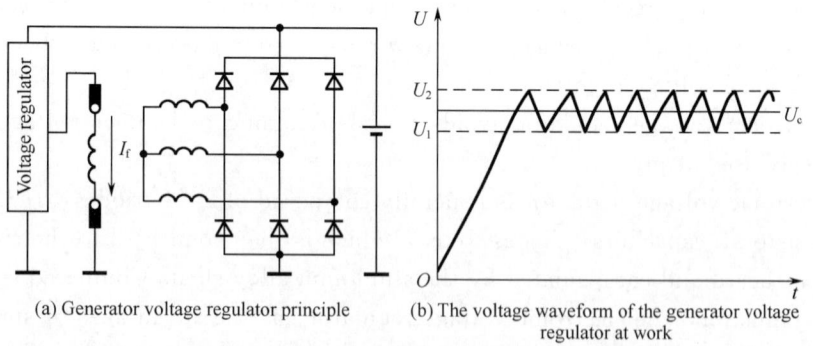

(a) Generator voltage regulator principle (b) The voltage waveform of the generator voltage regulator at work

Figure 3-18　Fundamentals of Voltage Regulator

The theoretical and experimental results show that the rate of rise of the voltage of the generator after the magnetic field is strengthened is different from the rate of fall of the voltage of the generator after the magnetic field is weakened.

2. Type of alternator regulator

According to the working principle of the alternator, for a generator, the voltage can only be adjusted by changing the speed and the magnetic flux of the generator. And the magnetic flux depends on the current of the excitation winding. Therefore, the voltage of the generator is regulated by controlling the excitation current.

There are many types of voltage regulators. They can be divided into two categories by the nature of components: contact type (also known as electromagnetic vibration type) and

electronic type, of which, the contact type can be divided into odd-electrode and even-electrode by the number of contacts, and the electronic type can be divided into three types: triode, integrated circuit and thyristor. According to the form of grounding, they can be divided into internal ground type (matching with the use of internal ground alternator) and external ground type (matching with the use of external ground alternator). At present, the external ground type is widely used.

Examples of the models of voltage regulators are as follows. FT126C means 12V even connection mechanical electromagnetic vibration regulator, FT is mechanical electromagnetic vibration type (FID is electronic type, JFT is triode type); 1 is voltage grade 12V (2 is voltage grade 24V); 2 is even (1 is odd, 4 is triode, 5 is integrated circuit); 6 is the sixth design (refers to design serial number); C is deformation code (deformation code is represents by letter A, B, C in sequence).

(1) Contact voltage regulator.

The basic principle of contact voltage regulator. The contact voltage regulator works in the form of electromagnetic vibration. The excitation current of the magnetic field winding is controlled by the electromagnet controlling the opening and closing of the contact, and the voltage of the generator is adjusted. Therefore, the contact voltage regulator is also called as electromagnetic vibration voltage regulator. The contact voltage regulators are divided into odd-electrode contact voltage regulator and even-electrode contact voltage regulator.

Contact sparks can not be completely eliminated when the contact voltage regulator is working. The contact is easy to ablate and causes high failure rate and short service life. The sparks produced when the contact vibrates can also cause radio interference. In addition, the structure of the contact voltage regulator is complex, and the vibration frequency of the contact is low. As a result, the contact voltage regulators are now rarely used in modern automobiles.

(2) Electronic voltage regulator.

The electronic voltage regulator avoids the shortcoming of contact voltage regulator, which is widely used at present.

The electronic voltage regulator is generally composed of $2 \sim 4$ triodes, $1 \sim 2$ stabilizers and some resistors, capacitors, diodes, etc., which is then connected to the circuit by the printed circuit board and encapsulated by the aluminum alloy shell. Compared with the contact voltage regulator, the electronic voltage regulator has the advantages of small volume, light weight, quick response, non-contact ablation and long service life.

① The basic principle of the electronic voltage regulator. Different types of electronic voltage regulators produced by different manufacturers have different circuit structures and component compositions, but the basic principles are the same. The electronic voltage regulator uses the on-off characteristics of the triode to adjust the excitation current of the generator through the change of the relative turn-on and cut-off time of the triode. The basic circuit of the electronic voltage regulator is shown in Figure 3-19.

The generator voltage flows through the voltage divider composed of R_1 and R_2, and applies a certain proportion of the voltage to the stabilizer VD. VD is connected or disconnected according to the variation of the generator voltage. The VT_1 is a low-power triode, which acts as an amplifier. The connection or disconnection of VT_1 is controlled by VD. The high-power triode VT_2 is used to control the excitation current. When VT_2 is connected,

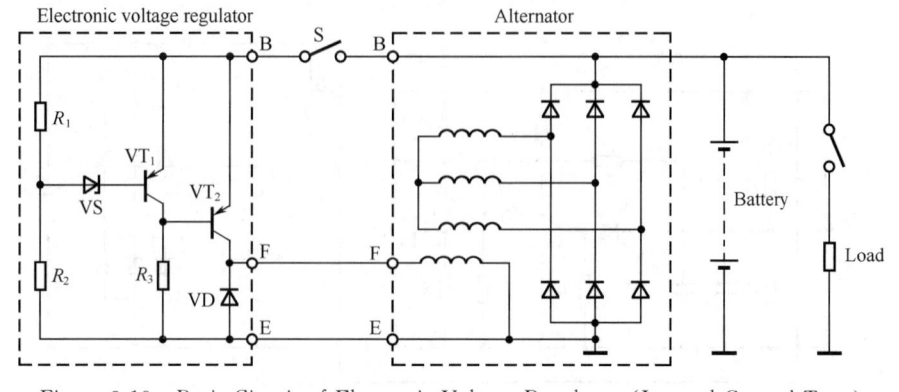

Figure 3-19   Basic Circuit of Electronic Voltage Regulator (Internal Ground Type)

the magnetic field winding circuit of the generator is connected, when VT_2 is disconnected, the excitation circuit is cut off. The setting of the circuit parameters makes both VT_1 and VT_2 work in the on-off state.

When working, before the generator voltage reaches the regulating voltage, the partial voltage on R_1 is lower than the conductive voltage of VD. If VD is disconnected, then VT_1 is disconnected. When VT_1 is disconnected, the base electrode potential of VT_2 is very low, which makes VT_2 have high enough forward bias voltage to saturate conduction and connect the generator excitation circuit. When the voltage of the generator rises to the set regulating voltage, the partial voltage on R_1 reaches the conductive voltage of VD, both VD and VT_1 are connected. After VT_1 is saturated and connected, the base electrode and the emitter electrode of VT_2 are short-circuited, VT_2 is cut off without forward bias voltage, generator excitation circuit is cut off. When the generator has no excitation current, its electromotive force and terminal voltage drop rapidly. When the partial voltage on R_1 is not enough to maintain VD to be connected, VD is cut off, and VT_1 is cut off. After the cut-off of VT_1, the VT_2 is connected and the excitation circuit of the generator is turned on. The process is repeated so that the voltage of the generator is maintained at the set regulating voltage value.

When the speed of the generator increases, the rate of rise of the generator voltage increases, the rate of drop decreases, the cut-off time of VT_2 controlled by the regulator increases relatively, and the average excitation current of the generator decreases, thus the voltage of generator is stable.

② Triode voltage regulator. The so-called triode voltage regulator refers to an electronic regulator made of discrete electronic components welded to a printed circuit board. The printed circuit board is fixed in the stamping iron box or the aluminum box. Sometimes, the silicone rubber is added in the box to facilitate the fixing of the components and the heat dissipation of the triode. An example of a triode voltage regulator is shown below.

JFT106 triode voltage regulator. The circuit board of JFT 106 triode voltage regulator is encapsulated in the aluminum alloy shell, which is suitable for external ground alternator. The circuit is shown in Figure 3-20.

JFT106 triode voltage regulator belongs to the external ground triode voltage regulator. The regulating voltage is 13.8~14.6V. It can be matched with the external ground 9-tube alternator of 14V and 750W. It can also be matched with the external ground 6-tube alternator of 14V and power less than 1,000W. The regulator has "+" "F" and "−" 3 terminals,

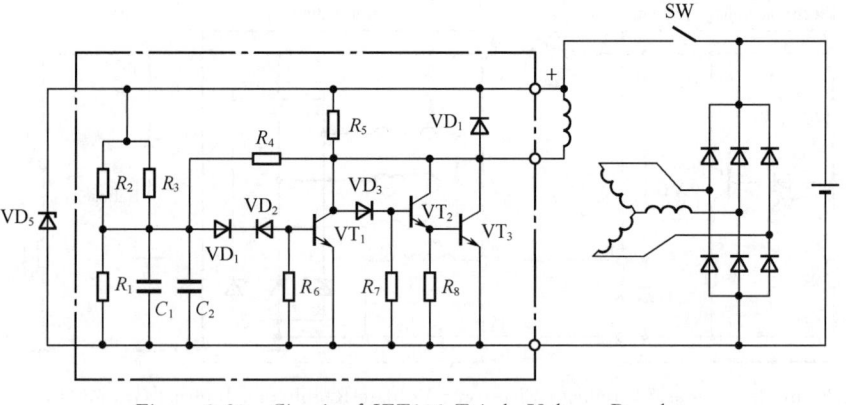

Figure 3-20   Circuit of JFT106 Triode Voltage Regulator

in which the "$+$" and "F" terminals are connected to the excitation winding of the generator, and the "$-$" terminal is grounded.

The working principle of JFT106 triode voltage regulator is as follows: Turn on the ignition switch SW, the battery supplies current to the triode voltage regulator through the ignition switch. First of all, the battery to provides bias current through R_5, VD_3 and R_7 to the composite tubes VT_2 and VT_3, so that the composite tubes VT_2 and VT_3 are conductive. The excitation circuit is (separate excitation): battery positive electrode $\rightarrow$ ignition switch SW $\rightarrow$ excitation winding $\rightarrow$ VT_3 $\rightarrow$ battery negative electrode. After the engine starts, the excitation circuit is changed from separate excitation to self-excitation, and the excitation circuit is: generator positive electrode $\rightarrow$ ignition switch SW $\rightarrow$ excitation winding $\rightarrow$ VT_3 $\rightarrow$ generator negative electrode. When the output voltage of the generator reaches the adjusted value, the terminal voltage of R_1 will reverse breakdown stabilizer VD_2, make VT_1 connected, VT_2 and VT_3 disconnected. The excitation current will decrease rapidly, and the output voltage of the generator will decrease accordingly. The output voltage of the generator will drop, the terminal voltage of R_1 will drop, VD_2 is cut-off, VT_1 is cut-off, VT_2 and VT_3 are connected again, and the output voltage of the generator will rise again. When the output voltage of the generator reaches the adjusted value, VD_2 is broken down reversely, VT_1 is connected, VT_2 and VT_3 are disconnected, the output voltage of the generator drops again. The process will be repeated, so that the output voltage of the generator is controlled and maintained at the specified adjusted value.

The other elements act as follows.

R_3 is an adjustable resistor with a resistance value of 1.3~13kΩ. Reasonable selection of R_3 can improve the stability of the regulator.

C_1 and C_2 are filter capacitors, which can make the voltage at both ends of VD_2 transit smoothly, reduce the influence of the pulsation by the generator output voltage, reduce the operating frequency of the triode and reduce the loss.

VD_1 and VD_3 are temperature compensated diodes, which can reduce the influence of temperature on the working characteristics of triode.

VD_4 is a continuous current diode, which can protect VT_3 from transient over-voltage short-circuit in the excitation winding when the VT_3 enters the cut-off.

R_6 is used to limit the breakdown current of VD_2, protect VD_2, and is the bias resist-

ance of VT_1.

R_4 is a positive feedback resistor, which is used to increase the conversion speed of the triode and reduce the loss.

③ Integrated circuit voltage regulator. The so-called integrated circuit voltage regulator refers to an electronic voltage regulator consisting of a chip integrated with several electronic components on a substrate and having all or part of the functions of the generator voltage regulator. Compared with the triode voltage regulator, the integrated circuit voltage regulator has the advantages of compact structure, small volume, high voltage regulation precision and low failure rate. The integrated circuit voltage regulator is often installed in the internal of the generator, which is also known as the integral generator.

The working principle of the integrated circuit voltage regulator is exactly the same as the working principle of the triode voltage regulator. It inducts the output voltage signal of the generator through the stabilizer, and controls the excitation current of the generator by the switching characteristic of the triode, to keep the output voltage of the generator constant. Integrated circuit voltage regulators can be divided into generator voltage detection mode and battery voltage detection mode by the way of voltage signal inpu.

a. Generator voltage detection mode. The principle circuit of the generator voltage detection mode is shown in Figure 3-21. The voltage added to the voltage dividers R_1 and R_2 is the voltage U_L of the generator excitation output end L, and the output voltage of the generator is U_B. Because $U_L=U_B$, the voltage of the voltage regulator detection point P is added to the stabilizer VDW_1, and the voltage U_P of the voltage detection point P is proportional to the terminal voltage U_B of the generator, so the circuit is called the generator voltage detection circuit.

Features of the generator voltage detection circuit: The distance of the generator to the detection circuit is close, so they may not be connected by a wire. The circuit is directly connected to the generator output end, which is reliable and does not cause the detection circuit can not detect the signal. The disadvantage of this detection mode is that when the connection wire between the generator and the battery has a large voltage drop due to poor contact, it will lead to low voltage at the end of the battery and insufficient charging.

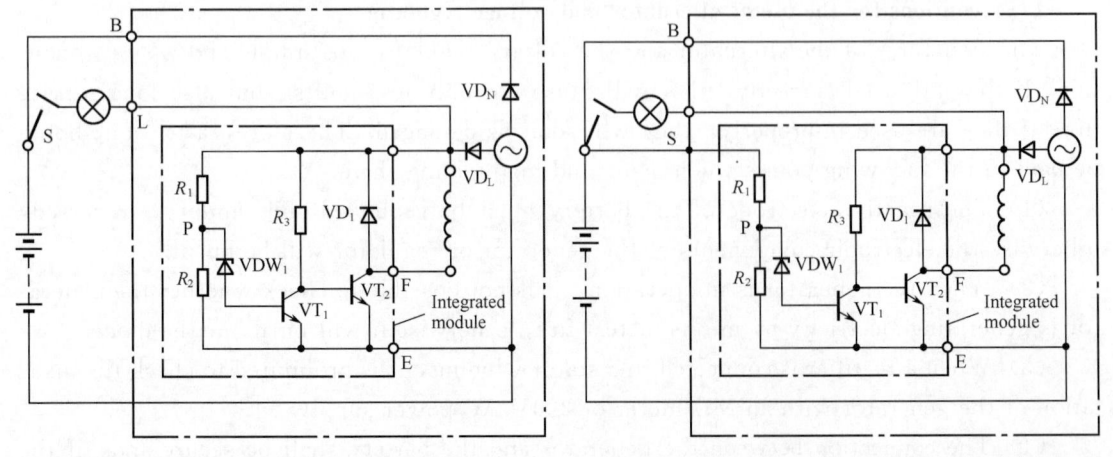

Figure 3-21　Generator Voltage Detection Circuit　　　Figure 3-22　Battery Voltage Detection Circuit

b. Battery voltage detection mode. The principle circuit of the battery voltage detection mode is shown in Figure 3-22. The voltage added to the voltage dividers R_1 and R_2 is the ter-

minal voltage of the battery. Because the reverse voltage added to the stabilizer VDW_1 through the detection point P is proportional to the terminal voltage of the battery, the circuit is called the battery voltage detection circuit.

Compared with the two basic circuits, if the generator voltage detection circuit is adopted, one generator lead-out line can be omitted. The disadvantage is that when the voltage drop between point B in the principle circuit of generator voltage detection and the positive electrode of the battery is large, the charging voltage of the battery will be low, which makes the battery under-charged. Therefore, generally, high-power generator should adopt the regulator of battery voltage detection circuit.

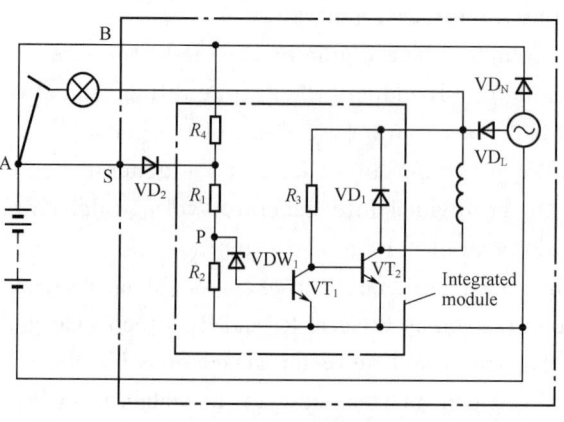

Figure 3-23　Battery Voltage Detection Circuit of the Actual Use

When the battery voltage detection mode is adopted, the generator voltage will be out of control because the terminal voltage of the generator can not be detected when the circuit is broken between point B and the positive electrode of the battery or between point S and the battery. In order to overcome this shortcoming, measures should be adopted on the circuit. Figure 3-23 shows the circuit of the battery voltage detection mode used in practice. In this circuit, a resistor R_4 and a diode VD_2 are added between the voltage divider of the regulator and the generator point B, so that when the circuit breaks between point B and the positive electrode of the battery, the terminal voltage U_B of the generator can be detected due to the presence of R_4, so that the regulator can work normally and the generator voltage can be prevented from being too high.

(V) Use and maintenance of alternator and voltage regulator

1. Precautions for the use of alternator and voltage regulator

The structures of the alternator and the voltage regulator are simple and easy to maintain. If they are used correctly, that will cause not only less faults, but also long service life; if they are used improperly, they will soon be damaged. Therefore, attention should be paid to the following points when using and maintaining them.

(1) The negative electrode of the battery must be grounded and cannot be reversed, otherwise the electronic components of the generator or regulator will be burnt.

(2) When the generator is in operation, it is not possible to check whether the generator is generating electricity by means of test fire, otherwise it will burn out the diode.

(3) When a rectifier is connected to a stator winding, it is prohibited to check the insulation of the generator with an $M\Omega$ meter or 220V AC power supply.

(4) The connection between the generator and the battery shall be secure and, if the connection is suddenly disconnected, an overvoltage will occur and cause damage to the electronic components of the generator or the regulator.

(5) When the alternator or the regulator fails, it shall be overhauled and repaired im-

mediately. It shall not be operated continuously.

(6) The regulator must be controlled by the ignition switch. When the generator stops turning, the ignition switch should be disconnected. Otherwise, the magnetic field circuit of the generator will be always connected. It will not only burn the magnetic field coil, but also cause the battery deficit.

2. Precautions for maintenance of alternator and voltage regulator

The following checks shall be carried out regularly when the alternator is in use.

(1) Check the generator drive belt.

① Check the appearance of the drive belt. Check whether there is no crack or wear by naked eyes. If there are cracks or wear, it should be replaced.

② Check the deflection of the drive belt. The deflection of the new belt is 5~10mm and that of the old belt is 7~14mm when applying 100N on the two transmission wheels.

(2) Check the connection of wires.

① Whether the wiring is correct or is reliable.

② The generator output end wiring screw must be added with a spring pad.

(3) Check whether there is noise during operation.

(4) Check whether the power is generated.

① Observe whether the charging indicator light is on or not. If the charging indicator light is always on, it indicates that the generator or regulator is out of order, or that the charging indicator light circuit is out of order, it should be repaired in time.

② The voltage is measured with a multimeter DC voltage gear. Measure the terminal voltage of the battery when the generator is not turned, and record the voltage value, start the engine and raise the speed to the idle speed, measure the terminal voltage of the battery, if it is higher than the original voltage value, it means that the generator works normally, if the measuring voltage does not always rise, it indicates that the generator or the regulator has a fault, it should be repaired in time.

(5) When the generator or the regulator is found to be out of order and needs to be removed from the automobile for overhaul, firstly turn off the ignition switch and all electric devices, remove the battery negative-electrode cable, and then remove the wire connector on the generator.

(6) It is better to use special tools when on-board maintenance and inspection are carried out. When determining whether the fault location is in the generator or in the regulator, and the regulator is short-circuited, we should note that the voltage of the generator will be out of control and the voltage may reach 16~30V, so the experiment should be controlled in a short time, or the automobile electrical equipment should be used as the load of the battery. When the circuit fault is not ruled out, the new regulator should not be replaced. Doing so may damage the new regulator.

(VI) Fault diagnosis of charging system

1. Introduction of the charging system circuit of Santana 2000 series automobiles

The charging system circuit of Santana 2000 series automobiles is as shown in Figure 3-24. The output terminal B_+ of the current rectifier circuit of the alternator is connected with the starter 30 terminal by a red wire. Three magnetic field diodes and six rectifier di-

odes constitute a three-phase bridge full-wave rectifier circuit, which becomes a magnetic field current rectifier circuit. Its output terminal D_+ is connected to the terminal D_4 of the socket D of the central relay with a blue wire passing through the single terminal connector T_1 next to the battery. The internal is connected with the A_{16} inside the central relay box. The terminal 30 of the ignition switch is connected with the positive electrode of the battery through the single terminal socket P of the central relay box. The terminal 15 of the ignition switch is connected with the terminal 14 in the rear socket of the dashboard by a black wire (which is not shown in the figure, we can refer to the original automobile circuit diagram), and then through the resistors R_1 and R_2 in the printed circuit of the dashboard and the charging indicator light and the diode, is connected to the terminal 12 in the rear socket of the dashboard, and is connected to the central circuit board A_{16} with a blue wire.

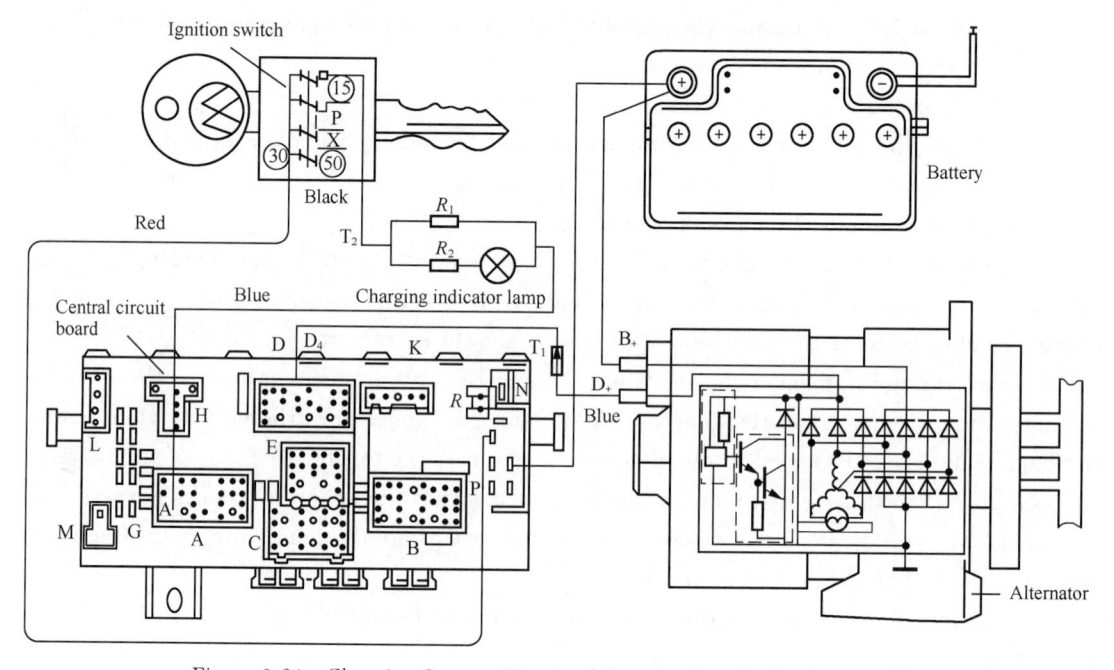

Figure 3-24   Charging System Circuit of Santana 2000 Series Automobiles

The charging indicator light and the current path of the excitation winding of the generator are: battery positive electrode-terminal P of central relay box-inside the central relay box-terminal P of central relay box socket-ignition switch terminal 30-ignition switch terminal 15-resistor R and charging indicator light-diode-terminal A_{16} of central relay box-inside the central relay box-terminal D_4 of central relay box-single terminal connector T_1-alternator terminal D_+-excitation winding inside the generator-electronic regulator power tube-ground-battery negative electrode.

When the voltage is higher than the battery voltage, the current is supplied directly to the excitation winding by 3 excitation diodes D_+.

2. Fault diagnosis of charging system

The faults of the charging system can be reflected according to the working condition of the on-board ammeter or charging indicator light. When the charging system is out of order, it should be overhauled in time to troubleshoot it, so as not to cause more losses.

The common faults of the charging system include do not charge, the charging current

is too small, the charging current is too large, the charging is unstable and so on. The faults may be caused by generator belt slip, generator fault, regulator fault, magnetic field relay fault, circuit break or short circuit in each connection line of the charging system, as well as faults of battery, ammeter, charging indicator light, ignition switch and so on. When diagnosing the faults of the charging system, the relationship between all parts of the system should be taken into account, the instruction manual and the wiring diagram should be read carefully, and the fault point should be found step by step according to a certain check steps.

(1) Do not charge. When the engine is running at a medium speed or above, the fault appears as that the ammeter indicates the continuous discharge or the charging indicator light is still on, indicating that it does not charge. The locations and causes of the faults are shown in Table 3-1.

Table 3-1   The Locations and Causes of the Fault without Charging

Location of fault		Cause of fault	Elimination method
Fan belt		Too loose or broken	To replace
Ammeter or indicator light		Damaged	To replace
Generator	Stator winding	Open-circuited or grounded	Recommend to replace the generator assembly
	Excitation winding	Open-circuited or grounded	Recommend to replace the generator assembly
	Slip ring or carbon brush	The slip ring is seriously ablative, dirty or cracked, and the carbon brush is excessively worn and stuck.	It can be repaired by welding and machining, and the carbon brush can be replaced.
	Rectifier	De-welding of diode	The failure of the de-welding can be repaired by re-welding, or the rectifier assembly can be replaced
Regulator		Transistor regulator is damaged	To replace the regulator
External line		Open-circuited or loose terminal	To turn on the circuit and tighten the terminal

(2) The charging current is too small. If the engine speed is gradually raised from low speed to medium speed, the fault shows that the light is dim when turning on the headlight or the volume is too small when pressing the horn, the ammeter indicates the discharge, indicating that the charging current is too small. The locations and causes of the fault are shown in Table 3-2.

Table 3-2   Locations and Causes of Small Charging Current

Location of fault		Cause of fault	Elimination method
Fan belt		The tension is not enough	To tension as required
Generator	Stator winding	Interturn short circuit	Recommend to replace the generator assembly
	Excitation winding	Interturn short circuit	Recommend to replace the generator assembly
	Slip ring or carbon brush	The slip ring is mildly ablative of, dirty or cracked, or the carbon brush is worn unevenly or in poor contact	To use fine sandpaper to polish the slip ring, replace the carbon brush and carbon brush spring.
	Rectifier	Individual diode is damaged	For the press-mounted diode, it can be replaced individually, otherwise the rectifier assembly can be replaced
Regulator		Transistor regulator is damaged	To replace the regulator
External line		The terminal is loose or in poor contact	To tighten the terminal

Item Ⅲ   Overhaul of Charging System   **055**

(3) The charging current is too large. When the engine speed is above the medium speed, the fault shoes that the ammeter indicates the large current charging (above 30A), battery electrolyte is consumed too fast and we can smell odour, ignition coil is overheated, distributor contacts are easy to ablative, light are easy to burn out, indicating that the charging current is too large.

The fault locations and reasons are as follows.

① The regulator regulates voltage too high or out of control, and the low-speed contact of the mechanical regulator is ablated.

② Generator "+" terminal and magnetic field terminal are short-circuited.

③ The battery is running out of power and the battery is short-circuited inside.

(4) Charging is unstable. When the engine is running normally, the fault phenomenon is that the ammeter on the automobile indicates the charging, but the needle swings to and fro, suddenly large or small, which indicates that the charging is unstable.

The fault locations and reasons are as follows.

① The generator belt is too loose, and beats or the pulley is out of circle.

② The internal wiring of the generator is loose and the contact is not good.

③ The generator brush wear too much, the elasticity of the brush spring drops or the brush spring is broken, the slip ring is dirty or out of circle.

④ The regulator contact is not good, and the magnetic field line contact is not good.

(5) Fault diagnosis process of the charging system. When the automobile engine is running, the working condition of the charging system is indicated by the charging indicator light. During the operation of the automobile, when the charging indicator light indicates that something is abnormal, it indicates that the charging system is out of order and should be diagnosed and eliminated in time. Here we introduce the fault analysis method of the charging system of Nissan Tiida as an example. The fault diagnosis process of Tiida charging system is shown in Figure 3-25.

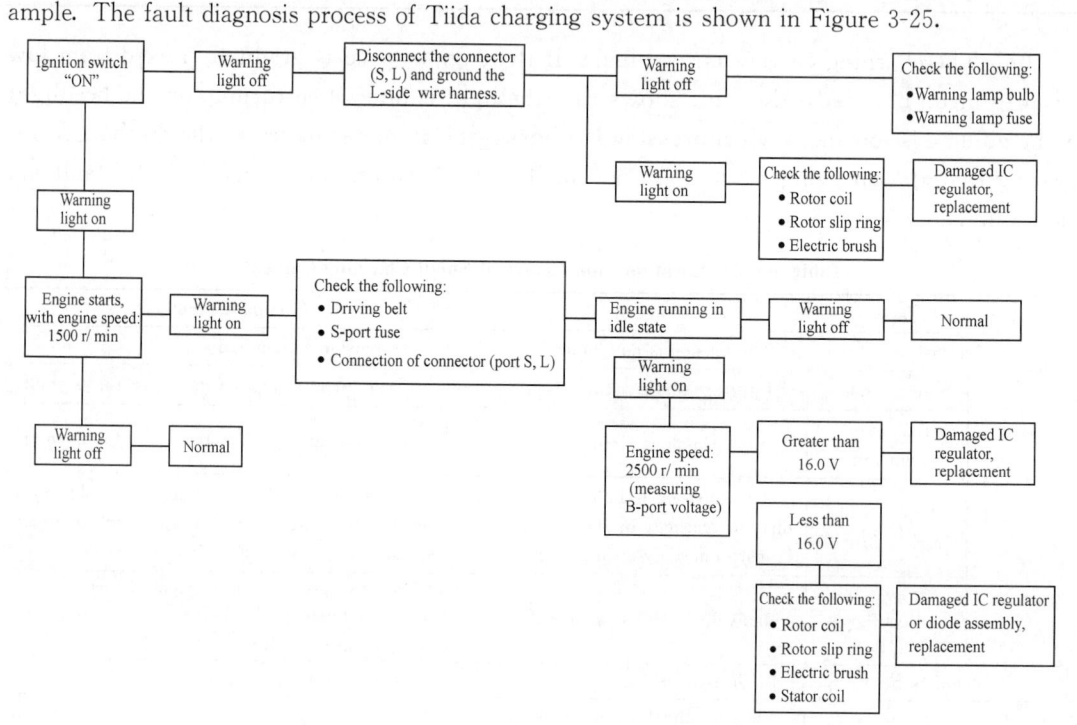

Figure 3-25　Fault diagnosis Process of Tiida Charging System

Note:

① If the charging system fails and the test results are normal, check the "B" port connection (check the tightening torque and the voltage drop).

② Check rotor coil, rotor slip ring, brush and stator coil. Replace the faulty parts if necessary.

III. Item Implementation

(I) Maintenance requirements for the charging system

① Through the implementation of this item, we should be able to disassemble and adjust the generator and the regulator of the charging system, and grasps the steps and methods of fault diagnosis and detection of the charging system.

② The item should be equipped with silicon rectifier alternator, engine hot test bench, electrical test bench, battery and other devices, with screwdriver, wrench, pliers, oil basin, brush and other disassembly and cleaning tools, with multimeter, spring scale, dialgage, V-shaped iron and other testing instruments, with automobile charging system circuit diagram and other data.

(II) Implementation steps

1. Non-disassembly detection of alternator

When the charging system is out of order, the generator should be removed from the automobile if it is checked to make it clear that the alternator is out of order. A further check is required to determine whether the alternator fails and where the location of the alternator is.

(1) Measure the resistance or voltage between the terminals. When the generator is not disassembled, the resistance or voltage between the terminals can be measured by a digital multimeter, which can be used to determine whether the generator is out of order. The method is to measure the resistance between generator terminals F and E by the resistance gear of the digital multimeter, and then measure the single-directional conductive voltage between generator terminals B and E by the diode gear of the digital multimeter. The measured values were recorded and compared with the corresponding standard values. The reference values between the terminals are shown in Table 3-3.

Table 3-3　Reference Values between Terminals

Alternator model		Between F and E/ Ω	Between B and E/mV		Between N and E/mV	
			Forward direction	Reverse direction	Forward direction	Reverse direction
Brush	JF13, JF15, JF21	5~6	500~700	∞	500~700	∞
Brushless	JF22, JF23, JF25	19. 5~21				
	JFW14	3. 5~3. 8				
	JFW28	15~16				

① The resistance between F and E. If it exceeds the specified value, it may be that the brush has bad contact with the slip ring; if it is less than the specified value, it may be that

there is a turn-to-turn short circuit or ground fault between the excitation windings; if the resistance is zero, it may be that there is a short circuit between the two slip rings or that there is a ground fault on the terminal F.

② The voltage between B and E. If the forward and reverse voltages measured twice are $500 \sim 700$mV and ∞, respectively, it can be considered that there is no fault; if the positive and negative values measured twice are ∞, it is indicated that there is a failure in the rectifier diode, which needs to be disassembled; if the indicator value is 0, it is indicated that there is a diode with different polarity broken down, which needs to be disassembled.

If the alternator has a neutral tap (N) terminal, the diode gear of the digital multimeter is used to measure the forward and reverse voltages between N and E and between N and B, so as to determine whether the fault is in the positive electrode tube or negative electrode tube.

(2) Observation of the output voltage waveform with an oscilloscope. When the alternator is out of order, the waveform of its output voltage will be abnormal. Therefore, according to the output voltage waveform, it is possible to judge whether there is a fault in the diode and stator winding inside the alternator. The waveform of output voltage in case of various faults of alternator is shown in Figure 3-26.

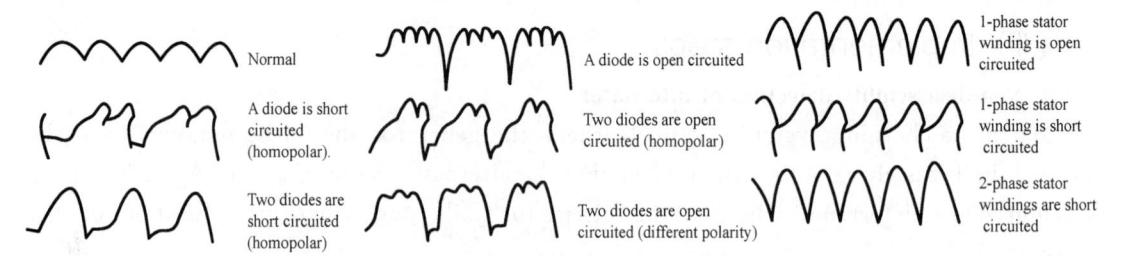

Figure 3-26   Waveforms of Output Voltage of an Alternator in Case of Various Faults

2. Disassembly of generator

(1) The removal of the generator from the automobile.

① Disconnect the negative electrode terminal cable of the battery. Before disconnecting the negative electrode cable of the battery, a record is made of the information stored in the ECU and other components, such as DTC (fault diagnosis code), selected radio channel, seat position (with memory system), steering wheel position (with memory system), etc.

② Disconnect the generator cable and connector (the generator cable is directly led out from the battery, there is an anti-short circuit cover on the terminal).

③ Disconnect generator connector. Disconnect the connector pawl and hold the connector to disconnect the connector.

④ Remove the generator. Unscrew the mounting bolt of the generator and remove the drive belt. Note, pulling the drive belt to move the generator will damage the belt. Remove all mounting bolts of the generator and then remove the generator. Because, the installation parts of the generator have shaft sleeves for positioning, the connection is tight. For this reason, shake the generator up and down for disassembly.

(2) Decomposition of the generator.

① Remove the generator pulley, clamp the generator on the bench vice, and remove the pulley by the method shown in Figure 3-27.

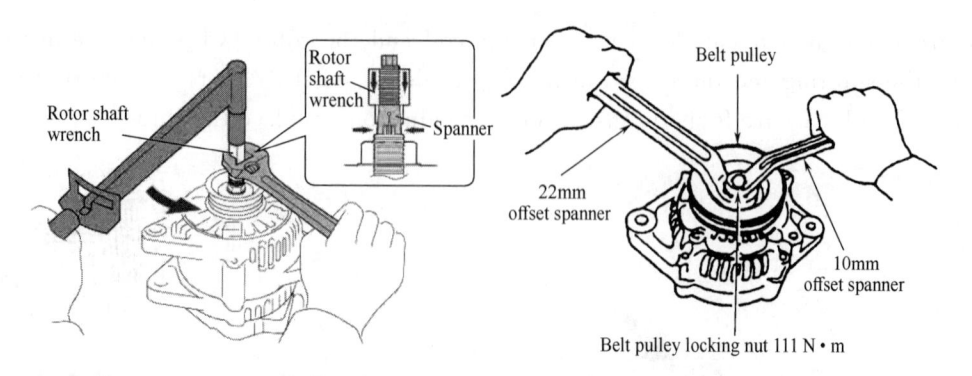

Figure 3-27　Disassembly of Pulley

② Remove the rectifier end cover. Since the seat and the rotor bearing are combined in one, a special tool is needed to disassemble it. When removing the end cap of the rectifier, hook the pawl of the special tool, as shown in Figure 3-28.

③ Remove the generator rotor. Remove the rotor from one end of the active seat by hammering it with a hammer. Note that when hammering the rotor, the rotor will fall off, so a piece of cloth should be spread out below in advance, as shown in Figure 3-29.

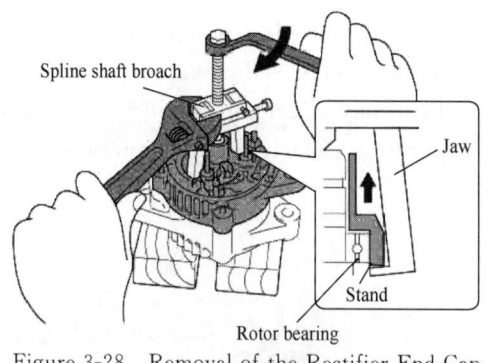

Figure 3-28　Removal of the Rectifier End Cap

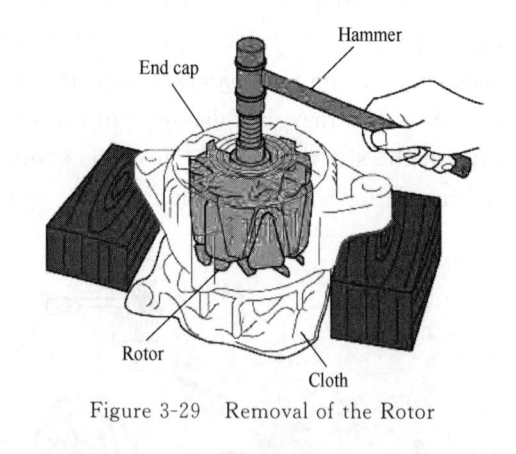

Figure 3-29　Removal of the Rotor

3. Overhaul of components of alternator

(1) Overhaul of the rotor.

① Visual inspection. Check how dirty or ablative the slip ring is, as shown in Figure 3-30. When rotating, the slip ring contacts the brush so that the current is generated. The sparks produced by the current produce dirt and ablation, which can affect the current and degrade the performance of the generator. Clean the slip ring and the rotor with a cloth and a brush. Replace the rotor assembly if dirt and ablation are evident.

② Inspection of the slip ring. Use a multimeter, as shown in Figure 3-31, to check whether the slip rings are conductive, and the rotor is a rotating electromagnetic body with a coil inside. Both ends of the coil are connected to the slip ring. Check whether the slip ring is open or not can be used to detect whether the inside of the coil is open or not. If problems are found in insulation or conduction, replace the rotor.

③ Inspection of the insulation between the slip ring and the rotor. Check the insulation between the slip ring and the rotor with a multimeter, as shown in Figure 3-32. There is an insulation state between the slip ring and the rotor to cut off the current. If the rotor coil is

Item Ⅲ　Overhaul of Charging System　**059**

short-circuited, the current flows between the coil and the rotor. Checking the insulation between the slip ring and the rotor can be used to detect whether there is a short circuit in the coil. If problems are found in insulation or conduction, replace the rotor.

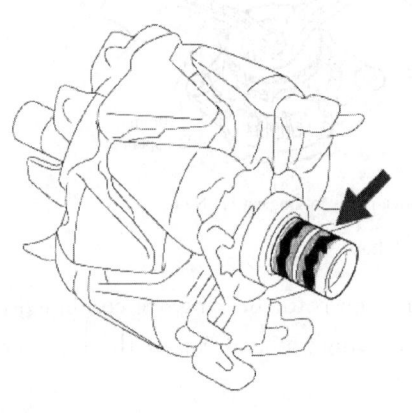

Figure 3-30　Check Whether the Rotor is Dirty or Ablative

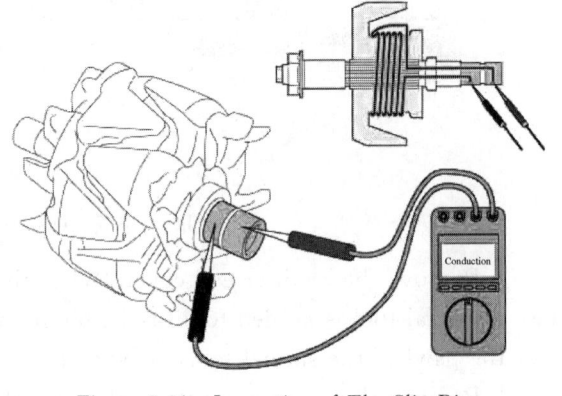

Figure 3-31　Inspection of The Slip Ring

④ Measurement of the slip ring. Measure the outer diameter of the slip ring with a vernier caliper, as shown in Figure 3-33. Replace the rotor if the measured value exceeds the specified wear limit. When rotating, the slip ring contacts the brush, causing the current to flow. So when the outer diameter of the slip ring is less than the specified value, the contact between the slip ring and the brush is insufficient, which may affect the stability of the current circulation. The result may reduce the power generation capacity of the generator.

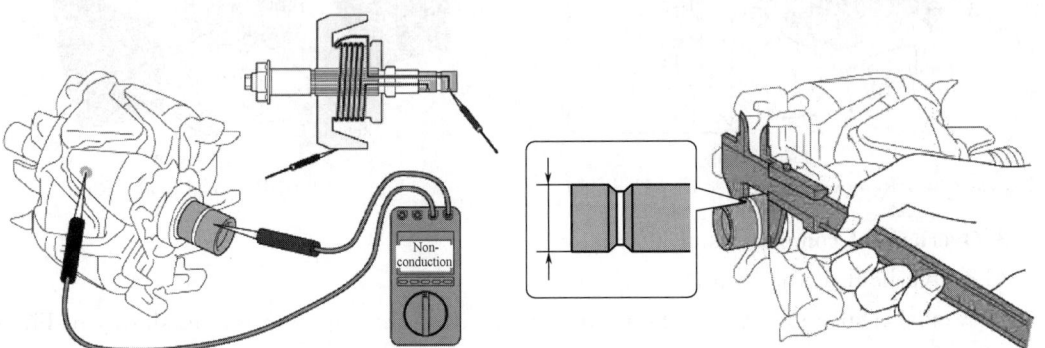

Figure 3-32　Inspection of the Insulation between the Slip Ring and the Rotor

Figure 3-33　Measurement of the Slip Ring

(2) Detection of rectifier. Use the diode test mode of the multimeter to detect, as shown in Figure 3-34. When measuring between terminal B and terminal P1 to P4 of the rectifier and exchanging the test wires, check whether the rectifier can be connected from a single direction. Change the connection mode between terminal B and terminal E, the measuring process is the same as above.

(3) Detection of brush. Measure the length of the brush with a vernier caliper, as shown in Figure 3-35. Measure the length (of the brush) in the middle of the brush, as this is where the wear is most severe. The slip ring contacts the brush and turns into an current as it rotates. Therefore, when the length of the brush is shorter than the specified value,

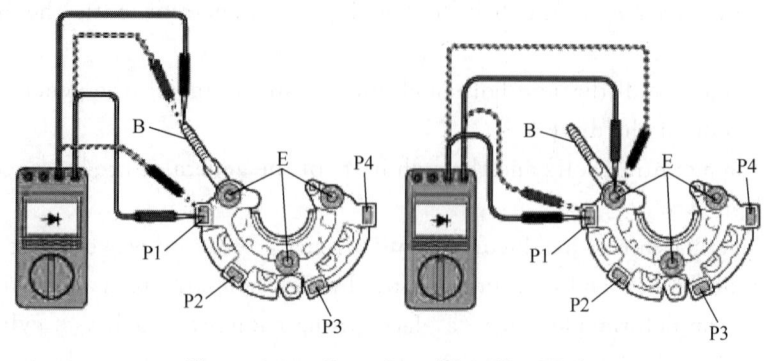

Figure 3-34　Detection of Rectifier Diode

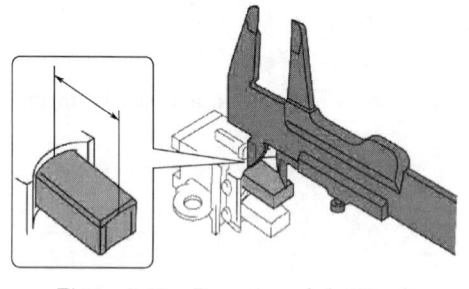

Figure 3-35　Detection of the Brush

the contact will deteriorate, affecting the flow of the current, resulting in decreased power generation performance of the generator. If the measured value is less than the standard value, replace the brush and the brush holder.

(4) Detection of stator.

① Check whether the stator is open. Use an ohmmeter to check whether the two ends of the coils of the alternator are connected, as shown in Figure 3-36. If they are not connected, the drive end frame assembly should be replaced.

② Check whether the stator is grounded. Use an ohmmeter to check whether the coil wire and the drive end frame are connected, as shown in Figure 3-37. If they are connected, the drive end frame assembly should be replaced.

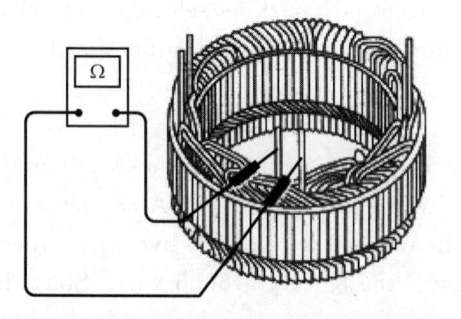

Figure 3-36　Check Whether the Stator
is Open or Not

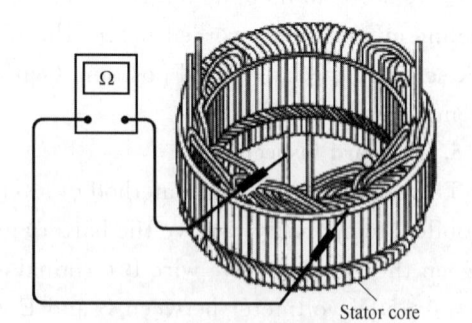

Figure 3-37　Check Whether the Stator
is Grounded

4. Assembly of alternator

(1) Installation of the generator.

① Slide the shaft sleeve until the surface and bracket are flat (one end of the tube connection), slide the shaft sleeve of the generator mounting part outward with a hammer and a copper rod, so as to install the generator.

② Preliminarily install the generator, so that it passes through.

③ Preliminarily install bolts.

④ Install drive belt.

⑤ Adjust the tension of the belt by moving the generator with the handle of the hammer.

⑥ Tighten and install through bolts and bolts to firmly install the generator.

(2) Installation of the drive belt.

① When the mounting bolts and through bolts of the generator are loosened, the belt is installed on all pulleys.

② Use a lever (hammer handle or hub nut wrench, etc.) to move the generator to adjust the tension of the belt and then tighten the through bolts. Note that the tip of the lever is held against a non-deformable place (a place strong enough), such as a cylinder cover or cylinder block. Place the lever in a position that is not easy to deform the generator and is closer to the adjusting bracket than the center of the generator.

③ Check the tension of the drive belt and tighten the bolt.

(3) Connection of the generator cable.

① The cable of the generator is connected straightly so as not to damage the terminal of the generator.

② Install the positioning nut.

③ Install anti-short circuit cover.

(4) Connection of the generator connector.

① Hold the connector body, then connect the connector.

② Make sure the pawl is firmly connected.

(5) Connection of the negative electrode terminal cable of the battery.

① Connect the negative electrode cable of the battery straightly so as not to damage the battery terminal.

② Restore automobile information. After the inspection process is completed, the automobile information recorded before the work is restored, such as selected radio channel, clock setting, steering wheel position (with memory system), seat position (with memory system), etc.

5. On-board inspection

The on-board inspection method of alternator is to turn off the ignition switch on the automobile, temporarily remove the battery ground wire, connect a $0\sim40A$ ammeter in serial between the generator live wire B terminal and the original wire of the live wire, then connect a $0\sim50V$ voltmeter between B and E, connect the battery ground wire. Start the engine, accelerate the engine, when the generator speed is $2,500r/min$, the voltage should be more than 14V or 28V, the current should be about 10A. At this time, turn on the headlight, wiper and other electrical appliances, the current should be about 20A, indicating that the generator works normally.

6. Detection of voltage regulator

When a regulator is used for an alternator, the voltage level of the alternator must be the same as that of the regulator, and the type of ground of the alternator must be the same as that of the regulator. The power of the regulator must not be less than that of the generator, otherwise the system will not work properly.

(1) Detection of the ground type of the voltage regulator. The positive electrode of the adjustable DC power supply is connected to the "B" (or "+") end of the regulator, and

the negative electrode is connected to the "E" (or "−") end of the regulator, one end of the small bulb is connected to the F, the other end is temporarily suspended, and the voltage of the regulated power supply is adjusted to 12V (28V regulator is adjusted to 24V).

① Put one end of the small bulb hanging on the power supply "B", turn on the switch S, if the light is on, the regulator is grounded externally. If the light is not on, turn off the switch S and go to the next step.

② Put one end of the small bulb hanging on the ground end "E", turn on the switch S, if the light is on, the regulator is grounded internally. If the bulb is not on in either case, the wiring is faulty or the regulator is damaged.

(2) Test of the performance of the regulator. The voltage regulator is wired according to the type of ground, as shown in Figure 3-38, Figure 3-39. After connecting the circuit, the adjustable DC supply voltage is adjusted to 12V (14V regulator) or 24V (28V regulator). Turn on switch S, at this point the bulb should shine, and then gradually increase the voltage, the brightness of the bulb should increase with the voltage. When the voltage rises to the regulated voltage (14V regulator is 13.5~14.5V, 28V regulator is 27~29V), if the bulb goes out, the regulator is of good performance, if the bulb always shines, the regulator is damaged.

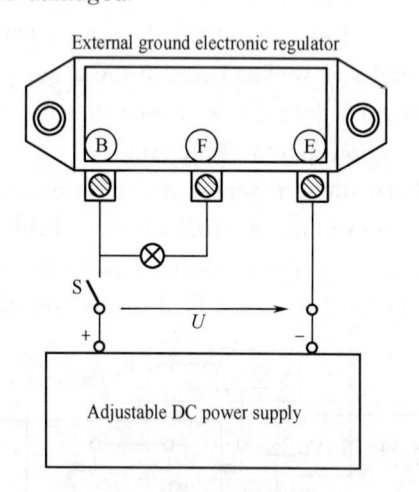

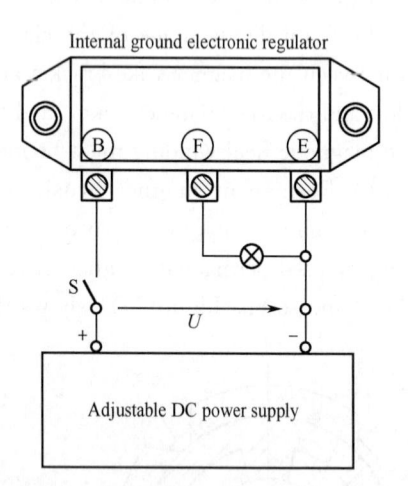

Figure 3-38　Measurement of the Performance of the Externally Grounded Triode Voltage Regulator

Figure 3-39　Measurement of the Performance of the Internally Grounded Triode Voltage Regulator

IV. Knowledge and Skills Expansion

(I) Other types of generators

Ordinary alternators need to use a brush and slip rings to direct the excitation current into a rotating magnetic field winding. During working, the brush may occur excessive wear, the brush may be stuck in the frame, the brush spring may fail, and the slip ring may be dirty, which will make the brush and slip ring in poor contact. This is one of reasons causing the generator do not generate electricity or do not generate electricity normally. Brushless alternator can overcome this defect of common alternators, so it is applied in the automobile. At present, brushless alternator has claw electrode type, exciter type, inductor type, permanent magnet type and other types.

Item Ⅲ　Overhaul of Charging System　**063**

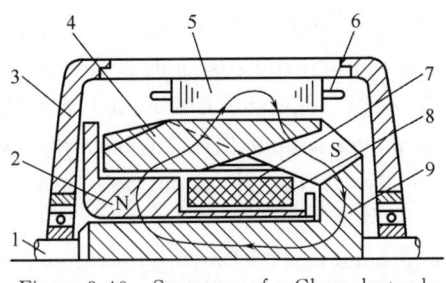

Figure 3-40   Structure of a Claw-electrode
Brushless Alternator

1—Rotor shaft; 2—Magnet yoke bracket;

3—End cover; 4—Claw electrode; 5—Stator core;

6—Stator winding; 7—Non-magnetic connection ring;

8—Magnetic field winding; 9—Rotor magnet yoke

(1) Claw-electrode brushless alternator. Figure 3-40 shows the structure of a claw-electrode brushless alternator. It is characterized in that the magnetic field winding 8 is fixed on the rear end cover 3 by a magnet yoke bracket, only one of the two claw electrodes is directly fixed on the rotor shaft, and the other claw electrode 4 is fixed on the front claw electrode by a non-magnetic connection ring 7. When the rotor rotates, one claw electrode drives the other claw electrode to rotate, and when the fixed magnetic field winding is connected to direct current, the magnetic field generated magnetizes the claw electrodes, one claw is N, the other one is S, and the closed magnetic circuit is formed by air gap and stator core. When the rotor rotates, an alternating magnetic field is formed in the stator. The three-phase armature winding produces three-phase AC electromotive force and then outputs DC after being rectified by the three-phase rectifier circuit.

The main disadvantage of the claw-electrode brushless alternator is that there are additional gaps between the magnet yoke bracket and the claw electrodes as well as between the magnet yoke bracket and the rotor magnet yoke, and there are more magnetic leakage, so the excitation capacity of the magnetic field winding must be increased when the output power is the same.

(2) Permanent magnet brushless alternator. Permanent magnet brushless alternator uses a permanent magnet as rotor magnetic electrode to produce rotating magnetic field. The commonly used permanent magnet materials are ferrite, chrome-nickel-cobalt, rare earth cobalt, Nd-Fe-B and so on. Figure 3-41 shows the structure of the Nd-Fe-B permanent magnet rotor.

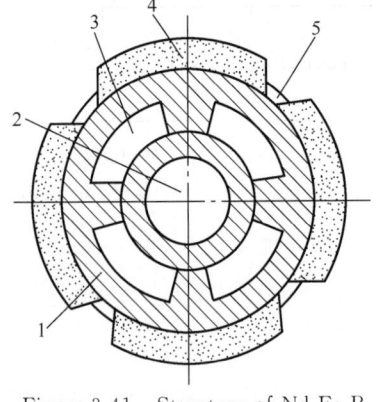

Figure 3-41   Structure of Nd-Fe-B
Permanent Magnet rotor

1—Magnet yoke; 2—Rotor shaft;

3—Vent; 4—Permanent magnet;

5—Epoxy resin adhesive

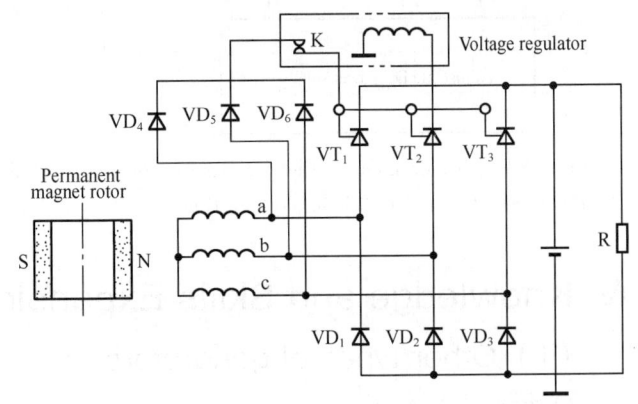

Figure 3-42   Circuit Principle of the Voltage Regulator of
a Permanent Magnet Brushless Alternator

The magnetic field strength of the permanent magnet brushless alternator is constant, so it is impossible to stabilize the voltage by adjusting the excitation current of the magnetic field winding like other types of alternators. Figure 3-42 shows the circuit principle of the

voltage regulation for a permanent magnet brushless alternator.

The three-phase half-controlled bridge rectifier circuit formed by three diodes VD_1, VD_2, VD_3 and three thyristor VT_1, VT_2, VT_3 outputs direct current, and the three-phase bridge rectifier circuit formed by VD_1-VD_6 provides the trigger voltage to the thyristor control electrode. The circuit is connected with the contact K of the voltage regulator in serial, the K of the voltage regulator is normally closed, and the electromagnetic coil is connected to the output end of the generator in parallel. The principle of the voltage regulation is as follows.

When the voltage regulator contact K is closed, the thyristor control electrode gets a forward trigger voltage and is connected, and the rectifier bridge outputs a three-phase full-wave rectifier voltage. When the rectifier voltage of the generator rises to the set upper limit with the speed increase, the magnetic force produced by the voltage regulator coil disconnects the contact K, the thyristor is cut off because the control electrode loses the forward trigger voltage, the generator voltage drops rapidly; when the generator voltage drops to the lower limit, the voltage regulator contact is closed again because the magnetic force produced by the coil weakens, and the thyristor gets the forward trigger voltage again an d is connected. The generator terminal voltage rises rapidly so repeatedly that the generator output voltage fluctuates within a fixed range.

Permanent magnet brushless alternator has the advantages of small size, light weight, convenient maintenance, high specific power and low-speed charging performance. If the performance of the permanent magnet material is further improved, the permanent magnet brushless alternator will develop more rapidly.

(3) Water-cooled alternator. Water-cooled alternator uses water instead of fan for cooling. Water-cooled alternator is shown in Figure 3-43. The main heating part of the alternator is stator, and the key cooling part of the water-cooled alternator is stator and coil winding. The front end cover and the rear end cover of the generator are made of aluminum and have water channel slots. The stator and coil windings are fixed and sealed with synthetic resin, and the aluminum enclosures are used between the stator and the rotor to separate them from the water channel. The water channel is connected with the inlet

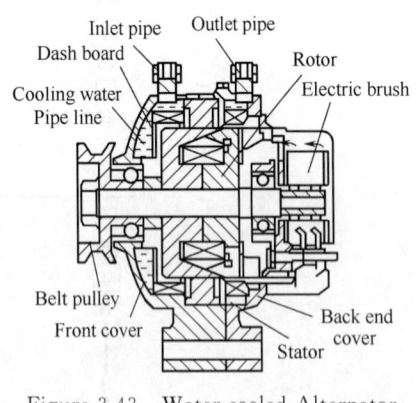

Figure 3-43   Water-cooled Alternator

and outlet pipes, and the inlet and outlet pipes are respectively connected with the engine cooling water system. Thus, when the engine is running, the cooling water circulates under the drive of the engine pump, and passes through the generator shell, so as to effectively cool the stator coil winding and the stator core, as well as other heating parts such as rotor, internal regulator and bearing.

The water-cooled alternator has good low-speed charging characteristic. The water-cooled alternator can greatly restrain the temperature rise of stator, rotor and regulator, and increase the excitation current accordingly. The larger the excitation current is, the higher the output voltage is. The water-cooled alternator have no fan, and there is no noise

from the generator fan. At 3,500r/min, the noise of the water-cooled alternator is 15dB lower than that of the air-cooled alternator. The water-cooled alternator has higher sealing requirement and higher cost than the air-cooled alternator. At the same time, because it is connected with water pipes, the installation and arrangement are restricted and the degree of freedom is reduced.

(II) Circuit diagrams of the generators of some brand automobiles

The circuit of Nissan Tiida charging system is shown in Figure 3-44.

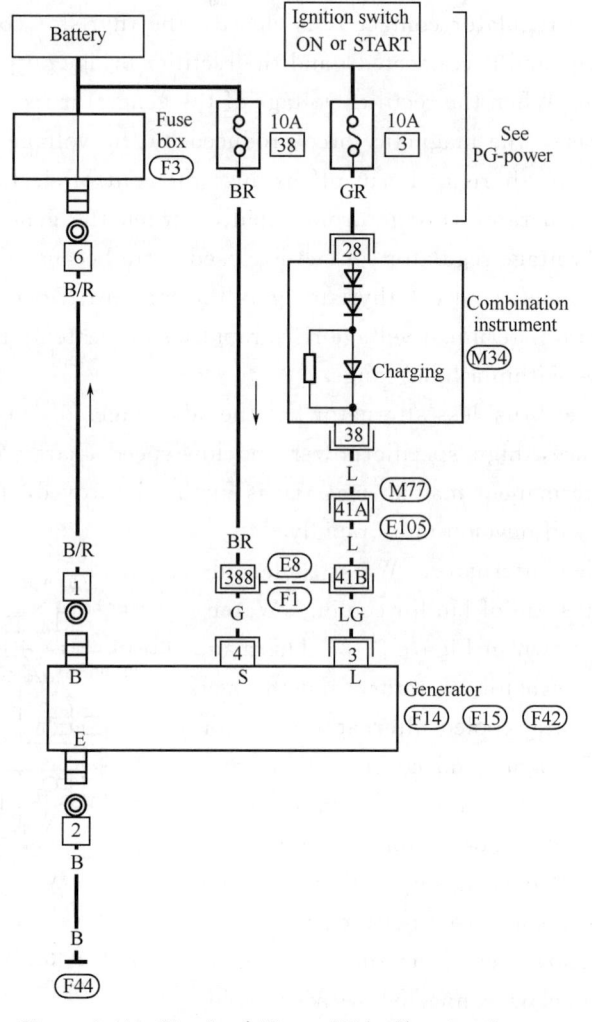

Figure 3-44　Circuit of Nissan Tiida Charging System

The circuit of Audi charging system circuit is shown in Figure 3-45.

(III) Power management system

The power management system is also called the on-board power grid management system, which is responsible for the distribution and management of electrical energy, so that the start-up performance of the automobile and the service life of the battery have been obviously improved and prolonged. With the development of the automobile, the number of electronic and electrical components used in automobiles is increasing, and the traditional

066 Automobile Electrical Equipment Maintenance

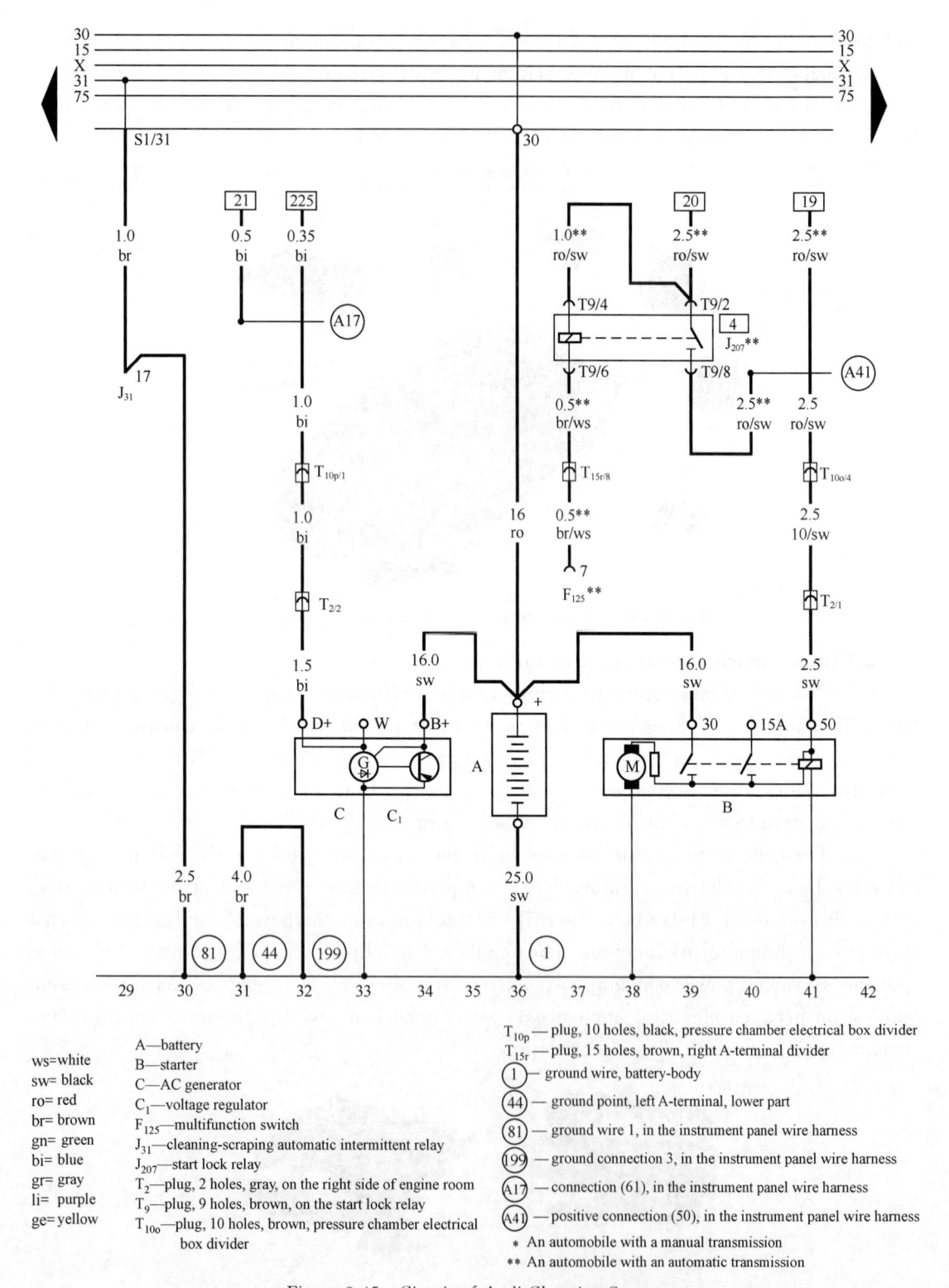

Figure 3-45   Circuit of Audi Charging System

ws=white
sw= black
ro= red
br= brown
gn= green
bi= blue
gr= gray
li= purple
ge=yellow

A—battery
B—starter
C—AC generator
C_1—voltage regulator
F_{125}—multifunction switch
J_{31}—cleaning-scraping automatic intermittent relay
J_{207}—start lock relay
T_2—plug, 2 holes, gray, on the right side of engine room
T_9—plug, 9 holes, brown, on the start lock relay
T_{100}—plug, 10 holes, brown, pressure chamber electrical box divider

T_{10p} — plug, 10 holes, black, pressure chamber electrical box divider
T_{15r} — plug, 15 holes, brown, right A-terminal divider
(1) — ground wire, battery-body
(44) — ground point, left A-terminal, lower part
(81) — ground wire 1, in the instrument panel wire harness
(99) — ground connection 3, in the instrument panel wire harness
(A17) — connection (61), in the instrument panel wire harness
(A41) — positive connection (50), in the instrument panel wire harness
* An automobile with a manual transmission
** An automobile with an automatic transmission

central relay box mode has been difficult to meet the demand of power supply for medium-end or high-end automobiles. Therefore, the new on-board power grid management system comes into being, for example, BMW, Audi, Volkswagen and other medium-end or high-

end automobiles are equipped with on-board power grid management system.

1. Composition of on-board power grid management system

The on-board power grid management system is mainly composed of fuse box, relay box and central electrical control unit J519, as shown in Figure 3-46.

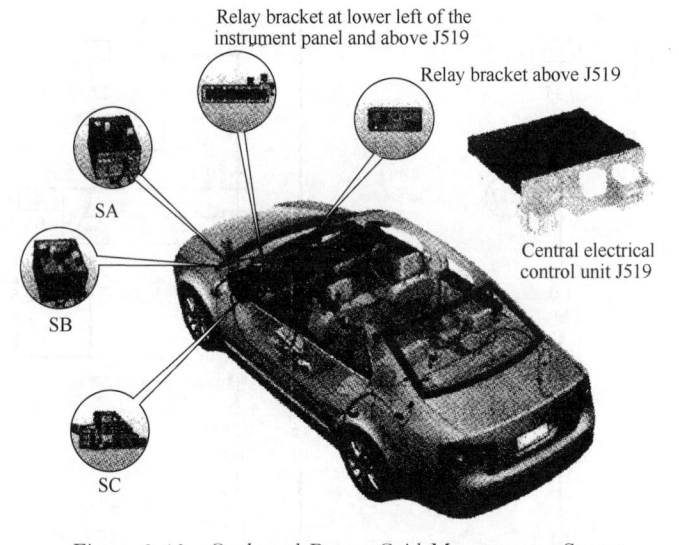

Figure 3-46　On-board Power Grid Management System

2. Central electrical system control unit

(1) Power load management, External light control and detection of light defects, Internal light control, Heating control of rear window, Comfortable light control (function of leaving home and coming home), Steering signal control, Power supply terminal control (30, 15, 75), Pre-working control of fuel pump, Control of lighting indicator light (58d), Generator excitation function, Wiper motor.

(2) The comparative advantages between the central electrical control unit and the central relay box. As shown in Figure 3-47, comparing Sagitar central electrical control unit J519 with Bora central relay box, the J519 not only realizes the power supply, but also has more powerful monitoring function. The details are as follows: stronger control of electrical appliances; saving power consumption; monitoring of electrical appliances; electronic communication between electrical appliances; power management; programmed setting; convenient repair; with self diagnosis function.

(a) Bora central relay box　　　　　(b) Sagitar central electrical control unit

Figure 3-47　Comparison between Bora Central Relay Box and Sagitar Central Electrical Control Unit

3. Electric load (power) management

(1) Purpose of power management. To ensure that the battery has enough power to

068 Automobile Electrical Equipment Maintenance

make the engine start and run smoothly, the control unit is evaluated based on the following relevant data: engine speed, battery voltage, DF signal of generator. On the premise of ensuring safe running, turn off the electric devices with comfortable function properly, as shown in Figure 3-48.

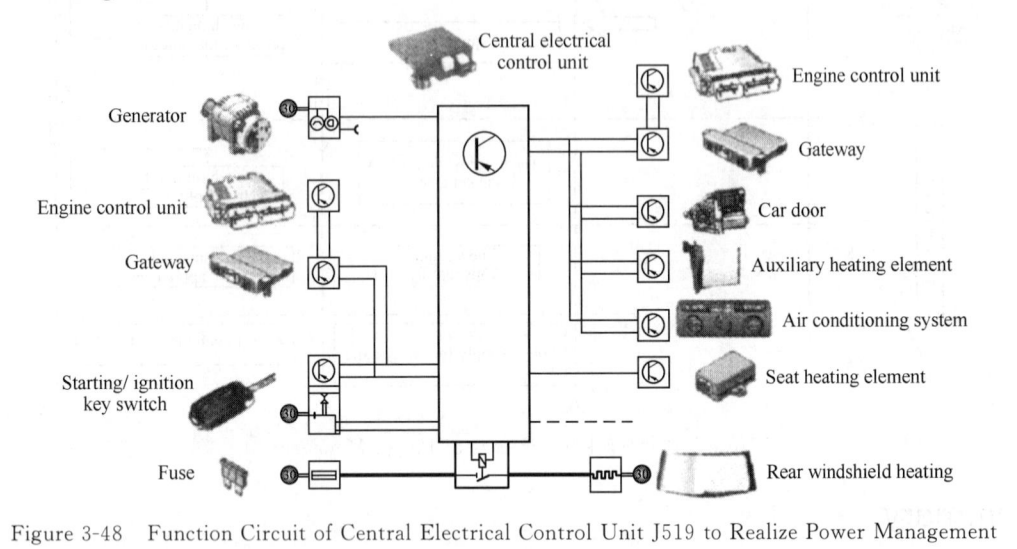

Figure 3-48   Function Circuit of Central Electrical Control Unit J519 to Realize Power Management

（2）Mode of power management. There are three modes of power management in the central electrical control unit J519, as shown in Table 3-4.

Table 3-4   Three modes of power management

Management Mode 1	Management Mode 2	Management Mode 3
Line 15 is connected and the generator is in working condition	Line 15 is connected and the generator is shut down	Line 15 is disconnected and the generator is shut down
If the battery voltage is below 12.7V, the control unit requires the engine idle speed to be raised If the battery voltage is below 12.2V, the following appliances will be turned off: seat heating, rear window heating, rear-view mirror heating, steering wheel heating, foot pit lighting, door handle lighting, reduction in energy consumption of fully automatic air conditioning or air conditioning shutdown, information entertainment system shutdown and warning of shutdown	If the battery voltage is below 12.2V, the following appliances will be turned off: reduction in energy consumption of fully automatic air conditioning or air-conditioning shutdown, foot pit lighting, door handle lighting, upper/lower automobile lights, leaving home function, information entertainment system shutdown and warning of shutdown	If the battery voltage is below 11.8 V, the following appliances will be turned off: inside light, foot pit lighting, door handle lighting, upper/lower automobile lights, leaving home function; information entertainment system

Note: 1. The difference between these three modes of management is that electric appliances are shut down in different order.

2. In Mode 3, some electrical appliances will be immediately switched off.

3. If the condition of shutdown is canceled, the electric appliances will be reactivated.

4. If an electric appliance is shut down for power management reasons, there is a fault in the J519.

（3）The working process of power management. The central electrical control unit J519 implements the working process of power management as shown in Figure 3-49.

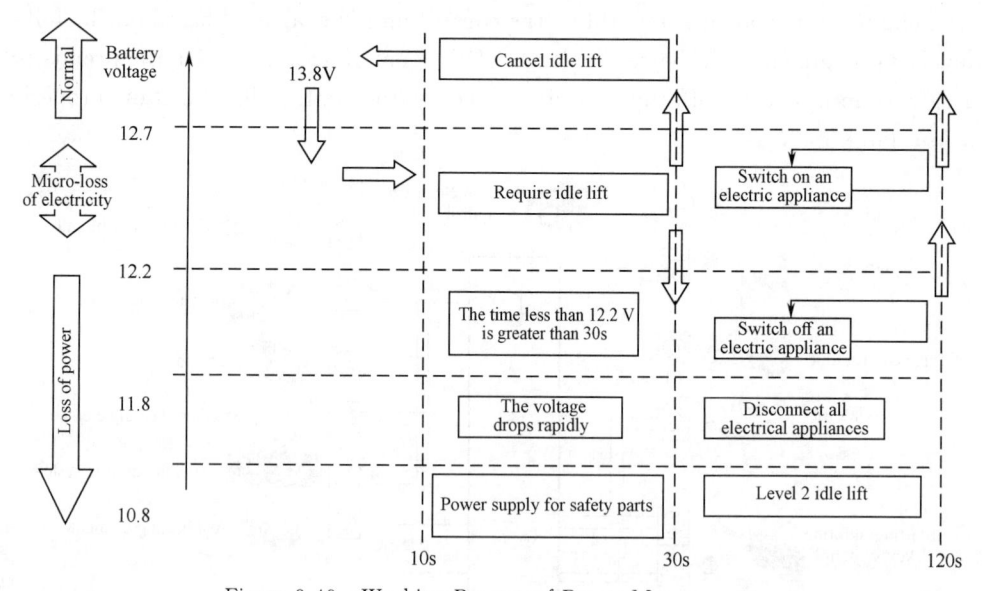

Figure 3-49   Working Process of Power Management

Summary

(1) The alternator is mainly composed of a rotor, a stator, a rectifier, a front end cover, a rear end cover, a pulley and a fan.

(2) The basic principle of the alternator to generate he alternating current is the principle of electromagnetic induction. The alternator uses a rotor that produces a magnetic field to rotate so that the magnetic flux passing through the stator windings changes, creating an AC induction electromotive force in the stator windings.

(3) The function of the alternator regulator is to automatically adjust the voltage of the generator when the engine speed changes so as to stabilize the voltage of the generator to meet the requirements of the automobile electric devices.

(4) No-load test and load test shall be carried out after the maintenance of the generator, and the minimum speed corresponding to the rated voltage of the generator under no-load and full-load conditions shall be measured to determine whether the generator is working normally.

Thinking and Practice

(1) Please briefly describe the composition and structure of the automobile alternator.

(2) Please briefly describe the excitation process of the silicon rectifier generator.

(3) Please briefly describe the working process of the charging system according to the circuit diagram of the Audi charging system.

(4) How to test the automobile charging system? Please briefly describe the testing process.

Item IV

Maintenance of Starting System

I. Scene Introduction

When a FAW weichi car turns on the ignition switch to start gear, only the starter runs slowly and a "crack" sound can be heard at the flywheel, while the engine cannot start normally. After overhaul, the single clutch tooth end face of the starter is worn seriously, which causes the engine to be unable to start. This example makes it necessary for us to study the common faults of the automobile starting system and the starter.

II. Related Knowledge

(I) Overview of starting system

The automobile engine is generally an internal-combustion engine. The starter supplies the crankshaft starting torque of the internal-combustion engine to the internal-combustion engine, so that the internal-combustion engine enters the self-running state. The minimum starting speed of gasoline engine is $50\sim70$r/min. The role of the starter (commonly known as the motor) is to start the engine. After the engine starts, the starter stops working immediately. The common starting modes of engine are manual starting, auxiliary gasoline engine starting and electric starter starting. At present, most of the transport vehicles have been started by electric starter. The starting mode of electric starter is started by direct current motor through transmission mechanism. It has the advantages of simple operation, small volume, light weight, safety and reliability, fast starting and repeatable starting. This kind of electric starter is generally referred to as starter. The starter is mounted on the seat hole at the front end of the automobile engine flywheel shell and is bolted.

1. Composition of starting system

The starting system consists of a battery, a starter and a starting control circuit. As shown in Figure 4-1, the starting control circuit includes a starting button or an ignition switch, a starting relay, etc.

The starter, under the control of the ignition switch or the starting button, converts the electrical energy of the battery into mechanical energy and drives the engine crankshaft through the flywheel gear ring. To increase torque and facilitate starting, the transmission ratio of the starter to the crankshaft is as follows: the gasoline engine is generally $13\sim17$, the diesel engine is generally $8\sim10$.

2. Classification of starter

(1) Classification by the manner in which the magnetic field is generated.

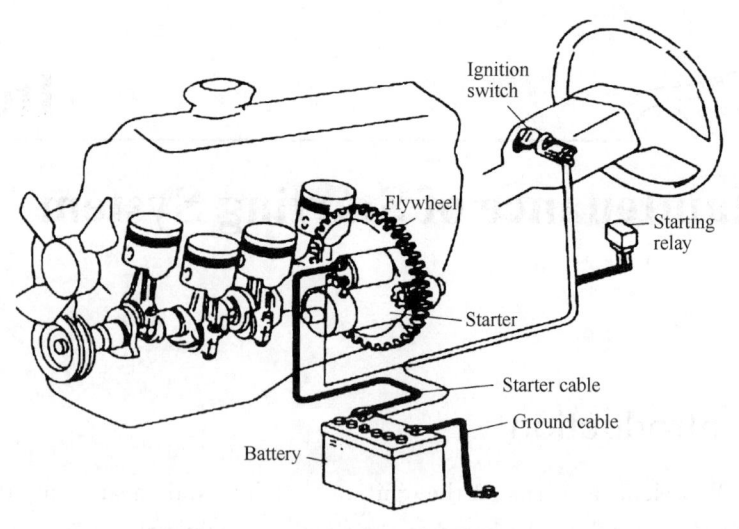

Figure 4-1   Assembly of Starting System

① Exciting starter. The magnetic field is produced by the field coil, which is used to start large and medium-sized engines.

② Permanent magnet starter. The permanent magnet starter takes the permanent magnet material (ferrite or iron boron) as the magnetic electrode. Since there is no magnetic electrode winding in the motor, the starter structure can be simplified and the volume and mass can be reduced correspondingly. It is used when starting small and medium-sized engines.

(2) Classification by control mechanism.

① Direct-controled starter. Direct-controled starter connects or disconnects the main circuit by the main circuit switch which is directly controlled by the pedal or the hand-pull lever linkage, so it is also known as the mechanical starter. Although this method is simple in structure and reliable in operation, it is seldom used because it is required that the starter and the battery are close to the cab, and are limited by the installation layout, and the operation is inconvenient.

② Electromagnetic controled starter. Electromagnetic controled starter connects or disconnects the main circuit by the starting button or ignition switch to control the relay, and then by the relay to control the main switch of the starter. This method can realize long-distance control, easy to operate, and is widely used in automobiles at present.

(3) Classification by the meshing mode of the transmission mechanism.

① Inertia meshing starter. When the starter rotates, the meshing pinion automatically feeds into the flywheel gear ring by inertia force. After starting, the pinion is automatically separated from the flywheel gear ring by inertia force. This kind of meshing mechanism is simple in structure, but it can not transfer large torque, and its reliability is poor, so it is seldom used.

② Forced meshing starter. Forced meshing starter is driven by manual or electromagnetic force to force the pinion into the flywheel gear ring. The meshing mechanism is simple in structure, reliable in action and convenient in operation, and is still used today.

③ The armature mobile starter. The armature mobile starter relies on the force of the

magnetic flux of the starter magnetic electrode, which causes the armature to move along the axis and causes the pinion to bite into the flywheel gear ring. After starting, the armature is returned by the return spring and the drive gear is pulled out of the flywheel gear ring. This meshing mechanism is mostly used in high-power diesel automobiles.

④ Gear mobile starter. The gear mobile starter is works as that an electromagnetic switch drives the meshing rod mounted in the armature shaft hole and causes the pinion to bite into the flywheel gear ring.

⑤ Deceleration starter. The deceleration starter also relies on the electromagnetic suction to push the one-way clutch so that the pinion is nipped into the flywheel gear ring. The structure of the deceleration starter is characterized by the installation of a first-stage reduction gear between the armature and the drive gear (generally, the speed ratio is 3~4). Its advantage is that it can use a small motor with high speed and low torque, so that the volume of the starter is reduced, the mass is reduced by about 35%, and it is easy to install; the starting torque of the starter is improved, which is beneficial to the start of the engine; the armature shaft is short and not easy to bend; the structure of the reduction gear is simple and efficient, which ensures its good mechanical properties and is convenient to disassemble and repair.

(Ⅱ) Construction of starter

The starter consists of a series-wound DC motor, a transmission mechanism and a control mechanism, as shown in Figure 4-2.

(1) Series-wound DC motor. The function of the motor is to convert the electrical energy of the battery into mechanical energy to produce electromagnetic torque.

(2) Transmission mechanism. Transmission mechanism is also known as starter clutch, meshing device. The role of the transmission mechanism is to make the pinion on the starter shaft into the flywheel gear ring at the start of the engine, and transfer the torque of the starter to the

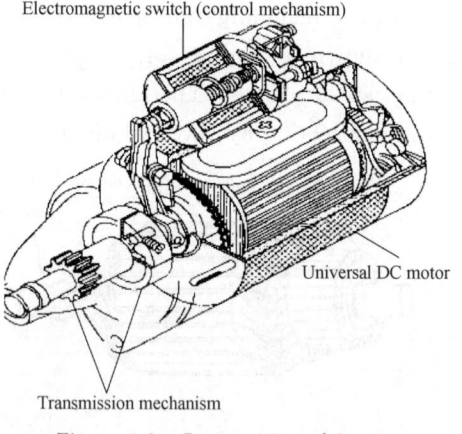

Figure 4-2　Composition of Starter

engine crankshaft; after the engine starts, the pinion and the flywheel gear ring can be automatically released.

(3) Control mechanism. The function of the control mechanism is to connect and disconnect the circuit between the motor and the battery.

The overall structure of the starter is shown in Figure 4-3.

(Ⅲ) DC motor

1. Construction of series-wound DC motor

The series-wound DC motor is the main component of the starter. Its working principle and characteristics determine the working principle and characteristics of the starter. The series-wound DC motor is mainly composed of armature (rotor), magnetic electrode (stator), brush holder and shell.

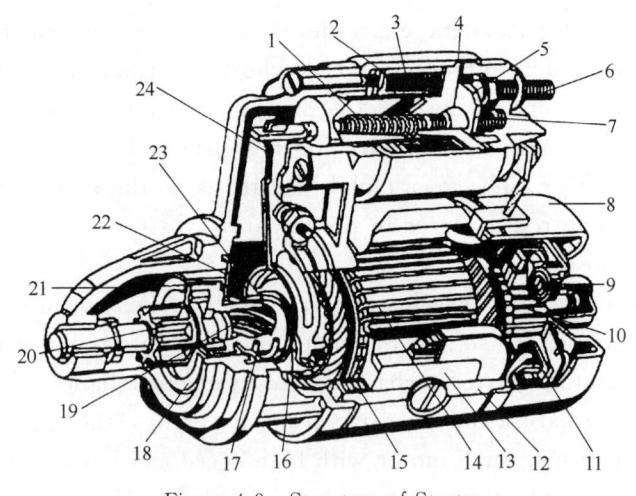

Figure 4-3   Structure of Starter

1—Return spring; 2—Hold coil; 3—Suction coil; 4—Electromagnetic switch shell; 5—Contact; 6—Terminal;
7—Contact disc; 8—Rear end cover; 9—Brush spring; 10—Commutator; 11—Brush; 12—Magnetic electrode;
13—Magnetic electrode core; 14—Armature; 15—Excitation winding; 16—Moving bushing; 17—Buffer spring;
18—One-way clutch; 19—Armature shaft spline; 20—Drive gear; 21—Cover; 22—Brake disc;
23—Drive sleeve; 24—Shifting fork

(1) The armature. The armature is the rotor part of the motor that produces the armature torque, including the armature shaft, commutator, armature core, armature winding, as shown in Figure 4-4. To obtain enough torque, the current through the armature winding is 200~600A. Therefore, the armature winding is made of copper wire with a thick rectangular section by wave winding.

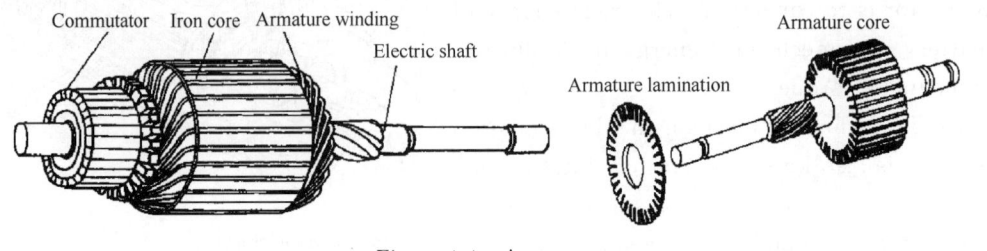

Figure 4-4   Armature

The ends of each coil of the armature winding are welded to the commutator plate, and the current of the battery is introduced through the commutator and the brush. The commutator is made of by overlapping commutator plates and mica plates. To avoid the short circuit caused by brush worn powder falling into the commutator plates, the mica between the commutator plates of the starter generally have not to be cut low. Generally, the starter mica plate for imported car is lower than steel plate. When overhauling, if the depth of the slot between the copper plates of the commutator is less than 0.2mm, a saw blade shall be used to cut the mica plate to the required depth.

(2) Magnetic electrode. The function of magnetic electrode is to produce magnetic field, and the magnetic electrodes are divided into separate excitation type and permanent magnet type. Automobile starter usually uses 4 magnetic electrodes, 2 pairs of magnetic electrodes are interleaved on the motor stator inner shell, the stator and the rotor core form the magnetic force line loop, as shown in Figure 4-5. The shell made of low carbon steel

plate is a part of the magnetic circuit.

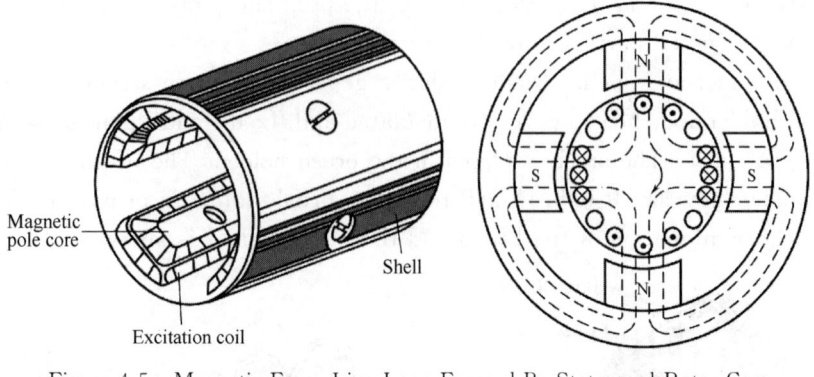

Figure 4-5　Magnetic Force Line Loop Formed By Stator and Rotor Core

（3）Excited magnetic electrode. There are 4 excitation windings, some of the 4 windings are in series with each other and then in serial with the armature winding, and some are in series with the armature winding after each 2 are in series and then in parallel, as shown in Figure 4-6.

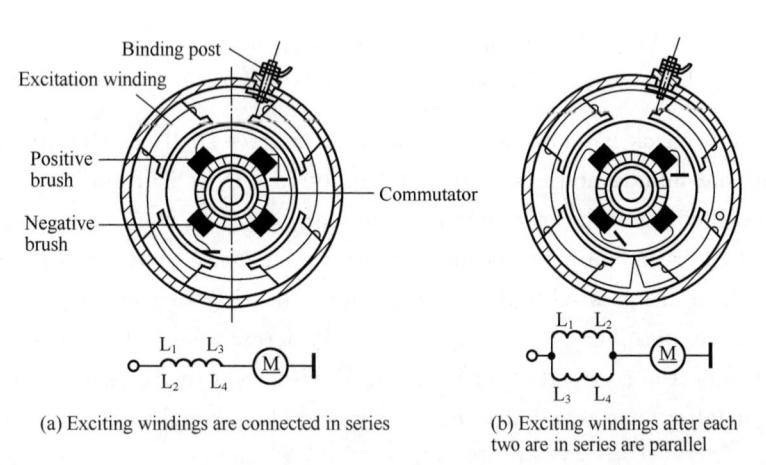

(a) Exciting windings are connected in series　　(b) Exciting windings after each two are in series are parallel

Figure 4-6　Connection of Excitation Winding

As shown in Figure 4-7, one end of the excitation winding is connected to the insulated terminal of the shell, and the other end is connected to two non-ground brushes. When the starting switch is switched on, the circuit of the starter is: battery positive electrode → terminal 1 → excitation winding 4 → non-ground brush 6 → armature winding → ground brush 5 → ground → battery negative electrode.

（4）Permanent magnetic electrode. The permanent magnet magnetic electrode adopts permanent magnet, which can save material and reduce the radial size of the motor magnetic electrode. The strip permanent magnet can be stuck on the inner surface of the shell by cold bonding

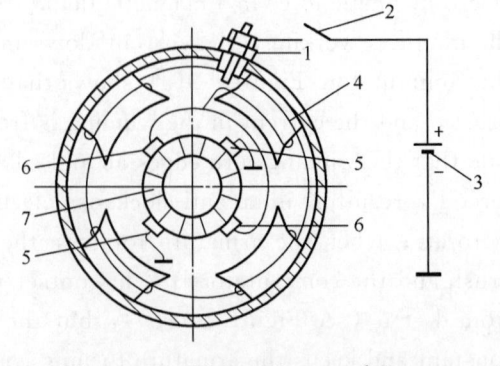

Figure 4-7　Wiring Diagram of Starter

1—Terminal; 2—Starting switch; 3—Battery;

4—Excitation winding; 5—Ground brush;

6—Non-ground brush; 7—Commutator

Item Ⅳ　Maintenance of Starting System　**075**

or uniformly fixed on the inner surface of the starter shell by sheet spring. Due to the limitation of the structure size and the performance of the permanent magnet material, the power of the permanent magnet starter is no more than 2kW.

(5) Brush holder and shell. Brush holder is generally a frame structure, in which the positive brush holder and the end cover are insulated and fixed, and the negative brush holder is directly grounded. The brush is placed in the brush holder. The brush is made of copper powder and graphite powder. It is brownish red. The brush holder is provided with a flexible disc spring. The combination of the brush and the brush holder is shown in Figure 4-8.

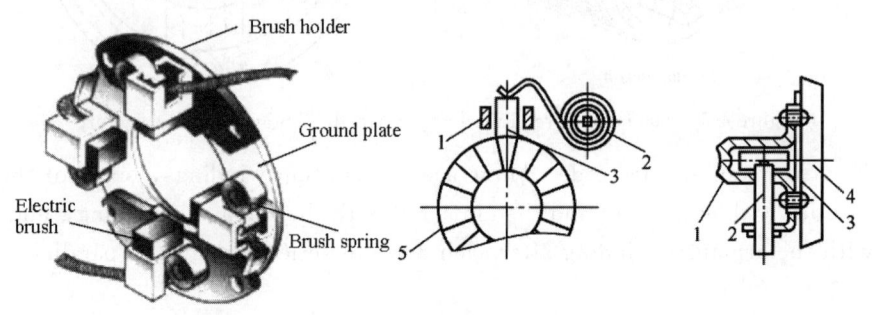

Figure 4-8　Combination of Brush and Brush Holder
1—Frame brush holder; 2—Disc spring; 3—Brush; 4—Front end cover; 5—Commutator

There are four check windows at one end of the starter shell, with only one current input terminal in the middle and connected internally to one end of the excitation winding. There are two end covers, the front one and the rear one. The front end cover is pressed by steel plate, and the rear end cover is made of gray cast iron, showing a notch cup shape. The centers of them are pressed with bronze graphite bearing sleeves or iron-based oil bearing sleeves, and the peripheries has 2 or 4 assembly screw holes. The brush is mounted in the front end cover, the rear end cover is provided with a shifting fork seat. The cover has a flange and an installation screw hole, and a screw hole for tightening the middle bearing plate.

2. Working principle of series-wound DC motor

The series-wound DC motor is based on the principle that a live conductor is subjected to electromagnetic force in a magnetic field. Its working principle is shown in Figure 4-9. When the motor is working, the current flows into the armature winding through the brush and the commutator. Figure 4-9(a) shows that the commutator A is in contact with the positive brush, and the current in the winding is from a → d, which is determined by the left-hand rule that the winding turn edges ab and cd are subjected to the action of the electromagnetic force F, resulting in an anti-clockwise electromagnetic torque M which causes the armature to rotate; when the armature rotates, the commutator A is in contact with the negative brush and the commutator B is in contact with the positive brush, the current is changed from d → a (see Figure 4-9(b)), but the direction of the electromagnetic torque remains constant and keeps the armature turning counter-clockwise.

Thus, the commutator of a DC motor converts the direct current supplied by the power supply into the alternating current required for the armature winding to ensure that the direction of the electromagnetic torque generated by the armature remains constant and that it

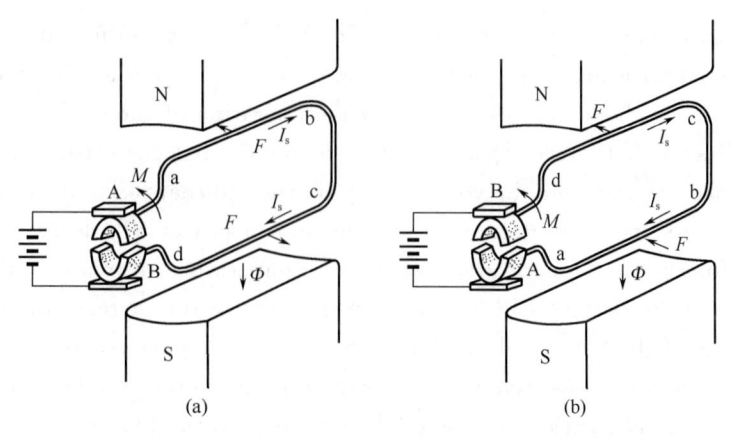

Figure 4-9   Working Principle of Series-wound DC Motor

produces directional rotation. To make the actual DC motor produce the electromagnetic torque which is large enough and the speed is stable, many coils are wound around the armature, and the copper plate of the commutator is increased accordingly.

3. Working characteristics of starter

(1) The characteristics of a DC motor in operation. The greater the current in the motor, the greater the torque produced by the motor. The higher the speed of the motor, the greater the back electromotive force produced in the armature coil and the lower the current.

A comparison of the indicators of the starter during the initial start-up period and the start-up period is shown in Table 4-1.

Table 4-1   Indicators of Starter During Initial Start-up Period and Start-up Period

Item	Stage	
	Initial start-up period	Normal start-up period
Motor speed	Lower	Higher
Motor current	Larger	Smaller
Torque produced by motor	Larger	Smaller
Back electromotive force in armature	Smaller	Larger

(2) Power characteristic. The law that torque M, speed n and power P of DC series-wound motor change with armature current is called the characteristic of DC series-wound motor. The starter characteristic curves are shown in Figure 4-10, of which, the curve M, n and P represent the moment characteristic, the speed characteristic and the power characteristic respectively.

In practice, there are many factors that affect the power of starter, so the starter must be properly maintained. The main influencing factors are as follows.

① The influence of contact resistance and conductor resistance. The bad contact between the brush and the commutator, the weak tension of the brush spring and the poor connection between the wire and the battery terminal will increase the resistance; and the excessive length of the wire and the small cross-sectional area of the wire will also cause a large voltage drop. The starter works with a particularly high current, which reduces the starter power. Therefore, it is necessary to ensure that the brush is in good contact with the commutator, that the wire

Item Ⅳ   Maintenance of Starting System   **077**

connection is firm, that the length of the wire from the battery to the starter and the wire of the battery ground wire are shortened as far as possible, and that the wire with enough cross-sectional area is chosen to ensure the normal operation of the starter.

② The influence of battery capacity. The smaller the battery capacity, the greater the internal resistance, the greater the voltage drop on the internal resistance, so that the voltage supplied to the starter will decrease, and the starter power will decrease.

③ The influence of temperature. When the temperature decreases, the capacity and terminal voltage of the battery will decrease sharply due to the increase of the viscosity and internal resistance of the battery electrolyte, and the starter power will decrease significantly. Therefore, in winter, effective thermal insulation measures should be taken for batteries, for example, do not park the automobile outdoors overnight, etc.

(Ⅳ) Transmission mechanism and control mechanism of starter

1. Transmission mechanism of the starter

The transmission mechanism of a starter generally includes a one-way clutch and a shifting fork of the drive gear.

When the starter is not working, the drive gear and the flywheel gear ring are disengaged, as shown in Figure 4-10(a). When the engine starts, press the button or the starting switch, the coil is energized to produce an electromagnetic force that draws the core and pushes the shifting fork out of the clutch so that the drive gear fits into the flywheel gear ring, as shown in Figure 4-10(b) and (c). After the engine starts, as long as the button or the switch is loosened, the coil is cut off, the electromagnetic force disappears, under the action of the return spring, the core exits, the shifting fork returns, the shifting fork head pulls back the clutch under the sliding condition, drives the gear out of the flywheel gear ring.

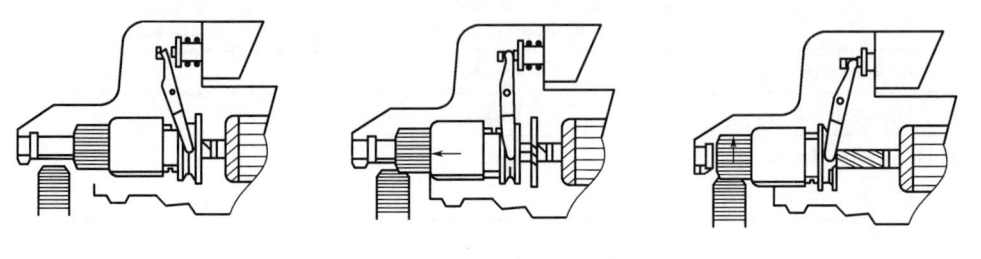

(a) The starter does not work   (b) The electromagnetic switch is energized   (c) The electromagnetic force of the main switch pushes the pinion into the mesh by means of a shifting fork

Figure 4-10   Working Process of Starter Transmission Mechanism

The main structures of one-way clutch (overrunning clutch) are roller type, friction plate type and spring type.

(1) Roller clutch. The roller clutch is constructed as shown in Figure 4-11. The drive gear and the shell are made into one body. The shell is provided with a cross block and 4 sets of rollers, pressure caps and springs. The cross block is fixedly connected with the spline sleeve, and the bottom of the shell and the shell are buckled and sealed with each other. The outer part of the spline sleeve is provided with a meshing spring and a lining ring, and the end is provided with a dial ring and a circlip. The whole clutch assembly is arranged on the spline part of the motor shaft, which can be moved axially and rotated with the shaft. Be-

tween the shell and the cross block, 4 wedge-shaped grooves with different widths are formed. The grooves are respectively equipped with a set of roller, pressure cap and spring. The diameter of the roller is slightly larger than the narrow end of the wedge groove and slightly smaller than the wide end of the wedge groove. Therefore, when the cross block is rotated as the active part, the roller rolls into the narrow end, and the cross block and the shell are clipped tightly so that the torque can be transmitted between the cross block and the shell. When the shell is rotated as an active part, the roller rolls into the wide end. If it is relaxed and skidded, the moment cannot be transmitted.

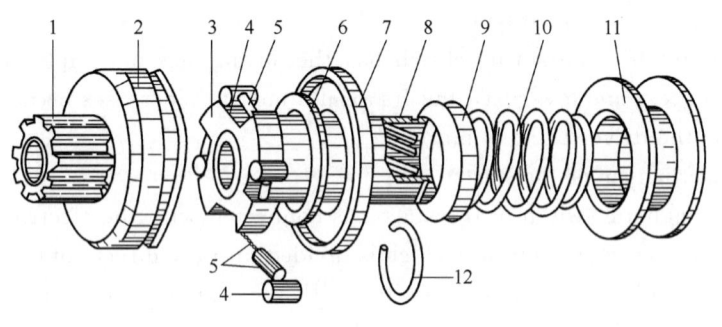

Figure 4-11   Construction of Roller Clutch

1—Drive gear; 2—Shell; 3—Cross block; 4—Roller; 5—Spring; 6—Washer; 7—Protecting cover;
8—Spline sleeve; 9—Spring seat; 10—Mesh spring; 11—Dial ring; 12—Clip spring

The working principle of the roller clutch is as follows. As shown in Figure 4-12(a), when the engine is started, the clutch is pushed along the spline by a shifting fork to drive the gear into the engine flywheel gear ring. Because the cross block is in active state and rotates with motor armature, 4 sets of rollers roll into narrow end of the slot to press the spline sleeve and the shell tightly, so the torque of the motor armature can be transferred from the cross block through the clutch shell to the drive gear, so as to drive the engine flywheel gear ring to rotate and start engine. As shown in Figure 4-12(b), after the start of the engine, the speed of the flywheel gear ring is higher than that of the drive gear, and the cross block is in a passive state, which cause the roller to enter the wide end of the slot and roll freely, only the drive gear rotates at high speed with the flywheel gear ring, and the speed of the starter armature does not rise, thus preventing the danger of the armature scatter by overrunning. After starting, due to the function of the shifting fork return spring, the clutch is returned by the dial ring, and the drive gear is completely separated from the flywheel gear ring.

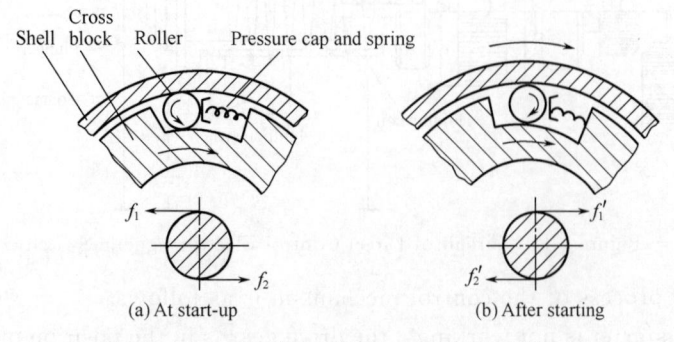

Figure 4-12   Working Principle of Roller Clutch

The roller clutch has the advantages of simple structure, strong and durable, small volume, light weight and reliable operation, so it is widely used. The disadvantage is that it can not be used in the high-power starter.

(2) Friction plate clutch. Friction plate clutch has the advantages of transmitting high torque and preventing overload from damaging the starter. It is widely used in high-power starter. But because the friction plate is easy to wear and affect the starting performance, it is necessary to check, adjust or replace the friction plate frequently. In addition, this kind of clutch structure is more complex, consumes more material, consumed more time for processing, and is not easy to maintain.

(3) Spring clutch. The spring clutch has the advantages of simple structure, simple manufacturing process and low cost, but its axial dimension increases because the number of cycles needed by the drive spring is more.

2. Control mechanism of the starter

The electromagnetic switch of the starter is connected with the electromagnetic shifting fork and controlled by the stop iron, which is divided into the direct control electromagnetic switch and the control electromagnetic switch with the starting relay. The structure of the electromagnetic switch is shown in Figure 4-13.

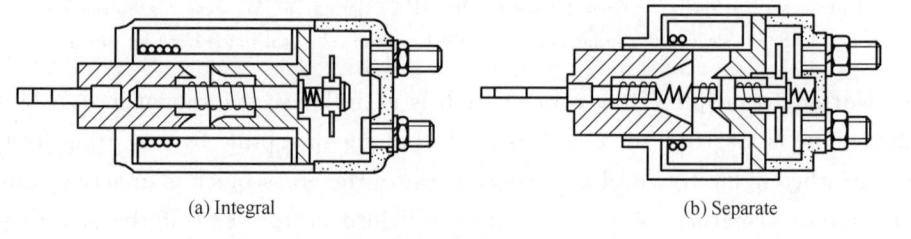

(a) Integral   (b) Separate

Figure 4-13　Structure of Electromagnetic Switch

(1) Direct control electromagnetic switch. In the automobile circuits with a starter power less than 1.2kW, the current in the suction coil and the holding coil is directly controlled by the ignition switch, as shown in Figure 4-14.

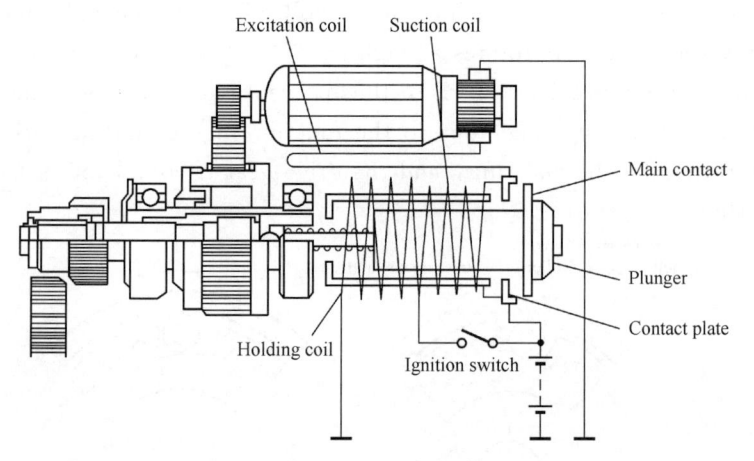

Figure 4-14　Circuit of Direct Control Electromagnetic Switch

The working process of the control mechanism is as follows.

① When the starter is not working, the drive gear is in the position of disengaging from

the flywheel gear, and the contact disk in the electromagnetic switch is separated from each contact, as shown in Figure 4-14.

② When the starting switch is switched on, it is divided into three stages.

Stage 1 is the attraction phase, as shown in Figure 4-15, the suction coil (the traction coil, the pull coil) and the holding coil work at the same time and the current loop is: battery (＋) → ignition switch → suction coil → excitation winding → ground → battery (－) → holding coil → ground → battery (－).

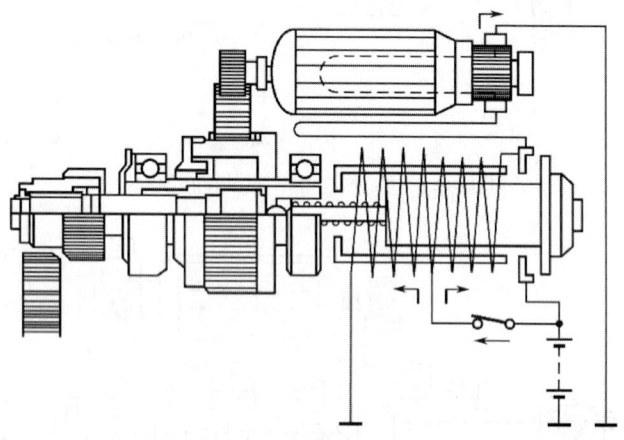

Figure 4-15　Suction Coil (traction coil, pull coil) and Holding Coil Work at the Same Time

At this time, the magnetic field direction of the suction coil is the same as that of the holding coil, the movable core under the action of electromagnetic force overcomes the elastic force of the reset spring to move inward, presses the push rod to make the contact disk of the starter main switch close to the contact, at the same time, drives the shifting fork to push the drive pinion to mesh; When the drive pinion is almost fully meshed with the flywheel gear ring, the contact disk has been connected to the contact, the starter main circuit is connected. Its current loop is: battery (＋) → ignition switch → electromagnetic switch contact → excitation winding → ground → battery (－).

The powerful torque produced by the DC motor is transmitted to the engine flywheel gear ring through a one-way clutch in the engaging state.

Stage 2 is the holding stage, as shown in Figure 4-16. When the main switch is switched on, the suction coil is short-circuited by the main switch, the current disappears, and the movable core remains in the suction position under the action of the electromagnetic force of the holding coil.

After the engine starts, the line speed of the flywheel rotating exceeds the line speed of the drive pinion of the starter, and the one-way clutch slips, thus avoiding the danger of the armature winding form scattering at high speed.

Stage 3 is the disconnection stage, as shown in Figure 4-17. When the starting switch is released, the starting control circuit is disconnected, but the electromagnetic switch internal suction coil and holding coil get current through the still closed main switch. Because the magnetic field direction of the suction coil is opposite to that of the holding coil and weakens each other. The movable core in the action of reset spring quickly return to make drive pinion out of mesh, main switch cut off, starter stop, and start end.

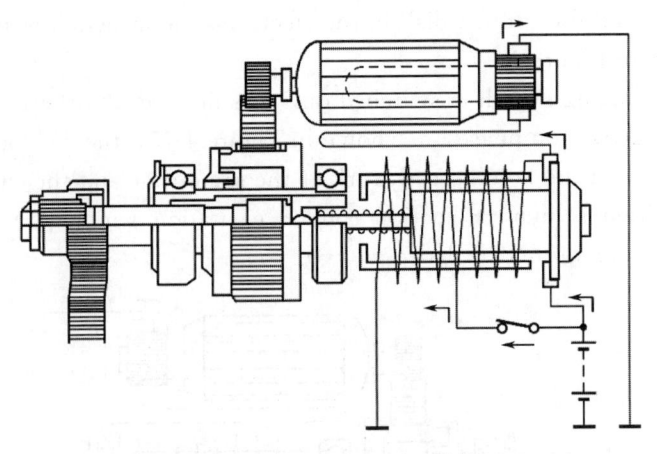

Figure 4-16   Magnetic Holding Stage

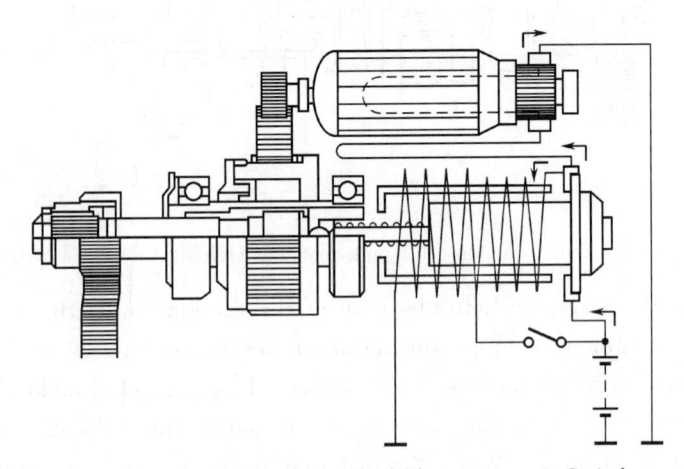

Figure 4-17   Power-off Status of Electromagnetic Switch

(2) Control electromagnetic switch with starting relay. The circuit of the control electromagnetic switch with starting relay is shown in Figure 4-18.

When the engine starts, turn the ignition switch key to the starting gear. After the starting relay is energized, the movable arm is sucked down to make the contact close, the electromagnetic switch coil circuit is connected, and the starter is put into operation. After the engine starts, just release the ignition switch key, the ignition switch automatically turns back to the ignition work gear, the starting relay coil is disconnected and the contact is opened, the electromagnetic switch is then disconnected, and the starter stops.

By using the starting relay to control the electromagnetic switch, the current of the starting contact through the ignition switch can be reduced, the contact can be avoided from ablation and the service life can be prolonged. After improving the control circuit, the starting relay on some automobiles can stop the work of the starter automatically and protect the safety.

(V) Control circuit of starter

1. Starting system circuit controlled directly ignition switch

The circuit of the Santana series automobile starting system is shown in Figure 4-19.

The working process is as follows. The ignition switch is switched to the second gear,

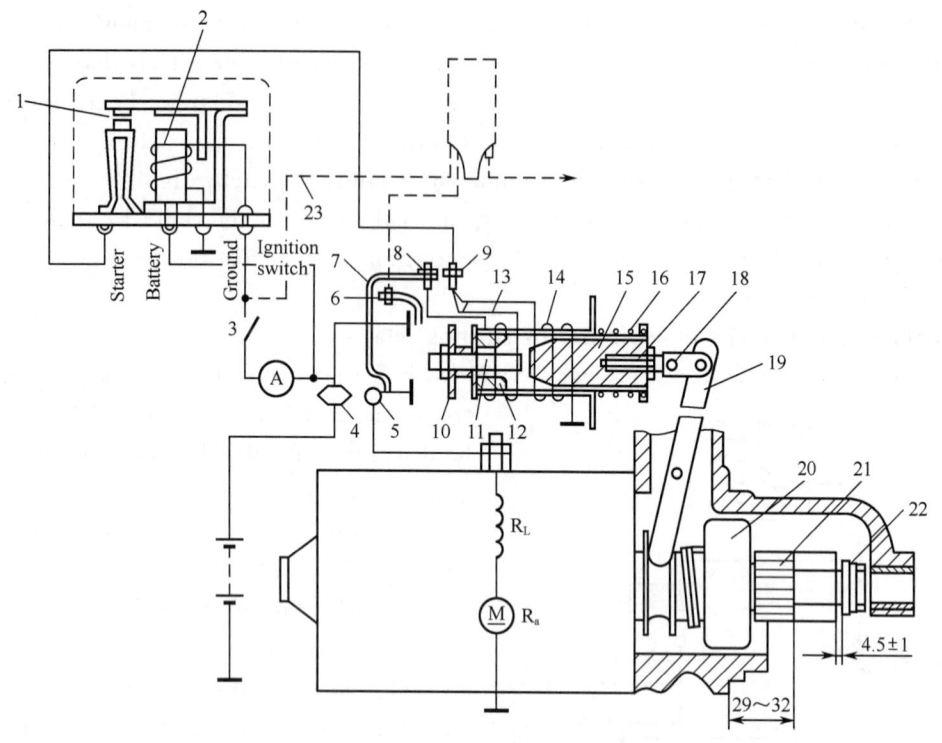

Figure 4-18   Circuit of the Control Electromagnetic Switch with Starting Relay

1—Starting relay contact; 2—Starting relay coil; 3—Ignition switch; 4,5—Main terminals;
6—Additional resistance short wire terminal; 7—Conducting plate; 8—Suction coil terminal; 9—Starter terminal;
10—Contact disc; 11—Push rod; 12—Fixed core; 13—Pull coil; 14—Holding coil; 15—Movable core;
16—Reset spring; 17—Adjusting screw; 18—Hitch yoke; 19—Shifting fork; 20—Roller clutch;
21—Drive gear; 22—Thrust nut; 23—Ignition coil additional resistance wire

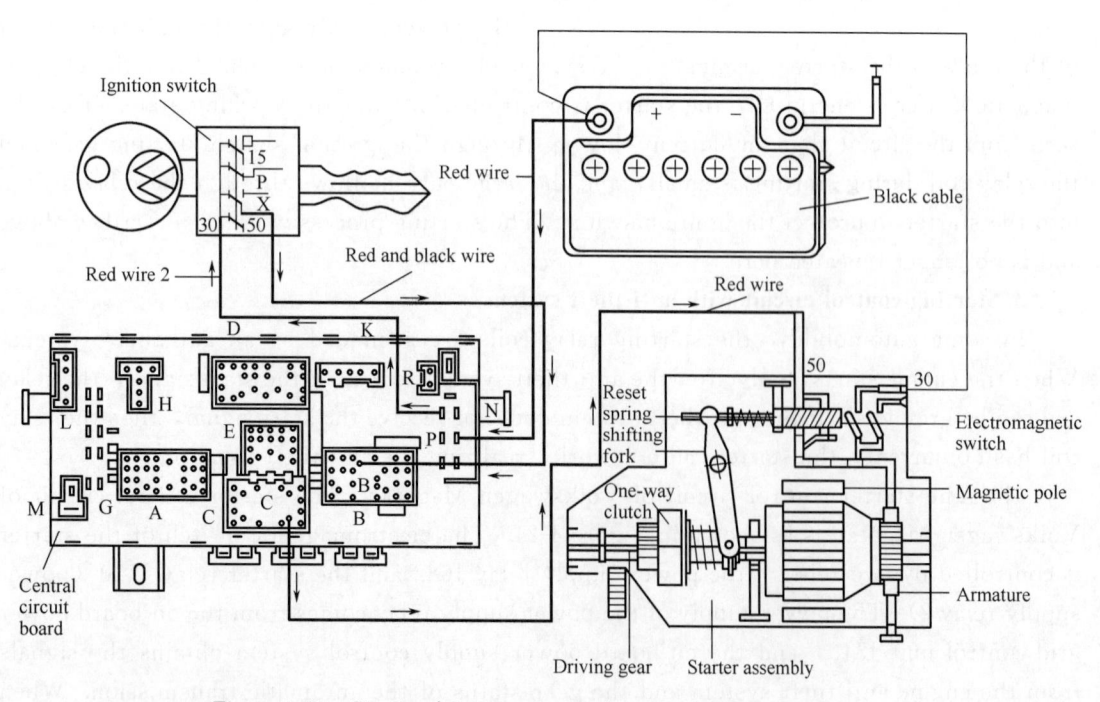

Figure 4-19   Circuit of Santana Series Automobile Starting System

Item IV   Maintenance of Starting System   **083**

and the terminal 30 is connected to the terminal 50, so that the electromagnetic switch of the starter is energized and the starter is in working condition. Its circuit is: battery positive terminal → red wire → single terminal socket terminal P of central circuit board 16 → internal circuit of the central circuit board → single terminal socket terminal P of central circuit board → red wire 2 → ignition switch terminal 30 → ignition switch→ ignition switch terminal 50 → central circuit board terminal B8 → internal circuit of the central circuit board → central circuit board internal circuit board C18 terminal → starter terminal 50 → into the electromagnetic switch.

2. Starting system circuit controlled by starting relay

When the starter with power over 1.5kW works, the current flowing through the electromagnetic switch coil is over 40A, it can not be directly controlled by the ignition switch, otherwise it is easy to burn the inside of the ignition switch. Therefore, the contact of the starting relay is often used as the switch, and the starting gear of the ignition switch only controls the control current of the starting relay coil (no more than 1A generally). Figure 4-20 shows the starting system circuit of the Toyota VIOS.

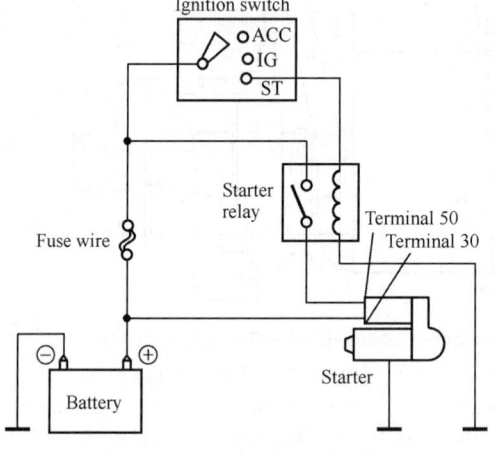

Figure 4-20　Starting System Circuit of Toyota VIOS Automobile

When the engine is started, the starting gear of the ignition switch is connected, the electromagnetic coil of the relay is energized, so that the contact is closed, and the current of the power supply goes through the contact of the relay to the starter terminal of the starter electromagnetic switch. After the electromagnetic switch is energized, the starter is controlled to enter the working state. It can be seen from the circuit that the current flowing through the ignition switch starting gear and the relay coil during starting is small, and the large current flows through the relay switch into the starter to protect the ignition switch. The starting process works as described above and is no longer repeated here.

3. Starting control circuit with anti-theft system

In some automobiles, the starting relay coils are grounded by an anti-theft system. When the engine starts, only after the anti-theft system sends out the start signal, the relay coil can be grounded. If the anti-theft system does not receive the start signal, then the relay coil has no current, the starter can not work, realizing the anti-theft function.

(1) The starter control circuit of Volkswagen Magotan. The starter control circuit of Volkswagen Magotan is as shown in Figure 4-21. The electromagnetic switch of the starter is controlled by two relays, the power supply relay J682 and the starter relay J710 (power supply relay 2). The power supply of the power supply relay comes from the on-board power grid control unit J519, and the on-board power supply control system obtains the signals from the engine anti-theft system and the gear status of the automatic transmission. When the anti-theft system does not send the starting signal normally, or the automatic transmis-

sion gear is not in P/N, the starting relay J682 can not be connected. Therefore the starting relay J710 can not be connected, the engine can not start, and the control of the electromagnetic switch of the starter can be realized.

(2) Working process. When the engine starts, under the condition that the automatic transmission is placed in P or N and the antitheft system sends out the starting signal, the ignition switch is placed in the starting gear, the electromagnetic coil of the starter relay J710 is energized, the normally open contact of the relay is closed, and the current of the power supply passes through the contact of the relay to the starter terminal of the starter electromagnetic switch. After the electromagnetic switch is energized, the main circuit of the starter is connected. The starter rotates and drives the engine at the same time.

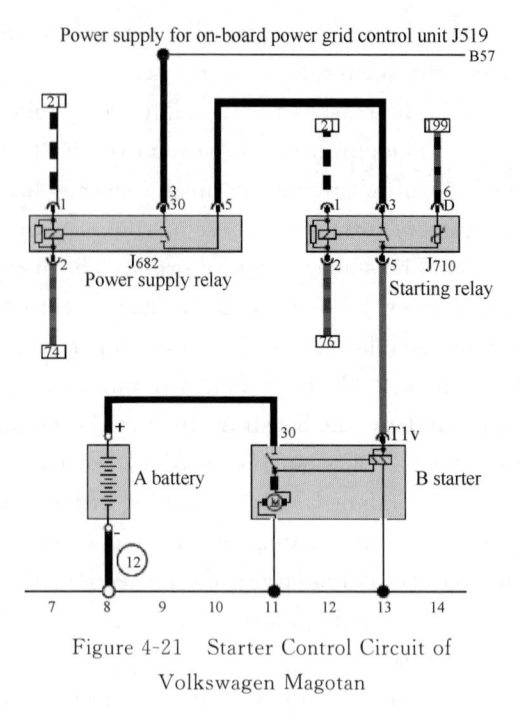

Figure 4-21　Starter Control Circuit of Volkswagen Magotan

(Ⅵ) Correct use of the starter

(1) The starting time of the starter shall not exceed 5s per start, and the next start shall be done after 15s, so that the battery can be restored. If there is a third start, the start shall be done after 15 minutes on the basis of checking and troubleshooting.

(2) Insulation measures shall be taken when starting in winter or at low temperatures.

(3) After starting the engine, the starter control circuit must be cut off immediately so that the starter stops.

Ⅲ. Item Implementation

(Ⅰ) Requirements for the implementation of the starting system

① Through the implementation of this item, we should be able to disassemble and adjust the starting system, and grasp the steps and methods of fault diagnosis and detection of the starting system.

② The item shall have materials such as the automobile that completes the item and the circuit diagram of the automobile.

③ Equipment and instruments. Starter, battery and other equipment; all kinds of screwdrivers, sharp-nosed pliers, torsion wrenches, bench pliers, etc. ; multimeter, vernier caliper, dialgage, V-shaped iron, spring scale and other testing instruments.

(Ⅱ) Implementation steps

1. Fault diagnosis of starting wire detection and starting system

(1) Diagnosis of the non-working fault of the starter of the starting system with starting protection.

① The phenomenon of the fault. When the ignition switch is turned to the starting gear, the starter does not rotate.

② The reasons for the fault are as follows.

a. The power supply system is out of order. The storage capacity of the battery is seriously insufficient and too much power is lost; the connection between the starter cable and the battery terminal is loose or the terminal is oxidized.

b. The starter is out of order. The suction coil or the holding coil of the starter electromagnetic switch is grounded, open-circuited or short-circuited. The electromagnetic switch contact is ablative, or due to improper adjustment, the contact disk is in poor contact with the contact; Magnetic field winding or armature winding is open-circuited, short-circuited or grounded; the brush is stuck in the brush holder, the spring is broken, etc. ; the commutator has oil stain, is ablative, worn, or produces grooves.

c. Combined relay is out of order. Starting relay coil is broken, short-circuited or grounded; the starting relay contact is ablative or has oil stain; the air gap between core and contact arm is too large; the protection relay contact is ablative or has oil stain.

d. The ignition switch is out of order. The starting gear is out of order.

e. Fuse.

③ Fault diagnosis method. Turn on the headlight and observe the brightness of the light before the starting switch is switched on. If the light is dim, it may be caused by excessive power loss of battery or loosening of the connection wire. In the normal condition of the battery, the non-working fault of the starter is diagnosed as shown in Figure 4-22.

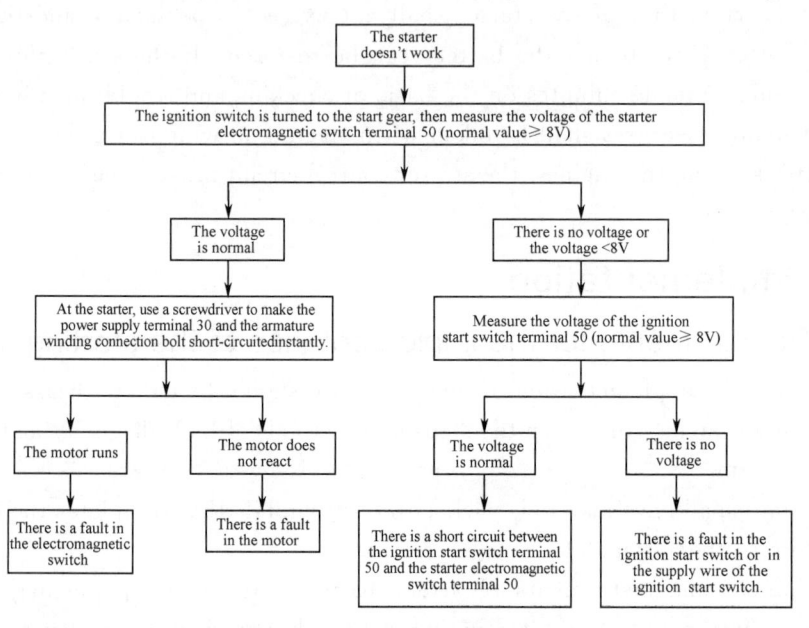

Figure 4-22 Diagnosis Method for Non-working Fault of the Starter of
Manual Transmission Automobile

(2) Fault diagnosis of starter not working in automatic transmission vehicle.

① Fault phenomenon: Press the brake pedal, the automatic transmission is in P or n gear, the ignition switch is turned to start gear, the starter does not respond.

② Cause of failure: The reasons for the fault are as follows.

a. Automatic transmission multifunction switch fault.

b. Automatic transmission control unit faulty.

c. Poor contact or open circuit of relevant circuit.

③ Fault diagnosis method.

For an automatic transmission automobile, firstly, we shall make sure that the automatic transmission is in N or P. Under the premise that the battery has the electricity, each wiring and each ground wire of the starter electromagnetic switch are in good contact, a wire may be used to short connect terminals 30 and 50 in the starter. If the starter does not work, then the fault is in the starter itself (at this time, we can further diagnose the fault, with a thick wire in the starter to instantaneously short connect terminal 30 and armature joint, if the motor rotates, then the fault is in the electromagnetic switch; otherwise, the fault is in the inside of the motor); if the starter works, we need to further carry out the diagnosis in the starting relay. Under the premise of confirming that each wiring is in good condition and the ignition switch starts and supplies power normally, special instruments (such as VAG1551 or VAG1552) can be used to diagnose the multi-function switch and control unit of the automatic transmission. If there is no fault, the fault is in the starting relay.

(3) Failure to operate the starter.

① Fault phenomenon: When starting, the engine speed is too low to start.

② The reasons for the fault are as follows.

a. The battery is out of power.

b. The wire is not in good contact or the terminal is oxidized.

c. The starter itself is out of order.

d. The engine turns with too much resistance.

③ Fault diagnosis method. In the case of correct use of engine oil and proper V-belt tensioning, fault diagnosis can be performed according to Figure 4-23.

2. Disassembly of starter

(1) Disassembly of the starter from the automobile.

① Disconnect the negative cable of the battery. Before disconnecting the negative cable of the battery, record the information stored in devices such as ECU.

② Remove the starter cable, remove the anti-short circuit cover, the starter cable positioning nut, and disconnect the starter cable at the starter terminal 30. Since the starter cable is connected directly to the battery, it has an anti-open circuit cover.

③ Disconnect the starter connector, press the pin of the connector, and then hold the connector body to disconnect the connector.

④ Remove the starter, remove the starter mounting bolt, and then shake the starter to remove it.

(2) Breakdown of the starter.

① Remove the electromagnetic switch assembly, as shown in Figure 4-24. Disconnect the lead and remove the positioning nut and disconnect the lead. Remove 2 nuts and pull the electromagnetic starter switch to the rear. Pull up the top of the electromagnetic starter switch and remove the plunger hook from the drive rod. Remove the electromagnetic switch.

② Remove the starter yoke assembly, as shown in Figure 4-25. Remove 2 bolts, remove the commutator end cover, separate the starter shell from the starter yoke, and re-

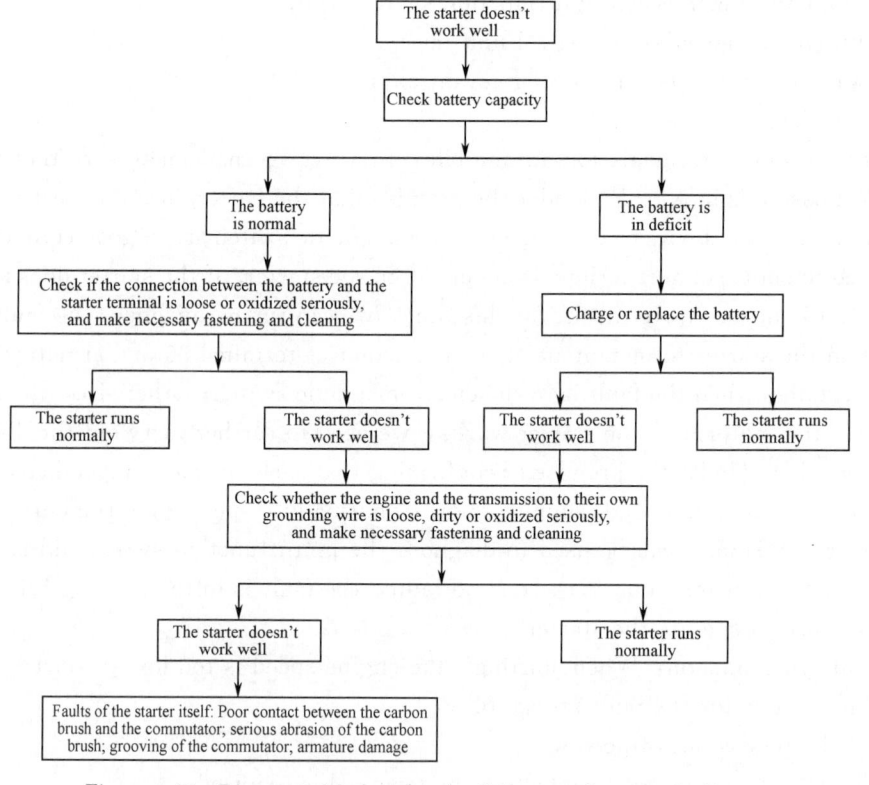

Figure 4-23   Diagnosis Method for the Failure to Operate the Starter

move the drive rod.

③ Remove the starter brush spring.

④ Removal of starter clutch.

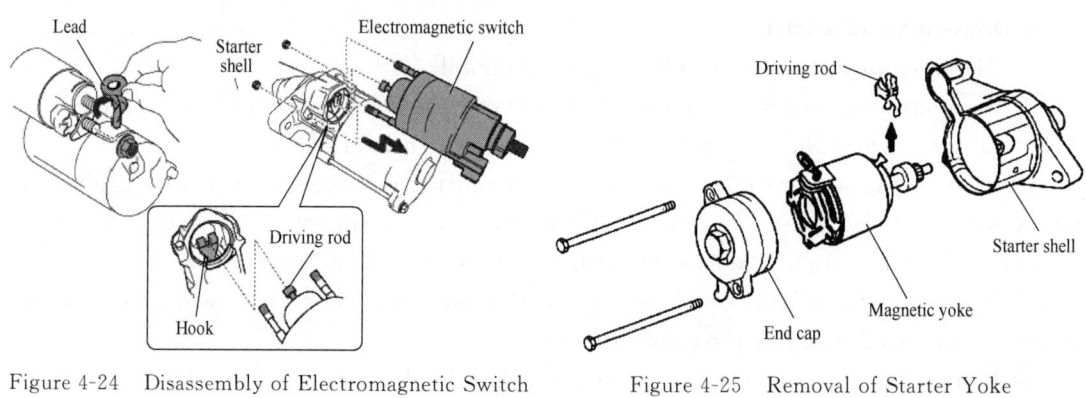

Figure 4-24   Disassembly of Electromagnetic Switch

Figure 4-25   Removal of Starter Yoke

3. Overhaul of various parts of the starter

(1) Overhaul of the rotor.

① Visual inspection. check whether the armature coil and commutator are dirty or burned. By self-rotating, the armature coil and the commutator contact the brush, and then turn on the current. Therefore, the commutator of the starter is easy to get dirty and burn out. When the commutator gets dirty and burnt, it interferes with the current and interferes with the normal operation of the starter. Clean the armature assembly with a cloth or a brush.

088 Automobile Electrical Equipment Maintenance

② Inspection of the starter armature insulation and conduction, as shown in Figure 4-26. Perform the following checks with a multimeter. Insulation between the commutator and the armature core. The state between the armature core and the armature coil is insulated, and the commutator is connected with the armature coil. If the parts are normal, the state between the commutator and the armature core is insulated.

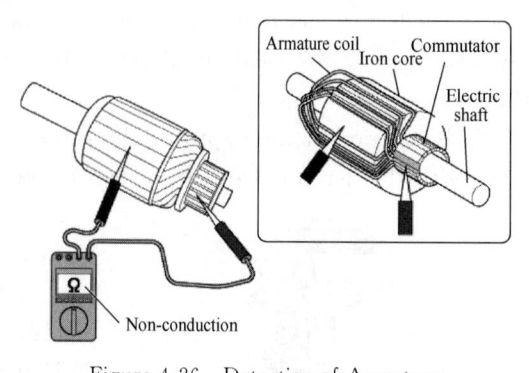

Figure 4-26   Detection of Armature

The conduction between commutator plates is shown in Figure 4-27. Each commutator plate is connected through an armature coil. If parts are normal, the state between commutator plates is conductive.

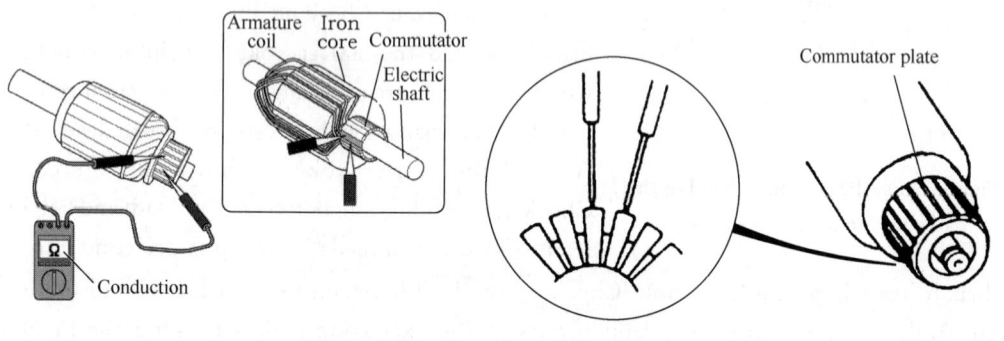

Figure 4-27   Detection of Commutator

③ Round runout inspection of commutator. Check the beat level of the commutator with a micrometer, as shown in Figure 4-28. The contact between the commutator and the brush will be weakened as the amount of the commutator beats becomes larger. As a result, a failure may occur. For example, the starter fails to operate.

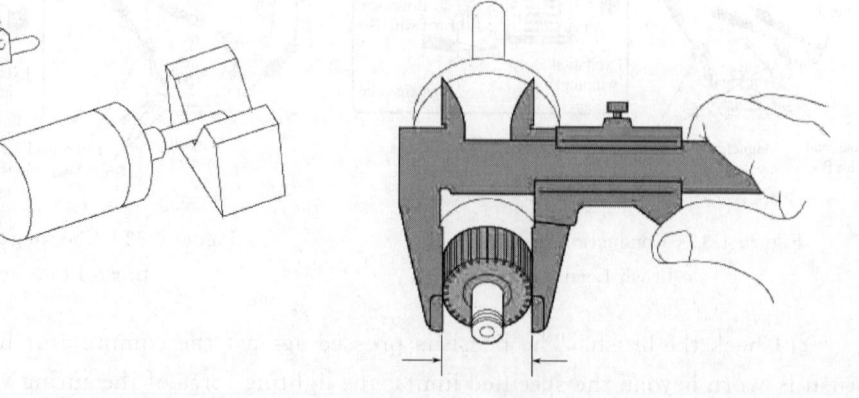

Figure 4-28   Round Runout Inspection of Commutator

Figure 4-29   Inspection of the Outside Diameter of the Commutator

④ Inspection of the outside diameter of the commutator. Measure the outside diameter of the commutator with a vernier caliper, as shown in Figure 4-29. Because the commutator is in contact with the brush when it rotates, it is subject to wear and tear. If the measured

Item Ⅳ   Maintenance of Starting System   **089**

value exceeds the specified wear range, contact with the brush will become weaker, which may lead to poor electrical circulation. As a result, the starter may be unable to turn and other faults may occur.

⑤ Inspection of the depth of the groove, measure the depth between the commutator plates with the depth bar of the vernier caliper, as shown in Figure 4-30.

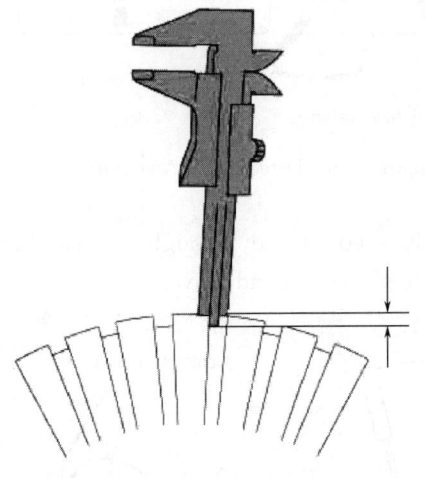

Figure 4-30　Inspection of the Depth of the Commutator Groove

(2) Overhaul of the stator.

① Check the excitation coil.

a. Check the conduction between the brush lead (group A) and the lead with a multimeter, as shown in Figure 4-31. Two brush leads in group A are conductive and two brush leads in group B are not. Checking the conduction between the brush lead and the lead is helpful to determine if an open circuit occurs in the excitation coil. Checking the insulation between the brush lead and the starter yoke is helpful to determine whether a short circuit occurs in the excitation coil.

b. The insulation between the brush lead (Group A) and the starter yoke is shown in Figure 4-32. Check the conduction between the lead and all brush leads. Two brush leads in group A are conductive and two brush leads in group B are not. Checking the lead between the brush lead and the lead is helpful to determine if an open circuit occurs in the excitation coil. Checking the insulation between the brush lead and the starter yoke is helpful to determine whether a short circuit occurs in the excitation coil.

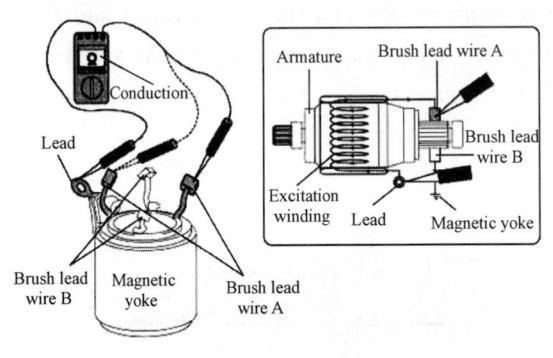

Figure 4-31　Conduction Inspection of Brush Leads

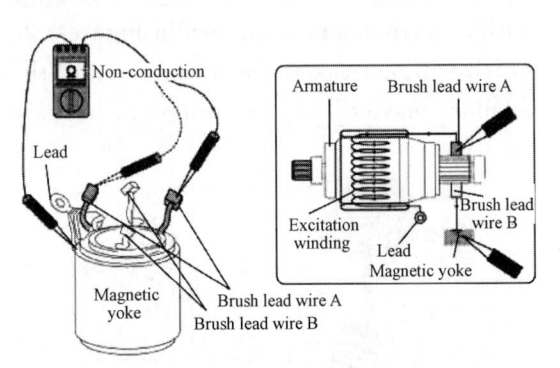

Figure 4-32　Checking the Insulation of Brush Leads and Yoke

② Check the brush. The brush is pressed against the commutator by a spring. If the brush is worn beyond the specified limit, the lighting force of the spring will be reduced and the contact with the commutator will be weakened, which may causes the current to flow unsmoothly and the starter unable to turn. Clean the brush and measure the brush length with a vernier caliper, as shown in Figure 4-33.

Note:

a. Measure the length of the brush in the middle of the brush because this part is the

most worn.

b. Use the top of the vernier caliper to measure the length of the brush, because the worn part is circular.

c. If the above measured values are below the specified values, replace the brush.

③ Check clutch. Turn the starter clutch by hand to check if the one-way clutch is locked, as shown in Figure 4-34. The one-way clutch transmits torque in only one rotating direction. In the other direction, the clutch is idle and does not transmit torque.

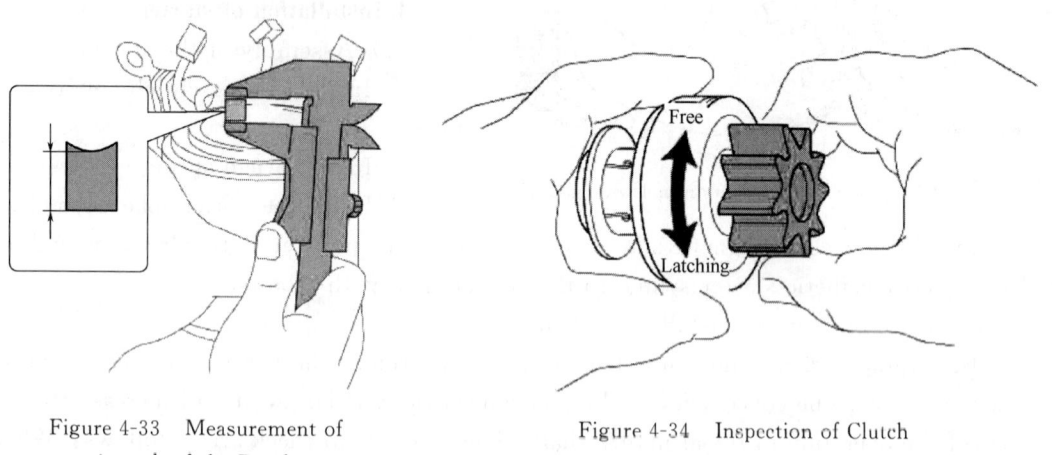

Figure 4-33　Measurement of
Length of the Brush

Figure 4-34　Inspection of Clutch

（3）Inspection of the electromagnetic switch.

① Check the electromagnetic switch and press the plunger with a finger. After releasing the finger, check whether the plunger returns smoothly to its original position, as shown in Figure 4-35.

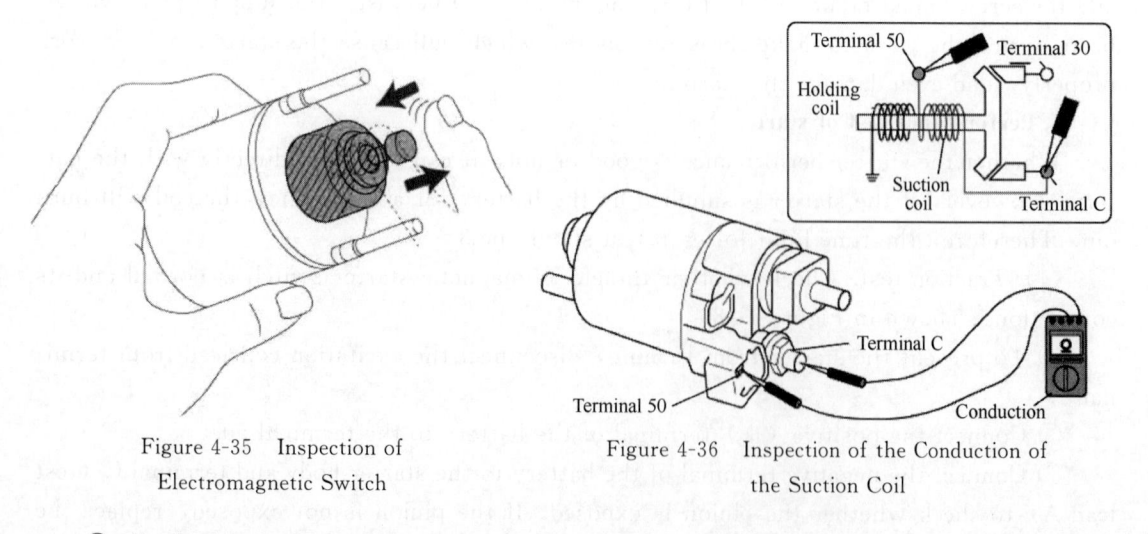

Figure 4-35　Inspection of
Electromagnetic Switch

Figure 4-36　Inspection of the Conduction of
the Suction Coil

② Check the conduction of the electromagnetic switch, as shown in Figure 4-36. Check the conduction between terminal 50 and terminal C with a multimeter. If the traction coil is normal, the two terminals are conductive to each other. If the traction coil is disconnected, the plunger cannot be introduced.

③ Check the conduction between the terminal 50 and the shell, as shown in Figure

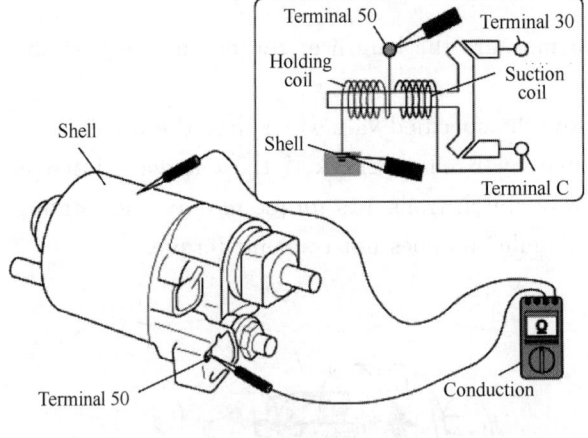

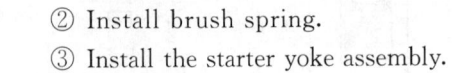

Figure 4-37　Conduction Inspection of Holding Coil

4-37. If the holding coil is normal, the connection between the terminal 50 and the switch body is conductive. If the holding coil is disconnected, the plunger can be pulled, but cannot be maintained, so the pinion is repeatedly extended and returned.

4. Installation of starter

(1) Assembly of the starter.

① Install starter clutch sub-assembly.

② Install brush spring.

③ Install the starter yoke assembly.

④ Install the electromagnetic starter switch. Hook the plunger to the drive rod and install the electromagnetic starter switch to the starter shell with 2 bolts.

(2) Precautions for the installation of the startor.

① Be careful to check the concentricity of each bearing. The bearings of the armature shaft are not easy to be concentric, if the non-concentricity is large, it will increase the resistance of the operation of the armature shaft. The methods to check are as follows: When each shaft neck is matched with each copper sleeve, it can be rotated freely without any apparent clearance. After installing the front end cover, turn the armature again, the armature also should rotate flexibly, otherwise the bearings are not concentric.

② Every copper sleeve, armature shaft neck, keyway thrust washer and other friction parts should be lubricated with oil. Fix the screws on the intermediate bearing support plate, and the screws must be provided with spring washers. Otherwise, the support plate will vibrate during the work to make the screw loose, which will cause the starter can not work properly, and even damage the starter.

5. Performance test of starter

Whether the starter performance is good or not, it can be tested directly with the battery. However, if the starter is supplied by the battery for a long time, the coil will burn out. Therefore, the time limit for each test should be 3~5s.

(1) Traction test. Check whether the electromagnetic starter switch is normal and its connection is shown in Figure 4-38.

① To prevent the starter from turning, disconnect the excitation coil lead from terminal C.

② Connect the positive (+) terminal of the battery to the terminal 50.

③ Connect the negative terminal of the battery to the starter body and terminal C (test lead A) to check whether the pinion is exposed. If the pinion is not exposed, replace the electromagnetic starter switch assembly.

(2) Holding test.

① Check to see if the holding coil is normal.

② After the traction test, when the pinion is out, disconnect the test lead A from terminal C. Check the pinion to see if it stays out.

092　Automobile Electrical Equipment Maintenance

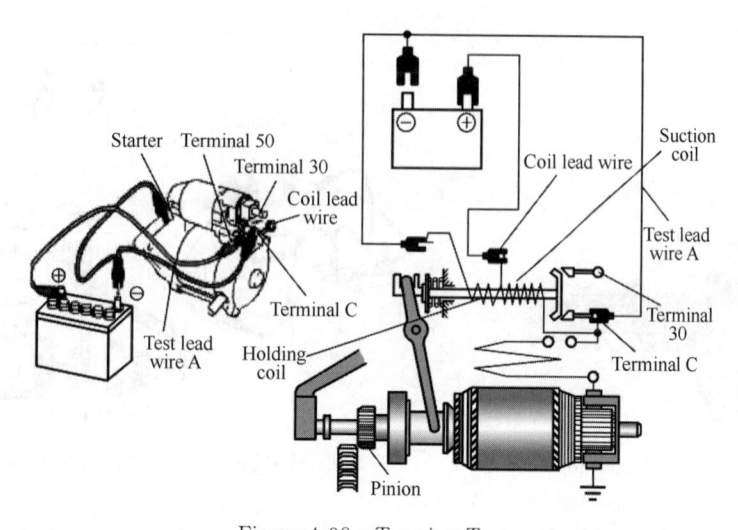

Figure 4-38   Traction Test

③ Disconnect the test lead A （which connects the negative electrode of the battery and terminal C）, disconnect the current flowing into the traction coil from terminal C, and allow the current to flow only into the holding coil. If the pinion fails to stay out, replace the electromagnetic starter switch assembly, as shown in Figure 4-39.

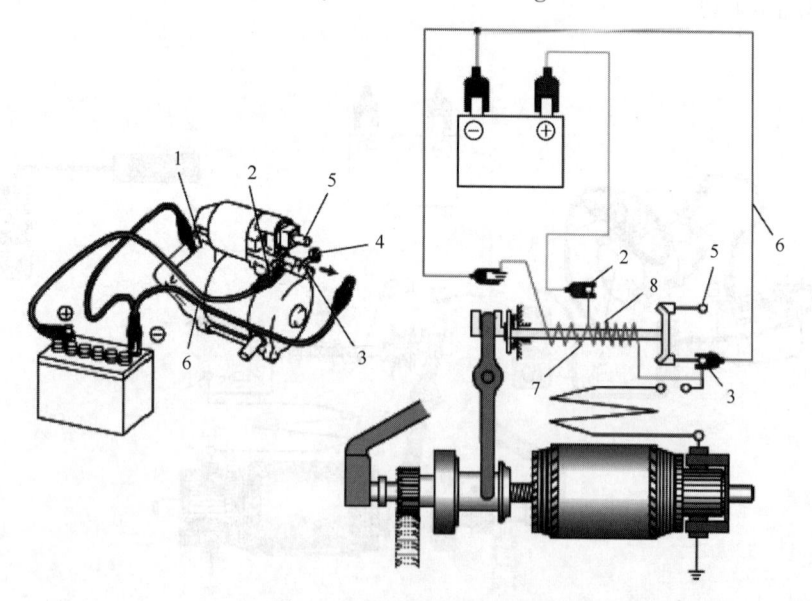

Figure 4-39   Holding Test

1—starter; 2—terminal 50 grounding post; 3—terminal C; 4—coil lead;
5—terminal 30 grounding post; 6—test line a; 7—holding coil; 8—suction coil

（3）Check the pinion clearance. Check the extension of the pinion, as shown in Figure 4-40. Measure the clearance between the pinion and the stop ring while maintaining the test condition. If the gap is beyond the specified range, replace the electromagnetic starter switch assembly.

（4）The pinion return test. Check whether the pinion returns to its original position, as shown in Figure 4-41.

After the holding test is finished, when the pinion is out, disconnect the ground wire from the starter body. Make sure the pinion returns to its original position.

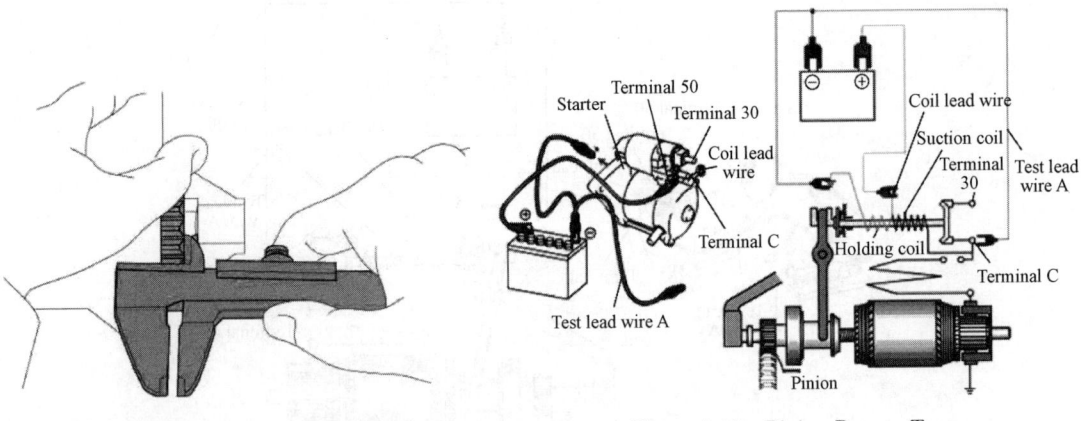

Figure 4-40   Pinion Extension Check   Figure 4-41   Pinion Return Test

(5) No load test. Check the contact of the electromagnetic starter switch and the contact between the commutator and the brush.

① Fix the starter between the aluminum plate or the cloth with a pliers.

② Connect the excitation coil lead detached to terminal C.

③ Connect the positive (+) terminal of the battery to terminal 30 and terminal 50, as shown in Figure 4-42.

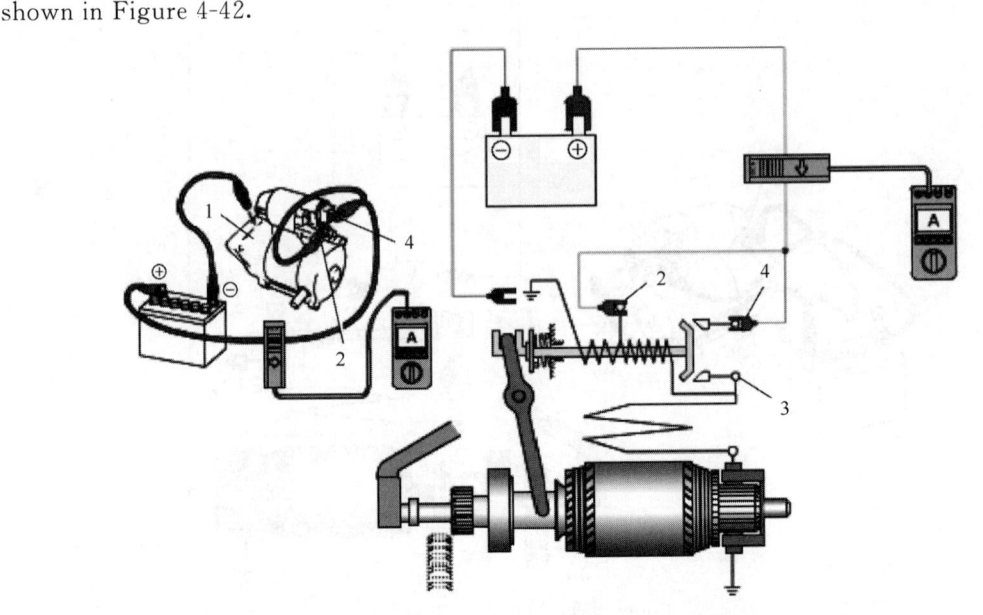

Figure 4-42   No-load Test

1—starter; 2—terminal 50 grounding post; 3—terminal C; 4—terminal 30 grounding post

④ Connect the multimeter between the positive (+) terminal of the battery and terminal 30.

⑤ Connect the negative (−) terminal of the battery to the starter body and turn the starter.

⑥ Measure the current flowing into the starter. The specified current of 11V is less than 50A, as shown in Figure 4-43.

Note:

In the no-load test, the current varies slightly with the starter motor, sometimes even

094   Automobile Electrical Equipment Maintenance

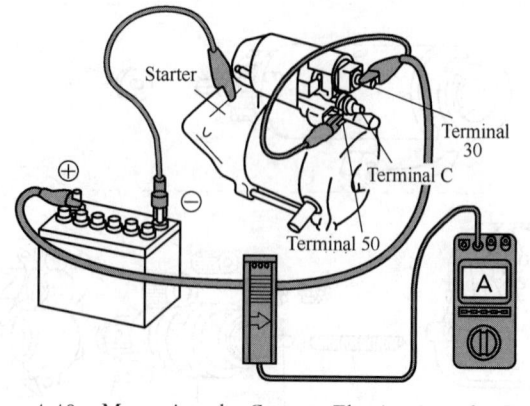

Figure 4-43   Measuring the Current Flowing into the Starter

200-300A current can be used. Consult the maintenance manual in advance. Be sure to use ammeters and leads of sufficient capacity.

IV. Knowledge and Skills Expansion

(I) Structure of deceleration starter

The structure of the deceleration starter is characterized by the installation of a reduction gear between the armature and the drive gear. The deceleration ratio is generally 3~4. The reduction gear reduces the speed of the starter, increases the output torque, and drives the pinion. Therefore, the starter can use small, high-speed, low-torque motor, which can reduce the size of the starter, reduce the weight of the starter, improve the starting performance and reduce the burden of the battery. The deceleration mechanism of the deceleration starter can be divided into three types by structure: external meshing type, internal meshing type and planetary gear meshing type.

1. External meshing deceleration starter

The idle wheel is used as the intermediate drive between the armature shaft and the drive gear of the starter, and the electromagnetic switch core is in the same axis with the drive gear, which directly drives the drive gear into the meshing without the need of a shifting fork. Therefore, the shape of the starter is quite different from that of the common starter. Figure 4-44 shows the external meshing deceleration starter for the Toyota series automobiles. Some external meshing deceleration mechanisms do not have idle wheels in the middle, and the drive gears must be moved by a shifting fork to engage.

The drive center distance of the external meshing deceleration mechanism is larger, therefore, due to the limitation of the starter structure, the reduction ratio can not be too large, and it is generally applied to the small power starter.

2. Internal meshing deceleration starter

The drive center distance of the internal meshing deceleration starter is small, so it can have a larger reduction ratio, so it is suitable for large power starter. But the drive gear of the deceleration mechanism of the internal meshing deceleration starter still has to be engaged by pilling with a shifting fork. Therefore, the shape of the starter is similar to that of the common starter. Figure 4-45 shows the working principle of the domestic QD254 internal meshing deceleration starter.

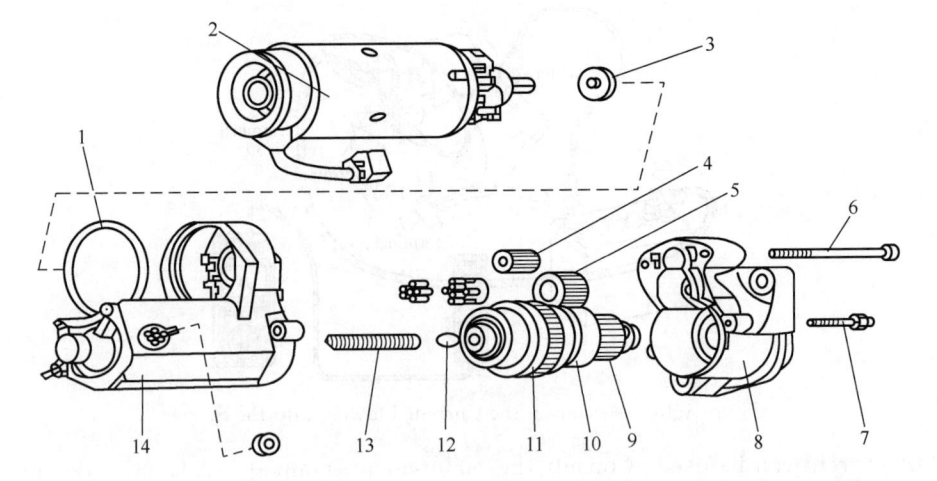

Figure 4-44　External Meshing Deceleration Starter for Toyota Series Automobiles

1—O rubber ring; 2—Motor; 3—Felt; 4—Drive gear; 5—Idler wheel; 6—Tension bolt;
7—Bolt; 8—Drive shell; 9—Drive gear; 10—One-way clutch; 11—Driven gear;
12—Ball; 13—Return spring; 14—Electromagnetic switch

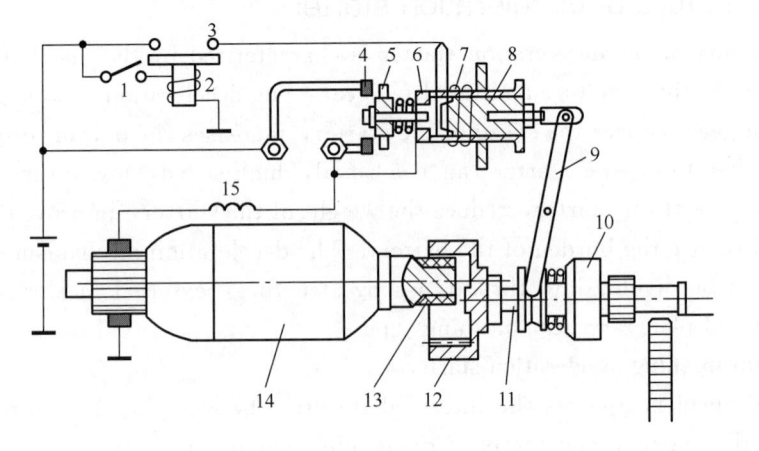

Figure 4-45　Working Principle of QD254 Internal Meshing Deceleration Starter

1—Starting switch; 2—Starting relay; 3—Starting relay contact; 4—Main contact; 5—Contact disc; 6—Suction coil;
7—Holding coil; 8—Movable core; 9—Shifting fork; 10—One-way clutch; 11—Screw spline shaft;
12—Internal meshing reduction gear; 13—Drive gear; 14—Armature winding; 15—Excitation winding

3. Planetary gear meshing deceleration starter

Planetary gear meshing deceleration starter has compact structure, large transmission ratio and high efficiency. Since the output shaft is concentric with the armature shaft and the coaxial armature shaft has no radial load, the size of the whole machine can be reduced. In addition to the planetary gear meshing reduction mechanism, the axial position structure of the planetary gear meshing deceleration starter is the same as that of the common starter, so the accessories can be used universally. The planetary gear meshing deceleration starter is shown in Figure 4-46. The device is provided with 3 planetary gears, 1 sun wheel (armature shaft gear) and 1 fixed inner gear ring, and its meshing relation and output path are shown in Figure 4-47. The planetary gear bracket is a disk with c certain thickness, the disk and the drive gear shaft are made into one body. The three planetary gears are mounted on the

disk together with the gear shaft, and the planetary gears can rotate flexibly on the shaft. One end of the drive gear shaft is provided with a screw key tooth, which is matched with the screw key groove in the clutch drive duct.

The sun wheel is made of 11 teeth, pressed on the armature shaft, and keeps meshing with the three planetary gears. The plastic-cast inner gear ring has 37 teeth, and the three planetary gears roll on it. The outer edge of the inner gear ring is raised and embedded in a pit on the rear end cover to keep it fixed. The reduction ratio of the gear is

$$i = 1 + Z_s / Z_e = 1 + 37/11 \approx 4.4$$

Of which Z_e——the number of the teeth of the sun wheel;

Z_s——the number of the teeth of the inner gear ring.

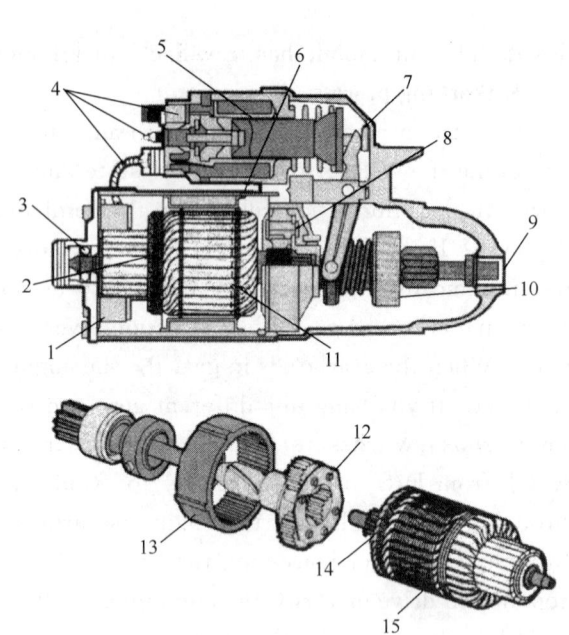

Figure 4-46　Planetary Gear Meshing Deceleration Starter
1—Carbon brush; 2—Welded connection; 3—Ball bearing; 4—Terminal and wire; 5—Movable core; 6—Permanent magnet; 7—Shifting fork connecting mechanism; 8—Planetary gear reducer; 9—Ball bearing; 10—Clutch; 11—Armature; 12—Planetary gear bracket; 13—Fixed gear; 14—Sun wheel; 15—Armature

(Ⅱ) Start/stop system

1. The role of the start/stop system

When the intelligent start/stop system is used, the engine automatically shuts down when the automobile is stationary in case of a red light. The ignition switch remains on during downtime. When necessary, the engine starts again automatically. With the ignition switch on, the intelligent start/stop system is automatically activated. When diving an automobile with the start/stop system in a congested urban road, it is helpful to save fuel and reduce CO_2 emissions.

2. Basic operating conditions for the start/stop systems

The driver's door must be closed. The driver fastens his seat belt. The engine hatch is

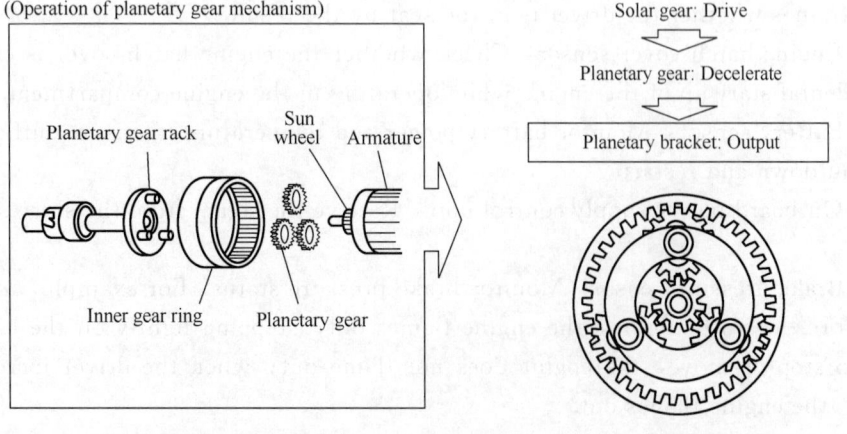

Figure 4-47　Core Relation and Output Route of Planetary Gear

closed. The automobile has travelled four kilometers since the last stop.

3. Working process

(1) An automobile equipped with an automatic gearbox.

Brake the vehicle to a standstill state and step on the brake, The engine will be shut down. In the information column on the combined instrument display, the indicator light is displayed. If the foot is removed from the brake, the engine starts again. The start/stop system indicator light goes out. Other information about the automatic gear selection lever, the engine is turned off in gear selection lever position P, N and D/S or tiptronic operation mode. When the gearbox is in gear P, the engine remains closed if the foot is removed from the brake. If you hang in a different gear and release the brake, the engine starts again. If the gearbox switches to the R reverse gear during downtime, the engine starts again. Switch from D/S to P gear quickly to avoid unnecessarily starting the engine as it passes through gear R. Whether the engine is turned off or not, you can control it by yourself through lowering or increasing the braking force. If you only tread on the brakes during a stop-and-go drive or turn, the automobile will not stop when stationary. If you step on the brake heavily, the engine is shut down.

(2) An automobile equipped with a manual gearbox.

Switch to neutral when the automobile is stationary and release the clutch. The engine will be shut down. In the information column on the combined instrument display, the start/stop system indicator light appears. If you press the clutch pedal, the engine starts again. The start/stop system indicator light goes out.

4. Description on parts

(1) Starter: Automobiles with a start/stop system are equipped with a powerful starter.

(2) Engine speed sensor: The engine speed sensor can identify the closing position (angle position) of the ignition switch so that the engine can be restarted quickly.

(3) Engine control unit: Start/Stop Coordinating Procedure: Enter all state variables (driver operation, environment and security status, system status)

(4) Battery: The AGM (Absorbent Glass Mat) battery with higher deep cycle resistance is installed.

(5) Seat belt latch sensor: Check whether the driver's seat belt is fastened; the system determines whether the driver is in the seat by the result.

(6) Engine hatch cover sensor: Check whether the engine hatch cover is closed. Prevent accidental start-up of the engine while operating in the engine compartment.

(7) Battery sensor: Monitor battery power and temperature to ensure sufficient power during shutdown and restart.

(8) On-board power supply control unit: Receive the signal from the start/stop system button.

(9) Brake pressure sensor: Monitor brake pressure status. For example, after normal brake before the traffic lights, the engine flames out; stepping lightly on the brake pedal, such as to stop or move, the engine does not flame out; when the driver increases brake pressure, the engine flames out.

5. Matters needing attention

Always turn off the start/stop system when wading through the water to prevent the engine from accidentally turning off and starting again to damage the engine cylinder by water intake; the closing button of the start/stop system is at the automobile center console.

Summary

(1) Most of the DC motors used in the starters are series-wound DC motors, because the characteristics of the series-wound DC motors can meet the requirements. The characteristics of the starter depend on the characteristics of the DC motor, while the series-wound DC motor is characterized by large starting torque and soft mechanical characteristics.

(2) Due to the high speed of the starter under light load or no-load, it is easy to cause "scatter" accidents, so it is not allowed to operate the series-wound DC motor with large power under light load or no-load.

(3) When the armature current is close to 1/2 of the braking current, the output power of the motor is the largest and the maximum power is the rated power.

(4) The main factors affecting the starter power are: contact resistance and wire resistance, battery capacity, temperature.

Thinking and Practice

(1) Why should no-load test and full-load test be done after assembling the starter?

(2) Is there any change in the current direction of the suction coil and the holding coil in the electromagnetic switch of the forced meshing starter under electromagnetic control before and after starting? Why?

(3) What are the advantages and disadvantages of the three types of clutch: roller type, friction plate type and spring type?

(4) What are the gaps in the starter that need to be adjusted? Why is it necessary to ensure the correct clearance of these parts?

(5) How to use the starter reasonably?

Item Ⅳ   Maintenance of Starting System   **099**

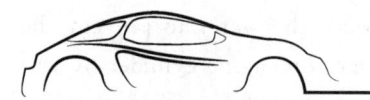

Item V

Maintenance of Ignition System

I. Scene Introduction

A Dongfeng Peugeot 206 car can reach 70km /h when it is cold, and when the automobile is running at the high temperature, the maximum speed can reach 40km/h. After overhaul, it is found that the reason is that the three-cylinder spark plug ceramic body is broken, which causes electricity leakage. This case is a typical example of a ignition system in which the engine is underpowered because a cylinder does not work.

The compressed combustible mixture in the cylinder of the gasoline engine is ignited by high-voltage EDM, and the function of producing EDM is realized by the ignition system. The work of the ignition system directly affects the quality of fuel combustion, which has an important influence on automobile power, fuel economy, working stability and emission pollution.

II. Related Knowledge

(I) Overview of ignition system

1. Type and development of ignition system

Ignition system plays an important role in gasoline engine. There are many types of ignition systems. The ignition systems are divided by the different power supply into battery ignition system and magneto ignition system. When the engine is working, the battery or the generator that supplies electricity to the ignition system is called the battery ignition system, while the magneto that provides electricity to the ignition system is called the magneto ignition system. The modern gasoline engines all use the battery ignition system.

The ignition system of the gasoline engine must store the energy obtained from the power supply before producing EDM, so that it can be released in an instant to produce high-voltage EDM. The ignition systems of gasoline engines can be divided into inductive energy storage ignition system and capacitive energy storage ignition system by the elements storing energy. The inductive energy storage ignition system stores the ignition energy in the inductor coil (ignition coil) in the form of magnetic field energy; the capacitive energy storage ignition system stores the ignition energy in the capacitor in the form of electric field energy. The ignition systems of gasoline engines generally belong to inductive energy storage ignition system.

According to the different control mode of ignition advance angle of gasoline engine ignition system, the development of the ignition systems can be divided into three stages: tradi-

tional ignition system, triode electronic ignition system and computer-controlled electronic ignition system.

(1) Traditional ignition system. The traditional ignition system is also called mechanical contact ignition system, which uses mechanical contact to control the ignition advance angle, and uses mechanical centrifugal device and vacuum device to adjust the ignition advance angle automatically. To ensure the ignition sequence, the traditional ignition system uses distributor to distribute power to each cylinder when the engine works.

The traditional ignition system has the advantages of simple structure and low cost and was first used in gasoline engine. However, due to the existence of mechanical contact, its ignition energy is low, its working reliability is poor, and it is sensitive to spark plug carbon and has large interference, which can not meet the requirements of modern automobile development. At present, the traditional ignition system has been replaced by the electronic ignition system with good ignition performance, reliable work and high control precision of ignition advance angle.

(2) Triode electronic ignition system. The function and the working principle of the triode electronic ignition system is basically the same as that of the traditional ignition system, but the element that controls the ignition advance angle, the circuit breaker is replaced by the electronic igniter, which uses the conduction and cut-off of the triode to control the on-off of the first winding circuit of the ignition coil, while the conduction and cut-off of the triode is controlled by the signal produced by the ignition signal generator. General electronic ignition system still retains mechanical centrifugal and vacuum ignition advance angle automatic adjustment device.

According to the structure principle of the ignition signal generator, the common inductive energy storage electronic ignition systems for gasoline engines are divided into three types: electromagnetic type, Hall type and photoelectric type. The ignition signal generator of the electromagnetic electronic ignition system uses the electromagnetic induction principle to produce the ignition signal; the ignition signal generator of the Hall electronic ignition system uses the Hall effect principle to produce the ignition signal; the ignition signal generator of the photoelectric electronic ignition system uses the photoelectric effect to produce the ignition signal.

(3) Computer-controlled electronic ignition system. In the computer-controlled electronic ignition system, the ECU (electronic control unit) controls and corrects the ignition advance angle, and even the distributor is canceled, so that it is an all-electronic ignition system. Because computer-controlled electronic ignition system reduces and even canceled the mechanical device compared with other ignition systems, the control precision of ignition advance angle is improved, the energy loss is less, the radio interference is less, and the work is more reliable.

Ignition system not only has the function of ignition advance angle control, but also has the function of explosion control, power-on time control and so on. With the development and popularization of automobile electronic control technology, the application of ignition system is more and more.

2. Function of ignition system

The ignition system has been developed for many years. Although there are many

types, the modern electronic-controlled ignition system is different from the traditional contact ignition system in appearance, but their functions are the same. The ignition system mainly has the following three functions.

(1) Producing an electric spark sufficient to puncture the spark plug gap. The ignition system must be able to generate a high enough breakdown voltage to break through the electrode gap of the spark plug, produce an electric spark with sufficient energy, ignite the air, fuel mixture, and maintain a long enough spark time to ensure the full combustion of the air and fuel mixture. In order to ensure the reliable ignition of the engine, the spark energy above 100 MJ should be guaranteed when the spark plug jumps.

(2) Controlling the ignition advance angle to suit the working condition of the engine. The ignition system must be able to adjust the ignition advance angle in time as the engine speed and load change and its working conditions change, so that the engine can ignite at the most appropriate time in all cases.

(3) Distributing electric sparks. For a multi-cylinder engine, the ignition system must deliver an electric spark to the correct cylinder at the right time of the compression stroke to start the combustion process.

(II) Basic construction and overhaul of the ignition system

1. Basic composition of ignition system

The overall layout of the ignition system is shown in Figure 5-1. It is mainly composed of power supply (battery), ignition switch, ignition coil, distributor. As shown in Figure 5-2, these components constitute two interconnected circuits: primary and secondary circuits. The primary circuit is a low-voltage circuit and the secondary circuit is a high-voltage circuit.

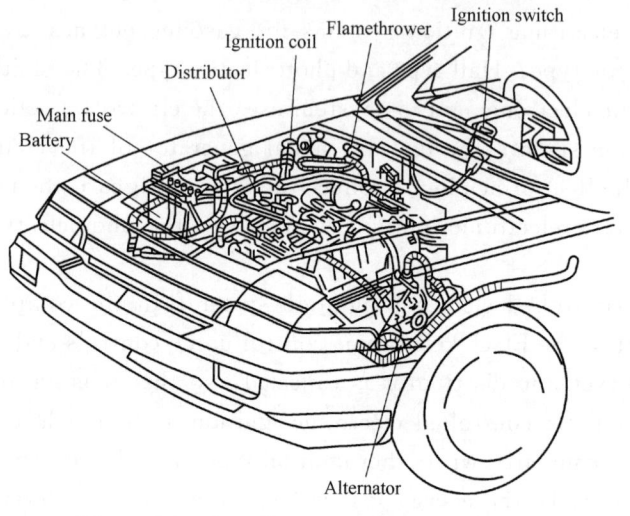

Figure 5-1   Overall Layout of Ignition System

(1) Primary circuit. When the ignition switch is switched on, the current flows from the battery through the ignition switch and the primary loop resistor to the primary winding of the ignition coil. The current then flows through some kind of switching device and is grounded. The switching device is controlled by the trigger device in the electronic way or in mechanical contact way.

The current in the primary winding of the ignition coil produces a magnetic field. The

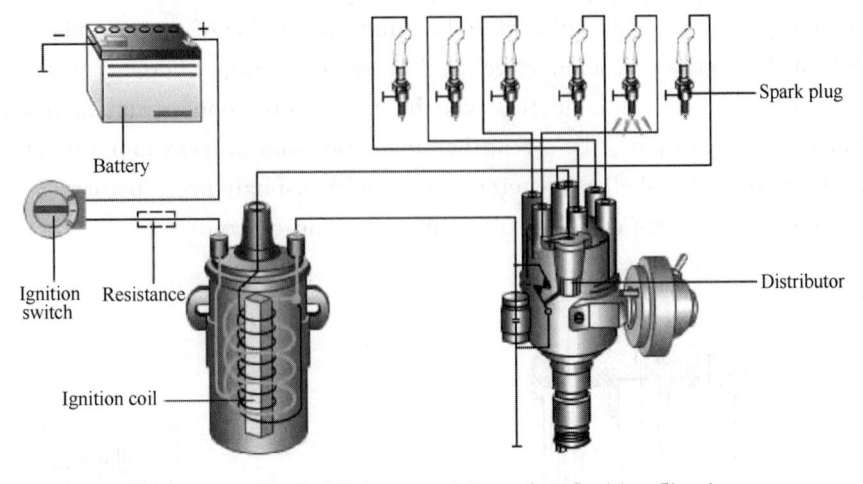

Figure 5-2 Typical Primary and Secondary Ignition Circuits

switching device or the control module cuts off this current at a predetermined time. At this point, the electromagnetic field in the primary winding disappears and the high-voltage pulse is induced on the secondary winding, which is then connected to the secondary circuit of the ignition system.

Some ignition systems are connected in series with an additional resistor between the ignition switch and the ignition coil terminal to provide the ignition coil with an appropriate amount of voltage and current. Now, many ignition systems no longer use additional resistors, and they provide 12V voltage directly to the ignition coil.

(2) Secondary circuit. The secondary circuit is used to provide a high-voltage pulse to the spark plug. In the past, the ignition system used a distributor to achieve this function. Now, to improve fuel economy and reduce pollution emissions, most automobiles use a ignition system without the distributor.

In the distributor ignition system, the high-voltage pulse generated by the secondary coil passes through the high-voltage wire from the ignition coil to the distributor. In the distributor, according to the ignition sequence of the engine, this high voltage is assigned to the spark plug of each cylinder by a group of high voltage dividers.

2. Structure and overhaul of the ignition coil

(1) The structure of the ignition coil. The ignition coil is the basic element to convert the low-voltage electricity of the power supply into high-voltage electricity. According to the structure of magnetic circuit, the ignition coil can be divided into open magnetic circuit ignition coil and close magnetic circuit ignition coil.

① The open magnetic circuit ignition coil. The structure of the open magnetic circuit ignition coil is shown in Figure 5-3. The ignition coil generally has two low-voltage terminals, and the two low-voltage terminals are marked with "+" and "−" symbols respectively.

The center of the open magnetic circuit ignition coil is an core made of silicon steel sheets. An insulated cardboard sleeve is arranged on the outside of the core. The first winding and the second winding of the ignition coil are layered around the sleeve. In the second winding, the enameled wire with a diameter of 0.06~0.10mm is wound around 11,000~23,000 turns, and in the first winding, the high strength enameled wire with a diameter of 0.5~1.0mm is wound around 230~270 turns. Because the passing current of the first wind-

Item V Maintenance of Ignition System **103**

ing is large and the heat is more, it is wound around the outside of the second winding to facilitate the heat dissipation. A conductive steel sleeve is arranged between the ignition coil winding and the shell, with an insulating bakelite cover on the upper part and a porcelain insulating seat on the lower part. To strengthen insulation and prevent moisture from sinking into the ignition coil, the shell is generally filled with asphalt or transformer oil, so the open magnetic circuit ignition coil is also called a wet ignition coil.

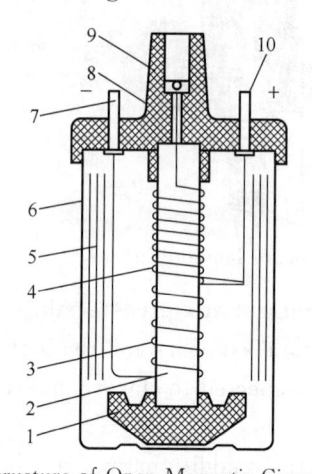

Figure 5-3　Structure of Open Magnetic Circuit Ignition Coil

1—Insulation seat; 2—Core; 3—First winding;

4—Second winding; 5—Conductive steel sleeve;

6—Shell; 7—Low voltage terminal "−"; 8—Bakelite cover;

9—High voltage terminal; 10—Low voltage terminal "+"

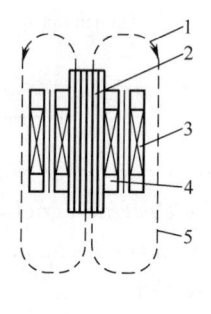

Figure 5-4　Magnetic circuit of Open Magnetic Circuit Ignition Coil

1—Magnet wire; 2—Core;

3—First winding; 4—Second winding;

5—Conductive steel sleeve

When the first winding circuit of the ignition coil is connected, the core is magnetized and its magnetic circuit is shown in Figure 5-4. Because the upper and lower part of the magnetic circuit needs to pass through the air, the outer part needs to pass through the conductive steel sleeve in the shell to form the loop, the core itself cannot form the loop (so it is called the open magnetic circuit ignition coil). The open magnetic circuit ignition coil has high magnetic resistance, high magnetic leakage loss and low energy conversion efficiency.

② Close magnetic circuit ignition coil. The structure and the magnetic circuit of the close magnetic circuit ignition coil are shown in Figure 5-5. The core of the close magnetic circuit ignition coil is a "日" shape, which constitutes a close magnetic circuit. To reduce the hysteresis of the core, a small air gap is left in the magnetic circuit. In the shell of the close magnetic circuit ignition coil, thermosetting resin is used as filler, so it is also called dry ignition coil.

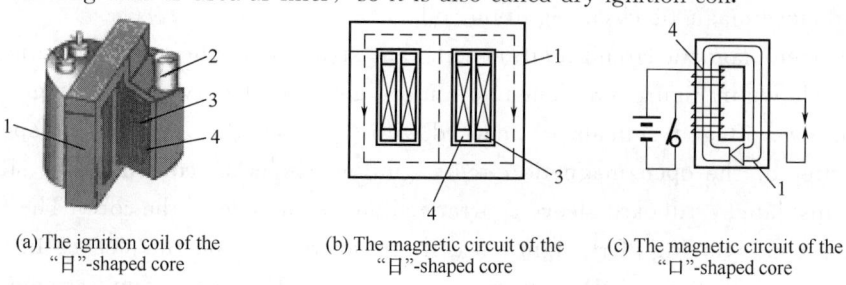

(a) The ignition coil of the "日"-shaped core

(b) The magnetic circuit of the "日"-shaped core

(c) The magnetic circuit of the "口"-shaped core

Figure 5-5　Structure and Magnetic Circuit Indication of the Close Magnetic Circuit Ignition Coil

1—Core; 2—High voltage jack; 3—Secondary winding; 4—Primary winding

104　Automobile Electrical Equipment Maintenance

Compared with the open magnetic circuit ignition coil, the close magnetic circuit ignition coil has low magnetic resistance, low magnetic leakage loss and high energy conversion efficiency. In addition, the shell of the close magnetic circuit ignition coil is usually molded by hot-melt plastic injection, and the filler is made of thermosetting resin, so that its insulation and sealing property are better than that of the open magnetic circuit ignition coil. With the increasing miniaturization of the volume of the close magnetic circuit ignition coil, it can be installed directly on the distributor cover, which not only eliminates the high voltage wire between the ignition coil and the distributor, but also makes the structure of the ignition system more compact. Therefore, it is widely used in the electronic ignition system.

(2) Overhaul of the ignition coil.

① Appearance inspection. To observe the appearance of the ignition coil, if there is dirt or corrosion of the terminal, it should be cleaned and then checked; if the bakelite cover is damaged, the terminal is loose, the shell is deformed, the filler overflows, the contact of the high-voltage socket is not good, the ignition coil should be replaced.

② Inspection of insulation properties. The resistance value between any terminal of the ignition coil and the shell measured by a multimeter should not be less than 50MΩ, otherwise it indicates that the insulation of the ignition coil is not good and the ignition coil should be replaced.

③ Inspection of winding resistance. The resistance value of the first winding and the second winding of the ignition coil shall be measured by the resistance gear of the multimeter. The resistance value shall be in accordance with the regulations, otherwise the ignition coil shall be replaced.

3. Structure and overhaul of distributor

The function of the distributor in the traditional ignition system is to turn on or off the primary circuit of the ignition coil, so that the secondary ignition coil produces a high voltage electricity, and sends the high voltage electricity to each cylinder spark plug according to the working order of the engine at the optimal ignition time. The composition of distributor in the traditional ignition system, as shown in Figure 5-6.

The distributor in the common electronic ignition system has the same structure as the distributor in the traditional ignition system, but its circuit breaker is replaced by the ignition signal generator. The distributor still has the traditional distributor, the mechanical centrifugal ignition advance angle automatic regulator and the vacuum ignition advance angle automatic regulator.

(1) Distributor. The function of distributor is to distribute the high voltage electricity produced by the ignition coil to spark plugs according to the ignition sequence of each cylinder of the engine, which is composed of distributor cover, distributor rotor and high voltage wire. The distributor is mounted above the circuit breaker. In the center of the distributor cover is a high-voltage wire jack, which is provided with a spring-loaded brush, which is pressed on the conductive plate of the distributor rotor by its spring. The central jack of the distributor cover is surrounded by each cylinder high-voltage sub-wire jack, which is connected with the side electrode in the distributor cover by the metal sleeve, and the side electrode is connected with each cylinder spark plug respectively through the high-voltage sub-wire. The distributor rotor is mounted on the rotor of the ignition signal generator at the top

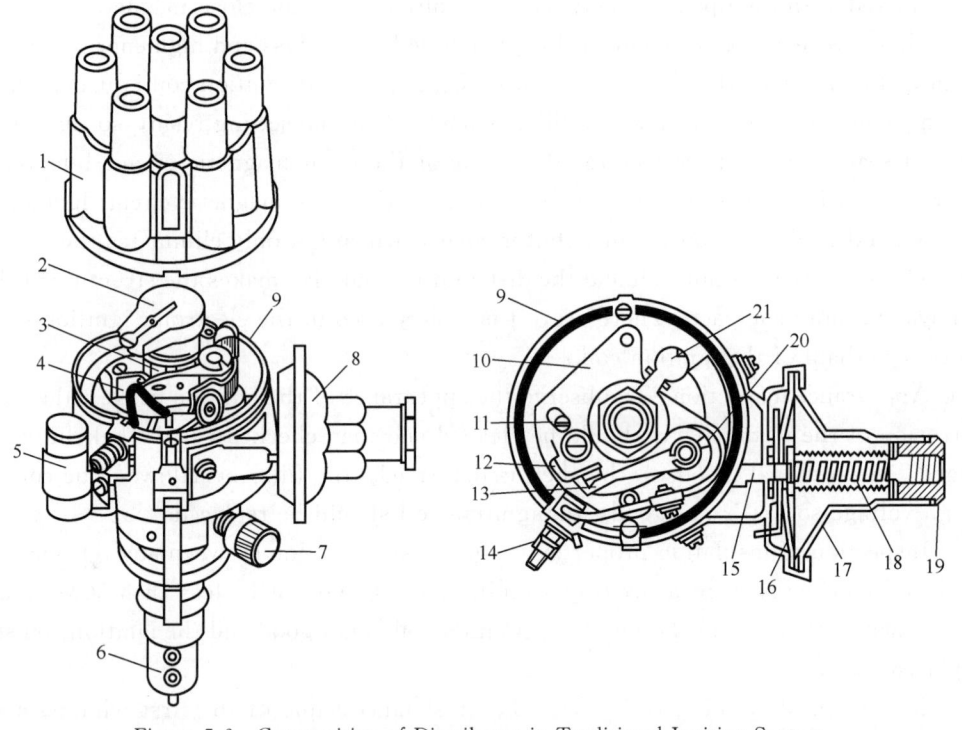

Figure 5-6　Composition of Distributor in Traditional Ignition System

1—Distributor cover; 2—Distributor rotor; 3—Cam; 4—Contact and circuit breaker bottom plate assembly;
5—Capacitor; 6—shaft joint; 7—Oil ring; 8—Vacuum advance mechanism; 9—Distributor shell; 10—Movable
bottom plate; 11—Eccentric screw; 12—Fixed contact and bracket; 13—Movable contact arm; 14—Terminal;
15—Drawbar; 16—Clapboard; 17—Vacuum ingition advance angle automatic regulator; 18—Spring;
19—Nut; 20—Contact arm spring; 21—Felt and clamping collar

of the cam. When the engine is working, the distributor rotor rotates with the rotor of the ignition signal generator. There is a copper conductive plate riveted on the top of the distributor rotor, and the gap between the end of the distributor rotor and the side electrode is 0.2~0.8mm. When the circuit breaker contact is opened, the high voltage electricity produced by the ignition coil jumps from the conductive plate of the distributor rotor to its opposite side electrode, and then is sent to the spark plug electrode by the high-voltage sub-wire.

The distributor works under high voltage, which is the part with high failure rate in the ignition system. The main common faults are leakage of distributor cover, bad contact between central jack brush and the conductive plate of the distributor rotor, leakage of distributor rotor, etc. The contents and methods of the overhaul of the distributor are as follows.

① Inspect the distributor cover by eyes, if the inside of the cover is dirty, it should be cleaned, if there are cracks on the cover, it should be replaced.

② Check the insulation performance of the distributor cover. As shown in Figure 5-7 (a), the resistance value between the sockets of the distributor cover should be measured with the resistance gear of a multimeter. The resistance value should not be less than 500 MΩ, otherwise the insulation performance is not good, the distributor cover should be replaced. The automobile jump fire method can also be used, as shown in Figure 5-7(b), pull out all the high-voltage sub-wires on the distributor cover, the central high-voltage wire is plug into any high-voltage sub-wire jack, and plug a high-voltage sub-wire in jack adjacent

to the sub-wire jack, so that its end from the cylinder body is 3-4mm, and then dial the circuit breaker contact arm, to see if there is a spark between the sub-wire end and the cylinder body. If the spark is jumped, it indicates that the high-voltage sub-wire jack checked has been broken down and leaked. Then follow the method mentioned above to check if there is any leakage between other high-voltage sub-wire jacks. This method can also be used to check whether there is leakage in the central high-voltage wire jack and each high-voltage sub-wire jack. Where no sparks is skipped, it indicates the insulation is good; if sparks skip, it indicates there is a breakdown and leakage in the central high-voltage wire jack and each high-voltage sub-wire jack, and they should be replaced.

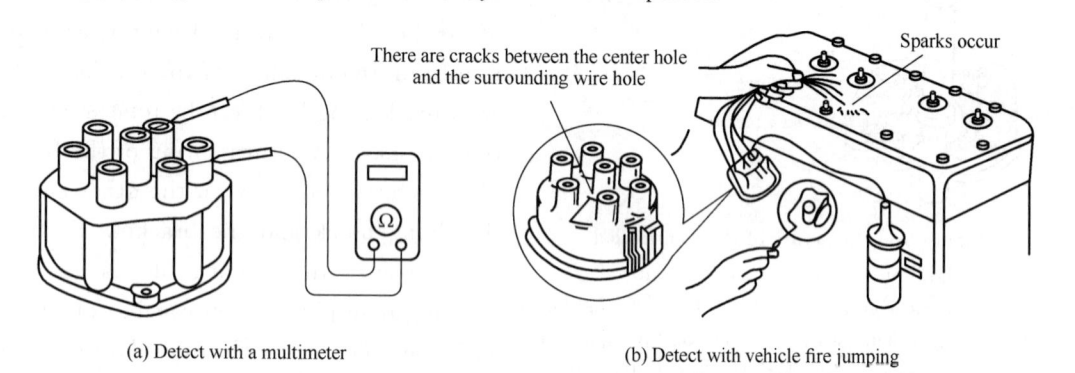

(a) Detect with a multimeter   (b) Detect with vehicle fire jumping

Figure 5-7   Measurement of Insulation Performance of Distributor Cover

③ Check whether the brush in the central jack of the distributor cover is elastic, stuck or worn, replace the distributor cover if necessary.

④ Check whether there is a crack in the distributor rotor, the conductive plate is ablative, the installation is not stable, and replace the distributor rotor if necessary.

⑤ Check whether the distributor rotor is leaking, as shown in Figure 5-8. A multimeter can be used (see Figure 5-8 (a)). The inspection method is the same as the distributor cover. The resistance between the electrode plate of the distributor rotor and the insulator should not be less than 500 MΩ. Otherwise, the distributor rotor is leaking. The automobile jump fire method can also be

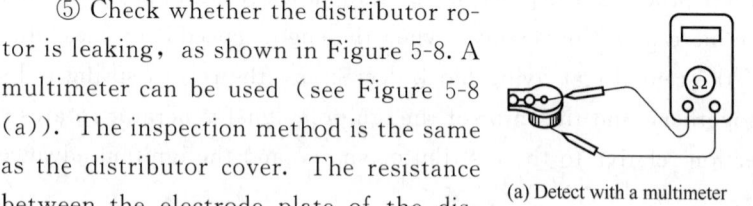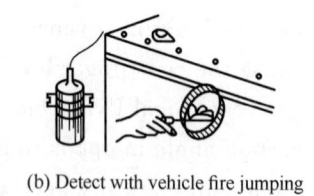

(a) Detect with a multimeter   (b) Detect with vehicle fire jumping

Figure 5-8   Check Whether the Distributor Rotor is Leaking

used [see Figure 5-8(b)]. Firstly, put the distributor rotor back on the cylinder cover, so that its conductive plate (metal part) is contacted with the cylinder cover, and then one end of the high-voltage wire is 6~8mm away from the seat hole of the distributor rotor, at the same time the ignition switch is connected. A screwdriver can be used to switch the circuit breaker contact, make it 1 open and 1 closed. At this point, if there is a spark between the high-voltage wire end and the seat hole of the distributor rotor, it indicates that the distributor rotor is leaking, it should be replaced.

(2) Centrifugal ignition advance angle regulator. The function of the centrifugal ignition advance angle regulator is to adjust the ignition advance angle automatically according to

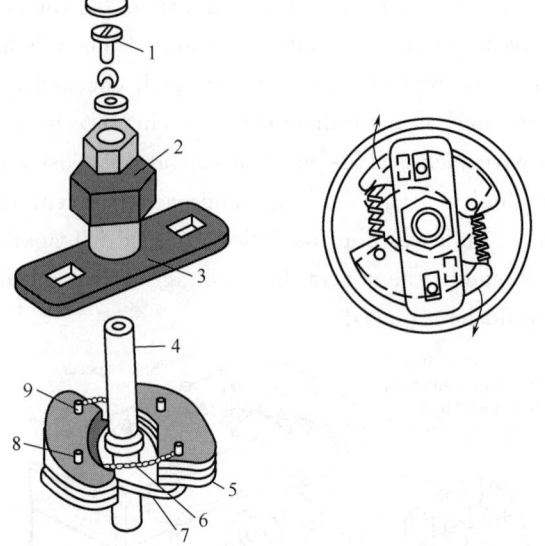

Figure 5-9   Structure of the Centrifugal
Ignition Advance Angle Regulator
1—Cam fixing screw and washer; 2—Cam; 3—Shifting
plate; 4—Distributor shaft; 5—Centrifugal flying block;
6—Spring; 7—Bracket; 8—Pin; 9—Pin

the change of the engine speed. The centrifugal ignition advance angle regulator is installed in the lower part of the bottom plate of the distributor, and its structure is shown in Figure 5-9.

The bracket of the centrifugal ignition advance angle regulator is fixed on the distributor shaft. Two centrifugal flying blocks are arranged on the bracket. The one end of the centrifugal flying block is arranged on the pin shaft of the bracket. The centrifugal flying block can be rotated around the pin shaft. A return spring of the flying block is arranged between the other end of the flying block and the bracket. Each of the two centrifugal flying blocks has one shifting plate pin, which can be connected with the hole on the shifting plate to drive the ignition signal generator rotor.

When the engine speed is increased, the centrifugal flying block is swung outward around its pin axis under the action of centrifugal force, and the shifting plate pin on the centrifugal flying block pushes the shifting plate along with the rotor of the ignition signal generator to turn a certain angle relative to the distributor shaft in its rotation direction, so that the ignition signal generator produces the pulse signal automatically ahead of time, that is, the ignition advance angle increases. Conversely, when the engine speed decreases, because the centrifugal force of the centrifugal flying block decreases, the return spring pulls the centrifugal flying block together, and the rotor of the ignition signal generator rotates a certain angle in opposite direction relative to the distributor shaft, and the ignition advance angle automatically decreases.

The common faults of the centrifugal ignition advance angle regulator include that the spring fails, the shifting plate pin and the shifting plate jack on the centrifugal flying block is worn, loose or stuck, etc. The contents and methods of overhaul are as follows.

① Check whether the centrifugal flying block can be swung flexibly or not, whether the centrifugal flying block is fit with the pin shaft, the shifting plate pin and the shifting plate normally, and repair or replace them if necessary.

② Use a spring scale to measure the elasticity of the return spring of the centrifugal flying block, and replace the return spring of the centrifugal flying block when necessary.

③ Check the performance of the centrifugal ignition advance angle regulator (that is, the relation between the ignition advance angle adjustment and the rotation speed) on the special test bench. If it doesn't meet the requirements, we can trigger the return spring bracket of the centrifugal flying block to adjust the spring pre-tightening force, and replace the return spring of the centrifugal flying block if necessary.

(3) Vacuum ignition advance angle regulator. The vacuum ignition advance angle regulator is installed on the outside of the distributor shell. Its function is to adjust the ignition advance angle automatically according to the change of engine load. The working principle of the vacuum ignition advance angle regulator is shown in Figure 5-10. A clapboard is arranged in the shell of the vacuum ignition advance angle regulator. The air chamber on the left side of the clapboard passes through the atmosphere. The clapboard is connected with the movable bottom plate in the distributor with a pull rod. The air chamber on the right side of the clapboard is provided with a clapboard return spring, which is communicated with the vacuum opening of the vacuum tube near the throttle through. When the opening of the engine throttle (i. e. the load) is reduced, the vacuum of the vacuum opening increases, so that the clapboard overcomes the force of the clapboard return spring to arch to the right, and the movable bottom plate in the distributor is pulled by the push rod to turn a certain angle counterclockwise. Because the movable bottom plate in the distributor is rotated with the stator assembly of the ignition signal generator, and the rotating direction is opposite to the rotating direction of the rotor of the ignition signal generator, the ignition signal generator produces the pulse signal ahead of time, the ignition advance angle increases. Conversely, when the engine load increases, the clapboard arches to the left under the action of the clapboard spring, and the ignition advance angle decreases.

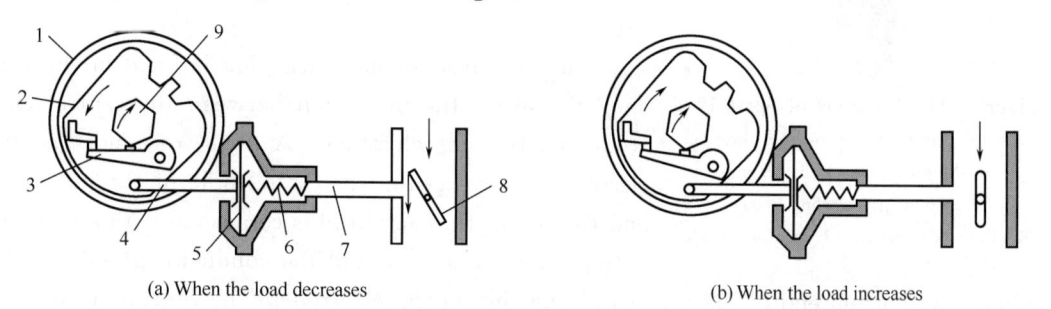

(a) When the load decreases   (b) When the load increases

Figure 5-10   Working Principle of Vacuum Ignition Advance Angle Regulator
1—Distributor shell; 2—Circuit breaker movable bottom plate; 3—Contact; 4—Push rod; 5—Clapboard;
6—Return spring; 7—Vacuum tube; 8—Throttle; 9—Cam

When the engine is in the idle condition and the throttle is in the minimum opening position, the vacuum opening is above the throttle. At this point, the vacuum degree is almost 0, and the clapboard return spring pushes the clapboard to minimize the ignition advance angle to meet the requirement of small or non-advance ignition advance angle in the idle condition of the engine.

The common faults of the vacuum ignition advance angle regulator include the spring fails, the clapboard is broken, and the circuit breaker movable bottom plate is stuck, etc. The contents and methods to overhaul the vacuum ignition advance angle regulator are as follows.

① Check whether the clapboard is broken, whether the spring fails, whether the connection between the push rod and the movable bottom plate is loose, whether the movable bottom plate is stuck or not, whether the vacuum pipe joint thread is in good condition, and if necessary, repair and replace them.

② Blow or inhale on the side of the vacuum tube to check the tightness of the vacuum

ignition advance angle regulator. If air leakage occurs, the vacuum ignition advance angle regulator assembly should be replaced.

③ Check the performance of the vacuum ignition advance angle regulator on the special test bench. When a vacuum pump is applied to the regulator at a fixed speed, the ignition advance angle should conform to the standard, otherwise, the gasket at the vacuum tube joint of the regulator can be increased or reduced, and the pre-tightening force of the clapboard return spring can be adjusted.

4. Structure and overhaul of spark plug

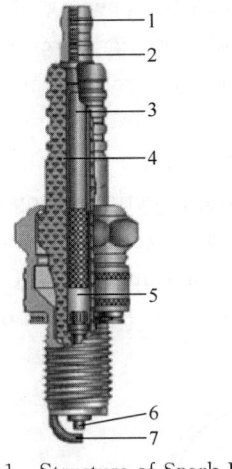

Figure 5-11   Structure of Spark Plug
1—Iplug nut; 2—Connecting thread;
3—Metal screw; 4—Insulator;
5—Conductive sealing glass;
6—Central electrode; 7—Side electrode

(1) Structure of the spark plug. All types of ignition systems use spark plugs, which introduce the high-voltage current generated by the ignition coil into the combustion chamber in the form of an arc and ignite the mixture. The spark plug consists mainly of a metal rod (steel core), a porcelain insulator (an insulator capable of conducting heat), and a pair of electrodes (one of which is insulated in a porcelain insulator, called a central electrode, and the other is grounded on a shell, called a side electrode). The structure is shown in Figure 5-11.

The insulator of the spark plug is fixed in the steel shell to ensure the insulation between the central electrode and the side electrode. A metal rod and a central electrode are arranged in the central hole of the insulator, and the top of the metal rod is connected with a sub-high voltage wire plug nut, and the conductor glass is sealed between the bottom end of the metal rod and the central electrode. The central electrode is made of nickel-manganese alloy and has good high temperature resistance, corrosion resistance and conductivity. The lower end of the shell is a curved side electrode, which maintains a certain gap away the central electrode. The gap size is determined by the automobile manufacturer. The spark plug shell is threaded to fit the spark plug on the engine cylinder cover. The copper sealing washer can be used for sealing and heat transfer. Many automobile spark plugs have a resistor between the terminal at the top and the central electrode, which reduces radio-frequency interference and thus avoids radio noise. It is important to note that voltage from radio-frequency interference can also interfere with or even damage the on-board computer. Therefore, if the automobile is equipped with a resistance spark plug when leaving the factory, a resistance one must be used when replacing the spark plug.

(2) Thermal characteristics of the spark plug. The spark plug has different thermal properties and is used in different working conditions. While the engine is running, most of the heat from the spark plug is concentrated on the central electrode. Because the side electrode is mounted on the cylinder by thread, the heat of the side electrode diffuses rapidly. The heat transfer path of the spark plug begins at the central electrode, passes through the insulator to the shell, then from the shell to the cylinder head, and the coolant circulating in the cylinder head absorbs the heat. The thermal properties of the spark plug are deter-

110 Automobile Electrical Equipment Maintenance

mined by the length of the insulator below the contact between the insulator and the shell. Hot and cold spark plugs are shown in Figure 5-12. For example, the insulator skirt of the hot spark plug is longer, the heat transfer path is longer, and the electrode temperature is higher. The insulator skirt of the cold spark plug is short, the heat transfer path is short, and the electrode temperature is low. The thermal properties of the domestic spark plug are expressed by the calorific value calibrated by the length of the spark plug insulator skirt, the calorific value code of the spark plug is 1～11, the spark plugs with the cal-

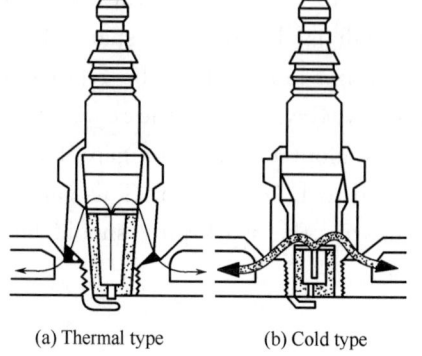

(a) Thermal type   (b) Cold type

Figure 5-12   Hot and Cold Spark Plugs

orific value code of 1～3 are hot spark plugs, these with the calorific value code of 4～6 are medium spark plugs, and these with the calorific value code of 7～11 are cold spark plugs.

When the engine works, the temperature of the spark plug insulator skirt has a great influence on its performance. If the temperature is too low, the gasoline or lubricating oil that falls on the spark plug insulator skirt is easy to form carbon deposition and causes the spark plug to leak electricity and do not jump fire; If the temperature is too high, it is easy to cause engine to burn early or detonate. When the temperature of the spark plug insulator skirt is kept from 500 to 700℃, it can not only make the oil particles fallen burn immediately, but also can not cause early combustion or knock combustion of the engine, which is called the self-cleaning temperature of the spark plug.

In order to ensure the normal operation of the engine, different engines should be equipped with spark plugs with different calorific values. For engines with low compression ratio and low power, the spark plug is easy to be contaminated by carbon deposition under the condition of continuous low speed operation. In this case, a hot spark plug shall be used. For the engine with high compression ratio and large power, the engine runs at a very high speed for a long time. In order to prevent early combustion or knock combustion due to high temperature, the cold spark plug is often used.

(3) Overhaul of spark plug. The spark plug works in high-temperature and high-pressure environment, and is subject to the corrosion of additives in the fuel. It is easy to damage parts. The common faults of spark plugs are insulator breakage, electrode ablation, carbon deposition, electrode gap misalignment, etc.

During the inspection, attention should be paid to whether the connection between the spark plug shell and the insulator is solid and reliable. If the thread and the insulator of the spark plug are found to be cracked or the shell is not firmly connected to the insulator, a new spark plug should be replaced. Or the spark plug insulation resistance should be measured with a multimeter. The measurement of the spark plug insulation resistance is as shown in Figure 5-13. The resistance should be 10 MΩ or greater; Check whether the central electrode is burned and the welding of the side electrode is open or off, if the above are found, a new central electrode should be replaced. Check whether there is carbon deposition. The carbon deposition inspection of the spark plug is as shown in Figure 5-14. When the carbon deposition of the spark plug is light, a copper wire brush or a soft wire brush can

be used to clean. When the carbon deposition is serious, the insulator is cracked, or the electrode is ablative, the spark plug shall be replaced. The cleaning of the spark plug is as shown in Figure 5-15. The gap between the electrodes of the spark plug is 0.7~1.0mm. In recent years, to meet the requirements of engine for exhaust gas purification, thin combustion is adopted. , and the gap of the spark plug has a tendency to increase, some have increased to 1.0~1.2mm. This gap can be measured by a feeler. If the gap does not meet the standard, the spark plug should be replaced, or a special tool is used to make an adjustment.

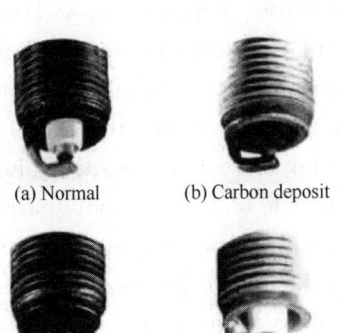

(a) Normal   (b) Carbon deposit

(c) Oil pollution   (d) Overheat

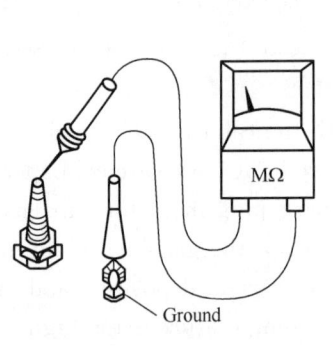

Figure 5-13　Measurement of the Spark Plug Insulation Resistance

Figure 5-14　Carbon Deposition Inspection of Spark Plug

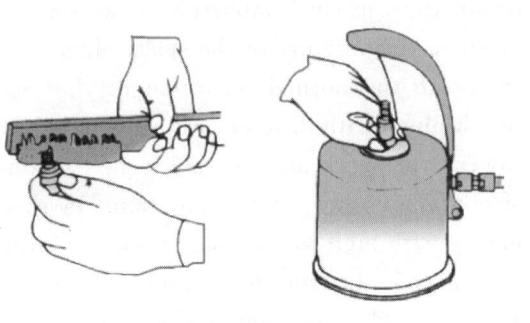

Figure 5-15　Cleaning of Spark Plug

The working condition of the spark plug is usually inspected by short circuit method, that is: when the engine is running at low speed, the wire between the high-voltage ignition wire of the spark plug to be tested and the cylinder is short-circuited or broken, at this time, if the engine has obvious jitter and unstable operation, it indicates the spark plug works well; otherwise, the spark plug is damaged.

(Ⅲ) Construction and maintenance of computer-controlled ignition system

1. The function of the computer-controlled ignition system

The computer-controlled ignition system is also called microcomputer-controlled ignition system. The computer-controlled ignition system is another major progress behind the use of contactless electronic ignition system. The characteristics is to change the mechanical adjustment of the ignition advance angle into the electronic control mode, increase the knock con-

112　Automobile Electrical Equipment Maintenance

trol, improve the engine power, economy and reduce emissions pollution by making the engine obtain the optimal ignition time. In the engine control system, ignition control includes three aspects: ignition advance angle control, power-on time (closing angle) control and knock-proof control.

(1) Ignition advance angle control. In a computer controlled ignition system, the ignition advance angle is controlled according to two basic conditions: during engine start-up and during normal operation, as shown in Figure 5-16.

When the engine is first started, its speed is low (generally below 500r/min), and the intake pipe pressure signal or intake gas signal is not stable. A fixed ignition advance angle, called the initial ignition advance angle, can be preset by the ECU according to the engine operating characteristics. That is to say, when the ECU detects that the engine is in start-up, it controls the ignition of each cylinder according to the preset initial ignition advance angle. The control signals detected by the ECU are mainly engine speed signal (Ne) and start up switch signal (STA). The setting of the initial ignition advance angle varies with the engine, but is generally about 10° before the piston reaches the TDC in the compression stroke.

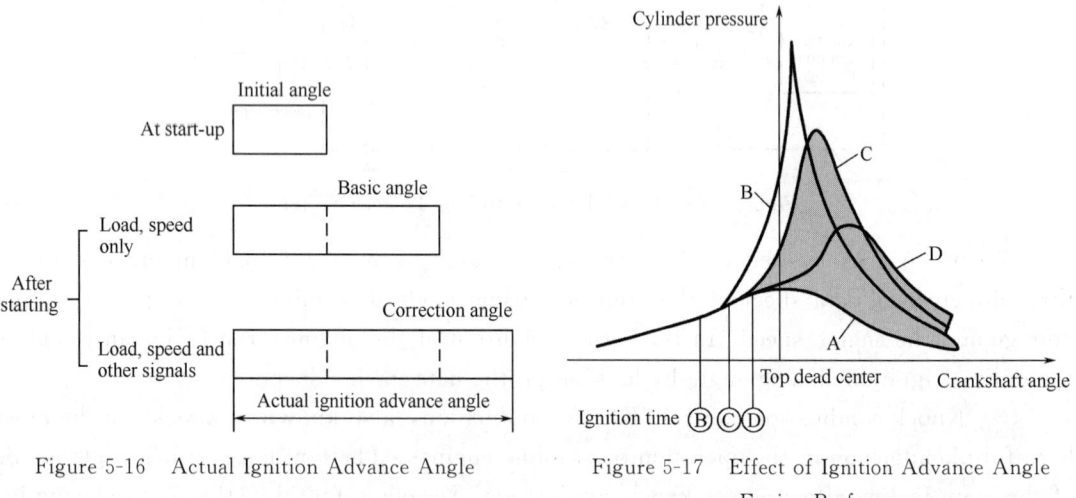

Figure 5-16　Actual Ignition Advance Angle

Figure 5-17　Effect of Ignition Advance Angle on Engine Performance

When the speed and the load of the gasoline engine are fixed, the power and the fuel consumption vary with the ignition advance angle, as shown in Figure 5-17, the appropriate ignition advance angle allows the engine to do the most mechanical work per cycle (shadow part under C curve). In order to achieve the best comprehensive performance, such as power, economy and emission, the engine should be ignited at the optimal ignition advance angle under various working conditions. The optimal ignition advance angle data of the engine under different working conditions is determined by experiments and stored in ECU. When the engine is in operation, ECU determines the basic ignition advance angle according to the engine speed and load signal, and modifies it according to other relevant signals. Finally, the ignition advance angle is determined and the ignition indication signal is output to the electronic ignition controller to control the operation of the ignition system.

(2) Power-on time control. To control the power-on time is to control the ignition closing angle. The size of the closing angle depends on the speed of the engine and the supply

voltage of the power supply. Under different speed, different supply voltage, it should ensure that there is a certain primary power-off current. With the increase of the engine speed, the closing angle should be increased properly to prevent the ignition difficulty caused by the decrease of primary power-off current and the decrease of ignition coil energy storage. When the power supply voltage changes, it will affect the primary power-off current. When the voltage drops, the value of the primary current can be reduced during the same power-on time, and the primary circuit should be switched on earlier, that is, to increase the power-on time (closing angle), as shown in Figure 5-18.

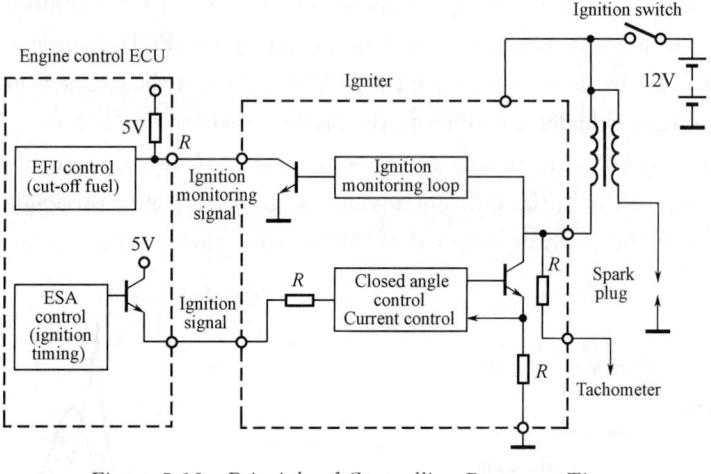

Figure 5-18   Principle of Controlling Power-on Time

When the ESA system controls the closing angle, the main ECU memory stores a three-dimensional data sheet of the ignition closing angle determined by the power supply voltage and the engine speed. In the actual condition of the engine, the ECU can calculate the optimal ignition closing angle by looking up the data in this sheet.

(3) Knock combustion control. Knock combustion, also known as knock, is the most harmful phenomenon in the operation of gasoline engines. The ignition advance angle is one of the main factors affecting the knock combustion. Delaying ignition (that is, reducing ignition advance angle) is the most effective measure to eliminate knock combustion. In the ignition system, ECU determines the knock combustion and the intensity of knock combustion according to the signal of the knock combustion sensor, and gives a feedback control to the ignition advance angle according to the result, so that the engine is on the edge of knock combustion, which can not only prevent the knock combustion, but also effectively improve the engine power and economy.

2. Fundamentals of computer-controlled ignition system

(1) Basic composition. The computer-controlled ignition system consists of various sensors, electronic control units (engine, ECU) and an ignition actuator, as shown in Figure 5-19. Sensors are devices used to detect information about various operating conditions associated with engine ignition. The ignition actuator is composed of an electronic igniter, ignition coils, a distributor and a spark plug. Some engines have no igniters, and the ignition control circuit is in the engine (ECU). Although the structures of the ignition systems manufactured by different automobile manufacturers in different years are different, but

114   Automobile Electrical Equipment Maintenance

there are many same aspects. The function of each component is shown in Table 5-1.

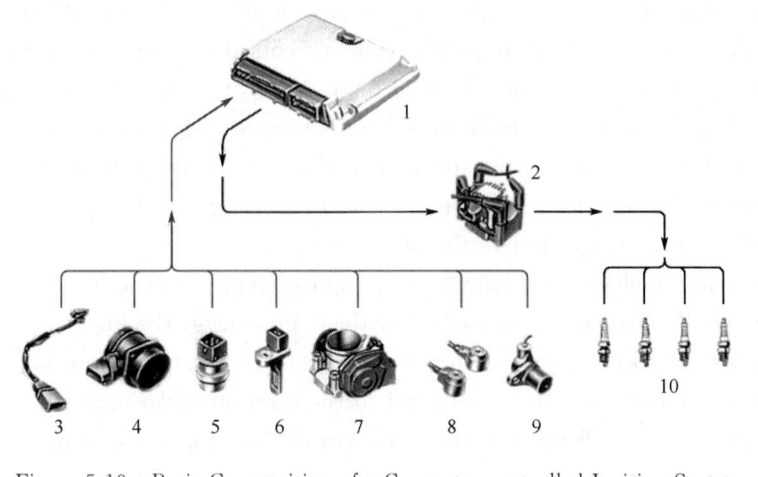

Figure 5-19   Basic Composition of a Computer-controlled Ignition System

1—Engine ECU; 2—Ignition controller and ignition coil; 3—Hall sensor; 4—Air flowmeter;

5—Coolant temperature sensor; 6—Intake temperature sensor; 7—Throttle position sensor;

8—Knock sensor; 9—Crankshaft position sensor; 10—Spark plug

Table 5-1   The Function of Each Components of a Computer-controlled Ignition System

Composition		Function
Sensors	Air flow meter	Measure air intake
	Inlet absolute pressure sensor	
	Crankshaft position sensor	Measure crankshaft angle(engine speed)
		Measure crankshaft angle reference position
	Throttle position sensor	Input ignition advance angle correction signal to main ECU
	Water temperature sensor	Measure the cooling water temperature of the engine
	Starting switch	Measure if the engine is in start-up condition
	Idle starting switch	Measure whether the shift lever of the automatic transmission is placed in N and P
	Speed sensor	Measure the speed and input the speed and the model to the main ECU
	Air conditioning switch A/C	Check the working state of the air conditioner(ON or OFF)
	Knock combustion sensor	Detect the knock signal of the engine
	Power supply voltage sensor	Input power supply voltage signal to main ECU
Actuating mechanism	Electronic igniter and ignition coil	According to the ignition control signal output by the main ECU, control the on-off of one side circuit of the ignition coil, to produce the second side high voltage to ignite the spark plug. At the same time, feedback the ignition confirmation signal IG_f to the ECU.
	Engine controller	According to the input signal of each sensor, calculate the optimal ignition advance angle and transmit the ignition control signal to the electronic igniter.

（2）Basic working principle. When the engine is running, ECU continuously collects the engine speed, load, cooling water temperature, intake temperature and so on, and compares them with the best control parameter stored in the computer memory, to determine the optimal ignition advance angle and the best conduction time of the primary circuit under this condition, and give the instruction to the ignition control module.

The ignition control module controls the conduction and cut-off of the primary circuit of the ignition coil according to the ignition instruction of the ECU. When the circuit is switched on, the current flows through the primary coil in the ignition wire, which stores the ignition energy in the form of a magnetic field. When the current in the primary coil is cut off, a very high induction electromotive force (15~30kV) will be produced in the secondary coil, which will be sent to the spark plug of the working cylinder by the distributor, the ignition energy will be released instantly, and the mixture in the cylinder will be ignited quickly, and the engine will complete the work process.

In addition, in the electronic-controlled ignition system with the function of knock combustion control, ECU also determines whether the engine occur the knock combustion or not and the strength of the knock combustion according to the signal of the knock combustion sensor, and carries on the closed-loop control to the ignition advance angle.

① Main sensor signal. When the electronic-controlled ignition system works, the main sensor signals required are crankshaft position sensor signal (Ne signal) and camshaft position sensor signal (G signal).

The Ne signal refers to the engine crankshaft angle signal, which is a pulse signal obtained by shaping and converting the signal produced by the crankshaft position sensor. In the electronic-controlled ignition system, the Ne signal is mainly used to measure the ignition advance angle and power-on time. When ECU calculates the ignition advance angle or the power-on time, its control precision must be accurate to 1° crankshaft angle. At present, the maximum speed of gasoline engines is more than 6,000r/min. When the engine works normally, the time of 1° crankshaft angle is very short. It is difficult to produce 1° crankshaft angle signal with a sensor. Taking the electromagnetic induction crankshaft position sensor installed in the distributor as an example, the rotor generally has 24 teeth, the crankshaft can only transmit 24 Ne signals to the ECU by rotating 720° per time, and the signal period is 30° crankshaft angle. It is obvious that the signal can not be used to directly control the ignition advance angle and the power-on time. Therefore, in the electronic control system of the engine, a microcomputer system with high speed computing is used to convert the Ne signal generated by the crankshaft position sensor into 1° crankshaft angle signal by frequency division.

The G signal is a discriminating signal of the piston running to the position of the TDC of compression. It is a pulse signal obtained by shaping and converting the signal produced by the camshaft position sensor. In the ignition system, the G signal is mainly used to determine the datum for measuring the ignition advance angle. The G signal is generally a pulse signal whose period is equal to the working interval angle, and when the G signal occurs, it is not the time when each cylinder piston runs to the TDC of the compression, but a fixed crankshaft angle before the TDC of the compression and 70° before the TDC. For camshaft position sensors of some engine, the crankshaft rotating every 2 turns can produce 2 signals, which corresponds to the TDC of the cylinder 1 compression and the TDC of the exhaust, called G_1 signal and G_2 signal.

When the engine is working, the ECU can't control the ignition advance angle if it can't receive the G signal and can't determine the datum for measuring the ignition advance angle. In order to prevent fuel waste or other accidents, the failure protection system will auto-

matically stop the operation of the electronic control fuel injection system, the engine can not start. For an engine with 2 signals generated by the camshaft position sensor as every 2 turns of the crankshaft, as long as one G signal (G_1 signal or G_2 signal) is normal, the electronic-controlled ignition system can work normally, so this kind of engine has high reliability.

② Control principle of ignition advance angle. The control method of the ignition advance angle by the ignition system is different at the start of the engine and after the start of the engine. In the starting process of the engine, the engine speed changes greatly, and because the speed is low (generally lower than 500r/min), the absolute pressure sensor signal or the air flow meter signal of the intake pipe is unstable, the ECU can not calculate the ignition advance angle correctly. Usually, the ignition time is fixed at the set initial ignition advance angle. At this point, the control signals are mainly engine speed signal (Ne signal) and starting switch signal (STA signal). During the start-up of the engine, the initial ignition advance angle set is pre-stored in the ECU, the setting value varies with the engine, generally about 10°.

When the engine is running normally after starting, ECU first determines the basic ignition advance angle according to the engine speed signal and load signal, then modifies it according to other relevant signals, finally determines the actual ignition advance angle, and outputs the ignition control signal to the executive element (ignitor) to control the operation of the ignition system. When the ECU determines the basic ignition advance angle, the angle is different under engine idle and non-idle conditions.

The determination of basic ignition advance angle in idle condition. When the engine is idle, the ECU determines the basic ignition advance angle according to the throttle position sensor signal (IDL signal), engine speed sensor signal (Ne signal) and air conditioning switch signal (A/C signal), as shown in Figure 5-20. The basic ignition advance angle when the air-conditioner works is larger than that when the air-conditioner is not working.

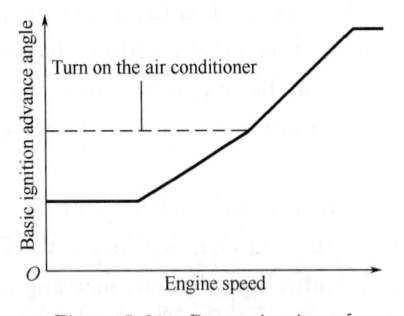

Figure 5-20 Determination of Basic Ignition Advance Angle in Idle Condition

The determination of basic ignition advance angle in non-idle condition. When the engine starts in other conditions except the idle condition, the ECU determines the basic ignition advance angle according to the engine speed signal and load signal (air intake or basic fuel injection per turn), and the basic ignition advance angle at different speed and load is stored in the ECU memory. The basic ignition advance angle control model is shown in Figure 5-21.

When the engine is other conditions except the idle condition, the signal controlling the ignition advance angle mainly includes intake pipe absolute pressure sensor signal (PIM signal) or air flow meter signal (VS signal), engine speed signal (Ne signal), throttle position sensor signal (IDL signal), fuel selection switch or plug signal (R-P signal), knock combustion signal (KNK signal), etc. According to the octane number of fuel, when there are 2 data sheets of basic ignition advance angle in ECU memory, the driver can choose through the fuel selection switch or plug according to the octane number of fuel used. In the electronic-controlled ignition system with the function of knock combustion control, the ECU also has the data dedicated to the ignition advance angle of knock combustion control.

Item V Maintenance of Ignition System **117**

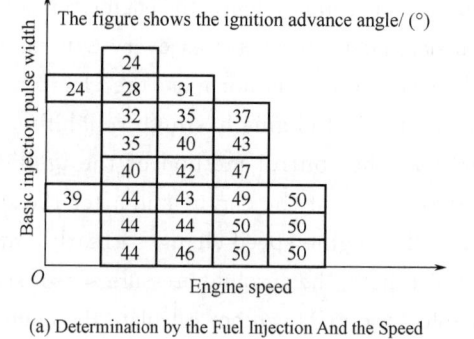

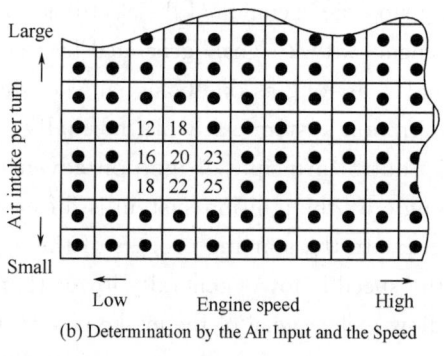

(a) Determination by the Fuel Injection And the Speed

(b) Determination by the Air Input and the Speed

Figure 5-21　Control model of Basic Ignition Advance Angle

Correction method of ignition advance angle after engine start-up. In different engine control system, the correction method of ignition advance angle is different, there are two main methods.

a. Correction coefficient method. For example, in the Nissan ECCS system, the actual ignition advance angle is equal to the product of the basic ignition advance angle and the correction coefficient of the ignition advance angle, i. e.

Actual ignition advance angle＝basic ignition advance angle×the correction coefficient of the ignition advance angle

b. The method to correct the ignition advance angle. For example, in the Toyota TCCS system, the actual ignition advance angle is equal to the sum of the initial ignition advance angle, the basic ignition advance angle and the corrected ignition advance angle.

Actual ignition advance angle＝initial ignition advance angle＋basic ignition advance angle＋corrected ignition advance angle

The correction coefficient or the corrected ignition advance angle is stored in the ECU. When the engine is working, the ECU calculates the actual ignition advance angle according to the initial ignition advance angle, the basic ignition advance angle and the correction factor (or the corrected ignition advance angle).

Correction of the ignition advance angle after start-up. When the engine is running normally after start, the correction of the ignition advance angle varies with the engine. The main correction items are as follows.

a. Correction of the cooling water temperature. The correction of the cooling water temperature can be divided into warm-up correction and overheat correction.

During heating the engine after it starts at low temperature, with the increase of the cooling water temperature, the combustion speed of the mixture is accelerated, the crank-shaft angle of the combustion process is reduced, and the ignition advance angle should be reduced as shown in Figure 5-22. The shape and advance angle of the correction curve vary with the model. Warm-up correction control signals mainly include cooling water temperature sensor signal (THW signal), intake pipe absolute pressure sensor signal (PIM signal) or air flow meter signal (VS sig-

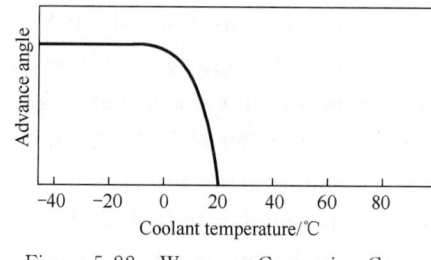

Figure 5-22　Warm-up Correction Curve of the Ignition Advance Angle

nal), throttle position sensor signal (IDL signal) and so on.

When the engine is working, the knock tendency increases with the increase of the cooling water temperature. When the cooling water temperature is too high, the ignition advance angle must be corrected to avoid knock combustion, as shown in Figure 5-23. When the engine is in idle condition (IDL contact is connected), the cooling water temperature is too high, which is usually caused by slow burning speed, the too large crankshaft angle of combustion process, so to avoid engine overheating for a long time, the ignition advance angle should be increased to improve the burning speed and re-

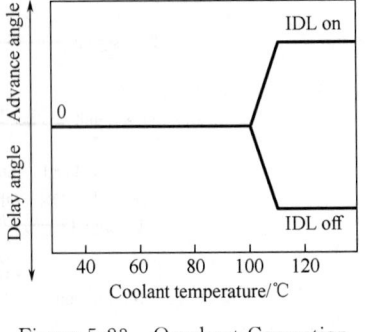

Figure 5-23   Overheat Correction Curve of the Ignition Advance Angle

duce the heat loss. When the engine is in other conditions except idle condition (IDL contact is disconnected), if the cooling water temperature is too high, the ignition advance angle should be reduced properly to avoid knock combustion. Overheat correction control signals mainly include cooling water temperature sensor signal (THW signal), throttle position sensor signal (IDL signal) and so on.

b. Idle stability correction. During idling, the engine speed will change with the change of load and other factors, the ECU must correct the ignition advance angle according to the difference between the actual speed and the target speed, so as to keep the engine running steadily at the specified idling speed, as shown in Figure 5-24. The idle stability correction control signals mainly include engine speed signal (Ne signal), throttle position sensor signal (IDL signal), speed sensor signal (SPD signal), air conditioning switch signal (A/C signal) and so on.

c. Air-fuel ratio feedback correction. Because the air-fuel ratio feedback control system adjusts the quantity of fuel injection according to the feedback signal of the oxygen sensor to realize the optimal air-fuel ratio control, the change of the fuel injection will inevitably change the engine speed. To stabilize the engine speed, the ignition advance angle should be corrected according to the fuel injection, as shown in Figure 5-25.

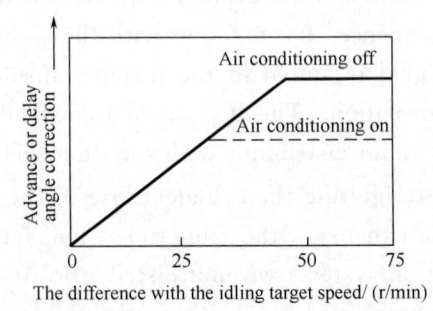

Figure 5-24   Idle Stability Correction Curve of the Ignition Advance Angle

Figure 5-25   Air-fuel Ratio Feedback Correction of the Ignition Advance Angle

For example, when the ECCS system is in a certain condition of the engine, the optimal ignition advance angle calculated by the ECU is 40° before the TDC, and the control principle of the ignition advance angle is shown in Figure 5-26. G signal converted by the po-

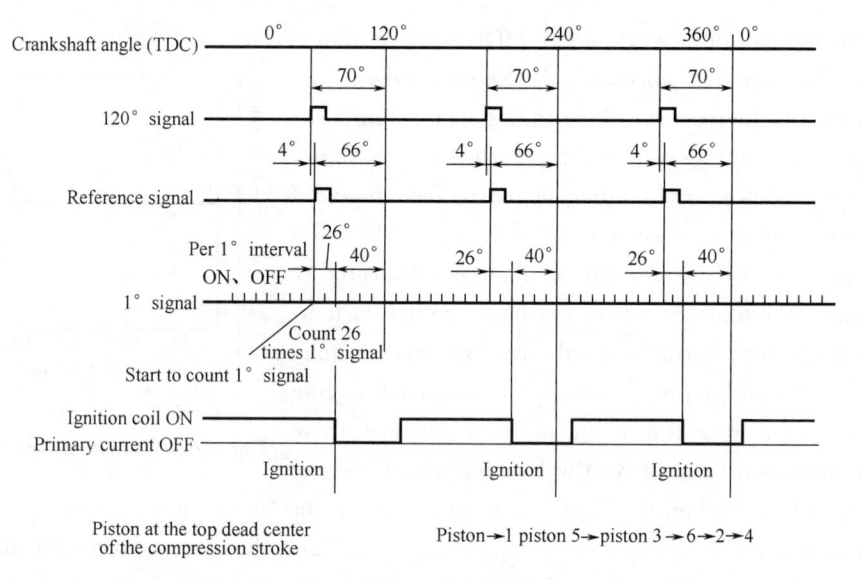

Figure 5-26　The Control Principle of Ignition Advance Angle

sition sensor of the camshaft is a pulse signal with the interval of 120° crankshaft angle (6-cylinder engine), the G signal is set at 70° before the TDC of the piston compression of each cylinder, and the reference signal set by the ECU is 4° behind the G signal, so the actual reference of controlling the ignition advance angle is 66° before the TDC. The ECU starts from receiving a G signal with an interval of 120°, that is to say, a cylinder piston is located 70° before the TDC of compression. Since the ignition reference signal G is 4°, the ECU starts from 66° before the TDC of compression and counts 26 (66−40＝26) 1° signals. At this point, the ECU sends a control signal to the igniter, making the first winding of the ignition coil power off, the second winding produce high voltage and send to the spark plug, which can ensure that the spark plug ignite at 40° before the TDC of the compression.

③ Control signal. In the electronic-controlled ignition system, the control signals from ECU to the igniter are IG_t and IG_d.

IG_t signal is an on-off control signal from ECU to the power triode in the ignitor.

IG_d signal is a discriminating cylinder signal in the ignition system without distributor sent by ECU to the igniter to ensure the ignition sequence. It, together with the G signal, determines the cylinder to be ignited. The IG_d signal is stored in the memory inside the ECU, which is actually the ignition sequence information. The IG_d signal is divided into IG_{d_A} signal and IG_{d_B} signal in the ignition system without distributor with simultaneous ignition mode. The simultaneous ignition mode refers to igniting the cylinder close to the TDC of compression and the cylinder close to the TDC of exhaust at the same time. This ignition mode is used in the some electronic-controlled ignition systems without distributor. It is effective to ignite the cylinder close to the TDC of compression, and it is ineffective to ignite the cylinder close to the TDC of exhaust (that is not work).

The ECU selects the IG_d signal state according to the G signal and the Ne signal to determine which cylinder is ignited. Taking the Toyota computer-controlled ignition system without distributor as an example, the ignition control signal output by ECU is shown in Figure 5-27, and the status of the IG_{d_A} signal and the IG_{d_B} signal is shown in Table 5-2.

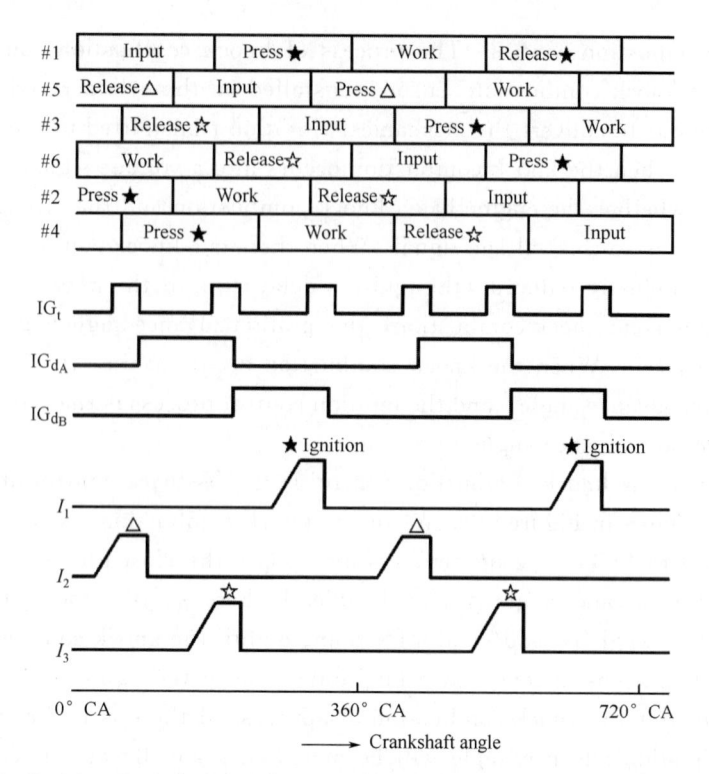

Figure 5-27　Ignition Control Signal Output by ECU in Toyota Computer-controlled Ignition
System without Distributor

Table 5-2　Status of the IG_{d_A} Signal and the IG_{d_B} Signal

S/N	Signal state		Cylinder ignited
	IG_{d_A} signal	IG_{d_B} signal	
1	0	1	1 and 6 cylinders ignited
2	0	0	2 and 5 cylinder ignited
3	1	0	3 and 4 cylinder ignited

④ IG_f signal. IG_f signal refers to the ignition confirmation signal sent to the ECU by the igniter after the ignition is completed.

In the electronic-controlled fuel injection system, the drive signal of the injector also comes from the position sensor of the crankshaft. If the ignition system fails to ignite the spark plug, the position sensor of the crankshaft will work normally and the injector will still spray oil as usual. In order to prevent the phenomena such as excessive fuel injection, fuel waste, difficulty in re-starting the engine or overheating of the three-element catalytic reactor during driving, the ignitor should return the ignition confirmation signal (IG_f signal) to the ECU in time when the ignition process is completed.

When the engine works, after the ECU sends the ignition control signal (IG_f signal) to the igniter, if the ECU can not receive the ignition confirmation signal (IG_f signal) returned for 3~5 times, the ECU determines that the ignition system is out of order, and forcibly stops the electronic-controlled fuel injection system to continue the fuel injection, so that the engine is flamed out

⑤ Knock combustion control. The process of knock combustion control is shown in Figure 5-28. The knock combustion sensor is installed on the cylinder body or the cylinder cover. Its function is to convert the mechanical vibration transmitted to the cylinder body or the cylinder cover when the knock combustion occurs into a voltage signal to the ECU. The ECU determines whether the engine has a knock combustion and the strength of the knock combustion according to this voltage signal. When there is a knock combustion, the ignition advance angle is gradually reduced (the ignition delays) until the knock combustion disappears. When there is no knock combustion, the ignition advance angle is gradually increased (the ignition advances). When the knock combustion occurs again, the ECU gradually reduces the ignition advance angle, and the ignition control process is the process of repeatedly adjusting the ignition advance angle.

The essence of the knock combustion control is the feedback control of the ignition advance angle, as shown in Figure 5-29. When the knock combustion sensor inputs the knock combustion signal to ECU, the ignition system adopts the closed-loop control mode, and reduces the ignition advance angle at a fixed angle. If there is still a knock combustion, then the ignition advance angle is reduced at a fixed angle until the knock combustion disappears. The ignition system keeps the engine working under the current ignition advance angle within a certain time after the knock combustion disappears. If there is no knock combustion in this time, the ignition advance angle will be increased gradually at a fixed angle until the knock combustion occurs again, and then the above process is repeated.

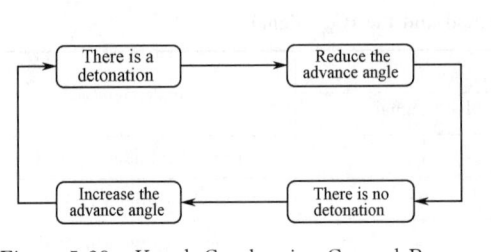

Figure 5-28   Knock Combustion Control Process

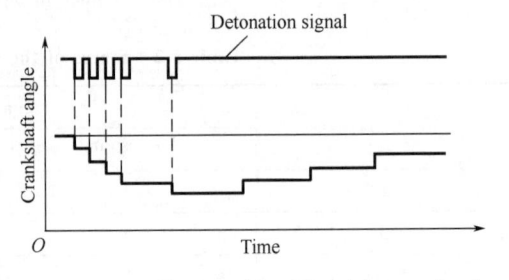

Figure 5-29   Change of Ignition Advance Angle During Knock Combustion Control Process

When the engine load is small, the tendency of the knock combustion is almost 0, so the ignition system takes the angle open-loop control mode in this load range. When the engine load exceeds a certain value, the ignition system automatically turns into closed-loop control mode. When the engine is working, ECU determines the engine load according to the throttle position sensor signal, so as to determine whether the ignition system adopts open-loop control or closed-loop control.

(3) The main circuits of the computer-controlled ignition system.

① The circuit of generating the ignition confirmation signal (IG_f signal). When the primary current of the ignition coil is cut off, the back electromotive force is generated to trigger the circuit of generating IG_f signal, which outputs an ignition confirmation signal (IG_f) to the ECU, and the IG_f signal is also called the ignition safety signal.

In an EFI engine, the driven signal of the injector is from the speed and the crankshaft position sensor. If the ignition system fails to ignite the spark plug, and the sensor works

properly, the injector will continue to inject fuel. To avoid this phenomenon, when IG_f signal is not fed back to ECU for $3 \sim 6$ times in a row, ECU determines that the engine has been turned off at this time and sends an instruction to the fuel injection control circuit of the EFI system to interrupt the fuel supply so as to prevent the waste of fuel, the difficulty of restarting and the overheating of the three-element catalytic converter when driving.

② Overvoltage protection circuit. When the power supply voltage of the automobile is too high, the circuit will cut off the power transistor in the igniter amplifier circuit to protect the ignition coil and the power tube.

③ Closing angle control circuit. The closing angle, also known as the connection angle, is the turning angle of the crankshaft during the energizing of the primary circuit of the ignition coil.

The closing angle control circuit can control the turn-on time of the power tube in the igniter, that is, control the turn-on time of the primary circuit of the ignition coil to ensure that the secondary circuit produces a suitable ignition high voltage.

④ Lock protection circuit, also known as engine stop power protection circuit. If the engine is turned off and the ignition switch is still on, generally when the turn-on time of the ignition coil and the power tube exceed the predetermined value, the circuit controls the power tube to cut off, cutting off the current in the primary circuit to protect the ignition coil and the power tube from burn-out and avoid unnecessary power consumption.

⑤ Constant current control circuit. It shall be ensured that the primary current of the ignition coil can reach the specified value (generally $6 \sim 7A$) at any speed and in a very short time, so as to reduce the influence of the speed on the secondary voltage and improve the ignition performance. At the same time, it can prevent the ignition coil from burning because of the large primary current, because the ESA system uses high-energy ignition coil, its primary circuit cancels the additional resistor, and the primary coil resistance is very small, the primary current can reach a large value from the beginning of power supply to the open circuit.

⑥ Detection circuit under acceleration state. When the engine speed rises sharply, the circuit detects this acceleration state and transmits the detected state signal to the closing angle control circuit, which leads the power tube to switch on early to increase the closing angle.

3. Typical computer-controlled ignition systems

The computer-controlled ignition systems can be divided into two categories: electronic-controlled ignition systems with a distributor and electronic-controlled ignition systems without a distributor.

(1) Electronic-controlled ignition system with a distributor. The main features of the electronic-controlled ignition system with a distributor are as follows: There is only one ignition coil, and the high voltage produced by the ignition coil is sent to the spark plug of each cylinder in sequence by the distributor in accordance with the working order of the engine.

(2) Electronic-controlled ignition system without a distributor. The electronic-controlled ignition system without a distributor is also known as direct ignition system, its main features are: The electronic control device is used to replace the distributor, and the high voltage electricity produced by the ignition coil is sent directly to the spark plug for ignition by the electronic ignition control technology. The quantity of ignition coils are more than that of the electronic-controlled ignition system with a distributor. The composition of the

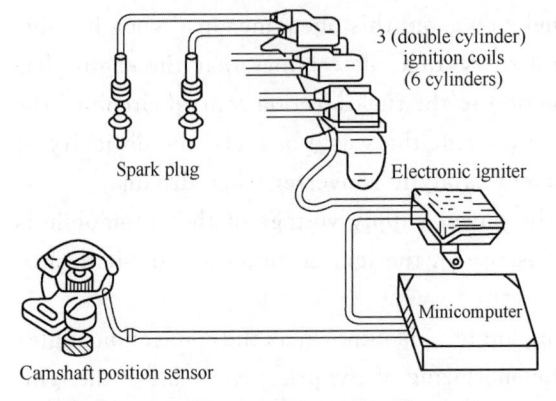

Figure 5-30 Composition of the Electronic-controlled Ignition System without a Distributor

electronic-controlled ignition system without a distributor is shown in Figure 5-30.

The electronic-controlled ignition system without a distributor has the same working principle and functions as the electronic-controlled ignition system with a distributor. The difference is that the electronic-controlled ignition system without a distributor has the function of electronic distribution, that is, when the engine is working, the ECU must not only output IG_t ignition control signal to the ignitor, but also transmit the cylinder discrimination signal IG_d stored in the ECU, to control the work order of multiple ignition coils and control the ignition of each cylinder ignition according to the working order.

According to the quantity of ignition coils and the distribution mode of the high voltage electricity, the electronic-controlled ignition system without a distributor can be divided into three types: independent ignition mode, simultaneous ignition mode and diode distribution ignition mode.

The circuit of the electronic-controlled ignition system without a distributor is shown in Figure 5-31. It is characterized by one ignition coil per cylinder, i. e. the number of ignition coils is equal to the number of cylinders.

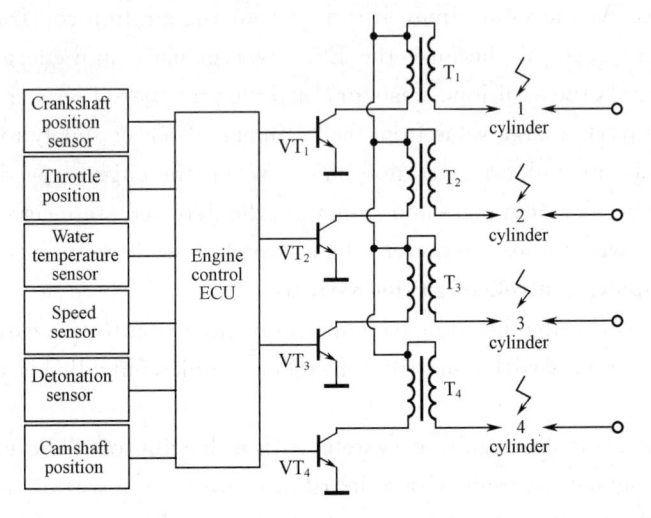

Figure 5-31 The Independent Ignition Mode Circuit of the Electronic-controlled Ignition System without a Distributor

Because each cylinder has its own independent ignition coil, the ignition coil has enough power-on time to ensure sufficient ignition energy even if the engine is running at a high speed. Compared with the electronic-controlled ignition system with a distributor, under the condition of the same engine speed and the same ignition energy, the current of the first winding circuit through the ignition coil in unit time is much smaller, the ignition coil is not

124 Automobile Electrical Equipment Maintenance

easy to heat up, and the volume of the ignition coil can be very small, and the ignition coil can be directly mounted on the spark plug.

4. Construction and maintenance of main components of the computer-controlled ignition system

The distributor and the ignition coil in the computer-controlled ignition system are basically the same as the common electronic ignition system. The main difference is that there is only a distributor in the distributor of the computer-controlled ignition system. The construction and maintenance of the distributor and the ignition coil are no longer detailed here.

(1) Igniter. In the electronic-controlled ignition system with a distributor, both the igniter and the ignition coil are assembled with the distributor, known as the integral ignition assembly. The main function of the igniter is to control the power on or off of the first winding circuit of the ignition coil according to the control signal of the ECU, and to transmit the ignition confirmation signal IG_f (also known as feedback signal or safety signal) to the ECU after the ignition is completed.

In use, connect the ignition coil and the wire harness connector of the igniter, measure the voltage between the corresponding terminals of the engine ECU with a multimeter or an oscilloscope, it should conform to the standard of Table 5-3, otherwise there is a fault in the ignitor or the ECU.

Table 5-3 Inspection Standard for Igniter

Test terminal	Inspection condition	Inspection standard
+B and ground	Ignition switch is "ON"	Battery voltage
IG_t and ground	Engine works	Pulse
IG_f and ground	Engine works	Pulse

(2) Knock sensor. The knock sensor is one of the main components of the electronic-controlled ignition system. Its function is to input the knock signal to the engine, control the ignition advance angle after processing the signal by ECU, to realize the feedback control of the optimal ignition advance angle.

The knock sensor can generally detect the vibration of the engine to know whether there is a knock and to get the strength signal of the knock. According to its working principle, it can be divided into two types: inductive and piezoelectric.

The knock sensor is usually mounted on the engine cylinder or on the spark plug. The installation location of the knock sensor is shown in Figure 5-32.

The quality of the knock sensor can by checking the resistance. When checking, it is necessary to unplug the wire plug of the knock sensor, and use the ohmmeter to detect the resistance between the terminal and the shell of the knock sensor, which should be ∞ (cut off); if the resistance is 0 (switch on), it indicates the inside of the knock sensor

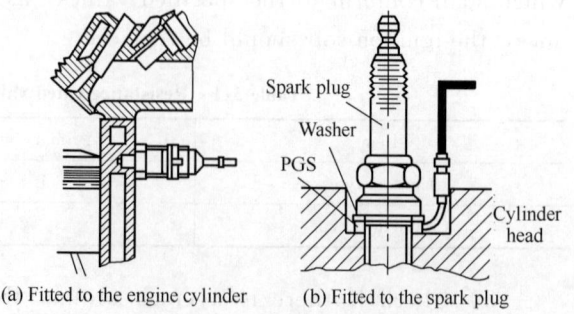

(a) Fitted to the engine cylinder   (b) Fitted to the spark plug

Figure 5-32 Installation Position of the Knock Sensor

Item Ⅴ Maintenance of Ignition System **125**

is short-circuited, it is necessary to replace the knock sensor. Or when the engine is in the idling condition, the knock sensor can be checked by an oscilloscope, the method is: disconnect the sensor wire harness connector, check the signal voltage between the sensor terminal and the ground with the oscilloscope, the pulse signal shall be output, otherwise it indicates the sensor is not good and should be replaced.

(3) Ignition control circuit.

The contents and methods of overhaul of ignition control circuit are as follows.

① After the ignition switch is connected, the voltage between the igniter$+$B terminal and the ground, as well as the voltage between the ignition coil$+$terminal and the ground shall be measured by a multimeter, which shall be the voltage of the battery, otherwise the power circuit is out of order.

② When the engine is idle, check the voltage signal between the IG_t terminal of the igniter and the ground, if it is normal, there shall be a pulse signal, otherwise the control circuit or the ECU is out of order.

③ When the engine is idle, check the voltage signal between the IG_f terminal of the ECU and the ground, if it is normal, there shall be a pulse signal, otherwise the igniter or the signal circuit is out of order.

Ⅲ. Item Implementation

(Ⅰ) Implementation requirements

1. It is necessary to have a Santana electronic-controlled engine training platform or related equipment, including a set of common tools, multimeter or oscilloscope, etc.

2. During the implementation of the item, attention must be paid to preventing the damage of the high voltage to the person and equipment, and the range or gear of the multimeter should be selected. For the inspection of igniter, attention should be paid to the instantaneous high voltage which can easily cause the triode to be broken down.

(Ⅱ) Implementation Steps

1. Ignition coil inspection

(1) Through maintenance, we shall ensure that the ignition coil insulation cover is clean, dry, nonleakage, and the wiring is correct.

(2) Check the ignition coil resistance. Remove all connecting wires and check the resistance of the primary and secondary windings of the ignition coil with a resistance meter, which shall conform to the specified values, as shown in Table 5-4. In case of non-compliance, the ignition coil should be replaced.

Table 5-4　Resistance rated value of Santana ignition coil

Item	Primary winding/Ω	Secondary winding/kΩ
Contact type	1.7～2.1	7.0～12.0
Contactless type	0.53～0.76	～3.5

(3) Check if there is a crack around the center jack of the ignition coil. If so, replace it.

2. Spark plug inspection

Check whether the spark plug has carbon deposition, whether the insulator is damaged, and whether the electrode gap is up to standard. Adjust the electrode gap if necessary.

3. Electronic igniter inspection

Check whether the wiring of the electronic igniter is correct, whether the ground is reliable, and whether the power supply voltage is normal. Determine whether the signal output of the electronic igniter is normal, if it does not meet the requirements, it should be replaced.

4. Inspection of Hall signal generator

The Hall signal generator and the ignition distributor are installed in one body. We should first check whether its input voltage is normal, if it is normal, we need to turn on the ignition switch, turn the distributor shaft, check whether its signal output voltage is in line with the requirements, otherwise it should be replaced.

Summary

(1) The ignition system can provide a very high voltage to the spark plug to break through the spark plug gap and form an air-fuel mixture in the spark ignition cylinder.

(2) The ignition system consists of two interconnected circuits, the primary circuit and the secondary circuit. The primary circuit provides a low voltage to the primary winding of the ignition coil to establish a magnetic field; the secondary circuit, when the primary circuit is disconnected, forms a high voltage pulse and sends the high voltage pulse to the spark plug.

(3) The distributor in the traditional ignition system contains a centrifugal or vacuum ignition advance device. The centrifugal advance device adjusts the ignition advance angle with the change of speed; the vacuum advance device rotates the signal plate in the direction opposite to the axial rotation of the distributor. The electronic spark advance cancels the centrifugal ignition advance device and the vacuum ignition advance device, while the ECU receives the input signal of the sensor and, on the basis of this, determines the optimal ignition time and sends the ignition signal to the ignitor so as to connect the secondary circuit at the required precise moment.

(4) Magnetic pulse sensor and Hall effect sensor are the most widely used crankshaft position sensors. They generate electrical signals at a specific point in the rotation of the crankshaft that trigger the switchgear to control the ignition timing.

Thinking and Practice

(1) How many types of gasoline engine ignition systems are there? Name three main functions of the gasoline engine ignition system.

(2) How does the ignition coil convert the battery voltage to a high voltage capable of causing the spark plug to ignite? How to check the ignition coil?

(3) What is the effect of the spark plug gap on the engine? How to adjust the gap?

(4) When discussing the composition of the ignition system, A says that the igniter is a part of the secondary circuit and B says that the spark plug belongs to the secondary circuit. Try to find out if their statements are correct.

(5) How many types of ignition signal generators are there in an electronic ignition system? What are the characteristics of each?

(6) What is the function of an electronic igniter? How to check its quality?

Item VI

Overhaul of Automobile Lighting System

I. Scene Introduction

A Shanghai Volkswagen Polo car after turning on the turn signal switch, the left and right steering lights are not shining. After the overhaul, it is found that the steering lights are out of order. Because the automobile light system is related to the safety of oneself and others, we can't ignore the overhaul of the automobile lighting system.

Automobile lighting system is divided into lighting system and signal system. The common faults of the automobile lighting and signal systems include safety burn-out, light bulb damage, relay burn-out, poor contact of switch or wire plug, etc., which make the lighting and signal systems can't work normally.

II. Related Knowledge

(I) Function, type and basic composition of the lighting and signal systems

1. Function of the lighting and signaling systems

The automobile lighting and signal systems can ensure the safe driving of the automobile in night, bad weather and complicated traffic conditions. The automobile lighting system is set up to ensure the safety and speed of the automobile under the condition of bad light. Generally speaking, the automobile lighting system is mainly used for lighting as well as for automobile decoration. With the increasing application of the automobile electronic technology, the lighting system is developing in the intelligent direction.

The automobile signal system is light (sound) signals (or signs) used by an automobile to indicate another automobiles or pedestrians, usually consisting of a steering signal device, a braking signal device, an electric horn, etc., to ensure the safety of the automobile.

2. Types and basic composition of the lighting and signal systems

The automobile lighting system is an essential equipment to ensure the safe driving of the automobile at night or in bad weather. The automobile lighting system can be divided into external lighting devices and internal lighting devices by its position and function. The external lighting devices include headlights, front fog lights, reversing lights and license plate lights; the internal lighting devices include a overhead light, reading lights, miscellaneous box lights, instrument and control button lights and luggage lights, etc.

128 Automobile Electrical Equipment Maintenance

In addition to the lighting system, there is a signal system used to indicate the intention or condition of the automobile to ensure the safe driving of the automobile in complex traffic conditions or the condition of the automobile. The signal system can be divided into external signal devices and internal signal devices. The external signal devices include steering lights, brake lights, tail lights, reversing lights and rear fog lights, parking lights, clearance lights and illuminator lights; the internal signal devices refers to the indicator lights in the instruments, which are used to indicate the working state of a system or warning, alarm light information, mainly have steering lights, low beam headlights/high beam headlights, lights to indicate oil pressure, charging, braking, water temperature, oil content, engine failure, airbag, ABS system, door closing prompt and so on.

In addition to the signal lights, the automobile signal system includes devices that emit sound signals, such as an electric horn, a buzzer, etc. The electric horn is used to send sound signals to external pedestrians or automobiles, and the buzzer can alert or alarm drivers to notice certain conditions or information of the vehicle.

(Ⅱ) Automobile lighting system

1. Headlight

The most important external light of the automobile lighting system is the headlight, which is used to illuminate the road and the environment ahead, to ensure the safe driving of the automobile in all weathers. The lighting effect of the headlight is directly related to the safe driving of the automobile at night. Therefore, the headlight is required not only to have bright and uniform lighting effect, but also to avoid dazzling the drivers who come in front and behind.

The headlight can be divided into 2-light headlight and 4-light headlight according to the installation quantity. The former is equipped with one headlight on the left and the other on the right, whose bulb generally uses double-filament bulb, with the outside of each using double-filament bulb, each lamp having low and high beams; and the latter is equipped with two headlights on the left and two headlights on the right. Generally, the outside is low beam, the inside is the high beam, while some headlights use double-filament light on the outside, that is, having both low and high beams.

The headlight can be divided into detachable headlight, semi-enclosed headlight and fully enclosed headlight by its structure. The detachable headlight is seldom used at present because the illumination effect is reduced by reducing the reflection ability due to poor air tightness and easy pollution of the mirror. For the semi-enclosed headlight, its lens is fixed with the mirror. The light bulb can be replaced from the rear of the mirror, and it is easy to maintain, so it is widely used. The fully enclosed headlight is also called a vacuum light. The mirror and the glass for lens are made into one, forming a bulb. The filament is welded to the base of the mirror. The reflecting surface of the mirror is vacuum aluminized and filled with inert gas. Because the fully enclosed headlight completely avoids the mirror from being polluted and from being not affected by the atmosphere, so its reflection efficiency is high, the illumination effect is good, the service life is long. It has obtained the rapid popularization; But when the filament burns out, the entire assembly shall be replaced, the cost is high, therefore its scope of use is limited.

Item Ⅵ Overhaul of Automobile Lighting System **129**

The automobile headlight is generally composed of a light source (light bulb), a mirror, and a lens (diffusing glass).

(1) The light source. At present, the light source used in the automobile headlight, that is the bulb type, includes ordinary incandescent light bulb, halogen tungsten light bulb and HID bulb, LED light-emitting diode, as shown in Figure 6-1.

(a) Incandescent   (b) Halogen Tungsten   (c) Halogen Tungsten   (d) HID Bulb   (e) LED Module
    Light Bulb   Light Bulb (I)   Light Bulb (II)   with Heat Sink

Figure 6-1   Bulbs for Headlight

With the development of automobile technology, the ordinary incandescent light bulb has been eliminated. Now the automobile headlights mainly adopt halogen tungsten light bulbs and xenon light bulbs. A halogen tungsten light bulb is a light bulb doped with a small number of halogen elements (such as iodine, bromine), from which tungsten and iodine atoms meet to form tungsten iodide compounds, and once the tungsten iodide compounds contact the hot filament (with a temperature more than 1,450℃), which will decompose into tungsten and iodine, tungsten will return to the filament, iodine will re-enter the gas. The cycle will repeat again and again, then, the filament almost does not burn and the bulb does not blacken, so it has a longer life and higher brightness than the traditional incandescent bulb, and is now widely used.

The HID (high intensity discharge) light is also known as high-voltage gas discharge light, which can be called heavy metal light or xenon light. The principle is that the UV-ant anti-ultraviolet quartz glass tube is filled with a variety of chemical gases, most of which are Xenon and iodide and other inert gases, and then the xenon in the quartz tube is ionized through the supercharger to boost the automobile 12V DC to 23,000V instantly, and a light source is produced between the two electrodes, which is called gas discharge. And the white super arc light produced by the xenon gas can improve the light color temperature value, close to the sun light of day. The current value required by HID is only 3.5A, the brightness is 3 times of that of the traditional halogen tungsten light, and the service life is 10 times longer than that of the traditional halogen tungsten light. The Xenon light not only greatly increases the safety and comfort of driving, and also helps to relieve the tension and fatigue of driving at night.

The structure and the principle of light-emitting of the LED light source make LED have a small volume, low power consumption (not more than 1W per unit), long service life (up to 100,000 hours), high brightness (color temperature close to 6,000K), low heat, environmental protection, energy conservation and durability and other unparalleled advantages, relative to the conventional light source. However, when the LED light overheats, there will be a light decay, so when it is used as a headlight, a heat sink and a cooling fan

are needed.

(2) Mirror. The surface of the mirror is shaped like a rotating paraboloid, generally made of 0.6~0.8mm thin steel plate, or made of glass or plastic. The inner surface is plated with silver, aluminum or chromium and then polished. At present, the inner surface of the mirror is usually vacuum aluminized. The function of the mirror is to reflect the reflected light of the bulb into a parallel beam, which greatly increases the luminosity by several hundred or even thousands of times to ensure sufficient illumination in the 150~400m range in front of the automobile.

(3) Lens. The lens, also known as diffusing glass, pressed by transparent glass, is a combination of a number of special prisms and lenses, with a circular or rectangular shape. The function of the lens is to refract the parallel beam reflected from the mirror, so that the road surface in front of the automobile has good and uniform illumination, as shown in Figure 6-2. Nowadays, the combination headlight of the automobile usually combines the mirror and the lens into one body, that is to say, the mirror, through the computer-aided design, can not only reflect the light, but also distribute the light reasonably.

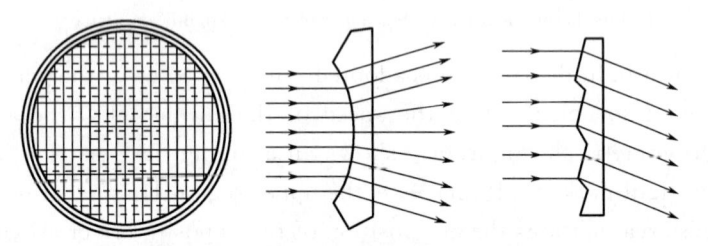

Figure 6-2   The Structure and Effect of the Lens

When a strong beam of light from the headlight suddenly enters a person's eyes, it will stimulate the retina, and there is no time for the pupil to shrink, the visual blindness occurs, which is called dazzle. When driving at night, a strong beam of light can dazzle the driver of the automobile on the opposite, which can easily lead to traffic accidents. To avoid this kind of phenomenon, the headlight takes the following measure to avoid dazzle.

① A double-filament bulb with a shading screen is used. Figure 6-3 is a double-filament bulb with a shading screen. For the kind of headlight using a double-filament bulb with a shading screen, its high beam filament is mounted above or front above the focus of the mirror. According to the principle of optics, the beams of light emitted by the high beam filament radiate into the distance. According to the principle of optics, the light emitted by the high-beam filament is concentrated and reflected by the mirror, and then radiate into the distance along the optical axis in the form of a parallel beam, so as to illuminate the road surface more than 150m in front of the automobile; there is a shading screen under the low beam filament, (also known as shading cover or beam deflector) to block

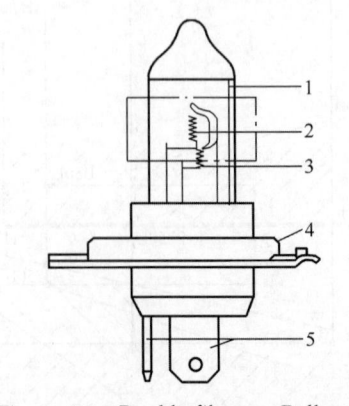

Figure 6-3   Double-filament Bulb with
A Shading Screen

1—Glass bulb; 2—Low beam light bulb;
3—High beam light bulb; 4—Light holder;
5—Socket

Item Ⅵ Overhaul of Automobile Lighting System   **131**

the light beam emitted by the low beam filament to the lower part of the mirror and elimi-nate the reflected upward beam. After the light emitted by the low beam filament is reflected by the mirror, most of the beam is tilted downward toward the road in front of the automo-bile, thus avoiding the dazzle of the opposite driver. Its high beam and low beam reflection effects are shown in Figure 6-4.

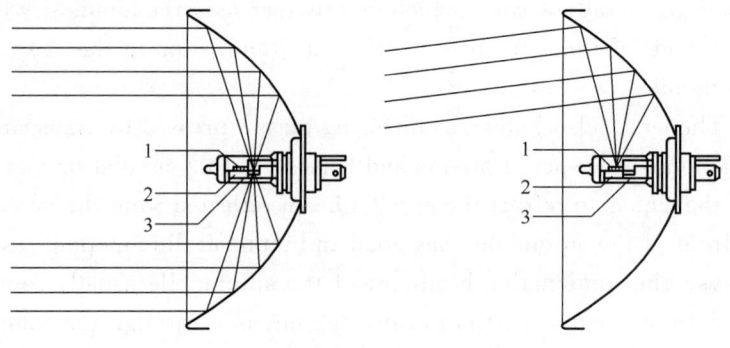

Figure 6-4 Reflection Effects of High Beam and Low Beam
1—Low beam filament; 2—Shading screen; 3—High beam filament

② Asymmetrical light distribution is adopted. In order to meet the goal of not only pre-venting dazzle, but also not affecting the speed of the automobile, the automobile head-lights are often asymmetrical. Figure 6-5 shows an asymmetrical distribution of light. We can see an obvious light-dark cutoff line, i. e. the upper region Ⅲ is a distinct dark area. The point B 50L in this area indicates the eye position of the opposite driver at a distance of 50m. Area Ⅰ, Ⅱ, Ⅳ below and about 15° above the right are a bright area which can effectively illuminate the road in front of the automobile and the sidewalks on the right. The lighting effect when meeting is shown in Figure 6-6.

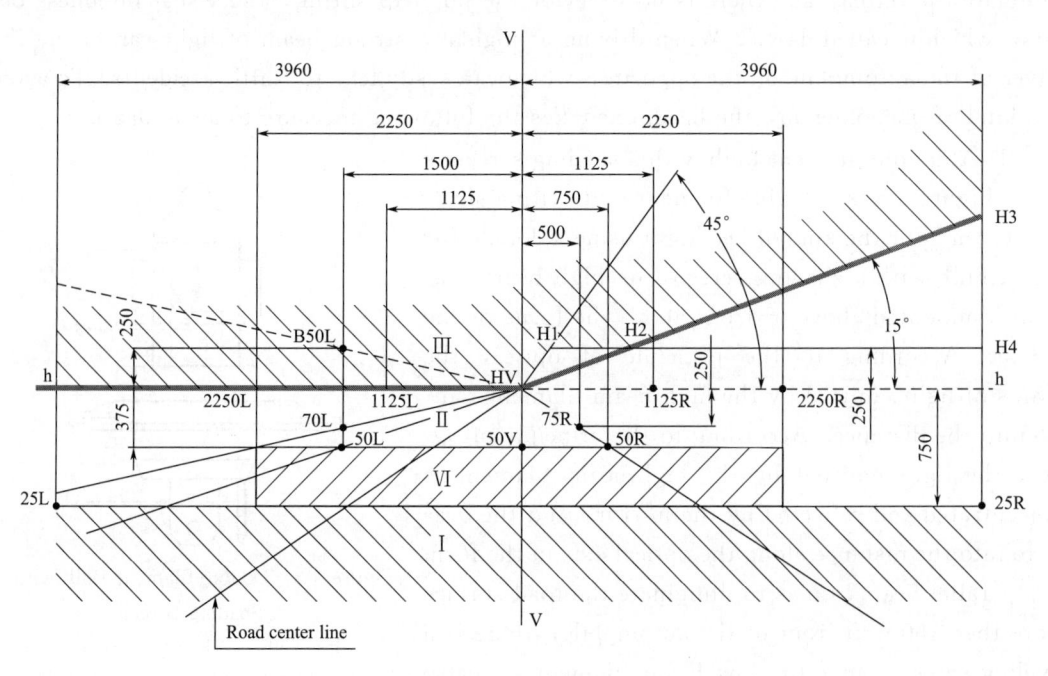

Figure 6-5 Asymmetric Light Distribution Mode

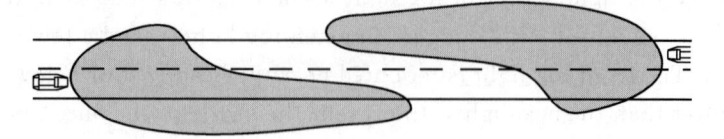

Figure 6-6　Lighting Effect of the Automobile Adopting Asymmetrical Light Distribution When Meeting

③ The light bulbs of some automobiles are just filaments, so use the change of the sun visor to prevent dazzle. The sun visor is controlled by an electromagnet to switch the high beam and the low beam.

④ The headlight automatic control system is adopted. The headlight automatic control system can automatically change the high beam to the low beam or the low beam to the high beam according to the brightness of the other automobile light. It has the advantages of automatic control, no driver control, small size, stable performance, reliability and high sensitivity.

The headlight automatic control system uses the speed sensor, the steering wheel angle sensor, the body height sensor, the infrared distance sensor, the photoelectric sensor (the environment light sensor) and the engine working state and the door state detection, to judge the automobile driving state, the road condition driven, the outside environment light intensity and the light real-time change situation, to transform the signal detected into the electric signal and to input the signal to the electronic control unit for judgment and processing, and then the unit issues the corresponding instruction to adjust the light, thus the headlight automatic control is realized. At the same time, the headlight automatic control system, during driving, detects whether each light works normally by detecting the feedback current signal of the power supply circuit of the each light and the input signal by the photoelectric sensor.

⑤ Precautions for the use of the headlight.

a. Keep the headlight lens clean, especially when driving in rainy and snowy days, earth and other dirt can reduce the lighting performance of the headlight by 50%. Some models are equipped with headlight wipers and water sprayers.

b. When two automobiles meet at night, turn off the headlight high beams and replace them with low beams to ensure safety.

c. To ensure the performance of the headlight, the headlight beam should be checked and adjusted after changing the headlight beams or after every 10,000km drive of the automobile.

d. Periodically inspect bulb and wire socket and ground for oxidation and looseness, ensure good contact performance of plug-in and reliable ground. If the contact is loose, when the headlight is switched on, the current shock will occur due to the on-off of the circuit, thus burning the filament, if the contact is oxidized, the brightness of the bulb will be reduced due to the increase of the contact voltage drop.

2. Fog light

Fog lights are divided into front fog lights and rear fog lights. Fog lights are mainly used to improve road lighting under heavy fog, heavy rain, heavy snow or dusty conditions. They not only help drivers to see the road clearly, but also help the automobile to be seen by

others. Therefore, the light source of fog light needs to have strong penetrability. Generally, automobiles are equipped with halogen tungsten fog lights, and a few are equipped with xenon fog lights. The front fog light is mounted near the headlight or below the front bumper where it is lower than the headlight, to prevent the dazzle of the oncoming vehicle driver, the front fog light beam is projected closer to the ground than the low beam.

The rear fog light is the light mainly used in the fog condition, observing from the rear of the automobile, to make the automobile more easy to be seen. Because the fog light has stronger penetrating power than that of the tail light, it can reduce the rear-end accident of automobile in bad weather to a great extent and prevent traffic accident. If the automobile is only equipped with a rear fog light, it is usually installed on the left side of the longitudinal plane of the automobile. The distance between the rear fog light and the brake light should be more than 100mm. Some are installed in the middle position under the bumper. The light color of the rear fog light is red, and the power of the bulb is 35W.

3. Other lights

(1) License plate light. Installed above or around the rear license plate of an automobile to illuminate the rear license plate, with a power of 5W, it can ensure that pedestrians can clearly see the words on the license plate in the rear 20m.

(2) Reversing light. Reversing light is a dual-purpose light used to illuminate rear road and to alert other automobiles and pedestrians when reversing. The color of the reversing light is white. When the driver hangs up the reversing gear, the reversing light is automatically switched on. The brightness of the light should illuminate a distance of 7.5m. The power of the light bulb is 28W.

(3) Door light. Door light, also known as indoor light, is used in automobiles or station wagons. Each door is provided with an independent door control switch or a micro-switch integrated in the door lock. When the door is open, the door light circuit is connected by the door control switch or micro-switch, and the door light is lit; when the door is closed, the door light circuit is disconnected by the door control switch or micro-switch, and the door light is extinguished. In order to facilitate the driver to go up, get off or turn on other devices and insert the ignition key, some door light circuits are also equipped with automatic delay time.

(4) Instrument and switch light. Instrument and switch light is mainly used to illuminate instruments and switches during night driving. The instrument and switch light provides convenient condition for the driver to check the instruments and operate the switches in time. The instrument and switch light is controlled by the automobile light switch.

(5) Overhead, reading light. The overhead light is mounted on the top of the cab and is mainly used for the interior lighting. The reading light is generally mounted next to the passenger seat for reading, providing sufficient brightness for the occupant without affecting the driver' normal driving and rest for other passengers in the automobile. At present, many automobile overhead lights can realize theater-type brightness control and delay-out control.

(Ⅲ) Automobile signaling system

1. Light signaling devices

(1) Steering signal light. The steering signal light is installed in the front and rear four

corners of the automobile. It is used to send the flashing signal of light and dark alternately when the vehicle is turning, parking, changing lanes and overtaking, and to provide the traffic signal to the automobiles, pedestrians and traffic police in front of the automobile. The light color of the front and rear steering lights is amber. The flash of the steering light is controlled by the flash relay. The frequency should be controlled at $1.0 \sim 2\,\mathrm{Hz}$ and the start-up time should be no more than $1.5\,\mathrm{s}$.

The flashing of the automobile steering light is realized by the flasher, which is usually divided into electrothermal type, capacitive type, vane type, mercury type, triode type, integrated circuit type and so on by the different structure and the working principle.

The electrothermal flasher, because of its poor working stability and short service life, the not obvious bright and dark of the signal light, is seldom used at present. At present, electronic flashers with simple structure, small volume, stable operation and long service life are mostly used, namely, triode type and integrated circuit type.

① Capacitive flasher. The capacitive flasher is composed of a capacitor connected by an electromagnetic relay. Its structure is different from that of the internal circuit, but the principle is basically the same. It is based on the charge-discharge delay characteristic of the capacitor. The control relay contacts are switched on and off at a certain frequency to make the steering light blink. The structure diagram of a typical capacitive flasher is shown in Figure 6-7.

The flasher contact K is kept normally closed by spring; the coil L_1 connected to the steering light circuit in series has a smaller resistance; the coil L_2 has a larger resistance, and one end of L_2 is connected to the moving contact through the relay core and the magnet yoke; the other end is connected to the fixed contact after connecting a capacitor C in series, and the L_2 and C circuits are connected in parallel with the contact.

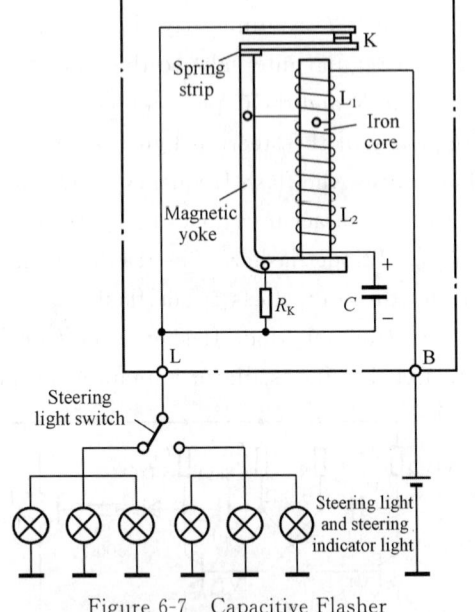

Figure 6-7 Capacitive Flasher

After turning on the switch of the steering light, the coil L_1 in the flasher is energized and the current path is: battery "+" $\rightarrow$ $L_1\rightarrow$ contact K $\rightarrow$ steering signal switch $\rightarrow$ steering light and steering indicator light $\rightarrow$ ground $\rightarrow$ battery "$-$". At this point, the L_2 and the C circuits are short-circuited by the contact, while the current passing through the L_1 is larger, and the electromagnetic force generated by the circuit causes the contact to open, thus, the steering light becomes dark immediately after it flashes.

After the contact is disconnected, the power supply is charged to the capacitor C, and the charging current path is: battery "+" $\rightarrow$ $L_1\rightarrow$ magnet yoke and core $\rightarrow$ $L_2\rightarrow$ C $\rightarrow$ steering light switch $\rightarrow$ steering light and steering indicator light $\rightarrow$ ground $\rightarrow$ battery "$-$". Because the resistance of L_2 is large and the charging current through the steering light is small, the steering light is dark. Although the charging current of C is small, the magnetic force in the same direction after the current flows through the L_1 and L_2 coils is enough to

overcome the elastic force of the spring and keep the contact open so that the steering light remains dark.

During the charging process, the terminal voltage of C increases and the charging current decreases. When the charging current is reduced to the magnetic force of the two coils not enough to overcome the elastic force of the spring, the contact is closed again. At this point, the current through the steering light increases and the light becomes bright. At the same time, the capacitor is discharged through the contact, and the discharge current path is: C "$+$" $\rightarrow$ L_2 $\rightarrow$ core and magnet yoke $\rightarrow$ K $\rightarrow$ C "$-$". Because the discharge current of C causes the magnetic field produced by L_2 to be opposite to that of L_1, which weakens the magnetic force of L_1, the contact can not be sucked open, so that the steering light remains bright.

In the discharging process, the discharge current of C decreases gradually and the magnetic field produced by L_2 decreases gradually. When the magnetic field produced by L_2 weakens to the magnetic field of the L_1 basically disappearing, the magnetic force of L_1 makes the contact open and the light darkens. Then again, the charging process is done, so repeatedly, C continuously charges and discharges, so that the contact is switched on and off at a regular interval, so that the steering light flashes at a certain frequency.

The R and the C parameters in the capacitor charge and discharge circuit determines the frequency of the steering light. In use, the R and the C parameters do not change much. Therefore, the flash frequency of the steering light is stable. The resistor R_K is in parallel with the contact to reduce the spark of the contact.

② Triode flasher. The triode flasher is divided into two types: the contact triode flasher and the contactless triode flasher.

a. Contact triode flasher. The so-called contact triode flasher is actually a hybrid flasher, that is, its oscillator is mainly composed of a triode and so on, and the steering light is driven by the electromagnetic relay (with contacts). The flash frequency of the steering light should be set at 65 ~ 120 times per minute, but it should be suitable within 70~90 times per minute; its turn-on/off ratio is 1 : 1; and it should have clear flash, stable operation and long service life.

b. Contactless triode flasher. The contactless triode flasher replaces the relay with a high-power triode and cancels the contacts, so it is also called an all-electronic flasher, whose structure is shown in Figure 6-8.

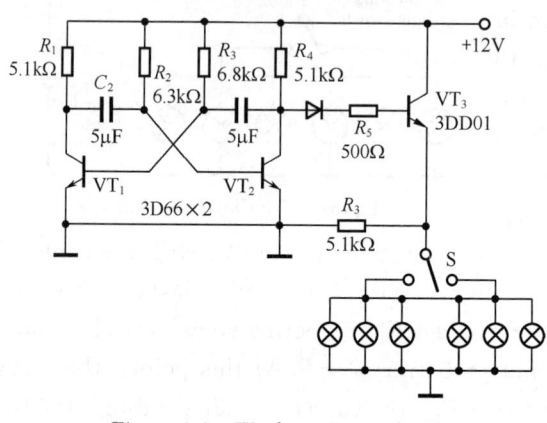

Figure 6-8　Working Principle of Contactless Triode Flasher

The circuit of the contactless triode flasher is a multivibrator, and its circuit structure is symmetrical, that is, $R_1 = R_4$, $R_2 = R_3$, $C_1 = C_2$, VT$_1$ and VT$_2$ are the same type of triode.

When the power supply switch is switched on, both VT$_1$ and VT$_2$ get forward bias voltage. Due to the dispersion of the triode parameters, that is to say, the parameters of

VT_1 and VT_2 can not be completely same, so one of them must be conductive first. If VT_1 is switched on first, the instantaneous potential of the collector electrode when VT_1 is conductive is reduced by the capacitor C_2, and the base potential of VT_2 is reduced, so VT_2 is cut off. At the same time, the power supply charges C_2 through $R_2 \rightarrow C_2 \rightarrow VT_1 \rightarrow$ ground, making the base potential of VT_2 is increased. When the base potential of VT_2 is higher than its turn-on voltage, VT_2 is switched on. Then, the potential of the collector electrode when VT_2 is conductive is reduced instantaneously by the capacitor C_1, VT_1 voltage, and the base potential of VT_1 is reduced, so VT_1 is cut off. At the same time, the power supply charges C_1 through $R_3 \rightarrow C_1 \rightarrow VT_2 \rightarrow VT_2 \rightarrow$ ground, making the base potential of VT_1 rise, when the potential of VT_1 is higher than its turn-on voltage, the VT_1 will be switched on. Thus VT_1 and VT_2 alternately switch on and off. If the steering light switch S is switched on at this time, when the VT_2 is switched on, the base potential of VT_3 is reduced, the VT_3 is cut off and the steering light is not on. When VT_2 is cut off, the base potential of VT_3 is raised, which produces the base current, VT_3 is on, turn on the steering light circuit, and the steering light is on. When the VT_2 is switched on, the VT_3 is cut off and the steering light goes out. The cycle will repeat to make the light flash.

③ Integrated circuit flasher. The difference between an integrated circuit flasher and a triode flasher is that an integrated circuit IC is used to replace a triode oscillator, which is also divided into two types: contact type and non-contact type.

Figure 6-9 shows a contactless integrated circuit flasher with a buzzer. It uses a high-power triode VT_1 to replace the relay of the contact flasher, and uses the switch function of the triode to control the turn-on and turn-off of the steering light. At the same time, the sound function is added, which constitutes the steering signal device of acoustooptic combination, to attract people's attention to the automobile steering and improve the safety.

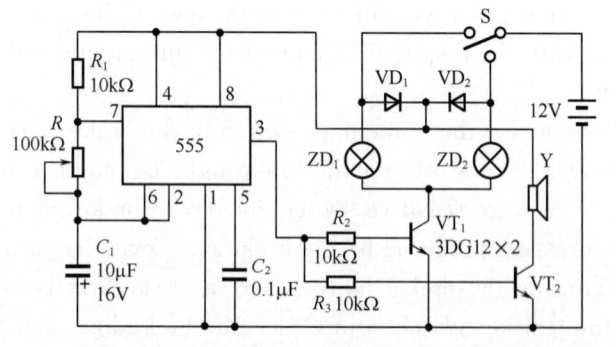

Figure 6-9　Working Principle of the Contactless Integrated Circuit Flasher with a Buzzer

When the steering switch S is switched on, the power supply charges the capacitor C_1 through VD_1 (or VD_2), R_1, potentiometer R, and the potential of pins 6 and 2 of the 555 integrated timer is gradually raised to high level. The logic function of the 555 timer shows that when pins 6 and 2 are high level, the output terminal 3 is low level. At the same time the pins 7 and 1 are switched on. Conversely, the output terminal 3 is turned to high level, the pins 7 and 1 are cut off. So at this point the output terminal 3 is low level, this low level is added to the base of VT_1 and VT_2, so VT_1 and VT_2 are cut off, so the steering light is not on, the buzzer is silent. At the same time, the pins 7 and 1 is conductive, capacitor C_1 discharges through potentiometer R, pins 7 and 1, so that the pins 6 and 2 are gradually re-

duced to low level, the output terminal to high level, so VT_1 and VT_2 are conductive, connected the circuit of the steering light and the buzzer, the steering light bright is on, the buzzer sounds. At the same time, due to the cut-off between pins 7 and 1, the power supply charges the capacitor C_1. As a result, the pins 6 and 2 become high level, the output terminal 3 become low level, VT_1 and VT_2 are cut off, the circuit of the steering light and the buzzer is cut off, so the steering light goes out and the buzzer stops ringing. At the same time, due to pins 7 and 1 are conductive, the capacitor starts to discharge again, so that the pins 6 and 2 are reduced to low level, the output terminal 3 is changed to high level, VT_1 and VT_2 are conductive again, the steering light is on again, the buzzer is ringing again. Over and over again, the steering light and sound signal is sent out. If the flash frequency does not meet the requirement, it can be adjusted by a potentiometer.

④ Flash relay integrated in control unit. At present, flash relays in many models are not independent, but are integrated in some control units, such as: automobile instrument control unit, on-board power supply control unit, and so on, respectively control the left front and rear steering lights, right front and rear steering lights. This kind of flash relay cannot be replaced and maintained separately.

(2) Danger alarm signal light. The danger alarm signal light is used for the automobile in case of emergency danger, which can turn on the front, rear, right and left steering lights at the same time to send out the warning signal. For safety, the power supply of the danger alarm signal light is not controlled by the ignition switch, and the danger alarm signal light can be turned on when the ignition switch is closed. It is safer for some models to turn on the steering switch after the danger alarm signal is on, then the light is turned into a one-sided flash.

(3) Brake light. Brake lights are used to indicate the braking or deceleration signals of an automobile. The brake lights are mounted on both sides of the rear. The two brake lights should be symmetrical with the longitudinal axis of the automobile and at the same height, the brake light is red.

Many automobiles connect the brake light switch to the brake pedal. When the brake is applied, the pedal moves downward and the brake light is on. In some automobiles, the brake light switch is a pressure-sensitive switch set in the brake main cylinder. When the brake is applied, the pressure produced by the brake main cylinder turns the pressure-sensitive switch on and lights up the brake light. After the fuse directly applies voltage to the brake switch, even the ignition switch is in OFF, the brake light can be turned on. When the brake light switch is closed, the voltage is added to the brake light. The brake lights on both sides of the automobile are connected in parallel, and the light bulb is connected to the circuit by grounding.

Some models not only turn on the brake light by the brake switch, but also control it by the brake pressure sensor in the Anti-lock Braking System (ABS), when the brake switch is damaged, step on the brake pedal, the brake light can also be lit, but it should be noted that if we step on the brake pedal slightly, the brake light will not be lit.

Most brake light systems use dual-filament bulbs that perform multiple functions. Usually, the filament (high-brightness filament) of the dual-filament bulb used for brake lights is also used for steering lights and danger alarm signal lights.

Nowadays, automobiles are also equipped with high-level additional brake lights (also known as high-level brake lights). High-level additional brake lights must be installed in the center line of the automobile.

(4) Clearance light. Clearance light is also called outline light, small light. It is installed in the front, rear, left and right edges of the automobile. In the middle and the outside of the cab of a large automobile, a pair of clearance lights is added to indicate the width of the automobile when driving at night. The clearance light sign is visible 300 m away at night. The front clearance light is white, and the back clearance light is mostly red.

With the clearance lights, the automobile can be seen as it enters the road from a fork in the road, and other drivers can estimate the length of your automobile accordingly. The front clearance light lens must be amber and the rear clearance light lens must be red. For the automobile with a curved corner-shaped lens headlight and a combined tail light, the part used as the lens shall also use the specified color.

(5) Tail light. The tail light is installed in the rear of the automobile. Its function is to indicate the position of the automobile when driving at night. The tail light is red. The tail light is also called the rear position light. When parking, it plays the role of the parking light. It is used to show the existence of the automobile.

(6) Reversing light. The reversing lights illuminate the road behind the automobile to alert automobiles and pedestrians to notice the reversing.

The manual transmission shell is equipped with a separate reversing light switch. The automobile with an automatic transmission that combines the reversing light switch with an Neutral safety switch.

2. Sound signaling device

(1) Electric horn. The function of the electric horn is to warn pedestrians and other automobiles. The sound level of the electric horn is 90~105dB (A).

(2) Buzzer. The buzzer, generally installed in the dashboard or instrument table, can sound a warning to the driver, such as to remind that the headlights are not turned off, the key is not pulled out, the door is not locked, and other information. Some automobile buzzers send out audible signals when reversing, warning pedestrians and automobiles behind the automobile.

Ⅲ. Item Implementation

(Ⅰ) Analysis of the circuit diagram of the control system for the headlight of the Volkswagen Bora and overhaul

1. Light control and detection system

(1) Classification of the light control system.

① According to the power supply mode, it can be divided into two kinds: control power supply and control ground.

② According to the control elements, it can be divided into light switch direct control, relay control and with light fault sensor control.

③ According to the lighting function, it can be divided into light exposure angle adjustment, light automatic opening, light closure delay, headlight cleaning and so on.

（2）Headlight control system.

① The light switch direct control. Figure 6-10 show the circuits of the headlight control system for a Volkswagen Bora.

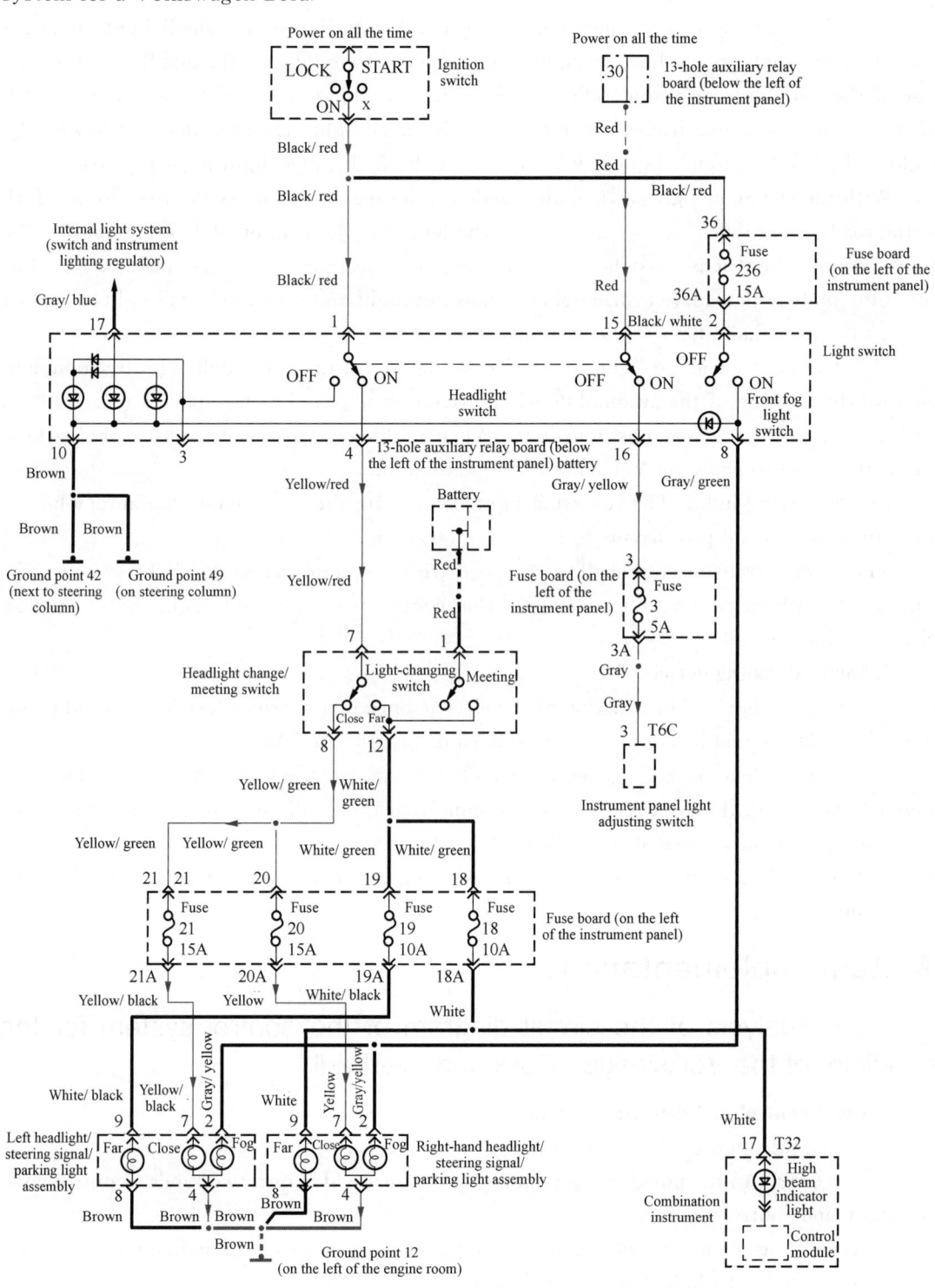

Figure 6-10   Circuit of the Headlight Control System for Volkswagen Bora
(light switch is in the low beam position)

140 Automobile Electrical Equipment Maintenance

The headlight control system of the Volkswagen Bora is directly controlled by the light switch. When the ignition switch is placed in ON, the light switch is placed in ON, the light switch "1 ♯, 4 ♯" terminal is in the on state, the power supply, through the ignition switch, the light switch, adds to the headlight switch. If the headlight switch is in the low beam position at this time, the power supply, through the low beam contact, the "21 ♯, 20 ♯" two fuses, provides power to the two headlight low beam filaments, respectively. Finally, a ground circuit is formed, and the low beam light is on. When the headlight switch is in the high beam position, the power supply, through the high beam contact, the "19 ♯, 18 ♯" two fuses, provides power to the two headlight high beam filaments. Finally, a ground circuit is formed, and the high beam is on. When the current headlight switch is transferred to the position of the meeting (overtaking), the power supply of the high beam is supplied by the "1 ♯" terminal of the headlight meeting switch, which is not controlled by the light switch.

② Relay control. The circuit of the relay control system is shown in Figure 6-11. The system adds the headlight control relay, the headlight light converter relay and the integrated relay, the light control switch and the light converter switch control are the signal line, which reduces the current of the switch contact and the control circuit. When the light control switch is placed in the HEAD, when the integrated relay receives the ground signal, the integrated relay controls the terminals of the headlight control relays "3 ♯ and 4 ♯" to close, the battery voltage, through the internal normal closed contact of the headlight light converter relay, and then two fuses, is added to the left and right low beam lights to form a circuit, the low beam light is on. When the light converter switch is placed in the high beam

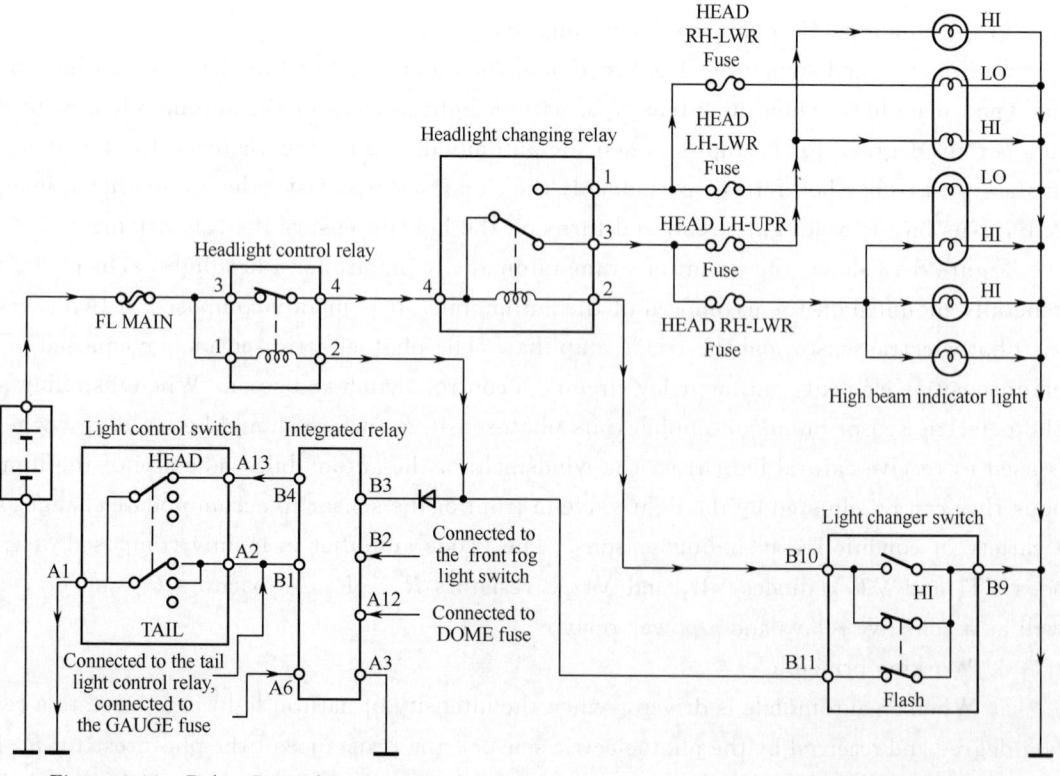

Figure 6-11　Relay Control System Circuit (light converter switch is in the high beam position)

position, the normally open contact of the front light converter relay is closed, the battery voltage, through the 3 # terminal of the front light converter relay, and then through two fuses, is add to 4 high beam and low beam indicator lights to form a circuit, the high beam and low beam indicator lights are on at the same time.

③ Light fault sensor control. The control system with a light fault sensor is shown in Figure 6-12. The system adds a light fault sensor, which can monitor the working state of the tail light. When any tail light has short circuit or broken circuit and the light bulb used is not up to standard, the light fault sensor will detect the abnormal working voltage and light up the fault indicator light to indicate the driver to repair.

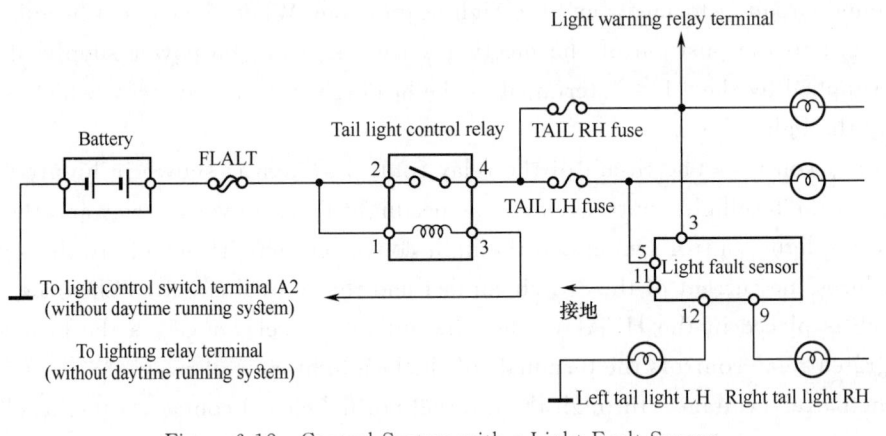

Figure 6-12　Control System with a Light Fault Sensor

2. Headlight control device

(1) Dim automatic luminaire for headlights.

① Function and structure. The function of the dim automatic luminaire is, during driving (not at night), when the intensity of natural light in front of the automobile is reduced to a certain degree, for example, when the automobile passes the viaduct, the forest path or the forest or bamboo forest, or suddenly the clouds are overcast, the luminaire automatically turns on the headlight circuit and turns on the light to ensure the safe driving.

Figure 6-13 shows the circuit of a dim automatic luminaire for a headlight. The device is generally mounted on the dashboard of the automobile. It is mainly composed of two parts: the photoelectric sensor and the triode amplifier. The photoelectric sensor is composed of a photosensitive element, a time-delay circuit, a control switch and so on. When installing an photoelectric sensor on an automobile, its photosensitive surface should be faced up, which is used to receive natural light from the windshield of the automobile. The size of the luminous flux can be adjusted by the light valve in front of the sensor to accommodate changes in a variety of conditions, including seasons. The triode amplifier is mainly composed of triodes VT_1 and VT_2, diodes VD_1 and VD_2, resistors $R_1 \sim R_9$, capacitors C_1 and C_2, as well as a sensitive relays and a power relay.

② Working principle.

a. When an automobile is driven, when the intensity of natural light is reduced to a certain degree and received by the photoelectric sensor, the resistance of the photoresistor R_2 in the sensor is reduced to a fixed value, it is sent to the triode amplifier with the output of the

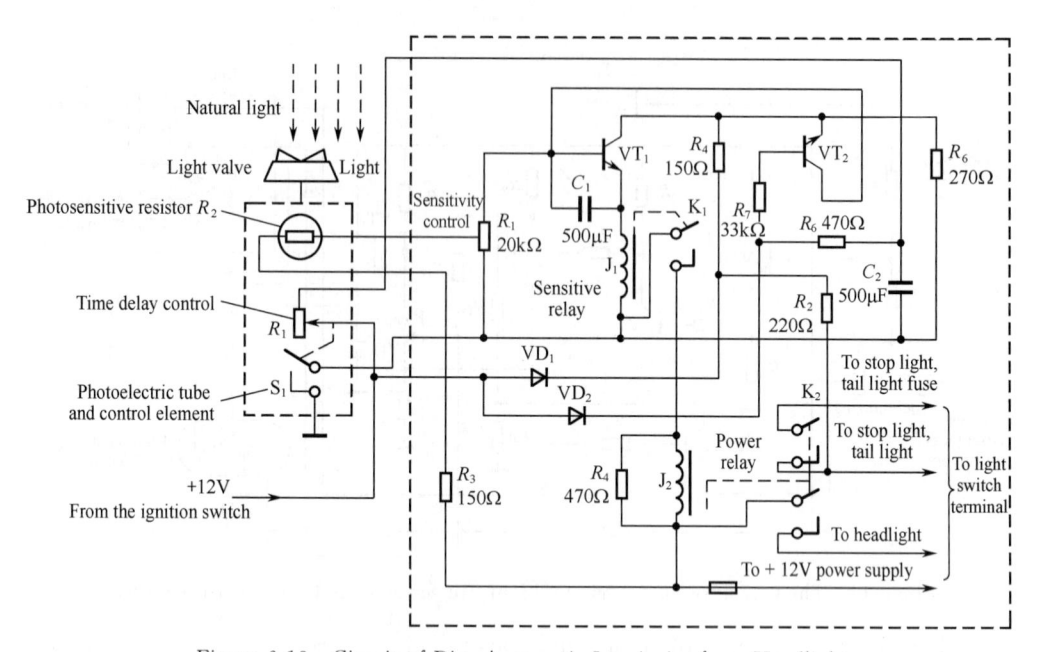

Figure 6-13   Circuit of Dim Automatic Luminaire for a Headlight

voltage (signal) that needs to be illuminated.

b. When the triode amplifier receives the output signal of the photoelectric sensor, the base position of the triode VT_1 drops rapidly, and the sensitive relay J_1 coil is connected.

c. When the relay J_1 circuit is connected, it produces electromagnetic suction to close the contact K_1. When K_1 is closed, the circuit of the power relay J_2 is also connected, so the switch is also connected by K_2, the circuit connecting to the headlight is connected, and the headlight is on. The function of the triode VT_2 in the circuit is time delay, that is, when the ignition switch is switched off, VT_2 keeps the VT_1 switched on until the voltage on the capacitor C_2 is reduced to insufficient to make the VT_2 switched on. After VT_2 is cut off, VT_1 is also cut off, due to the function of relay J_1 and J_2, the contact K_1 and the switch K_2 are open, so that the headlight is automatically extinguished. The delay time can be adjusted by potentiometer R_{10}.

(2) Automatic light converter for headlights.

① Function and structure. Automatic light converter for headlights is a kind of automatic control device which can automatically change light to high beam or low beam according to the brightness of counterpart automobile lights. In the night when the two automobiles drive oppositely, when they are $150 \sim 200$m away from each other, the light of the counterpart automobile is on the automatic light converter, the light is immediately and automatically changed from the high beam light to the low beam light, so as to avoid the dazzle of the other side driver caused by the high beam. After the two automobiles meet, the light converter automatically change the low beam light to the high beam light.

Figure 6-14 shows the circuit diagram of an automatic light converter with a photosensitive resistor. It is mainly composed of an electronic circuit, a photosensitive resistor and a relay. To prevent the electronic circuit failure so as to affect night driving, the light converter switch is also retained.

② Working process. The working process of the automatic light converter is as follows.

Item Ⅵ   Overhaul of Automobile Lighting System   **143**

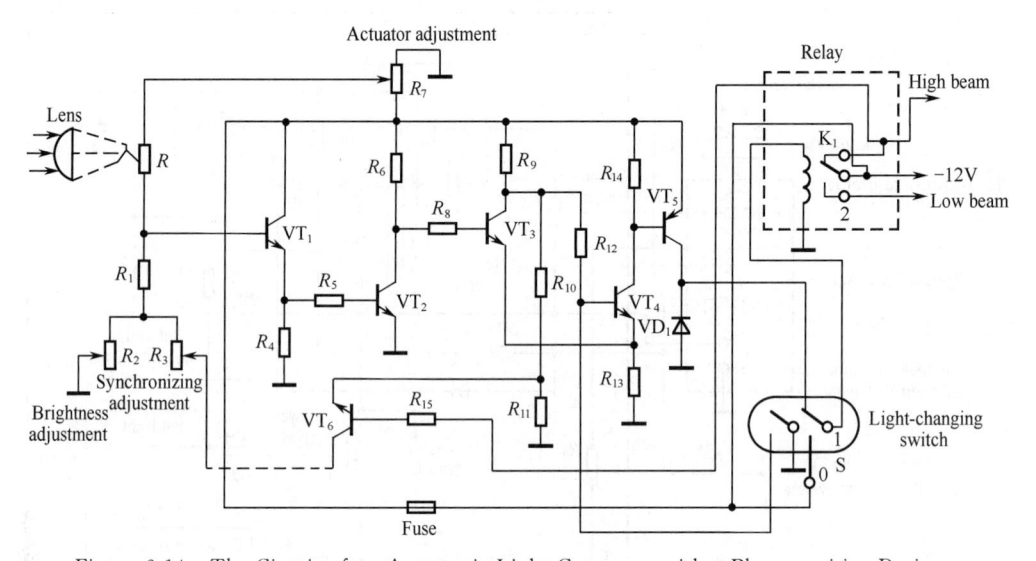

Figure 6-14   The Circuit of an Automatic Light Converter with a Photosensitive Resistor

a. When there is no automobile on the opposite side, there is no current in the relay J coil, contact K is in contact with the terminal of the high beam light, and the high beam light is on. When the automobile coming from the opposite side is $150 \sim 200 \mathrm{m}$ apart, the light is illuminated on the photoresistor R, which makes the resistance value of the photoresistor suddenly decrease, so the triode VT_1 gets the larger positive bias voltage and switches on, making the VT_2 get the forward bias voltage and switched on, and the base current of the VT_3 is short-circuited and the VT_3 is cut off, which makes the base potential of the VT_4 increase and the VT_4 is conductive. The base current of VT_5 is switched on, and VT_5 is connected and make the current pass through the coil of relay J, resulting in greater electromagnetic force to disconnect the contact and the high beam terminal 1, while connecting with the low beam terminal 2, the light changes from high beam to low beam.

b. After the two automobiles meet, the strong light acting on the photosensitive resistor disappears and the resistance value increases rapidly, which makes the forward bias voltage of the VT_1 of the triode decrease rapidly, the VT_1 is cut off, the base current of the VT_2 is cut off, and the VT_2 is cut off. Thus, the base current of VT_5 is cut off, VT_5 is cut off, the current in the relay J coil is cut off, the contact K is disconnected with the low beam terminal 2, and connected with the high beam terminal 1, and the work of the high beam light is resumed.

c. In the low beam state, the base potential of VT_6 is 0, so VT_6 is cut off and the shunt resistor R_3 is cut off, so the resistance of the branch is increased and the sensitivity is changed, which makes the circuit conversion appear lag phenomenon, which can effectively prevent the interference of stray light. If the electronic control part is out of order or damaged, we can use a pedal light converter to change the light. When stepping on the pedal light converter switch S, S is changed from "1" position to "0" position, so that the relay J coil gets current, produces electromagnetic force, makes contact K disconnect with terminal 1, connect with terminal 2, makes the headlight change from high beam to low beam. When the pedal is released to change the light, S returns from "0" to "1". The current in the relay coil is cut off, contact K is connected with the terminal "1" contact, the low beam

144   Automobile Electrical Equipment Maintenance

is changed to the high beam.

3. Headlight height adjustment system

The height adjustment of the headlight is also called the headlight beam level control. The lighting range of the headlight varies with the load of the automobile. When the load of the automobile is large, the headlight is closer to the ground, which makes the lighting range smaller. On the contrary, although the lighting range is larger, it will make the driver of the opposite automobile dazzle. In these cases, it is easy to cause safety accidents. To keep the light exposure distance constant, the light exposure is adjusted. There are two types of height adjustment for headlight, one is manual adjustment and the other is automatic adjustment.

(1) Manual adjustment of the height of the headlight. The manual adjustment switch of the height of the headlight is located near the headlight switch, as shown in Figure 6-15. The setting position of the adjustment switch is approximately equivalent to the following load states: 0—There are persons in the front of the automobile, the trunk is empty; 1—the automobile is full, the trunk is empty; 2—the automobile is full, the trunk is full; 3 the automobile is only a driver, the trunk is full. Turn the adjustment switch, and the servo motors in the two front headlight assemblies rotate to a pre-set headlight height. The circuit of the manual adjustment

Figure 6-15　Manual Adjustment Switch of the Height of the Headlight

of the height of the Shanghai Volkswagen Pora headlight is shown in Figure 6-16.

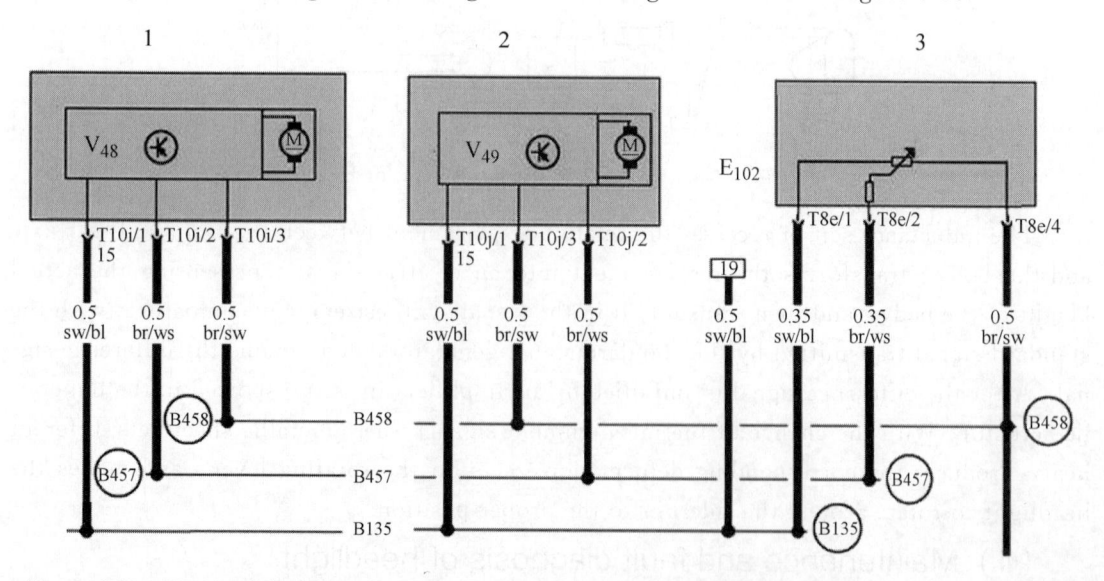

Figure 6-16　Circuit of the Manual Adjustment of the Height of the Shanghai Volkswagen Pora Headlight

1—Servo motor for adjusting left lighting distance; 2—Servo motor for adjusting right lighting distance;
3—Manual adjustment switch of the height of the headlight

(2) Automatic height adjustment of headlight. The height automatic adjustment system of headlight can adjust the exposure height automatically according to the data such as

Item Ⅵ　Overhaul of Automobile Lighting System　**145**

monitoring the centers of gravity in front and rear parts of the automobile. When the speed is relatively stable, the headlights automatically lower to illuminate the front under avoid causing the dazzle of the oncoming automobile driver; when the speed is fast, the headlights automatically raise, to obtain a wide field of vision to avoid danger. A schematic diagram of the height automatic adjustment unit of the Audi headlight is shown in Figure 6-17.

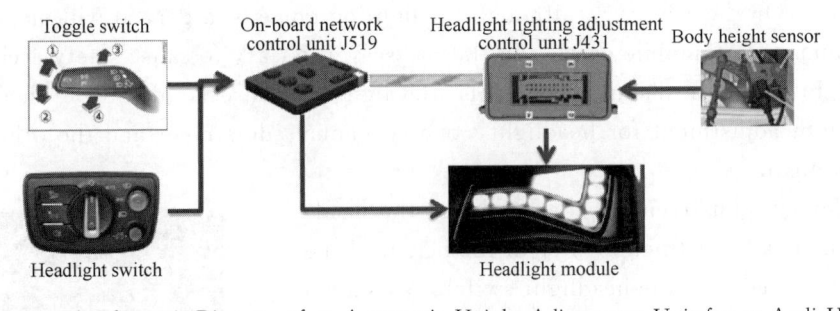

Figure 6-17　A schematic Diagram of an Automatic Height Adjustment Unit for an Audi Headlight

Figure 6-18 shows the working principle of the automatic adjustment system for the headlight produced by Bosch.

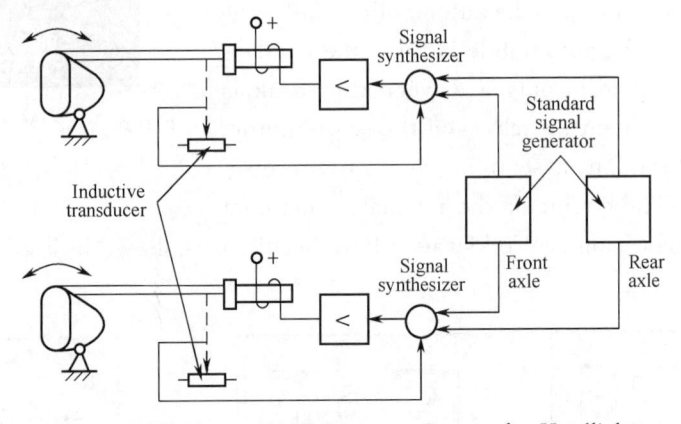

Figure 6-18　Automatic Adjustment System for Headlight

The inductance sensor receives the relative displacement between the front and rear axle and the body, transforms the displacement into an electric signal representing the actual height of the body, and then transmits it to the signal synthesizer, and compares it with the standard signal transmitted by the standard signal generator, and obtains the difference signal. After the difference signal is amplified by an amplifier, it is transported to the bimetallic actuator. With the change of the misalignment signal, the bimetallic sheet gets different heat, produces the corresponding deformation, acts on the rotating lever, and makes the headlight to rotate around the fulcrum to the proper position.

(II) Maintenance and fault diagnosis of headlight

1. Maintenance of headlight

If there is a little dust on the mirror, it can be blown clean with compressed air. If it can't blown away, it can be removed by different methods according to the different coating.

The mirror is chrome-plated and can be wiped gently by a soft skin dipping in a small amount of alcohol from the center of the mirror to the periphery in a spiral way.

If the mirror is silver-plated or aluminum-plated, it can be rinsed with cotton dipping in water (do not wipe). Then, it can be blown dry with compressed air.

Some mirror surfaces are coated a layer of very thin protective layer by the manufacturer. When wiping, do not destroy it. If the mirror often has dirt, the rubber seal should be replaced.

When replacing the headlight, because the halogen-tungsten bulb is hotter than a regular bulb when in use, and it will break if the oil or grease is glued to its surface. Moreover, salt in human sweat can contaminate quartz. Therefore, when changing the bulb, grab the flanged part to prevent the fingers from touching the quartz.

2. Fault diagnosis

The faults of the headlight mainly include that the headlight is not on, the high beam or the low beam is not on, the light is dim and so on. These faults are generally caused by bulb damage, filament burn-out, circuit break, switch failure and control failure, etc. See Table 6-1.

Table 6-1　Common faults and causes of the headlight

Fault phenomenon	Causes
All the lights are not on	The live wire between the battery and the main switch is short-circuited; the main switch of the lights is damaged; the main fuse of the power supply is fused; the electronic automatic transmission is damaged (for the electronic control headlight); the wires of the high beam or low beam are broken or not in good contact; the headlight is not grounded well
The high beam or the low beam is not bright	The light switch or automatic light converter is damaged; one wire of the high beam or the low beam is broken; one of the filament in the high beam or low beam filaments of the double-filament bulb is burnt-out; the light relay is damaged; the sensor is damaged
The headlights are dim	The fuse is loose; the wire joint is loose; the headlight switch or relay contact is in poor contact; the engine output voltage is low, the electrical devices is leaking, the load is too large
The front lights on one side are on and the front lights on the other side are dark	One side of the dark headlight is not in good ground or the light switch is in bad contact.
Bulbs often burn out	The output voltage of the generator is too high

3. Adjustment of headlight

There are usually two laws and regulations concerning the light distribution performance of automobile headlights: one is the European Economic Community (ECE) code matching performance standard; the other is the US FVMSS (Federal Motor Vehicle Safety Standard) 108 standard, which is equivalent to ECE code 76/756, that is, the SAE code lighting performance standard. ECE standards are more comprehensive and reasonable than SAE standards. In China, the national standard GB/T 7258—2017 *Motor vehicle operation safety technical conditions*, of which the headlight intensity and the beam irradiation position are specified as follows.

(1) The requirements on the position of the headlight beam.

① When a motor vehicle (other than a tractor for transportation) examines the position of the low beam of the headlight, the headlight shall be at a distance of 10m from the

screen, and the angle or center height of the light and dark cut-off line shall be $(0.6\sim0.8)$ H (H is the height of the reference center of the headlight); in the horizontal direction, the left-to-right deviation shall not exceed 100mm.

② For the four-light headlight, the adjustment of the high single-beam light requires that the height of the center of the beam on the screen should be $(0.85\sim0.90)H$, the horizontal position requires that the left light should not be more than 100mm to the left and 170mm to the right; the right light should not be more than 170mm to the right and to the left.

③ When a motor vehicle is equipped with a high and low dual-beam light, it mainly adjusts the low beam. For a light that can only adjust the high single beam, then adjust the high single beam.

(2) Light intensity requirements for headlights. The luminous intensity of the high beam of each headlight of a motor vehicle should meet the requirements of Table 6-2. When testing, its power supply system should be in charge state.

Table 6-2　Requirement for luminous intensity of high beam of headlight　　unit: cd

Item	Newly registered automobile			In-service automobile		
	One-light system	Two-light system	Four-light system	One-light system	Two-light system	Four-light[①] system
Automobile or trolley-bus.	—	15000	12000	—	12000	10000
Four-wheel agricultural truck	—	10000	8000	—	8000	6000
Three-wheel agricultural transport vehicle	8000	6000	—	6000	5000	—

① Two symmetrical light bulbs in a four-light motor vehicle are considered qualified when they meet the requirements of the two-light system.

(3) Light adjustment for ordinary headlights. Before adjusting or calibrating the headlight, the following inspection should be performed to ensure correct adjustment.

① If there is a thick layer of snow or mud on the automobile tires, they should be cleaned with high-pressure water.

② Make sure the tank is half full.

③ Check the spring and the shock absorber. If the spring or the shock absorber is damaged, the adjustment results will be affected.

④ Adjust all tire pressure to the specified value.

⑤ Before testing the headlights, the vehicle should be vibrated to stabilize the suspension by standing on the bumper and jumping a few times or pushing the front fender hard.

(4) Screen inspection method. The headlight beam can be inspected by the screen inspection method. The screen inspection method is introduced below.

① Park the automobile on a level ground and fill the wires with adequate pressure as required, remove all loads from the automobile (only one driver is allowed).

Stand a screen away from the headlight of the automobile s (m) (Note: Different models also require different values, please refer to the maintenance manual for details. Taking the Santana as an example, $s=10$m, $D=100$mm). Draw two vertical lines (each passing through the center of the headlight) and one horizontal line (equal to the height of the headlight) on the screen, as

shown in Figure 6-19. Draw a horizontal line lower D (mm) than H, which is intersected with the two vertical center lines of the headlights at point a and point b, respectively.

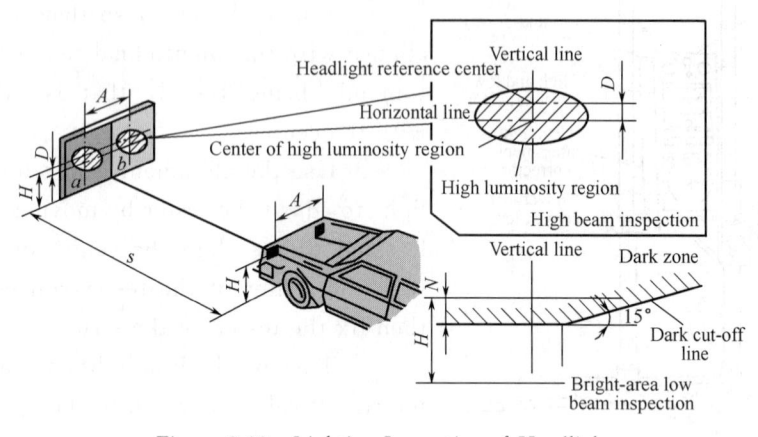

Figure 6-19   Lighting Inspection of Headlight

② Start the engine and rotate it at a speed of 2,000r/min (about 60% of the engine speed), i. e. to light up the headlight high beam without discharging the battery (some automobiles are adjusted according to the low beam, see the model manual for details).

③ When adjusting, one light should be covered and then check the other light to see if the beam is aligned to point a or point b (the center of light on the same side). Remove the headlight ring if it does not meet the requirements. Spin out the adjusting screw on the side, so that the beam can be adjusted in the horizontal direction, screw in or out the adjusting screw on the top, or adjust in the high and low direction (see Figure 6-20). After adjusting one light, adjust the other one in the same way so that the center of the beam is aligned at point b or point a.

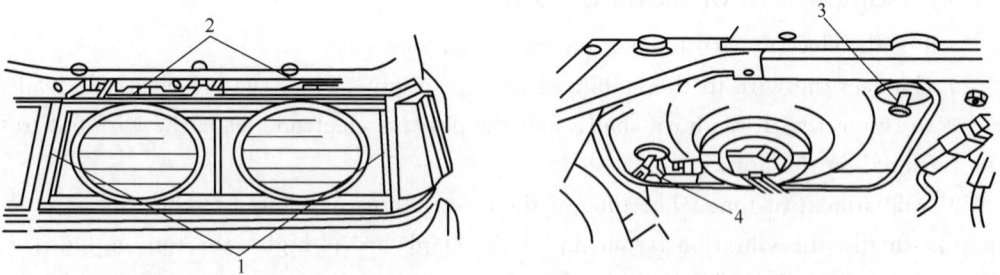

Figure 6-20   Adjustment Part of Headlight
1,3—Left and right adjusting screws; 2,4—Up and down adjusting screws

④ When the high beam light is adjusted, the low beam light should be turned on to check whether there is a clear light-dark cut-off line on the screen and whether the height is in accordance with the regulations. The provisions are as follows: for the automobile with the upper edge of the headlight not more than 1,350mm from the ground, on the screen 10m away from the headlight, the horizontal part of the light-dark cut-off line should be about $H/3$ lower than the reference center of the headlight.

(5) Adjust the headlight by means of a collector tester. The structure of the collector tester is shown in Figure 6-21, and its use method is as follows.

① The tester is placed vertically, the relative position of the automobile and the tester

Item Ⅵ   Overhaul of Automobile Lighting System   **149**

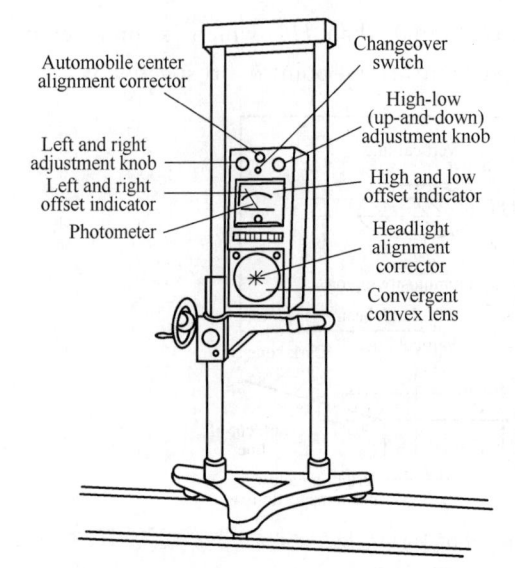

Automobile center alignment corrector
Changeover switch
High-low (up-and-down) adjustment knob
Left and right adjustment knob
Left and right offset indicator
High and low offset indicator
Photometer
Headlight alignment corrector
Convergent convex lens

Figure 6-21　Collector Headlight Tester

shall ensure that the distance between the tester collector lens and the headlight lens is 1m.

② Adjust the tester so that the calibrator is aligned with the longitudinal center line of the automobile being tested, that is, the alignment with the center.

③ Use the alignment calibrator of the headlight to adjust the tester by moving up and down, left and right, align the center of the headlight with the center of the tester collector lens, and then fix the tester on the strut.

④ Turn on the headlight and turn the photometric-optical axis switch to the optical axis position. The left and right, up and down offset indicator. Turn the left and right, up and down adjust the knob, so that the pointer of the left and right, up and down offset indicator indicates the central position (0).

⑤ Turn the photometric-optical axis switch to the photometric position, the photometer starts to work, read the photometer indication value and the scale value rotated of the left and right, up and down adjusting knob at this time, that is, the luminous intensity and the left and right, up and down offset of the optical axis are measured.

⑥ Adjust the left and right, up and down adjusting screw of the headlight, reset the scale of the adjusting knob of the tester to 0.

(Ⅲ) Adjustment of electric horn

(1) Fix the electric horn bracket on the bench vice.

(2) Connect the wire to the stabilized power supply. The negative electrode leads the wire out to connect with the horn shell, and the positive electrode leads the wire out to touch the terminal on the horn.

(3) Adjustment of tone. The tone of the electric horn is related to the core gap. When the gap is small, the vibration frequency of the clapboard is high, the tone is high; Conversely, the tone is low. The adjustment of the gap of the armature of the basin-shaped electric horn is shown in Figure 6-22. When adjusting, the locking nut should be loosened first, and then the volume adjusting bolt (core) should be rotated to adjust. Note that some automobile horns do not have tonal adjusting bolts.

(4) Volume adjustment. The volume of the electric horn is related to the current passing through the horn coil. When the contact pressure increases, the current flowing into the horn coil increases, causing the volume produced by the horn to increase, whereas the volume decreases. For the basin-shaped electric horn shown in Figure 6-23, the volume adjusting screw can be rotated (the volume increases when rotating the screw counter-clockwise). Don't overdo it when adjusting, just turn the adjusting nut 1/10 turn at a time. Note that some automobile horn volume adjusting screws are sealed with glue and cannot be seen directly from the back of the horn.

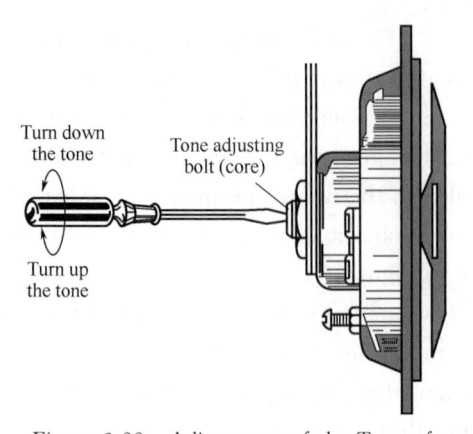

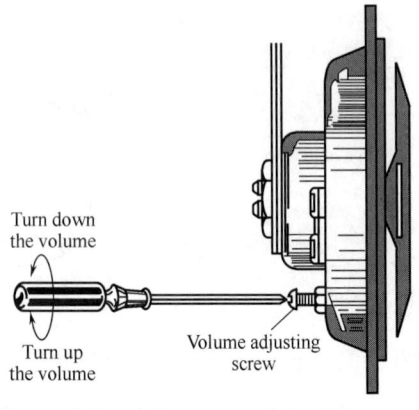

Figure 6-22　Adjustment of the Tone of
a Basin-shaped Electric Horn

Figure 6-23　Adjustment of the Volume of
a Basin-shaped Electric Horn

Ⅳ. Knowledge and Skills Expansion

(Ⅰ) Active steering system of lights

Usually, automobile headlights, regardless of brightness, have a certain lighting range. When turning at night, a "blind area" will occur due to the driving angle, which will affect the safety of driving in a certain degree. In the case of fixed lighting, this blind area is inevitable, so "AFS light follow-up steering system" came into being. It can automatically adjust the deflection of headlights according to driving speed, steering angle and so on, so that it can illuminate the "unreached" area in advance, provide all-round safety lighting, and ensure the safety of turning at night, as shown in Figure 6-24.

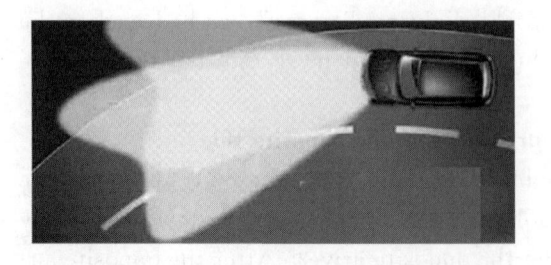

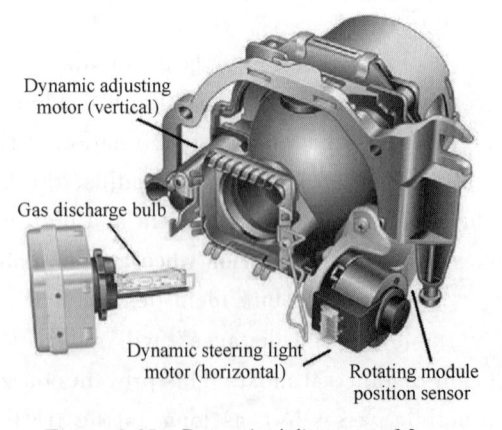

Figure 6-24　Turning of the Automobile
with AFS Function

Figure 6-25　Dynamic Adjustment Motor
(vertical) of the Magotan Headlight

The adaptive headlight can dynamically adjust the light when turning, and the projection module of the headlight is equipped with an motor which can change the direction of light exposure in the horizontal direction when the automobile is turning. The dynamic adjustment motor (vertical) of the Magotan headlight is shown in Figure 6-25. The headlight lens and bracket do not rotate. The angle of light rotation is about $15°$ on the inside of the turn direction and $7.5°$ on the outside, as shown in Figure 6-26.

Item Ⅵ　Overhaul of Automobile Lighting System　**151**

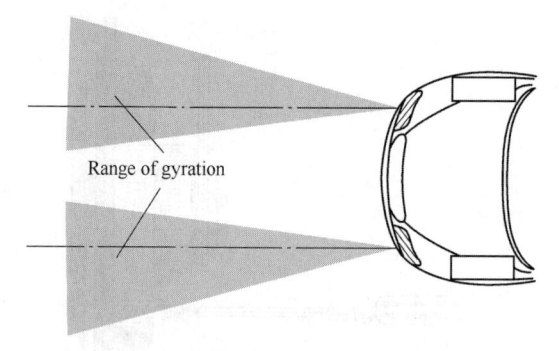

Range of gyration

Figure 6-26   Angle of Rotation of Headlights

This angle change allows the automobile to get better illumination when turning. At this point, the angle of rotation of the inner module in the light turn is twice that of the outer module. In this way, the maximum range of illumination can be obtained with the same intensity of light.

The angle does not return when the automobile is at rest. When the speed is less than 6km/h, the projection module in the headlight does not return. When the speed exceeds 10km/h, the angle of the light returning mainly depends on the angle of the steering wheel.

This can satisfy the legal requirement not to swing headlights while the automobile is stationary. At the same time, when the automobile accelerates at this low speed, the deflection of the headlight can be transferred evenly under the condition of constant steering angle.

(Ⅱ) Variable lighting distance of Audi A8

The function of "variable lighting distance" is as follows: When driving at night, it can ensure that this lane is adequately lit without causing dazzle to other automobile drivers. This function is developed on the basis of the high beam auxiliary system (the high beam auxiliary system can automatically identify whether to turn on the high beam and turn on or turn off the high beam accordingly under the current situation when driving at night).

Compared the high beam auxiliary system with the "variable lighting distance", the working difference is pure digital: That is to say, it switches directly from low beam to high beam. In contrast, this function of the "variable lighting distance" can be based on the traffic situation at that time, adjust the headlight range without level, so that the distance changes between the low beam and high beam.

1. Working condition when an automobile is driving from the opposite side

If the automobile identifies that an automobile is driving from the opposite side, the "variable lighting distance" will reduce the headlight range, which can be lowered to low beam distance at most. This prevents dazzle from the opposite driver. After the opposite automobile passes by, as long as the traffic conditions permit, the headlight range will increase, which can be increased to the high beam range, as shown in Figure 6-27.

2. Working condition when there is an automobile in front

If the automobile is approaching the automobile in front of it, the working condition of the system is roughly similar to that of the automobile in the opposite direction. In this case, the "variable lighting distance" function also reduces the headlight range continuously to prevent dazzle to the driver of the front automobile, as shown in Figure 6-28. If the automobile overtakes the front automobile, the headlight range will then increase, up to the distance of the high beam. Of course, only if the traffic conditions permit.

152 Automobile Electrical Equipment Maintenance

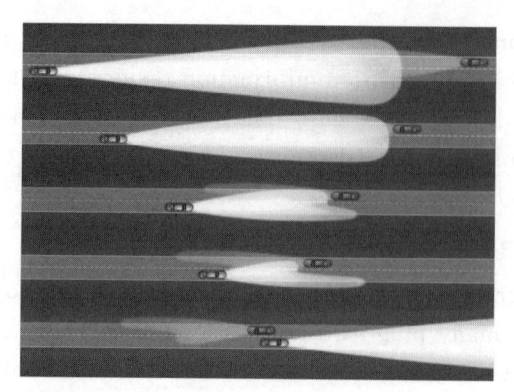 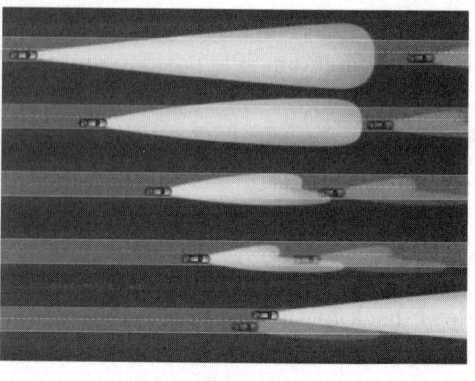

Figure 6-27　Working State of Incoming Automobile on Opposite Side

Figure 6-28　Working State of Automobile in Front of the Automobile

3. Fundamental

The current traffic condition is detected by the camera in the control unit J852 and analyzed in the arithmetic unit in the control unit. Image processing software searches for light sources in the camera image. The software in the control unit divides the identified light sources into the following categories: Headlights, Tail lights, Street lights, Other lights not related to this function.

If the light source can be accurately identified, the control unit J852 will determine the location of the identified automobile on the camera image and estimate the distance from the automobile. These two values are sent to the bend light and the control unit J745 by the extended CAN bus, as shown in Figure 6-29.

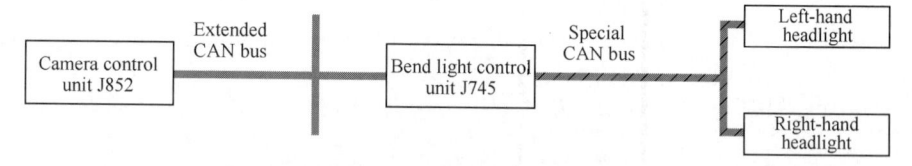

Figure 6-29　Basic Working Principle

Two headlights are equipped with rollers for adjusting the range of light. With the corresponding contour shape on the roller, the servo motor works to turn the roller so that the required lighting can be obtained as needed. The installation position of the servo motor is shown in Figure 6-30.

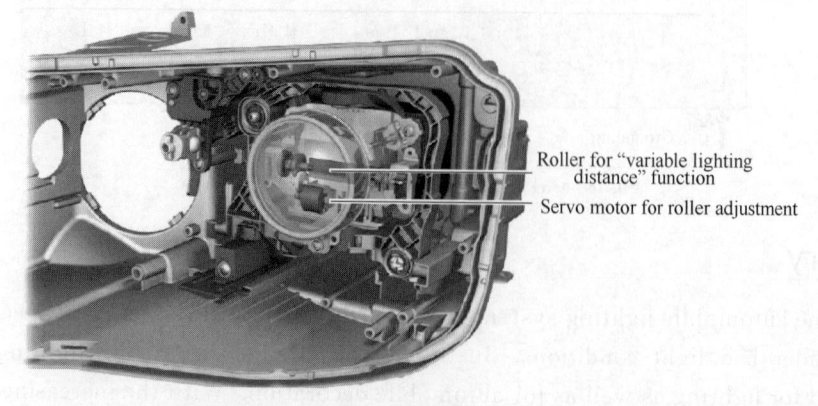

Figure 6-30　Installation Position of Servo Motor

The control unit J745 determines the position of the roller according to the two inputs of the identified automobile position and the distance. The position information required for the roller is transmitted to two headlights via a dedicated CAN bus. The headlight electronic system starts the servo motor according to the instructions of J745, so the driveway will get the ideal lighting according to the actual traffic condition.

(Ⅲ) LIN bus circuit for automobile light switch

Traditional automobile light switch integrates small lights, headlights, front fog lights, back fog lights and so on, so there are many plug-in terminals on the back of the switch, the related control circuit is complex. After the new automobile light switch adopts LIN bus control, the circuit is simple, and has self-diagnosis function.

All signals of switches, keys and regulators in the light switch are read by the power supply control unit through the LIN bus. In addition, the switch lighting and various functions of the indicator light instructions are transmitted from the power supply control unit to the light switch. The feedback line, also known as the redundant line, is introduced to be grounded through the circuit inside the switch to verify the correctness of the switch position. If the LIN line or feedback line is short-circuited or disconnected, the emergency lighting function of the power supply control unit is activated (the low beam is turned on) and a fault is recorded in the fault memory of the power supply control unit. The circuit of Audi light switch is shown in Figure 6-31.

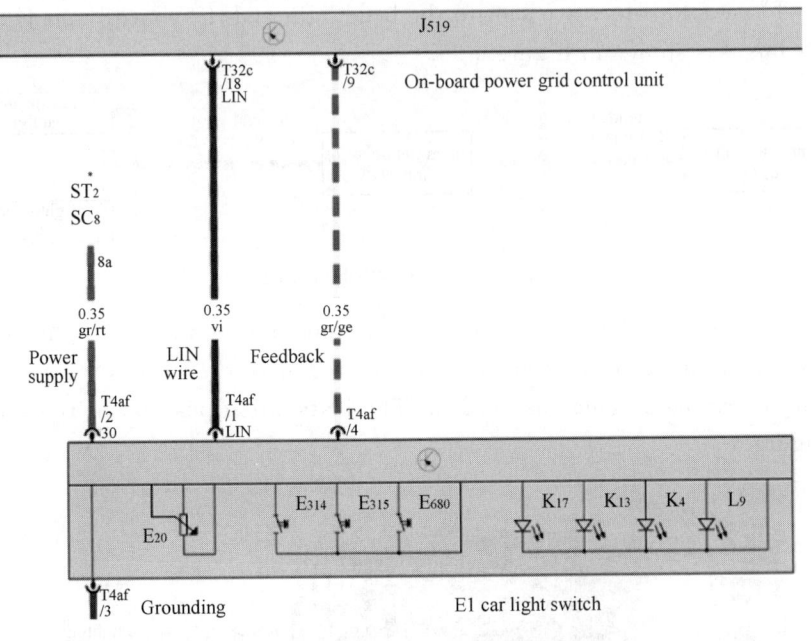

Figure 6-31   The circuit of Audi Light Switch

Summary

(1) The automobile lighting system is designed to ensure the safety and speed of the automobile under bad light conditions. In other words, the automobile lighting system is mainly used for lighting as well as for automobile decoration. With the increasing application

of automobile electronic technology, lighting system is developing in the direction of intelligentization.

(2) The automobile signal system is a light (sound) signal (or sign) used by the automobile to direct other vehicles or pedestrians, usually consisting of a steering signal device, a braking signal device, an electric horn, etc., to ensure the safety of the automobile.

Thinking and Practice

(1) What are the measures for headlights to prevent dazzle?

(2) Describe the circuit working principle of the steering signal system.

(3) What are the parts of the headlight? What is the function of the headlight relay?

(4) When does the fog light work? What are the characteristics of the fog light circuit?

(5) Briefly describe the adjustment method of the electric horn.

Item VII

Maintenance of Information Display System

I. Scene Introduction

A Volkswagen Jetta was found that when the automobile was filled with fuel, the fuel gauge showed a half-tank, which was not in accordance with the actual fuel quantity. This phenomenon is a common failure of the automobile information display system. The reason is generally the misalignment of the fuel quantity sensor, which needs to be replaced. Here we are going to learn about the common failures and overhauls of the automobile information display system.

II. Related Knowledge

The automobile information display system is mainly composed of the automobile instrument system and the automobile alarm information system. The automobile information display system is a dynamic reflection of the automobile running condition, is an interface of information exchange between the automobile and the driver, provides the necessary automobile running information for the driver, and is also an important basis for the maintenance personnel to discover and troubleshoot the failures.

(I) Automobile instrument system

1. Function of instrument

In order to keep the driver abreast of the various working conditions of the automobile, to ensure the driving safety of the automobile, and to detect and eliminate the faults of the automobile in time, all kinds of monitoring instruments and alarm information devices are installed on the automobiles now, which are all integrated on the dashboard to form the instrument assembly. Automobile dashboard is the most important and direct man-machine interface for information communication between the automobile and the driver. For automobile instrument, it should be not only reliable, earthquake-proof, impact-resistant, but also beautiful, accurate, clear and easy to read.

2. Classification of instrument

Automobile instruments can be classified by working principle and installation mode.

By the working principle, the automobile instruments can be divided into mechanical instrument, electrical instrument, analog circuit electronic instrument and digital electronic instrument. Traditional instruments generally refer to mechanical instrument, electrical instrument and analog circuit electronic instrument. With the development of information

156 Automobile Electrical Equipment Maintenance

technology and electronic technology, digital electronic instrument has the advantages of high integration and accuracy, high information content, good reliability and free display mode, which gradually replaces the traditional instruments.

By the installation mode, the automobile instruments can be divided into two kinds: separate instrument and combination instrument. Separate instrument is installed separately, which is common in early automobiles and racing automobiles. The combination instrument is to combine all kinds of instruments in the design, the structure is compact and easy to install. Most of modern automobiles use the combination instruments. The combination instruments can be divided into detachable type and integral non-detachable type.

Nowadays, the dashboard assembly of the automobile is generally divided into two parts, which generally refers to the platform consisting of the main dashboard in front of the steering wheel, the sub-dashboard and on the channel next to the driver and the instrument cover. On the main dashboard, the whole automobile monitoring instruments, such as speed meter, engine tachometer, oil pressure meter, water thermometer, fuel gauge, are integrated. Some instruments are also equipped with variable speed gear indication, clock, environment thermometer, road slope and elevation altimeter, etc. According to the current popular dashboard design style, the display and control parts of air-conditioning, audio, navigation, entertainment and other equipment are installed on the sub-dashboard to facilitate the operation of the driver. At the same time, it appears that the layout of the whole automobile is compact and reasonable.

The automobile instruments are installed in the most convenient position for the driver to observe, and display the information in the most clear, direct and simple way. The most prominent position on the main dashboard is used to indicate the most basic and important condition information of the automobile, as well as minor information by other indication forms. Generally, the automobile instruments have the most basic and important indication functions such as speed, mileage, engine speed, water temperature, fuel quantity, etc. , as well as the indication and alarm functions of engine electric control, light, power supply, safety, lubrication, brake, etc. For example, the instrument and its function of a Santana are shown in Figure 7-1.

3. Traditional automobile instruments

(1) Composition and classification. The fuel oil meter, water thermometer and oil pressure gauge in the traditional automobile instruments are all composed of indicator sensors, although the parameters measured and indicated are different.

The indicators are divided into electrothermal type (bimetallic sheet type) and electromagnetic type in principle. The electrothermal indicator is to use the heat generated by the electric heating coil to heat the bimetallic sheet, so that it is deformed to drive the corresponding indication of the pointer, it needs the intermittent pulse current; the electromagnetic indicator is to use the two vertical electromagnetic coils to magnetize the rotor through different current and magnetic field, the rotor drives pointer to indicate the corresponding indication value, it is a current ratio meter, so it needs continuous current signal.

The sensor is used in conjunction with the indicator, and its function is to extract the required parameter and turn the measured physical quantities into electrical signals. To measure different parameters, the sensors differ in structure. Sensors can be divided into

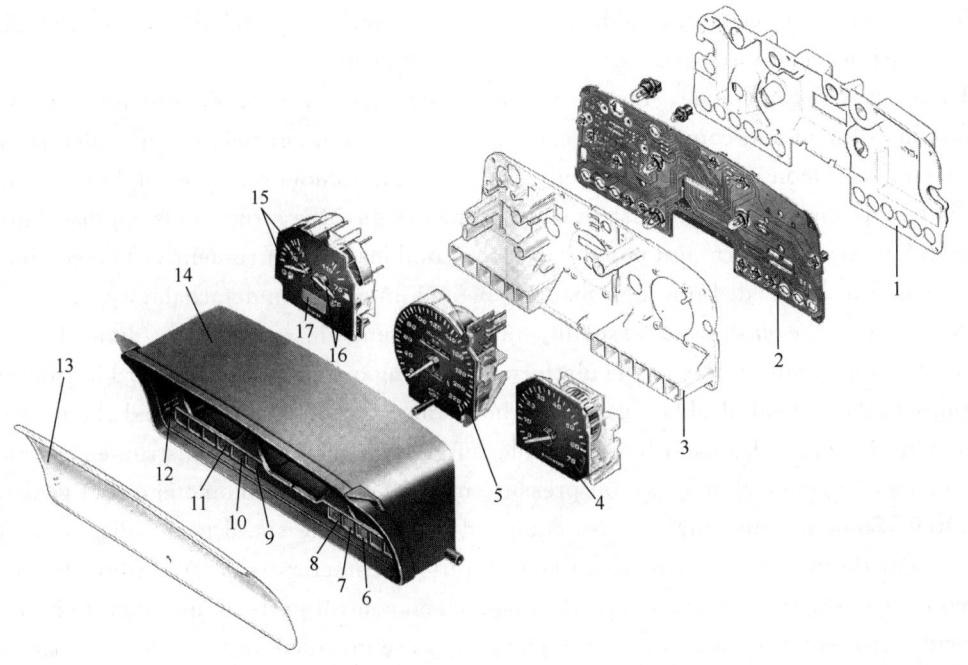

Figure 7-1   Instrument and its Function of a Santana

1—Back cover; 2—Circuit board; 3—Light guide board; 4—Engine tachometer; 5—Speed odometer; 6—Coolant
insufficient warning indicator light; 7—Rear air window electric heater indicator light; 8—Headlight indicator light;
9—Charging insufficient warning light; 10—Oil Warning indicator light; 11—Brake system failure and parking
brake indicator light; 12—Digital clock adjustment knob; 13—Transparent guard plate; 14—Dashboard;
15—Fuel gauge and signal light; 16—Coolant thermometer and signal light; 17—Digital clock

electrothermal type and variable resistor type. The electrothermal sensors provide intermit-tent pulse current signals, while variable resistor sensors provide continuously varying cur-rent signals.

By combining the above types of indicators and sensors, the following four different types of meters are produced.

Electrothermal indicator+electrothermal sensor.

Electrothermal indicator+variable resistor sensor.

Electrothermal indicator+variable resistor sensor.

Electromagnetic indicator+electrothermal sensor.

Among them, the first three combined forms are widely used in automobiles, such as common fuel gauge, water thermometer and oil pressure gauge.

① Fuel gauge. The fuel gauge is used to detect and indicate the amount of fuel in the fu-el tank. The fuel gauge consists of an indicator and a sensor. There are two common types of indicators, namely, the electromagnetic type and the electrothermal type, and the sensor is generally a variable resistor sensor. Some models are also equipped with a fuel alarm indi-cator to work with the fuel gauge.

② Water thermometer. The water thermometer is used to detect and indicate the work-ing temperature of the engine coolant. The water thermometer consists of an indicator and a water temperature sensor. The indicator is installed in the dashboard and has two types of structures, namely, electrothermal type and thermistor type. At present, in most

158 Automobile Electrical Equipment Maintenance

automobiles, the water thermometer and the water temperature alarm light are used simultaneously.

③ Oil pressure gauge. The oil pressure gauge is an instrument used to indicate the pressure of the main oil channel of the engine lubrication system and whether the system is working properly when the engine is in operation. The oil pressure gauge is usually composed of an indicator and an oil pressure sensor, and the pressure sensor is screwed to the main oil channel behind the oil pump. Common types of oil pressure gauges are electrothermal type, electromagnetic type and spring tube type. At present, many automobiles cancel the oil pressure gauge and use the oil pressure alarm device to replace the oil pressure gauge to monitor the oil pressure. The oil pressure alarm device is usually in the main oil channel of the engine lubrication system. When the oil pressure is below the normal value, an alarm signal is issued to the driver. It consists of an oil low pressure alarm light mounted on the dashboard and an oil pressure switch mounted on the main oil channel of the engine.

(2) Structure and working principle.

① Electrothermal indicator+electrothermal sensor.

The structure of the electrothermal water thermometer is shown in Figure 7-2. The indicator has the same structure as the indicator structure of the electrothermal oil pressure sensor above, except that the scale value of the dashboard is different.

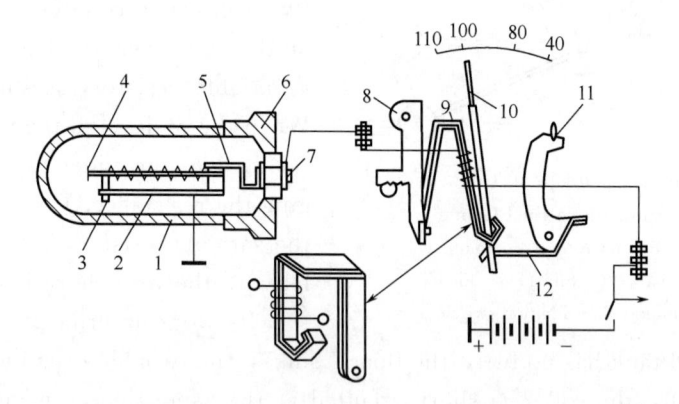

Figure 7-2　Structure of Electrothermal Water Thermometer

1—Copper shell; 2—Bottom plate; 3—Fixed contact; 4—Bimetallic sheet; 5—Contact sheet;
6—Shell seat; 7—Terminal; 8—Adjusting tooth fan; 9—Bimetallic sheet; 10—Pointer;
11—Adjusting tooth fan; 12—Spring

The water temperature sensor is a sealed sleeve with the bimetallic sheet 4, which is wound by the heating wire. The one end of the heating wire is connected with the indicator through the contact sheet 5 and the terminal 7, and the other end is grounded by a fixed contact 3.

The working principle of the water thermometer is similar to that of the oil pressure gauge. When the circuit is connected and the water temperature is not high, the bimetallic sheet in the water temperature sensor mainly depends on the heating wire to produce deformation, so the bimetallic sheet needs to be heated for a long time to separate the contact. After the contact is opened, due to the low temperature and fast heat dissipation around it, the bimetallic sheet is cooled quickly and the contact is closed. When the water temperature

is low, the contact works under the condition of long closing time and short disconnecting time, so that the current average value in the heating coil of the water thermometer is big, the deformation of the bimetallic sheet is large, driving the pointer to deflect to the right with a large angle, indicating the water temperature is low. When the water temperature is high, the temperature around the bimetallic sheet is high, the closing time of the contact is short and the breaking time is long, the current average of the heating coil of the water thermometer is small, the deformation of the bimetallic sheet is small, and the deflection angle of the pointer to the right is small, indicating the water temperature is high.

② Electromagnetic indicator＋variable resistor sensor. The electromagnetic indicator can be divided into non-core type and iron-core type in structure.

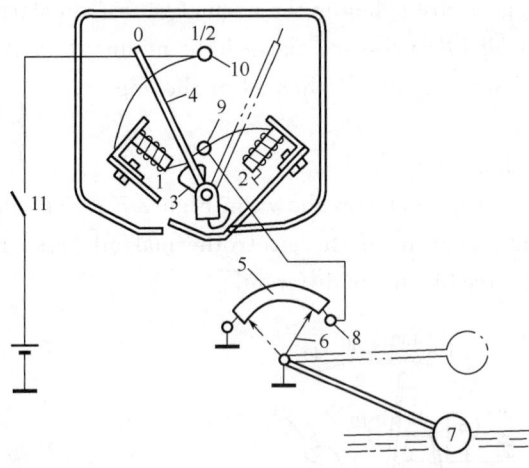

Figure 7-3 Structure and Circuit Connection of
a Core Electromagnetic Fuel Gauge
1,2—Coil; 3—Pointer rotor; 4—Pointer;
5—Variable resistor; 6—Slider; 7—Float;
8～10—Terminal; 11—Ignition switch

Figure 7-3 shows the structure and the circuit connection diagram of the core electromagnetic fuel gauge. The indicating oil gauge has a right electromagnetic coil and a left electromagnetic coil, the axes of which are 90° each other. On the core of the coil, the guide magnetic bend plate is fixed firmly, and a pointer rotor, a pointer, a small flywheel and a counterweight are installed on the pointer shaft. The sensor consists of a variable resistor, a slider and a float. When the oil level in the tank changes, the float drives the slider to move, thus changing the resistance. Coil 1 is in series with the variable resistor, and coil 2 is in parallel with the variable resistor.

Its working principle is as follows.

When the fuel tank has no fuel, the float 7 sinks, the variable resistor 5 is short-circuited by the slider 6, the coil 2 is short-circuited at the same time, and no current passes through. At this point, the current in the coil 1 reaches its maximum, producing the strongest electromagnetic force, attracting the pointer rotor 3 so that the pointer points to the "0" position.

When the fuel in the fuel tank increases, the float 7 rises and drives the slider 6 to slide, the resistance of the variable resistor 5 increases and the current in the coil 2 increases, while the current in the coil 1 decreases. Under the action of the synthetic magnetic field of the coil 1 and the coil 2, the rotor drives the pointer to deflect to the right, and the pointer points to the high scale position.

When the fuel tank is filled with fuel, the coil 2 has the greatest electromagnetic force. The pointer points to the "1" position. When the fuel tank is half full, the pointer points to the "1/2" position.

③ Instrument regulator. Because the change of the power supply voltage will affect the indicator value of the instrument, resulting in the error of the instrument value, so the circuit of the instrument should be equipped with an instrument regulator. The common instru-

160 Automobile Electrical Equipment Maintenance

ment regulators are bimetallic sheet type and integrated circuit type.

The integrated circuit instrument regulator mainly adopts three-terminal integrated regulator for automobile, which has the advantages of simple structure, low cost, good voltage stabilizing effect and long service life, so it is widely used. Figure 7-13 shows a three-terminal integrated circuit electronic regulator dedicated for the dashboard of a Santana and an Audi, 1 for the output angle, ⊥ for ground; 2 for the power input. The output voltage of the regulator is 9.5~10.5V.

(3) Speedometer. A speedometer is an instrument used to indicate the speed and mileage of an automobile. It consists of a speed meter and an odometer. The common speedometers are the magnetic induction type and the electronic type.

① Magnetic induction speedometer. Magnetic induction speedometer mainly uses magnetic induction principle to work, without circuit connection. The specific structure is composed of a permanent magnet, an aluminum cover, a shield, a dial and a pointer. The permanent magnet fastens with the drive shaft. The drive shaft is driven by a flexible soft shaft from the transmission output shaft. The pointer and the aluminum cover are fixed on the center shaft and the dial is fixed on the shell. When not working, the aluminum cover under the action of the balance spring, makes the pointer in the "0" position. When the automobile is running, the flexible hose from the transmission output shaft drives the drive shaft to rotate the U shaped permanent magnet, and the magnetic field generated by the eddy current is induced on the aluminum cover. This magnetic field interacts with the rotating magnetic field of the permanent magnet to produce torque, which causes the aluminum cover to turn a certain angle to the rotation direction of the permanent magnet until it is balanced with the reverse torque produced by the elastic force of the balance spring. The higher the speed, the greater the torque produced, the greater the angle at which the pointer swings on the dial, that is, the higher the indicated speed.

The odometer can indicate the total mileage and the single mileage data. The total mileage can only accumulate and can not return to 0. The single mileage indicator can return to 0 by the 0 button. The traditional odometer is mainly composed of turbine worm and counter wheel. When the automobile is running, the drive shaft drives the first counter wheel on the right side of the counter wheel (1/10km) via the turbine worm, and the transmission ratio of any counter wheel to the counter wheel on the left side is 10 : 1. The number displayed by this way is increased by decimal system, and is measured automatically in the automobile mileage.

② Electronic speedometer. The electronic speedometer consists of a speed sensor, an electronic circuit, a stepping motor, a speed meter and an odometer. Figure 7-4 shows the structure of an electronic speedometer.

The Audi 100 combination instrument is equipped with an electronic speedometer, which is based on the following principles.

The speed sensor, driven by a transmission, generates a pulse electric signal proportional to the speed of the automobile. The sensor consists of a reed switch tube and a rotor containing 4 pairs of magnetic electrodes, as shown in Figure 7-5. The magnetic rotor rotates per turn, the contact in the reed spring switch closes 8 times, resulting in 8 pulse signals. The higher the speed, the higher the signal frequency of the sensor. The function of

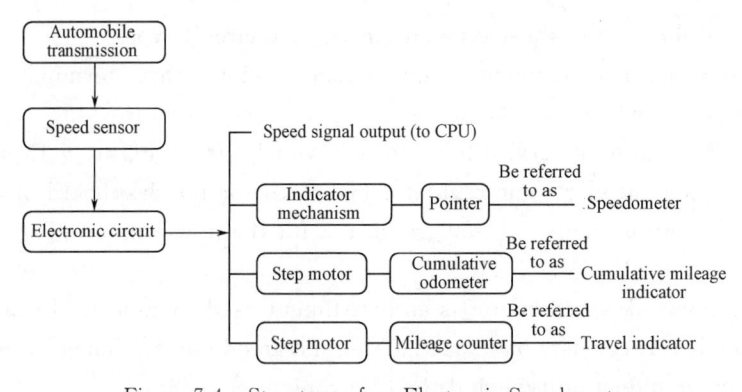

Figure 7-4　Structure of an Electronic Speedometer

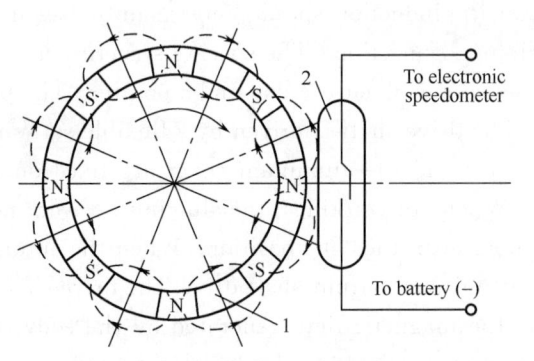

Figure 7-5　Audi 100 Electronic Speedometer Sensor
1—Magnetic rotor; 2—Reed spring switch

the electronic circuit is to shape and trigger the voltage with a fixed frequency sent by the speed sensor, and to output a current signal proportional to the speed. The electronic circuit mainly includes a regulator circuit, a constant current power supply drive circuit, a 64 frequency division circuit and a power amplifier circuit, as shown in Figure 7-6. The accuracy of the instrument is adjusted by resistor R_1, the initial working current of the instrument is regulated by resistor R_2, and the resistor R_3 and the capacitor C_3 are used for power filter.

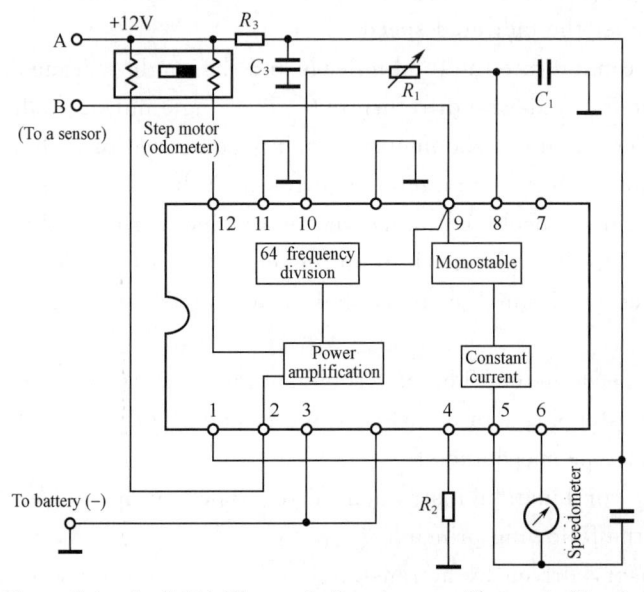

Figure 7-6　Audi 100 Electronic Speedometer Electronic Circuit

The speed meter is actually an electromagnetic ammeter. When the automobile is traveling at different speeds, the current signal output by the electronic circuit terminal 6, which is proportional to the speed, drives the pointer of the speed meter to deflect, thus indicating

162　Automobile Electrical Equipment Maintenance

the corresponding speed. The odometer consists of a stepping motor and a 6-bit decimal gear counter. The stepping motor is controlled by the controller in the electronic circuit to drive the counter to rotate, as shown in Figure 7-7.

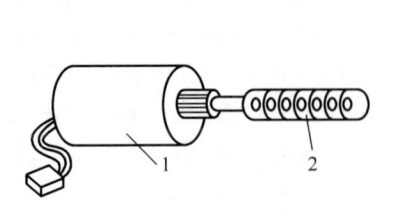

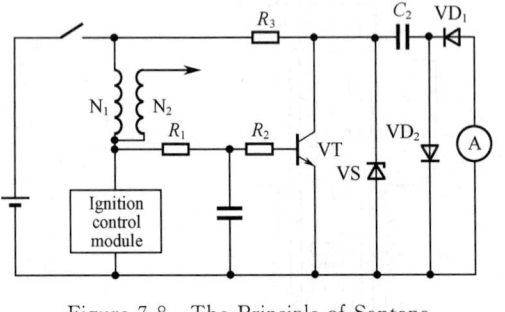

Figure 7-7   The driving of Audi 100 Odometer
1—Stepping motor; 2—Counter

Figure 7-8   The Principle of Santana
Electronic Tachometer Circuit

(4) Engine tachometer. The engine tachometer can intuitively display the speed of the engine under each working condition. The output of the torque of the automobile engine is closely related to the speed. The driver knows the running condition of the engine and can choose the shift time properly. With the suitable transmission gear and the throttle position, the vehicle can keep the best working condition. It is very beneficial to reduce the fuel consumption and prolong the engine life.

There are two kinds of engine tachometers: mechanical and electronic. The structure and working principle of the mechanical tachometer are basically the same as that of the magnetic induction tachometer. Electronic tachometer has many advantages, such as stable, simple structure and convenient installation, so it is widely used.

The electronic tachometer is generally composed of an indicator and a signal processing circuit, and some are equipped with an engine speed sensor. There are three ways to get the engine speed signal from the electronic tachometer: The signal is taken from the speed sensor mounted on the edge of the flywheel, the pulse signal is taken from the ignition coil and the sinusoidal AC signal is taken from the one-way stator winding of the alternator, because the engine speed is proportional to the frequency of these signals.

① Capacitor charge-discharge tachometer. The principle of the capacitor charge and discharge tachometer circuit (taking a Santana as an example) is shown in Figure 7-8. The engine speed signal is derived from the pulse signal generated when the primary current of the ignition coil is interrupted. Its working principle is as follows.

When the ignition controller makes the first side circuit turn on, the triode VT is in a cut-off state, and the capacitor C_2 is charged by the power supply. Its charging circuit is: positive electrode of the battery → ignition switch → R_1 → C_2 → VD_2 → negative electrode of the battery, constituting a circuit. When the ignition controller closes the primary circuit, the triode VT is switched on due to the increase of the base voltage. The capacitor C_2, through the triode VT, ammeter and VD_1 forms the discharge circuit, thus driving the ammeter. When the engine is working, the primary circuit is continuously on and off, and its on and off times are proportional to the engine speed. Therefore, when the first side circuit is continuously switched on and off, the capacitor C_2 is continuously charged and dis-

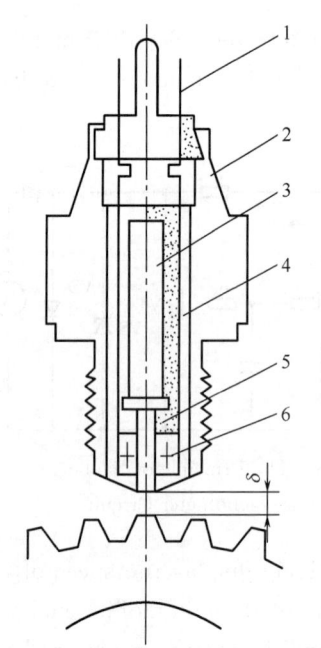

Figure 7-9　Structure and Principle of Magnetic Induction Speed Sensor

1—Terminal；2—Shell；3—Spindle；

4—Permanent magnet；

5—Core；6—Induction coil

charged，and the discharge current average is proportional to the engine speed，so the current average is calibrated to the engine speed.

② Electromagnetic induction tachometer. The electromagnetic induction tachometer consists of a speed sensor mounted on the flywheel shell and an indicator (including an electronic circuit) mounted on the dashboard. Figure 7-9 is the structural principle of a magnetic induction speed sensor，which consists of a permanent magnet，an induction coil，a spindle，a shell，etc.

As the flywheel rotates，the top and bottom of the teeth change periodically through the spindle continuously and the air gap，so that the magnetic flux passing through the spindle changes periodically，so the variable electromotive force is induced in the induction coil. The frequency of the variable electromotive force is proportional to the frequency of flux variation in the spindle and to the number of flywheel teeth passing through the spindle face.

The approximate sine wave frequency signal output by the magnetic induction speed sensor is added to the tachometer circuit. After being processed by the circuit, the rectangular wave with a certain amplitude and width is output，which is used to drive the milliammeter.

Since the input signal frequency is proportional to the number of flywheel teeth passing through the spindle，the frequency and amplitude of the signal is proportional to the engine speed，and when the speed increases，the frequency increases and the amplitude increases，so that the average current through the milliammeter increases，the swing angle of the pointer increases correspondingly，so the speed indicated by the tachometer is high.

4. Digital instrument

(1) Features of digital instruments. With the development of electronic technology and the increasing requirement of information and intelligentization of automobile，drivers need to know more and faster all kinds of information about automobile operation，and automobile instrument has become the terminal of information communication between automobile and driver. Because it is a trend of the times that all kinds of signals on the automobile are converted to digital signals for transmission and processing，the instrument of the automobile is naturally developing towards digital circuits. The basic differences between digital instrument and traditional instrument are that all kinds of signals are converted into digital signals for transmission，calculation and processing，and its instrument circuit is basically composed of integrated digital circuit.

The digital instrument is composed of a sensor collecting the working condition information of the automobile，an instrument control unit for single-chip microcomputer control and signal processing and a display system. The sensor transmits various working condition signals to the instrument control unit. The analog signals in these working condition signals are

164 Automobile Electrical Equipment Maintenance

usually converted to digital signals by A/D and then processed by the instrument control unit. The corresponding signals are then output to drive the stepping motor indicating device or display the corresponding indication values with data or graphics by a display device. For an automobile equipped with a multi-channel transmission system, the instrument is only one part of the system. The information used for the instrument display is often required by the engine ECU. The all sensor signals of the automobile are sent to the engine ECU, and then through the multi-channel transmission system to the instrument.

Digital instrument has self-diagnosis function. If the instrument fails, the fault code will be stored in the electric erasable memory of the combination instrument. After adjusting the code with the special instrument, the fault code can be read out, which is convenient for the maintenance personnel to diagnose the fault quickly.

(2) Display mode and display device of digital instrument.

① Display mode. The display forms of the digital instrument are analog and digital. Analog display form generally indicates a parameter by swinging the pointer on a fixed dial. The pointer can be either a real pointer driven by a stepping motor or a virtual pointer displayed by a liquid crystal display. Digital display form uses figures or bar graphics to replace the pointer graphic symbol. For example, an analog display tachometer works better than a digital display tachometer when the engine speed is raised or lowered. Since the driver does not need to know the exact speed of the engine, but the speed of the engine reaching the instrument red line. The digital display form is more suitable for displaying accurate data such as mileage, maintenance information and so on. As a result, many speedometers combine the analog (speed) display form with the digital (mileage) display form.

Figure 7-10 shows the full digital display instrument for the Audi A6L.

Figure 7-10　Full Digital Display Instrument for Audi A6L

② Display parts. There are many different types of instrument digital display devices used in automobiles, and each has its own characteristics. The most commonly used electronic displays can be divided into two categories: light-emitting and non-light-emitting. The light-emitting display is self-luminous, easy to obtain bright color display. The non-light-emitting display displays by reflecting environment light. The light-emitting display mainly includes vacuum fluorescent display (VFD), light-emitting diode (LED), cathode ray tube (CRT), plasma display (PDP) and electrochromic device (ECD). These can be used as automobile electronic displays, which can be either digital or graphic or analog pointer.

At present, the most commonly used digital instrument displays have the following three kinds.

a. Light-emitting diode. The light-emitting diode is the most widely used low-voltage display, its essence is a triode, and the structure is shown in Figure 7-11. The light-emitting diode has the advantages of fast response, long life, small volume and energy saving. The light colors of the light-emitting diode are red, green, yellow, orange, blue, white and so on, which can be used alone, or can also be used to form numbers, letters, light-emitting strips. The light-emitting diode on the automobile is generally used as a digital symbol field or a light bar graphic display with less points, backlight light source of warning lights or dashboard surface, kilometer meter pointer and LCD panel. Figure 7-12 shows a 7-character field display circuit consisting of a light-emitting diode.

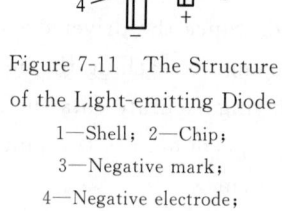

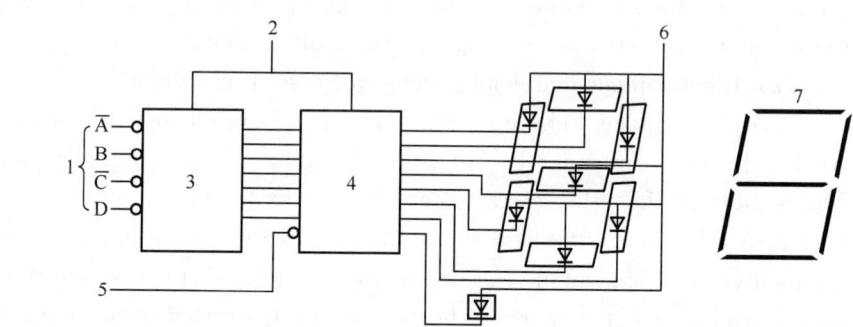

Figure 7-11　The Structure of the Light-emitting Diode

1—Shell; 2—Chip;
3—Negative mark;
4—Negative electrode;
5—Positive electrode

Figure 7-12　7-character Field Display Circuit Consisting of a Light-emitting Diode

1—Input terminal; 2—Logic circuit; 3—Decoder;
4—Constant current source; 5—Decimal point;
6—Light-emitting diode circuit; 7— "8" shape

Figure 7-13 shows a light strip graphic display consisting of a light emitting diode.

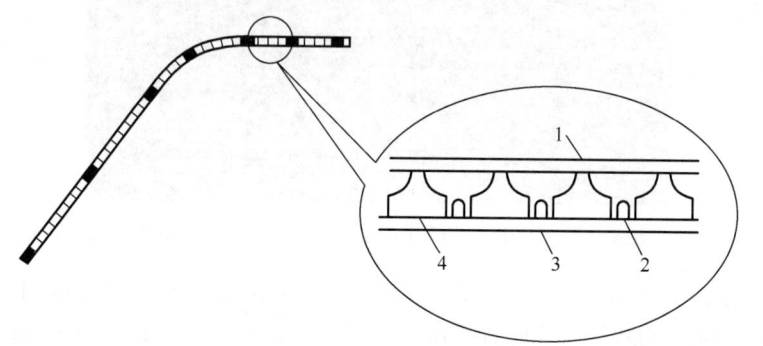

Figure 7-13　Light Strip Graphic Display Consisting of a Light Emitting Diode

1—Diffuser; 2—LED; 3—Printed circuit board; 4—Separator

b. Liquid crystal display. The structure and working principle are shown in Figure 7-14. There is a layer of liquid crystal between the front glass plate and the back glass plate. The outer surface is affixed with a vertical polarizer and a horizontal polarizer. The final surface is a mirror. The working principle of the liquid crystal display is: When the liquid crystal does not have an electric field, the molecular arrangement way of the liquid crystal can turn the light wave from the vertical direction of the vertical polarizer 90° into the horizontal light wave, and then by the horizontal polarizer back to the mirror, through the mirror back

166 Automobile Electrical Equipment Maintenance

to the original way, at this time, when we pass through the vertical polarizer to see the liquid crystal, the liquid crystal is bright. When an electric field is applied to the liquid crystal, the molecular arrangement of the liquid crystal is changed, which can not turn the light wave from the vertical direction of the vertical polarizer. Passing through the liquid crystal, the light wave is vertical and can not be reflected through the horizontal polarizer. When we pass through the vertical polarizer to see the liquid crystal, the liquid crystal is dark. In this way, the liquid crystal forms a character field. By controlling the power-on state of each character field, different characters can be displayed.

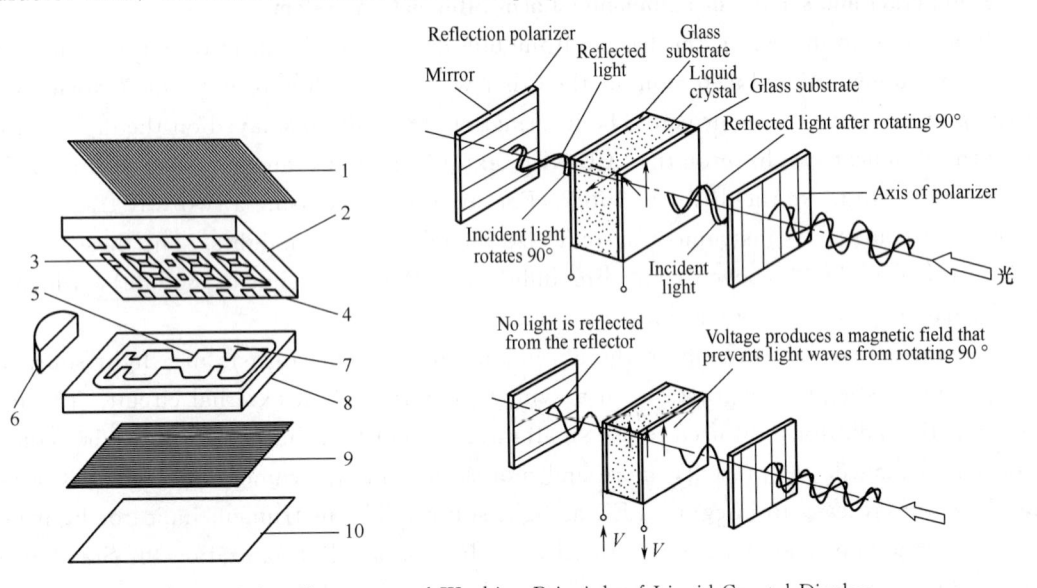

Figure 7-14　Structure and Working Principle of Liquid Crystal Display

1—Front polarizing plate; 2—Front glass plate; 3—Stroke electrode; 4—Terminal; 5—Back plate; 6—End seal;
7—Sealing surface; 8—Back glass plate; 9—Back polarizing plate; 10—Mirror

The liquid crystal display has low power consumption, flexible display information and clear indication, but because the liquid crystal is non-luminescent material, it is necessary to provide background light source for reading. The liquid crystal display is generally used for displaying meter mileage, clock or integrated information.

c. Vacuum fluorescent display. The light produced by the vacuum fluorescent display is like the picture tube in the TV. It is bright and clear. It is the most commonly used digital display. Its working principle is shown in Figure 7-15. The filament is essentially a coated resistance wire, the resistance wire is heated by current, and the coating produces free electrons. These electrons reach the anode through the fine wire mesh of the grid, and after impacting the fluorescent material in the corresponding section of the anode, it produces a blue-green light. The high voltage is ap-

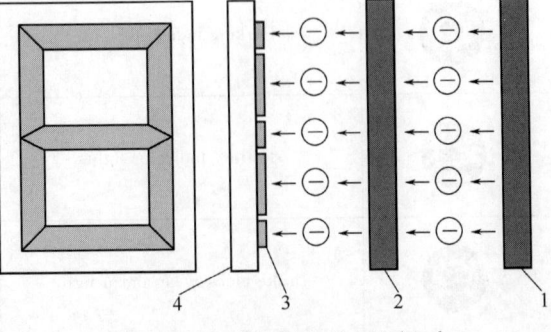

Figure 7-15　Working Principle of
Vacuum Fluorescent Display

1—Coated filament (cathode); 2—Grid;
3—Anode section; 4—Glass panel

Item Ⅶ　Maintenance of Information Display System　**167**

plied only on the anode plate to form a section of the characters to be displayed, and the instrument computer selectively energizes the section that needs to be displayed with light-emitting information, while the unenergized characters do not emit light, so that the instrument displays different digital information. The brightness of the vacuum fluorescent display can be changed by increasing or decreasing the accelerating grid voltage, and the higher grid voltage can increase the brightness of the display.

(Ⅱ) Automobile alarm information system

1. Function and symbol of automobile alarm information system

In addition to indicating the basic automobile driving condition information, the automobile instrument should also monitor the other working conditions and issue instruction or warning information to the driver. The information is usually displayed on the dashboard in the form of indicator light or on the LCD with text information, and some is accompanied by buzzing sound to make the driver to notice. For an automobile using a two-way transmission system, of course, its instrument system also includes indicator lights, but these systems are controlled by PCM (power control module) or BCM (body control module), which are usually part of a multi-way transmission system.

The indicating light system on the automobile instrument consists of a light source, a transparent plastic plate engraved with a symbol pattern and an external circuit. The light source of the indicator light used to use small incandescent light bulb, which can be replaced after it is damaged. At present, more and more electronic instruments use small volume, high brightness, easy to integrate LED as light source. The instrument indicator light generally uses the universal symbol specified by the International Organization for Standardization (ISO), which is easy to be recognized and understood by people all over the world. The common symbols are shown in Table 7-1.

Table 7-1   Common instrument indicator light and alarm information indicator symbols

Symbol	Description	Symbol	Description
	Door status indicator light		Water temperature indicator light
	Parking indicator light		Airbag indicator light
	Battery indicator light		ABS indicator light
	Brake block wear alarm light		Engine self-inspection light
	Oil indicator light		Fuel shortage alarm light

Continued

Symbol	Description	Symbol	Description
	Insufficient cleaning fluid alarm light		Seat belt indicator light
EPC	Electronic throttle indicator light	O/D OFF	O/D gear indicator light
	Front-and-rear fog light indicator light		Internal cycle indicator light
	Steering indicator light		Clearance indicator light
	High beam indicator light	VSC	VSC indicator light

When driving an automobile, the driver must develop a good habit of paying attention to the status of the indicator lights in time, and be able to take corresponding measures according to the meaning of each indicator light and the status of lighting or flashing, so as to use them correctly, maintain the automobile and drive safely.

2. The significance and principle of common automobile alarm information system

The composition and working principle of the automobile information indication and alarm device are different due to the different models. Here, the most common and important indicator lights and alarm lights are introduced.

(1) Status and failure indicator lights. The status indicator light is the most commonly used light signal, such as headlight high/low beam indicator light, front/rear fog indicator light, steering signal indicator light, clearance indicator light, dander alarm indicator light and so on. The lighting of the light signal indicator light is controlled directly by the light control switch of the external circuit, and some are controlled by relays.

Fault indicator light is often used for warning indication of driving safety-related systems, such as low tire pressure, failure of airbag, insufficient brake fluid, insufficient cleaning fluid, etc.

When the tire is under-inflated or burst, the tire pressure alarm light will be on. Some systems have red and yellow alarm lights, of which, the red alarm light will be on when the tire pressure is too low or when the tire burst, and the yellow alarm light will be on when the tire pressure is low. Some systems also make noises to inform the driver. The measurement of the tire pressure is calculated by measuring the difference of wheel speed when the

automobile is running straight, or by receiving the signal from the wireless pressure sensor installed in the tire valve core.

(2) Alarm light.

① The cooling system. The alarm information of the cooling system generally refers to the lack of coolant, low liquid level alarm and high coolant temperature alarm. The function of the high coolant temperature alarm light is that when the engine coolant temperature rises to a certain degree, the alarm light automatically lights up to alarm. The on-off of the high coolant temperature alarm light is usually controlled by the bimetallic temperature switch. When the temperature of the coolant is below 95~98℃, the active contact on the bimetallic sheet remains separate from the fixed contact, and the alarm light is off; when the temperature of the coolant is higher than 95~98℃, the heat deformation of the bimetallic sheet bends downward to a greater degree, so that the two contacts contact, turn on the alarm light circuit, and the alarm light is on to remind the driver.

② Lubrication system. The information indication and alarm of the lubrication system is generally to monitor oil pressure, oil temperature, oil level and oil quality and other conditions.

The oil pressure alarm light is used to remind the driver to pay attention to the abnormal oil pressure of the engine, indicating whether the oil pump can supply the parts of the engine with normal pressure. Some automobiles have both oil pressure gauge and oil pressure alarm light, but most automobiles only have oil pressure alarm light. The light is controlled by the oil pressure switch located in the engine lubrication system. The alarm switch of the oil pressure alarm device is arranged on the main oil channel.

Figure 7-16 shows the circuit of the clapboard oil pressure alarm.

③ Braking system. The information indication and alarm of the brake system include parking brake indication, low vacuum of brake system vacuum booster, low hydraulic pressure of brake line, insufficient brake fluid, excessive wear of brake block, fault alarm of ABS system, etc. Figure 7-17 shows the common brake fluid level alarm switch structure. If the brake fluid in the tank is less than the required amount, the float drops, the reed switch closes under the magnetization of the permanent magnet, and the alarm light is on during engine operation. This form of alarm switch can be installed in an liquid storage tank and other containers that need to detect liquid level and timely alarm when the liquid is insufficient.

④ Charging system. The charging indicator indicates the condition of the charging system. If the charging system fails, the light will be on when the engine is running. When the voltage of the generator reaches the normal charging voltage, the

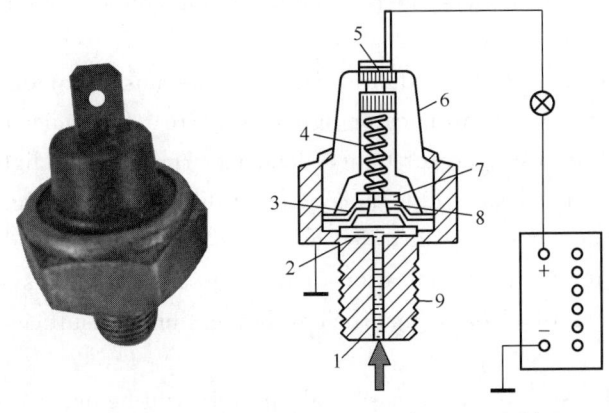

Figure 7-16　Circuit of Clapboard Oil Pressure Alarm

1—Engine lubricating oil; 2—Clapboard; 3—Insulated top block;
4—Spring; 5—terminal; 6—Insulation layer;
7—Moving contact; 8—Static contact;
9—Fixed screw opening

light will be off. If it is running normally, the light is on, it indicates that the charging system fails.

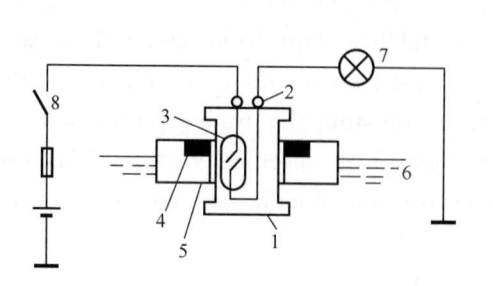

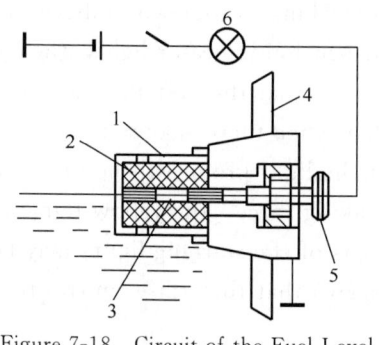

Figure 7-17　Structure of the Brake
Liquid Level Alarm Switch

1—Reed switch shell; 2—terminal; 3—Reed switch;
4—Permanent magnet; 5—Float; 6—brake fluid level;
7—Alarm light; 8—Ignition switch

Figure 7-18　Circuit of the Fuel Level
Alarm Light

1—Shell; 2—Explosion-proof metal mesh;
3—Thermistor; 4—Tank shell;
5—Terminal; 6—Alarm light

⑤ Fuel supply. The fuel quantity alarm light is used to monitor the fuel quantity in the fuel tank. When the fuel level drops below the specified value of the full tank oil level, the oil level alarm switch in the module closes and supplies power to the fuel level alarm light to make the alarm light on, it indicates the remaining fuel is insufficient. The common circuit of the fuel level alarm light is shown in Figure 7-18.

The device is composed of a thermistor fuel quantity alarm sensor with a negative temperature coefficient and a warning light. When there is more fuel in the tank, the thermistor is immersed in the fuel, the heat dissipation is fast, the temperature is low, and the resistance value is large. Therefore, the current in the circuit is very small and the warning light is not on. When the fuel is reduced below the specified value, the thermistor is exposed to the fuel surface, the heat dissipation is slow, the temperature is high, and the resistance value is small. As a result, the current in the circuit increases and the warning light is on.

⑥ The engine electronic control system. The engine electronic control system has the function of self-inspection, once it is detected that the engine electronic control system has a fault, the "Check Engine" indicator light on the instrument will be on to prompt the driver to enter the station in time for maintenance, and to store the fault code in the engine computer. The engine control computer monitors multiple systems in the engine and lights up the alarm light when a fault is detected.

⑦ Transmission and chassis. The transmission and chassis information indicator and alarm generally include transmission indicator light, transmission gear indicator light, drive status indicator light, air suspension indicator light, traction and stability control indicator light and cruise control indicator light.

The transmission indicator light is a part of the automatic transmission control system. If the control system fails, it will make the transmission work in fail-safe mode and be on to inform the driver that the transmission is not working properly.

The transmission gear indicator light can indicate the gear position of the transmission.

Item Ⅶ　Maintenance of Information Display System　**171**

Drive mode indicator light refers to that some four-wheel-drive automobiles are provided with a drive mode selection function. When the light is on, it indicates that the automobile is working in four-wheel-drive mode. When the air suspension is out of order, for the air suspension indicator light, the circuit will be grounded, and the indicator light is on, it indicates that the system is out of order. Traction and stability control indicator light means that when there is a problem in traction or stability control system, the light or the red light of the light group will be on, and when the system is adjusting the driving torque and the braking force, the yellow light will be on. In automobiles made specifically for Canada, the signs of the warning lights may be different. If the cruise control indicator light is on, it indicates that the cruise control function is enabled.

Ⅲ. Item Implementation

(Ⅰ) Fault diagnosis of coolant thermometer

(1) The pointer does not move.

Phenomenon: When the ignition switch is ON, the pointer does not move.

The reasons are as follows: The power cord of the coolant thermometer is broken, The coolant thermometer is out of order, The sensor is out of order, The wire from the thermometer to the sensor is disconnected.

Diagnosis: The diagnosis steps of the fault that the pointer of the electromagnetic coolant thermometer does not move are as shown in Figure 7-19.

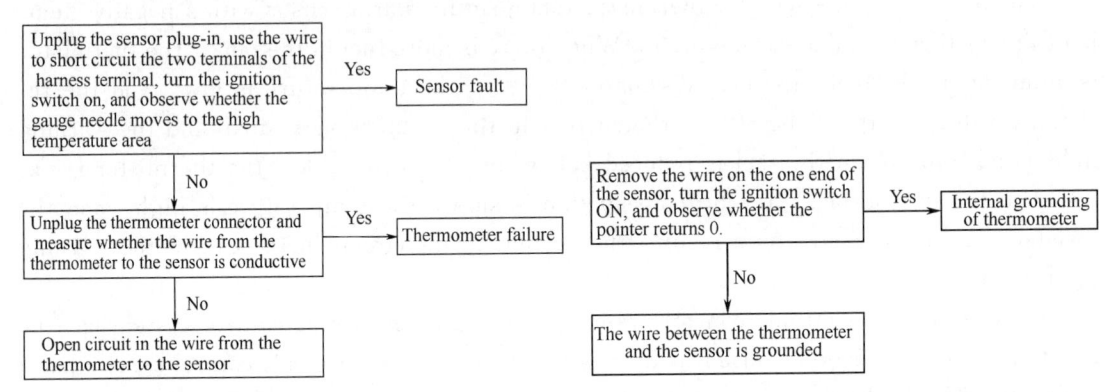

Figure 7-19　Diagnosis of the Fault that the Pointer of the Electromagnetic Coolant Thermometer does not Move

Figure 7-20　The Diagnosis of the Fault that the Pointer of the Electromagnetic Coolant Thermometer Points to the Maximum Value

(2) The pointer points to the maximum value and does not change.

Phenomenon: When the ignition switch is switched on, the thermometer pointer points to the highest temperature.

The reasons are as follows: The wire from the thermometer to the sensor id grounded, The inside of the sensor is grounded, The inside of the thermometer is grounded.

Diagnosis: The diagnosis steps of the fault that the pointer of the electromagnetic coolant thermometer points to the maximum value and does not change are as shown in Figure 7-20.

（Ⅱ） Fault diagnosis of fuel gauge

（1） The pointer always points at "1" (full of fuel).

Phenomenon: When the ignition switch is ON, no matter how much fuel there is, the pointer of the fuel gauge always points at "1" (full of fuel).

The reasons are as follows: The wire between the fuel gauge and the sensor is grounded, The inside of the sensor is disconnected, The inside of the fuel gauge is grounded.

Diagnosis: The diagnosis steps of the fault that the pointer of the fuel gauge always points at "1" are as shown in Figure 7-21.

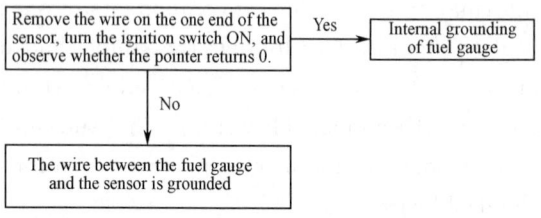

Figure 7-21　The Diagnosis of the Fault that the Pointer of the Fuel Gauge Always Points at "1"

（2） The pointer always points at "0" (no fuel).

Phenomenon: When the ignition switch is ON, no matter how much fuel there is, the pointer of the fuel gauge always points at "0" (no fuel).

The reasons are as follows: The inside of the sensor is grounded or the float is damaged, The wire from the fuel gauge to the power supply is disconnected, The inside of the fuel gauge is out of order.

Diagnosis: The diagnosis steps of the fault that the pointer of the fuel gauge always points at "0" are as shown in Figure 7-22.

（Ⅲ） Fault diagnosis of electronic speedometer

The common fault of the electronic speedometer is that it does not work.

Phenomenon: The pointer of the speedometer doesn't move when the automobile is running.

The reasons are as follows: The sensor is out of order, The instrument is out of order, The circuit is out of order.

Diagnosis: The diagnosis steps of the fault that the electronic speedometer does not work are as shown in Figure 7-23.

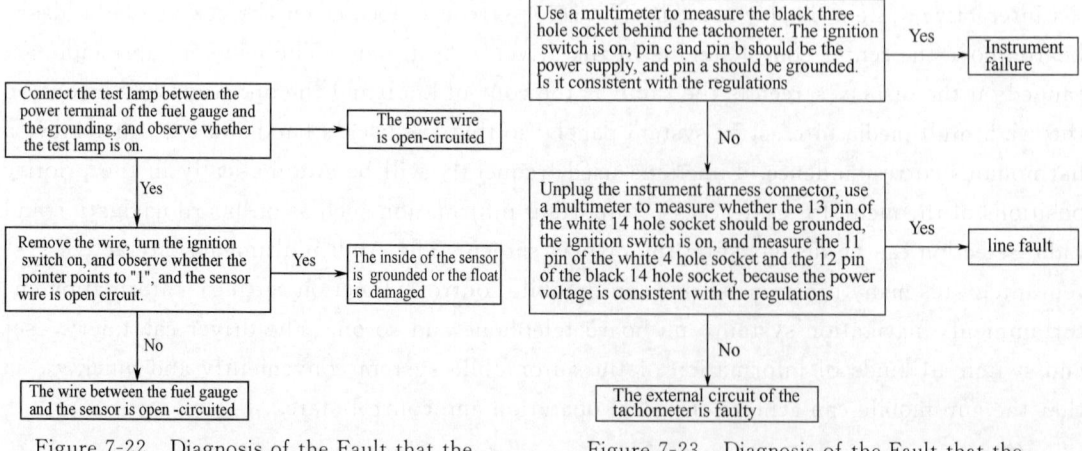

Figure 7-22　Diagnosis of the Fault that the Pointer of the Fuel Gauge Always Points at "0"

Figure 7-23　Diagnosis of the Fault that the Electronic Speedometer does not Work

IV. Knowledge and Skills Expansion

(I) The Audi multimedia interactive system

The Audi multimedia interactive system (MMI) cleverly combines the operations of all information entertainment components in one display screen and one operating system. Audi multimedia interface follows the simple and intuitive concept of operation, is an applicable auto part combining educational and entertainment. The Audi multimedia interactive system consists of two main elements: The Audi multimedia interactive system terminal at the central console and the black-and-white or color Audi multimedia interactive system display at the dashboard.

The control button is the main component of the Audi multimedia interactive system terminal (see Figure 7-24). The user can turn or press the button, which has 4 control keys around it. There are 8 function keys on the sides of the terminal, which can call the main menu directly (see Figure 7-25). The main functions of the system include entertainment, communication, information and automobile system control. The user can use 8 permanent assignment function keys to realize these functions. In each menu, the driver can turn/press the control button to activate the desired function.

Figure 7-24 Audi Multimedia Interactive System
Knob Controller

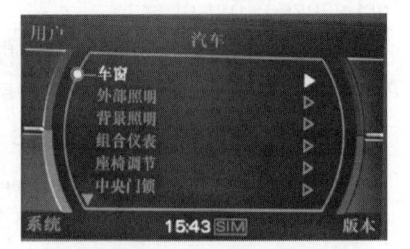

Figure 7-25 Main Menu of Audi
Multimedia Interactive System
Display Screen

The second component of the Audi multimedia interactive system is the Audi multimedia interactive system display screen. The color screen is located in the center of the dashboard above the center console and is in the driver's best view. The geometry principle arranged on the display screen is the same as the control knob and the operation key layout on the Audi multimedia interactive system panel, so that the user's hand and eye can achieve a harmonious correspondence. Functions used frequently will be automatically in the priority positions of the menu for easy access. Important information such as on-board navigation and radio selection can be displayed on the display screen. The Audi multimedia interactive system integrates many functions such as automobile control, function setting, information entertainment, navigation system, on-board telephone and so on. The driver can query, set and switch all kinds of information of the automobile system conveniently and quickly, so that the automobile can achieve the ideal operation and control state.

(II) Head-up display system

At present, many high-end automobiles use the head-up display system, which is an optical system that projects and displays the information of various automobile systems to

the extended driver's field of vision. If the driver wants to know these parameters, he doesn't have to change the head position obviously, just look at the road while sitting. Especially when driving at high speed on the freeway, it is safer.

The display of the head-up display system enables the driver to obtain important automobile information quickly and accurately. Using a special windshield on the automobile with a head-up display system can give the impression that: The contents of the head-up display system are not displayed on the windshield, but at a comfortable distance of 2~2.5m from the driver. The head-up display appears to be suspended above the hood of the engine. The working principle of the head-up display system is shown in Figure 7-26. The head-up display

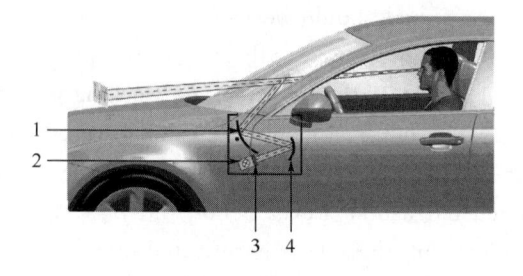

Figure 7-26　Working Principle of
Head-up Display System
1—Visual mirror; 2—Lighting unit;
3—TFT display; 4—Unadjustable mirror

system consists of a visual mirror, a head-up display control unit (see Figure 7-27), a TFT display and an unadjustable mirror. The information is projected onto the front windshield by refraction of light. Basic settings can be made for the display and the instrument lighting by means of the instrument lighting regulator (see Figure 7-28). The display brightness of the head-up display system will also change when the settings are changed.

Figure 7-27　Head-up
Display Control Unit

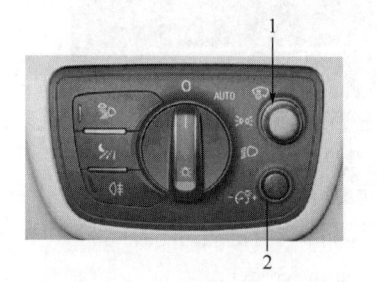

Figure 7-28　Operation and Settings Buttons of
the Head-up Display System
1—Head-up display position regulator; 2—Regulator
For the basic settings of the display and the instrument lighting

(Ⅲ) Electronic oil level height indication

Some high-end automobiles don't have oil gauges, but have an electronic ones.

1. Method of measurement

There are two methods to measure the height of oil level in the electronic oil level height display system.

Dynamic measurement is carried out when the automobile is driving. The important parameters to be measured are as follows: engine speed; lateral and longitudinal accelerations from the ESP-control unit; Hood contact switch signal; Engine temperature; After the above specific measurement values are met, the measurement results can be obtained.

Static measurement is carried out in the following circumstances: The ignition switch is switched on (to get the measurement results as soon as possible, the measurement process

begins when the driver opens the door. Engine oil temperature>40℃; Engine outage more than 60 seconds; In static measurement, the acceleration value of ESP-control unit should be taken into account (for the automobile parking on the slope). In addition, the parking brake signal should be used. If the oil level is low or high enough to damage the engine, then the instrument will give a prompt of too low or too high.

2. Installation position and working principle of the oil level height/oil temperature sensor

The oil level height/oil temperature sensor G266 (PULS oil level sensor) is screwed on the oil pan, and works according to the ultrasonic principle. PULS is an acronym for Packaged Ultrasonic Level Senor and is a closed ultrasonic liquid level sensor. The ultrasonic pulse from the sensor is reflected by the oil-air boundary layer, and the height of the oil level can be determined by the difference between the time sending a pulse and the time returning the pulse by referring to the acoustic speed.

The PULS oil level sensor is the basis of calculating the oil level display. The result can only be displayed on the combination instrument or the MMI display screen. So the previous use of oil gauge is eliminated. The oil level height on the instrument is indicated as shown in Figure 7-29. Engine Oil Level Display of Audi MMI Instrument as shown in Figure 7-30.

Figure 7-29　Oil level Height Indication
on the System

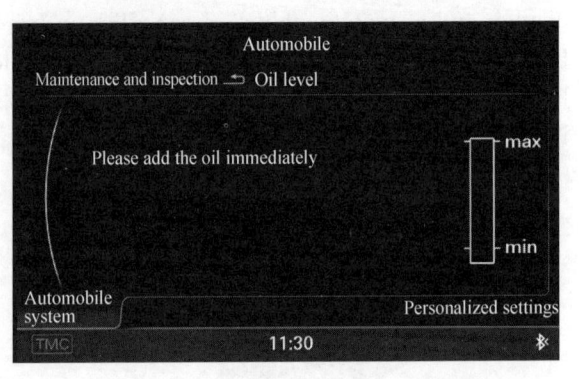

Figure 7-30　Engine Oil Level Display of
Audi MMI Instrument

(Ⅳ) Electronic park brake system (EPB)

At present, many models adopt the electronic park brake system instead of the traditional mechanical hand brake, but the indicator light on the instrument does not change.

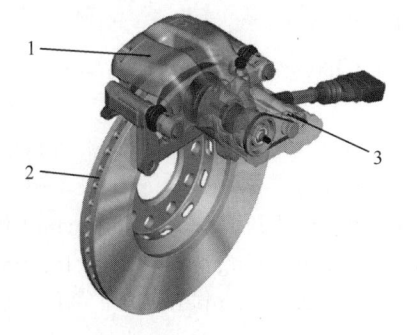

Figure 7-31　Rear Wheel Park Brake Assembly
1—Brake pliers; 2—Brake disc;
3—Electronic park brake motor

The system integrates the temporary braking during driving and long-time braking after parking to realize park brae. The brake lock automatically unlocks when the driver steps on the accelerator, which can relieves fatigue caused by stepping on the brake for a long time.

The main components of the system are an electronic park switch, an electronic park brake control unit (EPB) and park brake motors. The rear-wheel park brake assembly, shown in Figure 7-31, includes a park brake motor. When the

electronic park switch is pulled up, the electronic park brake control unit J540 drives the park brake motors V282 and V283 on the left and right rear brakes. The mechanical tensioning force of the brake shoe applied by the park brake motors through a drive shaft increases. When releasing the electronic park brake, it is necessary to turn on the ignition switch, step on the brake pedal, then press the electronic park switch, the electronic park brake control unit J540 drives the park brake motors V282 and V283 on the left and right rear brakes to release the mechanical tensioning force of the brake shoe.

For an automobile using an electronic park brake system, it is necessary to use a special diagnostic instrument to release the electronic park brake when removing the brake disc and the brake block of the rear wheel. When installing the brake disc and the brake block of the rear wheel, it is necessary to reset the electronic park brake with a special diagnostic instrument.

(V) Touch display system

With the development of science and technology, many high-end automobiles adopt touch-screen display system. The touch keyboard of a touch display system is usually displayed on the screen in analog form and can be operated by touching the keyboard with a finger, thus simplifying the process of selecting information.

The touch display system usually uses the infrared touch switch to detect whether the screen is touched. The principle of the infrared touch switch is shown in Figure 7-32.

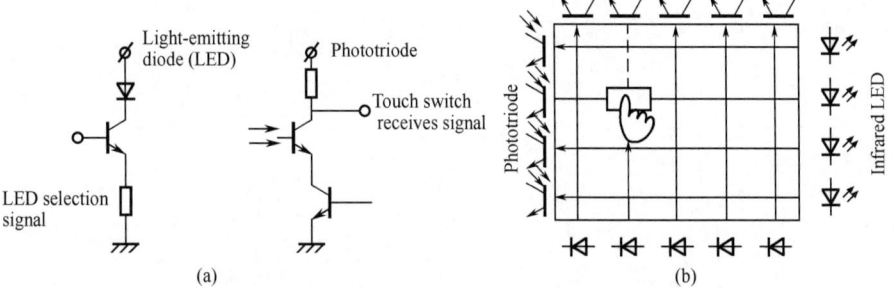

Figure 7-32   Principle of Infrared Touch Switch

At both ends of the display there is an infrared light-emitting diode and a photosensitive triode opposite to each other. When the display keyboard is untouched, the infrared light-emitting diode beam reaches the photosensitive triode to enable it to be connected. When the keyboard is touched, the infrared light-emitting diode light wave is truncated and the photosensitive triode is immediately cut off. The mixture of an infrared light-emitting diode and a photosensitive triode is placed in several places on the display, so the position of the keyboard touched on the screen is determined by the position of the photosensitive triode which is switched off.

Summary

(1) The automobile instrument can be divided into mechanical instrument, electrical instrument, analog circuit electronic instrument and digital electronic instrument by the working principle.

(2) Instrument regulator. Because the change of the power supply voltage will affect the indication value of the instrument, resulting in the error of the instrument value, so the

instrument circuit should generally be equipped with the instrument regulator.

(3) In addition to indicating the basic automobile driving condition information, the automobile instrument monitors some other conditions and issue to the driver instruction or warning information, which is usually displayed on the dashboard in the form of an indicator light or on the LCD in the form of a text message, and in some cases accompanied by a buzzing sound, to attract the driver's attention.

Thinking and Practice

(1) What are the common alarm messages for an automobile? Which systems can be detected?

(2) What are the common instruments in an electronic combination instrument?

(3) What are the common types of displays for electronic instruments? What are the display modes?

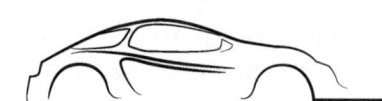

Item VIII

Overhaul of Automobile Auxiliary Electrical System

I . Scene Introduction

A Toyota Corolla, occurred the following faults: when pressing the right rear glass lift switch on the inside of the left front door, the right rear glass did not react, but when pressing the glass lift switch on the inside of the right rear door, then the right rear glass could rise and fall. It was found that the right rear glass lift switch in the combination glass lift switch on the inside of the left front door had been damaged after overhaul. The electric glass lift system is a subsystem of the automobile auxiliary electrical system. There are more and more kinds of automobile auxiliary electrical systems on the whole vehicle, so the overhaul of automobile auxiliary electrical system occupies a certain proportion in the common faults of automobiles.

II . Related Knowledge

To improve the safety, reliability and comfort of automobiles during driving, modern automobiles are generally equipped with some auxiliary electrical appliances, such as electric wiper, electric washer, electric window and door, electric seat, middle-control door lock system and so on. With the development of the automobile industry, the proportion of auxiliary electrical appliances is more and more big, and the performance is more and more perfect.

(I) Composition and classification of electric wiper

The electric wiper and cleaner is the standard configuration of the automobile, belonging to the auxiliary electrical appliances on the automobile, mainly used to clean and brush the rain, snow and dust on the windshield to ensure the visual effect of the driver. Some automobile headlights also have wiper and cleaner systems to ensure driving safety in rainy and snowy days, especially at night. The position of the element of the electric wiper and washer on the automobile is shown in Figure 8-1.

By the power, the wiper can be divided into electric wiper, pneumatic wiper and mechanical wiper. The electric wiper is widely used in automobiles nowadays. The basic composition of the electric wiper is shown in Figure 8-2. The wiper motor is mounted on the bottom plate, and the lever linkage mechanism is composed of the connecting rod swing rod, and the swing rod is connected with the wiper assembly (composed of the wiper arm, the wiper blade, etc.). When the driver presses the switch of the wiper, the motor starts and

the motor rotates through the deceleration and torsion of the worm gear, passing from the worm at the end of the shaft to the worm wheel, the eccentric pin on the worm wheel is connected with the connecting rod, and when the worm wheel rotates to swing the swing rod by the connecting rod, and then through the connecting rod, the wiper arm drives the wiper assembly back and forth to scrap the windshield.

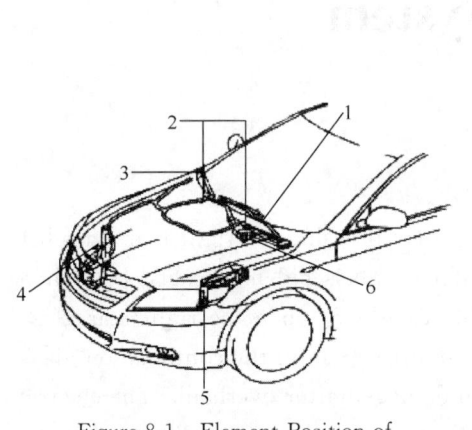

Figure 8-1　Element Position of
Electric Wiper and Washer
1—Front windshield glass left wiper assembly;
2—Nozzle; 3—Front windshield glass right
wiper assembly; 4—Storage tank and
cleaning pump assembly; 5—Fuse box;
6—Wiper motor assembly

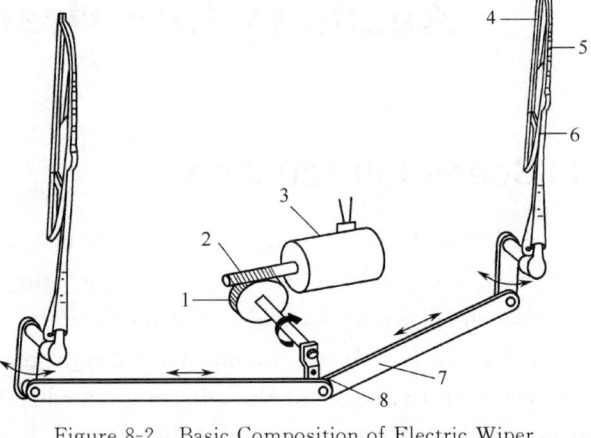

Figure 8-2　Basic Composition of Electric Wiper
1—Worm wheel; 2—Worm gear;
3—Motor; 4—Wiper blade;
5—Wiper blade holder; 6—Wiper arm;
7—Rod; 8—Rocker arm

The wiper can be divided into four types by the way of wiping, double-arm same-direction wiper, double-arm opposite-direction wiper, single-arm controllable wiper and common single-arm wiper.

The arms of some automobile wipers are equipped with water pipes, which is connected to the cleaner, when pressing the switch, there is water injecting to the windshield.

To avoid the wiper arm obstructing the driver's sight when the driver close the wiper. The electric wiper is usually equipped with an automatic reset device, which controls the wiper motor so that the wiper arm can be stopped at the bottom of the windshield at any time when the wiper is closed.

At present, the wiper used in automobile has three working gears: high-speed, low-speed and intermittent control. Among them, the intermittent control gear is generally to use the contact of the motor reset position switch and the charge and discharge function of the resistor and the capacitor to make the wiper wipe according to the a fixed period, that is, to stop 2~12s per action, the interference to the driver is less. In some automobiles, the wipers are equipped with an electronic governor, which is equipped with rainfall sensing function, and can automatically adjust the swinging speed of the wiper arm according to the rainfall. The wiper arm rotates quickly when the rain is heavy. The wiper arm rotates slowly when the rain is small. The wiper arm stops when the rain stops. The wiper used on the Audi A6 has the function of automatically adjusting the speed of the wiper arm according to the rainfall. The wiper motor control unit is shown in Figure 8-3. It integrates the rainfall sensor

and the wiper motor into the same shell.

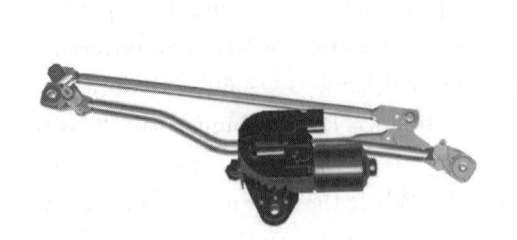

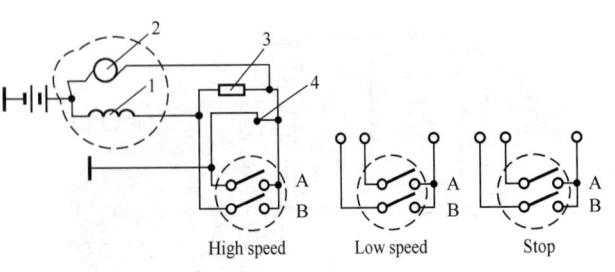

Figure 8-3　Wiper Motor Control Unit with
Automatic Speed Regulation Function

Figure 8-4　Working Principle of Excitation Wiper Motor
1—Motor excitation winding；2—Armature winding；
3—Additional resistor；4—Contact

(Ⅱ) Working principle of wiper system

The speed change of the electric wiper is realized by changing the speed of the motor. Automobile wiper motor is a micro DC motor, including excitation type and permanent magnet type. The permanent magnet motor has the advantages of simple structure, light weight, low noise, high torque and high reliability, so it is widely used.

1. The speed changing principle of excitation wiper motor

Generally, the excitation wiper motor has two speeds: low speed and high speed. It changes speed by changing the magnetic flux of the magnetic electrode, the principle of which is shown in Figure 8-4.

The excitation wiper motor has two switches, A and B, to control the wiper speed. When A is closed and B is open, the circuit of the motor excitation winding 1 is connected with an additional resistor 3 in series, so that the exciting current is reduced and the magnetic flux is weak. According to the characteristics of the motor, when the output torque is within a certain range, the magnetic flux is reduced and the speed of the motor is increased. At this time, the wiper works at high speed. When A and B are closed, the switch B makes the additional resistor 3 short-circuited, the exciting current does not pass through the additional resistor, the current increases, the magnetic flux increases, and the speed decreases. At this time, the wiper works at low speed; when A is open and B is closed, the current of the motor passes through the contact 4 which is controlled by the convex block on the worm wheel shaft, and the worm wheel rotates per cycle, the convex block opens the contact once. Usually when the wiper moves beyond the driver's horizon, the contact is disconnected, the power supply is cut off and the wiper stops working.

2. The speed changing principle of permanent magnet wiper motor

The structure of the permanent magnet wiper motor is shown in Figure 8-5. The worm gear speed changing device is mounted on the motor, with 2 magnetic electrodes bonded to the motor shell. The magnetic electrode adopts ferrite permanent magnet. It has the advantage of not demagnetizing, and its magnetic field strength cannot be changed. The end of the motor is provided with a plastic vent pipe to discharge the gas produced by arc discharge from the brush. A pair of main brushes B_1 and B_3 separated by $180°$ are pressed on the commutator (see Figure 8-6(a)). To obtain two speeds, usually the third brush B_2 is mounted in the motor. By changing the brush to change the number of conductors in series between

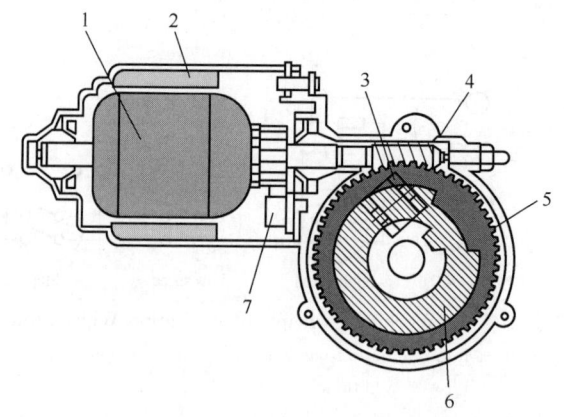

Figure 8-5　Structure of Permanent Magnet Wiper Motor

1—Armature; 2—Permanent magnet;

3—Contact; 4—Gear; 5—Worm wheel;

6—Copper ring; 7—Brush

the brushes, the speed can be changed. The principle of changing the speed is shown in Figure 8-6(b). The difference between B_1 and B_2 is $60°$, B_1 is a low speed brush, B_2 is a high speed brush, and B_3 is a high-low speed common brush. When the DC motor works, the back electromotive force is produced simultaneously in all the coils of the armature, that is $E = cn\phi$, which is opposite to the direction of the armature current.

To make the armature rotate, the applied voltage must overcome the effect of the back electromotive force. When the armature speed rises, the back electromotive force also rises correspondingly. Only when the applied voltage is almost equal to the back electromotive force, the armature speed becomes stable.

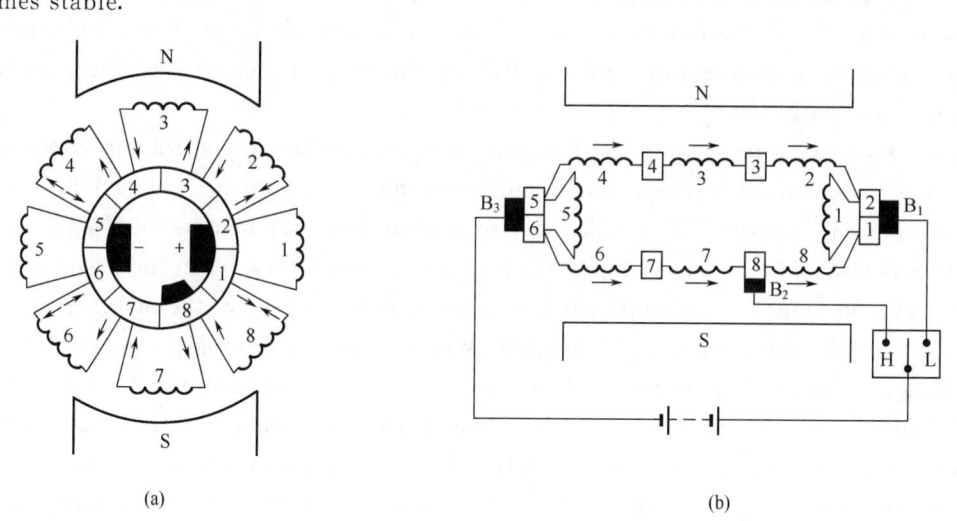

(a)　　　　　　　　　　　　　　　　　　(b)

Figure 8-6　The Speed Changing Principle of Permanent Magnet Wiper Motor

When the wiper switch is switched to low speed, i. e. S and L contact, the power supply voltage is added between B_1 and B_3. There are 2 parallel branches between the brush B_1 and the brush B_3. One branch is connected by coils 1, 6 and 5 in series; the other branch is connected by coils 2, 4 and 6 in series, that is, there are two branches between the brush B_1 and the brush B_3, each with three coils. After all the back electromotive force produced by these two branches is balanced with the power supply electromotive force, the motor rotates steadily. Because the back electromotive force of the coil with 3 coils in series is balanced with the power supply voltage, the speed is low.

When the wiper switch is switched to high speed, i. e. S and H contact, the power supply voltage is added between B_2 and B_3. At this point, one armature winding is connected by coils 2, 1, 6 and 5 in series, the other is connected by coils 3 and 4 in series. Among them,

182 Automobile Electrical Equipment Maintenance

the back electromotive force of the coil 2 is opposite with the back electromotive force in coils 1, 6 and 5, they are offset. So there are only 2 coils whose back electromotive force is balanced with the power supply voltage. Therefore, only the speed rises to increase the back electromotive force, the balance can be obtained. So the speed is higher at this time.

3. Reset principle of electric wiper

The reset principle of the electric wiper is shown in Figure 8-7. The wiper switch is provided with 3 gears, 0 gear for the reset, the wiper should be in this position when it is not working, I gear for the low speed, and II gear for the high speed. Four terminals are respectively connected to contact arm, low-speed brush B_1, ground and high-speed brush B_2. There is a copper ring embedded on the worm wheel, of which the larger piece is connected with the outer shell of the motor and grounded, the contact arm is made of elastic material, and one end of it rivets contacts that are respectively in contact with the worm wheel section or the copper ring.

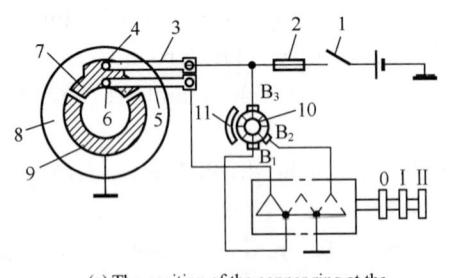 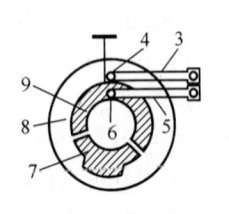

(a) The position of the copper ring at the return position of the wiper

(b) The position of the copper ring when the wiper is not in the return position

Figure 8-7　Reset Principle of Electric Wiper

1—Power switch; 2—Fuse; 3,5—Contact arm; 4,6—Contact; 7,9—Copper ring;
8—Worm wheel; 10—Armature; 11—Permanent magnet

When the power switch 1 is turned on and the wiper switch is pulled to I gear, the terminal 2 and the terminal 3 are connected by the wiper switch. At this point, the current from the positive electrode of the battery → power switch → fuse → brush B_3 → armature winding → brush B_1 → terminal 2 → wiper switch → terminal 3 → ground → negative electrode of the battery, forms a circuit, the motor runs at low speed.

When the wiper is pulled to the II gear, the terminal 3 and the terminal 4 are connected by the wiper switch. At this point, the current from the positive electrode of the battery → power switch → fuse → brush B_3 → armature winding → brush B_2 → terminal 4 → wiper switch → terminal 3 → ground → negative electrode of the battery, forms a circuit, the motor runs at high speed.

When the wiper switch is returned to the 0 gear, the terminal 2 and the terminal 1 are connected by the wiper switch. If the wiper blade does not stop at the specified position as shown in Figure 8-7(a), but stops at the common position as shown in Figure 8-7(b), the current passes through the positive electrode of the battery → the power switch → the fuse → the brush B_3 → the armature winding → the brush B_1 → the terminal 2 → the wiper switch → the terminal 1 → the contact arm → the copper ring 9 → ground, then the motor will continue to turn. When the wiper blade moves to the specified position as shown in Figure 8-8(a), the circuit is interrupted, but because of the inertia, the motor cannot stop im-

mediately, the motor runs in the form of a generator, the armature winding contacts the copper ring 7 via the contact arms 3 and 5 to form a circuit, and the armature winding produces a large inductive current, thus producing a braking torque, and the motor stops rotating rapidly so that the wiper blade stops at the specified position in the windshield.

The reset disc shapes of electric wipers produced by different manufacturers are different, but the function is the same.

4. Intermittent operation principle of electric wiper

When an automobile is driving in foggy or snowy day, if the wiper works continuously, the trace moisture and dust on the windshield will form a sticky surface, so that the glass is not only not clean, but will become blurred, affecting the driver's sight; at the same time, the drag on the wiper increases, affecting the life of the wiper. Nowadays, automobiles, through the installation of wiper intermittent control system, makes the wiper work intermittently according to a fixed period, so that the driver has a better vision.

The intermittent control system of the wiper is mainly composed of a pulse generating circuit (oscillating circuit), a driving circuit and a relay. The driving circuit, under the control of the pulse generating circuit, drives the relay to turn on and off the wiper motor to work intermittently.

The common wiper intermittent control circuit can be divided into two types: non-adjustable type and adjustable type.

(1) Non-adjustable intermittent control circuit. The non-adjustable intermittent control circuit of the wiper is realized by automatic reset device and electronic oscillation circuit. Figure 8-8 shows a schematic diagram of an non-adjustable intermittent control circuit formed by an integrated circuit, a pulse generating circuit and a driving circuit composed of NE555 and peripheral components.

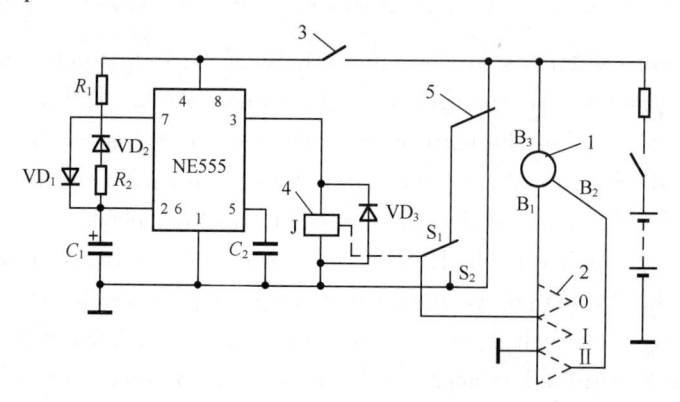

Figure 8-8　NE555 Intermittent Control Circuit

1—Wiper motor; 2—Wiper switch; 3—Intermittent wiper switch; 4—Relay; 5—Automatic stop switch

When the intermittent wiper switch is closed, the pin 3 of the NE555 integrated block outputs high potential, so that the relay J coil is energized, its normally closed contact S_1 is disconnected, and the normally open contact S_2 is closed, the wiper motor circuit, through the positive electrode of the battery → power switch → fuse wire → brush B_3 → armature winding → brush B_1 → wiper switch → relay normally open contact S_2 → ground → negative electrode of the battery, forms a circuit, and the wiper works. After the delay, the pin 3 of the integrated block outputs low potential, the relay is cut off, the normally closed contact

S_1 is closed, the normally open contact S_2 is open, if the wiper is in the stop position, the wiper will continue to work under the control of the automatic stop device, until the automatic stop switch is disconnected and the wiper blade stops in the original position. After a delay, the wiper repeats the above-mentioned working process to realize the cycle intermittent wiping action.

In addition to the intermittent control circuit of wiper composed of integrated circuit, there are non-stationary square wave generator and complementary intermittent vibration circuit which are composed of discrete components. As shown in Figure 8-9, which can reach the intermittent operation of wiper.

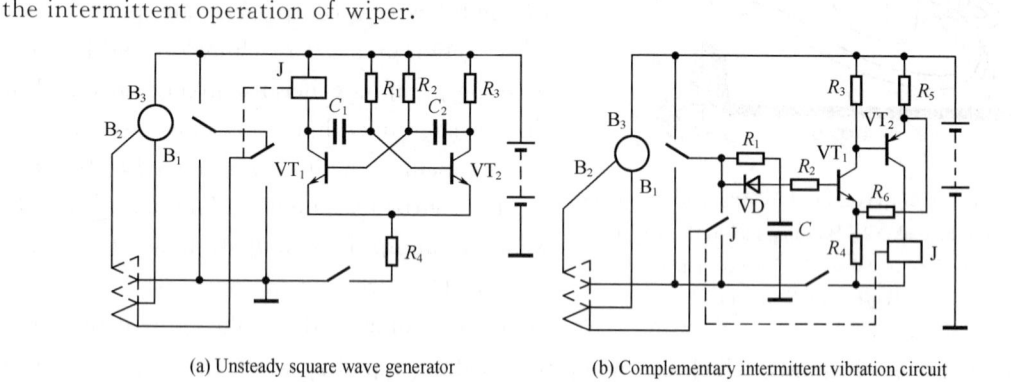

(a) Unsteady square wave generator   (b) Complementary intermittent vibration circuit

Figure 8-9　Control Circuit of Electronic Intermittent Wiper

(2) Adjustable intermittent control circuit. The wiper with adjustable intermittent control function in the event of rain, is driven by electronic controller drive wiper to rotate automatically. When the rain stops, the wiper stops automatically. The wiper speed can be automatically adjust according to the rainfall, and the interval time can also be adjusted. The driver does not need to worry about the adjustment, which is comfortable and convenient. Adjustable intermittent control circuit is usually composed of a rain sensor and a speed control circuit. The rain sensor may be a flow detection electrode or a photoelectric rain sensor [see Figure 8-10(a)]. The photoelectric rain sensor sends out the infrared ray, shoots on the window, the rain water causes the infrared reflection quantity to change, triggers the switch which connects the rain wiper, causes the rain wiper to run. This kind of rain wiper also can wipe slowly when the rain is light, and wipe quickly when the rain is heavy, as shown in Figure 8-10(b).

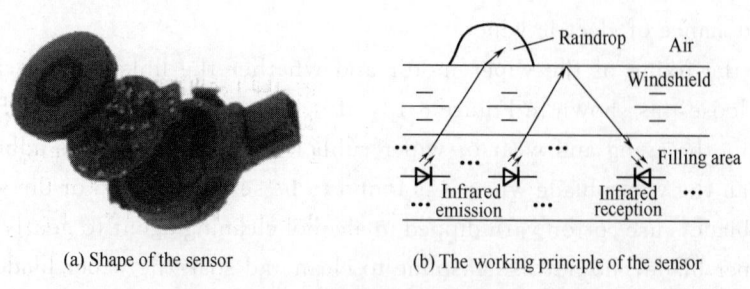

(a) Shape of the sensor   (b) The working principle of the sensor

Figure 8-10　Photoelectric Rain Sensor

(Ⅲ) Composition of the cleaning system

During the actual driving of the automobile, there will be a bit of dust floating on the

windshield glass, only using the wiper can not clean the glass. The windshield scrubber is used in conjunction with the wiper to make the windshield wiper work better and achieve a better wiping effect.

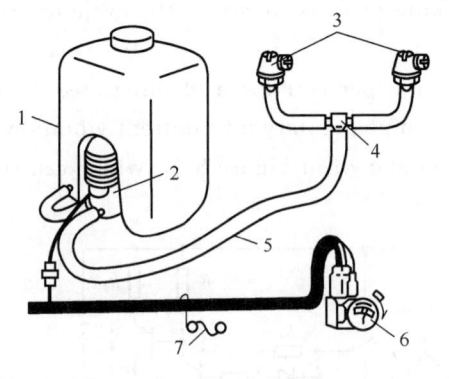

Figure 8-11   Composition of Windshield Scrubber
1—Storage tank; 2—Washing pump; 3—Nozzle;
4—Tee coupling; 5—Delivery pipe;
6—Wiper switch; 7—Fuse

The composition of the windshield scrubber is shown in Figure 8-11. It is mainly composed of a storage tank, a washing pump, a delivery pipe, a nozzle, etc. The washing pump generally integrates a permanent magnet DC motor with a centrifugal vane pump, with the injection pressure reaching $70\sim88$kPa. The washing pump is generally directly installed on the storage tank, but sometimes also installed in the pipeline. A filter is arranged at the inlet of the centrifugal pump. The nozzle of the washing pump is installed under the windshield. The direction of the nozzle can be adjusted according to the usage. The diameter of the spray is $0.8\sim1.0$mm, which can make the washing liquid spray in the proper position on the windshield. The continuous working time of the washing pump should not exceed 1min. For automobiles controlling wiping and washing separately, the washing pump should be opened first, and the wiper should be connected. After the spray stops, the wiper should continue to scrape $3\sim5$ times to achieve good cleaning effect.

(Ⅳ) Maintenance and troubleshooting of electric wiper and cleaner

According to the international driving safety survey: when driving on rainy days, the traffic accident rate is about 5 times higher than usual because of the blurred vision caused by the aging of the wiper blade. Therefore, good maintenance of the wiper is a necessary guarantee for safe driving in rainy and snowy days. It is recommended to maintain the wiper per 6 months or 10,000km, and the wiper blade should be replaced at least once a year. Since the cleaner is often used with the wiper, the cleaner should also be maintained while maintaining the wiper.

1. Maintenance of electric wiper and cleaner

(1) Maintenance of electric wiper.

① Check the fixing of the wiper motor and whether the linkage of each transmission mechanism is loose, as shown in Figure 8-12, if it is loose, it should be tightened.

② Examine the aging and wear of wiper rubber wiper blade and its adhesion to glass. Replace or clean the wiper blade when it is found to be seriously worn or dirty. When cleaning the wiper blade, use cotton yarn dipped in alcohol cleaning agent to gently wipe away the dirt on the wiper blade, do not use gasoline to clean and soak the wiper blade, otherwise it will be deformed and can not be used. The mouth of the wiper must match with glass angle, otherwise it should be polished or replaced.

③ After moistening the windshield with water, turn on the wiper switch, the wiper rocker arm should swing normally, and the motor should not make any noise. Switching the

186 Automobile Electrical Equipment Maintenance

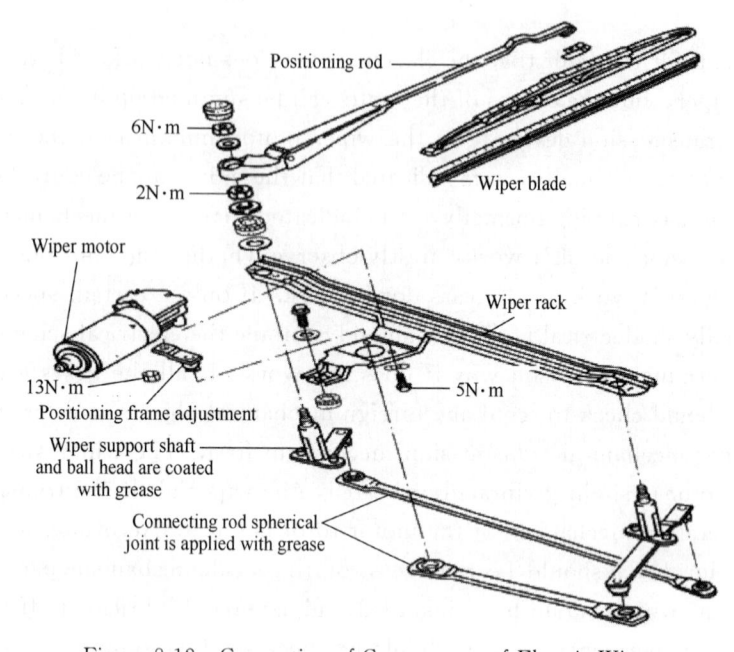

Figure 8-12　Connection of Components of Electric Wiper

gear switch, the wiper works at the corresponding speed, and can automatically reset. Otherwise, the wiper motor and related lines should be inspected.

④ After inspection, apply 2~3 drops of oil or grease to each moving hinge, and turn on the wiper motor switch again to make the wiper rocker arm swing, after the oil or grease is soaked into each working face, wipe off the excess oil or grease.

(2) Maintenance of cleaner.

① Check whether the pipe connection of the cleaner system is fastened. If it is dropped or loose, install it and fix it. If the plastic pipe is aging or broken, It should be replaced.

② Check the nozzle of the cleaner, clean brush can be used to clean the nozzle when it is dirty; press the spray switch, the nozzle should spray the cleaning liquid to the proper position on the windshield glass, as shown in Figure 8-13, otherwise the position of the nozzle should be adjusted, or the injection part and the circuit part should be overhauled.

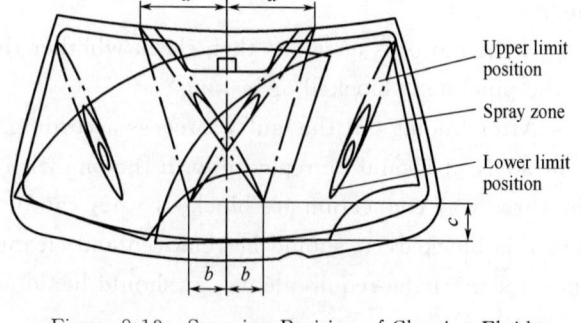

Figure 8-13　Spraying Position of Cleaning Fluid

③ The cleaning fluid should be selected according to the requirements of the original automobile, if the washing liquid is prepared by ordinary detergent and cleaning agent, in the winter, it should be removed to prevent the storage tank and the plastic pipe from damaged by freezing.

2. Common fault overhaul of electric wiper and cleaner

The common faults of electric wiper and cleaner are that the electric wiper doesn't work or is slow and weak, can't be reset, the cleaning system doesn't work or the injection pres-

sure is too low.

(1) Overhaul for the fault that the electric wiper does not work. There are many faults in the electric wiper, but the causes of the faults can be summed up in two aspects. Remove the mechanical transmission device from the wiper motor and turn on the wiper switch. If the motor does not run normally, it is indicated that the motor or the control circuit is out of order; if the motor is running normally, it is indicated that it is a mechanical fault.

If the electric wiper doesn't work, firstly observe whether the fault phenomenon is that one speed gear doesn't work or all gears don't work. If only a certain speed gear does not work, it is usually an electrical fault, we should combine the electrical schematic diagram of the wiper to determine the reason why it does not work. If all the gears are not working. Generally, we should check to see if any foreign mechanical objects interfere with the movement of the wiper mechanical transmission mechanism first. The wiper switch can be connected. If the motor is slightly vibrated or heated, the wiper blade the transmission mechanism, the deceleration mechanism or the motor rotor is stuck. According to the specific situation, the foreign body should be removed, or the local mechanism parts should be replaced. Then, the wiper should be re-installed, adjusted and lubricated. If the above faults are excluded, the wiper control circuit should be checked, for example, whether the power supply voltage is sufficient, whether the fuse is broken, whether the ground and the connection line is loose, whether the switch contact is good, etc., if all of the aforementioned are in good condition, the fault may be on the motor.

(2) Overhaul for the fault that the washer does not work.

When the windshield cleaner is not working, check whether the power supply voltage is too low, whether the motor connection of the cleaning pump is good, whether the ground is reliable, if there is a fault, it should be eliminated.

Then turn on the cleaning pump switch, touch the motor shell by hand. If the motor does not respond, then the cleaning pump motor has a fault, the motor should be dismantled.

If the motor is normal, then check whether the storage tank has cleaning fluid, whether the pipeline is blocked or leaking.

After finding out the fault, process according to the corresponding fault, if the pipeline is broken, it should be replaced with the one with the same specifications; if the nozzle and the three-way connection are blocked, they can be dredged by using a fine wire; if the filter screen is blocked, it should be removed and cleaned; if the cleaning fluid injection position does not meet the requirements, it should be adjusted; if the motor is damaged, it should be replaced.

(V) Composition and structure of electric windows

1. Composition of electric windows

The electric window allows the driver or the passenger to sit on the seat, uses the switch to make the glass up and down automatically, the operation is simple and is advantageous to the driving safety.

The electric window system consists of windows, window elevators, motors, relays, switches and so on. The structure of the Audi electric window is shown in Figure 8-14.

188 Automobile Electrical Equipment Maintenance

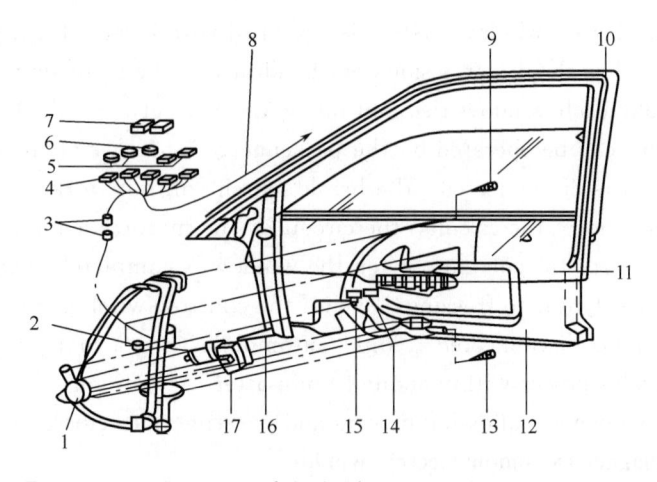

Figure 8-14　Structure of Audi Electric Window (driver side)

1—Window glass elevator; 2—Pad; 3—Motor socket; 4—Switch assembly socket; 5—Main switch; 6—Break switch of main switch; 7—Socket stand; 8—Wire harness; 9—Fixed bolt; 10—Window seal; 11—Front left window glass; 12—Window attachment bracket; 13—Fixed bolt; 14—Pad; 15—Window lock clip; 16—Fixed bolt; 17—Motor

2. Structure of electric window

In some automobiles, the electric window elevator is directly operated by the motor, while in others, the electric window elevator is operated by the driving mechanism so as to change the rotation of the electric automobile into the up-and-down movement of the window. There are two types of window elevators. One is a rope wheel electric window glass elevator, as shown in Figure 8-15. The other one is the cross drive arm type, as shown in Figure 8-16.

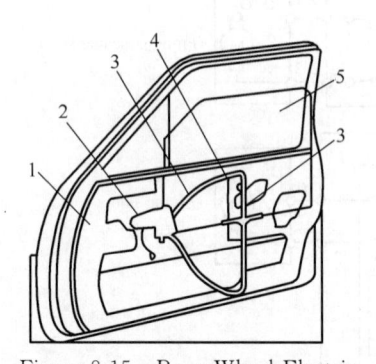

Figure 8-15　Rope Wheel Electric
Window Glass Elevator

1—Cover plate; 2—Permanent magnet
motor and reducer; 3—Guide sleeve;
4—Wire rope; 5—Window glass

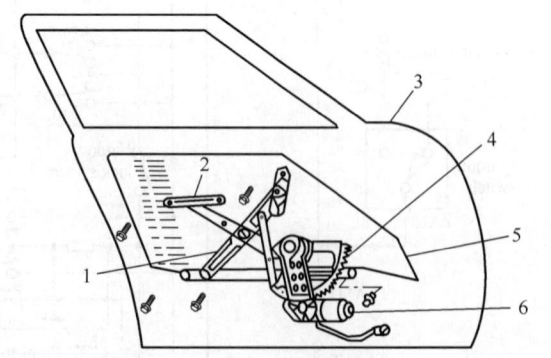

Figure 8-16　Cross Drive Arm Electric
Window Glass Elevator

1—Adjusting rod; 2—Support and navigation;
3—Door; 4—Drive tooth fan;
5—Automobile window glass; 6—Motor and socket

(Ⅵ)　Working principle of electric window

The motor used in the electric window is bi-directional, with permanent magnet type and double winding series excitation type. Each window is equipped with a motor that controls its rotation direction by means of a switch, causing the window to rise or fall.

Item Ⅷ　Overhaul of Automobile Auxiliary Electrical System　**189**

Generally, the electric window system is equipped with 2 sets of control switches. One set, on the dashboard or the driver's side door handrail, is the main switch, it is controlled by the driver to make each window rise and fall; Another set, installed on each passenger door, is sub-switch, can be operated by the passenger. A break switch is also installed on the main switch. If it is disconnected, the break switch will not work.

To prevent overload of the circuit, the circuit or the motor is equipped with 1 or more thermal switch to control the current, when the window is completely closed or the window glass can not move freely due to freezing, even if the control switch is not disconnected, the thermal switch will be disconnected. Some automobiles are also equipped with a delay switch, which provides power within about 10 min after the ignition switch is disconnected, or before the door is opened, allowing drivers and passengers to close the window.

1. Permanent magnet DC motor electric window

The permanent magnet DC motor is to change the current direction of the armature, so as to change the rotation direction of the motor, to make the window of the automobile rise or fall. Figure 8-17 shows the circuit of Lexus LS400 electric window control system.

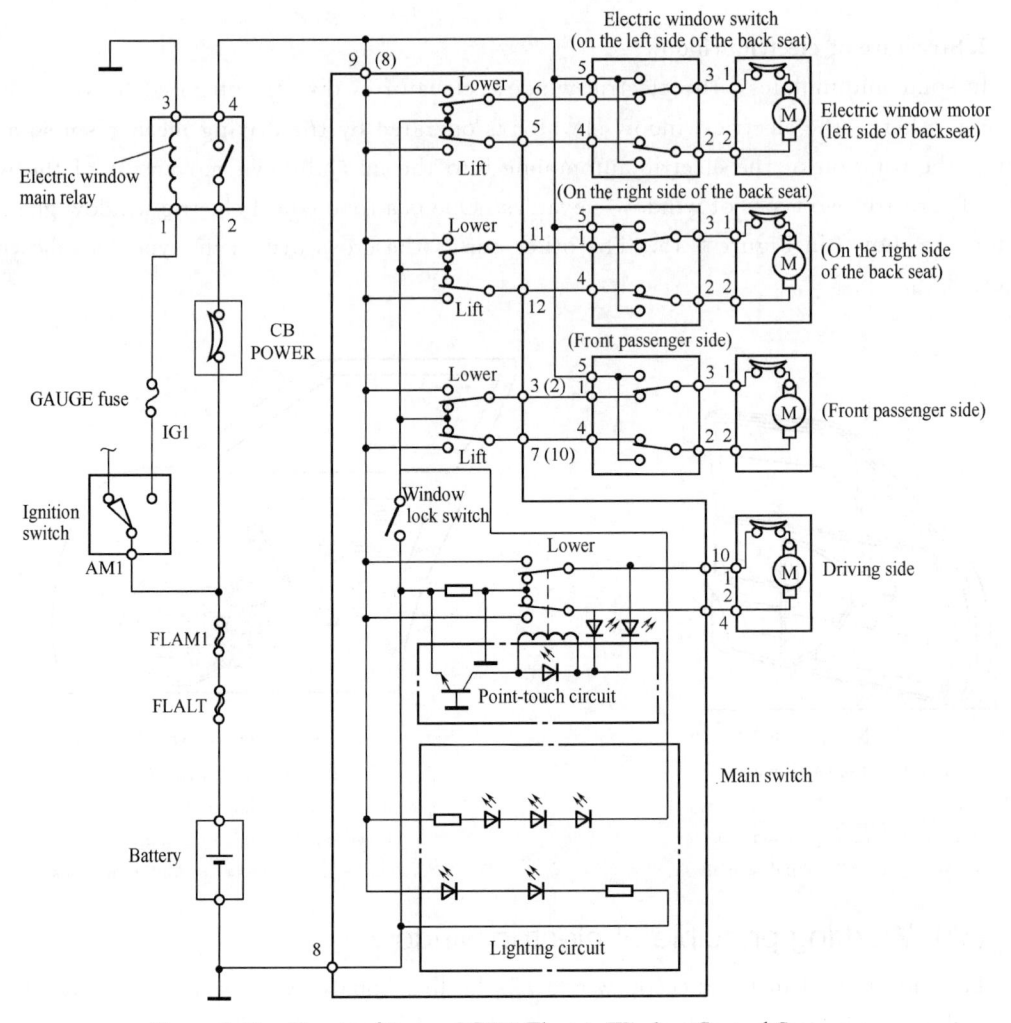

Figure 8-17   Circuit of Lexus LS400 Electric Window Control System

When the ignition switch is on the ignition gear, the main relay of the electric window works, the contact is closed, which provides power to the electric window; if the window lock switch on the main switch is closed, all windows can enter the working state at any time; if the window lock switch of the main switch is disconnected, only the driver side window can work. In addition, the window switch at the side of the driver is controlled by the point touch circuit, if the driver wants to make the window glass down, touch the drop switch, the window glass will automatically drop to the lowest point. During the drop process, if you want to stop the glass in a certain position, just touch the switch again.

2. Electric skylight

The electric skylight is mainly composed of a skylight assembly, a sliding mechanism, a driving mechanism and a control system. The skylight assembly comprises a skylight frame, a skylight window, a sunshade, a diversion channel, a drainage channel, etc. The electric window actuator is mainly composed of a motor, a transmission mechanism, a sliding screw and so on, as shown in Figure 8-18. When working, the motor drives the transmission mechanism so that the skylight slides open or tilts open.

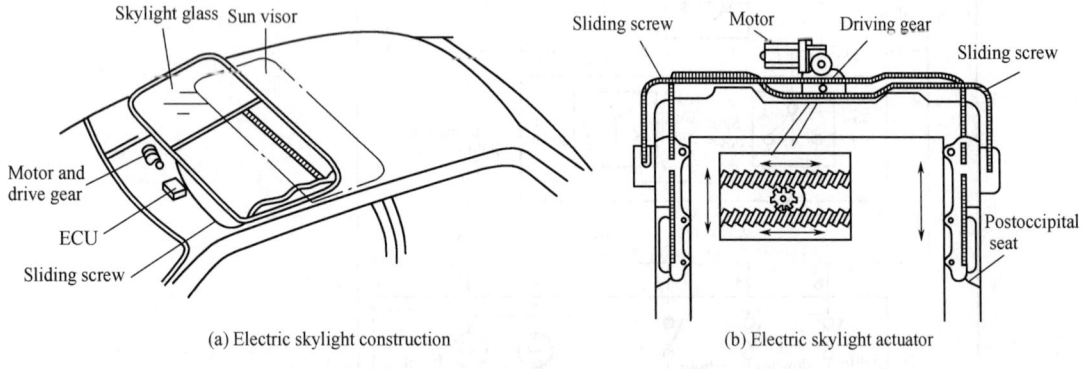

(a) Electric skylight construction   (b) Electric skylight actuator

Figure 8-18   Electric Skylight Structure and Actuator

The skylight control system mainly includes an electric window control switch, an electronic control unit (ECU), a relay, a limit switch and so on.

The skylight control switch has two functions: sliding opening and tilting opening, as shown in Figure 8-19. The slide switch has three positions: slide open, slide close and disconnect; the tilt switch also has three positions: tilt up, tilt down and disconnect. By driving the motor, the skylight rotates clockwise or counterclockwise, so that the skylight works in different states.

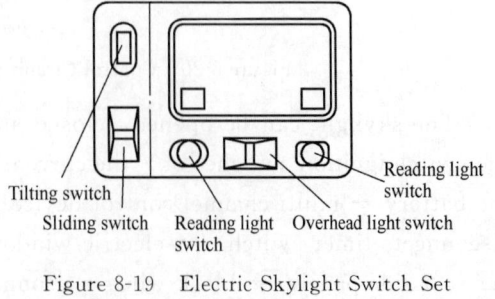

Figure 8-19   Electric Skylight Switch Set

The electric skylight glass has the function of blocking the sight (avoid being seen from outward to inside) and tilting back and forth. When the ignition switch is turned to the closed position without opening any door, the motor can still work for 10 minutes. The electric skylight control circuit of the Honda Accord is as shown in Figure 8-20.

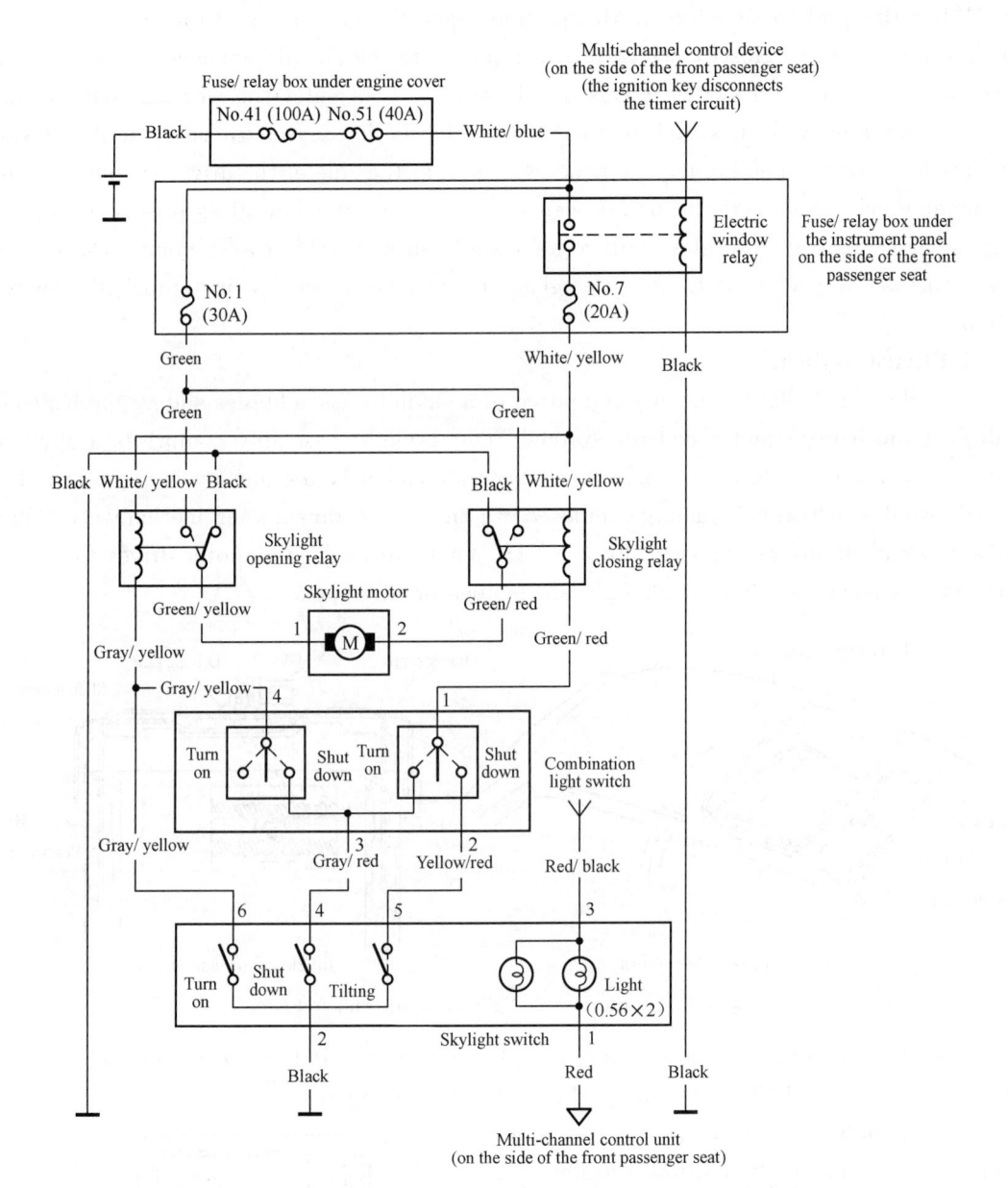

Figure 8-20   Control Circuit for Honda Accord Electric Skylight

The skylight can be opened, closed and tilted. For example, the open circuit, when the switch ignition switches on, the current in the circuit flows from the positive electrode of the battery → multi-channel control device (front passenger seat side) → (ignition switch disconnects timer switch) → electric window relay (fuse/relay box under the front passenger seat side panel) → black wire → ground → negative electrode of the battery, the electric window relay is connected.

When the electric skylight switch is in the open position, the current in the circuit flows from the positive electrode of the battery → black wire No. 41 (100A), No. 51 (40A) (fuse/relay box under the engine hood) → white/blue wire → electric window relay contact → fuse No. 7 (20A) (fuse/relay box under the dashboard on the front passenger seat

192   Automobile Electrical Equipment Maintenance

side → white/yellow wire → skylight opening relay coil → gray/yellow wire → skylight switch terminal 6 → skylight switch terminal 2 → black wire → ground → negative electrode of the battery. The skylight opening relay is connected to draw the contact to the left.

(Ⅶ) Fault diagnosis of electric window

(1) All windows can not be risen or fallen.

① Main causes of the fault: Fuse is broken-circuited; related relay and switch are damaged; the motor is damaged; the grounding point is corroded and loose.

② Diagnostic steps. Firstly, check whether the fuse is broken or not. If the fuse is good, we should switch the ignition switch on and check whether the voltage on the relay and on the terminal of the switch live wire is normal. If the voltage is 0, check if the ground wire is good. If the ground is bad, clean and tighten the ground wire; if the ground is good, the relay, switch and motor should be tested.

(2) One of the windows cannot be risen or fallen or can move in only one direction

① Main causes of the fault: The key switch is damaged, the motor is damaged, the connecting wire is broken, and the safety switch is broken.

② Diagnostic steps. If the window cannot be risen or fallen, firstly check whether the safety switch is working, whether the key switch of the window is working properly, and whether the motor of the window is running smoothly under clockwise and counterclockwise rotation. In case of fault, new parts should be repaired or replaced; in case of normal, the connecting wires should be checked. If the window can only move in one direction, it is generally caused by that the key switch fails or part of the wire is broken or connected wrongly, we can first check whether the wire connection is normal, and then overhaul the switch.

Ⅲ. Item Implementation

(Ⅰ) Overhaul of automobile auxiliary electrical system

① Through the implementation of this item, we should be able to disassemble and adjust the wiper and the cleaner, and master the steps and methods to diagnose and detect the faults of the wiper.

② The item should have the data such as automobile wiper system, screwdriver, wrench, multimeter and other disassembly and repair tool box, automobile wiper circuit diagram, etc.

(Ⅱ) Implementation steps

1. Fault diagnosis of the electric wiping and cleaning system

The fault diagnosis process of the electric wiping and cleaning system is shown in Figure 8-21.

2. Removal of the electric wiping and cleaning system

Removal of the electric wiper and cleaner may be carried out in accordance with the operating procedures recommended by the manufacturer manual and maintenance manual. This

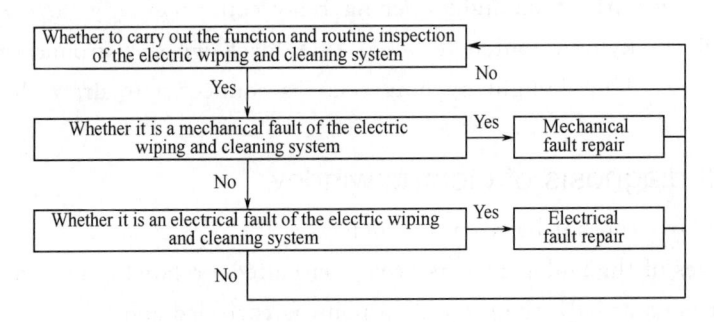

Figure 8-21   Fault Diagnosis Process of the electric Wiping and Cleaning System

item only provides the assembly and disassembly steps of Audi A6 electric wiper and cleaner, for reference only.

When dismantling, we should first remove the relevant parts that have to be disassembled, finally dismantle the wiper motor system, remove the wire harness connector, remove the connecting rod mechanism and motor assembly connecting bolt, etc. Be careful when disassembling to prevent damage to the permanent magnet inside the motor.

3. Overhaul of the electric wiping and cleaning system

(1) Overhaul of the linkage mechanism of the wiper.

① Check the wiper blade assembly. Whether the wiper blade is aging, whether the wiper arm is deformed. If the wiper blade is aging and the wiper arm is deformed, they will be replaced.

② Check the transmission mechanism. Whether the connecting rods and other transmission parts are bent or deformed. If they are deformed, they will be corrected; if the deformation can not be repaired, they should be replaced.

③ Check whether the joint parts, such as the connecting balls, are well lubricated and seriously worn. In the case of poor lubrication, lubricants should be added; in the case of severe wear, they should be repaired or replaced.

(2) Overhaul of control wires and switches. A multimeter can be used to detect the on-off of the wiper and cleaner combination switches when they are in each gear position. In the case of a wire problem, the corresponding wire should be reconnected; in the case of a fault caused by poor contact or burn-out of the internal contact of the switch, they should be dismantled for repair or be replaced.

(3) Overhaul of wiper motor assembly.

① Check whether the worm wheel and the worm gear change mechanism are worn or not, they should be replaced if the wear is serious.

② Check brush height, it should not be less than 8mm, otherwise it should be replaced.

③ Check whether the surface of the motor commutator is ablative, if it is ablative, use a fine gauze to polish, if the ablative or wear is serious, it need to be replaced or reprocessed to meet the requirement.

④ Check whether the magnetic field coil is short-circuited, open-circuited or badly grounded. If so, the coil should be replaced or rewound.

⑤ Check whether the armature shaft is bent and whether the clearance between the shaft and the bearing meets the requirements, otherwise it should be replaced.

(4) Overhaul of the cleaner system.

① Check whether the cleaning fluid in the storage tank is sufficient, otherwise the cleaning fluid should be replenished.

② Check whether the pipe is unobstructed or leaking, otherwise it should be replaced, reconnected and sealed.

③ Check whether the nozzles, the three-way connection and the filter screen are blocked, otherwise a fine wire can be used to dredge the nozzles and three-way connection, the filter screen needs to be cleaned.

4. Installation and adjustment of the electric wiping and cleaning system

The installation of the electric wiping and cleaning system is opposite to its disassembly step. It is recommended to follow the operation steps recommended by the manufacturer manual and the maintenance manual.

When installing, pay attention to the return of the wiper blade; do not spill out the cleaning liquid in the spray bottle, if it is spilled out, the standard cleaning fluid should be added; the connection of the spray pipe should be reliable; adjust the position of the nozzle according to the data provided by the manufacturer.

After installation, the motor should be connected to the power supply, the combination switch should be switched to different gears for inspection, the system should work normally, run smoothly, reset well, wiping clean. It is worth noting that, during inspection, do not just use the wiper to prevent it damaging.

5. Inspection of power supply wires for electric windows

Taking the Santana as an example, the electric window device used in the Santana 2000 is composed of a rocker key switch, a transmission mechanism, a elevator and an electric motor. The control circuit is shown in Figure 8-22. The key switch E_{39}, E_{40}, E_{41}, E_{32}, E_{53} are placed on the switch panel on the central channel panel. The yellow key switch E_{39} is a safety switch, which can make the rear window switch E_{53} and E_{55} do not work; E_{40}, E_{41}, E_{52} and E_{54} are left front, right back, left back and right back door glass lift switches respectively. To make the glasses of the left and right back doors can be raised and lowered independently, E_{53} and E_{55} key switches are set on the two back doors respectively. V_{14}, V_{15}, V_{26} and V_{27} are left front, right front, left back and right back window motors respectively. The motor is permanent magnet DC motor, with the normal working current of $4\sim15A$. The motor is equipped with overload circuit breaker to avoid overloading. The time-delay relay J_{52} ensures that after the ignition switch is disconnected, the window circuit is disconnected after about 50s. It is convenient and safe to use. The automatic relay J_{51} is used to control the left front door window motor.

The principle of tip control is as follows.

After the ignition switch is connected, the time-delay relay J_{52} is connected with the C-way power supply, its normally open contact is closed, the P in the key switch is grounded through the contact, and the P_+ is connected with the A-way power supply through the fuse S_{37}, at this time, pressing the key switch can make the window motor turn.

(1) Delay control after engine flames out. When the ignition switch is turned off, the

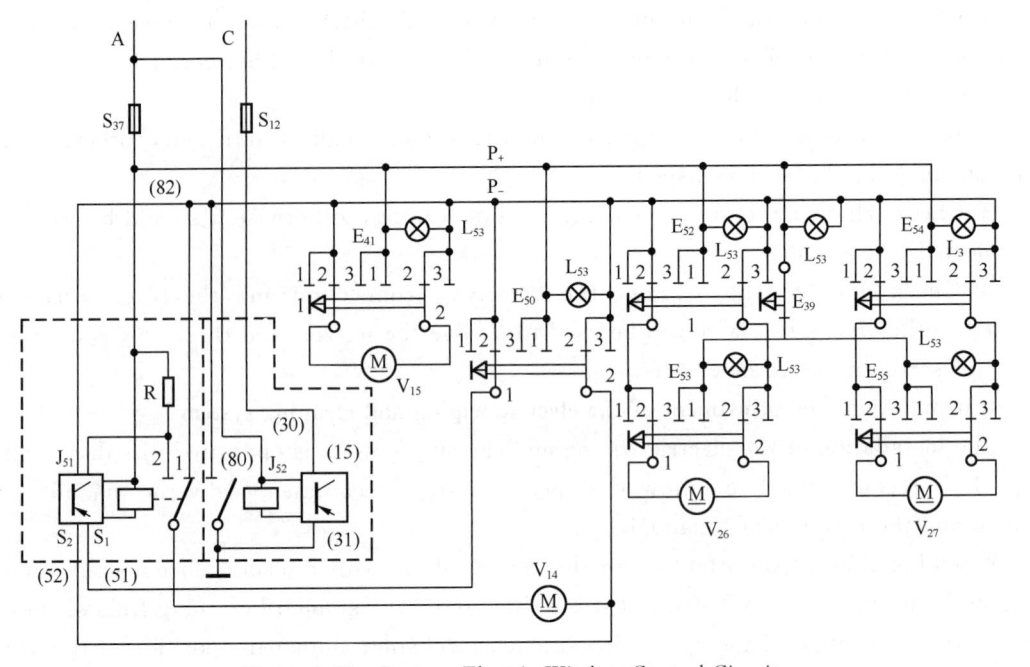

Figure 8-22　Santana Electric Window Control Circuit

C-way power supply is disconnected, and the time-delay relay J_{52} is powered by the A-way power supply. After the delay of 50s, the relay contact is disconnected, the ground wire of the key switch is cut off, and all the key switches are out of control.

(2) Control of the back window motor. The window motors of the left and right back doors each have two key switches E_{52}, E_{53} and E_{54}, E_{55}, E_{52} and E_{54} are installed on the central channel panel for driver control, E_{53} and E_{55} are respectively installed on the two back doors for backseat passenger control. The 2 switches of the same back door are connected by cascade. When the 2 switches are pressed at the same time, there is no control function. Only when one switch is pressed, there is control function. When the safety switch E_{39} is pressed, the normally closed contact of E_{39} is disconnected and the power supply of the control switch E_{53} and E_{55} on the back door is cut off, making them losing the control to the corresponding window motors, playing the role of protecting children's safety.

① The rising of the window glass. When the safety switch E_{39} is not pressed, the E_{52} (E_{54}) is placed in the rising position, and the window motor V_{26} (V_{27}) rotates clockwise, driving the left back (right back) window glass up, at this point, the circuit is: A-way power supply → fuse S_{37} → E_{52} (E_{54}) → E_{53} (E_{55}) → left back (right back) window motor V_{26} (V_{27}) → E_{53} (E_{55}) → E_{52} (E_{54}) → P → J_{52} contact → grounding → negative electrode of the power supply; If the left back (right back) window E_{53} (E_{55}) up key is pressed, the window motor V_{26} (V_{27}) can also drive the window glass up, at this time, the circuit is: A-way power supply → fuse S_{37} → P_{+} → E_{39} → E_{53} (E_{55}) → left back (right back) → window motor V_{26} (V_{27}) → E_{53} (E_{55}) → E_{52} (E_{54}) → P → J_{52} contact → grounding → negative electrode of the power supply.

② The falling of the window glass. When the safety key switch E_{39} is not pressed, the E_{52} (E_{54}) or E_{53} (E_{55}) is placed in the falling position, the direction of the armature cur-

196　Automobile Electrical Equipment Maintenance

rent of the window motor V_{26} (V_{27}) is opposite to the rising, the motor rotates counterclockwise, driving the left back (right back) window glass down.

(3) Control of the front window motor. The right front window motor V_{15} is controlled by the key switch E_{41}, while the left front door window motor V_{14} is controlled by the key switch E_{40} and the automatic relay J_{51}, and they have the tip automatic control function.

① The rising of the windows. Press the up key of the key switch E_{41}, the window motor rotates clockwise, driving the right front window glass rising, its circuit is: A-way power supply → fuse S_{37} → P → E_{41} → window motor V_{15} → E_{41} → P → J_{52} contact → grounding → negative electrode of the power supply; press the up key of the key switch E_{40}, P_+ and P are respectively connected to the input terminal S_2 and S_1 of the automatic relay J_{51} by E_{40}. At this point, the contact of the automatic relay J_{51} is closed, the contact 2 is broken, the window motor V_{14} rotates clockwise, the left front window is rising, the circuit is as follows: A-way → fuse S_{37} → P → E_{40} → window motor V_{14} → J_{51} normally closed contact 1 → P → J_{52} contact → grounding → negative electrode of the power supply, key switch E_{40} resets, the above circuit is cut off, and the motor V_{14} stops.

② The falling of the window. When pressing the down key of the key switch E_{41}, the window motor V_{15} rotates counterclockwise and drives the right front window down. The current path is opposite to that of the rise. When pressing the down key of the key switch E_{40}, $P_|$ and P are respectively connected to the input terminal S_2 and S_1 of the automatic relay J_{51}. At this point, the contact 2 of the automatic relay contact J_{51} is closed and the contact 1 is disconnected. The circuit is as follows: A-way power supply → fuse S_{37} → P_+ → sampling resistor R → J_{51} contact 2 → window motor V_{14} → E_{40} → P → J_{52} contact → grounding → negative electrode of the power supply, the current direction that flows through motor V_{14} is opposite to that of rising, the motor rotates counterclockwise and drives the glass down. When releasing the hand, the E_{40} resets, the contact of J_{51} also resets (contact 2 is disconnected, contact 1 is closed), the above circuit is cut off, and the motor stops.

③ Tip automatic control When the time pressing the down key of the key switch $E_{40} \leqslant$ 300ms, the automatic relay J_{51} will automatically judge it as a tip drop operation, so the relay acts, making contact 2 close. The current direction flowing through the window motor V_{14} is the same as that of the normal falling operation time, the motor rotates counterclockwise, and the window is lowered. If the current direction of the E_{40} during the lowering is the same as the normal drop operation time, the motor rotates counterclockwise and the window drops. If the rising key of the E_{40} is not pressed during the lowering, the contact 2 of the relay J_{51} will always be in closed state until the glass drops to the end, the motor V_{14} stops, at this point, the armature current will increase. When the current increases to about 9A, the voltage on the sampling resistor R makes the relay J_{51} move and the contact 2 disconnect, automatically cutting off the power circuit of the window motor, the motor stops; if during the lowering, the up key of the E_{40} is presses, relay J_{51} will judge it as the end of the operation, the contact 2 is disconnected, the window motor V_{14} stops. In this way, the left front window can be stopped at any position by the tip control of the key switch E_{40}.

If all windows do not fall, a window can not rise or fall or can only move in one direc-

tion, the corresponding fuse, voltages of relevant relays and related switch live wire terminal, and the motor should be checked according to the circuit working processes described above.

6. Inspection and maintenance of mechanical mechanism of electric window

(1) Removal of the electric window glass elevator. The construction of the electric window glass elevator is shown in Figure 8-23.

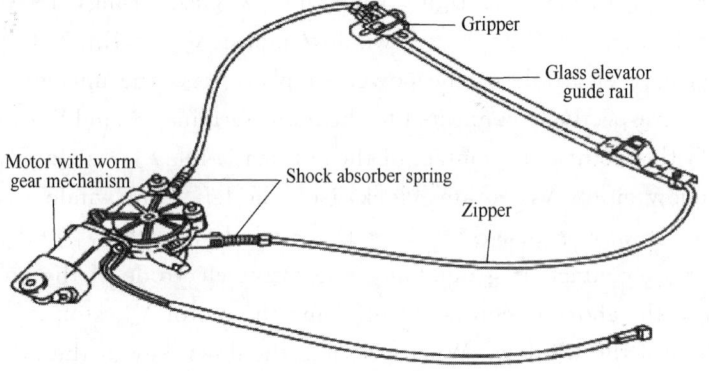

Figure 8-23   Construction of Electric Window Glass Elevator

① Separate the electric window glass regulator wiring plug.

② Use tie band 1 to connect and fix the drive cover 2 and the plastic bearing cover at 2 steel wire outlets (where the safety device faces the bulge) (pointed by the arrow), fix the drive cover 2, tighten the screw 3 (pointed by the arrow), during the whole repair process, it is not allowed to remove the tie band 1, otherwise it is impossible to repair, as shown in Figure 8-24.

③ When removing the drive cover 1, allow the drive cover 1 and the drive shell 2 to tilt slightly against each other. Pull the coil drum (inside the drive cover 1) out of the drive shell 2 along the direction of the arrow by hand. Do not damage the sealing line, as shown in Figure 8-25.

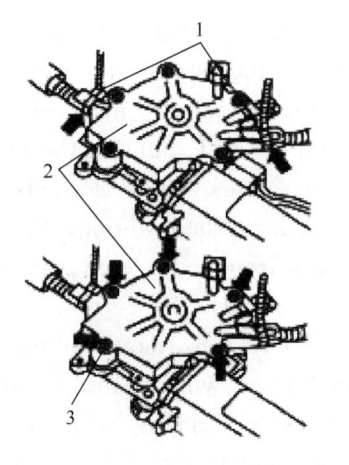

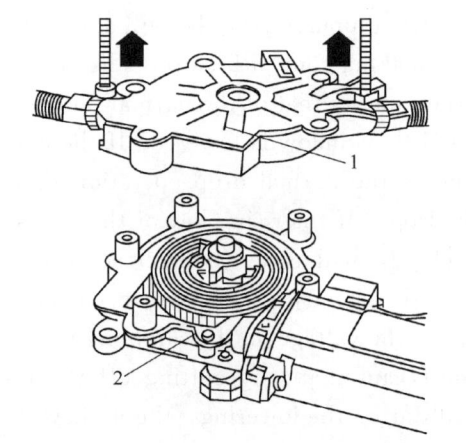

Figure 8-24   Breakdown of Electric Window
Glass Elevator（Ⅰ）
1—Tie band; 2—Drive cover; 3—Screw

Figure 8-25   Breakdown of Electric Window
Glass Elevator（Ⅱ）
1—Drive cover; 2—Drive shell

(2) Assembly of electric window glass elevator.

① When replacing the new driver, follow the direction of the arrow to remove the protective cover 3 which prevents dust and damage caused by transportation from the new drive, pay attention to ensure that the flange seal gasket and 3 support forming parts 2 are on the drive shell 1 (keep the surface clean, use special grease, do not allow dust and dirt on it), pull the 3 support forming parts 2 out along the direction of the arrow from the drive shaft 4. The rubber forming pad 5 must remain in the drive shell 1, as shown in Figure 8-26.

② Put the 3 support forming parts 1 into the coil drum 3 inside the drive shell 2, 3 cushioning parts must be carefully placed into the gap of the coil drum 3, and the drive shell 4 of the electric window glass elevator is combined with the coil drum 3 along the direction of the arrow. The gap on the rubber forming pad in the driving shell 4 must be aligned with the 4 clamps of the 3 support forming parts 1. When installing, the gear in the flange seal gasket 5 and the drive shell 4 can be coated with a layer of grease if necessary to prevent it from falling out, the drive shell 4 is connected with the coil drum 3, but can't contact each other, the clamp 6 can be moved slightly to change the position of rubber forming pad to achieve mutual coordination (screw meets torque requirement), as shown in Figure 8-27.

③ Tighten the screws (torque 3N·m) according to the order, install the window glass elevator to the front of the positioning bracket, carry out the function inspection, and cut off the excess tie band (preventing to produce scraping noise).

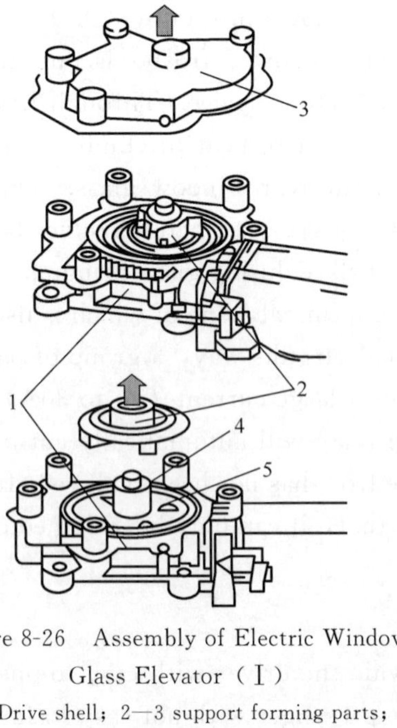

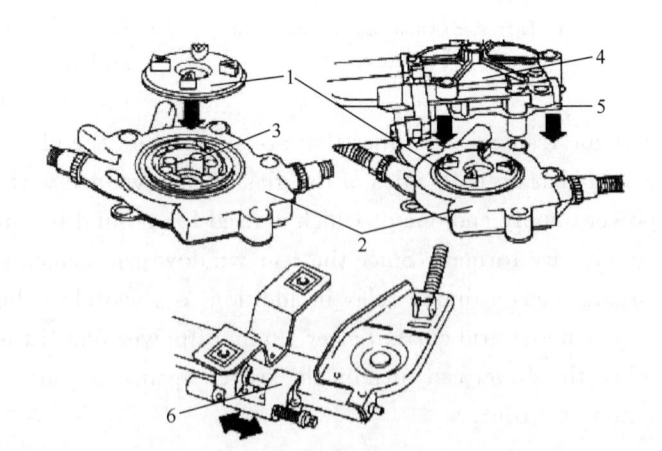

Figure 8-26　Assembly of Electric Window
Glass Elevator（Ⅰ）

1—Drive shell；2—3 support forming parts；
3—Protective cover；4—Drive shaft；
5—Rubber forming pad

Figure 8-27　Assembly of Electric Window
Glass Elevator（Ⅱ）

1—3 support forming parts；2—Drive shell；
3—Coil drum；4—Drive shell；
5—Sealing gasket；6—Clamp

(3) Precautions during maintenance.

① Because the electric window and the central door lock, the electric antenna share the ground wire, if the ground wire is not handled properly, it will lead to the failure of the central door lock.

Item Ⅶ　Overhaul of Automobile Auxiliary Electrical System　**199**

② When dismantling and installing the electric window, we must pay attention to the correct installation position, all the bolt connection holes are oval holes, positioning the front window up and down must not be interfered.

③ The dimension precision of the door guide slot will seriously affect the service life of the window elevator motor.

④ Pay attention to the sealing and dust-proof of the door. The inner panel of the door has a layer of plastic protective layer. If it is broken, it will cause dust to enter the window. If it is broken seriously, it will interfere with the movement of the electric window.

IV. Knowledge and Skills Expansion

(I) Window defrost device

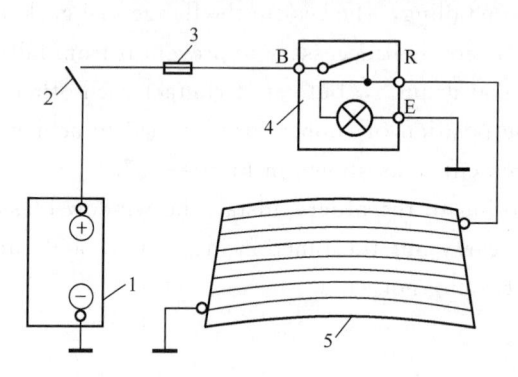

Figure 8-28   Rear Window Defroster
1—Battery; 2—Ignition switch; 3—Fuse;
4—Defroster switch and indicator light;
5—Defroster

In cold seasons, the moisture in the air tends to form tiny raindrops (fog) or frosts on the windshields of automobiles. In automobiles equipped with air-conditioning or heating devices, hot air can be blown to the front and side windshields through defrost doors to prevent moisture from condensing or melt the frosts. The rear window glass needs a defroster to defrost, as shown in Figure 8-28.

The rear window defroster is one kind of electric grid heating device. Through heating, it produces the micro-heat to eliminate the fog and frost on the rear window glass. The 5 in Figure 8-24 is a group of parallel silver-bearing ceramic transmission lines that are sintered on the glass surface during glass forming. There is a busbar on both sides of the glass, each welded with a terminal, one of which is used for power supply and one of which is used for ground terminal. In this way, a group of parallel circuits are formed. Since the rear window grid consumes a large current (up to 30A), the circuit needs a timing relay in addition to a switch. The relay will automatically cut off the rear window grid current after 10min of power-on. If the frost has not been removed after 10 min, the driver can turn on the switch again, but after that, it can only be switched on for 5 min at a time.

(II) Electric seat

The main function of the automobile seat is to provide the driver with easy-to-operate, comfortable and safe driving position, and to provide the passenger with not easy-to-fatigue, comfortable and safe riding position.

The seat, which serves as a link between people and automobiles, are increasingly required for their installation, and have evolved from fixed seats in the past to today's multi-functional power-regulating seats.

The adjustment of the seat is developing towards multi-function, which makes the safety, comfort and operability of the seat improve day by day. There are many kinds of seat

adjustments, and they can be combined in different ways, for example, the electric seat with 8 kinds of adjustment functions, its movement modes are seat front and back adjustment, up and down adjustment, up and down adjustment of the front section of the seat, backrest tilt adjustment, side back support adjustment, lumbar support adjustment and pillow up and down, forward and backward adjustment.

The forward and backward adjustment of the electric seat is 100~160mm, and the adjustment of the front and back section of the seat is 30~50mm. The total travel time is 8~10s.

1. Structure of electric seat

The electric seat generally consists of motors, transmission devices and control circuits for the seat, as shown in Figure 8-29.

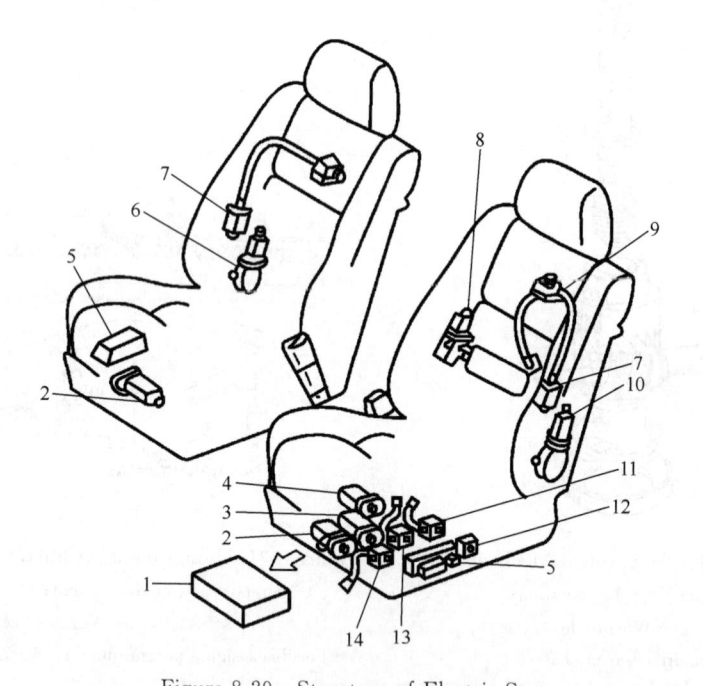

Figure 8-29   Structure of Electric Seat

1—Electric seat ECU; 2—Sliding motor; 3—Front vertical motor; 4—Rear vertical motor; 5—Electric seat switch;
6—tilt motor; 7—Headrest motor; 8—Waist pad motor; 9—Position sensor (headrest);
10—Tilt motor and position sensor; 11—Position sensor (rear vertical); 12—Waist pad switch;
13—Position sensor (front vertical); 14—Position sensor (slide)

(1) Motor. The number of motors depends on the type of the electric seat, usually a two-direction moving seat with two motors, a four-direction moving seat with four motors, up to six motors. Most electric seats use permanent-magnet motors, which operate the motors by switch to move in different directions. To prevent motor overload, most permanent magnet motors are equipped with circuit breakers.

(2) Transmission device. The rotary motion of a motor changes the spatial position of the seat by means of a transmission (mechanism).

① Height adjustment mechanism. As shown in Figure 8-30, the height adjustment mechanism is composed of worm shaft, a worm wheel, a spindle, etc. When adjusting, the worm shaft is driven by the motor, which drives the worm wheel to rotate so as to en-

Item Ⅶ   Overhaul of Automobile Auxiliary Electrical System   **201**

sure that the spindle is spinning in or out, so as to rise and fall the seat.

② Longitudinal adjustment mechanism. As shown in Figure 8-31, the longitudinal adjustment mechanism consists of a worm gear, a worm wheel, a rack, a guide rail, etc. The rack is mounted on the guide rail. When adjusting, the motor torque, through the worm gear, transfers to the worm wheel on the two sides, through the rack on the guide rail, driving the seat to move forward and backward.

③ Backrest tilt adjustment mechanism. The adjustment mechanism consists of 2 adjusting gears and connecting rods. When adjusting, the motor drives the adjusting gears at both ends to rotate, adjusting gears are linked with the connecting rod linkage, by the action of the connecting rods, the backrest inclination is adjusted.

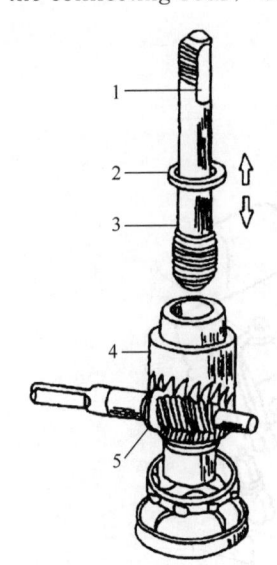

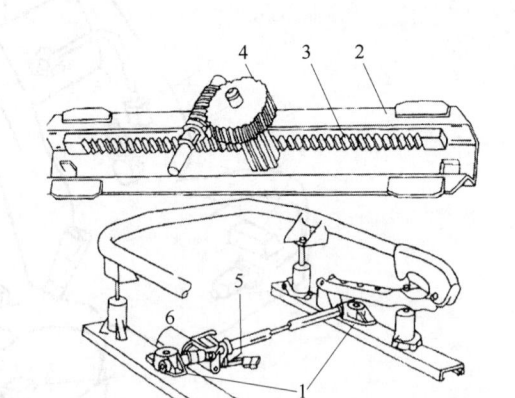

Figure 8-30　Height Adjustment Mechanism
1—Milling plane; 2—Thrust shim;
3—Spindle; 4—Worm wheel;
5—Flexible drive worm shaft

Figure 8-31　Longitudinal Adjustment Mechanism
1—Support and guide element; 2—Guide rail;
3—Rack; 4—Worm wheel;
5—Feedback signal potentiometer; 6—Adjustable motor

(3) Control circuits for electric seats. There are 8 kinds of modes to adjust the driver seat of Guangzhou Honda Accord: adjusting up and down for the front section; adjusting up and down for the back section; adjusting forward and backward; tilt adjustment forward and backward, as shown in Figure 8-32.

Through the electric seat adjustment switch, we can complete different adjustment functions, such as up and down adjustment of the front section of the electric seat, the circuit is as follows.

① Adjust up. When the up and down adjustment switch of the front section of the electric seat is at the "up" position, the current in the circuit is: battery → black wire → No. 42 (100A), No. 55 (40A) (fuse/relay box under engine cover) → yellow \ green wire → No. 2 (20A) (fuse \ relay box under the dashboard on the side of the front passenger seat) → red wire → electric seat switch terminal B2 → up and down adjustment switch terminal A3 of the front section→ red \ yellow wire → up and down adjustment motor terminal 1of the front section → up and down adjustment motor of the front section → up and

down adjustment motor terminal 2 of the front section → red wire → A4 → B5 → black wire → ground → negative electrode of the battery. The up and down adjustment motor of the front section starts. The front section of the seat moves upward.

② Adjust down. When the up and down adjustment switch of the front section of the electric seat is at the "down" position, the current in the circuit is: positive electrode of the battery → black wire → No. 42 (100A), No. 55 (40A) (fuse/relay box under the engine cover) → yellow/green wire → No. 2 (20A) (fuse/relay box under the dashboard on the side of the front passenger seat) → red wire → electric seat switch terminal B2 → electric seat switch A4 → red wire → up and down adjustment motor terminal 2 of the front section → up and down adjustment motor of the front section → up and down adjustment motor terminal 1 of the front section→ red/yellow wire → A3 → B5 → black wire → ground → negative electrode of the battery. The up and down adjustment motor of the front section starts. The front section of the seat moves downward.

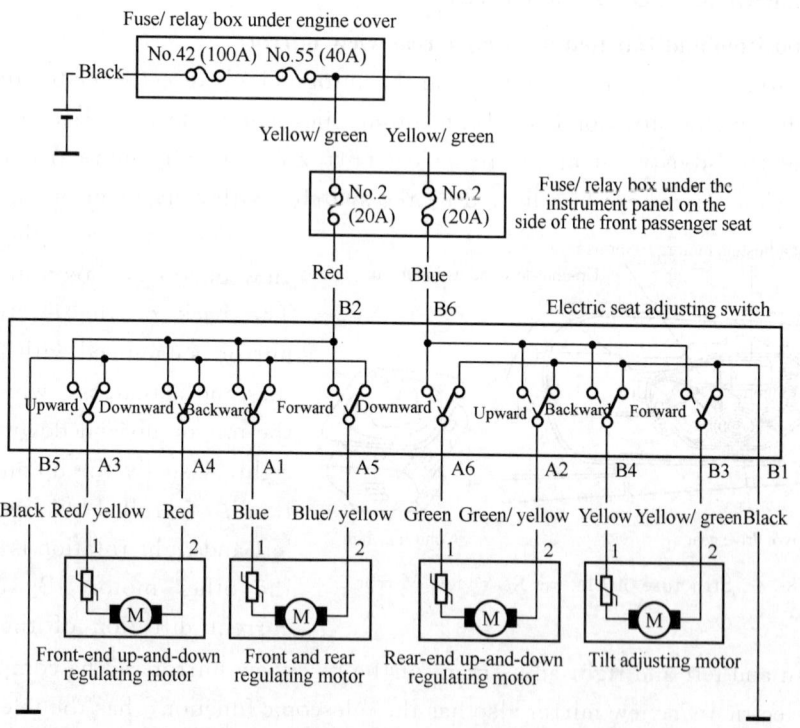

Figure 8-32   Electric Seat Circuit for Guangzhou Honda Accord Driver Seat

2. Electric seat with storage function

The electric seat with storage function is controlled by microcomputer. It can store the selected seat adjustment position. When using, the seat will automatically adjust to the pre-selected seat position by pressing the specified key switch. The control of the electric seat with storage function is shown in Figure 8-33.

The system has a memory, and the storage device controls the set position of the seat by 4 potentiometers. After the seat position is set, the driver presses the memory button, the electronic control device stores these voltage signals as a benchmark for re-positioning. When in use, only press the button, we can adjust the seat position according to the re-quirements of the stored seat position.

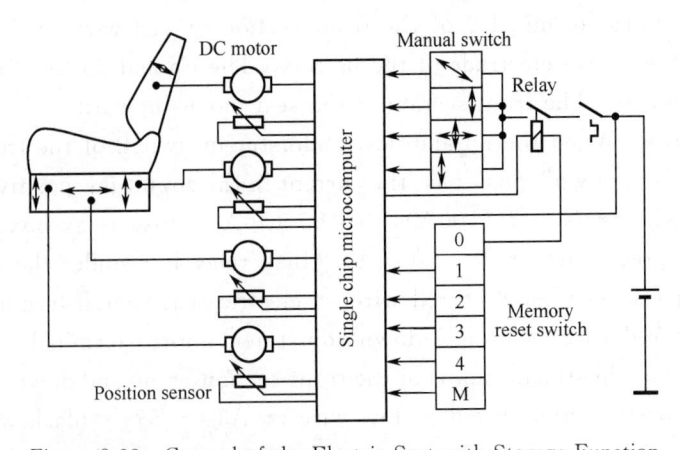

Figure 8-33　Control of the Electric Seat with Storage Function

(Ⅲ) Electric rear-view mirror

1. Composition and function of electric rear-view mirror

The position of the rear-view mirror on the automobile is directly related to whether the driver can observe the situation behind the automobile, and is closely related to the safety of driving. And the adjustment of the rear-view mirror is generally more troublesome. The electric rear-view mirror can be adjusted by the switch, with convenient operation.

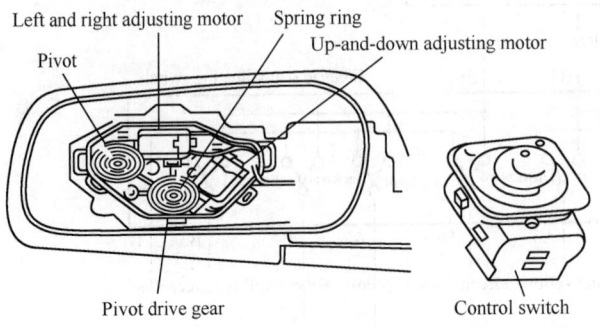

Figure 8-34　Structure of Electric Rear-view Mirror

The structure of the electric rear-view mirror is shown in Figure 8-34. The back of the electric rear-view mirror is equipped with 2 sets of motors and actuators, which can rotate the mirror up and down and left and right. Usually the up-and-down rotation is controlled by a motor, and the left-and-right rotation is controlled by the other motor. By changing the current direction of the motor, the up-and-down and left-and-right adjustment of the rear-view mirror can be completed.

Some electric rear-view mirror also has the telescopic function, has the telescopic switch to control the telescopic motor to work, causes the entire rear-view mirror to turn out or retracts.

2. Working principle of electric rear-view mirror

Figure 8-35 shows the circuit of the telescopic electric rear-view mirror control system for the Toyota Crown. When adjusting, firstly, choose the rear-view mirror to be adjusted by the left/right adjustment switch. For example, when adjusting the left mirror, the switch is turned to the left, at this time, the switch is respectively connected with contact 7 and 8 contact, and using the control switch can complete the up and down or left and right adjustment of the mirror. When adjusting it upward, we can push the control switch to the upper side. At this point, the control switch is combined with the up contact and the left up contact respectively. The circuit is positive electrode of the battery → fuse → ignition

204　Automobile Electrical Equipment Maintenance

switch → control switch up contact → left/right adjustment switch → contact 7→ left mirror motor → contact 1→ electric mirror switch contact 2→ control switch left up contact → electric mirror switch contact 3→ negative electrode of the battery, and the left mirror motor operates to complete the adjustment process. Other adjustment processes are similar to the upward adjustment process, which can be completed by switching on different switches.

The telescopic function of the electric rear-view mirror is controlled by the telescopic switch, which controls the relay to act and makes the telescopic motor of the left and right mirrors work to achieve the telescopic function.

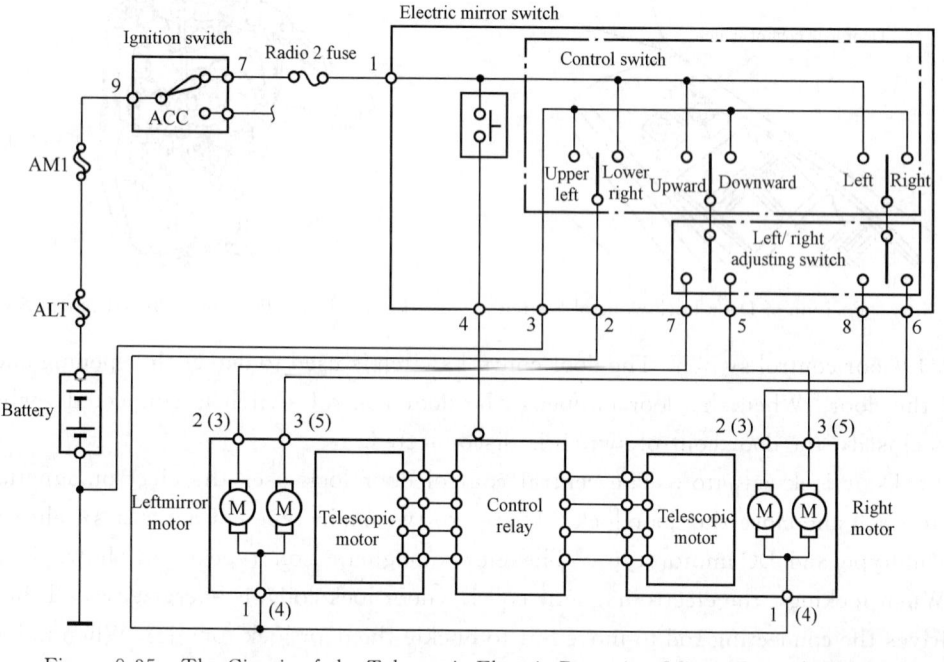

Figure 8-35　The Circuit of the Telescopic Electric Rear-view Mirror Control System for the Toyota Crown

(Ⅳ) Central control door lock system

The central control door lock is a kind of device which can control the door closing and opening at the same time through the switch on the cab door.

The central control door lock and the anti-theft system is an important part of modern automobile, which makes the use of the automobile more convenient and safe. The central control door lock and the anti-theft system are two systems which are interrelated and different. The realization of the anti-theft function depends on the normal work of the central control door lock. The automobile with the anti-theft system can greatly reduce the probability of theft.

The function of the control door lock in automobile is to increase the convenience and safety of automobile. The central control door lock is mainly composed of a control part and a executive part. The control part mainly includes a door lock switch and a door lock control relay.

(1) Door lock control switch. The door lock control switch is generally mounted on the handrail inside the driver side front door. All doors can be locked and opened simultaneously

through the door lock control switch. Figure 8-36 shows the position of a Toyotan automobile door lock control switch.

(2) Key control switch. The key control switch is mounted on the outside lock of the left front door and the right front door, as shown in Figure 8-37. When the door key is used to open or lock the door from the outside of the automobile, the key control switch sends the opening or locking signal to the door lock control ECU to open or lock the door.

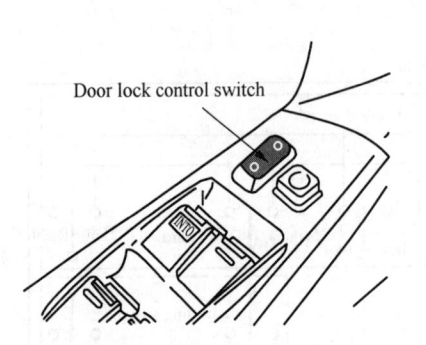

Figure 8-36　Position of Door Lock Control Switch

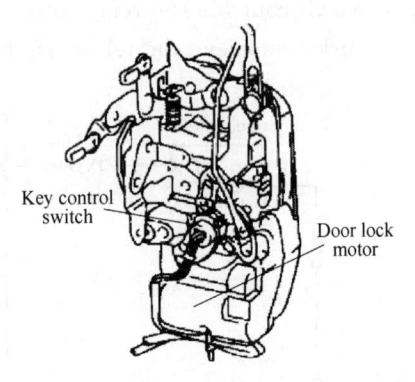

Figure 8-37　Position of Key Control Switch

(3) Door control switch. The door control switch is used to detect the opening and closing of the door. When the door is open, the door control switch is connected; when the door is closed, the door control switch is disconnected.

(4) Door lock actuator. The central control door lock uses the electromagnetic drive mode to open and close the door lock. There are two main types of actuators: electromagnetic coil type and DC motor type. The electromagnetic coil type is as shown in Figure 8-38. When locking, the electromagnetic coil L (door lock coil) is energized, and the armature drives the connecting rod to move left to buckle the door lock tongue; When unlocking, the electromagnetic coil U (unlocking coil) is energized, and the armature drives the connecting rod to move to the right to disengage from the door lock tongue.

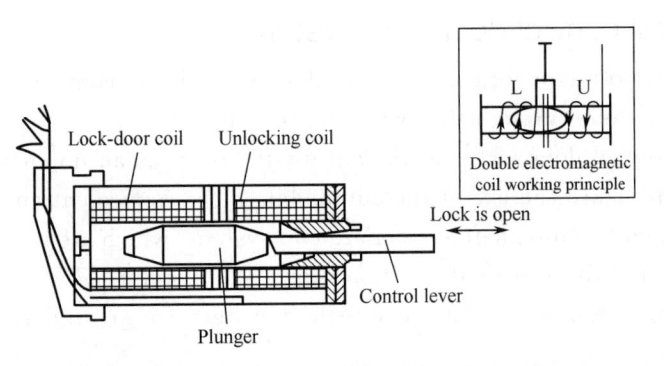

Figure 8-38　Electromagnetic Coil Lock Actuator

The connecting rod of the DC motor actuator is driven by a reversible DC motor, which makes use of the clockwise and counterclockwise rotation of the motor to lock the door and open the door.

(5) Door lock connecting rod control mechanism. The door lock connecting rod control mechanism is shown in Figure 8-39. When the door lock motor (or other actuator) is in op-

206　Automobile Electrical Equipment Maintenance

eration, the door lock is manipulated by the door lock connecting rod to lock or open the door.

The following functions can be realized after the automobile is equipped with the central control door lock.

① Central control. When the driver locks the door, the other doors are locked at the same time, and the driver can open all the doors through the door lock control switch.

② Separate control. In addition to the central control, the occupant can still use the mechanical spring lock of the door to open or close the door.

③ The key possession preventive function. If the door is locked and the key is still inserted in the ignition switch, all the doors will open automatically.

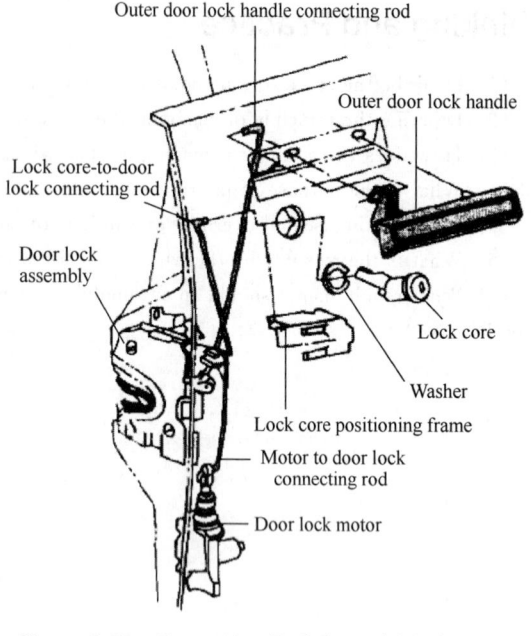

Figure 8-39　Connecting Rod Control Mechanism for Door Lock

④ Safety function. When the key is pulled out and the door is locked, the door can not be opened by the door lock control switch.

In addition, some models also have speed control function, automatic function and so on.

The remote central control door lock system is also called key-free access system. Its function is to add a remote control switch to the door lock system, and open and close the door by operating the wireless remote control device, which provides a convenient means for the driver.

Summary

（1）The electric wiper and cleaner are the standard configuration of the automobile, belonging to the auxiliary appliances on the automobile, mainly used for cleaning and brushing the rain, snow and dust on the windshield to ensure the visual effect of the driver.

（2）The windshield scrubber is mainly composed of a storage tank, a washing pump, a pipe, a nozzle, etc.

（3）The electric window with the permanent magnet DC motor is to change the current direction of the armature of the permanent magnet DC motor so as to change the rotating direction of the motor and make the window of the automobile rise or fall.

（4）There are two kinds of transmission mechanisms of electric window glass elevator, which are steel wire drum type and cross drive type.

（5）There are 2 sets of motors and actuators on the back of the electric rear-view mirror, which can control the up, down, left and right rotation of the mirror.

（6）The electric seat is generally composed of electric motors, transmission devices and control circuits for the seat, and some have a storage function.

Thinking and Practice

(1) Describe the composition and structure of the wiper.

(2) Describe the principle of changing the speed of the permanent magnet motor of a wiper.

(3) How does the permanent magnet electric wiper realize automatic return?

(4) What is the purpose of intermittent control of electric wiper? How to achieve intermittent control?

(5) Describe the use and overhaul precautions of electric wiper and cleaner.

(6) What is the reason why the wiper does not work after the power is turned on?

(7) What requirements should an automobile seat meet? What adjustment function does an electric seat generally have?

Item IX

Analysis of Circuit Diagram of Automobile Electrical System

I. Scene Introduction

A car, its left rear electric door lock failed. After overhauling, it is found that it was caused by the breakage of the wire from the left B-pillar to the left rear door trim plate due to the frequent opening and closing of the door. If we can't analyze the circuit diagram of the electrical system skillfully, we can't solve the practical problem quickly.

II. Related Knowledge

(I) Type of automobile circuit diagram

With the development of automobile electronic technology, the matching automobile circuit diagrams become more and more complicated. Therefore, how to read automobile circuit diagrams quickly and accurately is becoming more and more important. The automobile circuit diagrams have the partial circuit diagrams and the whole automobile circuit diagrams. Partial circuits are local circuits or unit circuits, usually including power supply circuit, start circuit, ignition circuit, lighting circuit, signal and instrument circuit, etc.; Whole automobile circuit is automobile electrical circuit. Usually all kinds of electric devices on the automobile are connected with each other reasonably according to their respective working characteristics and relations by various switches, fuses and other devices to form a whole circuit. At present, there are many kinds of automobile circuit diagrams, the circuit diagrams are definitely different according to the models. To sum up, the automobile circuit diagrams mainly include circuit diagram (wiring diagram), circuit schematic diagram, wire harness diagram.

1. Automobile electrical wiring diagram

Usually according to the appearance of automobile electrical devices, corresponding graphic symbols are used to make reasonable wiring. The wiring diagram is the true reflection that the electrical devices are connected with each other by wires. The installation position, shape and wiring route of the electrical devices connected are the same as the actual situation. It is easy to judge and troubleshoot the electrical faults of the automobile by using the electrical wiring diagram. Usually, the left of the diagram represents the front part of the automobile, and the right represents the rear part of the automobile. At the same time, most of the electrical devices in the diagram are represented in the shapes of physical outlines, giving a sense of reality. The function of the automobile electrical wiring diagram is to show the position of each original part on the electrical wiring diagram and the color, diame-

ter and direction of the whole automobile wires, to find out when the circuit is being over-hauled, to establish the logical check step on the electrical schematic diagram through the failure phenomenon and the analysis of the electrical schematic diagram, and then to carry out the concrete implementation on the electrical wiring diagram through the instructions of the electrical wiring diagram.

The advantages of the automobile electrical wiring diagram are that the appearance and actual position of the electrical device are all the same as that on the automobile. When loo-king for the wiring, the branch and the contact in the wire are easy to find, and the route of the wire is basically the same as the actual use of the wire bundle on the automobile; The disadvantages are that the wires are dense and crisscrossed. When reading the diagram and finding out and analyzing fault, it is very inconvenient. It can not reflect the internal struc-ture and working principle of the circuit.

The key points to read the wiring diagram are as follows.

(1) To have a definite understanding of the structure and principle of the electrical devices used in the automobile, and to have a clear understanding of its electrical device specifications.

(2) To identify the name and quantity of all electrical devices in the automobile and their actual locations on the automobile by reading.

(3) To know the number and name of the terminals of each type of electrical device, and understand the practical significance of each terminal.

2. Automobile circuit schematic diagram

The circuit schematic diagram is a more concise circuit drawn with specified graphic symbols according to the standards established by the state or relevant departments. The cir-cuit schematic diagram, also known as circuit sketch, are usually simplified according to electrical wiring diagrams. The function of this kind of diagram is to express the working principle and connection state of the circuit, without regard to the shape and position of the electrical device and the actual situation of the wire route. The electrical devices in the dia-gram are represented by symbols (more special symbols are stated by a diagram). The dia-gram is useful for understanding the working principle and process of electrical devices and for analyzing and judging the probable location of faults. The circuit schematic diagram of Shanghai Volkswagen POLO is shown in Figure 9-1.

The automobile circuit schematic diagram is the basic diagram of reading automobile electrical wiring diagram, wiring harness diagram and analyzing the working principle of au-tomobile circuit and judging the general position of fault.

The connection relationship described by the circuit schematic diagram is only a func-tional relationship, not the actual connection wire, so the circuit schematic diagram can not replace the wiring diagram.

The key points to read the schematic diagram are as follows.

(1) To identify which terminals of the electrical devices are respectively connected to which terminals of which electrical devices.

(2) To know the direction of the sub-line in which the circuit device is located.

(3) To know the structure and function of switches, fuse devices, relays on sub-lines.

3. Automobile wire harness diagram

The automobile wire harness diagram is mainly used to show which electrical wires con-

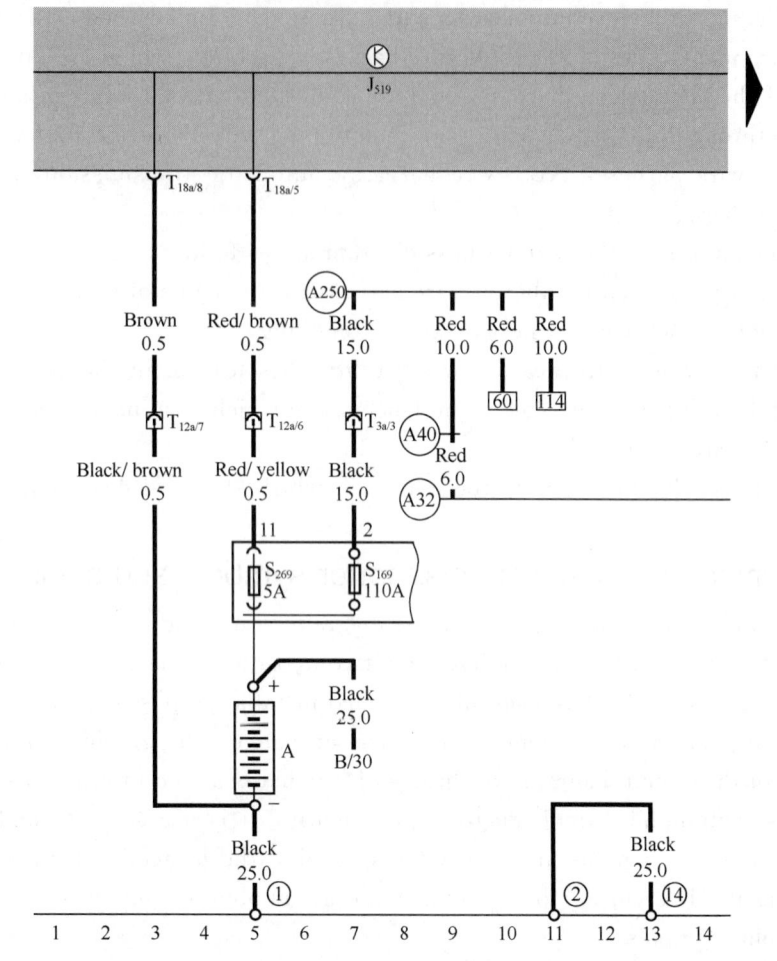

Figure 9-1　Circuit Schematic Diagram of Shanghai Volkswagen POLO

verge together to form the wire harness, and where to connect with and so on. There are many kinds and quantities of wires on automobiles. In order to ensure reliable installation, all kinds of wires with the same direction are often bundled into cables and wire harnesses. The wire harness shape diagram reflects the wire harness shape which has been made, so it is also called the wire bundle shape diagram. The diagram often indicates the name of the electrical device linked to each wire in the harness, and some also indicate the length of each wire. The wire harness diagram is a kind of circuit manifestation that highlights the assembly mark. It is helpful for installation and maintenance, but it can't show the direction of the wire and the circuit is simple.

If the wire harness diagram is used with a wiring diagram or a circuit schematic diagram, it will play a greater role, as shown in Figure 9-2.

The wire harness diagram is usually divided into main wire harness diagram and auxiliary wire harness diagram. The main

Figure 9-2　Automobile Wire Harness Diagram

Item IX　Analysis of Circuit Diagram of Automobile Electrical System　**211**

wire harness diagram is divided into chassis wire harness diagram and body wire harness diagram. There are many types of auxiliary wire harness diagrams, which are mainly used for the branches of the main wiring harness, and are connected with all kinds of auxiliary electrical devices (through plug-in), such as air-conditioning wire harness, roof wire harness, electric window wire harness, ABS wire harness, automatic transmission wire harness, electric seat wire harness, etc.

The key points to read the wire harness diagram are as follows.

(1) To identify the total number of wire harnesses, the name of each wire harness and the actual location of each wire harness on the automobile.

(2) To identify which electrical devices the branches lead to in the automobile, how many wire each branch has, their colors and labels, and which terminals of the electrical devices the branches are connected to.

(3) To identify which connectors there are and which electrical devices they should be connected to.

(Ⅱ) Common graphic symbols, letter symbols and signs

The automobile circuit diagram is a simple diagram to use the graphic symbols and the letter symbols to represent the automobile circuit composition, the connection relation and the working principle, without considering its actual installation position. To make the circuit diagram universal and convenient for technical exchange, the graphic symbols and the letter symbols of the circuit diagram are these with the national and international standards. To read and use automobile circuit diagram proficiently, it is necessary to understand the meaning of the graphic symbols and the letter symbols, the principle of marking and the method of using it. Therefore, to understand the automobile circuit diagram, we should master the graphic symbols.

1. Graphic symbols

Graphic symbols (Table 9-1) are divided into three types: basic symbols, general symbols and detail symbols.

(1) Basic symbols. The basic symbols can not be used alone, do not represent an independent electric appliance, only explain some characteristics of the circuit. For example, "$-$" means DC, "$\sim$" means AC, "$+$" means the positive electrode of the power supply, "N" means the negative electrode of the power supply, and "N" means the neutral wire.

(2) General symbols. A general symbol is a simple symbol used to represent a product and the characteristics of such a product. For example, ⊛ is a general symbol of the indicating instrument and ⊡ is a general symbol of a sensor. The general symbol, in broad sense, represents all kinds of components. In addition, it can also indicate a specific component without additional information or function, such as general resistor, capacitor, etc.

(3) Detail symbols. A detail symbol represents a specific electrical component, which is derived from a combination of basic symbols, general symbols, physical symbols, and literal symbols. For example, ⊛ is a general symbol of the indicating instrument, when it is used to represent the type and characteristics of current and voltage of the instrument, the "$*$" is replaced with "A" and "V", then it becomes a detail symbol. Ⓐ represents an ammeter, and Ⓥ represents a voltmeter.

212 Automobile Electrical Equipment Maintenance

Table 9-1 Common graphics symbols

S/N	Name	Graphic symbol	S/N	Name	Graphic symbol
I . Common basic symbols					
1	Direct current	—	6	Neutral point	N
2	Alternating current	∿	7	Magnetic field	F
3	AC/DC	∿ (with bar)	8	Ground	⏚
4	Positive electrode	+	9	Alternator output connector	B
5	Negative electrode	—	10	Magnetic field diode output	D+
II . Connection of wire terminals and wires					
11	Contact	●	17	A electrode of the plug	—
12	Terminal	○	18	Plug and socket	—<
13	Connection of wires	—○-○—	19	Multi-electrode plug and socket (3-electrode)	(3 plugs)
14	Branch connection of wires	⊤	20	Connected connector	—◻—
15	Cross connection of wires	+	21	Disconnected connector	(disconnected)
16	A electrode of a socket	—⊂	22	Shielded wire	—⊖—
III . Contact switches					
23	Make(normally open)contact		32	Pull operation	⊐- -
24	Break(normally closed)contact		33	Rotary operation	⌐- -
25	Contact first open and then closed		34	Push operation	E- -
26	Intermediate disconnected two-way contact		35	General mechanical operation	○- -
27	Double make contact		36	Key operation	△- -
28	Double break contact		37	Thermal actuator operation	⌐- -
29	Single-break double-make contact		38	Temperature control	[t]- -
30	Double-break single-make contact		39	Pressure control	[P]- -
31	Manual control in a general case	⊢- —	40	Brake pressure control	[BP]- - - -

Item IX   Analysis of Circuit Diagram of Automobile Electrical System   **213**

S/N	Name	Graphic symbol	S/N	Name	Graphic symbol
41	Liquid level control		52	Thermal switch make contact	
42	Cam control		53	Thermal switch break contact	
43	Linkage switch		54	Thermal automatic switch break contact	
44	General symbol of a manual switch.		55	Thermal relay contact	
45	Positioning switch (non-automatic reset)		56	Rotary multi-gear switch position	
46	Button switch		57	Push-pull multi-gear switch position	
47	Button switch can be positioned		58	Key switch(all position)	
48	Pull switch		59	Multi-gear switch, ignition, starting switch, instantaneous position is 2, which can automatically return to 1 (that is, gear 2 can not be located)	
49	Rotary, knob switch				
50	Level control switch				
51	Oil filter alarm switch		60	Throttle switch	

Ⅳ. Electrical components

S/N	Name	Graphic symbol	S/N	Name	Graphic symbol
61	Resistor		67	Sliding contact potentiometer	
62	Variable resistor		68	Instrument lighting dimming resistor	
63	Piezo-resistor		69	Photosensitive resistor	
64	Thermistor		70	Heating element; electric plug	
65	Slide line rheostat		71	Capacitor	
66	Shunt		72	Variable capacitor	

Continued

S/N	Name	Graphic symbol	S/N	Name	Graphic symbol
73	Polar capacitor		87	Fusible wire	
74	Through-core capacitor		88	Circuit breaker	
75	General symbol of a semiconductor diode		89	Permanent magnet	
76	Stabilized voltage diode		90	General symbol of operating device	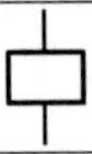
77	Light-emitting diode		91	One winding electromagnet	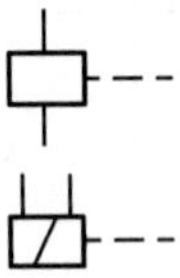
78	Bidirectional diode (variable resistance diode)	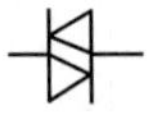			
79	Three-electrode crystal thyristor		92	Two-winding electromagnet	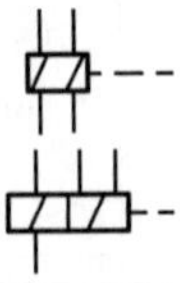
80	Photoelectric diode				
81	PNP type triode		93	Different direction winding electromagnet	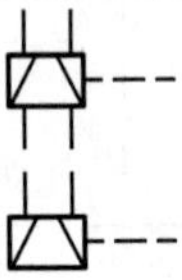
82	Collector nozzle shell triode (NPN)				
83	Piezoelectric crystal with two electrodes		94	Contact normally open relay	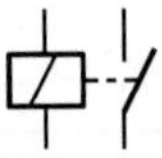
84	Inductor, coil, winding				
85	Core inductor		95	Contact normally closed relay	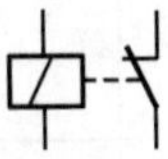
86	Fuse				

V. Meters

S/N	Name	Graphic symbol	S/N	Name	Graphic symbol
96	Indicating instrument	*	103	Tachometer	T
97	Voltmeter	V	104	Thermometer	t°
98	Ammeter	A	105	Fuel gauge	Q
99	Voltmeter and ammeter	A/V	106	Speedometer	V
100	Ohmmeter	Ω	107	Clock	
101	Watt meter	W	108	Digital clock	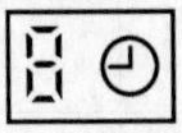
102	Oil pressure gauge	OP			

Continued

S/N	Name	Graphic symbol	S/N	Name	Graphic symbol
VI. Sensors					
109	General symbol of the sensor	 *	116	Air flow sensor	 AF
110	Thermometer sensor	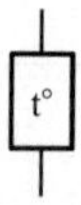 t°	117	Oxygen sensor	 λ
111	Air temperature sensor	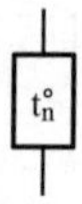 t_n°	118	Knock sensor	 K
112	Water temperature sensor	 t_w°	119	Speed transducer	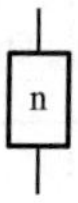 n
113	Fuel gauge sensor	 Q	120	Velocity transducer	 V
114	Oil pressure gauge sensor	 OP	121	Air pressure sensor	 AP
115	Air quality sensor	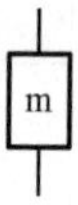 m	122	Brake pressure sensor	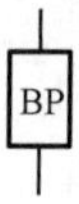 BP
VII. Electrical devices					
123	Lights, signal lights, instrument lights, indicator lights		129	Speaker	
124	Two-filament light		130	Buzzer	
125	Fluorescent light		131	Alarm or electric siren.	
126	Combination light		132	Signal generator	 G
127	Preheating indicator	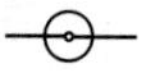	133	Pulse generator	 G
128	Electric horn	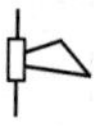	134	Flasher	 G

216 Automobile Electrical Equipment Maintenance

Continued

S/N	Name	Graphic symbol	S/N	Name	Graphic symbol
135	Hall signal generator		153	Thermal relay	
136	Magnetic induction signal generator		154	Intermittent wiper relay	
137	Temperature compensator		155	Anti-theft alarm system	
138	General symbol of solenoid valve		156	General symbol of antenna	
139	Normally open solenoid valve		157	Transmitter	
140	Normally closed solenoid valve		158	Radio set	
141	Electromagnetic clutch		159	Internal communication liaison and music system	
142	Idle speed adjusting device controlled by motor		160	Transceiver	
143	Overvoltage protection device		161	Wireless telephone	
144	Overcurrent protection device		162	General symbol of microphone	
145	Heater(defroster)		163	Ignition coil	
146	Oscillator		164	Distributor	
147	Converter		165	Spark plug	
148	Photoelectric generator		166	Voltage regulator	
149	Air conditioner		167	Speed regulator	
150	Filter		168	Temperature regulator	
151	Voltage regulator		169	Series excitation winding	
152	Smoke igniter		170	Shunt or separately excited winding	

Item IX   Analysis of Circuit Diagram of Automobile Electrical System   **217**

Continued

S/N	Name	Graphic symbol	S/N	Name	Graphic symbol
171	Brush on a collector or commutator.		183	Electric antenna	
172	DC motor		184	DC servo motor	
173	Series excitation DC motor		185	DC generator	
174	Shunt DC motor		186	Star-connected three-phase winding	
175	Permanent magnet DC motor		187	Three-phase winding connected by triangle	
176	Starter(with electromagnetic start)		188	Alternator with star-connected stator winding	
177	Fuel pump motor, washing motor		189	Alternator with triangle-connected stator winding	
178	Transistor electric gasoline pump		190	External voltage regulator and alternator	
179	Heating timer		191	Integral alternator	
180	Electronic ignition unit		192	Battery	
181	Fan motor		193	Battery pack	
182	Wiper motor				

For symbols not specified in the standards, the basic symbol, general symbol and detail symbol given in the standard can be selected, and the combination principle specified can be derived to form the graphic symbol of the complete component or device, but it must be explained in the blank of the drawing. Table 9-2 combines the general symbol of the antenna with the general symbol of the DC motor to form the graphic symbol of the electric antenna.

Table 9-2　An graphic symbol examples of the combination of electric antenna

Graphic symbol	Description
	General symbol of an antenna.
	General symbol of a DC motor.
	Derived symbol of a electric antenna

(4) Principles for the use of graphic symbols.

① First of all, the preferred type is selected.

② When the condition is satisfied, the simplest form is adopted first, but the graphic symbol must be complete.

③ In the same circuit diagram, the same graphic symbol is used in the same form.

④ Symbol orientation is not fixed, and on the premise that it does not change the symbol meaning, the symbol may be rotated or placed by image according to the needs of the layout of the diagram, but words and orientations must not be inverted.

⑤ Generally, there is no terminal code in the graphic symbols. If the terminal code is a part of the symbol, the terminal code must be drawn.

⑥ A wire symbol can be represented by lines of different widths, for example, a power supply line (main circuit) can be represented by a thick solid line, and a control and protection line (auxiliary circuit) can be represented by a thin solid line.

⑦ Generally, the connection line is not a part of the graphic symbol, and the orientation can be arranged according to the actual needs.

⑧ The meaning of a symbol is determined by its form and can be reduced or magnified as needed.

⑨ A graphic symbol represents a normal state in which there is no voltage or external force.

⑩ The letter and physical symbols in a graphic symbol shall be regarded as part of the graphic symbol. When the use of these symbols can not satisfy the annotation, it can be supplemented in accordance with the relevant provisions.

If the specified graphic symbol is not used in the circuit diagram, it must be explained.

2. Switch and warning light sign

The automobile dashboard and the steering column are usually equipped with many switches, alarm lights and indicator lights. To distinguish functions, a variety of graphic symbols are often engraved on the surface, and some imported vehicles are represented in English letters. These graphic signs are commonly used internationally, most of them are figurative and concise, which we can know their function by only glancing it.

To avoid distracting the driver, the indicator lights and alarm lights are not on when the system they indicate is working properly. When the system is not working properly, the indicator lights and alarm lights that represent the working conditions of the system are on. The alarm light is red usually, indicating that the situation is urgent and needs timely maintenance, such as brake pressure low alarm light, engine overheat alarm light, oil brake indicator light and so on. There are also indicator lights which belong to normal working condition, such as steering light (green), headlight (blue).

The indicator lights and the alarm lights mostly use the small power light bulbs (1～3.5W), also use the light-emitting diodes (adding the suitable current limiting resistor). The indicator lights and the alarm lights do not light up under normal working conditions. If the light bulb is damaged, it will also cause illusions. Therefore, when the ignition switch is switched on and the engine is not started, most of the indicator lights and the alarm lights can be checked, such as charging indicator light, oil pressure alarm light, SRS indicator light, etc. Some need to use special inspection switch and add a lot of isolation diodes to

Item IX   Analysis of Circuit Diagram of Automobile Electrical System   **219**

check.

See Table 9-3 for some switches and warning lights on the automobile.

Table 9-3 Switch and alarm light signs

S/N	Graphic or letter symbol	Description	S/N	Graphic or letter symbol	Description
1		Ignition switch(4 gears): Lock the steering wheel 0-OFF or(S) Accessory 1-ACC or(A) Ignition,instrument 2-IGN or(M) Start 3-START or(D)	6		Choke closing indication: when the automobile starts under a low temperature, the choke is closed,and the indicator light is on. The choke should be opened in time after starting, otherwise the engine will be black smoke
2		Ignition switch(3 gears): Lock 0-OFF or(S) Work 1-ON or MAR Start 2-START or AVV	7		The light is on when the throttle is closed
3		Power switch for a diesel automobile: 0-OFF disconnect 1-ON connect 2-START start 3-ACC Accessory 4-PREHEAT Preheat	8	VOLT AMP CHARGE 电压(伏特)表 电源(安培)表	Battery charging indicator light:when the generator does not produce electricity, the light is on;when the generator produces electricity normally, the light is off.
4		Ignition switch(5 gears): 0-LOCK lock the steering wheel 1-OFF disconnect 2-ACC Accessory 3-ON connect 4-START preheat	9	WATER OVER HEAT	Water temperature alarm light: when the coolant temperature is too high,the alarm light is on
5	CHECK	Engine fault code display light (self-diagnosis): when electronic-controlled engine fuel injection and ignition sensor and computer are out of order, the light is on, the fault code can be tuned out by a person or an instrument, to find out the fault quickly	10	OIL-P	Oil pressure alarm light: The light will be on when the oil pressure is too low

Continued

S/N	Graphic or letter symbol	Description	S/N	Graphic or letter symbol	Description
11	 FUEL	Fuel deficiency alarm light; when the fuel is insufficient, the alarm light will be on	21	 kPa	Vacuum indicator light
12	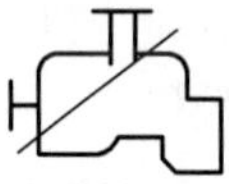	Diesel engine stop oil supply (flameout) pull rod (button) sign	22	SRS	Airbag indicator light
13	 (P) PKB	Stop brake indicator light; The light will be on when the hand brake is working	23	TRAC	Traction control indicator light
14	 (!) BRAKE AIR	Low brake gas pressure alarm; when the brake fluid level is low, the brake system failure alarm light will be on	24	CRUISE	Cruise indicator light; when the device works, the light will be on and the fault code will be displayed when there is a fault
15	r/min RPM	Engine tachometer	25	AIR SUSP	Electronic adjusted air suspension indicator light
16	km/h	Speedometer	26	O/D OFF	O/D OFF//light will be on when the overspeed gear is exited
17	20:08	Digital display clock	27	VOLT	Voltmeter
18	 COOLANT LEVEL WATER LEVEL	Coolant level indicator light; When the level of the cooling system is below the specified value, the alarm light is on	28	EXP TEMP	Too high exhaust temperature alarm
19	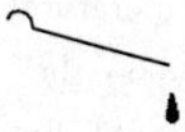	Oil level indicator light; when the engine oil quantity is less than the specified value, the alarm light is on	29		Steering light indicator light
20	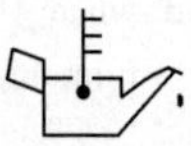	High oil temperature alarm light; when the oil temperature exceeds the specified value, the alarm light is on	30		Emergency alarm indicator light; When an automobile is in a traffic accident and calls for help or need other vehicles to avoid the situation, the left and right steering lights should flash at the same time

Item IX   Analysis of Circuit Diagram of Automobile Electrical System

Continued

S/N	Graphic or letter symbol	Description	S/N	Graphic or letter symbol	Description
31	BEAM	Headlight high beam indicator light	41	PASS / HI / L / R	Steering light and overlight switch: L-Left Steering; R-Right Steering; PASS-Overtaking; HI-High Beam; LO-Locating Intermediate (Low Beam)
32		Headlight low beam indicator light			
33		Light switch indicator light: It can be connected with clearance light, taillight, instrument, license plate light, etc.	42		Rotating light marks: rotating warning light switch sign of the roof of a police automobile, ambulance, fire truck
34		Automobile clearance light switch indication	43	BELT	Seat belt indicator light: When the ignition switch is switched on and the seat belt is not fastened, the light is on or accompanied by a buzzer
35		Stop brake light switch indication; When the hand brake works, the indicator light will be on	44	HEAT / GLOW	Electric heating plug indicator light; when starting at room temperature, it will be on for 0.3s, the automobile can be started directly; before starting at low temperature, it will be on for 3.5s, which means " waiting for preheating", and when the light is off, the automobile can be started.
36		Rear fog light switch indicator light			
37		Front fog light switch indicator light			
38	TEST	Check switch for the light bulbs of indicator lights and alarm lights	45	GLOW	Preheating plug (electric or flame preheating plug) indicator light; when starting at room temperature, it will be on for 0.3s, the automobile can be started directly; before starting at low temperature, it will be on for 3.5s, which means " waiting for preheating", and when the light is off, the automobile can be started.
39	R	Reversing light switch indication			
40		Indoor light (ceiling light) switch indication			

Item IX Analysis of Circuit Diagram of Automobile Electrical System   223

Continued

S/N	Graphic or letter symbol	Description	S/N	Graphic or letter symbol	Description
46	DIFF LOCK	Differential lock chain indicator light; it must be taken off when the automobile turns	53	(symbol)	Distributor front bridge access indicator light; When the off-road vehicle is fully driven, the light will be on
47	(symbol)	Exhaust brake indicator light; When the automobile goes down a long slope, plug the exhaust pipe and use the engine resistance to slow down the automobile, step on the clutch and it will be automatically released when refueling	54	KPa	Air filter blocking indicator light
48	EXH-BRAKE	Exhaust brake indicator light; When the automobile goes down a long slope, plug the exhaust pipe and use the engine resistance to slow down the automobile, step on the clutch and it will be automatically released when refueling	55	(symbol)	Hydraulic torque converter switch indicator light
			56	(symbol)	Excess water alarm light for diesel oil strainer
			57	HORN	horn button mark
49	(symbol)	Battery level indicator light	58	(symbol)	Smoke lighter sign; Press the cigarette lighter handle to turn on the circuit, the heating body burning red (about a few seconds) automatically pops out to light a cigarette
50	(symbol)	Trailer brake indicator light			
51	(symbol)	Brake shoe wear over-limit alarm light	59	(symbol)	Engine hood opening handle indication
52	ABS	Anti-lock brake indicator light; When the key is on at the start gear or the speed is under 5~10km/h, the light will be on; when the ABS is out of order, the alarm light will be on and the fault code can be displayed (with tools)	60	TRUNK	Luggage hatch cover open handle or electric button indication
			61	DOOR	Alarm light for the not closed door; set this light on the dashboard
			62	(symbol)	Cushion heating indicator light

Continued

S/N	Graphic or letter symbol	Description	S/N	Graphic or letter symbol	Description
63		Indoor light door control gear: When the door is closed, the indoor lights will be off. In addition, there are hand-controlled long time bright gear(ON) and disconnection gear(OFF)	72		Head light wiper washing switch indication
			73		Window glass lift switch: UP; DOWN
64	P R N D 2 L	Automatic transmission gear indicator light	74	A/C	Air conditioning system refrigeration compressor opening indication
			75	FAN	Air conditioning system blower indication
65	ECTPWR	Electronic-controlled automatic transmission has 2 kinds of shift modes which have been programmed: That is, Normal mode (Normal) and Power mode (Power). When power mode is selected by switch, the indicator light will be on.	76	VENT	Air conditioning system ventilation blower (FACE) gear
			77	HEAT	Air conditioning system heating(blowing foot)gear
66		The heater switch indicates, the defrost line indicator light and the switch indication: usually heated by rear-window toner	78	BI-LEVEL	Air-conditioning system double-layer (upper cold and lower heat)gear
67		Windshield wiper indication	79	DEF-HEAT	Air conditioning system defrosting and heating (blowing feet)gear
68	WASHER	Windshield washing switch indication	80	DEF	Windshield defrosting and defogging indication
69		Windshield wiper washing switch indication	81	Outside	Instruction for opening outside fresh air circulation outlet (FREESH)
70		Rear window wiper indicator light and switch sign	82	Inside	Instruction for opening inside fresh air circulation outlet (REC)
71		Rear window washing switch indication			

224 Automobile Electrical Equipment Maintenance

Continued

S/N	Graphic or letter symbol	Description	S/N	Graphic or letter symbol	Description
83		Cab Lock: When the tilting cab returns position, it does not reach the required locking state, the alarm light will be on	86		Sign of up and down adjustment and left and right adjustment switch of the rear-view mirror
84	EXH TEMP	The light will be on when the exhaust temperature exceeds a certain limit	87	AIR MPa	Air pressure gauge: It is commonly used in pneumatic brake system for double-line air pressure indication
85		Rear-view mirror heating indication	88		Air filter blocking signal alarm light

3. Letter symbol

The letter symbol is composed of the type (name) letter code and the function (status, feature) letter code of the electrical devices, devices and components. For the preparation of technical documents in the field of electrical technology, it may also be marked on or near electrical devices, devices and components to indicate the names, functions, status and characteristics of the electrical devices, devices and components. In addition, it can be used in combination with basic graphics symbols and general graphics symbols to derive new graphics symbols.

There are two kinds of letter symbols: basic letter symbols and auxiliary letter symbols. The basic letter symbols are divided into one letter symbol s and two letter symbols.

(1) Basic letter symbols.

① One-letter symbols. One letter symbols divide electrical devices, devices and components into 23 categories by the Latin alphabets, each of which is represented by a special one letter symbol, such as "C" for capacitors, "R" for resistors, etc.

② Two-letter symbols. A two-letter symbol is composed of a one letter symbol representing a category and another letter, and its combination shall be listed by the letter symbol in the front followed by another letter, such as "R" for resistance, "RP" for potentiometer, "RT" for thermistor; "G" for power supply, engine, generator, "GB" for battery, "GS" for synchronous generator, generator, "GA" for asynchronous generator.

(2) Auxiliary letter symbols. Auxiliary letter symbols represent the functions, status, and characteristics of electrical devices, devices, components and circuits. For example, "SYN" means synchronization, "L" means restriction left or low, "RD" means red, "ON" means closure, "OFF" means disconnection, and so on.

(3) Rules for the use of letter symbols.

① One letter symbols should be preferred.

② Only when the use of one letter symbols can not meet the requirements, it is necessary to further divide the categories, then the two letter symbols are adopted to describe the electrical devices, devices and components in more detailed and more specific way. For ex-

ample, "F" represents protective devices, "FU" represents a fuse, and "FV" represents a voltage-limiting protection device.

③ Auxiliary letter symbols can also be placed at the back of a single-letter symbol representing a category, such as "ST" for starting, "DC" for direct current, and "AC" for alternating current. In order to simplify the letter symbol, if the auxiliary letter symbol is composed of 2 letters, it is allowed to combine only its first letter, such as "MS" for synchronous motor, and "S" in "MS" for the first letter of the auxiliary letter symbol "SYN" (synchronous). Auxiliary letter symbol can also be used separately, such as "QN" for connection, "N" for neutral line, "E" for ground, "PE" for protection ground, etc.

4. Reading of a graphic symbol or letter symbol

For a basic component, its graphic symbol is the same as its letter symbol, such as resistor, capacitor, lighting, battery, and so on.

At present, there is no unified standard of graphic symbols and letter symbols for automobile electrical devices in the world. The graphic symbols and the letter symbols used by various automobile manufacturers are different from the standard ones. This makes it difficult to read the circuit diagrams, but the basic structure of the graphic symbols is similar. So long as we understand their differences, we can avoid reading errors. The following examples illustrate the differences between different models in the automobile circuit diagram when representing the graphic symbols of the same component.

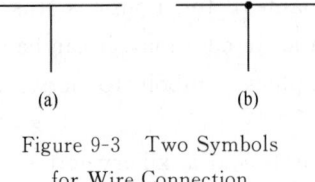

(a)   (b)

Figure 9-3   Two Symbols
for Wire Connection

Figure 9-3 shows two forms of wire connection. Shanghai Santana and Nanjing lveco take the form shown in Figure 9-3(a), while Citroen Fukang and Tianjin Xiali take the form shown in Figure 9-3(b).

Automobiles are equipped with silicon rectifier generators and voltage regulators, some with built-in, some with external, even the same structure, different models may use different circuit graphic symbols.

Figure 9-4 shows the graphic symbol for the silicon rectifier generator installed in the Fukang; Figure 9-5 shows the graphic symbol for the silicon rectifier generator installed in the Xiali (as specified in the national standard).

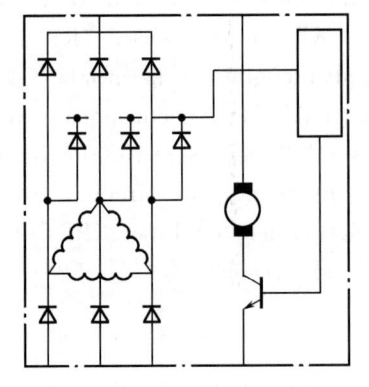

Figure 9-4   Graphic Symbol of the Silicon
Rectifier Generator Installed in Fukang

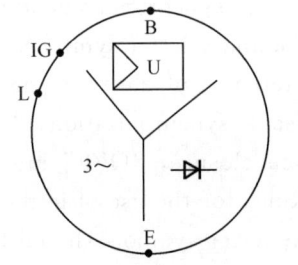

Figure 9-5   Graphic Symbol of the Silicon
Rectifier Generator Installed in Xiali

Nowadays, automobiles are equipped with starter for starting engines, and the structures of small and medium-sized starters are basically the same, but in the circuit diagram of different models, the symbols used are very different. Figure 9-6 is a graphic symbol for the starter of Tianjin Xiali; Figure 9-7 is a graphic symbol for the starter of Fukang.

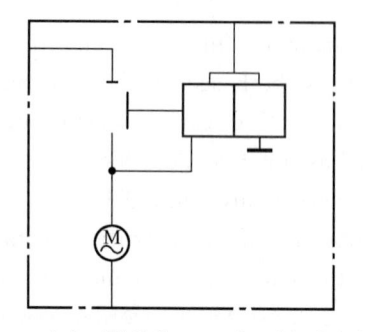

Figure 9-6   Xiali Starter Graphic Symbol

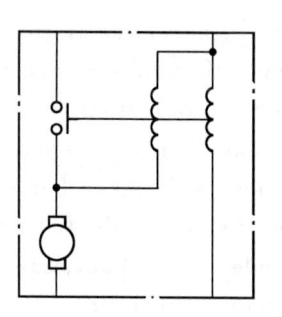

Figure 9-7   Fukang Starter Graphic Symbol

In many automobiles, there are 3-gear 4-terminal ignition switches, which are represented by box symbols. There are two symbols for the terminals and the gears, as shown in Figure 9-8; Shanghai Santana uses another symbol which is quite different from the previous two, as shown in Figure 9-9.

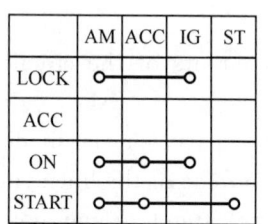

Figure 9-8   Spark Switch Graphic Symbol

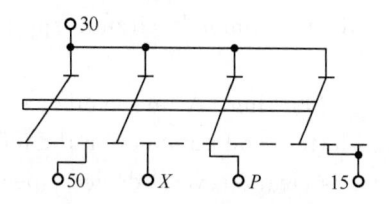

Figure 9-9   Shanghai Santana Spark Switch Graphic Symbol

From the above examples, we can see that there is no unified standard for the graphic symbols of automobile circuit at present. Most of the domestic automobile manufacturers adopt the industrial standards of electrical technology, while most of the joint-venture automobile manufacturers follow the original standards of foreign countries. Therefore, we should sum up our experience in the process of reading, and find out the similarities and differences of the graphic symbols used in different circuits, which can improve our speed of reading.

(Ⅲ) Key points for drawing and reading automobile circuits

1. Key points for drawing and reading the schematic diagram of automobile circuits

(1) The principle of drawing the schematic diagram of the automobile circuits.

① Method of representation of components. An important feature of the circuit diagram is that the components are represented by the graphic symbols specified in the national standard.

To facilitate the analysis and inspection of the circuit, in addition to the use of graphic symbols to represent the components in the circuit diagram, we should also indicate the item

code next to the graphic symbols. If necessary, we should also indicate the main technical parameters of the component next to the graphic symbols.

② The arrangement of graphic symbols. In the electrical system, there are a large number of components driving parts and driven parts using mechanical connection, such as relays, button switches, photoelectric couplers, etc.

③ The arrangement of circuits and wires. The arrangement of the circuit requires a clear graphic effect. The arrangement of each circuit must be based on the principle of left-to-right and top-to-bottom, and the marking method, using direct line, without crossing point, without changing the direction, should be used as much as possible.

④ Boundary lines and borders. The parts of the circuit are limited by dotted lines or border lines to indicate the functional or structural properties of the instrument components. In automobile electrical devices, a dotted line is used to indicate a non-conductive border in an instrument or an electrical appliance. This diagram may not be in accordance with a shell or may not be used to indicate an instrument ground wire.

⑤ Section identification. Section identifiers are marked on the lower edge of the circuit diagram, which is helpful to find the circuit parts more conveniently. There are three possible ways of marking.

a. Mark from left to right with continuous numbers at the same distance.

b. Mark the contents of the circuit section.

c. Combine the above two methods.

Most automobile circuits specify the contents of the circuit section in the circuit diagram.

⑥ Marking. A line symbol in a device, part, or circuit diagram can be annotated by using letters and numbers on the left or lower side of the line symbol. If the definition of the device is clear, several devices specified in the standard may not be annotated.

(2) Key points for reading the schematic diagram of the automobile circuit.

The main features of the circuit schematic diagram are as follows.

① It has a complete concept of the whole automobile circuit. It is not only a whole automobile circuit diagram, but also a local circuit diagram which is connected with each other.

② The concept of high and low potential is established on the diagram. The negative electrode ground potential is the lowest, expressed by the bottom wire in the diagram; the positive electrode live wire potential is the highest, expressed by the top wire. The current flow is basically from top to bottom.

③ The zigzag and intersection of wires should be minimized as much as possible. The layout should be reasonable, the diagram should be concise and clear, and the graphic symbol takes into account the shape and internal structure of the components, which is easy to analyze.

④ The interrelation of the circuit system is clear.

The key points for reading the schematic diagram of the automobile circuit are as follows.

① We should read the illustration carefully for several times. The illustration indicates the names of all electrical devices on the automobile and their digital codes. Through reading the illustration, we can preliminarily understand which electrical devices are installed on

the automobile, and then find out the electrical devices in the circuit diagram through the digital codes of electrical devices, and then further find the connection, control relationship. In this way, we can understand the characteristics and composition of the automobile circuit.

② We should keep electrical graphic symbols in mind. The automobile circuit diagram uses the electrical graphic symbol to express its composition and working principle. Therefore, it is necessary to keep in mind the meaning of the electrical graphic symbol to understand the schematic diagram of the circuit.

③ We should memorize the marking symbol of the circuit. To facilitate the drawing and reading of automobile circuit diagrams, some electrical devices or their terminals are given with different marking codes. For example, "B" or "+" is used for the terminal connected to the power supply, "SW" is used for the terminal connected to the ignition switch, "S" is used for the terminal connected to the starter, "L" is used for the terminal connected to the light, "N" is used for the neutral point terminal of the generator, and "F" is used for the magnetic field terminal of the generator, "D+" is used for the output terminal of the excitation voltage and "B+" is used for the output terminal of the generator armature.

④ We should remember the loop principle firmly. Any complete circuit consists of a power supply, a fuse, a switch, electrical devices, wires, etc. The current flow must start from the positive electrode of the power supply, go through the fuse, switch, wire and then to the electric devices, and then go through the wire or ground to the negative electrode of the power supply to form the circuit, then this circuit is correct, otherwise it is read wrong or check wrong.

We can follow the current flow direction of the circuit, starting from the positive electrode of the power supply, to the electric devices, switch, back to the negative electrode of the power supply; we can also follow the reverse direction of the current of the circuit, starting from the negative electrode of the power supply (ground), through the electric devices, switch, returning to the positive electrode of the power supply; we can also start from the electric devices, find its control switch, connection, control unit in turn, then arrive at the positive electrode of the power supply and ground (or the negative electrode of the power supply). In particular, when querying less familiar circuit, the latter is more convenient than the former. In practical application, we can choose different train of thought based on the concrete circuit. But one point is worth noting: With the wide application of electronic control technology in automobile, most circuits have both main circuit and control circuit. When reading, the two circuits should considered.

⑤ We should remember the polarity of the ground. All circuits of automobile electric appliances are negative electrode ground.

⑥ We should grasp the function of various switches in the circuit diagrams. For a multi-layer multi-gear terminal switch, the function of each layer and each gear should be analyzed step by step according to the layer, the gear and the terminal. Some electric devices are controlled by more than two single-gear switches (or relays), some by more than two multi-gear switches, the working state is more complex. When there are more switch terminals, firstly, grab one or two terminals from the power supply, then analyze which gear the electric device connected with other terminals is located one by one to find out the control rela-

tionship.

For the combination switch, the actual circuits are centralized, and in the circuit diagrams, they are drawn in the respective local circuits according to the function. We should carefully read it when in such case.

⑦ We should master the initial state of the switch and relay. In the circuit diagram, all kinds of switches and relays are drawn according to the initial state, that is, the button is not pressed, the switch is not connected, the relay coil is not energized, the contact is not closed (normally open contact) or not opened (normally closed contact), this state is called the original state. When reading a diagram, we can not totally analyze it according to the original state, otherwise it is difficult to understand the working principle of the circuit, because most of the electric devices change the circuit through the change of the switch button relay contact, and then realize different circuit functions. Therefore, the analysis of working state must be carried out. For example, a wiper achieves intermittent low-speed high-speed wiper function by changing the wiper switch gear, and the three working states of the circuit must be turned on.

⑧ We should master the position of the electrical devices in the circuit diagram. In the automobile electrical system, there are a large number of electrical devices are electromechanical such as various relays, as well as multi-layer multi-gear switch. When representing some electrical devices in the circuit diagram, to make the drawing simple and easy to read, some manufactures use the centralized representation, semi-centralized representation, and separate representation to reflect the connection of the circuit according to the actual situation.

We should remember the interrelationships between local circuits. The whole automobile circuit consists of power supply circuit, charging circuit, ignition circuit, starting circuit, lighting circuit, auxiliary circuit and so on. From the whole automobile circuit, each local circuit except the shared power circuit, is relatively independent. But there is also an inherent connection between them. Therefore, when reading, it is necessary to be familiar with not only the composition, working process and current flow path of each local circuit, but also the connection and interaction between each local circuit. This is a necessary condition to quickly locate the fault location and troubleshoot it.

⑨ We should be good at consulting and finding information. Due to the appearance of new automobile electrical devices and their use in the automobile, the automobile circuit diagram changes greatly. For those who do not understand the circuit, they should be good at consulting relevant personnel, good at finding information, until they understand.

⑩ We should start from simple circuits firstly. Some local circuits of some automobile circuit diagram may be more complex, we can not understand at first, we can temporarily put them away. After we understand other local circuits, we can further read them by combining the circuit diagrams understood with the relevant information related to the circuits.

⑪ We should browse the whole diagram and frame each system. To understand the automobile circuit diagram, we must first master the basic functions and electrical characteristics of each electrical component that makes up the circuit diagram. On the basis of approximately mastering the basic principles of the whole automobile circuit, a separate electrical

system can be framed so that we can easily grasp the main functions and features of each part.

When framing each system, we should neither miss the components of each system nor draw the components of other systems. The rule is that only the power supply and the total switch are shared by electrical systems, and any other system should be a complete and independent electrical circuit, that is, including power supply, fuse, switch, electric appliance, wire, etc. And the circuit is from the positive electrode of the power supply through the wire, fuse, switch to the electrical appliance, ground, and finally to the negative electrode of the power supply, otherwise the system diagram framed is not correct.

2. Key points for drawing and reading the automobile wire diagram

(1) Principles for the drawing of automobile wire diagrams. The wire diagram of automobile circuit pays more attention to the actual position of each electrical device on the automobile in drawing method. Although it is difficult to read, as long as we master the methods, we can read the drawing, and we can change the wire diagram into the circuit diagram. The features of the wire diagram are: because the shape and the actual position of the electrical device are the same as the original automobile, when looking for the wire, the branch in the wire and the contact are easy to be found out. The direction of the wire is basically same as the actual direction of the wire harness on the automobile.

The drawing principle of the wire diagram is as follows.

① The components, parts, assembly, devices and other items in the wiring diagram are represented by their simplified shapes (such as circles, squares, and rectangles), and are often represented by circular symbols when necessary for the convenience of reading.

② In the wire diagram, the terminal is represented by the terminal symbol.

③ The wire is indicated by a continuous line or a broken line. The continuous line is a continuous solid line used to indicate the actual existence of a wire between the terminals; The broken line is a broken solid line used to indicate the actual existence of a wire between the terminals and to indicate the direction at the broken place.

(2) Key points for reading the automobile wire diagram.

① We should know the structure and working principle of the electrical device used in this automobile, and be clear about the specification of the electrical device.

② We should identify the name and quantity of all the electrical device in the automobile and its actual installation position on the automobile by reading.

③ We should identify the number and name of the terminals of each type of electrical device, and understand the practical significance of each terminal by reading.

The reading of the wiring diagram can be carried out in three stages: browsing, drawing and sorting out.

3. Key points for drawing and reading automobile wire harness diagram

(1) The principle of drawing the automobile wire harness diagram. The automobile wire harness diagram is mainly in the form of wire harness, with fewer lines on the diagram, and the expression of the connection between the parts is the main content. The drawing principles of the wire harness diagram are as follows.

① The automobile wire harness diagram is composed of several wire harnesses, including main wire harness and auxiliary wire harness. The wire harness diagram shows how

Item IX Analysis of Circuit Diagram of Automobile Electrical System **231**

many branches there are on each wire harness, how many wires there are on each branch, and the colors and stripes of the wires.

② The number of electrical appliances on the automobile is large and complex. To make the wiring accurate, each connection point is marked with the code of the terminal.

③ The length of the wire harness includes the total length of the wire harness, the length of each branch and the distance between the ends of the wires.

④ Because there are many wire harnesses, the wire harness and the wire harness, the branch and the wire harness, the branch and the electrical devices are all connected through the plug-in device, we should indicate the number of the wires on the plug-in device, the specific position of each wire in the plug-in device hole, the specific shape of the plug-in device on the diagram.

(2) Key points of reading the automobile wire harness diagram. A wire harness diagram is a branch chart drawn by the automobile manufacturer after it arranges the actual wires on an automobile and collect the relevant wires together to form a bundle. The characteristics of the wire harness diagram are as follows: In the diagram, the serial number of each wire, the name of the electrical appliance connected and the name of the terminal, the serial number of each plug and socket are indicated. As long as the installation operator connects the wires or the plug-in device to the corresponding electrical terminal or connector according to the serial number indicated on the diagram, the installation of the whole automobile wire is completed. The wiring is simple and convenient for installation and maintenance, but it cannot indicate the direction of the wire.

Key points for reading the wire harness diagram are as follows.

① To identify the number of the wire harnesses on the automobile, the name of each wire harness and the actual location of each wire harness on the automobile.

② To identify the branches on each wire harness leading to which electrical device in the automobile, how many wires each branch has, their colors and labels, and which terminals they connect to.

③ To identify which plug-in devices there are and which plug-in devices on the electrical devices they should be connected to.

The reading of the wire harness is basically same as that of the wire diagram.

(Ⅳ) Common knowledge of automobile circuit overhaul

1. Fault diagnosis and overhaul process of automobile circuit

The fault diagnosis and overhaul for the automobile circuit usually have the following steps. The process is shown in Figure 9-10.

(1) To hear the customer's description of the fault. To know faults phenomena and situations and circumstances in the event of the fault in detail, including the following information: model, climatic condition, symptom of fault, operating condition, maintenance condition and whether added other accessories after purchasing it.

(2) To identify symptoms of the fault. To run the system and carry out road tests if necessary. To check to see if the customer's response is true, and pay attention to the post-run phenomena. If the fault can not be reproduced, the fault simulation experiment can be carried out.

(3) To read the circuit of the system and analyze the principle of the related circuit. To read the circuit and the related data carefully, to draw the system circuit related to the fault phenomena, to make clear the working principle of the circuit and the working current direction of the system, to make the correlation analysis of the system circuit to reduce the fault diagnosis scope.

(4) To analyze the causes of the fault. The possible causes of the fault should be analyzed in detail. According to theoretical analysis and working experience, the possible causes of the fault should be checked from easy to difficult.

(5) To carry out detailed diagnosis and repair of the circuit. To select the appropriate diagnostic testing devices and tools to diagnose the fault point and repair it.

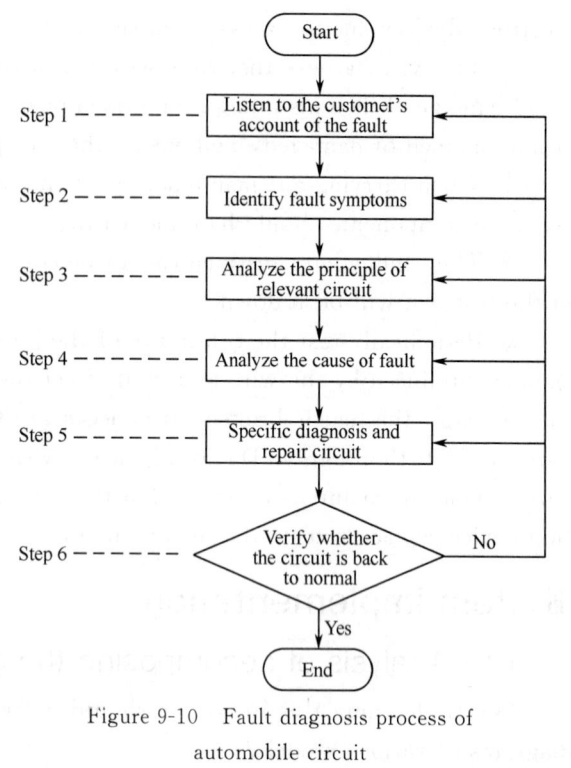

Figure 9-10　Fault diagnosis process of automobile circuit

(6) To verify whether the circuit is returned to normal. After the circuit is overhauled, run the system in all modes to ensure that the system is operating normally under all operating conditions and that no new faults are caused during diagnosis and repair.

2. Precautions for automobile circuit overhaul

The first principle of overhauling the automobile circuit overhaul is not to replace wires, electrical devices and connect wires at will, which may damage the automobile or cause fire due to short circuit or overload. At the same time, we should pay attention to the following matters.

① When disassembling the battery, we should first remove the negative electrode cable of the battery. When installing the battery and when disassembling or installing the battery cable, we should make sure that the ignition switch or other switches have been closed. Do not reverse the polarity of the battery.

② To avoid damaging the triode by the current overload, an ohmmeter and the low resistance ohms gear of the multimeter under $R \times 100$ should be used for detection.

③ When removing and installing components, power should be cut off. If there is no special instructions, the distance of the component pin to the welding point should be more than 10mm, so as to avoid electric soldering iron ironing components, and it is suitable to use an electric soldering iron with constant temperature or power less than 75W.

④ The wire harness near the vibrating part shall be fixed with a clip, and the slack part shall be tightened so as not to cause the wire harness to come into contact with other parts due to the vibration.

⑤ Electrical devices should be lightly held or placed, so as not to cause damage to the

Item IX　Analysis of Circuit Diagram of Automobile Electrical System　**233**

electrical devices due to excessive impact load.

⑥ The wire harness that rubs with sharp edge should be wound with adhesive tape to avoid damage. When installing it at a fixed position, we should ensure that the wire harness is not clamped or damaged, and ensure that the plug-in device is firmly connected.

⑦ When carrying out maintenance, if the temperature exceeds 80℃, the temperature-sensitive components should be removed first.

⑧ The conductivity test pen cannot be connected to a live circuit, otherwise, the light in the test pen will burn down.

⑨ Periodically test the continuity of the jumper wire itself with an ohmmeter. The resistance produced by the wire joint will affect the correctness of the fault diagnosis.

⑩ After the fuse is broken, it is necessary to find out the cause of the fault and eliminate the fault thoroughly. Do not replace it with a fuse with a higher specification rating. Be sure to read the maintenance manual or the user manual, and confirm that the circuit protection device replaced meets the requirements.

Ⅲ. Item Implementation

(Ⅰ) Analysis of decomposing the general automobile circuit diagram

(1) By learning this item, we should be capable of decomposing and analyzing circuit diagrams of various models.

(2) The item shall have a general automobile circuit diagram, a multimeter, a drawing tool and a common circuit detection tool, etc.

(Ⅱ) Implementation steps

1. Know the symbolic meaning in VW circuit diagram

The symbolic meanings in the VW circuit diagram are shown in Table 9-4.

Table 9-4　Symbolic meaning in VW circuit diagram

S/N	Graphic or letter symbol	Description	S/N	Graphic or letter symbol	Description
1		Fuse	4		Dynamo
2		Battery	5		Ignition coil
3		Starter	6		Distributor(mechanical)

Continued

S/N	Graphic or letter symbol	Description	S/N	Graphic or letter symbol	Description
7		Distributor(electronic)	19		Variable resistor
8		Spark plug	20		Thermistor
9		Heater heating resistor	21		Resistor
10		Solenoid valve	22		Thermal time control valve
11		Motor	23		Relay
12		Two-speed wiper motor	24		Relay(electronic control type)
13		Manual switch	25		Warm air regulator additional air valve
14		Thermal switch			
15		Manual button switch	26		Diode
16		Mechanical control switch	27		Voltage-regulator tube
17		Pressure switch	28		Light-emitting diode
18		Manual multi-gear switch	29		Pointer instrument

Item IX   Analysis of Circuit Diagram of Automobile Electrical System   **235**

Continued

S/N	Graphic or letter symbol	Description	S/N	Graphic or letter symbol	Description
30		Electronic controller	42	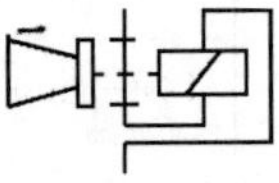	Horn
31		Pointer clock	43		Plug-in
32	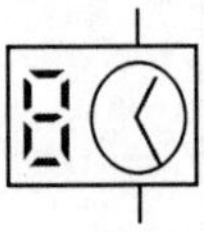	Digital clock	44		Multi-hole plug-in
33	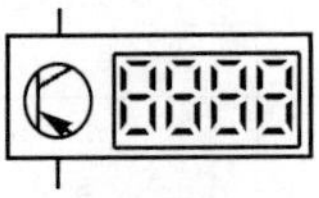	Multi-function display	45		Wire distributor
34	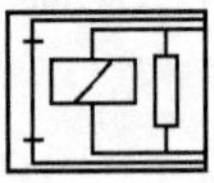	Buzzer	46		Detachable wire connection
35	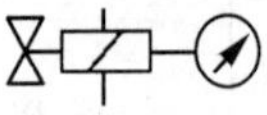	Fuel indicator	47		Non-detachable wire connection
36	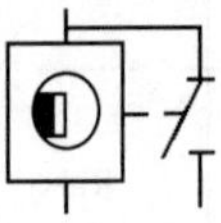	Velocity transducer	48		Connection within a component
37		Incandescent light	49		Resistance wire
38		Double filament incandescent light			
39		Interior light	50	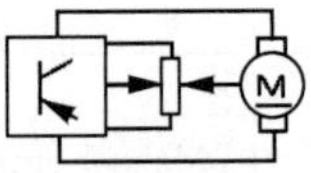	Light regulating motor
40	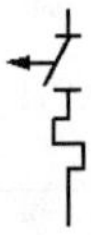	Cigarette lighter	51	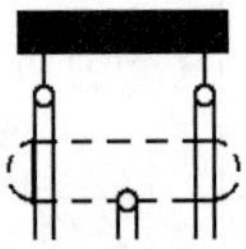	Top dead-end sensor (induction sensor)
41	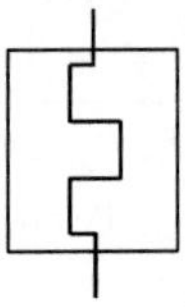	Rear window heating device	52		Sliding contact

2. Know the features of VW circuit diagram

(1) The circuit is arranged vertically. The power line is "+" for upper end, "−" for lower end. The circuits of the same system are collected together from left to right, and arranged by the order of power supply circuit, starting circuit, ignition circuit, intake preheating circuit, instrument circuit, lighting circuit, signal and alarm device circuit, wiping and cleaning device circuit, electric rear-view mirror circuit, electric window circuit, central control door lock circuit, air conditioning circuit, horn circuit.

(2) The broken line code method is adopted to solve the intersecting problem. When some complex electrical devices (such as headlights) work, they will involve the ignition switch, light switch and light changing switch, and other distribution devices, and these three switches are not in the same line. If they are drawn by the traditional drawing method, we should draw some horizontal lines to connect them, so that there are more horizontal lines on the diagram, which increases the difficulty of reading. So in the circuit diagram, we can use the "broken line code method" to solve it, in which the number in the box at the connection end of the wire is used to indicate the circuit number of the wire connected with it, for example, 98 indicates the wire connected with the circuit number 98.

(3) The circuit diagram of the whole automobile is divided into 3 parts. The top part represents the central relay box circuit, which indicates the position, capacity, relay position number and pin number of the capacitor. The middle part is the electrical components and connecting wires of the automobile, and the bottom horizontal line is the ground wire.

(4) The positive electrode of the power supply in the whole automobile electrical system is divided into 3 channels (30, 15, X). Wire 30 is directly connected with the positive electrode of the battery, which is called the constant live wire. When the engine stops, the electrical device that needs to work is connected to wire 30. Wire 15 is connected to the positive electrode of the battery when the ignition switch is located in "ON" and "ST" position. It is called the ignition switch control live wire. It is mainly used for providing power to the small power electric devices controlled by the ignition switch. The wire X is the unloading wire. When the ignition switch is located in the "ON" position, it is controlled by the intermediate relay. When the ignition switch is placed in the "ST" position, the intermediate relay does not work. The high-power electric devices (such as fog light, wiper, etc.) are connected with the wire X. If you forget to turn off these high-power electric devices when starting the engine, they will automatically power off to ensure the smooth start of the engine.

(5) The whole circuit is centered on the relay box. The electrical circuit of the automobile is controlled by the central circuit board as a center, most of the fuses and relays are installed on the front of the central circuit board, the plugs and sockets are installed on the back of the circuit board, the English letter is the position code of the socket, and the Arabic number is the terminal code of the wire harness plug. According to the code at the junction point between the wire and the lower frame line of the central circuit board on the circuit diagram, it can be found which wire is in which wire harness and is connected to which jack.

3. An example of VW circuit analysis

The recognition method of VW circuit diagram is shown in Figure 9-11.

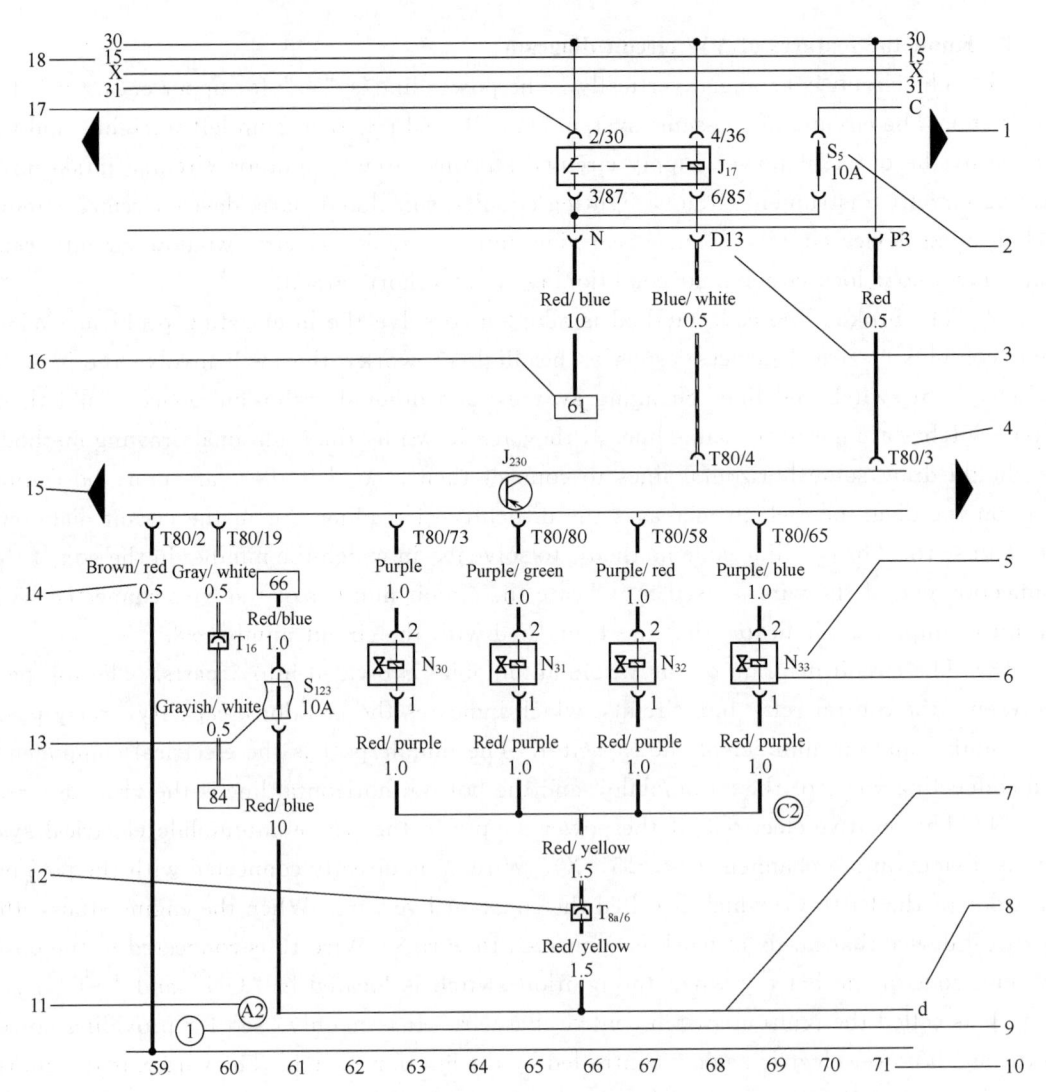

Figure 9-11　Recognition Method of VW Circuit Diagram

1—Triangle arrow, indicating that it is connected to the next page of circuit diagram; 2—Fuse code, S5 indicates that the fuse is located in the 5th position of the fuse seat, 10A; 3—Plug connection code of wire in the central circuit board, indicating the connection of multiple pins or single pin and the position of the wire. "D13" denotes the terminal of the wire at the position of socket D No. 13 on the central circuit board; 4—Terminal code, "80/3" means the terminal number of the connector on the electrical component 80, 3 is the terminal position code; 5—Electrical component code, the name of the component can be found under the circuit diagram; 6—Electrical component symbol, see the circuit diagram symbol specification; 7—Internal connection (thin solid line), the connection is not a wire, but a hinged point indicating the internal circuit or wire harness of a component; 8—Indicating the route of the internal wiring, and the letter indicates that the internal wire is connected with the internal wire marked with the same letter in the circuit diagram on the next page; 9—Ground point code, under the circuit diagram we can find the location of the code ground point on the automobile; 10—Circuit connection number, this sign is used to locate the wire in the circuit diagram; 11—The hinged point code in the wire harness, we can find under the circuit diagram in which wire harness the hinged point is located; 12—Plug-in, the plug-in T8a/6 represents the sixth pin terminal on the 8-pin a-plug-in; 13—Additional fuse code, "S_{123}" means No. 123 fuse on the central distribution box, 10A; 14—The color and cross-sectional area of the wire, "brown/red" means the main color of the wire is brown, the auxiliary color is red, "2.5" means that the cross-section of the wire is 2.5mm2; 15—Triangle arrow indicates that the electrical component is connected with the previous page circuit diagram; 16—Indicates where the wire is going and the number in the box is 61, indicating that the wire is the same as the wire of the circuit code 61. (The number in the box of the wire at the circuit code 61 is the circuit code 66 of this wire); 17—The terminal number of relay and controller and the relay board, "2/30" means the number 2 jack of the relay socket on the relay board, and "30" means the terminal No. 30 on the relay; 18—Wire code. "30" means constant live wire and "15" means small capacity live wire when the ignition switch is switched on, "X" means a large-capacity live wire powered by a unloading relay when the ignition switch is switched on, "31" indicates the ground wire; "C" is the internal wiring of the central distribution box.

238　Automobile Electrical Equipment Maintenance

4. An example of VW circuit reading

The Jetta radiator fan control circuit is shown in Figure 9-12.

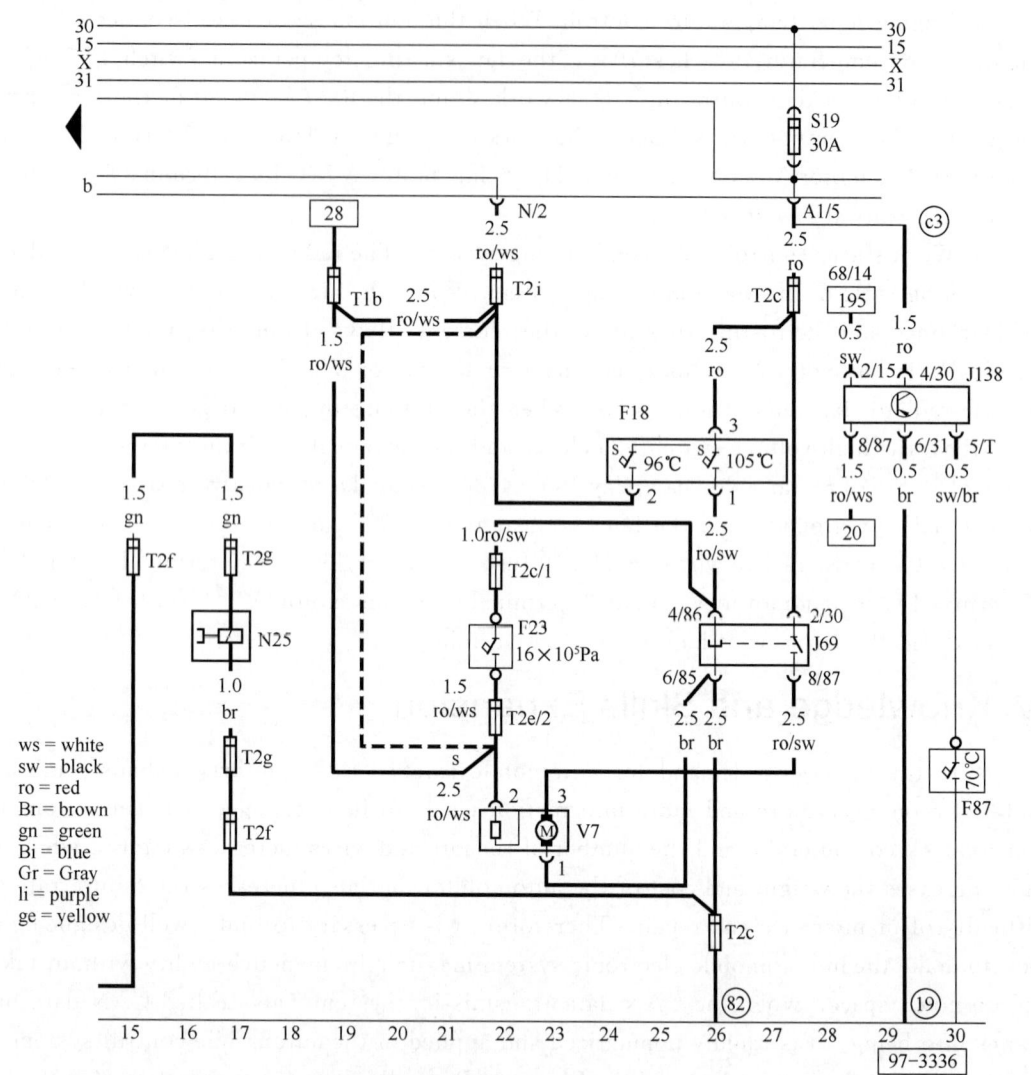

Figure 9-12　Jetta Radiator Fan Control Circuit

F18—fadiator fan thermal switch; F23—high voltage switch; J69-fan two-gear relay; J138—fan starting control unit;

N25—air conditioning electromagnetic clutch; T1b—single hole plug; T2c—2 hole plug (before engine room);

T2e—2 hole plug (before engine room); T2f—2 hole plug (before engine room);

T2g—2 hole plug (before engine room); T2i—2 hole plug (before engine room); V7—radiator fan;

F87—fan starting temperature switch; 82—ground point, inside the left front wire harness

① Cooling water temperature control. When the coolant temperature in the radiator reaches 92~97℃, the double-temperature switch F18 is connected to gear 1 (96℃ switch is closed). The circuit is: relay box (30 constant live wire) → No. 19 fuse (30A) → relay box A1/5 → F18 (No. 3 terminal) → F18 (No. 2 terminal) → fan motor V7 (No. 2 terminal) → fan motor V7 (No. 1 terminal) → ground, and the fan runs at a low speed (1, 600r/min). When the temperature exceeds 97℃, the double-temperature switch F18 is connected to gear 2 (105℃ switch is closed), the fan gear 2 relay J69 works, the circuit is: relay box (30 constant live wire) → No. 19 fuse (30A) → J69 (2/30 terminal) → J69 (8/

87 terminal) → fan motor V7 (No. 3 terminal) → fan motor V7 (No. 1 terminal) → ground, and the fan runs at high speed (2400r/min).

② Engine room temperature control. When the ignition switch is disconnected, if the engine room temperature reaches 70℃, the fan starting temperature switch F87 will be closed, the fan starting control unit J138 works, and the 8/87 terminal of the fan starting control unit J138 outputs the voltage. The working circuit is: J138 (8/87 terminal) → T1b plug-in → fan motor V7 (No. 2 terminal) → fan motor V7 (No. 1 terminal) →ground, and the fan runs at low speed.

③ Work status control of air-conditioning system. The radiator fan is also controlled by the working state of the air-conditioning system. When the air conditioning switch is in the refrigerating and defrosting position, the current flows from the relay box (N/2 terminal) → fan motor V7 (No. 2 terminal) → fan motor V7 (No. 1 terminal) →ground, and the radiator fan runs at low speed. When the pressure in the refrigeration line rises to 1. 6 MPa, the high-voltage switch F23 closes and the current flows from the relay box (N/2 terminal) → F23 → fan two-gear relay J69 (4/86 terminal) → fan two-gear relay J69 (6/85 terminal) → ground, and the fan two-gear relay J69 is sucked to close, the circuit is: relay box (30 constant live wire) → No. 19 fuse (30A) → J69 (2/30 terminal) → J69 (8/87 terminal) → fan motor V7 (No. 3 terminal) → fan motor V7 (No. 1 terminal) → ground, and the fan runs at high speed (2400r/min).

Ⅳ. Knowledge and Skills Expansion

With the increasing demand for automobile safety, ride comfort, exhaust emissions and fuel economy, more and more information needs to be exchanged between automobile controllers (computers), and the number of sensors and wires increases rapidly, which not only increases the weight and cost of the automobile, but also increases the failure rate and difficulty of maintenance and repair. Therefore, it is necessary to find a well-designed solution to make the in-automobile electronic system maintain its maneuverability without taking up too much space, when the CAN data transmission system (also called CAN data bus) comes into being, it is rapidly popularized and applied in the automobile control system. In China, such as Audi A6, Passat BS, Polo and Pora all adopt CAN data bus. CAN is the abbreviation of Controller Area Network, which means that the controllers connect each other through the bus and carry out data exchange, connect the engine management computer, the body (such as combination instrument, door control and skylight, etc.) control computer, air-conditioning computer, lighting control computer and entertainment system control computer through the data bus, then it can realize the sharing of sensor data and computer data, simplify the structure and improve the control efficiency. This is the use of CAN data bus to connect each control unit, forming the on-board network system, is the application of computer network system in modern automobile.

The Bora, uses two sets of CAN data transmission systems in power transmission system and comfort system (see Figure 9-13).

1. An overview of CAN data transmission system

CAN data bus is one kind of data transmission form between each control unit, it forms each control unit as a whole, all the information is transmitted along two wires, independ-

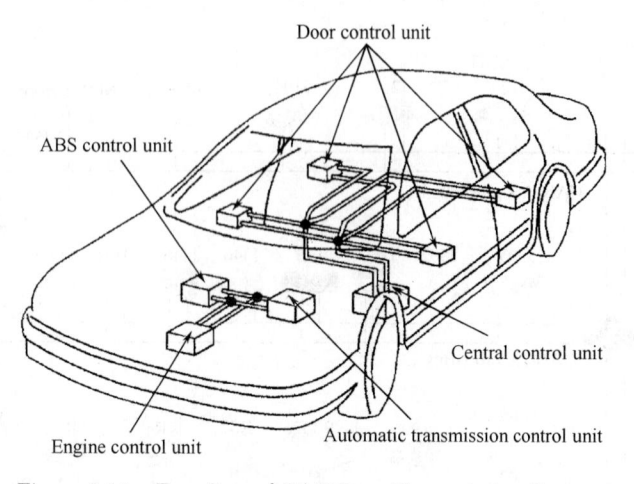

Figure 9-13   Two Sets of CAN Data Transmission Systems

ent of the number of control units and the amount of information involved, thus solving the problem that the number of plugs on the wire and control unit increases with the increase of the new information, and the problem that each information needs different wire can also be solved. Therefore, the home-made automobile Bora, Polo have applied the CAN data bus system, the concrete advantages are as follows.

(1) If the data is extended to add new information, simply upgrade the software.

(2) The control unit monitors the transmitted information in real time and stores the fault code after the fault is detected.

(3) The use of small control unit and small control unit jack can save space.

(4) To minimize sensor signal wires, high-speed data transmission can be achieved between control units.

(5) CAN data bus conforms to the national standard, so data transmission between different control units can be applied.

2. The composition and structure of CAN data bus

(1) Composition and structure.

In the CAN data transmission system, a CAN controller and a CAN transceiver are added to each computer, and two CAN data buses are connected externally to each computer. The two computers in the system that act as terminals are also equipped with a data transfer terminal (sometimes the data transfer terminal is installed outside the computer), as shown in Figure 9-14. In addition to the data transmission line, other components are placed inside the control unit, and the function of the control unit remains unchanged.

(2) The role of the principal component.

① CAN controller. The function of CAN controller is to receive the data from the microprocessor in the control unit, process the data and transmit it to the CAN transceiver. The CAN controller also receives the data received by the transceiver, processes the data and transmits it to the microprocessor in the control unit.

② CAN transceiver. The CAN transceiver is a combination of transmitter and receiver. It converts the data provided by CAN controller into electric signal and sends it through data bus. At the same time, it also receives the data of bus and transmits the data to CAN controller.

Item IX   Analysis of Circuit Diagram of Automobile Electrical System   **241**

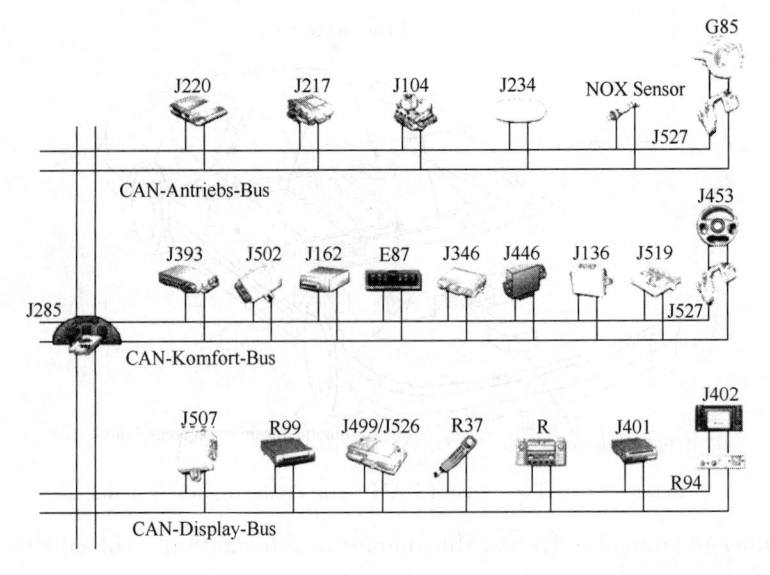

Figure 9-14   CAN Data Bus

③ Data transmission terminal. The data transmission terminal is actually a resistor. It prevents the online end of the data from being reflected back, which can affect the transmission of data.

④ Data transmission wire. The data transmission wire is a two-way data wire used to transmit data, which is divided into CAN-high and CAN-low data wires. With a designated receiver, the data is sent to each control unit through a data bus, and each control unit receives it and calculates it. In order to prevent external electromagnetic interference and external radiation, CAN bus uses two wires wound in one, the potentials on the two wires are opposite, if the voltage of one wire is 5V, the other wire is OV, the total voltage of the two wires is a normal value. In this way, CAN bus is protected from external electromagnetic field interference, while CAN bus radiation is neutral, i. e. no radiation.

3. The transmission principle and process of CAN data bus

(1) The principle of transmission. The transmission principle of the CAN data bus is similar to that of teleconference to a great extent. A user 1 (control unit 1) "speaks" the data to the network, while other users "listen" to the data. When a control unit considers the data useful to it, it receives and applies the data, while other control units may ignore the data. Therefore, the data in the data bus do not have a specified receiver, but is received and calculated by all the control units.

(2) The transmission process. The specific transmission process of the data is shown in Figure 9-15.

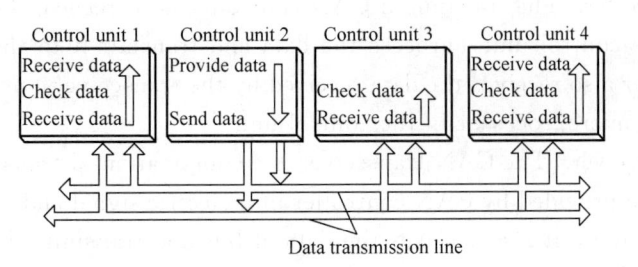

Figure 9-15   Data Transmission Process

The control unit provides data to the CAN controller for transmission. The CAN transceiver receives data from the CAN controller and converts it into an electric signal and sent it out. All the control units that form a network with CAN data bus become receivers. The control unit detects the received data to see if they are needed by its function. If the data received is important, it will be recognized and processed and, conversely, ignored. For example, the engine computer sends data to a computer CAN transceiver, which receives the data from the engine computer, converts the signal and sends it to the controller of the computer. Other computer transceivers in the CAN data transmission system receive this data, but it is necessary to determine whether the data is needed, if not, the data will be ignored.

Summary

(1) The automobile circuit diagram comprehensively reflects the principle of the automobile circuit, the connection relation and the position and other information, is the indispensable maintenance technical data for automobile maintenance, and has provided the maintenance technical personnel how to carry on the fault diagnosis when the automobile electrical system is broken down. To correctly reading the automobile circuit diagram is a basic skill of the maintenance technical personnel to diagnose and eliminate the electrical system faults.

(2) There arc many kinds of automobile circuit diagrams. However, as long as we master the reading rules of automobile circuit diagrams, and select some typical whole automobile circuits for comprehensive and in-depth analysis, we can fully master the basic skills of reading automobile circuit diagrams.

Thinking and Practice

(1) What are the reading points of a automobile wire diagram?

(2) What are the common circuit symbols in automobile circuit diagrams?

(3) What are the characteristics of the VW circuit diagram?

(4) How to diagnose and repair overhaul automobile circuit faults?

(5) What are the precautions for overhauling the faults of automobile circuits?